D1169068

PRAISE FOR

CONFIDENCE MEN

"No book about the Obama presidency appears to have unnerved the White House quite so much as *Confidence Men* by Ron Suskind, a Pulitzer Prize–winning journalist who has developed a niche in the specialized art of parting the curtain on presidential dealings." —*Chicago Tribune*

"The White House says Suskind talked to too many disgruntled former staffers. But he seems to have talked to a lot of gruntled ones, too. The overarching portrait of chaos, lack of intellectual depth, and absence of political wisdom, from a Pulitzer Prize–winning former reporter at this paper, rings true." —Peggy Noonan, *Wall Street Journal*

"Suskind makes you see Obama's potential all over again, he makes you mourn that it has so far been underrealized, and then, in the end, he rekindles the word that has been mocked relentlessly by the president's opponents: *hope*. Journalism like this is all too rare in an age in which reporters trade their critical faculties for access. And it's even rarer that skeptical reporting is turned into something lasting." —*Esquire*

"An authoritative window on the inner workings of the administration and a useful management primer on how not to run an organization. . . . *Confidence Men* is crammed with interesting detail." —*Fortune*

"Like all of Suskind's recent books, *Confidence Men* doesn't just expose the secret goings-on that explain so much about how our government works. It also makes so much of the mainstream press coverage look shallow and credulous by comparison. . . . Time and again, Suskind's revelations have initially been pooh-poohed by reporters who couldn't re-create his reporting—and then much later were recognized as being utterly correct." —Dan Froomkin, *Huffington Post*

"Suskind's book often reads like Halberstam's *The Best and the Brightest*. . . . But the quagmire isn't a neo-Vietnam like Afghanistan—it's the economy, and the casualties are measured in lost jobs."

—Frank Rich, *New York* magazine

"The work that went into *Confidence Men* cannot be denied. Suskind conducted hundreds of interviews. He spoke to almost every member of the Obama administration, including the president. He quotes memos no one else has published. He gives you scenes that no one else has managed to capture."

—Ezra Klein, *New York Review of Books*

"Ron Suskind's book is . . . the one that makes the most sense. . . . The shudder-inducing bits of *Confidence Men* come when the team is too optimistic about how its policies will play out. The confidence allows them to move on too quickly. It seeps into every other mistake."

—*Slate*

"The book paints a harsh, stark portrait of a president in over his head. . . . Suskind makes a compelling case that Obama was able to win the election because he was talking to the right people . . . but when it came to choosing his administration, he went with a different group."

—*Daily Beast*

"Written in sharp, cinematic scenes, in which just about all the main players in the administration from the president down are captured in full-blooded, un-censored conversation, *Confidence Men* sprawls across the multiple crises, inher-ited and self-inflicted, of the opening two years of the Obama presidency. . . . Suskind's central thesis deserves to be taken seriously."

—*Financial Times*

"Suskind does a magnificent job explaining the way an economy centered on debt has decimated the middle class and made the top 1 percent of Americans impossibly wealthy. . . . Suskind describes a leader pulled off course by his staff. But we still don't know where Obama wants to take us."

—Joan Walsh, *Salon*

"This narrative . . . keeps you reading long after you've absorbed the White House's petty criticisms about the book. The portrait of Obama that emerges here is sympathetic, even though Suskind addresses the president's failings. . . . Though the book toggles between Washington and Wall Street, the freshest material comes from Suskind's deep access to the West Wing."

—*Bloomberg News*

"Ron Suskind's account of the Obama administration is a marker of our times. It reveals a president of the United States unable to perform responsibly the duties of his high office and the costly consequences. . . . Suskind's contribution to this tale of woe is to give us a fine-grained picture of Obama's passive place in deliberations."   —*Huffington Post*

"The book that every former Obama enthusiast is reading is Ron Suskind's *Confidence Men*. . . . This is a formal piece of journalism by a reporter with deep inside sources. . . . Indeed, the book represents some sort of watershed, a formal measurement of the distance between the perception of a vaunted political figure and the reality."   —Michael Wolff, *GQ*

"This inside account of the Obama economic team contains enough damning on-the-record quotes to give it the ring of truth, despite White House efforts to discredit the narrative of infighting and missed opportunities. Read it and weep. It reminds me of the post-Iraq invasion books that documented a similar failure to rise to the enormity of the problem, whether the insurgency was in Iraq or on Wall Street."   —Eleanor Clift, *Newsweek*

CONFIDENCE MEN

**WALL STREET, WASHINGTON, AND
THE EDUCATION OF A PRESIDENT**

RON SUSKIND

HARPER PERENNIAL

NEW YORK • LONDON • TORONTO • SYDNEY • NEW DELHI • AUCKLAND

HARPER ● PERENNIAL

A hardcover edition of this book was published in 2011 by HarperCollins Publishers.

CONFIDENCE MEN. Copyright © 2011 by Ron Suskind. All rights reserved. Printed in the United States of America. No part of this book may be used or reproduced in any manner whatsoever without written permission except in the case of brief quotations embodied in critical articles and reviews. For information address HarperCollins Publishers, 10 East 53rd Street, New York, NY 10022.

HarperCollins books may be purchased for educational, business, or sales promotional use. For information please write: Special Markets Department, HarperCollins Publishers, 10 East 53rd Street, New York, NY 10022.

FIRST HARPER PERENNIAL EDITION PUBLISHED 2012.

Designed by Leah Carlson-Stanisic

Library of Congress Cataloging-in-Publication Data has been applied for.

ISBN 978-0-06-143046-6 (pbk.)

12 13 14 15 16 OV/RRDH 10 9 8 7 6 5 4 3 2 1

CONTENTS

PART I

THE TWO CAPITALS

SEPTEMBER 17, 2010

PRESIDENT BARACK OBAMA DANCES LIGHTLY DOWN THE FOUR marble steps to the Rose Garden and across the flagstones to a waiting lectern. He still glides, elegant and purposeful, in that tall man's short-step—a ballplayer returning to the court after a time-out.

Today, September 17, 2010, he has committed to putting some "points on the board," in the sports parlance of Rahm Emanuel, his chief of staff. The president needs to show the country that he hasn't lost his game, the ineffable confidence, the surety of stance and delivery that propelled a man with little political experience to scale cosmic heights and to realize what felt, on Election Day, like democracy's version of the moon landing.

Through recent history, America has considered itself something of a providential miracle, a country that kept finding reasons to believe in its Manifest Destiny. That faith, sorely tested over the past several decades, found itself restored with dizzying ebullience when Barack Obama and his beautiful family stepped onto the stage in Chicago's Grant Park as America's First Family. It was a sensation of such intensity as to startle many across the country and around the world into believing in the promise of America, the original and long-burning beacon of the democratic ideal.

The legacy of that moment is ever more found in the lengthening shadow it casts. In the nearly two years since, Barack Obama, like an archangel returned to earth, has been forced to walk the flat land and feel its hard contours. What, if anything, it has awakened in him remains unclear—at present, he is clearly struggling to get his bearings. And yet it is impossible to see the president and not search out signs of that man from Grant Park, who strode so boldly across history's confetti-strewn stage.

On this warm late-summer afternoon, with Congress out of session, Obama has convened the press to announce the launch of a new agency,

the Consumer Financial Protection Bureau. It has been designed to protect American consumers from the predations of the financial services
and banking industry, which over the past couple of decades has grown
vast and insatiable by inventing, for the most part, new ways to market,
sell, and invest in debt.

The woman standing awkwardly at Obama's left hip, Harvard Law
School professor Elizabeth Warren, has become the nation's town crier
on the subject of bankruptcy and debt. In the two years since the economic crisis, she has emerged from nowhere to trumpet the story of how
debt was turned into a velvety weapon, how engorged financial firms de-
ceptively packaged it, sold it as securities, and extracted usurious profits
from American consumers, especially those in America's once-vaunted
middle class. The notion of a consumer financial product agency, a free-
standing, independently funded entity like the Federal Communications
Commission, was originally hers, unveiled in an article she published
in the spring of 2007. The truth is that no one much cared for the idea,
until her unheeded concerns turned up at the center of the worst financial
meltdown since the Great Depression.

So today is a long-delayed victory for Warren—almost. Somehow
nothing in the Rose Garden is quite as it seems. The president praises
Warren, whom he says he met at Harvard Law School, as though they
are old friends. They're not, and Warren only became a professor at Harvard Law the year after Obama graduated from it. In fact, over the past
two years, while Warren has seen herself lionized on magazine covers
and in prime-time interviews as a leading voice for tough, restorative reforms, the president seems to have been studiously avoiding her. Part of
the problem, clearly, is that she has been acting the way people expected
and hoped that man from Grant Park would.

This has caused discomfort not only for the president, but also for
his top lieutenants, including the boyish man in the too-long jacket at
Obama's right hip, bunched cuffs around his shoes, looking more than
anything like a teenager who just grabbed a suit out of his dad's closet.
That's Treasury secretary Tim Geithner, looking sheepish. Only those
in his inner circle at Treasury, though, can precisely read what's behind
that expression: a string of private efforts across the past year to neutral-
ize Warren. The previous fall, Geithner huddled with top aides to develop what one called an "Elizabeth Warren strategy," a plan to engage

with the firebrand reformer that would render her politically inert. He never worked out a viable strategy—a way to meet with Warren without drawing undesirable comparisons—and so, like the president, he didn't.

What the Treasury Department did do, unbeknownst to Warren, was embrace demands from the banking industry to create a bureau under the condition that Warren would not be allowed to lead it. But as the financial-reform bill moved to a vote in early summer, industry lobbyists were so aggrieved at the idea of an agency—they felt it unsupportable under any conditions—that they didn't bother to call in their chits on Warren.

In fact, they played it just so. The industry managed to get the proposed agency shrunk into a bureau that would live under the auspices of the Federal Reserve, the government's greatest mixed metaphor of public purpose and private self-regard, representing as it does the dual interests of a sound monetary policy and the health of the banking industry. Beyond that, the bureau's rules can be vetoed by a two-thirds majority of a panel of other financial regulators—an indignity of institutionalized second-guessing known to few other agencies.

But after financial regulatory reform legislation passed in July, the prospect of Warren at the bureau's helm quickly grew into a movement: complete with Internet write-in campaigns, online petitions, flurries of editorials, and even a viral rap video—certainly a first in the history of appointing government regulators.

Warren would seem the easiest of choices. Since his earliest days on the campaign trail, Obama had spoken passionately about restoring competent government, and with it competent regulators. With the midterm elections less than two months away, he could have used a confirmation battle over Warren to draw a much-needed distinction between his administration and those, mostly Republicans, who dared to side publicly with America's big banks and financial firms. Warren's celebrated ferocity looked tailor-made to revive Obama's vast grassroots campaign network. Like an encamped army with nothing to do, the foot soldiers of the campaign had fought among themselves a bit, eaten the leftover rations, and then drifted back to private life. Field commanders still in touch with the White House signaled by midsummer that a Warren confirmation battle would rally the troops and, according to one, "at least show what we stand for." On the other side was the financial services industry, which hurled nonspecific attacks at Warren, claiming she was arrogant, disrespectful, and power-hungry. It had begun castigating Obama as "antibusiness," a charge the industry asserts would be definitively confirmed by the appointment of Warren.

In mid-August, Warren was finally called in to meet with the president. Obama began their sit-down saying, "This isn't a job interview." It wasn't. The president had already decided what he was going to do, in a managerial style that had become his trademark: integrating policy options and political prognostication into a prepackaged solution—announced before the game even started.

Combatants over a Warren nomination will never take the field. Shuffling papers on the lectern in the Rose Garden, Obama says, with a few passive locutions, that Warren will be on the search committee to find someone to run the bureau:

"She was the architect behind the idea for a consumer watchdog, so it only makes sense that she'd be the, um . . ." He stumbles briefly, as though the text is pulling him off balance. ". . . She should be the architect working with Secretary of Treasury Geithner in standing up the agency." He adds that she'll be an adviser to both him and Geithner and "will also play a pivotal role in helping me determine who the best choice is for director of the bureau."

That's basically it. None of the troops are energized, and anyone who feared the financial debacle might produce a true innovation, a rock star regulator, is left unruffled.

The press conference ends with reporters shouting as the president turns to leave. One yells above the rest, "Why didn't you put her up for confirmation?"

A moment later the president walks from the Rose Garden to the basement of the White House. Having finished with Geithner and Warren, he strolls unaccompanied, free of handlers and Secret Service, through a long subterranean hall on his way to the Situation Room.

"Hey, Alan, how you doing?" he pipes up, spotting Assistant Secretary of the Treasury for Economic Affairs Alan Krueger coming the other way. Krueger carries an additional title, held over from the nineteenth century: chief economist of the United States.

"Just fine, Mr. President," a somewhat surprised Krueger responds. "In fact, today's my birthday."

The two men stop to chat for a moment at the entrance to the White House mess. The president has grown to appreciate Krueger's input over the past eighteen months. A Princeton professor and frequent stand-in for Geithner at Obama's morning economic briefing, Krueger is something of an oddity in the upper reaches of government: he's an actual researcher. Typically, high-ranking economists do their substantive, elbows-deep research in the earlier stages of their careers. Not Krueger. Not only had he been publishing groundbreaking studies up until joining the administration in January 2009, but he had also gone so far as to commission targeted research over the past year, using Princeton funds and resources when he found the government's research apparatus too slow.

The current economic crisis, he felt, was too thorny and too unusual not to study with fresh eyes and first questions. Characterized by both rock-bottom interest rates and a catastrophic deleveraging spiral, the crisis defied most historical precedents from which actionable policies might be drawn. And the White House needed nothing so much as a stream of creative remedies, one right after the next.

The administration undershot the crisis, convincing itself by the summer of 2009 that the economy had turned the corner and, at the same time, recognizing that it would be a jobless recovery of stunning disparities, with restored GDP growth alongside fast-rising unemployment. In fact, internal administration projections in June 2009, with unemployment having risen to 9.5 percent, noted that joblessness would average a whopping 9.8 percent in 2010. Krueger and others began to work furiously to find innovative ways that the government might stimulate job growth. Being a close friend of both National Economic Council chairman Larry Summers, who was his graduate adviser at Harvard, and Office of Management and Budget director Peter Orszag, whom he mentored at Princeton, made Krueger one of the few people to whom both of Obama's top economic advisers deferred. All to no avail. After the stimulus bill was passed in February 2009, little else happened on the jobs front for a year and a half. Proposals were talked to death without resolution; the few that were adopted tended to lack a coherent political strategy to make them legislative reality. The day before, the Census Bureau had announced that poverty had hit a fifteen-year high. Even the *Wall Street Journal*'s editorial page had bemoaned that middle-class incomes dropped a stunning 5 percent between 2001 and 2009, a lost decade laying claim to the country's worst economic performance in half a century. Unemployment stood at precisely the 9.8 percent the administration's prognosticators had foretold.

Obama, who was at the center of this dispiriting process, tries to keep things light and breezy in the hallway with Krueger. He seems improbably ebullient, wanting to talk.

"So, how old?"

"A little older than you," Krueger says. "Just turned fifty."

Obama steps back, appraisingly.

"Fifty? You're looking pretty good for fifty."

He means it. Krueger notices for the first time that the president, a year his junior, has really aged in office, bits of gray hair now sprinkling his crown, wrinkles growing around his eyes. Krueger is about to say, "Well, my job's easier than yours," but he catches himself and instead goes with "You should see me on the basketball court." Maybe this will win him an invitation to one of Obama's famous five-on-fives.

None forthcoming, and Obama closes it out. "So what are you doing for your birthday?"

"Going back to Princeton," Krueger says. He's a breath away from adding: *soon for good*.

He's through with D.C. He has decided to return home a day after the midterms, exhausted for sure, but more than that, tamping down the sense of missed opportunity. As the two men part, he can't help but wonder if Obama feels the same way. How could he not?

———

Waiting in the Oval Office are Jann Wenner, the founder of *Rolling Stone* magazine, and his executive editor, Eric Bates. They have been there for an hour, since just before the Elizabeth Warren event, waiting and preparing for an interview with the president. *Rolling Stone*, failing to score an Obama interview since the campaign, has nonetheless gone through a renaissance in the past two years, dealing some of the most forceful criticisms of Wall Street and Washington and the collusion between the two, with targeted shots directed at both Goldman Sachs and Obama himself.

So, for the president, today is all about forcefully answering the charge from the progressive community—and a great many independents—that what got him elected has not been evident in his governance. The administration's strategy is to emphasize that the distance between the hopes of Grant Park and the trimmed ambitions of legislative pragmatism is not a fissure, rupture, or acquiescence, but rather the hard reality of governing in a partisan era. All the better for those words to appear in an organ of criticism, which is why *Rolling Stone* was chosen.

Obama enters his famous office and compliments Wenner, the stylish, aging hipster, on his colorful socks: "If I wasn't president, I could wear socks like that." Then he settles himself into a wing chair between marble busts of his heroes, Abraham Lincoln and Martin Luther King, Jr.

Obama is ready to rebut criticisms head-on. But the questions today do not pose much of a challenge, beginning with standard fare about the state of the economy he inherited and Republican obstinacy that, the president notes, reared up a day before his inauguration even, when he learned that the Republican Caucus would vote as a bloc against the stimulus package, even though it included tax cuts and other features they'd asked for.

Fifteen minutes have passed before he gets the first tough question, about how his "economic team is closely identified with Wall Street and the deregulation that caused the collapse."

The president gives a revealing response, noting that while Tim Geithner and the proud and obstreperous Larry Summers never actually worked for Goldman Sachs, "there is no doubt that I brought in a bunch of folks who understand the financial markets, the same way, by the way, that FDR brought in a lot of folks who understood the financial markets after the crash, including Joe Kennedy, because my number-one job at that point was making sure that we did not have a full-fledged financial meltdown."

To compare Geithner and Summers to Joe Kennedy is a reach. Kennedy was so instrumental for Roosevelt in setting up the Securities and Exchange Commission because he knew Wall Street from the inside as a master operator, had made all the money he could ever need, and, crucially, was bursting with zeal to move into the public sector and never look back, even if it meant that his old colleagues from Wall Street wouldn't invite him to dinner ever again. There has been no one remotely like this in a position of real power under Obama—especially not Summers or Geithner. The irony of Obama's Joe Kennedy reference is that a comparable figure, in equal measures expert and unencumbered, is precisely what he has needed, and lacked. This is something Obama surely knows at this point.

There are more answers of this sort going forward: clever—respectfully acknowledging opponents' positions, even those with thin evidence behind them, that then get stitched together into some pragmatic conclusion—but hollow. With today's Warren announcement also part of the broader counterattack on progressives' criticisms, the president then unabashedly champions Warren, speaking as though he has named her head of the bureau. A light bit of chat about Paul McCartney and the Obama girls closes out the lengthy (hour-and-change) interview. Obama bids the visiting journalists adieu and leaves to confer with aides outside the office.

Then suddenly he's back, enlivened and ready to say something—as if the person the journalists had sat with for the last hour in the Oval Office was not the person he'd intended for them to meet.

"One closing remark that I want to make: It is inexcusable for any Democrat or progressive right now to stand on the sidelines in this midterm election. There may be complaints about us not having certain things done, not fast enough, making certain legislative compromises. But right now, we've got a choice between a Republican Party that has moved to the right of George Bush and is looking to lock in the same policies that got us into these disasters in the first place, versus an administration that, with some admitted warts, has been the most successful administration in a generation in moving progressive agendas forward. The idea that we've got a lack of enthusiasm in the Democratic base, that people are sitting on their hands complaining, is just irresponsible."

He continues, passionate, punching the air, throwing some jabs at 527s and the Roberts Court, which had freed companies to spend at will, without disclosure, as political actors, leaving Democrats heavily outspent in the current midterm campaign. Then he brings it to a crescendo.

"We have to get folks off the sidelines. People need to shake off this lethargy, people need to buck up. Bringing about change is hard—that's what I said during the campaign. It has been hard, and we've got some lumps to show for it. But if people now want to take their ball and go home, that tells me folks weren't serious in the first place."

The speech he's referring to "during the campaign" was witnessed by only a few hundred people. It was the darkest moment of his run, in early October 2007, after an American Research Group poll put him 33 points behind Hillary Clinton, with only three months to go until the all-important Iowa Caucus. Obama gathered his National Finance Committee, the campaign's top givers, in the auditorium of a Des Moines hotel for a do-or-die meeting. He explained to them that they were running a different kind of campaign, a genuine from-the-bottom-up, grassroots effort, that it had never been done before, not like this, and that it took time for those roots to take hold. The heavy hitters nodded: fine, they understood the concept. But it wasn't working. The dispiriting national polls were one thing, but a recent *Des Moines Register* piece had Obama running third in Iowa.

Obama listened to them air their doubts for an hour or so before responding. Then his gaze, filled with the flinty resolve of tough love, swept over the crowd.

"Did you think I was kidding when I said this was the unlikely journey? I never said this was going to be simple or easy. You thought this would be simple? Change is never simple. Change is hard." He dug deep, his voice dropping to a whisper. "Listen, I know you're nervous. I understand. But if you're nervous, I'll hold your hand. We're going to get through this together. I promise we will. And if we can win Iowa, we'll win this country." Many of those in the room, among them not a few Wall Street financiers, cheered, moisture creeping into their eyes. They opened their wallets, one last time, giving a campaign on life support a final transfusion. Of course, he did go on to win Iowa and "win this country."

Now Obama is in the depths again, but there's no one's hand to hold. No one, outside of a few people in this iconic building, understands what the past two years have held, or what they've revealed to this man and those gathered tightly around him.

By being himself—an alluring and inspiring self, supremely confident yet expressing humility, speaking powerfully of grabbing history's arc and bending it toward justice—Obama became the first black president. But more and more, walking the halls of this building, he doesn't feel like himself—someone who could bring people together, who could map common ground and, upon it, build a future.

Disputes among his top advisers have become so acute, so fierce, that the president has had to step in and mediate many of them himself. He's not getting what he needs to manage this daunting job, and some advisers have become convinced that his lack of experience, especially managerial experience, may be his undoing; that, at a time of peril, the president may simply not be up to the demands of this moment. But his gratitude for those who've ushered him to power, and have walked with him through battle, gets in the way of tough love, at least with those closest to him. There are top aides he's wanted to remove for months or even longer, but can't seem to. He knows he should, that no organization can run without accountability.

But today, as he runs between events and interviews—struggling to square the circle between pitiless reality and high ideals that, on Election Day, allowed him to claim kinship with FDR—President Obama is feeling oddly buoyant.

In the past few days, he's caught a break. The mayor of Chicago decided not to run for reelection. That means his chief of staff, Rahm Emanuel, will be seeking "other opportunities" and the president won't have to worry about firing him.

All taken care of. Emanuel will be out by month's end to resume his political career. Many other top advisers are now planning their exits.

After that, maybe Obama can at least attempt a fresh start, a next chapter. There's no perch, anywhere, like the presidency, with the daily burdens of office, the weight of history—and all in a fishbowl, with the world, some of it malevolent, watching every move. Which is why a president who doesn't feel quite like himself often portends a crisis of leadership. But change presents opportunity—always—and the ground is now shifting beneath Obama's feet. And soon enough, the president of the United States may get a chance to resume his conversation with the men whose busts stare from the cabinet behind his favorite wing chair, looking, with icy grandeur, over his narrow shoulders.

2

THE WARNING

SENATOR BARACK OBAMA SLIPPED OUT OF THE SWELTER OF AN unbearable Washington day—August 1, 2007, with the temperature nosing up toward a hundred degrees—and into the nondescript, six-story building a few blocks from the U.S. Capitol. This office, his campaign headquarters, abuts Armand's Original Chicago Pizzeria, and with windows open to catch a faint breeze, the air inside smelled of baked dough and marinara.

And a pinch of doubt. Running for president was turning out to be harder than Obama had figured, which was not to say he'd expected it to be easy. He said all the time that "change is hard" for anyone, and he included himself. But the nature of the challenges seemed to surprise him, demanding that he narrow the scope of his personality and exhibit more discipline than even he, a disciplined man, was accustomed to.

What had become clear to those at campaign headquarters and beyond was that the senator had lost his early rhythm, his perfect pitch. This sort of thing happened; Babe Ruth led the league in strikeouts the same year he hit sixty homers. But everything had been going so well. Obama's ascent was already one of the most astonishing in modern political history: from lowly state senator to presidential candidate in just three years.

He had become a sensation on the power and perfect cinema of a few brilliant speeches. First, the show-stealing turn at the 2004 Democratic National Convention: "I stand here knowing that my story is part of the larger American story . . . and that, in no other country on earth is my story even possible." Then his declaration of candidacy on a freezing February day in Lincoln's own Springfield, Illinois: "If you sense, as I sense, that the time is now to shake off our slumber, and slough off our fear, and make good on the debt we owe past and future generations, then I'm ready to take up the cause, and march with you, and work with you. Together, starting today, let us finish the work that needs to be done, and

usher in a new birth of freedom on this earth." Heady and stirring, with
the artful finish that yoked together two of Lincoln's most famous lines.

But it was hard to know how even Lincoln's rhetorical genius would
have met the awesome challenge of modern politics: to explain hugely
complex problems and offer first-step solutions in all of sixty seconds.
Hillary Clinton could do it just like Lincoln split wood: steady and true,
swing by swing, as the clock ticked—fifty-four seconds . . . fifty-five . . .
fifty-six—her final summarizing sentence would hit its period and leave
her three seconds to step back and consider what she had said, as though
it had all just dawned on her. Obama watched her, on stage after stage,
suppressing his amazement. He found the demands confounding and
unreasonable, and he responded with a professorial mien, oddly uncertain, offering what felt like introductions to dissertations never to be
completed.

The prepared speech, meticulously crafted and delivered, was his
forte. So that very August morning, he led with his strength—a finely
wrought policy address to highlight his one major difference with Clinton and most of the Democratic field: early opposition to the Iraq War.
The contours of the current foreign policy debate turned out to have
been mapped back in October 2002, when members of Congress, among
them Clinton, authorized the invasion of Iraq. The then-unknown Illinois state senator spoke out against the decision at the Federal Plaza in
Chicago. Little noted at the time, Obama's speech was cited exhaustively
through the first seven months of his presidential campaign, particularly
its Lincolnesque finish: "We ought not, we will not, travel down that
hellish path blindly. Nor should we allow those who would march off and
pay the ultimate sacrifice, who would prove the full measure of devotion
with their blood, to make such an awful sacrifice in vain." To summon
the dreadnought term "in vain," even as the country marched to war
back in 2002, was indeed audacious. Hoping to make the leap from debating highway bonds in Springfield to debating the country's future at
the heart of the national fray, Obama astutely noted that the deaths in
wars of necessity were materially different from those in wars of choice,
and that the latter carried a distinct and dangerous moral liability.

While the country had moved in Obama's direction, granting him
precious political capital, to be president he would have to go beyond a
simple antiwar stance to paint his own compelling picture of "America in
the world." Hence the morning's address, given at Washington's Wood-

row Wilson Center, covering everything from "getting out of Iraq and onto the right battlefield in Afghanistan and Pakistan" to "restoring our values and securing a more resilient homeland." The speech was tough, hawkish even, and doubled down on his offhand comment from a month back—criticized by Clinton as naïve—that he would reverse Bush's policy of refusing to negotiate with rogue states, including Iran. "Presidents," he said, "can't only meet with people who will tell them what they want to hear. President Kennedy said it best: 'Let us never negotiate out of fear, but let us never fear to negotiate.'"

An audience of former national security officials and veteran reporters, definers of the conventional wisdom, responded that he was no Jack Kennedy. They swiftly connected his speech's opening statement of support for a Wilson Center scholar imprisoned by the Iranians with its summation that "Iran presents the broadest strategic challenge to the United States in the Middle East in a generation." By early afternoon, online and cable news pundits were saying that Obama was now openly threatening the Iranians.

"Did I say I was going to bomb Iran? Did you hear me say that?" Obama groused into the speakerphone, as he settled into the second-floor conference room at campaign headquarters.

"No, Barack," said the crackling voice of Dan Tarullo, a top Treasury official under President Clinton, now advising Obama on the economy. "I definitely didn't hear you say that—or anything like it."

Obama exhaled in frustration, drawing sympathetic nods from a group of economists gathered around the conference room table. It was two o'clock and they had booked the room for the next two hours, an eternity in the minute-by-minute scheduling of a campaign. Even before the lukewarm response to that morning's speech, the reason for today's meeting was clear: attention-grabbing domestic policies looked like the only way his campaign was going to generate forward motion. Obama needed some—and fast. An NBC News/*Wall Street Journal* poll released the day before showed Hillary Clinton with a 21-point lead.

Obama grabbed a water bottle, nodded to his economic team leader, Austan Goolsbee, and settled into that mindful, Zen hyper-focus that had, since his law school days, impressed just about everyone who saw it.

Goolsbee opened the meeting by running through a few top items—relations with China, capital gains taxes—then guided the discussion over to free trade. There was no real sense of urgency to any of this, however, and for seemingly good reason. GDP growth was still strong, unemployment was at 4.7 percent, and inflation was low. With the Fed keeping interest rates low, credit continued to flow so cheaply that few could refuse borrowing. Goolsbee took advantage of a small lull in the conversation to introduce a newcomer to the group.

Alan Krueger—at that point a top economic adviser to Hillary Clinton—was doing a bit of candidate shopping today. The value of the Princeton professor, to any candidate, was not only his contacts but his ecumenical appeal at having managed to retain the respect of both warring kingdoms of economics: the rationalists, with their abiding faith in the profitable mathematics of market efficiency, upon which much of the financial and political realms still relied; and the behaviorists, led by Krueger's Princeton friend Daniel Kahneman, who'd teased out the subtle biases that impel seemingly sensible actors to act against their best long-term interests. The latter group was clearly on the rise.

Krueger broke out a set of packets from his briefcase that showed why. The country, relying ever more singly across three decades on unregulated markets and the "wisdom of crowds"—of each rational economic actor, from steelworker to housewife to CEO, acting in his or her own best interest—was displaying dangerous imbalances. Certain groups were racing forward, increasing their lead. Many others, falling farther and farther behind. There were countless debates about whether the economy was in a postindustrial transition that revealed the lights of Joseph Schumpeter's "creative destruction," soon to yield more robust and widely distributed prosperity, or of simply destruction that increasingly profited those who were already ahead, as in a marathon where only the leaders got to grab cups at the water table.

Krueger passed around copies—eighteen slides, each a chart of blazing, graphed insight. Taken together, the charts dug beneath the standard confidence-affirming economic indicators to reveal underlying fragility in the U.S. economy.

The first chart, "Growing Together (1947–1973) vs. Growing Apart (1973–2005)," might have been called "A Crisis of the American Dream." It showed the glory days, those first twenty-five years after World War II, when real income for all families grew at nearly 3 percent a year and the highest increases flowed to those at the bottom, in greatest need. Since 1973, the chart showed, income growth had been negligible, less than 1 percent annually, for four-fifths of all families. The top 5 percent of the country had done very well, with family income rising about 2 percent a year, but real hourly wages had fallen for almost everyone else, failing even to keep pace with inflation.

Other charts looked at the fortunes of specific demographic groups, showing their earnings increasingly driven by educational attainment, a strengthening area for women. Men, on the other hand, had seen a dramatic downdraft in almost every measurement since 1983, including a startling decline in job stability for all age groups.

Krueger put it to Obama bluntly. The American workforce was on an unsustainable course: overworked, heavily stressed, inadequately insured against rising health costs, and moving more deeply into debt each year. Other economists at the table jumped in to say that household debt, commonly between 30 and 50 percent of GDP, had more than doubled since 2000, to almost *100 percent* of GDP. Savings rates, usually around 10 percent of income, were now negative. Like a car with rusted axles, the group agreed, the American worker needed to hit just one deep pothole—a big medical bill, a broken furnace, a salary cut, a lost job—and the wheels would come off.

"And the weakest link in this chain is the country's male workforce," Krueger added, explaining that men had been steadily dropping out of the labor market since the early 1990s. The losses had been stanched and obscured in part by the housing boom, which had brought with it plenty of construction jobs.

Obama turned to Goolsbee.

"But aren't we already seeing excess capacity in housing?" he asked. "Aren't values starting to plateau?"

Then everyone at the table had something to say. Talk about housing values will do that. The presumption still existed that real estate prices were special, defying basic laws of economic gravity, but this view had begun to erode. Federal Reserve chairman Ben Bernanke had claimed a few weeks before that losses resulting from the subprime mortgage mess would not exceed $100 billion, about one-third the size of the 1990s savings-and-loan crisis, and spoke of how the Fed's two-decade, liquidity-above-all policy would keep credit flowing and continue to buoy residential and commercial building, at least for now.

Obama took a swig from his water bottle and sat up, ramrod straight.

"Okay, in year two of my administration, when the housing bubble finally bursts, I come to you guys as my economic advisers and say, 'What do we do!' Well, what *do* we do?"

Feeling suddenly like advisers to the president, the group burst into a debate about where ten million low- to moderately skilled male workers might go. Obama mentioned his energy policy, the current core of his domestic platform.

"Tops, we'd be producing just two million jobs, in all the areas: wind, solar, all renewables," Goolsbee said. "And some of that will be offset by expected job losses in the oil sector, if we ever get that far."

It was a disappointing number. Others groped around for "sunrise" industries that might catch fire, with a targeted government subsidy lighting the match. It did not take long to settle on the health care sector, which was growing steadily as the population aged. That was where the jobs would be: nurse's aides, companions to infirm seniors, hospital orderlies. The group bandied about ideas for how to channel job-seeking men into this growth industry. A need in one area filling a need in another. Interlocking problems, interlocking solutions. The Holy Grail of systemic change.

But Obama shook his head.

"Look, these are guys," he said. "A lot of them see health care, being nurse's aides, as women's work. They need to do something that fits with how they define themselves as men."

For a politician, Obama laid claim to a heavy dose of the writer's sensibility: an inclination to look, deeply and unsentimentally, at the inner workings of the human heart. As the campaign kicked up, this side didn't appear very much, or certainly not as often as it did a decade before, when he finished writing *Dreams from My Father*, a book in which he deconstructs himself, piece by piece, and then rebuilds the corpus to display an extraordinary map of identity—with its many conflicts and comforts—in the modern world.

This writerly instinct still popped up in times of need, and with it, a sort of empathetic acuity.

As the room chewed over the non-PC phrase "women's work," trying to square the senator's point with their analytical models, Krueger—who was chief economist at the Department of Labor in the mid-1990s at the tender age of thirty-four—sat there silently, thinking that in all his years of studying men and muscle, he had never used that term. But

Obama was right. Krueger wondered how his latest research on happiness and well-being might take into account what Obama had put his finger on: that work is identity, that men like to build, to have something to show for their sweat and toil.

"Infrastructure," he blurted out. "Rebuilding infrastructure."

Obama nodded and smiled, seeing it instantly. "Now we're talking. . . . Okay, let's think about how that would work as a real centerpiece."

No longer sitting back, the senator proceeded to guide a discussion on how the nation's decaying infrastructure was the Achilles' heel of the U.S. economy; how the electrical grids people were building in Hong Kong and Mumbai were superior to ours; and how the states were strapped for cash, with tight budgets and statutory spending limits, leaving only the federal government to take up the cause. "Don't even get me started about potholed highways and collapsing bridges," Obama said. They talked logistics and scale: how to fund it, how to make it a sweeping national effort.

And there it was: the mind of a man who hoped to be president, showing how it bent toward integration; coolly fitting disparate, competing analyses into a coherent whole and then seasoning this with a dollop of trenchant human insight. And just like that, a policy to repair the nation's infrastructure was born. The federal government, in partnership with the private sector, would call upon the underemployed men of America to rebuild the country, and in doing so restore their pride.

That such sweeping public works take time did not seem to be a disqualifier. Obama, Krueger, and the others believed they had what they needed to design and execute a well-considered plan to address the frailties of the U.S. economy and its workforce by building what the country desperately needed.

Systemic problem, an integrated solution. This sort of thing got the senator fired up. And now he was ready to go.

"Gotta preside over the Senate in fifteen minutes," Obama said, spirits visibly lifted. He grabbed his jacket and glided to the door. "Good meeting. Real good."

Three hundred miles north, at the Stamford, Connecticut, headquarters of UBS, Robert Wolf looked through a glass partition from his office, which hung like an emperor's balcony above the largest trading floor in the world. Below was a carpeted coliseum—a pit, two football fields long, of financial combat. The four-o'clock bell had just rung, ending market activity for the day and leaving an army of traders and assorted assistants to mill about, filing paperwork and straightening up.

Wolf loved this moment: the end of a trading day. Though now chairman and chief operating officer of UBS Americas, the U.S. operation of the Swiss financial giant, Wolf was still a trader at heart. He missed the trading floor, its staccato beat and mathematical finality, and he missed this moment, when the day's scorecards were tallied.

Back in 1984, Wolf got his start at the Salomon Brothers trading desk right out of the University of Pennsylvania, where he played fullback. Work on the floor had felt like another contact sport. Trading stocks and bonds, Wolf discovered, was still just a game of inches—going head-to-head with someone on the other side of a trade. He made money fast, a bit quicker off the mark than others and able to match hustle with top-drawer math skills. When huge sums started flowing through the market in the mid-'80s, Wolf and his colleagues made one hell of a haul. But it was one hell of a haul by that era's standards, certainly not enough for the mad men who had taken over trading operations at UBS.

Or so Wolf now thought, as he watched the traders steer through the sprawl of cubicles below him. Had people just gotten so greedy, so lightheaded from excess, that they had started calling new plays from the huddle?

Sure, he could think like a trader, but he was now a boss, a big one, above it all, and he needed to think well beyond each trading day, or even each quarterly report. Something had gone terribly wrong and, weeks before, in mid-July, he began digging through UBS's books, looking for clues. He found that the company's overall leverage ran at nearly sixty times capital. That meant for every dollar in core capital, UBS had borrowed almost $60 to bet with, and a huge amount of this had gone into the era's risky new financial confections, especially those exotic securities attached to the mortgage market. Wolf knew that leverage was Wall Street's dangerous addiction: it made the highs higher and the lows deadly. On the right side of a trade, leverage greatly multiplied your winnings. But as July progressed, Wolf began to wonder if he wasn't gazing at a new definition of the wrong side.

Although the housing market had begun slipping into distress by mid-2006—with rising foreclosures forcing the largest mortgage origina-tor, Countrywide Financial, to spiral out of control in 2007—UBS traders had not been deterred from buying nearly $3 billion in mort-gage-backed securities from JPMorgan in just the past month. Those securities were largely a particular kind of derivative—the term for anything that derives its value from an underlying asset—called collat-eralized debt obligations, or CDOs. Their value was based on pools of bundled mortgages. These mortgages looked, in theory, like reasonable investments. Historically, the risk in the mortgage market tended to be driven by local or regional issues: a factory closing could dramatically raise mortgage defaults in a town, just as the downturn of some large industry could bump up foreclosures in a region. By bundling together thousands of mortgages from across the country, that risk could be di-versified. They were also sliced into tranches, a tower of different levels of anticipated risk, based on measures such as loan-to-value ratios or the credit rating of the borrower. What was the chance that mortgages in every part of America—small mortgages and jumbos; prime borrow-ers, with fine credit, and so-called subprimers—would all go south at the same time?

"Only a remote possibility" was the official view inside most of the large financial firms, which tended to hold CDOs at the top of the tower that the rating agencies stamped AAA. Beyond that, their confidence in being able to handle such risk with complex hedging strategies—the algorithmic articles of faith Wall Street had been resting on for years—was still intact. Home values may drop, along with the CDOs resting on them, but at some price, buyer and seller would meet. All the major trading positions, at all the big firms, were hedged to handle every step down that ladder.

But something, Wolf felt, was amiss, something that stretched beyond trading strategies being deployed inside of each of the Wall Street firms. After he dropped his son off at summer camp in late July, as he watched the highway's dotted line pass under his Mercedes, his mind raced. What if everyone were wrong, in the same way, at the same time? As soon as he got home he wrote a confidential note to the other top executives at UBS:

On my 7 hour drive back from Maine, I had a lot of time to think about the current situation in the markets. I think that there is more than an outside chance of a fed ease—yes—a fed ease—(which few are calling for) to resolve the current problems. If price discovery continues to be unattainable in both the subprime, structured CDO and lower quality markets, and if bridges become non-liquefiable, then what we have is a "financing" dilemma. With balance sheets in the dealer communities very heavy and accurate pricing a non-starter, the Fed may need to ease to prevent an asset valuation free fall and bring liquidity into the marketplace. Just a different perspective than what many market pros are forecasting.

Different indeed. Not that there wasn't fear building on Wall Street. But in five terse sentences, Wolf had called it: *a panic was ahead*. A "financing dilemma" is investment-speak for bankruptcy and ruin. What kills investment firms, especially those living on borrowed money, is funding long-term assets, such as mortgages, with short-term liabilities, or loans, and then not being able to replace, or "roll over," those short-term debts. Wall Street is the engine of this long-versus-short financing, but, since the 1970s, much of America had followed their lead. The company that financed its operations out of revenues—that old virtue of spending what you've got—was a rarity, especially among the large corporations. They all lived on short-term paper of every variety and flavor imaginable—paper that relied on the broad confidence in Wall Street and the nation's largest banks, which had become increasingly interconnected and indistinguishable. Wolf saw what others were just waking up to: that this banking/finance sector had become the land of the dead—or undead—with firms needing short-term infusions of capital to survive each night's rollover of debt, while not being able to stand the sunlight of "price discovery" of the diminished value of their long-term assets, such as CDOs. Once this don't ask, don't tell situation became clear to all, fear would reign, credit would start to freeze, and the Fed would have to step in by lowering interest rates to infuse new blood into the system as a whole.

Lower interest rates prompt everyone, everywhere, to roll over debts of all kinds by replacing whatever is on their balance sheet with its equivalent at a lower rate. Making this the central tool of national policy was an innovation of previous Fed chairman Alan Greenspan, who followed every financial tremor—the 1987 market crash, the 1991 savings-and-loan crisis, the meltdown of Long-Term Capital Management in 1998, the bursting of the technology stock bubble in 2000—with a cut in rates. That's what Ben Bernanke would have to do, Wolf wrote his colleagues, to boost the whole system. Or, more specifically, to keep large banks and financial houses from having to acknowledge that the declining value of hundreds of billions or more in unsellable assets meant they were already insolvent. Who would loan money to a dead company? Mostly unwitting pedestrians by way of their 401(k)s, in investment funds, pension funds, and retirement accounts of all stripes, or in the new infusions of debt they'd take on, at that slightly lower rate, through their credit cards and second mortgages—debts that, more and more, would never be paid back, because the point, for so many Americans, had not been their ability to pay debts, but just to carry them, for one more day. They'd been flocking to Wall Street's debt rollover party for years—a rate cut means a whole new set of invitations—though few would realize it had become a vampires' ball. They'd be devoured so Wall Street could live another day.

In the long run, though, there is a problem with this model. The country—even the world—is only so big. The amount of money saved is finite. At some point, even vampires starve. They simply run out of fresh blood.

———

That night, just a few hours after his economic briefing and turn presiding over the U.S. Senate, Barack Obama stood in front of the television, a man transfixed.

It was like an omen, though he didn't believe in such things. That same afternoon, in one of the most substantive economic policy meetings of his candidacy, he had come up with an anchor for his domestic policy, a sweeping proposal to rebuild the country's crumbling infrastructure with the labor of a group whose fortunes were uncertain: America's working-class men. It was government's responsibility to ensure that the physical foundations of the country, on which its economy and way of life rested, were sound. The bridges and dams, the electrical grid, the highways—the condition and upkeep of these things could not be left to the private sector and profit motive alone. They never had been. If government did not step up soon, disaster would surely ensue.

Now, flashing across the screen, one such disaster unfolded before Obama's very eyes. During the evening rush hour, an eight-lane bridge across the Mississippi River in Minneapolis had collapsed, throwing some rush-hour drivers into the river 115 feet below and stranding others, by the hundreds, on the warped spans of wobbling roadway. Traffic cameras had recorded the moment of collapse, and now a national drama played out on television as emergency workers, guided by a post-9/11 response plan—in the event of a terrorist attack on the bridge—attempted to pull survivors from the water and rescue the stranded drivers.

A yellow school bus, with sixty kids on a field trip to a water park, dangled its wheels over a severed crag of roadway. A teacher kicked open the back door and carried the kids, one by one, to safety. In some ways it was what all presidents must stand ready to do: carry those in need to safety.

Reggie Love, Obama's body man, ducked into the room. "Time for that call, Senator."

Obama picked up the phone.

"Wolf, you there doing what a husband's supposed to do?"

Though they had known each other for only ten months, the two men had taken a shine to one another. They had met the past December, when Obama came to Manhattan to deliver a dinnertime speech on child poverty. That afternoon he'd stopped by the Midtown office of aging hedge fund guru and Democratic stalwart George Soros, who had assembled a dozen of New York's top Democratic contributors. Obama had decided to run for the presidency only days before and had yet to announce. These money men—and they virtually were all men—were officially uncommitted, though most were expected to land in Hillary's camp. Obama held forth in front of the group, talking about his vision for the country. Wolf was impressed and handed the senator his business card. Obama then surprised Wolf, calling him the next day. He said they should get together after the holidays, and they did. For two hours, over dinner in D.C., they talked about everything—Wolf's life story, Obama's hopes and goals—and found they were a good match: Obama, cerebral and cool, yet very much a guy's guy; Wolf, a shoe salesman's kid with a footballer's build, Mensa-level math skills, and a big laugh. Wolf flew back to New York and went wild—called in every chit, grabbed Wall Street colleagues by the shirtsleeves, and, along with dialing for dollars, held two fund-raisers for Obama in New York, which netted the senator $500,000 apiece.

Obama may have been 20 points behind, but largely because of Wolf and his merry band—many of them the smart ethnic kids whose trading culture had come to dominate Wall Street—he was beating Hillary in the so-called money primary.

So the candidate was happy on this Wednesday night to call Wolf, who passed his cell phone across the linen tablecloth on the outdoor terrace at L'Escale, a pricey French restaurant in Greenwich, Connecticut.

"Happy Birthday, Carol," Obama purred to Wolf's wife. "If he's not treating you like a queen, you call me. I'll straighten him out."

"No, Barack," she said, clearly elated. "Tonight he can do no wrong."

The sun danced across the gentle waves of Long Island Sound three days later, on a warm Saturday morning, August 4, as the Wolfs stepped aboard a vessel owned by Sal Naro, Robert Wolf's buddy and former employee.

Naro had left UBS in 2005 to start a hedge fund, Sailfish, and had done well enough that the Wolfs and another couple—David Shulman, head of municipal bond trading at UBS, and his wife—were now making their way across the wide deck of a 110-foot Lazzara, a European-style yacht with four staterooms, a library, and an onboard water desalinator. It was supposed to be a two-night cruise, three days of floating bliss, but Wolf could tell right away that something was wrong.

"Jesus, are you okay, Sal?" Wolf asked, grabbing Naro, also a former college football player, by his thick biceps. "You look like someone just killed your best friend."

"The world's coming to an end, Wolfie," Naro said, putting down his cell phone. "The nightmare is here."

Naro laid it out for Wolf, talking rapidly, trader to trader, terror in his voice. He had been on the phone nonstop for the past week and a half, since mid-July, when the French global insurance group AXA quietly released a notice that it was changing its policy on redemptions for its money market funds. Over the past forty years, money market funds had become the place where individuals and institutions deposited their excess cash, as they once had in banks. Searching for a solid, steady yield like everyone else, these funds naturally invested in CDOs, stamped with their triple-A ratings. AXA recognized that the expected drop in the value of their CDOs would mean enough decline in overall value that their money market funds would soon be worth less than the original contributions. AXA wanted to avoid a panic, and so it proceeded coyly, telling clients they could sell shares in AXA's bond fund, which the company would buy back and hold until the price returned to an acceptable level. Keen observers such as Naro, who had spent twenty years in fixed income, saw clearly that this was not an isolated incident. AXA had invested in the same way as everyone else. It was just the first to own up to it. Others would soon follow suit and then . . . panic.

Sailfish was leveraged ten to one, modest for a hedge fund and much less than many of the broker-dealers such as Lehman Brothers and UBS. But Naro's crisis would soon be everyone's, and so he had to hurry. It started, and ended, with the phrase "You have to hold your own shit." No one would want to sell CDOs in a declining market as buyer interest fell off. So, instead, you held your bad assets and tried to unload everything else at a high enough price that it could offset the perilous combination of your leverage and the declining value of your "shit," which would eventually have to be "marked" publicly as . . . well, shit. If you couldn't sell the gems of your portfolio, quietly, quickly, and at a reasonable price, you might well go bust.

This was the drop in "asset values" Wolf had written about in his memo. The panic he mentioned was starting to take hold, and spread, even faster than he had predicted. As the couples settled in on the peaceful aft deck of the yacht—which Naro had named *Le Rêve*, French for *The Dream*—its owner was screaming. A manager at Sailfish, who had meticulously built up profitable positions for the fund, was hesitating. He couldn't bear to give up his gems, so to speak, at just *any* price: to sell into a thin market, with few buyers. So he was allegedly "painting the market," a legally questionable (though rarely prosecuted) activity where a trader stealthily makes a flurry of purchases in one area to create the illusion of buying activity and thereby draw other buyers in before dumping his securities. Naro was now screaming at the manager's boss, whom he told to fire the SOB and take over the trading himself.

"Do you hear me? You fire the fuck, and you dump it all yourself, at whatever price you can get!"

Of course, Naro was actually living inside the "financing dilemma" that Wolf had foretold and that others were quietly fearing as credit tightened all spring and summer. Sailfish couldn't roll over its debt. It needed cash, and fast. So it sold securities, to raise cash as collateral for loans. Naro had been on the phone for days trying to borrow $800 million from JPMorgan. After a week of asset dumping, the value of his funds, which had performed well for much of the year, was slipping fast. They had dropped more than 10 percent in just a few days. Once that became known, his investors would flee. Simply put, Naro was fighting for his life.

As *Le Rêve* slipped from the mouth of Long Island Sound and into the open Atlantic, Wolf was trying to keep the conversation upbeat. So was Shulman, who later would settle a civil suit brought by the New York attorney general for alleged insider trading arising out of his own panicked selling. They were supposed to be sailing the East Coast for three days. The boat was loaded with gourmet food and fine spirits, and the wives, all friends, had been looking forward to this for much of the summer. Naro's wife had already excused herself to try to calm her husband down. Wolf, summoning what good cheer he could, talked about his kids and generally kept things light.

But it was impossible. They were holed up together on the boat, where Sal's screams of pain into his cell phone echoed across the blue waters. Wolf excused himself and made for the terrace atop the ship, with its small onboard swimming pool.

Naro spotted him. "Wolfie, where the hell are you going?"

"Where am I going? I'm going to call Barack to tell him a shit storm is coming."

"I'm dying here, and he's calling Obama," Naro grumbled to his wife, turning back to his phone.

Wolf paused on the pool deck. He had spent plenty of time with Obama, but he'd never seen himself as someone who should be giving the candidate advice. The senator had plenty of smart advisers. That wasn't Wolf's role. He was just a supporter—who sometimes joked he had a "nonsexual crush" on the skinny guy. He would have taken a bullet for the senator.

Now he saw a bullet coming, and he knew he was seeing it early—maybe before anyone else close to Obama.

"Hey, happy birthday, young man," Wolf said a moment later into the phone. It was Obama's forty-sixth.

The two chatted and laughed for a few minutes, talking a little sports, as they often did, and asking after each other's wives and kids. Then Wolf took a deep breath.

"I hate to bring you bad news on your birthday," he said, "and you know I've never advised you; that's not my role. But you need to see what I'm seeing, from where I sit."

Then Wolf laid it out, straight and simple: how UBS was leveraged up, more than most, but certainly not in a class alone; how all the big shops—Lehman, Goldman, Morgan Stanley, Citigroup, Merrill Lynch, and Bear Stearns—were living on short-term credit, leveraged to the hilt, which "means they have no margin, no cushion, to take a significant loss." Then he described the nightmare's haunting spirit: all those derivatives bets on mortgage-backed securities.

Obama was quiet, taking it in, asking for a definition of this, an explanation of that. Wolf knew this stuff backward and forward—he had lived it—and he was gaining confidence with every active verb.

"Listen, Barack, this isn't about natural ups and downs of economic cycles, of growth followed by recession and then rebound. I think what we're looking at could be a once-in-a-lifetime kind of thing."

He needed to say it more clearly.

"This is a market-driven disaster that could crush Wall Street and with it the whole U.S. economy."

Wolf paused, suddenly self-conscious, high atop the flying deck of a sparkling era soon to end.

"I mean, Barack, I just thought you should know."

"Happy birthday, huh?" Obama said, ever cool. He paused for a moment. "Hey, Robert, you're an adviser now. Call Austan Goolsbee. Okay? And let's keep talking, you and me, just like this. Deal?"

"Deal."

———

Barack Obama had been given that rarest of gifts: a glimpse of the future. The rest of the world, the political world at least, was still rooted in the past.

The senator was slated to speak that night in Atlanta, at the Southern Christian Leadership Conference, an organization founded in 1957 by a young reverend named Martin Luther King, Jr., in the wake of the Montgomery Bus Boycott. Soon after its founding, it had become the organizing fist of Southern clergy—those fierce, clear-eyed pastors who would march into bayonets and swinging billy clubs leading prayers. Fifty years later Obama would stand before them as an emblem of what they had achieved.

King himself, in the last years of his life, turned his attention to what he termed "economic justice." In his 1967 book, *Where Do We Go from Here*, he championed a "guaranteed income" to turn the country's impoverished into active consumers with enough to live modestly. He wrote that "the contemporary tendency in our society is to base our distribution on scarcity, which has vanished, and to compress our abundance into the overfed mouths of the middle and upper classes until they gag with superfluity. If democracy is to have breadth of meaning, it is necessary to adjust this inequity."

King's attempt to make a moral case for not just equality before the law, but a greater equality of distribution, led some civil rights leaders such as Bayard Rustin to break with him. He appeared to be crossing into dangerous, uncharted territory. Undeterred, King gave a speech at Washington's National Cathedral on March 31, 1968, reaffirming that equal opportunity and economic possibility were issues of moral reckoning.

"One day we will have to stand before the God of history, and we will talk of things we've done," King said that night. "Yes, we will be able to say we have built gargantuan bridges to span the seas. We built gigantic buildings to kiss the skies . . . It seems to me I can hear the God of history saying, 'That was not enough! But I was hungry and ye fed me not. I was naked and ye clothed me not.'"

A few hours before, the leadership of the SCLC persuaded King to return to Memphis to support the striking garbage workers. King was reluctant to go, but felt, he told aides, that the need "to push forward the nonviolent struggle for economic justice" was too great.

He booked rooms at the Lorraine Motel and left Washington for Tennessee.

Barack Obama, in just a few days, had caught sight of an emerging catastrophe that would again draw together the issues of economics and justice. No one in Washington's power structure had been presented with a similarly dire and credible prediction from an actual captain of a Wall Street bank, the latter group having too much at stake for that level of candor.

And such a "market-driven" tidal wave would surely be headed for the dense shoreline that, only days before, Krueger and the economists had so aptly described: rickety structures—freshly painted with easy credit, but rotted beneath—that housed so much of the country's economic livelihood. Did government, in its weakened state, have the power to hold a catastrophe at bay? If such a tidal wave wreaked devastation, might it recast basic moral equations by which power and wealth had long been distributed, and perhaps even herald a rebirth of the public ideal?

When King spoke of giving democracy its full "breadth of meaning" by altering economic inequity, he was in the midst of his own struggle with a certain duality—between the transcendent character who stood at Lincoln's feet to tell of "a dream . . . deeply rooted in the American Dream" and the man who spent the ensuing years of his life walking the flat earth struggling to conjure the righteous actions with which to make real that earlier day's effusion of noble purpose. A week after that National Cathedral speech, King's death in Memphis would leave behind the image of a man, as familiar now as an old friend, giving voice to an expansive dream, perhaps big enough to bridge America's own duality between noble ideal and, at times, ignoble action—between principle and practice, word and deed.

Obama acutely understood how people painted their longings onto his welcoming presence, yearnings he would try to harness in the service of tangible change. If he could manage it, he might finally cash King's promissory note—to stand, his right hand raised, on the other end of the Mall—as the culmination of a centuries-long struggle for civil equality and as the torchbearer for King's second dream, of equality of opportunity upon which to found a truer democracy. Obama had seen the longing in the eyes of his crowds, and though he had not yet found a way to tap this longing, he understood, on some level, that his fortunes rested on how he could craft his narrative and himself into a sure vessel for that hunger.

The forces of change were now in play. Obama finished up the conversation with Wolf, his Wall Street informer, and turned his attention to polishing that night's speech. Like so many he had given, it would strive to conjure the spirit of King—or at least the spirit embodied in that well-worn image of the man. But now those hard questions of economic justice gathered around him, those questions of the second, less familiar King. They gathered in the air like the clouds of a coming storm.

SONNY'S BLUES

EIGHT MONTHS AFTER ROBERT WOLF SOUNDED THE ALARM FROM the flying deck of *Le Rêve*, Barack Obama found himself in Manhattan, tucked in the backseat of a black SUV, the UBS chief by his side, dodging potholes on Third Avenue. They had been talking regularly since Obama's birthday, and in many ways Wolf had turned out to be the gift that kept on giving.

UBS had taken heavy losses that fall, and Wolf, ahead of the curve in grasping the nature and implications of the crisis, had seen himself promoted to president and CEO of UBS Americas. In the meantime he had been working with Obama to demystify the machinery of Wall Street. Alongside the intellectually nimble Austan Goolsbee, Wolf was part of a team that helped Obama and his twenty-six-year-old speechwriter, Jon Favreau, draft a prescient speech on the country's financial perils, which the senator had delivered at NASDAQ in mid-September. It had all been there in the speech: a new framing of the country's financial dilemma.

"Amid a crisis of confidence, Roosevelt called for 'a reappraisal of values,'" Obama had begun. "He made clear that in this country . . . 'the responsible heads of finance and industry, instead of acting each for himself, must work together to achieve the common end.'" It was this idea of common cause, the senator continued, that we needed to restore. Then he laid out a plan of attack: to investigate the subprime market, ensure transparency in trading, and regulate the rating agencies. Everything flowed from the underlying point that no one can exercise sound fiscal judgment "if the information is flawed, if there is fraud or if the risks facing financial institutions are not fully disclosed." With this speech, Obama had suddenly leapt ahead of everyone in Washington—at very least the other presidential hopefuls, out stumping through the cornfields of Iowa. There was concern inside of Obama's camp about what his many Wall Street contributors would think about the speech, and then surprise at how they'd embraced it. It was a damn nice rundown, Obama thought, one of his best, highlighting what was only just dawning on the national consciousness: that Wall Street and Main Street had grown inextricably and dangerously intertwined.

The NASDAQ speech received scant coverage. Obama was trying, at that point, not to show signs of desperation, but the circumstances were even testing his preternatural calm. He told Valerie Jarrett, the Chicago businesswoman who'd introduced him and Michelle and had become his close personal adviser, that he needed her in Iowa, and she put aside her business commitments to be at his beck and call. At least now he would have someone to commiserate with in the worst moments, such as the September night when he called the home of an Iowa power broker, someone whose support he needed, only to have the man's teenage daughter answer, saying, "I'm really busy with my homework," and then hang up. He turned to Jarrett, wondering if this could get any harder.

It would, and then there'd be a first break. Finally, an opening.

In November, during a nationally televised debate in Philadelphia, Clinton bungled a question on whether she supported New York governor Eliot Spitzer's plan to give driver's licenses to illegal immigrants. She'd fudged and flip-flopped, as the other candidates piled on. At last she'd lost her storied composure, bitterly remarking to moderator Tim Russert, "You know, Tim, this is where everyone plays gotcha!" The next day she'd compounded the slip-up, releasing a video of the other candidates—all men, of course—ganging up on her, implying that the attack had more to do with sexism than her front-runner status.

Maybe it was Clinton-fatigue in the end. Or maybe Americans just like a hard-fought contest and the story of an underdog comeback. Whatever its cause, this shifting tide would carry Obama to victory in Iowa two months later, to yet another occasion for delivering a brilliant speech on national television and summoning his particular brand of magic. As he stepped onto a stage in Des Moines the night of his triumph, the gaze of the nation adjusted itself and refocused. Before them was a black man, who had just won in a 95-percent-white state, thundering, "We are one nation, we are one people, and our time has come!"

The cheers of "O-ba-ma! O-ba-ma! O-ba-ma!" rose like a roaring surf, such that he had to stop and wait, and flash the thousand-watt smile—couldn't help himself—before going on, proceeding to talk about expanding health care coverage, cutting taxes on the middle class, and ending the war in Iraq. But as he continued in his distinctive manner—

precise and lyrical, heartfelt and gently clipped—the audience waited for him to move past these policy points, for him to weave his story once again into the broader story of the nation and thereby make his victory theirs.

In three paragraphs Obama wove it tight:

"Hope is what led a band of colonists to rise up against an empire. What led the greatest of generations to free a continent and heal a nation. What led young women and young men to sit at lunch counters and brave fire hoses and march through Selma and Montgomery for freedom's cause.

"Hope"—the cheers drowned him out—"hope is what led me here today. With a father from Kenya, a mother from Kansas, and a story that could only happen in the United States of America. Hope is the bedrock of this nation. The belief that our destiny will not be written for us, but by us, by all those men and women who are not content to settle for the world as it is—who have the courage to remake the world as it should be.

"That is what we started here in Iowa and that is the message we can now carry to New Hampshire and beyond. The same message we had when we were up and when we were down, the one that can change this country—brick by brick, block by block, calloused hand by calloused hand—that together, ordinary people can do extraordinary things. Because we are not a collection of red states and blue states. We are the United States of America. And at this moment, in this election, we are ready to believe again."

Clinton would fight on, drawing on her seasoned political skills, her pluck, and a crack staff, but there was no way she, or anyone, could ultimately match, or in the end catch, Obama. Not now. Not after his come-from-behind victory and dazzling speech in the Iowa heartland. He had officially become a vessel for hope, an emblem of the very comeback a bruised and battered nation, emerging from a dark decade, pined for. As his crowds began to swell, the question became one of whether this brilliant construct, a man who seemed to fuse together so many disparate elements of the wildly diverse country, could handle the waterfall of inchoate yearnings crashing down on him.

This question was put to the candidate soon after, when in March a YouTube clip of his longtime spiritual leader, Chicago reverend Jeremiah Wright, became an overnight cable news sensation. The clip showed Wright, a man who had officiated at Obama's wedding and his daughters' baptisms, swapping out "God bless America" with "God damn America" in a fit of wild-eyed, white-robed histrionics.

Obama was compelled to respond to Wright's tirade, and he did, once again in an extraordinary speech. The address spoke directly to where he, Obama, fit in the nation's struggle with the "original sin" of slavery and its bitter harvest of racial strife. But it did something far more profound in placing the candidate at the meeting point of a still largely segregated America, in a unique position to speak hard-nosed yet sympathetic truth to black and white America alike. From this vantage point, Obama seemed to promise, implicitly, to heal the wounds that still divided us. Those well-worn stanzas about a father from Kenya and a mother from Kansas were now widened into a full symphonic expression of unity overcoming mistrust. Obama paired Reverend Wright's angry rants to the dark suspicions of his beloved grandmother—"who would often express fears of black men and uttered stereotypes that made me cringe"—explaining that he could not "disown" either one. They "are both a part of me," he said, just as it was clear that they were both part of a still-divided nation aching for wholeness.

The YouTube video of the speech soon replaced Wright's on the media loop, closing the issue. It was, however, a moment of growth for the emerging candidate. Though, later, many would claim credit for approving the race speech, all Obama's top aides advised against his giving it. They said either don't do it now, or don't do it at all. Obama shucked them off, all of them. He knew what he could do from a dais. He told them he'd need a weekend to write it; their job was to prepare the terrain for him to deliver it.

In the yin of crisis, he seemed to spot the yang of opportunity.

Which was what Obama was hoping to do today, a cool early-spring day in Manhattan, as he raced toward Cooper Union, a major economic speech in hand and Robert Wolf at his side. The intervening eight months since Wolf's early warning had played out in ways neither man could have imagined. By this time, late March 2008, everyone was eager to get close to Obama. But Wolf had been there, a true believer, before the senator won the nation's popularity contest. That counted for a lot. The two had developed an easy rapport in the meantime and discussed loan securitization with the same chummy informality they enjoyed when talking about the Bulls and Knicks.

As an adviser, Wolf had been quietly upping his game, passing along to Obama the analyses of UBS's economists and staying up nights to do his own research, digging beneath the era's accepted wisdom. In another memo to his fellow bosses at UBS, this one in January, Wolf predicted that the financial markets would soon collapse, causing a severe recession with at least two quarters of starkly negative growth. He had a bleaker view than most, both at UBS and inside Team Obama, but the presidential candidate listened to him attentively as he ran through his analysis.

"Barack," Wolf now quipped, "you're doing pretty much the same speech you did in the fall—when no one gave a shit."

"No doubt," Obama agreed. "But a lot has changed since then."

No doubt.

Just two weeks before, on March 16, JPMorgan agreed to buy Bear Stearns, which was teetering on the brink of collapse, for a measly $2 a share. Sweetening the deal was the Fed, which guaranteed to fund up to $30 billion of Bear Stearns' least liquid assets. Now, as the new Democratic front-runner arrived at Cooper Union, site of a famous 1860 speech that catapulted Lincoln toward the presidency, crowds and press clogged the streets of Lower Manhattan: another emergency, another big speech.

Standing above the rest, lighthouse tall, was a grinning Paul Volcker. Volcker had been hovering around the campaign since the prior summer, but having endorsed Obama only in January, this would be his debut as an official adviser. Over the years, the eighty-year-old former Fed chairman had become a figure of grumbling, unassailable credibility. His decision to tighten the money supply in the early 1980s had plunged the country into a recession, but also finally ended a decade of stubborn inflation. Though a hugely controversial decision at the time, it was now seen as the tough-love approach that laid the groundwork for years of economic growth. Volcker had nonetheless been replaced by Reagan in 1987 for not being a strong proponent of deregulation. It had been, and still was, Volcker's view that without serious "rules of the road," backed by the law, firms would find ways to profit that put the markets at risk. It turned out to be a prophetic stance, from the 1987 market crash on, and proved only more so in the current election year. Volcker now saw reregulation as a matter of the country's economic survival.

Since his victory in Iowa, Obama had been drawing top economic talent from both parties. Volcker's graybeard twin today was William Donaldson, a Republican who served under Nixon and Reagan and was George W. Bush's 2003 pick to head the SEC. On the other side of the ideological aisle was economist Laura Tyson, former Council of Economic Advisors chair under Clinton and one of the few leading figures to predict disaster from a soon-to-burst housing bubble. Next to her was Robert Reich, the peripatetic former labor secretary, who collided with Bob Rubin and his minions in the early days of the Clinton administration. Robert Wolf and Austan Goolsbee rounded out the team.

The advisers all agreed on at least one thing: the disequilibrium of consumption and production in the United States had led Wall Street and the federal government, in their dicey modern partnership, to overcompensate with easy credit, which had led to underpriced risk across the economic landscape. The team was racking their brains for what to do about it. No one was quite sure how to deleverage the world's largest economy.

The speech, like Obama's best, managed to weigh the ideological with the pragmatic. He could simultaneously mix neo-Rooseveltian rhetoric ("a free market was never meant to be a free license to take whatever you can get, however you can get it") with the practical endorsement of competent governance ("We've put in place rules of the road to make competition fair and open, and honest, we've done this not to stifle but rather to advance prosperity and liberty"). The subject didn't carry the deep personal insights, and subtle confessions, that his race speech did, but within months his analysis would form a starting point for reforms.

"The concentration of economic power and the failures of our political system to protect the American economy and the American consumers from its worst excesses have been a staple of our past: most famously in the 1920s, when such excesses ultimately plunged the country in the Great Depression. That is when government stepped in to create a series of regulatory structures, from FDIC to the Glass-Steagall Act, to serve as a corrective, to protect the American people and American business."

The latter, Glass-Steagall, was, in essence, repealed in 1999 when the Gramm-Leach-Bliley Act, with support from Bill Clinton's team of Bob Rubin acolytes, led by then–Treasury secretary Larry Summers, withdrew the original provision preventing bank holding companies from owning other financial companies. In particular, it affirmed the recent merger of Citigroup and Travelers, two unique financial entities that would not have been able to consummate their merger, a vast entity that Rubin would soon sit atop as chairman.

Obama now spoke of repairing and restoring a regulatory framework. In particular, he envisioned a broad swath of new regulations that would be able to properly monitor the chimerical nature of Wall Street. Across the board, he saw a new structure of oversight, from increasing the purview of the Federal Reserve to setting in place consumer protections based on a broader principle that "we need policies that once again recognize that we are in this together. And we need the powerful, the wealthiest among us—those who are in attendance here today—we need you to get behind that agenda."

The coverage of the speech, this time, was heavy and laudatory. Obama remarked several times from the dais, "As I said last fall at NASDAQ . . . ," and the point was lost on no one. He had called it, just as he had with Iraq. He'd been ahead of the pack, ahead of everyone, and only now were events and consensus catching up to him. Interviewers lined up, cheek to jowl—Charlie Gibson of ABC, Maria Bartiromo of CNBC, staff writers from the *Times* and *Journal*. Obama seemed to have taken his game to another level: in the zone, every shot a swish.

"Barack Obama's speech on the financial crisis was a remarkable breakthrough," gushed Robert Kuttner, the tough-minded editor of *The American Prospect*. Kuttner had, up until then, been reserved in his enthusiasm for Obama. But no longer. "First he connected all the dots—between the complete dismantling of financial regulation, the declining economic opportunity and security for ordinary people, the current financial meltdown, and the political influence of Wall Street as the driver of these changes. Astounding! I wish I had written the speech. It is this kind of leadership and truth telling that is the predicate for the shift in public opinion required to produce legislative change.

"The speech was Roosevelt quality: the president as teacher-in-chief," Kuttner continued. "Those who felt that Obama was capable of real growth that will transcend the campaign's early and somewhat feeble domestic policy proposals should feel vindicated. The speech was courageous, in that it goes well beyond the current Democratic Party consensus, and one can only wonder about the reaction of some of Obama's own financial backers."

Several of those financial backers were gathered two weeks later on April 11 in a hotel ballroom in Washington for a meeting of what might well be the world's most exclusive club: the Financial Services Forum. Its members were the CEOs of many of the very largest financial institutions in America. Together they controlled $20 trillion, roughly the annual GDP of the United States and China combined.

The forum's semiannual meetings usually drew a majority of the CEOs, but at this particular spring meeting in 2008, only about half of them had shown up. Many of those absent found themselves instead on corporate jets to China and the Persian Gulf, on their way to meet with the heads of those states' sovereign-wealth funds to plead for capital infusions. This close to Bear Stearns' implosion, the sense of urgency among Wall Street's top executives was so great that they had decided to pass up a private session with Treasury secretary Hank Paulson and Ben Bernanke to meet instead with Saudis and Kuwaitis and Chinese government officials. Paulson and Bernanke might tell them what the U.S. government would do in the event of a financial death spiral, but the Kuwaitis could tell the CEOs just how much, at today's prices, it would cost them to avoid this fate.

One forum attendee, however, was especially happy to be in the mix: Greg Fleming, Merrill Lynch's number two. He was just glad to still be employed at Merrill, the company that in 1914, with its first storefront offices, essentially invented the brokerage business in America. As he gazed now across the crowd of senior executives waiting for Ben Bernanke in the conference room at the venerable Willard Hotel, Fleming could not help but consider how much had changed in the past two years, since the spring of 2006.

Thinking back across those two years, he could neatly mark both time and distance traveled—for himself, his industry, and the wider country—with two dinners.

The first: in May 2006. That's when Merrill's headstrong CEO, Stanley O'Neal, took Fleming out to dinner to tell him he was planning to fire a friend of Fleming's. The executive, Jeff Kronthal, who was the head of fixed income at Merrill, had noticed that the number of new mortgage holders not making even a single payment—a typically tiny number, less than 1 percent—had more than doubled in just a few months. A longtime risk manager who had once worked at Salomon Brothers, Kronthal dug into some CDO bundles and saw just how dramatically underwriting standards had collapsed. He recommended that Merrill reduce its exposure in mortgage derivatives, which at the time was only $4 billion. But these mortgage derivatives were also the company's profit engine—as they were for the rest of Wall Street—and the risk-averse Kronthal stood in the way of those profits. O'Neal told Fleming he hoped to replace Kronthal with an executive whose background lay in sales.

Fleming strongly opposed the move, contending that Kronthal was a man of good character and that if he said there was a problem, O'Neal, who had no background in risk management, would do well to listen. By the time the entrées were served, the two men were sitting in tense silence. O'Neal eventually cut Fleming off midsentence to call for the check. Soon after, Kronthal was fired, and under O'Neal's management the company would go on to add an astonishing $50 billion in CDOs between the summer of 2006 and the late spring of 2007.

That latter date was around the same time that Fleming got a call about the second of the two dinners, this one with Barack Obama. Fleming, raised by two teachers in upstate New York, had been a lifelong Democrat. When his friend Mark Gallogly, the billionaire number two at Blackstone, the huge private-equity firm, called to say he was organizing a Washington dinner for Obama, Fleming jumped at the opportunity.

On June 20, 2007, two dozen executives slipped inconspicuously from Manhattan to D.C. and gathered in a private room at Johnny's Half Shell, a pricey spot on Capitol Hill known for its barbeque shrimp, Asiago cheese grits, and Maryland crab cakes, which run thirty bucks a pair. It was a first encounter with Obama for most of them, including Paul Volcker, who had expressed an interest in meeting the junior senator. Gallogly, who had been greatly impressed with Obama, sent the former Fed chair a packet of reading material on the senator, including his two books. Now, as Obama moved lightly through the crowd of money men, Fleming managed to score a little face time, chatting with him over drinks. The two men, both forty-five, seemed to hit it off. Fleming was a graduate of Yale Law School, and Obama, of course, Harvard Law, so naturally they had people in common.

As everyone seated himself for dinner, the group went around the table doing introductions: Larry Fink, one of the inventors of mortgage-backed securities, who was now head of the huge asset-management firm

BlackRock; Lehman CEO Dick Fuld; Gary Cohn, the sharp-minded chief operating officer at Goldman; the legendary Volcker. Then the head of fixed income and the putative number two at Bear Stearns took a stab at levity.

"I'm Warren Spector of Bear Stearns, the current scourge of Wall Street."

This drew appreciative laughter from the room. Obama laughed, too. The failure of Bear's two mortgage derivative–laden hedge funds had come in late spring, and since then debate had swirled around how the collapse should be viewed: as a one-off overreach in the mortgage derivative sector by Bear, or as the first of several implosions likely to hit mortgage derivative–heavy funds on Wall Street.

If it turned out to be the latter, of course, that would mean the end of the line for some of those currently sizing up Obama. So that would never track. This was Wall Street, after all, where the world's smartest people still flocked, where everyone's risk-management team was still the best in the business, every firm's traders still the most ingenious. Everyone knew there was trouble in mortgage-backed securities. But everyone in the room could still muster confidence, albeit with a bit of added effort. Financial innovation meant there was always a way to price and sell off risk, even for mortgage securities. The bottom line: those astronomical salaries for 2007—already looking like the best year Wall Street had ever known—were utterly justified. Or so the consensus went.

The night was set up so Obama could play for the thousands these men gave in campaign donations—and the many thousands more they could compel their colleagues and friends to give—and he didn't disappoint. He said, among other things, what they wanted to hear, that he believed unreservedly in private enterprise, the efficient and productive distribution of capital, and the "need for a strong financial sector." Fleming watched from across the table, sitting next to his good buddy Larry Fink, a billionaire, like many of the men in the room. Fleming wasn't in that league—not even close. But despite that, or because of it, he was ready to leap ahead of the pack, ever the self-made man. When questions over dessert turned to the only issue anyone there much cared about— whether Obama would raise taxes on the wealthy—Fleming jumped in: "I think, based on the way things have gone, it's ridiculous to think that taxes shouldn't go up." No one there would have said this, but suddenly just about all the financiers nodded. Obama smiled. You could all but see him making a mental note: Fleming.

Fleming was dining in Manhattan three months later with his family when the phone rang. He figured on ignoring it. It was his daughter's birthday, and they were planning to follow up dinner with a Broadway show. He looked down at his vibrating BlackBerry and read, "Unknown Number." He accepted the call.

"I was impressed with what you said at the dinner," Obama said, jumping right in. "Especially about taxes and everyone carrying their fair share."

A startled Fleming thanked the senator and, whispering an apology to his wife over the cupped mouthpiece, slipped outside the restaurant. They chatted for a few minutes, and Obama explained that he wanted Fleming to take a more significant role in his campaign, fund-raising and maybe more.

Fleming paused. In the few months since their dinner in D.C., he had become aware of just what a catastrophe Merrill was facing. It was only in the past month that he'd begun to realize he'd been more right than he had ever wanted to be: those mortgage derivatives could take the company down.

"Sorry," Fleming told Obama reluctantly. "There's going to be an awful lot going on at Merrill in the coming months." He explained that he had better not take on any extracurricular activities, though he would continue to be a contributor. The two men agreed to stay in touch, and Fleming wished Obama "all the luck in the world." Both men would need it.

A month later, in mid-October, Merrill chief Stan O'Neal was abruptly fired after the firm lost $2.3 billion in its third quarter. Fleming was named interim CEO, and about a month after that, in early November, the *Wall Street Journal* reported that Merrill had fraudulently handled its derivatives book. Fleming suddenly found himself in front of a crowded room of employees, reporters, and stock analysts. Greed had so quickly and thoroughly switched to fear—fear laced with a watch-your-back insecurity—that Merrill's future, with its stock plummeting, seemed to rest on a few careful words to the gathered mob. Fleming managed it with a quip and a disarming shrug. He would not try to deny any reports he hadn't had a chance to check out for himself. He said he was sure there was plenty going on inside of Merrill about which he was unaware.

It worked. In the court of public opinion, Fleming was granted the time to get up to speed on Merrill's inner workings, and the company's sliding share price stabilized. His saving grace was convincing deniability: he had made the wrong career choice. He was a traditional investment banker, an expert in assessing the value of financial companies for sales, mergers, and the like. As Wall Street's great debt-shuffling and power-trading operations grew to overwhelm the lower-margin business of actual investing, Fleming watched the raging river of fixed-income funds from across the world flow through the coffers of Goldman, Lehman, Bear, and eventually Merrill, on its way to slaking America's seemingly bottomless thirst for debt.

So it was credible that Greg Fleming, the odd man out in Stan O'Neal's regime, didn't know much about Merrill's main line of business. A few weeks later, after conducting his own investigation—using dozens of auditors, poring over months of trading—Fleming announced publicly that the *Journal* report on fraud at Merrill had been false. (The paper subsequently published a clarification.) Merrill soon hired John Thain, a former second-in-command at Goldman, to take over as its top executive. Fleming, after all, had crucial work to do as an investment banker: sell off Merrill's gems. Schmoozing in D.C. with top executives at the Financial Services Forum could, thereby, only be a good thing. Fleming was looking to unload Merrill's prime assets, after all, and here was a roomful of potential buyers. Merrill's position was not dissimilar to Sailfish's the prior summer. The firm was glutted with a cancer of mortgage securities, namely $54 billion in mortgage derivatives, an astounding $51 billion of which it had purchased since the spring of 2006. To sell them in a market with no buyers, where their value upon sale would be marked to nearly zero, was suicide. This meant the company, leveraged thirty to one, needed to build up cash to offset the tanking value of its CDOs by selling its most valuable assets.

As Bernanke now spoke, Fleming looked across the room, a plush little second-floor chamber in the Willard called The Nest. The Fed chairman was being circumspect, not saying very much. In the wake of Bear's collapse Bernanke had opened up the Fed's discount window to investment firms for the first time, and now the chairman ran a short tutorial on how investment houses would be treated differently from banks, which had been using the window almost since the Fed's creation in 1913.

It was not until the next session that afternoon that things picked up. Treasury secretary Hank Paulson arrived full of his famous manic energy. Most people in the room knew Paulson personally; until 2006 he had sat on the other side of the felt table, as the CEO of Goldman and himself a member of the Financial Services Roundtable. Today his message was that familiarity should not breed familial goodwill; contempt might be more appropriate.

Everyone should know that the Bear Stearns deal was a special case, Paulson said firmly, "and not something we *ever* intend to repeat." JPMorgan's number two exhibited a look of studied indifference as glances were cast his way. All the executives by now had had a chance to look over the sweet deal offered to JPMorgan chief Jamie Dimon to buy Bear Stearns. Now everyone, thinking of any kind of merger or consolidation, wanted a "Jamie Deal."

Paulson said that there'd be no help coming from the U.S. government, and that they should all be out looking for capital anywhere they could find it. A second message: deleverage, and do it fast. But he assured them this was only to shore up their cushions of capital for some unseen, and unknown, threat. Based on his read at Treasury, he said, things were on the mend. The housing bubble had burst, he stressed, and housing values would not be dropping much further. Not that some mortgage toxicity didn't still plague balance sheets, he acknowledged, but his bigger concern was the sluggish economy. He and President Bush had just pushed through a $168 billion stimulus in an attempt to jolt it. With stabilizing real estate values, a few more rate cuts, an opening up of the Fed discount window, and this stimulus package, the Treasury secretary said, "we should manage to get through this period just fine."

At one end of the table, Robert Wolf sat in silence. He knew this was what Paulson had to say. The whole game was about confidence, as it always was. Everything was fine—until it wasn't. The government wouldn't be coming to the aid of any more financial giants—until it did. Volcker and a few others who were encircling Obama were convinced the whole system was on the verge of collapse. Wolf wondered if he was the only one in this plush room who agreed.

The CEOs had a blind spot, Wolf thought. With all their leverage, all it would take is one bad week, one speed bump, and they would be facing catastrophe. He thought about challenging Paulson with a targeted question, but he held back. Why bother? Though he never publicized it, people in the room knew he was Obama's man. He had put his money on Team Obama washing away Team Bush, including Paulson and his gang. Wolf was waiting, betting on regime change.

Fleming, at the other end of the table, shook his head, thinking of all he had been through in the prior year. For Paulson to point to "strong fundamentals" was to miss the point. It was really about trust, a loss of basic trust that Wall Street was resting on anything resembling firm ground. One rumor, one false report in the *Wall Street Journal*, and a ninety-four-year-old firm like Merrill had been brought to its knees overnight. Fleming was especially unconvinced by the secretary's assertion that the real estate market had stabilized, that, as Paulson said, "the worst was over." Had Treasury at least put together a what-if strategy?

"Hank, what are you planning to do if the real estate situation happens to get worse, which of course it could, and bleeds through into the larger economy?" Fleming asked. "That could create real problems for quite a few large firms and trigger wider systemic issues."

Paulson glared at Fleming. This was precisely the sort of question, a worst-case-scenario question, that he had been steering the conversation away from.

"I'm not responding to that," Paulson said, his face growing red. Then he turned the heat on Fleming: "Listen, you better focus on Merrill! We'll worry about the larger economy, which is doing fine. You worry about your shop." He turned back to the larger group. "All of you should. We're done with capital assistance from Washington. You're on your own."

The room was quiet. No follow-up questions.

In the days that followed, Fleming sized up the landscape for mergers and acquisitions, as he had been trained to do . . . starting right at home. His most pressing mission would be to assess the value of Merrill's franchise and figure out what it might take to sell it. Word on the Street was that Lehman was in serious trouble. Fleming *knew* that Merrill was in trouble, but he also knew that there was only one institution with both the will and capacity at this moment to buy a large Wall Street investment house: Bank of America. One buyer, two banks. The question: Who would get there first?

After the Financial Services Forum meeting, Hank Paulson returned to Treasury. His department had tried to project the image of engagement and competence, but behind the scenes they were accomplishing little.

A top Treasury official who served under Paulson put succinctly what others would later reaffirm: "We mostly spun our wheels because there was no process at Treasury that could get much done. Everything had to be run through the frenetic, short attention spans of Hank. You needed to get him to focus, which was a battle, and then hold his attention with something catchy you said in the first sentence or that'd be that. Nothing would happen and weeks of work would be for naught."

The bottom line, the official added, was that "during the eight months since the credit markets first seized up, that first heart attack in August 2007, we at Treasury had done very little. Almost nothing, to be fair. We kicked into high gear for the frantic rush to sell off Bear Stearns, but that was an emergency. We had blown that time, those months when it was clear that real trouble was coming, and we'd done nothing of any real significance."

Now the clock was ticking. Several CEOs at the forum meeting had scheduled their trip to D.C. strategically. If they had to spend a day in Washington, it was going to be the day *after* the forum event, when the finance ministers of the G7 countries, seven of the world's largest economies, were in town. That night, April 11, there was going to be a dinner in Treasury's ornate "Cash Room," a grand two-story hall decked out with seven different types of marble. Under three sweeping brass chandeliers, Paulson and the G7 ministers dined with Jamie Dimon, John Thain, Morgan Stanley chief John Mack, Deutsche Bank CEO Joe Ackerman, and others.

Paulson later recalled how he went around the room asking each of them how they had ended up at this difficult juncture.

"Greed, leverage, and lax investor standards," John Mack said. "We took conditions for granted and we as an industry lost discipline."

The CEO of TIAA-CREF, the enormous teachers' pension fund, said the big funds used to think they "knew a lot more about these [mortgage-backed] assets" than they did. "But we've been burned, and until we see large-scale transparency in assets, we're not going to buy."

Mervyn King, a short-tempered British regulator, quickly grew impatient with this sort of talk. "You are all bright people, but you failed," he said. "Risk management is hard. So the lesson is we can't let you get as big as you were and do the damage that you've done, or get as complex as you were, because you can't manage the risk element."

King was half right—but only half. The banks had grown so big and fragile because they had created a host of profitable intermediary steps, separating risk from sound and sober assessment, from basic financial accountability. The risk had instead been passed around, sale by sale, until the marketplace itself held a kind of aggregated risk, a vast web of credit connections resting on nothing more solid than confidence.

Two top Treasury officials, Neel Kashkari and Phillip Swagel, had already created a memo on bailouts that they called the "Break the Glass" Bank Recapitalization Plan—a ten-page apocalyptic scenario outline that would later provide the rubric for TARP. Its idea was straightforward: Treasury would purchase toxic assets from the banks, unwind them using a private-asset intermediary, such as BlackRock, and then sell them to maximize value for the people who would ultimately be on the hook: the taxpayers.

Two days after the Cash Room dinner, Paulson looked at the memo with reticence. If they ever actually needed to implement the plan, he said, they would never get it through Congress. He was more skeptical of the plan's political viability than he was concerned about its effect on the economy. And if word got out, it could send the markets into a panic.

That was Paulson's dilemma. To act in a responsible, preparatory way would show what the government was planning to do in the event of an emergency. This is something that firms could then factor into their risk models, which would affect everything from how banks or nonbanks invested their capital to how they structured, and protected, their pay packages. It was enough that Bernanke had opened up his discount window to investment banks, probably the most dramatic shift in Fed policy since the Great Depression. If anything, now was the time to match federal largess with firm boundaries. He had to show confidence that he expected no more disasters, and wasn't planning for any more public funds to help Wall Street.

As a Christian Scientist, Paulson fell back on the old standard: God helps those who help themselves. The group agreed that the potential havoc that this "Break the Glass" plan could wreak on the market, even just in undermining confidence, meant it needed to be closely guarded.

In the meantime, Paulson would try to find market solutions to the impending disaster and preempt the gathering storm.

What he did do was pick up the phone and call Dick Fuld, CEO of Lehman Brothers, which looked next in line to fall after Bear.

"Dick," he said, cutting to the chase. "You really need to find a buyer."

———

What amazed Obama was how big the whole circus had become, and how fast.

By the third week in April, he was a global phenomenon, the focus of acute, almost frenzied attention, at the head of a wave.

It had built, strong and steady, since Iowa. But coming out of Cooper Union, he was a man touched by the gods—the toast of both coasts, the media, the intelligentsia, Hollywood, Washington, and even Wall Street, which still knew how to invest with targeted might when a growth stock hit its stride. He'd been tested on race, and temperament, and had passed brilliantly with his stunning speech. Race issue: check. He'd pulled together a bipartisan economic team and leapt ahead of the pack on dealing with the country's growing financial shakiness. Policy prescience: check.

To be sure, with each stride there was a hedged bet being laid down by Middle America, wary by nature of the Harvard-trained darling of the elites and the rising tenor of the enthusiasm he was stoking.

That skepticism was harvested with steady sure-handedness by Hillary Clinton, who was counted out after Obama's string of victories in January and February. No, she wasn't down, not yet. America loves a race, has a long history with buyer's remorse, and always liked Hillary best when she was fighting for her life—as the First Lady, living through an adultery nightmare, and many times since.

Obama wanted it to be over with. After his string of primary victories, he was way ahead on delegates, and ready to be the party's putative standard-bearer. He was tired. He craved sleep. He missed the girls. Let it be over.

But Texas and Ohio wouldn't let that happen on March 4. He lost them both, big states. Texas was no surprise. But Ohio, the bellwether state in so many national contexts, seemed within his grasp. If he could beat her there, it would end. It didn't, even after the Obama campaign spent nearly $20 million on media and organization.

Obama was crestfallen, but he stayed cool and steady. On the night of his Ohio loss, his senior staff was waiting for the strong words of criticism. They never came. The road was long, he told them; they were doing their best. Losses like this would happen; they'd eventually make it. The most pointed he got: an offhand comment leaving the Ohio postmortem meeting, when he told Axelrod, "Now, tell me again what $10 million in advertising [in Ohio] got us."

For some on the staff, this equanimity was just shy of amazing, even unsettling. Obama was changing—his eyes now on the prize. Looking out on mobs crushed against barricades, reaching to touch him, to be healed, the campaign's innermost circle started to use its nickname for him, Black Jesus. The pressure of hope and expectation, of almost religious fervor, seemed to quiet and settle him. To establish their bearings, that he was mortal, they'd tell stories of the sometimes tetchy, short-tempered candidate of a year before. A favorite was from June of 2007, when they were flying back and forth to Iowa while trying to squeeze in votes in the Senate. Obama was on the plane with Robert Gibbs and Reggie Love, grousing nonstop. This was foolish. Miserable. A waste of time.

Gamely, Gibbs stepped in.

"All right, Barack, just think of one thing you like about all this. Just one thing, and focus on it. Maybe that'll help."

Obama was unreachable. "There is not even one thing I can think of. Not even one."

"Well, I can tell you one thing, boss," said Reggie Love, the former Duke basketball player hired to be Obama's aide in 2006, who was regularly getting mobbed by girls in Iowa gymnasiums. "I'm loving this! Hope that helps."

"No, it doesn't, Reggie," the senator mumbled, unmoved even by this strong showing of empathic esprit de corps.

Now some senior staffers yearned for that grumbling guy, a guy they once knew, rather than the calm, Olympian presence looking down from on high, touching the outstretched hands of true believers.

Then, on April 22, the night of the loss in Pennsylvania, bemusement about their sainted candidate began to sour into concern. You can't win America just by taking the northeastern and California corridors, no matter how many times you appear on *Charlie Rose*. After a brutal six-week campaign, he'd lost Pennsylvania to Clinton by a whopping ten points. She was out of money, facing the precipice of a "mathematical impossibility" in delegates, but heroically unbowed. "Tonight, more than ever," she said, in her acceptance speech, "I need your help to continue this journey . . . We can only keep winning if we can keep competing with an opponent who outspends us so massively."

After Obama's concession, his inner circle flew to Chicago for a crisis meeting. Forget about delegate counts. She was showing, to one and all, how beatable he was. News reports began to trot out Bill Clinton's quote from January, about how the media were going easy on Obama, giving him a bye about voicing some generalized support for the Iraq War as a senator: "This whole thing," Bill Clinton groused, "is the biggest fantasy I've ever seen." Now the line, taken out of context, seemed to be a generalized critique of the Obama phenomenon.

Republicans, meanwhile, were offering their own version, mentioning how little experience Obama had doing anything other than managing his own one-man narrative.

In Chicago, at Obama's house, Pete Rouse and Valerie Jarrett conferred with their man. The rest of the team was gathering in the living room. The three of them stood near the kitchen, an ideal trio, in its way.

Valerie was the first among equals, with her role as part of the campaign but above it. As adviser, friend, protector, older sister, soul mate, and, in some ways, creator—the matchmaker, after all, of Barack and Michelle—she watched him evenly, asked how he was feeling. He didn't need to say much. She knew he was in there, trying to work through the complex equations of his place at the center of all this noise, and she was happy to see Pete.

Rouse was also separate from the campaign's senior staff, but with a role of unique consequence and clout. At sixty-one, he was Obama's Washington anchor—and a truly original character in the nation's capital. He was Tom Daschle's right-hand man, his chief of staff for twenty years, who rose—as Daschle became Senate majority leader in 2000—into a role that drew him the moniker "101st Senator."

When Obama won his Senate seat in 2004, Daschle was losing his, after twenty-eight years.

One coming, the other going, they became fast friends, and Daschle persuaded much of his staff, from Rouse on down, to move from the most powerful office in the Senate to that of the bright young man from Illinois. This was unheard-of. First off, skilled and seasoned staffs in the

Senate—and Daschle's was about the best—have never been known to be transferrable. But this one was. Daschle became Obama's mentor, with Obama's new chief of staff, Rouse, as his guide.

Obama leveled with them both when he arrived, telling Rouse, "I know what I'm good at and I know what I'm not good at. I can give a speech." He continued, "But I don't know how to build a large staff and negotiate the potential pitfalls of being a relatively high-profile new-comer to the Senate." They set up a game plan for Obama. Rouse was a legendary memo writer. He handed Obama a black notebook, the "Senate Strategy," laying out how Obama would stay quiet, work hard, and try to learn the rhythms of how laws are made. Options were developed based on whether he decided to run for president. But they are all thinking of when—when would he run.

Everyone was. So to map the realm of possibility, and build up favors in the event of a dash for the presidency, Obama went on the road in 2006. He gave speeches, and wooed the auditoriums and banquet halls as every Democratic senator's handsomest-ever friend, and that's before he opened his mouth. Then it was time for decisions and—in what would soon become a storied encounter—he and Daschle sat in the kitchen area of a pricey Washington restaurant. Obama wanted to know if Daschle thought he was ready, wondering if he shouldn't wait and get more experience. After all, Obama had only one year actually walking the halls of Congress before he went on the banquet circuit, and of course he needed a lot more experience before becoming president. But the system was busted, terribly, and in this age of 24/7 pie fights that pass for political discourse, having a thin record for others to shoot at, to attack, may have been the only way to move forward. Daschle had just finished a race where Republican John Thune and his ops research staff picked at Daschle's twenty-six years of votes like the vulture at Prometheus' liver. All Daschle did, day after day, was try to explain away mischaracterizations of his record trumpeted on cable, online, and in ads, until he collapsed in defeat.

And maybe it was true—that there was simply no way a senator with any experience could win the presidency anymore, considering that none had managed it since John F. Kennedy. Obama, of course, was never able to fully internalize that answer. Within a year, he was already focused singularly on the presidency. By early 2008 he had been running for elective office for much of his adult life, mostly as a one-man show.

Now, after Pennsylvania, his managerial nascence was showing—
and Pete Rouse, flying to Chicago, knew it.

He understood how Obama operated from moments when no one
was looking, how unflinchingly loyal he was to everyone around him—
grateful, really, that they were doing what they could on his behalf. His
instincts were to always push for consensus, and then affirm it, usually
with some trenchant twist that would make it his own. But Rouse knew
that Obama, comfortable reaching for the sweeping concept, and trying to spot paths of historical consequence, was fairly easily managed.
Which was what had been happening. He'd been deferring too much
to political consultant David Axelrod and David Plouffe, his campaign
director, and the wider staff. He was the candidate. They were the managers. So, fine, manage me. I've got plenty to keep me occupied.

Obama turned to Rouse, as the group beckoned from the other room.
"Pete, what can I do here that I'm not doing?"

"Barack," Rouse said, looking hard at his friend. "You need to take
ownership of this campaign."

Obama nodded. Ownership. Got it. That night was a big one in a
little-noted area that often defines the fortunes of leaders: management
skills. For all his intellectual firepower, Obama had none. Over the next
few hours, and next few days, a new structure was set up. There would
be a nightly phone call, led by Obama, with the senior staff, no matter
where he was or what else competed for his time. The agenda for each
night would be drawn up by Anita Dunn, who'd worked for everyone
from Jimmy Carter to Daschle, had run Obama's precampaign political
action committee in 2006, was now a political consultant, and had been
called on by Obama to assist the campaign in early 2007. Axelrod was
upset; he was being usurped. Despite his respect and affection for Axelrod—the man who had taken him to the Senate and now the precipice
of the Democratic nomination—Obama, with Rouse's support, insisted.
Dunn was in.

It was a lesson in management, care of Rouse. There are certain things
the boss needs. And if he doesn't demand them, it's no one's fault but
his own. The campaign righted itself from there. Obama began to understand the dynamic operating beneath him, some of it dysfunctional.
The nightly calls solved next-day problems before they occurred, and the
calls would be continued, religiously, through the presidential transition.

A first lesson. There would be many more to come.

Reflecting on this period in an Oval Office interview, Obama divided the management issue, like most others, along the great before-and-after divide of his life.

"I distinguish between the campaign and the presidency," he said. "In each one there were different phases. In the campaign, my management evolved partly because my position in the race evolved and my prospects evolved—in the same way that my secret service protection kept evolving." He described how his detail grew from eight agents to forty, after Iowa, to a "massive enterprise by the time I won the nomination," and that "the same was true of the campaign" staff.

The president ran through the campaign's evolution: the core team of David Axelrod and David Plouffe; the eventual need to bring in Pete Rouse and Valerie Jarrett, to make sure everyone was "more disciplined"; and onward through the primaries and into the general election, as the campaign grew and became more organizationally complex. To be sure, he, as the candidate, was the one being managed down to the frenetic minute. But he needed to "own" it and guide it. As president, atop the most complex managerial organism on the planet, it would become much more difficult.

Carmine Visone looked out of his twelfth-story window at one of Lehman Brothers' Midtown Manhattan offices. On a warm late-April day, they'd put out the awning and the outdoor tables at Bice, his favorite Italian restaurant.

This was his seasonal ritual, for years. Reserve the corner table on the street, and watch from his office window. And at the appointed time, see if his lunch date had arrived and been seated. He hated to wait. Now he'd always show up five minutes after his dining companion, usually someone from another investment bank or real estate trust, had settled in, just in time for the Pellegrino to be served. As the manager of Lehman's vast real estate portfolio, Carmine had, he felt, at fifty-nine, waited plenty in his life. Let the other guy fuckin' wait.

If Greg Fleming was in an ideal perch to see the debt mess and enter a strange kind of footrace with Hank Paulson for Bank of America's favor, Carmine was the guy who had been around long enough to see exactly what had gone wrong from the bottom up.

But he'd never have called himself an old-timer. That he'd worked hard to preserve his youth was understandable: he'd been at Lehman for longer than some of his current colleagues had been alive. It was a different company and a different world back in 1971, when he filled out his application for a job as a bookkeeper, working in Lehman's basement.

As a young tough on the streets of Brooklyn, Visone had gotten into his fair share of trouble, so it was a bit unexpected when he landed on his feet with a job at Lehman. His father was a bricklayer, an Italian immigrant who taught Carmine to assess value with the fundamental premise that "you're fucking worthless—you want to be something, you find something of value, take it into your hands, and hold on tight." As a young man and a big one at that, Carmine worked out furiously to transform himself, as a bodybuilder—he once won the "Mr. Tall Brooklyn" title—and then worked his way up from there. When he was made a managing director at Lehman in 1988, he had been at the company seventeen years.

Dick Fuld, who had joined the company in 1969, two years ahead of Carmine, took him aside.

"You know, Carmine," he said, "I think this will be the last time a guy like you is named managing partner."

Carmine wasn't sure if he meant it to be a compliment, but he knew what Fuld was saying. It didn't take a rocket scientist. By then, the entire baby boom talent pool had started racing to the Street, and most of them had never met a bricklayer.

"Thanks, Dick," Carmine said, taking it as a kind of congratulations.

There was more truth in Fuld's remark than the future CEO himself probably even realized. Certain differences between Carmine and his fellow managing partners would emerge only later. For one, Carmine couldn't embrace the idea that he was worth what he was getting paid. Looking over a bonus check in 1993 with his wife, Kathleen, he wondered aloud, "What more do we need?"

Like everyone in New York, he passed his share of homeless people on the street. Their ranks had grown over the years, he noticed. New York had become a city of startling disparities. If you really believed that compensation was a dollar vote on your intrinsic and indisputable value, you might have looked past them. After all, there must be some reason they were on the street and you were wearing a Zegna suit.

But Carmine couldn't manage it, couldn't in good faith agree with the market's decisions about how vastly different some lives were valued compared with others. So he and Kathleen rented a U-Haul truck, drove it to one of those giant supermarkets in suburban New Jersey, and loaded it up with food. Then they began driving the streets of New York passing out food to the hungry. Night after night, year after year, Carmine drove the streets in his trucks—first a van, then a panel truck, then a big one, with a cab and a trailer. At times he would stick around for a bit, after handing out the food.

"I like to watch them eat," he said to Kathleen one night. "That's my weakness, I guess. I need to touch something that's real, and there's nothing as real as hungry people having something to eat."

With a night-school degree from Pace University, Carmine made partner through a tireless career-long search for value—for something he could touch and convince others to invest in, something, or someone, that could pass his father's brutal crucible.

That was how he met Sonny. Sonny was Carmine's best client, one of Lehman's best, and for a time the largest converter of rental apartments into condominiums in the country. Sonny's story was classically American in its basic lesson about success: anyone can achieve it. Coming to the United States from Israel at eighteen, with no education beyond high school and no money to speak of, Sonny proceeded to give Horatio Alger a run for his money. For years Carmine told Sonny's story—a kind of nutritiously humbling fare—to younger colleagues, who he felt tended to draw untested self-confidence from their bonuses and prestigious degrees.

Sonny, on other hand, was a guy even Carmine's father would have loved. He and his brother started out leasing an apartment together in LA, driving cabs to make rent. It was the 1970s, and the concept of apartments "going condo" was just taking hold. Pooling cab fares, Sonny and his brother eventually took out a loan to buy their first condo—a single unit. They worked out the math of the transaction, bought another condo, and flipped it. In time they had moved on to purchasing a small building. In this way they gradually built up their assets. Then they had an idea: a plan to convert apartments in cities that hadn't yet caught the condo fever.

Their stratagem was ingenious. The brothers would go to a town such as Milwaukee, look at rental prices, and, from these, calculate how much a mortgage might cost. Then they would set an imaginary price— "Two-Bedroom Condos Starting at $195,000"—which is exactly what a quarter-page ad in the *Milwaukee Journal* would say the next day. The local number listed in the ad would go to an answering machine in some hotel room they'd booked for a few weeks. Sonny and his brother would be long gone, back to LA, and a local Wisconsinite they'd hired would check the machine after a week or two. If there were five messages, that was the end of it; seventy messages, however, meant they'd head back to Milwaukee looking for an apartment building to buy. This was how, city by city, Sonny spread across the country.

He had a rule that Carmine liked to quote: "Buy low. Sell low—and a little." It meant *don't get greedy*. You don't want to hold on to inventory; you want to move it. No one, after all, can predict the future.

By 2004, Carmine estimates, Sonny was worth a billion dollars. Carmine himself, at that point, was managing Lehman's $50 billion real estate portfolio. The portfolio had been built up over years and was not part of the more recent mortgage derivative free-for-all. No, these were properties Lehman owned or financed for select investors. There tended to be an owner of record, so to speak, that was either the bank or one of its customers.

As New York real estate had been steadily appreciating, Sonny had been buying it—until suddenly he wasn't. Carmine talked it over with his old pal, noting that the price for residential properties, $110 per square foot, still had some upside and might go as high as $140. Sonny agreed with him but said he'd had enough of all that. He told Carmine that he'd "done fine in New York and it was foolish to stay until the bitter end, looking for the very tiptop and then trying to get out before everyone else."

Carmine had always thought of Sonny as a brother, but as they rose together, a key distinction between their work lives emerged. Carmine, who had treated Sonny's money as though it were his own, was now investing huge sums for people he could only know so well—and many not at all.

"He pulled out, plain and simple, because it was *his* money," Carmine would later say. It meant the lenses through which Sonny and Carmine saw risk were wholly distinct. The two of them looked at the same numbers and saw them differently. Such was the power of incentive and—with one's own money on the line—disincentive. These divergent perspectives were by no means unique to Sonny and Carmine, but in this case the latter's up-the-hard-way sensibility could help him grasp the wisdom bound up in Sonny's viewpoint, and he was big enough to thank his friend for a lesson learned.

At this same moment in 2004, a nearly identical conversation was taking place inside the New York Federal Reserve, with Tim Geithner, its
youthful president, at the head of the table. In October 2003, at the age
of forty-two, Geithner was placed at the helm of the most powerful of
the institution's twelve branches, insofar as it oversees a collection of the
most powerful financial institutions in the world. The president traditionally convenes an advisory board made up of representatives from big
financial firms and top thinkers in various relevant fields. For the past
fourteen years, an anchor of the board was Robert Shiller, one of the era's
standout economists and someone in line, many would agree, for a Nobel
Prize. If Stockholm gives Shiller the nod, it would almost certainly be for
his pioneering work in behavioral economics, which helped the economist craft several books articulating how the succession of ever-growing
bubbles, since the 1980s, would end disastrously. But Shiller was also a
key developer of one of the practical tools most widely used by investors:
the Case-Shiller Index. Aside from having made Shiller wealthy enough
to do without the Swedish prize money, Case-Shiller charts and projects
changes in real estate values.

At his first advisory board meeting with Geithner presiding, in 2004,
Shiller described his data suggesting that home values, after having risen
steadily for nearly three decades, were inflated by 30 to 50 percent. He
focused specific attention on data he and his staff had unearthed showing
how, over the past century, rents had tracked with mortgage payments
in determining sale prices. In the early 1980s, as home values began their
precipitous rise, these two lines began to diverge. Shiller, a densely educated Yale professor, and Sonny, the high-school-educated Israeli émi-
gré, turned out to be brethren in teasing out and trusting a commonsense
measure, the cost of shelter, to use as a yardstick to assess what was real,
or unreal, in the buying and selling of property.

Around the table, the representatives from big financial institutions,
and many academics who'd grown wealthy advising those institutions,
looked on skeptically, figuring they had the mortgage planet properly
mapped and assessed. Yes, it was true that by 2004 the FBI had issued
a warning on the rampant fraud in mortgage underwriting. AIG was
already telling Goldman—which had many of its former, and future,
employees working at the Fed—that it was not going to underwrite any
more credit default swaps, the soon-to-be-famous "insurance without
reserves" that Wall Street firms and banks were selling to one another.

Goldman figured that would be fine. AIG was already on the hook for billions if the mortgage-backed securities went bad. Goldman would just get other clients to write the CDSs, and it had already started hedging and swapping against the CDOs it was packaging and advertising as "safe as cash" to the investing public.

Shiller was saying to one and all that the entire financial edifice, and the U.S. mortgage market, the bedrock of the country's economic safety and soundness, was resting on the mother of all bubbles. Sonny, had he been present, would have agreed.

Shiller recently recalled the meeting, how he "talked about the bubble and housing prices," something the professor talked about at all the meetings. But, after a few minutes that day, running through his thoughts, data, and expertise on the matter of real estate, "I had this feeling, the same feeling anyone has when they are kind of violating groupthink. Here I am, talking about the bubble in the advisory committee and after a few minutes starting to feel uncomfortable about it. I'm thinking, maybe I'm sounding flaky. 'Bubble' was not even in the textbooks then. There is a certain image we project of scientific objectivity in the economics profession and 'bubble' sounded like a newspaper term." Bubble, incidentally, is now a term economists use. And Shiller can hardly be faulted for wondering if the problem was what he was saying, or how he was saying it.

Geithner ignored Shiller's warning and summarily removed him from the board.

———

To be fair, Carmine did not dramatically change course after his 2004 conversation with Sonny, either. He had a business to run, and it was a matter of incentives. His were different from Sonny's.

For his part, Sonny stuck by the inner rigors that had brought him such success. He called Carmine in 2006 to tell his friend, "I'm done. I'm out. I have no more inventory."

Carmine was startled. "How's that possible?" he asked.

Sonny explained to him that all the buildings he had bought in the past few years had been converted into condos and that he had just returned from his thirtieth apartment building auction in the past six months.

"I got outbid thirty times in a row," Sonny said. "I'm not going to pay whatever it takes to buy a building. Based on the rents in an area, I know what a building is worth. I know this business, and it's stupid to pay more than something's worth, even if you know there's a greater fool who will buy it from you."

So Sonny took his ball, his billion dollars, and went home. Carmine had lost his biggest client, though he continued to consider what he called "Sonny's rules." By early 2007 he was seeing more and more clearly that they were rules to live by.

It was around this time that Carmine found himself on the shoreline when the real estate hurricane hit. In this case, it was the south Florida coast, where Lehman and its investors owned condominiums built during the construction boom of the past decade.

People had suddenly stopped showing up at their closings. Carmine noticed this, but it took him a few days to realize the full implications. Say someone, in March, signed a purchase and sale agreement for $900,000 for a South Beach condo, putting down 10 percent of the total price—in this case $90,000. When the closing date arrived in May, just sixty days later, and the lawyers and title company convened to complete the deal, the buyer simply wouldn't show. The reason was that the price of the condo had dropped so fast in the meantime that it now made more financial sense to lose the $90,000 than to own the damn thing. By the summer of 2007 more than half of the buyers in soft parts of the Florida market were no-shows at their closings.

By the end of the year, Carmine was in round-the-clock discussions with the owner-investors of these complexes. Several suggested cutting prices. If values were dropping that fast, they should try to lure buyers to their closings by lowering the sale price on the condos. The problem was that prices were dropping so fast that, as Carmine said, "It would cause riots in the buildings. Someone would say, 'I paid $900,000 two months ago for a unit that just got its price cut to $600,000. I'm gonna stop paying my mortgage. I'm gonna sue the developer.'"

Carmine sent along updates to his fellow managing directors and held the line. The other directors might have been shrewder in their methods of packaging and selling off debt, but it was not clear that they understood the dramatic fashion in which the mortgage values behind their CDOs were collapsing. They were relying on the safety of their tranches—the name for the way mortgages were bundled based on various flavors of perceived risk—and the credit default swaps the directors believed had insulated them from defaults. Carmine's office, just down the hall, was a wormhole into an older world, one in which investment banks could assess their real estate holdings, if they ever cared to, by actually visiting the physical buildings.

In his grounded, intensely terrestrial life, Carmine was privy to other portents, too. The economy officially slipped into recession in December 2007. The following spring, Secretary Paulson would tell anyone listening that economic growth for the coming quarters looked steady, if not strong. But by today, in the late spring of 2008, Carmine noticed that there were more hungry people on the streets of New York than he had seen in many years—maybe ever. He had upped the number of runs with his truck.

Some people are graced with a more complete view of the complex world. It's usually by happenstance; they cross invisible borders. Carmine, in his twisting path, was regularly visiting several disparate provinces in the wider country: on the Gold Coast of Florida, where those glittering condos stood empty along the endless beach; in his old Brooklyn neighborhood, where immigrants from Africa, South America, and the Caribbean were now trying to find footholds on the ever-slipperier shores of the American dream, by buying properties from his old Italian neighbors with "liar loans," meaning no documentation needed; on the streets of New York City, where the homeless and hungry, leading indicators of the recession, lined up at his truck; and, of course, the sight from his twelfth-floor Lehman office, with its view across Midtown Manhattan, from lofty tower to lofty tower, high above the hard pavement.

What Carmine and Sonny and Bob Shiller all saw was the outcome of a thirty-year effort to find new ways to increase leverage without assuming heightened risk, a process rather breathlessly called "financial innovation."

The experiment started in the late 1970s at Salomon Brothers, where Wolf and many other Wall Street titans had gotten their start. Salomon at the time was a bit like Florence in the early days of the Renaissance: they saw the world differently and then helped to make it so. The name of the Italian genius in this case was Lewis Ranieri, a rough-and-tumble trader at the mortgage bond desk, who saw debt, suddenly, with new eyes.

Governments and corporations had long been raising money by selling bonds, tradable on open, active markets. This had been going on and growing in sophistication for centuries. In the thirteenth century, governments first started floating bonds to raise money for wars. In the sixteenth century, in Italy, corporate bonds followed closely on the heels of the modern corporation. But as the successes of twentieth-century market economies brought with them higher standards of living and greatly expanded ownership, a third, vast new ocean of debt emerged: mortgages.

By the late 1970s, home mortgages in the United States totaled in the trillions of dollars, kicking off an explosive growth in interest payments. These payments flowed mostly into traditional commercial banks, savings and loans, and credit unions, institutions that since the Depression had been federally insured under the Glass-Steagall Act, which also kept them legally separate from investment houses and brokerages. In return for this security, these institutions accepted strict limits on how they could invest their assets. Their basic function was to assess creditworthiness and lend out money accordingly. Mortgages were thus one of the pillars of their business model. The so-called 3-6-3 rule governed a banker's work life: pay depositors 3 percent interest (short-term liability), lend their money out at 6 percent, and be on the golf course by 3:00 p.m. Banking was boring, prudent, and reliable, and because of this it could serve as a sturdy backbone for the U.S. economy.

But investors were less enthusiastic about the arrangement. If they hoped to invest in mortgages, they could do so only secondhand, by investing in the thousands of sleepy institutions that held all those American mortgages on their books. The genius of Ranieri and his colleagues—and a future Wall Street leader named Larry Fink, then at First Boston—was in developing a new way to invest in this untapped pool of mortgage debt. By breaking home mortgages down into different categories, based on characteristics such as loan terms (30-year fixed, 15-year adjustable, etc.) and borrowers' credit scores, they found they could assess the risk of default and the chance of a loan being repaid early. Once the risk was established, it could be priced into a security, and so the mortgage-backed security was born.

Even if someone had come up with the idea in, say, the early 1960s, it would have been impossible to implement any earlier than it was. As much as Ranieri's insight, it was the great leap forward in computing power, those famous supercomputers of the seventies, that made the MBS possible by allowing financial firms to aggregate and process the huge amounts of data that went into pricing risk. If the "profiling equations" that established a security's riskiness could be made sound, the prize was tremendous: a smorgasbord of investment opportunities, of virtually any risk profile of debt (and corresponding return), for every investor's taste. Ranieri believed that the market efficiencies gained through this process, of bringing together new communities of debt buyers and sellers, could reduce mortgage rates by as much as 2 percent. And the same securitization model could be easily extended to monthly payments made on cars, credit cards, insurance policies—on anything, really. Credit would be extended to an undiscovered country of borrowers, and the underwriters of the original loans would not even have to hold the debt on their books. They could sell it to the vast new world of creditors, and thereby free up more cash to lend. If this new lend-and-send idea caught on, it would make the stock market look small by comparison.

By 2008 it had. Those old-line activities of the financial industry—the challenging work of, say, identifying underappreciated value in public companies, made famous in the 1980s by value investors such as Warren Buffett and Fidelity's Peter Lynch—were by that point overwhelmed four to one by the new line of debt investments in "securities" backed by contractually mandated payments of all sorts of debt "assets": mortgages, credit cards, and car loans.

This shift, of course, didn't occur in a vacuum. In the early 1980s, just as the rating agencies first began to stamp mortgage-backed securities as sound investments, the wider economy began tipping away from its mid-twentieth-century equilibrium, and the demand for debt inside the United States steadily rose.

It was a perfect storm of trends: global outsourcing of jobs, with profits flowing back to senior managers, stockholders, and investors; increasing automation in the workplace; full-time jobs increasingly becoming temporary or contract labor; the steady decline of unions and resulting wage and benefit concessions; and the 1990s arrival of the Internet and software advances, allowing the fewer remaining workers to be that much more productive. All this created overall economic growth. The U.S. GDP, at roughly $14 trillion in 2007, was twice as large as it was in 1980. But that wealth flowed dramatically to the top, as real median wages stayed flat for nearly three decades. In 1980 the richest 1 percent of Americans received about 9 percent of overall income, roughly the same level it had been since World War II. By 2007 it was 23 percent—an income disparity not seen in the United States since 1928, a time of Robber Baron wealth, stock manipulation schemes, and vast poverty, where more than half of America still lived on farms and survived, with little security, off the land.

But now, in the new century, there was a financial relationship between the widening strata of American life. Despite Shakespeare's catchphrase "neither a borrower, nor a lender be," the vast majority of Americans who'd seen their incomes flatten were loaded up on cheap debt to fill the gap between earnings and rising expenses and to fuel consumptive desires. Rich folks were borrowing, too. The lenders were, in essence, those who'd caught the decades-long updrafts of the economy and had built up large investment portfolios, now heavily—and disastrously—invested in the miracle of debt securities, creating an enormous bubble.

Most bubbles, historically speaking, last between only a few months and a few years. When they pop, those caught within them feel the bite and amend their ways, regrounding themselves in a hard-eyed clarity on how to apply their limited means on items of greatest discernible value. Burning off wild-eyed overconfidence, or making one resistant to its purveyors, is the whole point of such retrenchment. It acts as a counterweight to what behavioral economists, such as Daniel Kahneman, have mathematically mapped since the early 1970s: a host of subtle human biases that make the upside look more likely than a downside of equal or even greater probability. While confidence has outdistanced pessimism over the past several centuries, accounting for an embrace of risk as an engine of human progress, the corrections are crucial.

But they are inconvenient, and hard to predict. That's where Greenspan, understanding this, established his greatest historical influence. He helped to ensure that, in each crisis, the rollover of debts—the "liquidity bridge" Wolf wrote of—would be supported by the federal government: a flood of liquidity that altered the ancient, commonsense physics between price and value, confidence and pessimism. The retrenchments, with all their cleansing effects, never really occurred. And the debt bubble, shifting its focus as needed, continued to grow. The practical effect of this by 2000 was a continued rise in borrowing, and corresponding debt, at the same time that the lowered Fed rates reduced the return on fixed-income investments, such as government bonds. It was, to reverse Churchill, the beginning of the end.

The era's victors—that 1 percent of the population hauling in 23 percent of overall income, and their kindred in other countries—had by 2001 started to hit a wall of their own. After the bursting of the Internet bubble, it was clear the stock market was an unattractive destination. Stocks were flat. Capital, lots of it, was suddenly very impatient. The great pools of money—investment funds, pension funds, government funds, corporate funds, amounting to $38 trillion of the world's acquired wealth by 2001—were searching for a safe, fixed-income yield. As Greenspan cut rates, and stressed that he planned to cut them further to continue to fuel America's debt-driven consumption—at that point accounting for 70 percent of GDP—that great river of money flowed more forcefully than ever into the U.S. market fueling that debt. American debt, in terms of MBSs and other mortgage-related derivatives, had become the preferred investment opportunity of the entire world.

The underlying truth was that these securities were less secure than their name or profiling equations suggested—far less secure, in fact. The idea that all mortgages couldn't drop at once was simply wrong. And many of the banks suspected it, even if, year by year, they weren't sure what to do about it. Clayton Capital, hired in 2004 by a host of large investment banks, noted that nearly 40 percent of all mortgages had significant underwriting "irregularities." The fundamental and ancient relationships that underlie credit, going back to passages in Deuteronomy—that borrower and lender enter a relationship that carries obligations on both ends—were severed by the firms originating mortgages, taking front-end profit, and selling the mortgages off into investment pools, defined mostly by their yield, that were then sold far and wide by the great marketing and influencing machines of Wall Street. Prudence, even common sense, had been bled out of the equation.

But that's what always happens when everyone is focused on what something can be sold for while ignoring the many other factors that define worth. It just had never happened on such a sweeping scale.

America, with its huge economy, found itself in the later stages of a vast pyramid scheme. By late 2006 it was clear that the U.S. mortgage market, as large as it was, could not absorb another drop of capital. The sluggishness of productivity gains and real economic growth in the United States had finally caught up with the eternal dream of home buying. Even with the government's public-private mortgage banks, Fannie Mae and Freddie Mac, guaranteeing roughly 80 percent of all mortgages, and for years encouraging the extension of debt to unsteady borrowers as part of a national bipartisan push to spread the "virtues" of home ownership, the mortgage market could not grow any further. Wall Street's remedy to this, since the saturation's start in 2004, was to create "synthetics," products that allowed investors to make naked bets without any tangible connection to the underlying asset. A thousand bettors could wager with one another on the fortunes of a single mortgage. Investors could buy CDOs that were simply bets on the fortunes of other CDOs. Then they began to use credit default swaps—something created, without guaranteed reserves, to lower the price (and risk) of sleepy corporate bonds in the 1990s—as faux insurance for CDOs. Of course, there was nothing sleepy about a CDO, with its towers of descending risk profiles and equations of how each level was expected to respond to shifting economic forces. Nothing sleepy about a synthetic CDO, based on bets over how those equations would perform. This new strain of CDS was more like a collateral standoff between so-called counterparties, a bit like those casinos that allow bettors to sign their houses over as collateral in exchange for more chips. The more collateral—and CDSs often used CDOs as their collateral—the more leverage was permissible as an added illusion of a "we're in this together" security. All that made the debt flow even more freely.

All this business created enormous fees. It was very profitable for investment banks and rating agencies. And virtually all of it happened in the shadows—a vast dark pool for financial derivatives that had virtually no transparent clarity for either buyer or seller. The middlemen, the investment banks, knew what they were dealing with.

But like it or not, they all still lived inside the wider U.S. economy, which had not been inventing and investing, saving and hustling, in its storied, robustly profitable way for many years. Those things are hard, and ever harder in the new global economy. They take time and grit and, sometimes, luck. And they actually fit with the ancient and immutable physics of investing: high risk, high reward; low risk, low reward. The country's native engines of innovation had been obsessed instead with a shortcut: the repackaging and expansion of credit into a vote of confidence in a better tomorrow. "Debt," a word broken down morphologically into underlying terms such as "denial" and "hope," had become potent currency in the world of politics, just as in its financial counterpart.

Civilizations rise and fall on confidence. America had figured out a way to borrow money to manufacture it.

INSIDE THE BUBBLE

W ITH HIS NOMINATION SECURE BY EARLY JUNE, BARACK Obama—now the putative leader of the Democratic Party— was faced with the most important decision since the declaration of his candidacy: choosing a running mate.

The guiding principle for the selection of a "number two" has long been a hard-eyed assessment of need—finding a person who will fill some perceived deficits in the politician topping the ticket. Geography, of course, usually carries the day. The denizen of a part of the country that looks with suspicion on the nominee: *He's not from here, he's not one of us, but he's chosen someone who is.* It was decided, not surprisingly, that Obama's greatest vulnerability was his lack of experience, especially in facing John McCain, who'd spent three decades on the national political stage. Obama, until so recently a midwestern state legislator, needed a partner who could claim long affinity with a part of America that was still largely foreign to him: the tiny nation-state of Washington, D.C.

To head up the search committee, Obama announced on June 4 that he had turned to someone who had long, intimate relations with Washington's most experienced players: Jim Johnson, the former head of Fannie Mae.

Johnson's gravity and profile were testimony to a host of hard truths— ones not found in high school civics texts—about the way the nation's capital has actually operated, at least for the past few decades.

Back in 1977, Johnson was executive assistant to Vice President Walter Mondale and went on to be Mondale's campaign chairman in his failed run against Reagan in 1984. Reagan's landslide was fueled in no small measure by the enthusiastic support he received from American business. Johnson—having to raise money for Mondale against Reagan's overwhelming advantage—acutely felt the change Reagan had brought to Washington: an official end to the adversarial relationship between government and business engendered by FDR during the Depression. That stance—of government acting as the no-nonsense traffic cop, enforcing the "rules of the road" for the great pursuit of economic advancement and profit—had been slowly buckling since 1971. That year, Richard Nixon imposed a 10 percent tariff on all imported goods as a response to the way economics had increasingly become a kind of "war by other means," as Clausewitz would put it, in the burgeoning, increasingly borderless global economy. It was a war that every American soon felt buffeted by with the oil embargo, gas rationing, and resultant "stagflation" of the 1970s, as Ford and then, more dramatically, Carter, increasingly saw government's role as nourishing the profits and protecting the franchise of America's signature industries. It wasn't until Reagan, though, that the laws guiding the conduct of business were themselves seen as the problem, and that government needed to "get out of the way," in Reagan's parlance, in every way possible, to unleash America's native, "can-do" spirit. Profits and patriotism were starting to become gently enmeshed.

Jim Johnson followed Mondale's crushing defeat with a trip north, to a managing director's post at Lehman Brothers. In 1991, suffused with exciting insights about risk management from Wall Street's first modern era of "financial engineering," he returned to Washington with some innovative ideas about how to breathe life into that slow-footed half-man/half-beast called Fannie Mae.

The Federal National Mortgage Association, known colloquially as Fannie Mae, was established by Roosevelt in 1938 to spread home ownership and more affordable housing to a still-beleaguered nation. The idea was for Fannie Mae to act as the builder and guarantor of a liquid, second-mortgage market that would disencumber the balance sheets of banks so they could make more housing loans. The government had been holding bids and creating short-lived specialty markets since the days of Alexander Hamilton, but creating a permanent entity that, in essence, held a monopoly over an industry—in this case second mortgages—was a new, somewhat uncomfortable role. So, in 1954, a federal statute turned Fannie Mae into something novel, a "mixed-ownership corporation," in which the federal government held controlling preferred stock while private investors could purchase common stock. In 1968 it officially became a publicly held corporation, to remove its debt and related activities from the federal balance sheet. But the federal guarantor's role remained. Fannie, and, in 1970, a sister entity called Freddie Mac—built to compete

with Fannie in the second-mortgage market in order to create some marketplace discipline—both carried the "full faith and credit" backing of
the United States, a security blanket that merited continued government
oversight of their activities while allowing them to borrow money more
cheaply than any potential competitor could.

Which is what they both did through the 1970s and 1980s, as the two
government-sponsored enterprises, or GSEs, bought and sold mortgages, and then mortgage-backed securities. By "backstopping" loans
that conformed to certain standards of sound underwriting, they lowered
the cost of those loans as a way to, in essence, reward prudence.

It wasn't until the early 1990s, under Johnson, that Fannie Mae began
to rethink the earnings potential of this arrangement. Wall Street was
working furiously, as it had been for a decade, to free its net income from
the consequences of risk. It was, after all, the core of their business model
to package, parcel, and sell off debt, getting transactional fees and a taste
of the debt service, while transferring burden of "default risk"—that
cold shower of propitious clarity for lenders since ancient times—to any
locale other than their own balance sheets.

But someone had to "hold the risk" and, through the 1990s, Jim
Johnson volunteered. Year by year, Fannie's and Freddie's balance
sheets became engorged with underpriced risk as the guarantor of nearly
80 percent of the U.S. mortgage market. Along the way, though, the
GSEs—and by association the U.S. government—were the guarantors
of Wall Street's business model and its vast profits.

There were, of course, a few people who noticed the perils of this
financial arrangement and waved their arms in distress, but they were
washed downstream on a fresh and frothy river of cash that was soon
surging though Washington. Johnson, who helped dig the canal, made
sure that water flowed wherever it was needed. Political action committees and campaign coffers of both parties, and all manner of causes, some
quite worthy, were recipients of Fannie's largess. Johnson became chairman of both the Kennedy Center for the Arts and the Brookings Institution, while Fannie and Freddie became the destination of choice for
former elected officials, assorted senior regulators, and anyone of consequence in D.C. with that patriotic can-do spirit and bills to pay. Meanwhile, Johnson and his deputy, Franklin Raines, were among a handful
of people in Washington who were graced with Wall Street–level compensation. And they did it the Wall Street way: justifying handsome

compensation by moving expenses off Fannie's balance sheet, an action that a government oversight agency later deemed improper, and under-reporting Johnson's pay at $6.2 million. In fact, it was $21 million. Ultimately, Johnson's haul from seven years running Fannie—he handed it off to Raines in 1998—was over $100 million.

The issue of compensation, though, was even more broadly applicable. Elected officials of both parties, watching the two-decade rise of the professional, managerial, and financial classes in America while most Americans saw their incomes freeze or decline, could compensate for those shifts by directing Fannie's might. From the mid-1990s forward, Fannie, by widening the types of mortgages it would guarantee, was the agent of the "American dream of home ownership"—a dream trumpeted by both Clinton and Bush—by extending mortgages to those who were, increasingly, on the wrong side of economic tides Washington felt it could do so little to reverse.

The price for those best intentions was to "bid out" the government's precious role as guarantor. While Wall Street created the models to separate risk from reward, the government's role as backstop—final recipient of the risk being passed to and fro between investors in debt—was crucial to the equation. By 2003, concern that the GSEs, at that point carrying $1.5 trillion in debts, could be capsized by a shift in the markets prompted the Bush administration to propose they be overseen by a division of Treasury that could set capital requirements for the giants based on market conditions. The subtext, of course—to curb the GSEs' lending standards—soon became a political struggle with populist overtones. Fannie's supporters rose up: policing Fannie in this way would mean less affordable homes for middle- and low-income Americans.

As is often the case, the debate was shaped by the distinctive voice of Representative Barney Frank, the Massachusetts Democrat and a member of the powerful House Financial Services Committee.

"Fannie Mae and Freddie Mac are not in crisis," he said at a hearing. "The more people, in my judgment, exaggerate a threat of safety and soundness, the more people conjure up the possibility of serious losses to the Treasury, which I do not see, I think we see entities that are fundamentally sound financially, and withstand disaster scenarios, and even if there were a problem the Federal government doesn't bail them out, but the more pressure there is there, then the less I think we see in terms of affordable housing." Did it matter that Barney's partner, Herb Moses, had worked at Fannie, a job Barney helped him get, or that his mother, the sainted Mrs. Frank, had received a $75,000 grant from Fannie for a foundation she ran that helped the elderly?

Probably not, but appearances notwithstanding, nothing was done as Fannie and Freddie took on more of Wall Street's risk. To be sure, the GSEs never pressed for the underwriting of subprime loans—which were defined by the fact that they didn't conform to Fannie's and Freddie's underwriting standards. But mixing of conforming and nonconforming loans into CDOs and other mortgage-backed securities brought the contagion directly into the Roosevelt-era's edifice to affordable housing for a battered nation.

What was clear by the fall of 2007 was that those best intentions worked only in a landscape where government and business were separate and distinct in their definition of core interests—one of public purpose, the other private endeavor. Once the government business partnership was stuck, with profits as a shared goal, it was just a matter of when the "mixed ownership corporation" would explode and how costly it would be.

When Jim Johnson was first asked to join up with Caroline Kennedy and Eric Holder to start some preliminary inquiries for a VP search in April, the former Fannie Mae CEO was already displaying signs of toxicity. Some smart analysts on Wall Street and a few at Treasury had begun running the numbers on Fannie and Freddie: their liabilities in the current environment were daunting and taxpayers could be on the hook if the federal government were forced to make good on the GSEs' precious guarantee. But as soon as Johnson was officially introduced on June 4 to head the VP search committee, McCain's campaign went on the offensive. It took just five days for reporters to discover that Johnson had gotten loans for some of his properties directly from Angelo Mozilo—the CEO of Countrywide, the huge mortgage underwriter at the center of the subprime mess.

"I think it suggests a bit of a contradiction," McCain chided Obama on Fox News, "talking about how his campaign is not going to be associated with people like that."

Two days later Johnson resigned his post, stressing it was unpaid and thereby voluntary—a statement showing his continued appreciation of the power of illusion. Tapping Johnson was a misstep for Obama, spurred on by his desire to pick a running mate who would ease his flight to a perch atop the nation's imperious and insular capital. McCain, of course, had spent many years in Washington as a boy—the son and grandson of famous admirals—and saw it change from the time he arrived as a freshman congressman from Arizona in 1983. In fact, he lived it, getting caught up in the signature scandal of the early 1990s savings-and-loan mess as one of the five senators accused of trading favors with failed S&L operator Charles Keating.

McCain could remember the post–World War II period in Washington, when the town was filled with plenty of lifelong public servants who didn't pine for private sector rewards or think about the perfect time to leave for lobbying work. It was to that era—and that ethic—that he spoke about passionately and publicly, expressing genuine shame and contrition about his dealing with Keating. It saved his political career, and he went on to be a crusader, certainly among Republicans, for campaign finance reforms. Obama and a campaign team heavy with Washington outsiders were showing a lack of acuity about the town they soon hoped to command, while McCain understood the ugly ways in which Washington had, from year to year, been debased. Yes, Jim Johnson knew everybody in Washington—and across decades he had helped fund the town's glorious, can-do lifestyle—but suddenly, no one could afford to know him.

The driver of the car pulled up to 32 Maple Hill Drive on June 9 and peered into the modest Tudor home for signs of life. The clock showed 7:00 a.m., and the air was already warm in anticipation of a hot summer day.

These early-morning pickups more often involved gated estates, where the crunch of tires on gravel announced the car service's arrival. In the world of high finance, rare was the curbside pickup. But then, Tim Geithner had never been party to the affluence that typically came with a career in the industry. He was often mistaken for an investment banker. Something about the quick smile, withdrawn just as quickly. After being put in charge of the New York Fed, he and his wife bought this relatively modest house in Larchmont, New York, in front of which a car engine now softly idled.

Inside the house, Geithner was getting ready for a wildly busy day. The driver might make the Fed building in thirty minutes if FDR Drive was clear, but even so, he would be cutting things close. Geithner's first morning call, with Goldman CEO Lloyd Blankfein, was scheduled for 7:45. John Mack from Morgan Stanley was set for 8:15, and Jamie Dimon of JPMorgan for 9:30, and by then Geithner would probably be running late for his speech at the Economic Club of New York. It was an insane schedule. It had been since Bear's collapse.

As the subprime crisis began to unfold, Geithner had joined with Hank Paulson and Ben Bernanke to decide, in a sense, the fate of the economy. He was the least high profile of the three but had become, all the same, increasingly central to the group's decision-making process. Just three months earlier it had been Geithner in the lead, setting up the Bear Stearns deal with JPMorgan.

While Paulson was still holding the line that Wall Street would have to take care of itself without the help of taxpayer money, Geithner was tending to his downside risk: having to answer the "what did you know and when did you know it" question.

The New York Fed chair had first become aware of the gathering economic storm in an August 2007 phone call. To Geithner's disbelief, the mortgage giant Countrywide, and leader of the subprime bonanza, was not going to be able to refinance its repo book.

"Repo" was industry-speak for "repurchase agreement," a growing practice in the financial sector by which firms borrowed and lent each other huge sums of money on short-term bases—a few weeks, a few days, sometimes just overnight. Like any other loan, collateral has to be put up to secure the loan. Like lots of firms of all types—banks, financial firms, industrial companies—Countrywide was using mortgage derivatives, such as CDOs, as collateral. At this point, Geithner, like virtually every other regulator, had only a passing familiarity with how repos were being used and how they'd grown since 2005. They were viewed as another kind of cheap, short-term lending, somewhere between commercial paper and a swap. And as with the credit default swaps, the participants in this arrangement were called counterparties. No one, in 2007 or even 2008, knew how big the repo market was.

"That was really interesting," Geithner later reflected, "because Countrywide had no idea what its exposure was, no understanding of what it had gotten into. And the fact that the market was unwilling to fund Treasuries if Countrywide was a counterparty was the best example of how fragile confidence was and how quickly it turned."

Translation: the market would not even lend Countrywide cash to buy Treasury bonds, the safest investment in the firmament. CDOs, MBSs, or similar types of mortgage-based collateral that Countrywide was using to roll over its repo loans were suddenly seen as impossible to value or sell in August 2007, meaning it was illiquid. The whole point of collateral is that it can be taken—the way the repo man repossesses your car after too many missed payments—and sold in liquid markets for cash. Collateral that is illiquid is no collateral at all. Countrywide's intended use for the borrowed funds—to go out, like Sal Naro, and buy Treasuries and shore up its balance sheet or to use them as collateral for emergency bank loans—was irrelevant. Its collateral was no good.

Geithner, at the time and looking back, saw this strictly in terms of confidence.

Confidence, in fact, was Geithner's currency. He viewed his role, then and later, as assuring confidence in the financial markets, by any means necessary, at whatever cost. His view was that the financial markets would engage in myriad transactions, all but matching the diversity of flora and fauna in the natural world. Knowing how all those transactions worked was daunting and unnecessary. His job, and that of the Fed, was to preserve widespread faith in the system's overall soundness.

"People on Wall Street watch each other," he explained. "It's like watching people leave a theater. As soon as a few people leave, the tone of the theater shifts. All these huge institutions start to pull back, and they watch each other pulling back and wonder, 'What's going on?'"

Whether there is actually a fire in this crowded theater, or just someone yelling "Fire!," the job of the regulator is to rush in with the hoses. Spray first; ask questions later. Over the weekend of March 14–16, 2008, as Bear Stearns imploded, Geithner had taken extraordinary measures to prevent a mass exodus from the Wall Street theater. Bear Stearns died because it could not roll over its repo book. Why? It was using mortgage-backed securities and related derivatives, still sporting their triple-A ratings from Moody's, as collateral. In its final weeks, other firms, getting jittery about Bear, were shorting the repo durations, from months to weeks to days. In its last week, Bear had to raise $50 billion a night in repos to replace the expiration of its day-to-day obligations and to fund operations. This is called "rolling your book" of debts. This is how financial firms die in this era. It's not from losses, or declining revenues. It happens when they can't roll their debts—essentially replacing old credit cards with new ones, every day.

The $30 billion federal backstop that ultimately clinched the Bear Stearns deal had been Geithner's handiwork, though Bernanke got the credit. They presented the circumstances of the rescue as a once-in-a-lifetime emergency that called for unorthodox action. But that was dead wrong. Saying this repeatedly only forced the actual players driving the financial markets to have to decide whether Geithner and Bernanke were lying or whether they were stupid.

Around 11:00 a.m., Geithner arrived at the Grand Hyatt Hotel on Park Avenue, speech in hand and fresh off his call to Jamie Dimon. He had given his talk the particularly dry title "Reducing Systemic Risk in a Dynamic Financial System." But dry was, on balance, a good thing in the world of high finance.

The Economic Club of New York had long been a prestigious audience for industry bigwigs and esteemed economists. Almost exactly two months earlier, on April 8, fresh off of orchestrating the Bear Stearns rescue, Geithner had sat front and center to hear Paul Volcker eviscerate the Fed's recent actions in that very deal.

The luncheon had been in honor of Volcker's eightieth birthday, the actual date of which was back in September 2007. The former Fed chairman stood behind the lectern, hunched and mumbling, delivering his first address at the club in thirty years. As he worked his way into the speech, however, he grew more impassioned, finally railing against those regulators who had allowed "excesses of subprime mortgages to spread into the mother of crises." His voice rose to a thunderous pitch as he declared, "The financial system has failed the test of the marketplace!"

An audience member later asked him if he predicted a crisis of the dollar.

"You don't have to predict it," Volcker retorted. "You're in it."

By the summer of 2008, gloom and doom had become popular position for economists, but Volcker was in a category of his own. Geithner valued the man's analysis and insight—everyone did—yet now he found himself implicated in exactly what Volcker found so reckless.

"The Federal Reserve," Volcker had continued, enunciating clearly and slowly to underscore the importance of what he was about to say, "has judged it necessary to take actions that extend *to the very edge* of its lawful and implied power . . . and in the process transcended long-embedded central banking practices and principles."

Was the former chairman implying that the Bear Stearns deal had been legally dubious? It was a tough criticism, coming from the venerable Volcker. The term "moral hazard"—describing the dangerous precedent of federal actions supporting reckless business practice—had become part of the Washington lexicon by this point. But that was still mostly noise. Volcker, on the other hand, just a month after the Bear Stearns rescue, was the first major voice to say that Bear Stearns was an investment firm free to make money as it saw fit, and to fail without pity. If this meant that the rest of Wall Street was forced, by existential fears, to suffer huge losses on its debt casino and start racing toward prudence to survive, so be it.

To think this way, you'd have to be able to imagine a world without Goldman Sachs.

Geithner, in this morning's speech, offered his response to Volcker: that the Fed's actions to shore up Bear Stearns and sell it to Jamie Dimon were sound and justified.

"The Fed made the judgment," he said, "after very careful consideration, that it was necessary to use its emergency powers to protect the financial system and the economy from a systemic crisis." He explained that they had done this "with great reluctance," but that it had seemed "the only feasible option" to avert the crisis. "Our actions," he continued, "were guided by the same general principles that have governed Fed action in crises over the years."

What came next were mostly statements followed by hedges, and assertions carrying qualifiers. He threw a bone to the moral hazard crowd—"the management of the firm and the equity holders" at Bear Stearns "suffered very substantial consequence"—and then called "for a comprehensive reassessment of how to use regulation to strike an appropriate balance between efficiency and stability," so the Fed and Treasury were not ginning up bailouts, weekend to weekend. Then he immediately walked away from this bit of "forewarned is forearmed" good sense to say that such a task would be "exceptionally complicated" and that "poorly designed regulation" might well "make things worse."

That last line—in 2008 and onward—would widen into Geithner's overarching dictum, a twist on Hippocrates and his doctor's oath: "first, do no harm."

After the speech—attended by a host of notable economists who were friends of Wall Street, including Martin Feldstein and Columbia Business School head R. Glenn Hubbard, chief of George W. Bush's Council of Economic Advisers—a wide delegation from Wall Street was slated to meet with Geithner in a closed session to discuss credit derivatives.

As a prelude of sorts to that gathering, Geithner finished his speech, arguably the most important of his career, with a final qualifier about the limits of what any public official could do about the ultimate issue: "Confidence in any financial system," he said, "depends in part on confidence in the individuals running the largest private institutions. Regulations cannot produce integrity, foresight or judgment in those responsible for managing these institutions."

Shortly after 2:00 p.m. he proceeded to the Fed's stately Liberty Room with executives from seventeen firms that represented more than 90 percent of credit derivatives trading, a market now with a nominal value of $68 trillion. Mentioning this meeting in his luncheon speech an hour earlier, he said they'd "outline a comprehensive set of changes to the derivatives infrastructure."

The meeting was attended by Geithner's full staff, along with executives from all the major banks. The New York Fed chief laid out his agenda for the group. Bullet point number one: The establishment of a central clearinghouse for credit default swaps.

This sounds like more than it was: a clearinghouse is just a place where, at each day's end, the swaps can be valued, as when someone goes to the closing on the purchase of a house. But clearinghouses tend to demand that counterparties in a swap put up collateral, or show the clearinghouse, like a casino, that they can cover their bets. A central clearinghouse for CDSs is not so much a solution to regulation of the wildly profitable and potentially destructive world of derivatives as it is merely a good start.

After the session finished, the Fed released a terse overview of the group's findings and commitments. There was no more mention of clearinghouses.

The waters were rising throughout the United States in the summer of 2008. Defaults on mortgages, car loans, and credit card payments were rising faster than they had at any point since the 1982 recession. Americans of every income level were quickly realizing that when bills are greater than income and credit gets scarce, the ground beneath your feet begins to liquefy.

The Obama campaign had scheduled an event to discuss this very issue for June 12, in Cedar Rapids, Iowa, when the water there began to rise, literally. Over the years, the Cedar River had been known to swell with heavy rains, but its hard red clay shoreline always held back the churning rapids. No one much bothered to sell flood insurance. Fire, yes; liability, of course. But everyone knew that the Cedar River rarely crested its bank.

Until now.

In her corner office overlooking the Harvard Law School quad, Elizabeth Warren watched the Iowa flood reports confirmed on Weather.com and CNN. She was supposed to be flying there the next day, but as dusk fell on the eleventh, she got the call: Cedar Rapids was out. The city was underwater.

"Dagummit," she whispered, her go-to epithet—not considered one of the more satisfying ones; a holdover from her "no cussin' allowed" Oklahoma upbringing. But she really was irked, since she had been looking forward to the trip for a while. Finally she would get to spend some substantive time with the candidate who had so piqued her curiosity and enthusiasm: Barack Obama.

The senator had had close friends at Harvard Law, such as Charles Ogletree, the esteemed African American law professor who had taught both him and Michelle. But with regard to Warren, the sense of connection to Obama was more a matter of shared interests, a mutual fascination with how the law affected people on society's bottom rungs, who might not know, off the top of their heads, just how many justices sat on the Supreme Court. At least it seemed to Warren that they shared this fascination. After two years spent working as a community organizer in South Side Chicago, Obama had attended law school in 1988, "to see," as he later explained, "how power really operated in America."

He found out—then spurned the road most took after law school, the well-worn path whereby a precious Harvard degree was traded in for a portion of that very power. Students such as Obama, the top students from top schools, generally went on to clerk for federal and appellate judges, the very best for Supreme Court justices. A few became professors, and an overwhelming majority took big salaries at corporate law firms. Obama instead returned to Chicago, armed with another credential to round out his core narrative as the wayward, loner kid who managed to rise up and seize one of the great prizes of the professional class: becoming editor of the *Harvard Law Review*. In Chicago, he started writing an autobiography—truly audacious for a thirty-three-year-old—and began his well-known journey in public life.

Thirteen years Obama's senior, Warren was a bit further along on her own unlikely journey, which she began as the lone daughter of a down-on-their-luck Oklahoma family, the Herrings, who lost everything in the Depression and never quite recovered. The route from there to her professorship at Harvard Law was anything but conventional: her first child at nineteen; the better part of a decade following her husband, a high school beau, from job to job; a Rutgers law degree picked up along the way; then single motherhood in Houston after leaving her husband.

But the really unlikely part, the bit that started Warren down the path to becoming a household name, came in 1979, when as a professor at the University of Houston she started researching how bankruptcy law was going to be reshaped in a federal legal overhaul that same year. She set out to prove what the business community was, at that point, incensed about: people gaming the system, irresponsibly running up debts and then discharging them in court.

The reality she found, however, traveling from one courthouse to the next, was altogether different from the one she'd expected, and far more complex: the filings came *overwhelmingly* from working people who had suffered from mishaps and bad luck—illnesses, deaths of family members and spouses, divorces, and economic downdrafts that often swallowed communities whole. Page after page, Warren started to recognize the shadows of a past she had long ago left behind, that of her own struggling family and the families she grew up with in Oklahoma. As with Obama, Warren's past and future suddenly came together in a powerful integration. Elizabeth Warren was once again Betsy Herring, native of Oklahoma City, up the hard way, now asking the country's judges and legal barons a tougher set of questions about the nature and cause of financial ruin.

That was how Warren got her start. Thirty years hence, she was one of the leading bankruptcy experts in America, and certainly the most visible.

But at this point, in June 2008, with Bear Stearns escaping a true melt-down, and the particulars of the coming crisis wholly foreign to most Americans, an expertise in bankruptcy law and consumer lending was not the sort of thing to get you a national soapbox. So Warren hoped to get her message out behind the scenes—and to one person in particular.

———

By midday on June 12, the crowd that had gathered at the Illinois Insti-tute of Technology, a smallish sprawl of aluminum and glass on Chica-go's South Side, was almost all reporters. One hundred and fifty of them, mostly with the traveling press, there to watch Obama and Warren chat with three Chicagoans in varying degrees of credit hell.

This was the event that the Obama campaign threw together in a mat-ter of hours, as downtown Cedar Rapids slipped beneath the water.

One by one, each citizen told a story—they were surprisingly con-ventional stories of people overwhelmed by debt—as Obama listened patiently, asking a question or two.

When Warren finally spoke up, she recounted the first time she'd met the senator—then an Illinois state senator—at a 2003 fund-raiser in Cambridge and how "he had me at 'predatory lending,'" a sure-laugh line. Then she and Obama ran through an array of the typical traps bur-ied in deceptive credit card agreements: teaser rates in the low single digits that suddenly jump to 30 percent, the arbitrary lowering of card-holders' credit limits in order to charge over-the-limit fees. Obama even appeared to know more than Warren about the details of one practice, called the "fair-play rule." Warren looked on at the senator in amaze-ment.

"In the interest of full disclosure," he admitted quietly, "I've gone through this. I've had credit cards."

Ears pricked, the reporters crowded in close. Throwing his lot in with those sitting around the table was a risky gambit. Their stories were the stories of millions across the country, but traditional judgment still looked down on those who took on debts they couldn't repay. But Obama, and Warren beside him, were a pair of winners, those who had risen from humble beginnings and managed to overcome obstacles and mishaps, and maybe even errors. It was a bold and empathetic statement, challenging a censorious culture: *Don't be too swift to judge*.

"We've just heard three examples of what I think most people would say is grossly unfair," Obama said, citing the three participants. "But this is not atypical." For good balance, he acknowledged the merits of the other side. "Part of why our debt crisis is so bad," he continued, "is that some folks are making reckless decisions—racking up big credit card bills by purchasing flat-screen TVs and other luxury goods that they know they can't afford." The qualifier, as always with Obama, was there to help him earn his conclusion—a nod at both sides' reasonableness in order to justify his authority in arbitrating between them. Here he was looking to redefine the basic notion of fairness. No mean task.

Warren, too, threw her weight behind a new framing. "We have a bunch of regulators in Washington," she explained, "who see their job as protecting banks and see you folks as little profit centers for them."

Then there was talk of Obama's proposal for a Credit Card Bill of Rights and his 2005 opposition to a bankruptcy bill, which had given banks additional advantages and taken away consumers' rights. All to the good, in Warren's book, but then, the true lines of advantage and disadvantage were tough to draw. During the thirty-year credit binge, who in power hadn't made money? Penny Pritzker, Obama's national finance chair, had run Superior Bank, a Chicago-area savings and loan that had been among the pioneers in predatory lending. Since Jim Johnson's resignation from Obama's vice presidential search committee a week before, the McCain campaign had been busy talking about his special mortgage deals with his friend Angelo Mozilo, the man responsible for running Countrywide into the ground.

Warren knew all this, and she also knew, from years of battle, how difficult it was to frame arguments for debtors' rights. No one had forced them to take money they couldn't pay back. How could you blame the creditor, filling people's desire for cash, even if it was just to set the interest hook into the debtors? Warren had come to view the whole system more elementally, in terms of its fundamental power imbalances. The average bank was strong, well funded, and skillful; the average consumer, much less so. Who was looking out for the little guy? No one, really.

But gazing now at Obama, who talked warmly, sympathetically, with those facing fiscal ruin, Warren couldn't help but wonder if the country might soon have a president who would fight, really *fight*, for the little guy. After bidding the day's three roundtable participants farewell, Obama called Warren over. He explained that he had another event, a speech at a nearby junior high school, but that he wanted to talk with her for a minute before he rushed off. Everyone kept their distance as the two spoke, leaving a wide perimeter.

"I want to thank you for doing this," Obama began. Then he looked at Warren intently. "So how did you think it went?"

She sighed, smiling. It had gone fine—better than fine. Would he not know that? She supposed he was really asking about how she thought he had connected with the guests in their distress.

"Frankly," Warren said, "I can't believe you understood all of this so well—what they felt each day and the stresses they faced, and really esoteric stuff, some things I barely know about how they get trapped in credit hell and can't get out."

Obama smiled. "I was talking to Michelle last night about what we were going to do today and I said, 'You know, we've been there. We walked through this when we were young and trying to get ahead. This is not stuff from the streets. This is something middle-class people face.'" He paused, as a thought seemed to take shape. "I haven't been living in this bubble very long," he said softly. "I'm in it now, but not that long ago I had a real life."

Elizabeth Warren would think about that man-in-a-bubble conversation all the way back to Cambridge and many times since. She would go on to become the country's top consumer advocate, and Obama its president. He would preside over the worst financial crisis in generations, one that would develop, in large part, because financial firms and other creditors had retooled their business models to bleed the country's consumers dry. But it would be a long time before Warren saw Obama again. He would go on to meet with hundreds of people in the meantime—financiers, bankers, Wall Street CEOs—but not her. And she would wonder, replaying that last conversation in her head, if it was really about the bubble or the character of the man inside the bubble, and if in Chicago she had seen what she hoped to see, rather than what was really there.

The pressurized bubble Barack Obama had entered by June 2008 demanded some seasoned tending. After Hillary Clinton's formal withdrawal that month from the race, professional managers were on their way.

Lawrence Summers had at this point been in exile from public life since his 2006 ouster from the Harvard presidency. In this last major job, he'd managed to lose the confidence of the university and its directors, most notably over comments suggesting that he held a discriminatory attitude toward women. At a meeting of the National Bureau of Economic Research in January 2005, Summers had opined that women's underrepresentation in the advanced sciences might be due to "innate gender differences." In the fallout that ensued, it looked suddenly like more than a coincidence that, during his time in office, Summers had overseen the tenure appointment of just four women to Harvard's Faculty of Arts and Sciences, out of thirty-two total appointments.

This flap would generally be cited as the cause of his dismissal, but the real story was a bit more complicated. Other Harvard presidents, after all, might have survived the incident. But then, most would also have been familiar with the many studies on the so-called stereotyped threat, the faulty seeing-is-believing tendency that's been shown to have a tightening effect at the highest ends of academic disciplines. Whether Summers knew about this research or not, in those comments at the NBER meeting for which he would later apologize, he certainly never mentioned it.

But this has been a pattern with Summers: to assume that his opinions in areas well outside his expertise are nonetheless sound. He trusts his analytical capacities to a remarkable degree, his ability to frame both sides of an argument and then decide which side is right. Many would say he trusts them to a fault. As he has aged, he has grown less troubled by being uninformed. This is at least what his friends say, while all the same pointing to his overall brilliance. His enemies—a substantial community by 2008—are less charitable. They point to the many instances in which Summers has marshaled powerful arguments for actions and policies that turned out to be disastrously wrong.

In an odd way, Summers's extraordinary self-confidence would grow both harder and more brittle as he spent time in the public sphere. The architecture of his personality, in this way, recalls that of Nixon and Henry Kissinger, or, more recently, Dick Cheney—all men who blurred the line between ends and means. On issues of domestic policy and economics, Summers has long been rising to a similar status.

"Like Rome," an old friend of Larry's said, "he has spread himself too thin and must ever be on guard to put down even the slightest challenge or insurrection in intellectual territories which he claims but can't hold."

By most accounts, Summers exhibited less of this pomposity at earlier stages of his career, when he was still on the upward thrust of his meteoric ascent. As the child of two economists, with two Nobel laureate uncles in the field, Summers was primed for a life among the top economic minds of academia. He spent the first five years of his life in New Haven, Connecticut, while his father taught at Yale, then moved with his family to Philadelphia when his father got a professorship at Penn. As a teenager, in the span of just *two years*, Summers would see his uncles Kenneth Arrow and Paul Samuelson each win the Nobel Prize in Economics.

The lofty standard set by his family threw Summers full tilt into a scramble up the academic meritocracy. During his adolescence, when left home alone, he would get a math problem from his parents. If they forgot to leave a problem for him, he would chase after them demanding one. He matriculated at MIT at age sixteen, starred on the debate team, got his PhD in economics from Harvard by his midtwenties, and received tenure at the tender age of twenty-eight, becoming one of the very youngest tenured professors in Harvard's 350-year history.

But for all his academic success, Summers did less well in his leadership roles. In the Clinton administration, he only really stepped out of Bob Rubin's shadow at the end of that president's second term. He then managed, in his own brief tenure as Treasury secretary, to preside over perhaps the most disastrous piece of deregulatory legislation since the Great Depression: the Financial Services Modernization Act of 1999 (also known as Gramm-Leach-Bliley), which, in undoing a major provision of Glass-Steagall, directly precipitated the "too big to fail" crisis nine years later. But it was as Harvard president that Summers provoked the most acrimony. Along with his knack for the public faux pas, he succeeded in antagonizing his bosses behind closed doors, specifically through meddling in the university's investment strategy for its multibillion-dollar endowment. In addition to championing Gramm-Leach-Bliley in 1999, Summers played a central role, that same year, in making sure the burgeoning derivatives market was left unregulated. When he became president of Harvard a few years later, his faith in derivatives was so great that it was all but indistinguishable from his expertise in how the products actually worked.

The result of this particular overreach came with merciless speed when Harvard lost nearly one-third of its endowment, largely because of investments in interest rate swaps and other derivatives. Summers had talked in 2003 about overseeing a period of expansion at Harvard "not unlike the growth of the early Renaissance." By 2005 the wildly over-committed university was freezing professors' salaries, cutting support staff, and canceling construction projects left and right.

It all boils down to the classic Larry Summers problem: he can frame arguments with such force and conviction that people think he knows more than he does. Instead of looking at a record pockmarked with bad decisions, people see his extemporaneous brilliance and let themselves be dazzled. Summers's long career has come to look, more and more, like one long demonstration of the difference between wisdom and smarts.

Not that Summers himself would admit this—or admit to having been wrong in more than a public relations sense. His disastrous foray into private investing at Harvard might have sidelined a lesser man, but by 2007, Summers was signed on at the hedge fund DE Shaw as an absentee consultant. Despite spending just one day a week at the fund, Summers was paid $5.2 million in his second year with Shaw, according to a report in the *New York Times*. He had now fulfilled one key goal he set for himself after leaving Harvard: to make money. Now it was time to burnish his image.

The idea of retiring from public life at age fifty-three, of receding into the private sector to make money hand over fist, was not enough for Summers. As the Bush era lurched to its ignoble end and a troop of resurgent Democrats took the field, Summers began putting considerable energy into writing columns for the *Financial Times*. They were state-of-the-world renderings, most of which looked at the global economy and the challenges it presented. The columns were artfully crafted bids for reappraisal, for the world to take another look at Larry Summers. He wanted back in the game.

But Obama already had a formidable team of economic advisers, several of whom claimed long, troubled histories with Summers dating back to the Clinton years. They knew him and they understood him too well. Yet somehow, in the ensuing shakeout, Summers would wind up with a coveted spot as head of the National Economic Council.

The real antecedent to Summers's blazing return to prominence was Obama's decision, in the week that Hillary conceded, to appoint Jason

Furman as head of the campaign's economic team. It was a job that Obama's friend and adviser Austan Goolsbee had wanted, and this fateful decision would open the door through which those Rubinite economists such as Summers would slowly slip back in. In his new role, Furman became the bottleneck between Obama and his other economic advisers, the gatekeeper deciding whom the senator spoke to. For Summers, the appointment could not have been more propitious. Furman had been a teenage phenom and Summers had known him for years. Now, with Furman advising Obama, Summers saw his opening.

According to those on the staff at the time, Furman and Summers had conversations to the effect that Furman could get Summers access to Obama's economic circle, but Summers would have to do the rest.

No problem. This was Summers's strong suit: conference calls—free-form, wide-ranging, and loosely organized. No one had Summers's rhetorical command, the skills of argument and persuasion he had been honing since his days on the MIT debate team. Summers would work his magic on the president-to-be, and in spite of all those trusted economic advisers on the team—such as Volcker, Goolsbee, and Wolf—Obama came slowly to invest confidence in what amounted to a Clinton-era redux, with Summers's brash voice carrying high above the rest.

––––––––––

If the opposite of certainty is doubt, humility must lie somewhere between the two. By August 2008, as hundreds of financial professionals gathered for their annual meeting in Wyoming, humility had finally begun to set in—albeit too little, too late.

Within a month, the financial system would begin its free fall, and those prudential voices that had urged caution and humility through the years would get, for their trouble, I-told-you-sos they'd just as soon have gone without. Hindsight is twenty-twenty, of course, but the truth of the 2008 crisis was that some had seen it coming a mile away. Foresight had not been wanting; it had been ignored. And though the early critics would be cast as outliers, if they were it was largely for having been shouted down by an arrogant, self-congratulatory consensus.

As Fed chairman Ben Bernanke stepped to the podium, in the shade of the nearby Teton Range, it was all too clear that the market in certainty had begun to correct.

"The financial storm that reached gale force some weeks before our last meeting here in Jackson Hole has not yet subsided," Bernanke said, opening a speech titled "Reducing Systemic Risk." The chairman continued: "Its effects on the broader economy are becoming apparent in the form of softening economic activity and rising unemployment."

This was hardly news to the attendees by this late date of August 22. After the past year—to say nothing of the past few months—it would not have been at all odd to see these staid central bankers trading their light beer and Chablis for a few stiff shots. The conference's same-time-next-year spirit was now clouded with uncertainty. How many of those now in attendance would be here next time around, and what sort of financial storm, at what battering force, would they be discussing then?

One audience member, a Wharton professor by the name of Gary Gorton, thought he had a pretty good idea.

It was Gorton's first time at the Jackson Hole conference, and though he had been invited as a guest presenter, he was there now as a Jeremiah.

The night before, he had spotted Bernanke at the cocktail reception and sidled up. The ever-polite Fed chairman nodded attentively as Gorton introduced himself. He wanted to alert Bernanke, to warn someone with power and sway, about what he had found in his research. But he wasn't quite sure now how to broach the topic.

Fishing for the right way in, Gorton heard himself say, "You're doing a great job for the country, and we're all behind you." Bernanke took the compliment graciously and listened as Gorton explained who he was. He managed to touch briefly on the journey that had brought him there, and thought he'd succeeded in piquing Bernanke's interest, one academic to another, but other revelers had crowded in before he could get to his main point: repos.

For a decade, Gorton had been studying the growth of the repo market and had become increasingly troubled by what he found. Firms were funding more and more of their operation with repos, often basic expenses and even salaries. The size of the repo market alone remained a mystery. Gorton and his colleague Andrew Metrick, a Yale professor who had that summer drawn Gorton from Wharton to a professorship in New Haven, estimated it could be a whopping $12 trillion, slightly more than all the bank lending in the United States. But repos were not the province of just banks, or mostly banks. Anyone with cash could do it. The largest repo vendors were the huge fund companies, such as Black-

Rock, Fidelity, and Pimco. Industrial companies did it, too (even if they didn't have large finance subsidiaries, as General Electric or General Motors did), as did manufacturers with significant cash flow. Everyone had become a bank. What concerned both men, though, was that any slight disruption—any small loss of confidence—threatened sweeping consequences for this so-called shadow banking industry. This was exactly what had happened to Bear Stearns, which found itself with no money to do business when confidence in the company flagged and its repo market dried up.

Especially worrisome was the way repos allowed companies to fund their off-balance-sheet activities. Repos made possible the vast world of shadow banking—a realm of operations and transactions hidden from the public and from shareholders. In shadow banking, firms had found a way to shift risky activities and liabilities off their books. With the ready spigot of repo money, they could then tailor their cash flows and balance sheets to create the illusion of health and stability. And as liabilities disappeared from their books, the amount of leverage the firms could operate with increased.

The prevalence of repos and their undisclosed nature meant it had become impossible to assess the country's financial stability. But even with Bear Stearns—toward the end, "dialing for dollars" each morning to fund its operation—regulators still did not seem to understand the severity of the situation. One whole point of repos was, after all, to escape notice: the agreements were typically made on a bilateral or tripartite basis, meaning the deal was struck and known about by just the two firms involved (borrower and lender) and occasionally a third, middleman firm. But Gorton and Metrick had an inside track.

Though a professor of finance at Wharton for nearly two decades, Gorton had been a regular consultant for AIG since the late 1990s. There he'd developed some of the models the firm used—and, in cases, misused—in its investment decisions, and he happened to be on AIG's trading floor on August 9, 2007, just a week after Barack Obama got his all-points alert from Robert Wolf, when the rest of the financial world saw a full-blown credit crunch unfold. Gorton saw the traders' shock and fear firsthand. It was palpable and frightening, and all driven by the shifting winds of confidence.

Gorton had left shaken. He returned to Wharton, put on his professorial robes, and began to cast a hard, cold eye at what had beset the financial markets. It was at this point that Metrick entered the picture. He, too, was an academic with a window on the inner operations of the finance industry. His father, Richie, was the deputy and so-called other brain to Alan Schwartz, the head of Bear Stearns at the end of its run. Andrew had spent Bear Stearns' final chapter visiting regularly with his father.

A "financing dilemma"—in Wolf's parlance—is the specific cause of death for Bear Stearns. As fears about the company's exposure to toxic CDOs grew in January and February of 2008, its repo book began to tighten. The repo deals Bear Stearns struck were with every type of company, financial and otherwise. If corporate treasurers have excess cash, they lend it as a repo, and then purchase it back. Their money gets parked in a repo, as opposed to being put in a bank, where the $100,000 of federal insurance—fine for an individual, and, after the coming crash raised to $250,000—is so small for a company as to be no insurance at all. The lender of a repo gets a tiny percentage of short-term interest, in the area of .03 percent a month, as well as collateral, which the recipient has to post. If there's a default on the repurchase, there's someone to call.

And there was no doubt, since 2005, that they'd pick up. That last part is a crucial addition to the repo equation. After many years of sustained lobbying, the financial industry pushed through a key provision in the 2005 Bankruptcy Act, which overhauled the U.S. bankruptcy system. All repos and swaps, like those soon-to-be-fatal credit default swaps, were exempt from bankruptcy's famous "automatic stay"—the defining provision, really, of bankruptcy, where all assets and liabilities are frozen as a company seeks the protection from creditors that bankruptcy court provides. Creditors then get in line at the court, with the most secure, or senior, creditors first, then unsecured creditors, and so forth. Repo and swap contracts, though, are exempt from the stay. They must be honored, even if a company goes bankrupt. That makes them the safest item on any balance sheet—safer, even, than cash accounts, which are frozen in a bankruptcy like everything else. In terms of debt, safe means cheap. Repos, thereby, became the cheapest, safest funding source available, and repo growth was dramatic after 2005.

In the specific case of Bear Stearns, the firm was using repos to fund many operations and most of its special investment vehicles—the legal vessels not noted on the company's balance sheets and which held CDOs and other exotic investments. This is the sort of creative license that repos offered financial engineers across corporate America, helping them craft earnings, especially at the end of each quarter, to hide losses, pump up their share price, or, maybe, make certain stock option-based compensation packages hit their strike points. An odd twist on the repo market that both Gorton and Metrick discovered is that repos, inexplicably, become more expensive at the end of each quarter—something both men feel is worth investigating. It might indicate that their prime value is in obfuscating a company's public disclosures, which would be fraud.

But even with the bankruptcy exemption, fears about Bear Stearns' condition tightened its repo "durations" dramatically as March 2008 approached. In the week of Bear Stearns' collapse, Metrick watched his father suppress panic as the firm's traders were rolling over a stunning $50 billion a night in repos. On Thursday night, March 13, 2008—three days before the Fed sold off the collapsing Bear Stearns to JPMorgan—Andrew's father and Alan Schwartz called Geithner's office to say that the firm needed to declare bankruptcy. They couldn't roll over their repo book by morning. Geithner told them to hold out one more day, and New York Fed officials made sure Bear got the overnight infusions it needed.

When Gorton and Metrick huddled before Gary's trip to Jackson Hole, and began to talk about the latest wave of fears rippling through the investment markets, their concerns deepened.

Repos, both men felt, had grown into the equivalent of demand deposits for lots of American businesses, especially those on Wall Street. If confidence in the ability of firms to make good on their repos dipped, creditors would all clamor for their money back at the same time, as in a classic bank run. The firms, which had invested in long-term, illiquid assets, would not have enough money at that point to pay back their borrowing. When Roosevelt saw that this had happened in regular old consumer banking, he created the Federal Deposit Insurance Corporation in 1935, to resolve failing banks and guarantee deposits. In the world of Big Finance, however, there's no equivalent, nothing half so sturdy, backing up a forbidding mountain of debtor commitments.

Gorton had written a ninety-page paper over the summer, which he intended to present the next day at Jackson Hole. The paper, titled "The Panic of 2007," investigated the causes of that crisis in more depth than just about any other document. The dynamic it described was like a glimpse into the future. Precipitating the crisis, he found, was a drop in the ABX, a newish index put together to get a handle on the CDO market. As the ABX began falling in early 2007, because so many CDOs had been funded by repos or used as collateral in repo transactions, fear spread quickly to the repo market.

If the collateral behind a loan loses its value, the loan suddenly becomes much riskier. In this way, as the CDOs lost value, the repo market dried up and companies began demanding greater collateral as security against a given repo. This meant firms needed to sell off lots of assets to get cash for basic needs, which drove down the market they were selling into even further.

This tightening in the repo market lasted through the fall of 2007, but somehow, by the next summer, it was still widely unrecognized as a central contributor to the year-end contraction in economic activity. When the much larger crisis of 2008 hit, only weeks later, the role of repos would again go underappreciated. Had they relied on repos less, the investment banks would surely have better weathered a crisis of confidence. Lehman's distinguishing feature—what would set it apart in sickness—was its bloated repo book.

Bernanke gave his speech that morning, August 22, and then left. Gorton went next.

"I thought my talk went badly," he recalled. "I just went up there with no notes and talked until time ran out—explaining modern capital markets, but not explaining why it was that way. I stopped abruptly because I ran out of time. The audience was people who had focused on inflation and interest rate policy for the last few decades. I must have seemed like an alien landing."

Gorton felt panic rising inside of him as he watched the attendees sit blithely through his Cassandra turn. He wanted to scream at them—or maybe just scream.

Afterward, as central bankers chatted and mingled, Gorton spotted Austan Goolsbee. He cornered him, mincing no words: "Obama should stand up and say, 'Look, everybody can't own a home—sorry. We have to do something about Freddie and Fannie right away, and here's what we plan to do.'"

Goolsbee nodded gamely, but he was busy. They never got to the "here's what we plan to do" part. Then Larry Summers walked by, a group of acolytes in tow, hanging on his every word.

Gorton followed the posse to a lunch with Mario Draghi, governor of Italy's central bank and a man on the short list to eventually head the European Central Bank. Draghi, the luncheon speaker, was talking generally about how to shore up regulations to better support financial stability. Summers asked him some questions, Gorton recalled, "with a kind of dismissive pomposity, like a sniffing English don."

At that point Gorton made for the door. He had had enough. As he booked a flight back east, he vowed to himself never to waste his time going to Jackson Hole again.

THE FALL

O N WEDNESDAY, SEPTEMBER 10, JOHN MCCAIN WOKE UP FEEL-
ing confident. Finally his campaign was picking up the kinetic energy it needed if he hoped to topple the Obama juggernaut. The polling
looked auspicious. Obama's summer lead had been eradicated. Of the
first fifteen polls covered that month by *Real Clear Politics*, Obama was
ahead in just four of them. McCain had shown ruthless, all-in political
savvy selecting Sarah Palin as his running mate, and he had timed the
announcement just so. The morning after his speech at the Democratic
National Convention, Obama awoke to McCain's startling, unexpected
choice. The ratings honeymoon that typically follows a lauded convention speech was cut abruptly short. Ten days later, Joe Biden, dumbfounded, merely asked, "Who is Sarah Palin?"

By the tenth, Palin had become a phenomenon. Obama had poured
fuel on the fire of Palin mania the day before, remarking in a speech,
"You can put lipstick on a pig, but it's still a pig." The McCain camp had
pounced on the comment, casting Obama's words as a crude and deliberate attack on Palin. The country's punditry had then seized on this read.
Words such as "anxious" and "concerned" had started to crop up in the
liberal chatter. Could McCain really win this thing?

But the Palin groundswell, and the broader battle for the White
House, would soon be overtaken by events even larger than the qua-
drennial election.

The banner headline across the top of that morning's *New York Times*
read: "Wall Street's Fears on Lehman Bros. Batter Markets." The article
quoted Malcolm Polley, chief investment officer at Stewart Capital Advisors, saying, "I think the market's telling you that if Lehman is going to
go away, Merrill is probably the next victim."

Reading the story, Obama couldn't help but realize that all those
conversations with his Wall Street contributors would now give him
a material advantage over most other politicians. Even if he couldn't

describe the particulars of a CDO, or the ABX index, he could talk the talk about the markets. And, indeed, the market-driven disaster had arrived.

A year before, when Obama asked his economic team how he should react to the bursting of the bubble in year two of his administration, it had only been a thought experiment. Despite Robert Wolf's prescient early warnings, the collapse had never really seemed all that imminent.

Thinking about Wolf's warning from the flying deck of *Le Rêve* on his forty-sixth birthday, Obama, in an Oval Office interview, reflected on how he had "had the benefit of a couple of friends who, for some time had been warning about the potential of a severe financial crisis because of what was happening in the mortgage markets.

"It was one of those situations where you knew an earthquake might happen but you couldn't necessarily time the week. When Bear Stearns happened, I think that was a signal that some of the predictions I had heard a year or two years previously, might come to pass.

"At that point, I don't think we still had a sense of how bad it might get. By the time you get to Lehman, obviously, people do have that sense.

"I can't claim that I had a crystal ball and understood what all the ramifications would be. I don't think anybody at that point understood how deep this went. The situation just of AIG, to take one example—the magnitude of the bets that had been placed—they were beyond, I think, my comprehension."

It was, similarly, beyond the comprehension of Obama's Wall Street patrons, many of whom had gathered at a restaurant in Denver the night before Obama's acceptance speech at the Democratic convention on August 28. There were, at that point, rumors about the possibility of the government having to take over its huge, public-private mortgage guarantors, Fannie Mae and Freddie Mac. What's the likelihood? someone asked. They went around the large, twenty-seat table. The vote? Fewer than half thought it could happen. Nine days later, on Sunday, September 7, it did, with Paulson stressing this was a special event, due to the federal guarantee that was still the defining feature of the mortgage giants. Similarly, the Congressional Budget Office had estimated in August that a government bailout of the mortgage giants could amount to $25 billion. To start the fateful second week of September, a CBO spokesman said that would be "optimistic."

Greg Fleming, of course, read the *New York Times* headline, too. He'd been secretly planning for this eventuality—that if Lehman went, Merrill would be next—since the late spring.

He had been busy selling off parts of Merrill to strengthen the firm's balance sheet. First was Merrill's sizable stake in Bloomberg, which the financial information and media conglomerate bought back for $6.8 billion. Next were nearly $30 billion in troubled mortgage-related assets that were sold for just $7 billion, a hit that lightened Merrill's toxic load, but pressured other firms, including Lehman, to further write down their assets. With Merrill's balance sheet now as good as it could possibly be, he turned his attention to the only potential suitor.

He had to get to Bank of America to make an overture first, but he couldn't involve Merrill CEO John Thain, who had made it clear he wasn't interested in selling the company that he'd just been brought in to lead. Ed Herlihy, Wachtell Lipton's top mergers and acquisitions lawyer, had worked with Fleming on various deals and had also been JPMorgan's lead counsel on the government-assisted purchase of Bear Stearns. Fleming decided that Herlihy, a close friend, could act as a discreet facilitator. Herlihy, who was also Bank of America's lead counsel, called Greg Curl, the bank's number two, and set up a dinner in New York for Fleming and Curl in late July.

Now the question was what to do next. Fleming went back and forth. To meet with a senior player at Bank of America to discuss a sale of his firm, without notifying his own CEO, was a fireable offense. On the other hand, if he didn't move now, Merrill might find itself in the abyss. Finally, Fleming could take it no more. The day of the dinner, he phoned Curl, also an old friend, and told him it wasn't going to work, that they couldn't meet, that he'd be crossing too many ethical lines. But before they hung up, Fleming deftly suggested that Bank of America was the only fit for Merrill; Curl said, from his side, that Bank of America would be interested in looking at such a deal. Message passed.

Now, sitting in his office as Lehman began to teeter, Fleming ran the endgame calculus: if Lehman went first, Paulson—no matter how often he said there'd be no government bailout—would be in a "too big to fail" nutcracker. He'd offer Curl and Ken Lewis—Bank of America's chief—anything they demanded to buy Lehman, a "Jamie Deal" plus. Government cash would go to facilitate that deal, while Merrill would be left without a suitor or government support. Panic began to set in.

By the next morning, Thursday, September 11, the financial markets around the globe were like an overweight man worrying about the tingling in his left arm and the tightness in his chest.

Hank Paulson got on the phone with Ken Lewis at Bank of America. He and Lewis had already chatted several times that week, as Paulson, talking the talk of the mergers and acquisitions banker he once was, tried to convince Lewis that Lehman was a good buy and the right fit for Bank of America. Lewis, despite his long-standing desires to buy a Wall Street bank, was coy.

Paulson, of course, was no longer Goldman's M&A banker in chief. He was the top domestic appointee of the United States, in an ornate office with a desk used by Alexander Hamilton. His problems in properly defining his role were, more broadly, dilemmas shared by the wider U.S. government. Over the past three decades, it had acted as partner and booster of the profits of large corporations, especially on Wall Street. Were the profits themselves the goal, or was there a large public purpose to government's engagement?

That question was now being posed. Neither Paulson nor President Bush provided an answer. Paulson's limited response since the spring was simply that Bear Stearns was a special event that would not be repeated. Even as the fears of financial contagion began to grip global markets since Fannie and Freddie's fall on Sunday, Paulson stuck to his script. The Treasury would not again be opening the government's accounts to help a private institution. A "market-based solution," he said, was the only path. They were on their own.

Ken Lewis, representing the only domestic hope for Lehman, didn't buy it.

He said that Bank of America would not help Lehman unless they received government assistance similar to the JPMorgan–Bear Stearns deal. Paulson appealed to what he hoped Lewis would see as a wider, even enlightened, self-interest: if Lehman fell, it would surely be bad for the financial sector at large, of which Bank of America, the nation's largest bank, was a flagship.

Not his problem. In fact, in a shakeout, Bank of America might pick up some deals. Lewis reiterated his desire for a "Jamie Deal," stressing that buying Lehman meant assuming tens of billions in troubled assets. If Paulson wanted Lewis to act in the "greater good," as a bulwark against "systemic risk," then the government would have to pay for it, period.

After all, Dimon didn't buy out Bear Stearns because of some wider interest in supporting his industry. He did it because of the Fed's role in guaranteeing $30 billion in toxic assets. Paulson said that doing that sort of a thing again would put the government on a slippery slope, that the markets had to remain sacrosanct as a basic principle, and that it wasn't going to happen. He and Lewis agreed to talk again, but as they clicked off, there was a chill on the phone lines.

What Paulson didn't realize: he'd been beaten to the punch by Fleming.

In a panic, Paulson and his Treasury team shifted their focus to the London-based Barclays, which was eager to widen its Wall Street footprint and had desires for Lehman. Paulson, Geithner, and Bernanke all huddled on a conference call to discuss a known hurdle: British banking regulators would have to approve such a deal, and fast. They were not known for either speed or decisiveness. Paulson groused, "The thing about these Brits is that they always talk and they never close" a deal. Worse, Paulson said he considered the person at the helm of Barclays, John Varley, a "weak man."

On that last score, Paulson had no worries. Barclays was being driven forward these days by its hard-charging number-two executive, Bob Diamond, an American who'd been a top executive at Credit Suisse First Boston and, before that, Morgan Stanley. Diamond had pulled together a tentative bid for Lehman. Paulson summarily got on the phone with Alistair Darling, who carried the staid and dusty title chancellor of the exchequer of Britain. Darling, along with Barclays, had been running their due diligence on Lehman, looking at balance sheets and projections, and were concerned by what they saw. Darling feared that an acquisition of Lehman would expose Barclays and, by extension, the UK economy to much more risk than they were prepared to accept. Paulson attempted to assuage Darling's concerns.

Still bluffing like a deal maker, Paulson cited Bank of America as a "backup buyer," even though talks with the Charlotte-based behemoth had already frosted. But Paulson's principal argument to Ken Lewis, that of systemic risk, carried even less purchase with a British-bank regulator. He needed to convince Darling that a Lehman failure could have ramifications across the pond. Yes, Darling felt, consequences that would be devastating if Barclays went down trying to effect a rescue.

Nonetheless, Paulson felt he'd made the case, a strong one, about the shared interests between the United States and Britain in a global financial system that all but mocked national borders and long-standing definitions of sovereignty. It had, in fact, been nearly two hundred years since Britain set the precedent for government's role in stopping a financial panic, firmly establishing the concept that certain institutions in a society were simply "too big to fail." It was, specifically, the Panic of 1825, when a financial bubble, grown large with speculation on textiles and shipping, burst, leaving many of the banks insolvent. Those in Parliament cried that the banks had been warned about overspeculation, which many bankers had profited from, and that they should be left to their own demise. As the panic spread, depositors crowded into bank lobbies and were turned away by bankers trying to hoard capital to stay afloat. The result: credit froze solid, commerce halted. After a weekend of heated meetings with the prime minister, his chancellor of the exchequer ordered the Bank of England's bailout of London's banks. The panic soon passed and all was well, until the next panic.

Now, as the U.S. government tried to avoid having to bail out financial institutions—which in this era acted like banks and then co-opted traditional banking functions with wild speculation—Hank Paulson and Tim Geithner felt that, in a crunch, the British would do what was needed.

———————

Obama was on a run through New Hampshire on Friday afternoon, giving a few speeches before flying back to Chicago for a precious weekend of downtime with Michelle and the girls. But already he sensed opportunity.

"The good news is that in fifty-three days, the name George Bush will not be on the ballot. But make no mistake: his policies will," he said to a large crowd at a gymnasium in Dover. "A few weeks ago, John McCain said that the economy is 'fundamentally strong,' and a few days later George Bush said the same thing. In fact, Senator McCain has said that we made 'great progress economically' over the last eight years. And here's the thing. I think they truly believe it."

Obama, from his many economic briefings, knew how wrong they were, and how, if a financial industry meltdown now further bruised the economy, such statements would seem nonsensical.

Working his phone nonstop between hits in New Hampshire, Obama got word that afternoon from his economic team that Paulson, Geithner, and representatives of all the major banks would be meeting briefly that evening and then all day Saturday and Sunday at the New York Fed headquarters. Wolf sent a note to Obama saying he'd be representing UBS. Obama was delighted; he'd have a source in the room. He told Wolf to make sure to give him regular reports over the weekend.

On Friday evening inside the New York Fed's large conference room, Paulson and Geithner sat across from the heads of Wall Street. It was a replay, with much higher costs and stakes, of what the banks had done in 1998, when Long-Term Capital Management imploded: they gathered to divide up the damage to keep the financial system from locking up, each taking a share of the hit, except for Bear Stearns. For a decade, Bear Stearns' intransigence was a bitter pill, making it a moment of prairie justice that the fifth-largest investment bank had its comeuppance in the spring. Now Paulson, who until so recently would have been sitting in the seat now occupied by Lloyd Blankfein, told the group that there would be "no government money" helping this time, and anyone who didn't cooperate—in a thinly veiled reference to Bear Stearns—"would be remembered."

Paulson counted on their dreading a domino effect, that if the contagion of fear spread, they'd go down, one after another.

But fear was a hard sell to this crowd: in fact, over the course of nearly a year, it had failed to conquer deeply ingrained hubris and self-regard. Like European monarchs in the centuries before democracy, the financial industry CEOs—like so many American CEOs whose behavior Wall Street had shaped and then rewarded with 1980s-forward "innovations" in compensation practices—acted as sovereigns, untouchable. It was clear since the late summer of 2007 that many of their institutions had been busily swapping and subbing debt—rolling it over, or keeping it invisibly tucked away far from their balance sheets—so they would not have to recognize their underlying insolvency. Vikram Pandit, presiding over the disaster that was Citibank, was sitting in a chair until recently occupied by Charles Prince, who had left in December with a compensation package worth $52 million. Bob Rubin, the bank's chairman, was in line for $126 million in compensation. Thain's predecessor, Stan O'Neal, had slipped out of a crippled Merrill the previous fall with a $72 million package. Hank Paulson himself, who oversaw Goldman's powerful, viral machinations in mortgage securities until his departure for Treasury in 2006, had left with a pay package worth $700 million.

John Mack of Morgan Stanley, looking up and down the table, asked where Dick Fuld was. Paulson said he was "in no condition to be helpful" right now. Some CEOs nodded.

Everyone in the room, men who knew one another as members of a club, understood the darkest scenario of dominos falling: that if Lehman, the fourth-largest investment bank, went down, then Merrill, the third-largest, would be next. After that, Morgan Stanley, the second-largest, and finally Goldman, at the top. Of course, the last three were all close to the same size, each of them three times the size of Lehman. But, in many ways, the more incisive disaster scenario might have put Merrill in its own special category of destructive capability, in terms of shattered confidence. Lehman, like the other investment banks, had only a small arm, $20 billion or so in assets, that came directly and regularly from the public—it was mostly an operator in funds, institutional trading, bank-to-bank operations, and a wide array of investment activities.

The biggest part of Merrill, conversely, was still its ninety-four-year-old consumer brokerage business, now called "wealth management." That business had grown with breakneck speed over the past thirty years as millions of savers moved from traditional banks to investment funds. Driving the migration was a combination of the government's 1970s creation of tax-exempt 401(k)s and IRAs, to encourage saving, and the 1980s heady rise in stocks. Merrill, always the biggest brokerage, was soon enough handling the life savings of a significant slice of the country, as traditional banks once did, and there was no going back. By 2008 it boasted fifteen thousand financial advisers handling four million customer accounts worth $1.5 trillion. That would be the nest eggs of more than ten million people.

But, of course, it isn't a bank. So, those accounts are not federally insured, as bank accounts have been since the Great Depression. That means Merrill was actually like a huge national bank . . . but in 1929.

No one was quite sure what would happen if Lehman went down—trading desks at the big houses were trying to figure that out on Friday, running what-if scenarios. But, being focused on Lehman—with Paulson saying first let's save Lehman, then we'll think about what happens next—no one thought much about how a Merrill collapse would have sparked a public panic: people lining up at brokerage houses, banging on the windows and maybe worse, just like they lined up at the locked doors of banks seventy-nine years before, on Black Tuesday.

Such on-the-ground insights—about the behavior of panicked customers or how fear spreads across landscapes far from Wall Street—was not in the line of sight of those at the table. They were mostly looking at one another, measuring themselves against the only men, maybe anywhere, they considered peers and competitors. John Thain, the former number two at Goldman, who after Paulson left was beaten out for the top job by Blankfein, was eager to continue as Merrill's chief, something he'd long wanted to be, and didn't see that his house was already on fire, with a weight of toxic assets every bit as bad as Lehman's.

So many of the dynamics of the crisis, in fact, were exacerbated by the ego-addled dance of the CEOs—over the years and in this very room—marking an era when the imperial chief executive often existed in a cloud city immune from accountability, even to quarterly earnings. Critics of astronomical CEO pay, and captive boards, in which CEOs supported fellow CEOs, often said the interests of chief executives were no longer woven with those of either shareholder or employee. The idea was get to be a CEO, by any means necessary, and you'd live in your own separate universe that defied traditional laws of business physics.

Even Dick Fuld, atop his Midtown office tower, couldn't imagine a world without Lehman. A week before, the Koreans were ready essentially to merge with Lehman. Once his subordinates had it all set, Fuld, who'd been kept at a distance, burst into the deal room pronouncing that they'd undervalued Lehman's real estate—that "plenty of those assets were good as gold"—ultimately scuttling the deal. Tonight, he was holed up atop his castle, where he'd presided for two decades, wrestling with wounded pride, and outrage—"Thain's worse off than we are!" he was yelling at subordinates, and "Hank will never let us go down." Paulson, and a few other CEOs in the know, were, meanwhile, livid at Fuld for having shooed away the Koreans.

Blankfein, for one, was concerned about how Lehman would pay its obligations to Goldman. Goldman, in fact, was owed money by many of the men in the room, having been early, and most active, in hedging and selling swaps on the great piles of toxic mortgage debt. For any banks wanting to restructure those debts, Goldman was poised like the sword of Damocles. Any attempts to restructure CDOs, to ease pressure on overburdened balance sheets, would trigger a contractual violation of the CDS contracts Goldman held, underwritten by AIG and other banks.

Jamie Dimon, who became CEO of JPMorgan in December 2005, was fortunate that his predecessor, Bill Harrison, expressed distaste in the late 1990s for the mortgage-backed securities and never wavered, even as JPMorgan's earnings sagged in the coming years compared with those of CDO-trading competitors. When Dimon took over in early 2006, with Harrison still chairman, he never loaded up on toxic mortgage securities, even though many of what would prove disastrous "innovations" in how to trade and account for CDOs occurred under Dimon's 1990s tenure at Citigroup. Now with the strongest balance sheet at the table, Dimon was looking for more "Jamie Deals," drawing suspicions from chairs on all sides.

Meanwhile, John Thain, sitting across from his old boss Paulson, and three seats down from his onetime rival Blankfein, wasn't even considering a world without Merrill. He'd just made it to the table. He wasn't going anywhere.

———

Greg Fleming, of course, was not a member of the CEOs club. Having spent two years enduring an array of cleansing ego-adjustments, he went home that evening to his home in Bedford, New York, ate a late dinner, and fell into fitful sleep. At 4:00 a.m. he awoke, and began wandering the halls of the silent house.

There were too many variables, too many to game. Padding barefoot in his kitchen, he found the world quiet and settled and coming into focus. Merrill needed to be sold this weekend or it would either die or be sold on its knees for a few bucks a share. A sense of panic began to rise from his gut. While Merrill had profited in recent years from exotic trading in CDOs, Fleming, after all, was overseeing the firm's old core business, "wealth management." He'd traveled the country, edge to edge, many times, talking to brokers at the big offices. Merrill was vastly, systemically woven into the global financial fabric, just like Lehman, but was significantly larger. Its accounts held the money of real people in the real country. Panic at trading desks and in corner offices was horrific, but nothing compared to angry mobs.

He put on a pot of coffee and grabbed a pad. He needed to move—now. Even though he'd received a come-hither nod of interest in early August from Bank of America, nothing could happen unless Thain were fully on board. He wrote down lines for what he would say to his CEO as soon as the sun came up.

The first call went in at 6:30 a.m. Thain was already in the back of a Town Car, on his way to New York City for the Saturday meeting at the Fed. He was surprised to hear from Fleming. The two men did not get along.

"What is it?"

"I think you need to talk to Ken Lewis."

"About what?"

"About a deal."

"What are you talking about? Greg, this really isn't the time."

"If you don't talk with Bank of America, I think this company is going to fail."

There was a pause on the other end.

"Go on," Thain said.

Fleming laid out the variables, all the scenarios of what might happen over the weekend, and how Merrill needed to move, today, not in spite of those uncertainties, but because of them. "It's Saturday. We have until Monday in early morning, before Asia opens, to get this done. If those markets open, and we don't have a buyer, we'll have the whole world breathing down our necks." He raced through a calculus of how Merrill's stock, currently $17, "could lose $15 in a day—and we'd be at $2. The next thirty-six hours is like eight years in deal land. Now's our moment."

"Greg, you're panicking," Thain said, dismissively.

Fleming was sitting on the front steps of his house, script in hand, and it was all slipping away. He made a desperate bid. "We need to do the right thing for our sixty-five thousand employees and the shareholders," he said evenly. "It's not about me and you and you being pissed about what I'm saying and how I'm saying it."

Silence. After years living under Stan O'Neal's explosive bravado, Fleming had become a survivalist, expert in managing the blend of insecurity and willed confidence common to the modern, wildly compensated, and ever more imperial CEO.

"Listen," he said to Thain, his voice softening. "You're going to be a hero if you save this company."

Thain cleared his throat. "Well, umm, that's not the focus." And, finally: "All right, I'll think about it."

A green light? Not really. But Fleming decided to see it as one.

He immediately called up Greg Curl, Bank of America's number two, and Ed Herlihy, the bank's lead lawyer at Wachtell Lipton. "We're on."

Curl and Fleming each began to pound through their contact lists, alerting and assembling their respective SWAT teams of lawyers, accountants, and key executives within each institution. The two number twos, both with a long history of buying and selling financial institutions, had to get their two number ones together to get things launched officially. They decided on a 2:30 meeting in the Bank of America apartment in the Time Warner Center, on Columbus Circle. Curl called Lewis in Charlotte and said he needed to be on the corporate jet to New York, and fast. Lewis, following CEO protocol, said he wasn't getting on any jet until he'd heard directly from Thain.

While the CEOs settled into the New York Fed to try to make Lehman saleable to Barclays—which, Paulson had informed them, was the sole potential buyer—an actual Wall Street deal, the last deal of the golden era, was taking shape.

Or almost.

Fleming was back on the phone to Thain.

"You've got to call Lewis."

"No way," said Thain. "I don't want to do it. I'll be at a tactical disadvantage."

Fleming was speechless. A tactical disadvantage? *It's these guys or nobody*, he wanted to shout at Thain. *Either they want Merrill or they don't.* He composed himself. "Look, you just have to tell him it's a beautiful day in New York and you're looking forward to seeing him. Talk about the weather."

Thain wouldn't budge—nope—and then he hung up.

Fleming was back on the phone with Curl, staking everything—"my reputation, my whole career"—on a guarantee that Thain would show up at that apartment by 2:30. But Curl had his own imperial CEO to deal with. Without a call, Lewis wasn't coming—and unless the call came quickly, Lewis would be hard-pressed to get to New York today.

But now Thain wasn't picking up. He was in the conference room at the Fed, looking over Lehman's books. The clock was ticking. A half hour passed; it was already past 11:00 a.m. Fleming had talked to his boss six times already that morning, and was now dialing into the ether every few minutes. Finally he called Ed Herlihy, Wachtell's lawyer, telling him, "this whole thing is about to collapse," because he couldn't get Thain on the phone. Herlihy paused. "He's sitting right next to me here," in the New York Fed conference room. "I think he just doesn't want to talk to you."

A few minutes later, Thain finally picked up. "I'm not happy with this Greg. I'm not happy with the way you're handling this!"

Fleming had nothing more to say. He pleaded, he begged.

"All right," Thain finally groused. "I'm going to call him just so I don't have to talk to you again!" And he hung up.

A few feet away, in the hallway outside the Fed conference room, Wolf looked for a quiet nook and punched in a number.

"Wolf, what have you got for me?"

"It's a fucking mess, Barack. Just getting our arms around the problem will be a feat."

Inside, he explained to Obama that they were, first, trying to figure out the depth of "the hole inside of Lehman"—meaning the value of its toxic assets and how far underwater that left the firm. Once that could be established—and the midday numbers looked to be about $70 billion— every bank would decide how much capital it was willing to put up to keep Lehman whole while it found a suitor. He said that the likely buyer was Barclays. But it would want only the profitable parts of Lehman. The toxic assets, in some of kind of bad bank, would have to be assumed by those in the room. Obama asked if they could accurately gauge the "depth of the hole," because "aren't lots of these securities difficult to value?"

Wolf said, yes, that was a problem, "especially considering how much stuff is not on the balance sheet" in terms of counterparty risks on instruments such as CDSs. "So what happens, Robert, on Monday morning if this doesn't work?"

"A shit storm, Barack. We'd have to take the company apart, piece by piece, but it would be a nightmare. They're in the middle of trading relationships all over the planet. The value of billions of financial instruments would go zero, because they can no longer be funded."

Wolf had been closely following the solvency-versus-liquidity game since the previous summer, and he had his eye on Wall Street's insurance broker, AIG. That was not just an intermediary's business, like much of financial services. Insurance was different—a miracle product invented in the 1600s after the then-newfangled "theory of probability" was matched with statistical breakthroughs to create the actuarial tables still used today. Insurance was, in fact, the only proven model to manage and price risk, a leap of progress as great as any in human history. Life, fire, flood, liability, maritime, property, and casualty—the familiar list of lines allowed for the modern economy to develop across three centuries, and AIG was the world's largest insurer. And now the most precarious, having strayed from core principles to sell the faux insurance of CDSs. For that there was no actuarial table, no informed oceans of data, but rather computer models assessing the probabilities of events yet to occur.

"I don't understand why no one is talking about AIG," Wolf told Obama. "There's no way they can survive, and the part of AIG that's gone bad, with all the CDSs, will pull down the side that still insures everything under the sun."

Wolf was being beckoned. He had to go. He'd call later, and Obama went back to his first quiet Saturday afternoon at home in three months.

As Thain prepared to meet Lewis at 2:30 uptown, he told Fleming, "I don't want to sell the company; they can buy 9.9 percent." At the New York Fed, Thain had been talking to Blankfein about Goldman Sachs taking a 9.9 percent stake, infusing some new capital into Merrill. He'd now decided that Bank of America would be convenient as someone for Goldman to bid against. Fleming was succinct: Bank of America wanted to buy the whole company or nothing, which is what Lewis soon told Thain at their 2:30 meeting when the Merrill CEO proffered his minority stake idea. The meeting was brief, perfunctory. Thain left Columbus

Circle to head back downtown to the Fed, and told Fleming to none-theless have the negotiations move on two tracks: one to sell the whole company, the other to sell a minority stake. Fleming nodded and ignored the directive.

Now, with the CEOs out of the way, he and Curl could actually start to cut the deal, something Wall Street still knew how to do, starting with a discussion of Merrill's earnings potential, with those fifteen thousand advisers and million of customers, who weren't going anywhere. Merrill also owned 50 percent of the giant asset manager and mutual fund company BlackRock, locked up in 1994 when Fleming, then a young Turk at Merrill, helped Larry Fink break his firm away from Blackstone, the huge private equity firm. How did those franchises fit with Bank of America's structure and product lines—were there synergies or overlap—and would their value be enough to counteract the heavy load of hard-to-value toxic assets built up by Merrill's other half, its trading operations? It was, in essence, old Wall Street versus new: traditional investment, mutual fund, and brokerage activities versus the new innovations of bets and bonuses based on high-stakes math competitions. Merrill remained valuable because in the trading frenzy of the past decade, no one had bothered to jettison its legacy operations.

Inside the large conference room at the New York Fed, the heads of the major banks looked up and down the table. CNBC was now openly speculating about Lehman's impending bankruptcy, as the CEOs were forced to do with Lehman's books what many had avoided doing at their own firms: look hard at dizzyingly complex asset-backed securities that a thirty-year debt fixation had bred and try to fix a value on credit default swap contracts linking all the banks in a daisy chain of disaster. Each of them was committed to kicking money into the Lehman hole, filling it, in essence, so Barclays would buy everything else. But had they really assessed all of Lehman's obligations? Everyone knew they hadn't. Who knew how many CDOs and CDSs Lehman had off its balance sheet, funded by overnight repos? Anybody's guess.

By the late morning on Sunday, after a sleepless night, Greg Fleming and Greg Curl were closing in on a final deal. Lewis had been peripherally involved. Thain, not at all. And that was the key. "This is it," Curl said. "It's $29 a share, a $50 billion acquisition. There is not a nickel more that we are willing to pay." It had been a night of insane brinksmanship inside Merrill, with factions forming and breaking up, price-per-share numbers flung in every direction—all the way down to $2 a share by some fearful Merrill advisers. Fleming immediately told Curl that $29 a share—a 70 percent premium to where the stock closed on Friday—would work. He now just had one call to make.

"John, it's done. We got them at $29!"

There was an unexpected silence on the other end.

"That's great," Thain said, "but I think we can get $30."

Fleming paused. A joke? "Come again?"

"I said we should go for $30. Call them back and get $30!"

Fleming felt the thread of sanity, the one that had helped him keep his cool over the most chaotic weekend of his life, tremble and break.

"*You* can call them back. Twenty-nine is it. I refuse to call them back."

How had a call that was supposed to be triumphant—euphoric, even—turned so acrimonious?

"You know what, Greg?" Thain shouted. "You are starting to piss me off!"

The line went dead.

It took a minute for Fleming to see it. It was just human nature. Thain had been notably absent from the biggest deal in his company's history. In fact, he had been the biggest obstacle to getting it done. Now he wanted to put his thumbprint on the final document so he could go on to say, "I made this happen."

A half hour later, Thain called back. "Yes, it's time to move," he said quietly, as though breaking out of a trance. He threw in some caveats to create the illusion of having been involved in the historic deal, and in the loss of his prized seat at the CEO table.

Fleming said, sure, those were easy additions. And thanked his dazed CEO. Fleming had survived in his career by sticking with businesses handling money and risk that had been around, in various forms, for a century. And this core of Merrill, soon to be part of Bank of America, would survive with him—a twenty-fifth-hour maneuver that averted probable catastrophe.

A few hours later, as news of the Merrill deal spread through Wall Street's back channels, Paulson and Geithner assembled the CEOs in the conference room. They'd just finished a round of midmorning conference calls with Darling and the British regulators.

They wouldn't approve the deal. Barclays was out. Paulson was incredulous. Darling told Paulson he didn't want to take on "the cancer" of a flailing Wall Street giant. Paulson, while frustrated, knew that for Lehman Brothers, the prestigious investment bank, liquidation had become inevitable. Now all Paulson, Bernanke, and the country could do was brace for impact.

The CEOs were quiet; Paulson and Geithner, grim. They hadn't listened carefully to what the British were saying when they'd all talked on Thursday. They'd slammed into a brick wall of "no."

In some ways, this officially ended a year of colossal failure for Paulson, Geithner, and Bernanke. There was very little new information about the nature of the financial crisis that had emerged since the fall of 2007. What was knowable then—with the most modest, government-sponsored inquiries—was simply magnified now: the U.S. financial system had been on the verge of collapse, ready to blow, for nearly a year. What had been done in that year was emblematic of the modern dilemmas of projecting confidence, whether or not it is justified. Bernanke set up a "liquidity facility" in the fall of 2007. It had lent hundreds of billions in what was all but free money to banks, shadow banks, investment houses, and other companies to prop them up while the market could somehow correct itself. Insofar as the program was successful, as a stopgap, it was because it was secret—a fundamental violation of long-standing principles of corporate accounting, where the source of each dollar is supposed to be clear. As to any structural solutions, both the Fed and the Treasury ducked, as did the Bush administration, because acknowledging the need for dramatic action and then forcing architectural changes in the system would have undermined "confidence in the markets." The Treasury's main contribution was a grant of $30 billion to Dimon to take over Bear Stearns, and little else.

In the panicked weeks of September, the only job of noteworthy public officials was to provide a buyer with the capacity to purchase Lehman Brothers. They mistakenly thought Barclays was such a buyer, even when their fellow regulators in the United Kingdom strongly suggested otherwise.

The entire "Lehman weekend" had been a waste of time.

The only bright spot was that it had kept John Thain occupied so Greg Fleming could sell the giant investment house out from under him, and avoid having Merrill collapse on top of Lehman.

After Paulson's mea culpa, all the CEOs slipped out to call their trading desks. *Unwind Lehman trades as quickly as possible.* That afternoon they'd all huddle to try to figure out how to control the damage to each of their firms.

Wolf slipped out and dialed Obama. "It's over, Barack. Lehman's dead. But this is probably just the start. AIG—they're bigger, more interconnected, and there's no way they'll survive."

"As bad as we thought it could be?" Obama said.

"Worse," said Wolf. "Much worse."

Dick Fuld of Lehman Brothers assembled his senior managers on Sunday afternoon and told them what they already suspected: the 158-year-old investment bank would have to file for bankruptcy the next day. Fuld was depressed and angry, but even more than that, as a Wall Street sovereign used to seeing reality bend to his will, he was in a state of shock. Speechless employees crowded his office on the thirty-first floor of Lehman's Seventh Avenue headquarters. As dusk settled, he tried to call Geithner at the Fed. They would never let Lehman fail. He was told Geithner was nowhere to be found.

At 1:45 a.m., a few hours into Monday, September 15, Lehman Brothers filed.

The prebankruptcy valuation of Lehman's assets was $639 billion, making it the largest bankruptcy in U.S. history—by a factor of six. (WorldCom came in next, at a mere $104 billion.) The numbers were off the charts: $40 billion in commercial real estate, $65 billion in residential real estate, another $100 billion tied up in CDOs, CDSs, and other exotic asset-backed securities and derivatives. And yet for all the attention paid to mortgage securities and their derivatives, the most shocking number of all was that Lehman carried $300 billion in repos and their equivalent—nearly 50 percent of its total holdings.

Carmine Visone went to work on Monday morning as he had every Monday morning for thirty-seven years. He had kept tabs on what was happening. It wasn't hard. Just turn on the television. Everyone sat in front of screens the previous week: the computer screens at their desks; the flat screens on the walls.

He and other senior managers were on the phone, cursing and scheming all weekend. Now he went to the office in a daze.

What is it like to stand inside a collapsing world? Things that seem so solid—solid like the earth, as regular as a sunrise—and then nothing?

Fleming had scored the one suitor. He went home on Sunday night, hugged his wife, and wept.

Carmine, in this game of acey-deucey, was left looking out his twelfth-story window. The crowds still flowed up and down Fifty-fourth Street. Most of the people and cameras were gathered at the larger Lehman Building, the headquarters—five wide blocks across town, and down nine, on Forty-fifth and Sixth.

The lunch crowd was gathered at Bice, someone sitting at Carmine's table. How many lunches, over how many years? He was a throwback all right: he'd given his whole life to this company. Thirty-seven years. He walked in at twenty-one, worked in bookkeeping. Now, in a flash, he was a sixty-year-old man facing however many years he had left as the butt of jokes, or worse. There'd be lawsuits—God, did he hate those fuckin' lawyers—and, worse, there'd be shame. Managing partner; real estate; Lehman Brothers. You've got to be kidding me. It's like a punch line.

How could he face the world—that world? So Carmine Visone started to work out the logistics. How to get the window open wide enough. That wouldn't be hard. He was as strong as three men; he could break it with his fist. He'd wait for an opening, to make sure he didn't hit anyone on the sidewalk. It was the honorable thing to do.

After some time passed—he isn't sure how long—he got up and looked out his door and into the wider office. A last look. The secretaries were crying, boxing up their stuff. He watched them. It was their home, too. And God knows, they had no cushion, most of them. He had a lot more than they did: money in the bank, plenty of it, and Kathleen, and the nice house in Jersey. And from there it wasn't far, along the chain of references that make up a life, to see the U-Haul truck and all those poor bastards he'd handed food to over the years, and how they thanked him and said, "God bless you," over and over, one cold night after the next. What would they all say if he jumped out a building as if he had nothing to live for?

And that's how all those hungry people returned the favor. Carmine Visone decided not to jump. With tears running down his cheeks, he began to pack up his box. After a few minutes, all he had left was to decide if he'd leave his jacket on its hanger behind the door. It didn't seem right to wear it out, like a guy in uniform with an appointment to keep.

He looked at the jacket for minute, maybe more. It had a nice stitch, was a good shade of gray for him, and well made. And he'd paid cash for it. Grabbing the jacket, feeling the soft fabric in his hand, he seemed to remember that this was a way to find worth in this world, usually in the things you could touch.

He threw the jacket into his box. He'd go out like he came in: in shirtsleeves.

THE RISE

T HE WEEK OF SEPTEMBER 15 WAS A WHIRLWIND IN AMERICA that spread across much of the globe—one of those rare moments when foundations are uprooted, shown to be insubstantial. Modern market economies, those steadily growing organisms that have generated stunning wealth over the past two centuries, showed their soft underbelly: trust. What is a dollar bill but a piece of paper that one trusts will be honored as legal tender? What is an investment bank but a legal entity that acts as a custodian and intermediary in the handling of money, or stands between parties in a trade? As buyers and sellers collide and couple in the vast global marketplace—with little to bind them beyond the self-interest of one party having money and the other needing it— the institution makes certain that everyone honors his obligations, or legal remedies are triggered. That's their essential function. When the financial institution itself can't honor its obligations, panic is uncorked. On Monday morning, clients of all kinds found that Lehman—or, more specifically, Lehman's London office, where $5 billion was housed— couldn't honor its obligations, not to everyone at once. Certainly anyone who has a passing knowledge of banking or finance, or who has seen *It's a Wonderful Life*, knows that the obligations to everyone cannot be met all at once. All the money, either deposited or invested, isn't sitting in a closet, neatly stacked. It's out there working, invested in this or financing that—a plain, known fact that no one wants to hear at the moment their money is unattainable and trust vanishes.

When the institution is America's fourth-largest investment bank, the fear, spreading like a contagion, is that other institutions anchoring the global financial system will not be able to honor their obligations. By midday, eastern standard time, other investment banks started to see clients pulling their money out, and worried that more would follow. On Tuesday, Moody's and Standard & Poor's downgraded ratings on AIG, the world's largest insurer, which was the guarantor of eight million insurance policies with a face value of $1.7 trillion, and tens of trillions in swaps between financial institutions. That same day, the Reserve Primary Fund, the venerable money market fund largely responsible for inventing the very concept, lowered its share price below one dollar—normally the guaranteed "a dollar in means a dollar back" net asset value for money market funds—and halted redemptions. This so-called breaking the buck caused redemptions to be frozen at other money market funds, the safest, banklike investments that form the core of the commercial paper market, the short-term loans that companies have long used to fund expenses.

On Wednesday the Federal Reserve announced it was lending $85 billion to AIG, to prevent the insurer's having to file for bankruptcy, and began its preparations, to be announced the next day, to guarantee all money market funds. Meanwhile, a fleet of banks had announced they were taking drastic measures. Washington Mutual put itself up for sale, Morgan Stanley and Goldman Sachs watched their usually rock-solid share price drop by double-digit percents, and Wachovia thought its prospects were bleak enough to enter merger talks with Morgan Stanley. In a seventy-two-hour span, the Dow plummeted an unprecedented 1,100 points.

Spreading from investment banking to insurance, money market funds, commercial paper, and then commercial banking, it was a run—no different from depositors converging on the doorsteps of banks in 1929—across the global financial system. In chaos lies opportunity, and in this case, the two candidates for president were afforded a rare chance to show the nature and posture and assuredness of leadership. It was here, in their responses to the crisis, that Obama and McCain would starkly diverge, in temperament and public approval alike. McCain started the week with the same line from a week before: "the fundamentals of the economy are strong." Coming on the very day of Lehman's collapse, this attempt at surety or consistency seemed redolent of Bush's brittle brand of stay-the-course resolve in the face of any disaster. It was a sign of either stubbornness or ignorance, two qualities that made McCain look like a doddering old man.

Speaking in Elko, Nevada, on the seventeenth, Obama managed to frame the crisis within the context of his campaign, yet not reduce its startling scope. "What we've seen the last few days," he asserted, "is nothing less than the final verdict on this philosophy, a philosophy that has completely failed. And I am running for president of the United States because the dreams of the American people must not be endangered anymore. It's time to put an end to a broken system in Washington that is breaking the American economy. It's time for change that makes a real difference in your lives."

Paulson had spent the weekend of crisis operating out of the Waldorf-Astoria hotel. By Thursday, September 18, the venue had changed back to Washington. He needed to sell lawmakers on the fact that the systemic risks the economy faced were not only catastrophic but imminent. At 3:30 p.m. he went to the White House and told the president that he intended to ask Congress for a huge sum of money with which to purchase toxic assets from the banks. Bush trusted Paulson on financial matters and gave his blessing to what would turn into the Troubled Asset Relief Program. Now it was a matter of winning over the legislators.

That evening, as a group of key policy makers gathered in Speaker of the House Nancy Pelosi's office, Paulson and Bernanke figured that their best shot at passing TARP was to terrify this group, to make them all feel what these two men had been feeling for a week. Not a man known for histrionics, Bernanke opened the meeting on a dramatic note.

"I am a student of the Great Depression," he began. "Let me state this clearly. If we do not act in the next few days, this will be worse than the Great Depression." He let the statement sink in, just long enough for Senator Chris Dodd to gasp audibly, before he continued: "Investors have lost confidence in our capital markets. It is a matter of *days* before we will witness a series of catastrophic failures."

It was Senate Majority Leader Harry Reid who finally broke the ice.

"The markets *were* up," he remarked, demonstrating a thoroughgoing ignorance of the situation. Paulson's blood, meanwhile, was boiling. The only reason the markets had rebounded at all was that Wall Street was anticipating a rescue plan at any minute! But Paulson knew he could not openly berate the lawmakers, even if they had no idea what they were talking about. He needed somehow to convince them that the issue's urgency was apolitical.

"This is a one-hundred-year situation," he explained. "We can't deal with it around the edges. There are a series of tactical things that need to take place or else all hell will break loose." He wasted no time on that minutia. "This needs to be done by next week. It will take a comprehensive approach to deal with illiquid assets on the balance sheets of these institutions. We are going to ask for the authority to purchase these toxic assets. This is neither a case of regulation or deregulation," he said, trying to distance himself from the image of the free-market demagogue that he knew the Democrats had of him. "The Treasury needs broad authority to purchase illiquid assets from the balance sheets of financial institutions. It goes beyond Wall Street. At bottom these are mostly home loans. If we take care of these illiquid assets, I believe it will stabilize the system."

"What is this going to cost?" Reid asked.

"I'm not entirely sure yet," Paulson said. "Somewhere in the hundreds of billions. Maybe five hundred."

"If you think we can pass a bill to give you $500 billion, you don't understand the Senate!" Reid shot back.

But the group had heard the desperation behind Paulson and Bernanke's words and they knew that if things were really that bad, Congress would rise to the occasion. Senate Minority Leader Mitch McConnell was especially emphatic.

"This sounds like it needs to happen," he said. "If that's the case, we should do this. We *can* do this."

Pelosi offered support from the House.

"We need to leave this room saying we *will* write a bill," she said.

John Boehner agreed. "This is a national crisis," he affirmed. "We need to rise above politics and show Americans we can work together. I will be here as long as it takes. Lock arms and get it done!"

But the group fell into two camps: those who took Paulson and Bernanke's proposal as the Word of God, who thought they should proceed full steam ahead, and those who took the opportunity to demonize Wall Street and to complain about more massive government spending. In this latter camp with Reid was Republican senator Richard Shelby, who complained that it was a "blank check" for the Treasury.

Barney Frank, chairman of the House Financial Services Committee, showed an incisive grasp of the issues at hand. "Who will be the operating entity?" he asked. "If we buy these assets, we will be the foreclosure agent. We need warrants."

"We keep talking about buying up these complex securities," Frank continued, "but we need to understand that at the bottom, these are made up of people's mortgages."

Just before the meeting broke, McConnell addressed what was clearly hanging over the politicians' heads. "I know this is an election year," he said, "and we need to be careful. As soon as this meeting lets out, we need to inform both presidential candidates and ask them not to politicize this debate."

As noble as McConnell's plea might have been, it was far too late. The crisis had already become wholly a political dogfight, and a full-fledged audition, for the presidency.

While Paulson and Bernanke were making their case for TARP on the Hill, John McCain was holding a rally in Cedar Rapids, Iowa, where the waters had finally receded. He was listening wearily to his running mate, who had gone from fresh new face to nationwide obsession almost overnight. She now threatened to swallow his campaign whole. Sarah Palin, for her part, was doing her best to redirect chants of "We want Sar-ah!" to enthusiasm for the top of their ticket, repeating a stale riff about the "courage" of the "maverick of the Senate." Still, the chant persisted, echoing off into the distant future: "We want Sar-ah!"

A thousand miles away, in Española, New Mexico, Obama was campaigning to one of the most evenly split electorates. The state had gone for Gore in 2000 and Bush in 2004, each time by razor-thin margins. Obama by this point had realized how heavily economic issues were weighing on voters' minds, and he tailored his speeches to the crisis. The next day, September 19, he would fly to Miami and kick off a weeklong blitzkrieg that would end, effectively, with him on his way to the presidency. From Florida, Obama endorsed the Fed-Treasury plan that Paulson had unveiled to the country only a few hours earlier.

"Today I fully support the effort of Secretary Paulson and Federal Reserve chairman Bernanke," he said, having by then talked to leaders from the previous day's meeting and heard that TARP was going to pass, and pass soon. "What we're looking at right now is to provide the Treasury and the Fed with as broad authority as necessary to stabilize markets and maintain credit."

McCain, meanwhile, had been running on unfettered markets and reduced government spending, two broad policies that TARP managed, at the same time, to contravene. He would be obliged to support TARP in the end. It was the only responsible stance, if an unpleasant one all the same. But Obama suspected that the program would meet with stiff opposition in McCain's party and that his opponent would find it all but impossible to do the responsible thing *and* please his base. This turned out to be right, as McCain couldn't manage to reframe the issues in a way that gave him a solid place to stand.

On the morning of September 19, Obama met with his economic team in Miami.

A shift in the group's composition and tone had taken place. Their previous meeting, on July 28, included JPMorgan's Jamie Dimon and Google CEO Eric Schmidt, two former Clinton secretaries in Bob Rubin and Bob Reich, and onetime Bush officials such as former SEC chairman Bill Donaldson and former Treasury secretary Paul O'Neill. But none of them carried the clout, at least not in the senator's mind, that Volcker did. Obama started that meeting as he always did, with "Paul, you go first."

This morning, though, Volcker had a scheduling conflict. He said he could stop by in Miami only briefly, before catching a plane to Europe. But if his presence wasn't required, he could take a different flight and be available on the phone, as some other participants would be. Obama told him the photo op would be preferable. In the previous weeks, during a series of phone calls with this group of free-floating bigfoots, Larry Summers had risen to the fore. Volcker stayed a few minutes, offering his symbolic value of a man behind Obama, and then slipped away, as the reporters and photographers exited.

Summers took charge. It was a matter of neither experience nor expertise that pushed him to prominence. Among those present in person or on the conference call, Bob Rubin had more experience in both government and business. Paul O'Neill had actually run an industrial company, Alcoa, and was more of an original thinker. Warren Buffett had vastly more expertise in how the world's markets actually worked. Summers was simply a master explainer, able to deftly boil down the complexities of matters economic and financial, and to put them in terms the nonexpert could understand. He was brilliant at cultivating the sense of control, even as events spun far beyond what could be managed with any certainty. That was his feat, an illusionist's trick calling for a certain true genius: he could will into being the confidence that eluded others—those less self-assured and, maybe sensibly, on humbler terms with the complexities of the world.

To top it all off, Summers believed in the basic soundness of the financial industry. He was sympathetic to liberal ideas but not an advocate of major, systemic change. It was a comforting prospect to think the messy crisis, so far beyond the ken of most politicians, could be solved with a one-off intervention and a few modest reforms thereafter. It would not entail big risks, either in getting the reforms wrong and dragging down the economy with them, or in alienating wealthy allies. Though it was exciting to consider the brazen readjustments championed by progressive economists, such actions had the potential to rock a boat already listing dangerously—and to make powerful enemies. Lacking decades of expertise in the rocket science of modern economics, what sort of leader laid claim to the confidence with which to remake the entire system in grand Rooseveltian fashion?

Oliver Wendell Holmes, Jr., famously remarked that Roosevelt matched "a first-rate temperament" with "a second-rate intellect," but it is undeniable that what Roosevelt lacked in probing, analytical brilliance, he more than made up for in those intangible qualities that distinguish leadership from technical expertise. He understood that the problems afflicting a nation are always in equal measure spiritual crises, and that there is never a clear distinction in politics between the practical and the symbolic. Obama, having risen to prominence on the strength of this very insight, would start disbelieving his own rhetoric as the economic crisis hit. It was, in more ways than one, a true crisis of confidence.

Larry Summers disagreed vehemently with Volcker on fundamental issues. Volcker saw the ad hoc response to each crisis—Bear Stearns, Lehman, Fannie and Freddie, AIG, and now possibly the car companies—as a dangerous program. "We can't keep doing this over a weekend!" he said in frustration at the July meeting, foretelling the disasters of September. Volcker saw that the credit system in the United States was broken. He thought they should set up a modern version of the Depression-era Reconstruction Finance Corporation, a government entity to guarantee smart, responsible lending to private companies. It was a way to slowly work the country off its high ledge of debt, Volcker said, and to kill off the business model of profitably selling debt without having to actually assume the risk, which then gets passed around like a hot potato. Across the table, Larry Summers just rolled his eyes.

The power of Summers's derision is well known, and in grappling with a financial industry that had spent the prior decade pressing farther down the rabbit hole of complex math and tortured modeling, there was currency to the idea that someone's expertise might be out of date. Volcker's entire appeal was his anachronism, an old-school focus on fundamentals, which helped him cut through the mind-numbing logic and technical details with which financiers justified their terrifically risky and profitable operations. Even as Summers ruffled feathers on the team, polluting the group's collegial atmosphere with his brusque, competitive manner, he was winning the battle for Obama's trust. They were already fencing, collegially, like peers. Once the reporters were shooed away in Miami, so that the real meeting could start, Summers's opening précis strayed into political analysis. "Larry, I didn't bring you here for political advice," Obama chided jovially, as Summers and others laughed. And then Summers pushed forward, taking charge. The senator's electoral lead widened as the country's crisis deepened and his cold-sweat moment arrived: he would have to lead the country through this darkness and back to light. In the midst of this crisis of confidence, Obama needed what Summers was offering.

On September 24, five days after the Miami meeting, John McCain suspended his presidential campaign. He said he was going to Washington to participate in the bailout talks. Obama didn't bite. If the crisis had brought on his cold-sweat moment, it had also given him the political window in which to make his move. When McCain called a White House meeting the following day, bringing together Obama, Bush, Paulson, and top party brass, an odd gambit to demonstrate his *own* leadership, Obama was by all accounts—from both Democrats and Republicans— the far better prepared of the two. Having spent a year among Wolf and his Wall Street patrons, Obama could talk finance like a pro.

"Obama delivered a thoughtful, well-prepared presentation, sketching the broad outlines of the problem and stressing the need for immediate action," Paulson later recalled. Others noted the senator's calm focus and even "presidential" demeanor.

Obama knew he had McCain on the ropes. His opponent had called the meeting as a sort of trap, and Obama had responded with an unmistakable smackdown. He spoke without notes—didn't need them—and a thought flitted through his mind: he knew this stuff.

"The Democrats will deliver the votes," he asserted with confidence. McCain had no rebuttal. He just listened, aloof and irritable at his own meeting, his discomfort palpable. Obama noticed this and pressed his advantage:

"I'd like to hear what Senator McCain has to say, since we haven't heard from him yet." That qualifier was a jab, small and calculated. It was the presidential election, after all, and Obama intended to win this thing.

McCain fumbled through a few platitudes and political nonstarters. He was clearly uncomfortable engaging in any kind of serious discussion on the topic, reading clumsily from the single note card he'd brought with him.

News reports and photos of the meeting—a true leadership audition, in a crowded room of official Washington —were soon circling the global media, offering what felt like an unmanaged glimpse into government's own assessment of who could best lead it through peril.

Here, in the Cabinet Room of the White House, Obama clearly won the prize of being the most presidential, followed by the oddly deferential Bush—who didn't say very much and seemed perplexed about why the meeting had been convened—and McCain, in a distant third, who looked confused, as if he had stepped off at the wrong bus stop. Like several seminal moments that preceded it—the convention speech in 2004, the Iowa victory speech, the brilliant dissertation on race—this was an instant when the public refocused its gaze. The African American senator with little experience indisputably looked and acted like a president in a time of crisis.

When the discussion broke, the two political camps huddled in separate White House enclaves. The Democrats retreated to the Roosevelt Room to talk through the sticky task of reconciling politics with what looked like a once-in-a-lifetime crisis. In the middle of this, an exasperated Paulson burst into the room, begging them not to attack TARP.

Pelosi for one had had enough. Her speakership had been built on a groundswell of anti-Bush fervor, and she not only vehemently disliked the president and his team, but also didn't *trust* them—their declarations or their motives.

"That's bullshit, Hank," she said.

Paulson knew the only answer here to Pelosi's aggressive politics was prostration. He genuflected, clasping his hands together, and put it on the line.

"I'm begging you," he said. "*Please* don't let this fail."

"I didn't know you were a Catholic," the Speaker remarked dryly.

The next night would see the first of three presidential debates, but it would hardly matter. As Obama and McCain argued in Oxford, Mississippi, the election had already been decided. Their conduct in the wake of the crisis was already showing in the polls. The weak numbers that had concerned Obama in the early part of the month were fading quickly. After September 25, the day he suspended his campaign, McCain would not lead again in a single major poll. The election had been clinched in ten days.

On September 29 the first incarnation of TARP failed in the House, 228–205. Just moments before the vote took place, Pelosi spent just two lines describing the bill before launching into a diatribe against the Bush administration.

"Seven hundred billion is a staggering number," she said, "but only a part of the cost of the failed policies of the Bush administration."

Paulson's plea had failed. It was all politics on the Hill.

"When President Bush took office," Pelosi went on, "he inherited President Clinton's surpluses, four years in a row of budget surpluses." As she continued, policy makers from both parties were working on their own multibillion-dollar stimulus plans, having come to a consensus on, at least, the necessity of action. "No regulation, no supervision, no discipline," Pelosi persisted, "and if you fail, you will have a golden parachute and the taxpayer will bail you out. Those days are over. The *party* is over."

Many Republicans would cite Pelosi's use of her platform to denounce Bush as their reason for voting against the bill. It was a circus. Wall Street traders watched in horror as the Dow plummeted an all-time, one-day record: 777 points. Obama took the vote in stride. It was one of the country's darkest hours and yet, in a little more than a month he would have the country feeling as good as it had in decades. But now, with the reality of victory in his grasp, Obama was left to contend with both an irony and a sobering truth. The former was that Obama's year and a half relentlessly courting Wall Street's titans, who had pocketed historic profits on the path to disaster, had inadvertently graced him with enough mastery of how money and risk were managed, and mismanaged, that he could best Bush and crush McCain in the Cabinet Room audition. All the better that none of the politicians gathered around the table seemed to recognize this much less bracing truth, known only to him and a handful of others: he wasn't ready.

––––––––

On October 13, Paulson summoned the CEOs of nine of the largest American banks to the Treasury Department's large conference room to deliver a surprise ultimatum.

Getting them to come—without telling them why—had been a feat. But it was simply too risky to offer advance warning of what he was attempting: his intentions might leak and then his gambit might fail, a combination that would kill the confidence-building—the faith that government had this crisis under control—that was the very point of the meeting.

The night before, while streams of urgent e-mail invites were being sent to an array of corner offices, Paulson met with Bernanke, Geithner, and Sheila Bair at his office to work through strategy. The goal was to get credit flowing again. The financial system was gripped with fear. Institutions were hoarding assets. Geithner had been pressing, cajoling, even threatening the various banks to merge—to pool capital, and then slash duplicative staffs, all to no avail. The CEOs were all in self-protective mode, trying to avoid messy marriages. Bernanke, meanwhile, had been secretly opening the Fed coffers to all manner of financial institutions, and some nonfinancials as well, in the United States and abroad. Since the previous fall, nearly $400 billion in virtually free money had been passed out by the Fed. Still, the economy was starved of capital, like a thirsty man living off drops of water. The original plan, to use TARP funds to repurchase toxic assets from the banks, had been deemed too slow. It could take months. Without credit, the system would seize—as it had during the Great Depression—and the consequences could be unimaginable. Those at Treasury often thought of the call with Jeff Immelt in the panic after Lehman's fall, when the General Electric CEO said that his company might not be able to fund operations and fill orders. The flow of credit, like blood through the circulatory system, is a precondition for the economy's survival.

So instead Paulson, Bernanke, and Geithner decided they would use capital injections, giving each of the largest banks multimillion-dollar welfare checks that they would commit to use expressly for lending.

Or, at least that was the plan. Bair, as was her way, was skeptical. "How are you going to get the banks to take the money?" she prodded Paulson at the planning session. Paulson said he would threaten them, and that the institutions that needed the capital would drag along the few that didn't. Why was it important for banks that didn't need a capital injection to agree to take one? For cover. Paulson said he'd tell them they must take it so that their less fortunate brethren wouldn't be marked as in desperate need of a government infusion. Such a decline of confidence in those institutions could trigger a "run."

At 3:00 p.m. on the thirteenth, a Tuesday, the bankers filed into the conference room, several of them grousing about why they had been summoned to D.C. Paulson attempted his ultimatum.

"Let me be clear: if you don't take it and you aren't able to raise the capital that they say you need in the market, then I'm going to give you a second helping and you're not going to like the terms on that."

He paused, and reached for the high ground: "This is the right thing to do for the country."

Geithner then rattled off the amount each bank would be given. Bank of America: $25 billion; Citigroup: 25; Goldman Sachs: 10; JPMorgan: 25; Morgan Stanley: 10; State Street: 10; Wells Fargo: 25.

The quid pro quo, Paulson stressed, was that the banks use this money to lend. Nods all around.

But this initial receptiveness dissolved when John Thain, now technically an employee of Bank of America, mentioned the CEO's version of the "third rail."

"What kind of protections can you give us on changes in compensation policy?"

The Treasury was giving the banks cheap capital, in the midst of a crisis, and Thain was asking if their bonuses would be safe? CEO arrogance, though now tinged with a bit more unspoken desperation, had restored itself. The CEOs started to push back. What would the government demand in return for this "investment"—influence over operations, corporate decisions, and strategies? Though Thain was no longer a member of that exclusive club, he could still play the part—now they all were.

If nothing else, this prompted Bank of America's actual CEO, Thain's boss, to assert his primacy.

"I have three things to say," Ken Lewis intervened. "There's obviously a lot to like and dislike about the program. I think given what's happening, if we don't have a healthy fear of the unknown, then we're crazy."

Secondly, he said, "if we spend another second talking about compensation issues, we've lost our minds!"

And, finally, "I don't think we need to be talking about this a whole lot more . . . We all know that we're going to sign."

Slowly the tension subsided and the group acquiesced. The CEOs one by one took the plunge, allowing the federal government to essentially take a stake in their companies. By 6:00 p.m., all the bankers signaled that their boards had either approved or soon would approve the proposal. Signatures poured in. The government had handed $125 billion to nine banks, without conditions. Lending? Paulson's assurance that the U.S. government would not intrude on the sovereignty of the banks receiving taxpayers' money would make the issue of what to do with the money a matter ultimately of CEO discretion.

Not every president gets an era. Bush "41" didn't. Reagan did, and of course FDR got his. Clinton yearned for his eight years in office to mark an era, but he sensed they fell short. He often said a president needed to have governed during a crisis to be considered "great." But clearly greatness calls for stiffer stuff than that. Bush II and LBJ got their eras, but in large part they saw their presidencies swallowed by titanic events, forces capable of crushing best-laid plans and magnifying their errors of judgment.

By November 3, the forty-third U.S. president had all but vanished. He had only a handful of public events scheduled for the final weeks of October and none for the first few days of November. Bush's 20 percent approval rating, the lowest on record for any president, stood as a testimony to the country's rejection of his prideful, intensely personal style of leadership. During the decades since Nixon, Republican politicians had found success in a particular model: stalwart, unreflective leadership that championed America's greatness at every turn and conceded nothing to their opponents. But Republican presidents had a tendency to turn away from party dogma by the end of their tenures. The term "Nixon to China"—referring most literally to the direct talks Nixon held with a Chinese leadership he had long reviled—is now a catchphrase for how a leader can move in an unexpected direction. Reagan, who won the presidency advocating tax cuts, saw in his second term that he had gone too far and reined in those cuts. Then he sat down rather amicably with Gorbachev, head of the "evil empire," to work on ridding the world of nuclear weapons. Even Bush the Elder went back on his "No new taxes" pledge in an effort to balance the budget—a decision that helped set the table for Clinton's budgetary success.

But Bush the Younger never made a similar leap. He watched the election approach from inside the White House, a pariah now across the land he had governed with will and nerve. He remained forthright, unwilling to apologize for anything that might have gone wrong during his eight years, uninterested in second-guessing himself. No, he was going into hiding, not planning to emerge from the White House. He voted by absentee ballot. The leader of the free world, head of the world's longest-standing democracy, would be staying home on Election Day. He had already mailed it in.

Eras end with a whisper, reflection, and the quiet drift preceding sleep.

But they start with a roar, the forceful declaration of a new dawn, different from all those that came before.

A wave was gathering force across the country on the night before the election. It had been gathering for weeks. The grass roots that had taken hold in Iowa a year before had steadily spread, gaining purchase from state to state, and by November 3, 2008, Team Obama was running through fields of tall grass, in city after city, town after town.

The senator would give the final speech of his campaign that night in Manassas, Virginia, and everything was clicking for him. David Axelrod, his campaign manager, worried now about the fact that he could not think of anything to worry about.

"I don't have much time to reflect on what's happening—to ask the *why* questions—and Barack doesn't, either," Axelrod said. But as he paced the carpet, he was reminded of the original *why* question that had gotten all this started.

It had come in December 2006. Obama, Michelle, and eight others were gathered in Axelrod's downtown Chicago office. If Obama was going to run, he had to decide soon. The group had laid out what the primary schedule would look like, alongside a thorough game plan for fund-raising and organization building. Insights and queries shot back and forth across the room.

But it was Michelle, Axelrod remembered, who stopped the show.

"You need to ask yourself *why* you want to do this," she said. "What are you hoping to uniquely accomplish, Barack?" Obama sat quietly for a moment, while everyone waited to hear what he would say.

"This I know," Obama said. "When I raise my hand and take that oath of office, I think the world will look at us differently. And millions of kids across the country will look at themselves differently."

Obama understood, from his own search for identity, how America's struggle with race was part of a larger story—a quest for dignity and hope that defined countless lives across the globe. This battered and downcast nation, he believed, was ready—eager, even—to prove the truth of its sacred oaths and, in so doing, prove itself once again to the broader world: liberty and justice for all. If through his own ambitions he could offer the country a chance to step forward, the country just might rise to the occasion and step with him into a brighter future.

And it had. You could see it clearly, at this highest peak of the journey, the last night of a historic twenty-one-month campaign. By 10:00 p.m., a hundred thousand people had gathered at the Prince William County Fairgrounds in Manassas. They had been gathering since midafternoon, matching, person for person, the largest crowd Obama had ever drawn.

Manassas lay on one of those border territories where the two Americas met, where the edge of D.C.'s suburbs bled into the real Old Dominion, where Starbucks gave way to gun shops, whole grains to grits. Under a dark and starless sky, people arrived from every direction, trekking miles on foot from the nearest parking spots, through a cool, misty bite of the November air. The crowds pressed thick along the fences, Americans of all backgrounds and skin colors huddling close. A special-ed teacher and her sister, who said, "I never felt this way. I just feel like he can save us," stood beside an American-born Rothschild, a big contributor who had met Obama at a fund-raiser and said she'd "never been the same." Down the row, a Virginian farmer, thick-necked, calloused, and brush-scrubbed after a day with his hogs, remarked that it was "a long way from the War of Northern Aggression, which my great-greats fought in, to here." But not so far. It was only about five miles from the battlefield where northern and southern troops first clashed in the battle of Bull Run to start the Civil War. One hundred and forty-seven years later, at 10:28 p.m., a black man stepped to the stage, the presidency within his grasp.

"What a scene, what a crowd," Obama said, half to himself, half to the roiling sea of humanity screaming in jubilation and waving American flags. He shook his head. "Wow."

The crowd seemed to swell with recognition. This is the way great speeches work: the call and the response. The giver receives, the receivers give, and they are one. With long-deferred dreams waiting in the wings, tonight, for the last time, the crowd could watch their hero reach, fingertips outstretched, for the great prize, and say, like a silent hymn, *So close, so close, and when you reach it, we will reach it, too.*

America believes it is a blessed nation, that its triumphs and misfortunes bear the imprint of higher purpose. Everyone in the crowd knew the heartrending final twist of the story, that Obama's grandmother—the tough Kansan lady who worked in a bomber factory through World War II and raised Barack—had died that day. Obama teared up in Charlotte in the afternoon, one lone drop on his cheek and his voice catching, just once, as he talked about her being "a very humble person and a very quiet person, she was one of those quiet heroes that we have all across America." He pushed through the swell of emotion. "In this crowd there are a lot of quiet heroes like that, mothers and fathers and grandparents who have worked hard and sacrificed all their lives. And the satisfaction that they get is seeing that their children, or maybe their grandchildren or great-grandchildren, live a better life than they did. That's what America is about."

A promised land—what it has *always* been about. It is through this self-conception that America has fit itself most powerfully into the greatest of human narratives: the journey narrative, of the elusive "up ahead," and of those who usher us forward with sacrifice and faith but cannot themselves cross over. So it seemed fitting in a way that "Toot," the quiet hero, could not "be there with us," as her black grandson, the boy she had loved so dearly, finally led the way into Canaan.

Obama reconciled himself to being a vessel for this narrative, although he knew its perils. So in Manassas he tried not to say too much about what he would do when, along with all those surging behind him, they reached this promised land. It was an idea, after all, more than a place. But in the hopeful electricity of the air, a careful-enough listener might have heard this tension, between symbol and reality, crackle softly. What substance of triumph to come, what feat of world-beating diplomacy or legislative derring-do, could shine as brightly as this victory of emblem and ideal?

"I have just one word for you," Obama intoned to the crowd. "Just one word, a single word: tomorrow. Tomorrow."

Then he ran through the obligatory riffs about policies encouraging "hard work and sacrifice," reinvesting "in our middle class" and giving everybody "a chance to succeed." But not too much of this. People didn't care to hear more than a few familiar cadences of these old platitudes of slow, steady progress and fair play. So he wrapped it up, this final campaign speech, by reaching back for his best stuff, a tale he hadn't told since Iowa and the primary, the story of down-and-out Obama, from back when "nobody gave us much of a chance."

It was really a preacher's riff—of being lost and finding redemption—and even if the audience tonight hadn't heard this particular story, they knew how it must turn out. So he worked it up, full of relish, recalling how he was limping along the campaign trail, town by town, at this point in South Carolina and without a prayer. He had somehow ended up in a field house in Greenwood on a rainy morning, about twenty people in the audience, and he was "coming down with a cold, and my back is sore," and "I am mad, I am wet, and I am sleepy."

"Suddenly I heard this voice cry out behind me. 'Fired up!' I'm shocked. I jumped up. I don't know what's going on, but everyone else acts as though this were normal, and they say, 'Fired up!' Then I hear this voice say, 'Ready to go!' And the twenty people in the room act like this happens all the time, and they say, 'Ready to go!' . . . I looked behind me and there is this small woman, about sixty years old, a little over five feet, looks like she just came from church, she's got on a big church hat . . . She looks at me and she smiles and she says, 'Fired up!'

"For the next five minutes she proceeds to do this. 'Fired up?' And everyone says, 'Fired up!' And she says, 'Ready to go?' And they say, 'Ready to go!' I'm standing there and I'm thinking, *I'm being outflanked by this woman. She's stealing my thunder* . . .

"But here's the thing . . . after a minute or so I am feeling kind of fired up. I'm feeling like I'm ready to go. So I join the chant. It feels good. For the rest of the day, even after we left Greenwood, even though it was still raining, even though I was still not getting big crowds anywhere . . . I feel a little lighter, a little better . . .

"Here's the point, Virginia: that's how this thing started. It shows you what one voice can do, that one voice can change a room. And if a voice can change a room, it can change a city. And if it can change a city, it can change a state. And if it can change a state, it can change a nation. And if it can change a nation, it can change the world."

That last part he said softly, his voice hoarse. Then he led them in the chant—"Fired up!" "Ready to go!"—thundering now as one hundred thousand voices, roaring through tears, sent their cries echoing across the old battlefield, just a few miles away, where the rebel yell once rang out to start a war and the century-long journey to King and then the path to Obama, cut across America to this night, full circle, in the long, fitful quest for a more perfect union.

Tonight would come about as close to that perfection as may be attainable. When the chants died down, Obama stood there and waved, calm as the thunderous din washed over him. Then his whole body seemed to exhale. Game over. He grabbed the water bottle from the lectern and downed it. Rippling in the air, claiming its place among our most essential, was that single word.

"Tomorrow."

Twenty-four hours later, a few minutes before 11:00 p.m., Barack Obama stepped onto the stage in Chicago's Grant Park as president-elect of the United States. The ground was trembling from the streets of Chicago to the fertile fields of Kansas; from Montgomery, Alabama, to San Francisco; from the Great Lakes to the coasts, and across the world. And there was something sobering, even ominous, in the shaking earth. It is one thing to rouse the passion of a people, but quite another to lead them.

You could hear a certain relief in John McCain's gracious concession speech, the half-contented sigh of a man who could now return to the self-deprecating, no-bullshit persona he liked best, without the fate of a nation resting on his shoulders. But for Obama, who had so powerfully joined hands with the country's yearning and beleaguered, the road ahead had only gotten more difficult. The yawning chasm now loomed between who he was and what he really intended to do.

It is a rare bond that allows a president and a nation to move as one. It forms when people, usually too busy to fuss over policy debates, see their leader as someone guided by a familiar internal compass, who will rise to meet the nation's crises in the same way they meet the challenges in their own daily lives. Policies suddenly become not just what the president does at some adviser's behest, to score a political point, but who he—or, someday, she—is. It is then that president and public enter their shared moment.

Bush rose up, harnessing his basic trust in emotion and impulse, to meet the first challenges of 9/11. But then he froze solid. The crisis, so unprecedented and fast-moving, demanded reappraisal as it unfolded and deepened. Bush, instead, kept returning to his own inner issues, his old battles and insecurities, which proved too static and too limited for the dictates of the moment. He needed to grow, and he didn't.

Obama's charmed journey would soon bring him to a similar crucible. But not just yet, not tonight. The crowds in Grant Park, those around the country and the globe, wanted for now to live in this shared moment, to live in their champion's victory and to make it theirs. It was no longer about tomorrow but about today.

And yet, inside Obama, another quality was at work, one that had remained largely hidden from view during the campaign—an anticipatory sharpness, a sensitivity to how his actions would be seen and his words taken. He tended to trust this instinct too much, to give in to his tendency to assert control, and this could cut him off from the dynamism of the present tense, from the shared moment, even though, as in Manassas the night before, it was often when he was at his best.

He had thought through this victory a thousand times before—what it would look like, what it would mean. But before he had even stepped to the stage, into that very moment for which he had been waiting his whole life, he grabbed Axelrod and told him to cancel the fireworks. Too celebratory. The country was in crisis, after all, and it was the wrong tone.

In this moment he had brought to ignition, his response was to manage expectations and gently tamp them down. The canceled fireworks would be just the beginning; the job promised to be one hell of a challenge. As Michelle and the girls walked back across the floodlit runway to the wings, Obama turned to deliver a speech that, from the start, would strike a subdued note. It was as much his manner as his words, which began memorably:

"If there is anyone out there who still doubts that America is a place where all things are possible, who still wonders if the dream of our founders is alive in our time, who still questions the power of our democracy, tonight is your answer."

And what did this answer consist in?

"It's the answer that led those, who have been told for so long, by so many, to be cynical and fearful and doubtful of what we can achieve, to put their hands on the arc of history and bend it once more toward the hope of a better day. It's been a long time coming, but tonight, because of what we did on this day, in this election, at this defining moment, change has come to America."

In speeches over the years, Obama had often referenced his favorite line of King's: "The arc of the moral universe is long but it bends toward justice." Everyone borrows from everyone else and pays homage to their heroes. But in Obama's rendering tonight, King's arc now bent "toward the hope of a better day," skewing in this bright direction for the simple fact of his election.

What change really had come, beyond the extraordinary fact of his arrival, was not clear—nor clarified in this speech. Instead, the president-elect retreated from his opening salvo, dialing back expectations:

"This victory alone is not the change we seek," he explained. "It is only the chance for us to make that change. And that cannot happen if we go back to the way things were. It cannot happen without you."

None of this kept anyone from weeping and cheering, not his avowals that the "road ahead will be long" or that our "climb will be steep." They were dancing in Kenya, and all across Africa. From South Side Chicago out across at least one country and continent, the streets filled with young and old, in inner cities and suburbs, gated communities and slums alike. It was a difficult world everyone lived in, each day, but tonight was the long-awaited counterpoint to all that, to the wars, the collapsing economy, and that growing sense, in the long Bush twilight, of being leaderless.

But you can miss the moment, even the one you've been waiting for your whole life.

Not that the crowd could be quelled or could see in Obama, in his Kennedy suit hanging perfectly from his angular shoulders, anything but the confidence of a true leader and the promise of better days, brighter skies. People were overcome. Even the ever-competitive Jesse Jackson, a few rows back from the stage—a man who carried King's bags and long thought *he* would be the man's heir onstage tonight—wept like a child, tears soaking his weathered face. It was no different on either side of him, or among those crowded a mile back from the first row. Everyone let the moment's emotion run through them.

Everyone except the man on the stage.

He had tried on his presidential voice, flatter and soberer than the night before, to see how it fit, to see if any posture or presentation, much less word or deed, could rise to meet the roaring hopes of this expectant crowd. But it hadn't fit—at least not like it had the night before in Manassas. And the theater of the campaign had suddenly given way to a sobering reality: he was going to be the president. Something in that lofty title, for all his demonstrable talents, didn't fit.

After five minutes of waving to the massed convulsions, Obama stepped down into the stage's tented wings, where Michelle, the woman who knew everything, knew him when he was Barry and sat up nights with him wondering what sort of life they could look forward to, raised her palm for a high-five, her face aglow.

He took her raised hand and gently lowered it. Not tonight, he whispered. Not tonight.

THE B-TEAM

T HE DAY AFTER THE ELECTION, OBAMA GOT UP EARLY, DONNED a sweatshirt and White Sox cap, and stepped out into a brisk Chicago morning. The autumnal tranquility of early November was already giving way to the frosty throes of winter in Chicago. He quietly slipped into the health club at a friend's apartment building and by 12:30 was at his desk in an office building near Hyde Park meeting David Axelrod and his transition chief, John Podesta.

A best-kept secret could now begin openly to bear rewards: Podesta had been meeting with the candidate since June to prepare him for a transition to the presidency. Word of this preemptive planning had been closely guarded to avoid the impression of entitlement to victory.

Obama said later that, because of the economic crisis, "In some ways, my presidency began in September of 2008." His words and deeds—consulting with Paulson about his efforts at Treasury, or meeting with congressional leaders about emergency measures—carried the weight of presidential engagements. At that point, he was almost like the leader of the opposition in a Parliamentary model, supporting ministers, like Paulson and Bernanke, in their emergency actions.

By late September, when polls started to show him pulling firmly into the lead, Podesta secretly called together former chiefs of staff to help Obama sketch out his presidential future.

They met in a Reno hotel. Two former Clinton chiefs of staff, Erskine Bowles and Leon Panetta, joined Podesta, also a former Clinton chief of staff, and a clutch of Obama's oldest and closest advisers, Jarrett, Axelrod, and Rouse. Also called in was William Daley—son of Chicago's former mayor, brother of its current one—who had been commerce secretary and deputy chief of staff to Clinton. He was now a senior executive at JPMorgan Chase. Each brought a list of potential appointees for senior positions, as well as their most incisive advice for the management challenges Obama was about to face.

"If I win, what advice can you guys give me" about how to proceed? Obama queried.

Erskine Bowles cut right to the chase. "Leave your friends at home," he said. "They just create problems when you get to Washington."

Jarrett and Axelrod looked on, dumbfounded.

The former chiefs nodded. They'd all been in White Houses where old friends or senior campaign aides found themselves lost and ineffective in managing a presidency. Panetta talked about the need for a strong chief of staff who could run the White House and, himself, command loyalty and accountability, but always be in sync with the president. Bowles agreed. "You can't run this operation on your own—you need to have someone solid you can rely on so you can be president." As this discussion progressed, Obama cut them off. "Sounds like you're talking about Rouse." There were smiles all around—everyone in the room was a Rouse fan—but Pete demurred. He said being chief wasn't right for him at this point for a variety of personal reasons. He felt he'd be better as the trusted guy Obama could call into the Oval Office to talk about tough issues, just one-on-one. "Well, not now," Obama nodded, "but maybe later."

The attendees then spent hours offering their best suggestions for the chief job and other senior positions. The name of Rahm Emanuel never came up.

He had not been a perfect friend to the Obama campaign. Caught between his allegiances to Obama and Clinton during the primary, he opted to "hide under his desk," in his words, rather than endorse either candidate, and never did much to assist in the general election.

In the ensuing six weeks, Obama had often thought of the Reno meeting. As one close adviser said, "I think he heard everyone in the room, but deep down he felt that his charm and intelligence would be plenty to handle these management issues, which of course often sneak up on presidents to show how important they can be."

By November 4, Obama had narrowed his chief of staff choices down to two names: Tom Daschle and Rahm Emanuel, who'd been recommended by the Chicagoans, including Axelrod.

Sitting that afternoon with Podesta and Axelrod, with the ink barely dry on his electoral victory, Obama knew that picking the chief of staff was job one. The position is widely recognized to be among the most powerful among nonelected officials in the executive branch, possibly in the entire government. The compare-and-contrast between the two men was simple: in Daschle, Obama would get a like-minded partner, calm, intelligent, and surprisingly firm; in Emanuel, the yang to his yin, someone excitable, action-oriented, and by certain accounts ruthless. Emanuel was in many ways Obama's antithesis, but as the campaign wore on, especially in the weeks leading up to November 4, it had become clear that Obama was leaning toward the pugnacious congressman.

Emanuel was, of course, a widely known entity, a D.C. fixture with a reputation for a two-fisted style of politics and boundless tactical energy. Though the fourth-ranking Democrat in the House, he had even loftier ambitions. It was universally known that he hoped to be the chamber's first Jewish Speaker. Two decades younger than Pelosi and her two deputies, who were all approaching seventy, Emanuel seemed a shoo-in to take the job one day.

But he also came with White House experience, having worked for Clinton as political director in the 1990s, in what everyone agreed had been a tumultuous tenure. Dubbed "the enforcer," Emanuel was at one point demoted for being abrasive, only to reemerge as the tactical force behind NAFTA. He went on to engineer a series of small-bore Clinton initiatives before leaving in 1998 to take a job in finance.

Like many Democrats in exile from the late '90s on, "Rahmbo," as he was jokingly known, monetized his talents. With no MBA and little business experience, he was nonetheless able to secure a job as a managing director at the investment bank Wasserstein Perella, which netted him more than $16 million during his brief tenure. Insofar as it was always clear that he'd return to government, the compensation makes sense, said one former investment chief, a fan of Emanuel's, who now works in Washington: "Paying someone who will be a future government official a lot of money for doing very little? On Wall Street we call that an investment."

By 2002, when he was elected to Congress, Emanuel already knew the upstart state senator with the funny name and presidential ambitions. They were not close friends but, like a pair of ions, had an opposites-attract quality that was instantly apparent. At a roast of Emanuel during a Chicago fund-raiser in 2005, Obama, cool and coy, with his flawless timing, zinged the emotive Emanuel, claiming the onetime ballet dancer had adapted Machiavelli's *The Prince* to dance, "with a lot of kicks below the waist." Obama went on to explain that the loss of a middle finger in a teenage mishap with a meat slicer had left Emanuel "practically mute." The crowd roared. But when he had finished with the barbs, Obama offered a concise, accurate description of his colleague.

"Rahm is a little intense," Obama had said. "He's strong, he's aggressive, he's emotional, he's moody."

Why Obama would want a right-hand man with these qualities—especially the last two—was puzzling to a few senior members of his campaign staff. One later remarked, "Rahm's all impulse and action, with very modest organizational skills. This was not a mystery to people who'd worked with him. Either Obama didn't know that, which is unlikely, or he didn't care."

The campaign's innermost circle, meanwhile, was all slipping into key roles. The three "senior advisers" would be David Axelrod, Valerie Jarrett, and Pete Rouse. Right behind them was a trio that had been with Obama since 2004: Robert Gibbs, who would become press secretary; Bill Burton, deputy press secretary; and Jon Favreau, now all of twenty-seven, as head speechwriter.

These decisions were all but foregone conclusions, but others would prove thornier. Obama's toughest calls, everyone knew, would concern his economic team.

In a single day of informed consent, the Windy City had become the de facto center of American politics. While President Bush and Washington plodded through a lame-duck season, Democrats were mulling over what they would do come January 20. Insiders and policy experts found themselves heading from Washington to Chicago, for a chance to bend the president-elect's ear.

The day after the election, Peter Orszag booked a flight to Chicago for the following week. He had much less personal experience with Obama than many of those—especially from the campaign—who hoped to score a position on the economic team. In the midst of the September crisis, Orszag—who held one of Washington's most influential jobs as head of the Congressional Budget Office—watched from afar as a veritable who's who of economists gathered around the senator. Despite his lengthy tenure in the capital, he'd met Obama on only a few occasions, but the young senator seemed to speak clearly to Orszag's "super-wonk" sensibilities.

Orszag was a bona fide academic phenomenon who blew through Princeton for his bachelor's (*summa*) and went on to get a master's while a Marshall Scholar at the London School of Economics, where he later received his PhD. He could think in numbers, talk in full sentences, and he worked nonstop, all of which impressed the era's ubiquitous mentor to young economists, Bob Rubin. Ever nearby through these years was another, even more accomplished Rubin protégé, twenty years past his wunderkind moment of becoming, at twenty-eight, one of the youngest tenured professors ever at Harvard. That of course was Larry Summers, who became Treasury secretary in 1999, around the time that Orszag was promoted to senior economic adviser to the president. When Larry and Peter met across the conference table in those days, staffers joked that the Treasury Department could add to tax receipts by selling tickets. They both felt entitled to "smartest guy in the room" honors—and, after all, how could there be two?

During the Bush era, when Summers began his stint as Harvard president, Orszag became a senior fellow in economic studies at the renowned Brookings Institution and then in 2005 became director of the Hamilton Project, a think tank within Brookings set up by Rubin to bring hard-eyed analysis to long-standing liberal positions.

That's when he first met Senator Barack Obama. After more than a decade in D.C., Orszag was no stranger to what he referred to as the "Senate gestalt." One custom obliged him to pick his seat only after a senator had picked his or her own. So when he walked into Obama's office, Orszag found himself standing around awkwardly, waiting for the senator to sit down.

Finally he asked, "Senator Obama, where should I sit?"

Obama looked at him perplexedly. "I sit where you aren't," he directed. "I'm not into this whole alpha-senator thing."

From there, it got even better. A policy geek, Orszag was prone to tangents and often lost listeners in his love of esoteric facts. So as the conversation with Obama wandered, Orszag, in typical fashion, found himself citing a vaguely relevant study out of the Brookings Institution. "I know exactly the study you're talking about," Obama interjected, catching the never-one-to-be-outwonked Orszag entirely off guard. "I thought it was interesting how . . ." And off he went.

Orszag was bowled over. There was simply no way Obama's staff had distracted him with such obscure policy studies. The guy was the real deal. There are few things as awing or as humbling to a professional whiz kid like Orszag as the realization that among the nation's senators, a group he was accustomed to having to sway toward intellectual sunlight, there was someone as smart as he was, if not smarter still.

These thoughts played through Orszag's mind as he made his way to Chicago for his job interview with the leader-in-waiting of the free world. Because of his day job, Orszag had to handle matters with the utmost delicacy: no calls to his office from anyone in the Obama campaign, only to his cell phone and only after work hours. He was, after all, in one of the last true honest-broker positions in the federal government, heading up the bipartisan Congressional Budget Office.

The "bipartisan" tag was hard-won and ever more the key to CBO's franchise. With its hundred number-crunching analysts—both Democrats and Republicans—the office served as Congress's official scorekeeper, offering the consensus view of a given law's impact on the federal budget. Not that everyone heeded CBO's projections, but at least someone was keeping score.

During his years in D.C., Orszag had come to be a leading expert on what, year by year, the government was recognizing as its greatest existential threat: the rising cost of health care. When he had arrived in Washington in the mid-1990s, in the wake of Clinton's failure to reform the health care system, Medicare and Medicaid spending—though only a fraction of what they would become—were already showing steady increases driven by rising medical costs. The cost of health care had, in short, moved onto the political radar. But in typical D.C. fashion, the problem could not really be confronted until it was matched with a politically viable solution.

So this was what Orszag looked for—and what he found. The place was Dartmouth College, in Hanover, New Hampshire, and the man was named Jack Wennberg.

A quiet revolution in medicine had begun in 1967. Wennberg, a headstrong and independent thinker, was settling in Vermont after a postgraduate stint at Johns Hopkins. His research interest had been piqued by President Johnson's recently established programs, Medicare and Medicaid, the data on which, in those days, were easily obtained, rich, and complete. By virtue of the large population these programs embraced, Wennberg found he could suddenly track medical outcomes across a vast sea of patients. What he found was startling. Thousands of risky and expensive procedures were being performed each year without any likely medical value.

This conclusion took a while to come to, but strong clues were evident from the very beginning. In a pair of demographically similar counties Wennberg looked at in Vermont, there were wide variations, he found, in the numbers of common procedures performed. Some were conducted two or three times as often in one county as in its neighbor. But despite this, there was virtually no variation in medical outcome. People got sick and died from the conditions in question at all but identical rates. Could this mean that some procedures had virtually no medical value? he wondered. The answer would turn out to be yes, and Wennberg, who was treated for years as a dangerous heretic by America's medical papacy, eventually founded the Dartmouth Atlas Project and a new school of "evidence-based" medicine.

By the early 2000s the medical establishment had reluctantly conceded the basic soundness of the so-called Wennberg Variation. The institute built around his early breakthroughs had in the meantime gathered similar data from across the country. The purview of evidence-based medicine had widened to embrace thornier issues about the stunning variance between both practice and cost. Some hospitals, for instance, were charging twice as much as others, with no discernable added value for patients. Certain procedures appeared to come into vogue based on revenues per hour, rather than on their provable medical value. Most damning of all were the supply-driven findings, which showed that the number of specialists in a given geographic area often determined the number of procedures performed there. Twice as many gynecological surgeons meant twice as many hysterectomies. The same correlations applied with orthopedic surgeons and back operations, cardiac surgeons and heart shunts, and so forth.

For Orszag this was evidentiary heaven. With accountability and data-driven rigor, Dartmouth's findings pointed the way toward improved treatment at lower cost. What could be better? Wennberg himself called medicine to that point "an unmanaged, evidence-free experiment." And it was time to bring both management and evidence to bear. The government, as the biggest single source of medical payments, was clearly the sole body with the will and power to do this. If it could embrace even a fraction of the Dartmouth methodologies, health care would be improved and the federal budget rescued.

By the time Orszag became head of the CBO in January 2007, he was carrying the Dartmouth charts to congressional meetings and preaching to anyone who would listen about the "evidence-based" cure for rising medical costs. Though he'd had only a few discussions with Obama during this period about health care, he was comforted to find that the senator knew about the Dartmouth revolution and could recite a variety of its key findings.

Now, even though his meeting was not until ten o'clock the next morning, Orszag couldn't help but be excited. The lame-duck Congress and administration had been phoning it in. The CBO's docket was relatively light, and Orszag had made it his 2008 goal to take a crack at breaking down the fiduciary metrics of health care reform. In only a month, in December 2008, CBO would release its own health care tome, offering one of the most detailed analyses of what reforming medical finances would look like.

The fiscal and evidentiary reform of health care consumed Orszag—so much so that now, on the plane to Chicago, he considered an ultimatum: he would accept the job offer only if Obama could look him in the eye and say that health care reform would top year one's domestic agenda. He had heard through back channels, namely from Rahm Emanuel and Jason Furman, that Obama's eyes were on this prize. But given the economic disaster of the last few months, Orszag was uneasy. Nothing was ever certain in politics, and his worries could be pacified only by his hearing it from Obama's mouth.

Deplaning in Chicago, Orszag flipped on his smartphone to check for e-mails and saw a note pop up from Michael Froman, Obama's transition team hiring chief: *Peter, the 10 a.m. meeting won't be necessary. You are good to go for OMB.*

Orszag was dumbfounded. *Good to go?* Surely Obama would want to at least chat before offering him such an important job. Orszag called Froman immediately.

"Michael," he said, "I'm already in Chicago. It might not be necessary for OMB, but I really want to meet with Obama."

Froman seemed surprised. "Hmm. Let me see what I can do," he said. "I'll call you right back." An instant later he did. "Okay! We'll do it. See you tomorrow."

"Great, thanks," Orszag managed, not quite sure what to think.

That night, he dined with Austan Goolsbee in Chicago, but his mind was elsewhere. The logistics of leaving CBO, a job he loved, for OMB weighed heavily on him. He thought about his life at home with his boys, a single dad. But the allure of opportunity ultimately drew him back in. "If I'm going to do this," he thought to himself again, "I need to know that health care is going to get done."

When he got to his meeting the next day, it took Orszag a few seconds to figure out why the shades in Obama's transition office were drawn on a cloudy mid-November day. Of course, a security measure—this was no ordinary job interview.

Obama was running five minutes late, so Orszag waited in a side office, feeling atypically nervous. OMB was a great opportunity, but he didn't really know the guy. Minutes later Obama wandered into the office with Reggie Love. The three made their way into his office.

"I want to be clear right off the bat," Obama began. "This is not a job interview."

It was a phrase he had fallen into the habit of using. It seemed intended to be both disarming and inviting, the kind of management guru–speak Obama might have culled from the Peter Drucker books he was known to favor. But considering the seriousness of today's interview, it couldn't help seeming contrived and more than a little precious. Obama, who appeared so at home with himself in front of large crowds, sometimes had trouble sounding as authoritative and confident in small settings. Admirers read this as humility; detractors saw it as awkwardness. As was so often the case, people saw in Obama largely what they wanted to see.

The pair moved now into the minutiae of policy specifics. While the budget would of course be Orszag's top priority, the conversation gravitated naturally to health care.

It took all of two seconds for Obama to say it: "I'm definitely committed to health care reform for my first year."

It was not just what he said that was convincing, Orszag recalled, but how he said it. His body shifted and settled with a kind of physical firmness. "He wanted health care reform to be his legacy," Orszag said later. Though he did not think much of it at the time, it was an odd ambition to have before even taking the oath of office; a touch early, perhaps, to be considering your legacy. But, if anything, a singular, anxious focus on history's arc had been evident in Obama since 1995, when he published his memoir at age thirty-three.

In any case, they both knew and agreed on the *whys* of health care reform. It was the *hows* that were trickiest and that now occupied their next half hour. The Dartmouth team had recently found that correcting for practice variation across the country could lead to as much as $700 billion per year in savings. The cost issue might very well be the key, both to expanding coverage and to selling the necessity of reform. Obama said he wanted Orszag to assume an expanded portfolio as OMB chief, serving as the administration's budget czar and also as the driving force behind health care reform.

The week after the election had been notably brutal for the flailing economy. The Dow dropped a stunning 411 points the morning of Orszag and Obama's meeting. Secretary Paulson had just made public a crucial decision regarding the recently enacted TARP: its $700 billion would no longer be put toward the purchase of the toxic "troubled" assets, as originally outlined, but be used instead to bail out the capital-short banking industry, with direct payments to troubled institutions.

But for all this, the two never really discussed economic policy. Here was Obama at his most ideologically focused and his most aloof, chatting with one of his first appointments to the economic team about health care while the economy caved in. Well, maybe that was okay, Orszag considered. Ahead of him in the appointment line, he'd heard, was Jack Lew, widely believed to be a lock for National Economic Council chairman.

This gave Orszag comfort. The NEC, created under Clinton in 1993 and first chaired by Bob Rubin, was designed as an apparatus for advising the president on economic matters. It would be a hugely important body in the midst of an economic crisis, and it called for a chairman with the greatest skill and wisdom, someone who could shape and nourish competing ideas about what to do to arrest the sliding economy and reverse its course. The quiet and brilliant Lew was a consensus favorite for the job. He'd been in Washington for decades, first as Tip O'Neill's top policy adviser and then as special adviser to Clinton. After a bunch of key posts in the Clinton White House, where he negotiated the Balanced Budget Act of 1997, Lew served as OMB chief for the last two years of the president's term. He was the perfect fit, and Orszag felt good knowing he would have such a strong team around him.

As the meeting began wrapping up, Obama casually solicited Orszag's opinion on the two men he was looking at for Treasury secretary: Larry Summers and Tim Geithner. Orszag was complimentary of both men, thinking that as long as Lew was quarterbacking the policy process from NEC, either would make an adequate secretary. Summers at NEC, acting primarily as an honest broker, didn't make sense for an economist of his strong opinions.

Now on the point of parting, Orszag summoned the courage to ask the one other question still tickling the back of his mind. He wanted to know if this White House would be more family-friendly than Clinton's West Wing, where the hours were long, often stretching into late nights.

"I'm not worried about your work ethic," Obama said.

As Orszag was left to wonder what exactly his future boss meant, and what question exactly he was answering, Obama walked his new OMB chief out of the office. They exchanged parting formalities, and Orszag reiterated his excitement about joining the team. As they shook hands, Orszag realized he was looking forward to getting to know the man behind the curtain more intimately. The air of change that seemed to hover around the president-elect was heady—intoxicating, even. As the two separated, Obama tossed off one last cryptic joke, poking fun at Orszag's pinstriped suit.

"All you economists dress the same!"

Obama's offhand queries to Orszag about who should head Treasury were more than idle chitchat. In the weeks following the election, the president-elect had been seriously weighing the various pluses and minuses of three major contenders: Geithner, Summers, and the aging Volcker.

But while Treasury secretary was the marquee job, it really came down to a more fundamental question of Team A versus Team B. The former, Team A, which had shepherded Obama to triumph, comprised Volcker, Goolsbee, Wolf, Reich, O'Neill, and Donaldson, all of whom were understandably confident of getting key jobs or advisory roles.

The heft and credibility that Volcker lent Obama's candidacy was hard to overstate. He had been there from the fall of 2007 on, offering the most powerfully disinterested guidance available, as an earthquake began to shake the U.S. financial system. Volcker had also been there at the birth of the contemporary economy, managing it as Fed chair from 1979 to 1987, and he seemed to know it like a parent might a child—a child who now, in adulthood, had gone terribly astray. Across those decades of maturation, Volcker had stayed actively involved, the independent-minded director of various companies and a steward of patient capital in his own investment work. From these vantages he'd watched how the management of money and risk had changed over the years.

Besides all that, he was an old guy, plenty robust, but free from the standard set of public and private ambitions. He had little care for money and had lived happily, working with his longtime assistant, and soon-to-be wife, Anke Dening. His tenure as Fed chair, meanwhile, so long overshadowed by Alan Greenspan's, was being appreciated afresh by the summer of 2008. As his successor, Greenspan had presided over two decades of a Miracle-Gro economy, in large part the result of cheap credit policies. When these turned out to have played a fundamental role in the 2008 crisis, the intelligentsia had swung back to Volcker, dusting off a record that suddenly looked like a finely aged vintage. Volcker's invaluable asset could be summed up in a single phrase: tough love.

The subtle and unsung value of the Volcker-led team was exactly the absence of what on Wall Street is called a "financial handle." Reich and Tyson were public intellectuals whose standing in the marketplace of ideas came from their scruples about accepting money from the broader marketplace. Wolf viewed his status, as Obama's buddy and top counselor with a job on Wall Street, as sacred. He would never even have thought to ask a favor of the guy, and as difficult as it might have been to place a UBS executive in a senior administration post, had the offer been made, Wolf told close friends, he would have left New York and done a "Nixon to China," turning against type to use his financial savvy to regulate the industry that had so long employed him. Donaldson laid claim to a similar sort of integrity, as a Republican free-market champion and longtime Wall Streeter who had undergone a tough-minded conversion.

But for all this, as the gravity of being elected president and the severity of the crisis bore down on him, Obama found himself leaning toward Team B. Sure, the other team brought to the table honesty and passion, but those bold visions of the campaign season had meanwhile resolved into the serious, often risk-averse business of actually governing. In the midst of a battering economic storm, it no longer seemed like the right time to be making waves.

What Volcker understood, which made him extremely dangerous in the eyes of the banks, was that in order to stabilize America's credit system, Wall Street's great debt machine would have to be dismantled. If the industry was going to center its business on consumer debt products such as credit cards and mortgages, or a vast matrix of complex business-to-business lending, it would have to be treated more like regular old commercial banks and savings and loans. Boom-bust cycles in equities markets were one thing. A lot of wealth was lost during the stock market crashes of 1987 and 2000. But these two crises had proven far more manageable than the present one. People felt poorer, but a lot of their losses were paper profits. When busts occurred in debt markets, however, the results were dire. Debt is a legal contract, and its interest payments don't budge. When payments can no longer be met, people lose their collateral—which is serious enough. But when the collateral itself loses value, creditors tend to realize losses they never guarded against. The collateral, after all, was the backstop. In the collapse of a big enough market—the housing market, say—the whole credit system can come crashing down with it.

Volcker also saw that the recent profitability of Wall Street was directly tied to the riskiness of its behavior: the banks and investment houses had been making money hand over fist by investing in the boom-bust cycle for debt. On the consumer end, debt was temporarily underpriced to make it more attractive, so people had assumed more than they could afford. On the far other end, with the sale of debt securities to major institutional investors and the like, the riskiness of underlying debts was masked and massaged through financial innovation until these ticking time bombs could be sold as rock-solid, high-yield securities.

Now that a lot of the bombs had gone off, it was time systematically to set off the rest, Volcker felt. How else could we feel safe moving forward? This meant accurately pricing the "toxic" mortgage-backed securities on which the credit system was resting. Even if prices were severely depressed, at least they would hit a floor. The result would be painful, no doubt, but moral hazard would be averted. And if executives who had sold the explosive debt products wound up in the streets, having to hire their own lawyers to fight off waves of legal suits, well, so much the better for discouraging such behavior the next time around.

The competing team in this drama could hardly have disagreed more strongly. Heavy on former Clinton officials, many of whom swore allegiance to the former Treasury secretary and Citigroup chairman Bob Rubin, Team B believed the crisis called for delicate actions in support of a fragile banking system. Who knew what would happen if you started pricing mortgage securities correctly—which banks might find themselves on the verge of insolvency, or in its grasp? Team B had been moving forward with tactical clarity since September: the Volcker-led group must be stopped. Several people had complained, directly to Obama or within earshot, about how Volcker mumbled, how he had lost a step over the years and might not be able to handle the heavy demands of the secretary job. Goolsbee was unknown to the public and did not inspire surety or have much gravitas. As for Reich, Tyson, and Donaldson, their strong, fiery words might disrupt the shaky market. The first priority, Team B stressed, was to stand up a facsimile of the old system, to get Wall Street up and running and to restore faith in iconic American institutions. Credit needed to start flowing again. After that—and it might take a year or two—everyone could talk about sweeping reforms.

Secretary Paulson had adopted Team B's approach, infusing banks with capital and giving Wall Street what amounted to an early victory. But the game had hardly begun. If the new president chose to surround himself with Volcker's A-Team, then a throw-them-out-on-the-street, rip-the-bandage-off scenario would be in the offing. The hopes of Rubin's B-Team—many of whom had turned high-ranking posts under Clinton into Wall Street riches—came to rest on the two men challenging Volcker for the Treasury secretary job: Summers and Geithner.

By the morning of November 11, when the president-elect had asked Orszag what he thought of the two candidates, they were in deep, side-by-side discussions with Obama. Several possible arrangements were taking shape, offering an early glimpse of Obama's managerial style and inclinations.

One possibility would be to put Volcker in the top job of Treasury secretary and make Geithner his deputy. Once the markets had stabilized and the big structural reforms—conceptualized and shepherded by Volcker—were under way, Geithner could move up into the secretary job. He was better on the implementation side of things anyway.

Obama liked Geithner personally. He brought youth and energy to the table and undisputed expertise on the particulars of the current crisis.

Though his roots with the Clintonite B-Team were deep—he had served as an undersecretary of the Treasury under both Rubin and Summers—his arrival on the national stage, as a member of the new administration, would make him Obama's man. When they met in October they chatted amiably for forty-five minutes, two charming but sometimes hard-to-read young men, both of whom had spent many youthful years overseas. After a few minutes, they figured out that Geithner's father, a director at the Ford Foundation, had briefly worked with Obama's mother, a coincidence that brought a warm glow to Obama. Geithner just needed a little seasoning.

On the other hand, Summers could just as easily lead the charge at Treasury, then move over to the Fed when Bernanke's term was up at the end of 2009. Summers told Obama he would be very interested in the Fed job, a unique and prestigious position on the world stage. Summers had watched his old friend Greenspan turn the chairmanship into a seat of extraordinary, dynastic power. In twenty years on the job, Greenspan could lay claim to having been the most powerful public official of his era. At only fifty-four years old, Summers saw in the Fed post the long final chapter to a storied career. When Summers moved over, Geithner would move up.

But then it all started to become complex math. The financial crisis was altering the country's professional landscape. Citigroup, made a home for so many former Clintonites by Rubin and others, suddenly went from esteemed financial behemoth to bumbling charity case. The financial meltdown revealed a host of sins and perfidies, and Citi seemed to have plenty of every variety. It had loaded up on toxic mortgage assets rather late in the game, received the initial $25 billion in bailout money, and then another $25 billion to keep it afloat. It had seen fit, along the way, to dole out stunning compensation, including the $126 million to Rubin over a period of eight years. The mélange of greed, incompetence, and bailout funds was toxic. As late as early September, Rubin was actually talking to Obama about a taking a job in the administration: a "dollar-a-year" position as a presidential adviser, with an office in the West Wing. Now he was persona non grata, at least in public. The same was increasingly the case for Jack Lew, who had been well compensated in the past few years at Citi. If congressional Republicans dug into some of the activities occurring in departments beneath Lew—even if he didn't know about them—it could get ugly. In mid-November, Lew reluctantly withdrew himself from consideration for the job he'd all but been offered: NEC chairman.

There was one other twist. The prospect of selecting Hillary Clinton as secretary of state—speculated publicly, and much discussed internally by the Obama team, with high hopes—was increasingly seen as a strike against Summers. If he were put at Treasury, the president's top two appointments would both be central actors of the Clinton era.

Obama began to reconsider the mix, with an eye on the close bond between Summers and Geithner, something neither had with Volcker. This friendship might turn into an asset, encouraging close coordination between the White House and Treasury, as they worked together through the crisis. Obama was initially worried that Geithner might assume an overly subordinate manner with Summers, who had once been his boss. But the remark, from someone who knew the pair well, that Geithner could stand up to Summers and tell him he was "full of shit" allayed Obama's worries. Both longtime tennis players, Summers and Geithner had played together for years, cementing a bond in athletic battle that Obama respected. He became enamored, as he thought about it, of the idea that Summers could spearhead economic debate within the White House while using his deep rapport with Geithner to keep the administration closely coordinated with Treasury's emergency activities.

When Obama suggested this arrangement, however, Summers demurred. Having once been Treasury secretary, he considered the NEC job a step down. He hinted that he might be less than ideal for the position, pointing out that his strong suit was not in evenhandedly distilling rival ideas into distinct, unbiased choices. This was what the NEC job demanded. Then, for good measure, Summers added conditions: he would manage all information regarding economic matters that passed to Obama, and he would be first among equals to replace Bernanke.

Obama accepted his conditions.

Many people with Obama's ear advised the president-elect against Summers, among them several members of Team A. They said he was too divisive, too combative, and, to their knowledge, never a consensus builder—that his brilliance was rhetorical rather than substantive, that he had abandoned original research two decades ago, and that his track record over the years in major decisions had been disastrous.

But for every voice testifying against Summers, there was one who said, simply, that he was brilliant and that the rest was irrelevant. Many of those voices came from Rubin's B-Team and from Wall Street, which should have set off an alarm. But their message and the timbre of their voices, full of confidence and loyalty, were in the end more comforting than those of the ragtag A-Team, whose love seemed suddenly too tough.

———————

For Christina Romer it was love at first sight.

She had seen the convention speech in 2004, and watched in awe the declaration of candidacy from the Illinois snows and his victory speech in Iowa.

But her teenage son was a Hillary supporter. She was dumbstruck.

"Yes, Hillary's fine. But have you seen the speeches?"

Romer loved the Cooper Union speech, but she was unsettled—as Hillary made her final push in Ohio and Pennsylvania, playing to union workers—to see Obama step back from his earlier statements in favor of NAFTA. She called up Austan Goolsbee, whom she knew from academic circles.

"Don't let him sink to that," she told Goolsbee, a fellow free trade enthusiast. "Have him broaden the discussion about displaced workers and what government can do to help them."

Soon enough she was sending Goolsbee a steady stream of materials, adding to the Obama campaign's economic potpourri her own notes and various handpicked academic reports. By June, however, Jason Furman had replaced Goolsbee as the campaign's top economic adviser. He was calling the shots now, and Romer found herself out of the loop.

That is, until a mysterious e-mail popped up in her account on November 16. She was sitting at her home in Berkeley with her husband, David, also an economics professor, when a note arrived from Michael Froman, with a strange tag: @NTT.org. She thought it might be someone looking for a job.

"If it's a job with Obama they want, I certainly can't help them," she thought.

On a whim, David decided to Google the name Froman. "I think you might want to respond to this one," he told her. "NTT stands for National Transition Team. Michael Froman is the head of hiring for the Obama transition team."

Curious just what in the world Froman might want, Romer made the call.

"What kind of a job would you be interested in?" Froman asked, sending a thrill of excitement through Romer. She played her cards close.

"Well, there are a few Fed governorships opening up," she noted.

"We had something else in mind," Froman said. It was the chairmanship of the Council of Economic Advisers.

Five days later Romer found herself on a plane to Chicago, like Orszag before her, on her way to meet the object of her political infatuation. But her excitement crowded out the obvious question: Why her? Obama had already surrounded himself with a healthy cast of top economic minds from the highest reaches of the private sector and academia. She had been an ardent supporter, sure, but hardly an instrumental adviser.

The answer would only begin to dawn on her later in her West Wing tenure. Obama had a woman problem: too few of them in key jobs. There was Valerie Jarrett, but she'd been a friend of Michelle's first. Speculation that Hillary would get the secretary of state job had begun circulating, but she wouldn't really garner the administration any diversity points. She was "Hillary," a single-name entity across the globe, and bringing her into the fold would be more about power than equal opportunity.

It was on a Friday, November 21, that Romer first entered Obama's curtain-sealed office in Chicago. Unlike Orszag, she was nervous about meeting Obama and she hadn't even come with any ultimatum or conditions about taking the Council of Economic Advisers job. She was just elated to get to know the guy.

But their first meeting would open on an odd note. "He said that it's clear monetary policy has shot its wad," Romer said, and that "we need to focus on fiscal policy."

Romer later said that this was her paraphrasing of what Obama said—that, upon reflection, she couldn't recall specifically what words the president used—but recalled being a bit startled by this strident bit of analytical jousting.

Not exactly, she thought. And, feeling immediately comfortable with Obama, she told him so. "No, you're wrong," she corrected him. "There's quite a bit we can still do monetarily, even with the historically low interest rates."

She described how, even with rates near zero, an expectation of coming inflation, and a rise in rates, prompts the use of cheap debt in more robust, and stimulatory, ways.

Women tapped for senior levels of government, even now, often wonder if they've been called upon, at least in some small measure, because of their gender. But any such concerns vanished in an instant for Romer, as she began what was, in essence, her first briefing of Barack Obama. The president-elect listened attentively to her disquisition on managing interest rate expectations. He had questions. Already, Romer had answers.

And, then the president-elect took the lead, turning the conversation to more familiar ground: Roosevelt. Romer, a scholar of the Depression, listened to Obama invoke FDR's example as a model of crisis management. He praised the way Roosevelt took charge of the situation and let everyone know that "I'll fight this thing with everything in my being. We'll put the people first." That, Obama added, "was how Roosevelt restored confidence."

Romer was impressed. With Rooseveltian fantasies dancing in her head, she said she would be honored to accept the job as chair of the Council of Economic Advisers. The president-elect had Rooseveltian fantasies of his own, and Romer later recalled that he seemed to understand that economic policies could often "have an impact beyond what was immediately quantifiable," that "for a president to forcefully take a stand could really affect confidence."

With a kind of giddiness, Romer recounted the meeting highlights to her husband. "He's even better than I expected," she announced.

But David Romer was more blown away by her brazenness than anything. "The first thing out of your mouth was 'No, you're wrong'?!"

On Monday, November 24, Obama unveiled his newly minted economic team. The headline names were Summers, Geithner, and Romer. It was a markedly different group, compositionally and ideologically, from the A-Team Obama had showcased throughout his campaign. Summers would take the NEC chair, Geithner the top job at Treasury, and Romer the head role at CEA. As for the members of Team A, they would find themselves exiled to the hastily crafted President's Economic Recovery Advisory Board.

For all the infighting and acrimony that would plague the administration after the inauguration, the atmosphere of the transition was one of surprising camaraderie. As one high-ranking official put it, "We were actually working as a team in December."

Never was this feeling so palpable as on November 30, when Larry Summers turned fifty-four years old. Spirits were high as they gathered to celebrate in the Chicago transition office; Geithner even brought cupcakes for the career curmudgeon. Following a hearty rendition of the Happy Birthday song, Summers, without missing a beat, launched into his own solo verse: "For he's an unpleasant fellow!"

Everyone laughed. Looking back, Orszag would later say, "It was one of those moments where we felt like whatever happened before, it was okay. It was one of those moments in one of those windowless conference rooms." There was something poignant about the self-awareness of the verse, something in the humility of self-deprecation that evoked a sense of new beginnings. The team had begun to gel, with good humor, around the quirkiness of its members.

The moment would not last.

Christina Romer was soon struggling to understand exactly what her role as head of the CEA entailed, and she was having serious reservations. The position, impressive as it had seemed, looked more and more insubstantial, a big title without much effective heft. In the coming months she would feel increasingly isolated in her job, excluded from the broader discussion by Summers, whose Kissingerian role at NEC had basically annexed her position in the sweep of its bureaucratic imperium. Later on she would go straight to Rahm Emanuel about the issue, although she had reservations about the president's chief of staff, too. For the time being, however, she worked with Larry as best she could.

She even had a degree of sympathy for the newly "mellowed" Summers. "He's just not very good at politics," she thought. "If he were the CEA chair, he would be saying the exact same things I am." The issue of the moment, as the inauguration inched closer day by day, was the stimulus package. It was the seminal debate of the transition. The figure being thrown around early in December was $300–400 billion, but Romer didn't have to crunch the numbers to know that wouldn't be enough.

"I think it should be bigger," she told Summers, as the two set to drafting the memo they would pass on to Emanuel.

"How much bigger?" Summers asked.

"Eight hundred, at least."

"I agree," Summers said, surprising Romer. Both of them knew that if the stimulus was going to have any real impact, it was going to need to be a politically unpopular number. They drafted the memo to include two options below $1 trillion. Romer pushed for a larger stimulus, at around $1.2 trillion.

"All of these stimulus options are set up to achieve eight percent unemployment," she exclaimed. "Since when is eight percent unemployment acceptable? We've spent the last few years at four percent!"

Romer, in preparing a report for Obama, included the perspectives of several big-name economists who supported a larger stimulus: Stiglitz and Tyson, along with Ken Rogoff, a highly respected Harvard professor. But $1.2 trillion was going to be a political nonstarter, and in a sign of his increasingly dominant role, Summers chose not to include it in the materials for the president-elect.

The fledgling transition team's first major stimulus meeting took place on December 16, in snowy Chicago. For all the fierce internal debate, there wasn't much the president-elect could do until January 20. Though his strong desire was to tackle health care in year one, Obama knew his first piece of legislation would have to address the financial crisis. Much of what ended up as the American Recovery and Reinvestment Act of 2009—the stimulus—was decided at this meeting.

All eyes were on Romer, who had spent much of her career studying the effects of government spending under FDR. She opened the meeting, taking to heart David Axelrod's message that the gravity of the situation could not be overstated.

"Mr. President, this is your 'holy shit' moment," she said in surprisingly strong language.

She was right. The crisis was that big. She clicked and brought up a PowerPoint slide—something Summers disliked ("Don't show what you are already saying anyway!")—describing the difference between a severe recession and a depression. Only through major intervention, she explained, firmness and earned certainty in her voice, could they hope to prevent the latter.

The effectiveness of stimulus spending was still considered the realm of unproven economics, but its detractors, in failing to take the "multiplier effect" into account, appeared to underestimate its value. Whatever dollar amount of stimulus passed through Congress would be only a fraction of the money actually added to the economy. Because Americans tended to spend more and save less than people in other countries, stimulus spending could be expected to go a long way, generating more actual value than it cost, as beneficiaries spent and the stimulus money passed from hand to hand.

Inside Team Obama there was almost no discussion of whether to undertake a stimulus, just of how large it ought to be. The number had grown quickly. Clinton had attempted to pass $16 billion in stimulus after taking office in what, at the time, was considered a huge piece of legislation. Before this election, $100 billion had seemed to be the number. But now, with the economy speeding off a cliff, Congress was working with numbers closer to half a trillion. The key would be to fill the output gap, estimated to be around $2 trillion. Romer stressed that because of the multiplier effect, the stimulus didn't need to be quite that large.

For his part, Obama was surprisingly aloof in the conversation. Like McCain during the September meeting with Paulson, the president-elect now seemed disconnected and less than in control of the process. As the economic team hashed out the minutiae of a plan and tried to settle on a number, Obama's contributions were rare.

"There needs to be more inspiration here!" he said at one point.

The team was sympathetic to Obama's position, which demanded that he somehow deliver on the high rhetoric of his campaign, but it was taken aback all the same by how out of place the comment seemed in the middle of a discussion of quantifiable outcomes.

The debate would ultimately hinge on whether the stimulus should exceed $1 trillion. As the resident expert, Romer had convincingly argued that $1.2 trillion would suffice. The forces pushing for a number in the billions, however, were strong. For one thing, there was the near-term issue of being able even to get such a monumental package through Congress. In the long run there was the worry of coming across as a tax-and-spend administration. As Peter Orszag said, "There was the concern that we would look wacko lefty."

Obama seemed persuaded that the stimulus did not need to exceed a trillion dollars. For him it was more about the symbolic content of the stimulus.

"What about smart grids?" he asked at one meeting.

The conversation then turned to an extended discussion with Carol Browner, Obama's top adviser on energy and the environment, about the limitations of eminent domain. A smart grid would need to be implemented district by district, which, as part of the stimulus, was entirely unfeasible.

Obama, frustrated, refused to let the topic go. "We need more moon shot," he said.

Members of the team were perplexed. How could the guy who had wowed them with his ability to synthesize ideas and move discussions forward get so hung up on something that everyone agreed was impossible? Yes, it was important for legislation to inspire, but couldn't they hash out a basic plan first? For the first time in the transition, people started to wonder just how prepared the man at the helm really was.

―――――――――

It was too cold to camp out, but people still tried, and some managed it. They had come to watch history unfold before their eyes, to be a part of its unfolding. Toughing out the brutally cold night seemed to bind them more closely to the historic moment, as hero participants. By midmorning, assembling in the sunless cold was a crowd many times the size of Grant Park's. Later estimates would put it at nearly two million, making it the largest gathering ever in the nation's capital.

The emotions of Election Night had widened and deepened, becoming, in light of the crisis, more urgent still. Everyone knew the economy had collapsed, losing three and a half million jobs over the past six months, a slide that showed no sign of slowing. But no one needed to see those numbers to know the country was in trouble. You could feel it. Things were out of control.

So people controlled what they could. For most of the two million, that meant finding a way to Washington, a place to stay, clothes warm enough for long exposure, and a path to the Mall through the teeming throngs. They had come to be inspired. That was what they needed and couldn't manage on their own. That's what presidents are for.

A year before, almost to the day, Obama had given an interview to the *Reno Gazette-Journal* that prompted a line of ongoing analysis and controversy. On the issue of which recent presidents had been "transformational," the senator had said that "Ronald Reagan changed the trajectory of America in a way that, you know, Richard Nixon did not and in a way that Bill Clinton did not. He put us on a fundamentally different path because the country was ready for it."

This prompted a dustup. During a debate the following week, Hillary

Clinton, smarting from the slight to her husband's tenure, accused Obama of "admiring Ronald Reagan."

Obama's response was almost legalistic: "What I said was—is that Ronald Reagan was a transformative political figure because he was able to get Democrats to vote against their economic interests."

Since then, there'd been a change in tense. Obama and others began to think more seriously about how Reagan had managed his transformative magic, how it might be created again and put to a different purpose.

Obama had been meditating on Reagan's presidency and legacy for a long time. In *The Audacity of Hope* he writes that "Reagan spoke to America's longing for order . . . our need to believe that we are not simply subject to blind, impersonal forces but that we can shape our individual and collective destinies, so long as we rediscover the traditional virtues of hard work, patriotism, personal responsibility, optimism and faith."

Fifteen minutes into his Inaugural Address, he echoed that passage in the central moment of his own speech: "Our challenges may be new, the instruments with which we meet them may be new, but those values upon which our success depends, honesty and hard work, courage and fair play, tolerance and curiosity, loyalty and patriotism—these things are old. These things are true. They have been the quiet force of progress throughout our history. What is demanded then is a return to these truths. What is required of us now is a new era of responsibility—a recognition on the part of every American that we have duties to ourselves, our nation and the world, duties that we do not grudgingly accept but rather seize gladly, firm in the knowledge that there is nothing so satisfying to the spirit, so defining of our character than giving our all to a difficult task."

Reagan's difficult task when he stepped to the lectern in January 1981 was similar, if less dire. Unemployment had eclipsed 7 percent, and inflation was averaging a startling 12.5 percent. Having won electoral support from conservatives for his stances on a host of social issues, Reagan was compelled to put all these aside when he took the oath of office and to focus instead on the economy. Fortunately for him this dovetailed with another theme of his campaign: reining in the growth of government and unleashing the power of the private sector. Or at least he could claim it did.

And this was just what he claimed, with considerable rhetorical skill, in his Inaugural Address, asserting brazenly that the country's troubles were for good reason "parallel and proportionate to the . . . unnecessary and excessive growth of government." Following this with the bold affirmation that we were "too great a nation to limit ourselves to small dreams," Reagan cast government as the bad guy, standing in the way of the country's hopes and aspirations. "In the days ahead," he continued, "I will propose removing the roadblocks that have slowed our economy."

While Reagan's address lacked a signature line like Kennedy's famous "ask not," it spoke to a shifting cultural current—to the individual and entrepreneur—laying a vicious right cross on the talk of shared sacrifice that dominated the late seventies: "We have every right to dream heroic dreams."

But Reagan's most remembered line—"In the present crisis, government is not the solution to our problems"—sounds today hedged and conditional, his qualification about not wanting to abolish government but "make it work, work with us, not over us," altogether tame.

Nearly thirty years later Obama would utter almost identical words during his inaugural speech, explaining that the "question we ask today is not whether our government is too big or too small, but whether it works." This was, in fact, the centerpiece of what he put forward as a remedy to our long list of ills. The speech was mostly that list—what had gone wrong and the country's history of overcoming challenges similar and even greater in their breadth. No one would ever forget attending Obama's inauguration, but for most of them the speech itself underwhelmed. They had come to be inspired, and he had denied them.

The next day would be Obama's first full one as president, and he would spend it diving full bore into the stimulus debate. On a conference call with Nancy Pelosi's office, he pushed for the very "inspiration" he had deliberately withheld the day before.

"This stimulus needs more inspiration!" he shouted into the speakerphone.

Pelosi and her staff visibly rolled their eyes. Inspiration works ideologically and rhetorically. It can consume and invigorate the masses, and get results when their ire or enthusiasm is then directed back at the permanent government. But day to day, in the clinch with the canny operators of Washington, inspirational gifts find no neat application.

Next to the speakerphone was that morning's *Washington Post*, so thick with photos and purple prose about the inauguration that it looked like a special collector's edition.

That's the way it was. The town was swept up in the power of a moment, of an African American man taking the oath of office before two million people, those who'd "seen it all" but still wept, and others who hoped to tell their grandchildren of this day.

But after covering nine presidencies, the dean of the city's press corps, *Washington Post* columnist David Broder, still spry at seventy-nine, managed to summon a kernel of hard perspective in the last line of his column that morning.

"What speeches can accomplish, they have delivered handsomely for Barack Obama," he wrote, in a gentle warning to the young president. "Now, it will depend on his deeds."

PART II

HOME ALONE

A NEW DEAL

Obama ascended to the presidency channeling FDR. Like the longest-serving American president, Obama also arrived in the middle of economic crisis—albeit several months, not several years, after it began. Just as Roosevelt's administration set the standard for progressive agendas in the prior century, Obama hoped his would build on that foundation and then raise its own high bar for progressive agendas in the young new century.

Roosevelt laid out a famously aggressive program for his first one hundred days in office, passing, in this period, many of the laws that now define his presidency. With a huge wind at his back, he saw Congress accede to virtually all his priorities. In addition to the Emergency Banking and Glass-Steagall acts, which rapidly stabilized the banking industry, he established the Civilian Conservation Corps and Tennessee Valley Authority and, in addition, passed the Farm Credit, Truth in Securities, and National Industrial Recovery acts, among others. A few of Roosevelt's signature laws would come later, but considering that his term in office lasted for more than twelve years, it is remarkable just how much of what now comprises Roosevelt's legacy came in his first three months.

The hundred-day precedent has been the legislative standard for presidents ever since, so much so that Hillary Clinton mapped out her hundred-day strategy during the primary campaign. Obama acknowledged that he'd been studying Roosevelt's first hundred days when he arrived at the White House, mentioning books—including *The Defining Moment*, an FDR biography by Jonathan Alter—he was reading. Like FDR, Obama had tools of action to work with: overwhelming popular support, Democratic majorities in both houses of Congress, and the latitude afforded by crisis.

Yet the transition's heavy pregame planning meant that much had already been sketched. The pre-inaugural blueprint for financial reform—at this point a closely held document—laid out a fairly conventional set of changes that preserved the current structure of the financial and banking industries while largely beefing up the power of regulators to try to spot systemically dangerous institutions before they created a crisis, and granting them "resolution authority" to handle collapses such as Lehman in an orderly, bailout-free way. The stimulus plan, at roughly $800 billion, was similarly shaped by mid-January to be a middle-ground proposal that could curry bipartisan support. The bill, called the American Recovery and Reinvestment Act of 2009, was actually less ambitious than it might have looked at first blush. It was something of a hodge-podge, a hastily built plan that reflected the competing and unresolved ideas coursing through the barely formed administration.

It wasn't as though the recession, and the need for stimulus, was itself a surprise. While the speed of the economic downdraft was startling, the question of how to construct an effective stimulus had been a subject of public discussion for almost a year.

Because states were so short on funds already, a lot of the money they'd receive would end up simply covering their normal budgetary outlays, saving the jobs of teachers, firefighters, and police officers. The tax cuts—going equally to all income strata in a nod to Republicans—were not as stimulatory as a host of other, more immediate direct-aid proposals in that many higher earners would use their bonuses to pay down debts or boost savings. Much of the infrastructure spending, meanwhile, was destined to languish unused, as it was made clear, even during the transition, that there were limits to how quickly money could be spent. Obama would own up to these concerns a year and a half later, admitting that he had learned "there's no such thing as 'shovel-ready' projects." Actually, he'd been warned of this well ahead of the bill's unveiling.

Even Alice Rivlin, the famously clear-eyed economic adviser from early in the Clinton administration, was sounding an alarm after the proposal's outlines became clear in late January. "A long-term investment program should not be put together hastily and lumped in with the anti-recession package," she said, in a widely covered speech at the left-leaning Brookings Institution. "The elements of the investment program must be carefully planned and will not create many jobs right away."

As a top official later said, looking back, "We should have spent more time thinking about where the money was being spent, rather than simply that there was this hole of a certain size in the economy that needed to be filled, so fill it. How each dollar is spent is almost as important as the gross number." Another senior White House official acknowledged that, while there was a need for speed in getting something passed, "there's no excuse for poor conceptualizing."

Hastily constructed policy was matched by miscalculations of political strategy: all the accommodations to conservative principles and practice in the plan were never exchanged for hard commitments. On the way to his inauguration, Obama got word that Republicans in the House had committed, as a bloc, to oppose his stimulus plan.

But that was all before he raised his right hand. Obama's predict-and-prepare navigation system—that finely tuned capacity to prefigure the outcomes, political and historical, before each footfall—would now begin to struggle with something that simply can't be predicted: what it feels like to be president.

Duly sworn in and pacing the Oval Office—ushered there by enthusiasts whose ardor seemed immune to his efforts at expectation management—Obama began, from his first minutes in office, to improvise with his new, just-elected identity.

He was, after all, now the president. But how should a president, especially an inspirational figure named Barack Hussein Obama, act in a time of crisis?

A day after the inauguration, the president's top domestic appointee took his first tentative steps into the blinding lights.

The demands of the job were daunting, greater, in many ways, than that of any recent Treasury secretary—and Tim Geithner's experience was mostly in back rooms with bankers.

This was clear during the transition, as it was obvious that there'd be a mismatch between Geithner's performance skills and the challenges that awaited him. There were several extended prep sessions for his confirmation hearings. Other key players during the transition, many of whom would soon assume their senior positions, fired questions at Geithner, attacking his recent action to bail out the banks, his positions on all but imponderable issues of regulation, his personal beliefs and history. "Are they really going to ask me this kind of stuff?" he groused after one heated exchange. Yes, and maybe worse, everyone agreed. Summers, feeling protective of anyone who once served under him in Clinton's Treasury Department, offered sage advice: "Don't anyone admit we did anything wrong," he said during the prep sessions. Summers was refer-ring to that administration's late-1990s moves to undercut what was left of Glass-Steagall and then block the regulation of derivatives. This stance, of course, was of sufficient import that it might have merited presidential review and some political analysis. Obama, after all, had selected for his top domestic officials two men whose actions had contributed to the very financial disaster they were hired to solve.

It wasn't as though Obama hadn't heard pointed concerns on this very issue. At a meeting in December of 2008, Byron Dorgan, the longtime North Dakota senator who'd been a leader of the Democrats, used un-usually direct language with the then president-elect about his top eco-nomic selections. "You've picked the wrong people," he said to Obama, citing Geithner and Summers, both of whom Dorgan knew. "I don't un-derstand how you could do this. You've picked the wrong people!"

Tim Geithner walked into the Hart Senate Office Building, just a block northeast of the Capitol Dome, for his 10:00 a.m. confirmation hearing on January 21. The city was still collectively hungover from its frigid revelry, with scaffolding being disassembled and mountains of trash be-ing hauled away. By the time Geithner arrived at his hearing it wasn't even thirty degrees outside, but the Obama team had been working over-time for weeks to make certain he received a warm reception that morn-ing from the Senate Finance Committee.

Again they turned to Paul Volcker, who sauntered into the hearing room on Geithner's heels to give the young regulator his endorsement, even if it gave committee members a glimpse of what a Volcker Treasury might have looked like. Volcker's assuredness was unmistakable. Fuss-ing with his microphone in response to Max Baucus's effusion of what a privilege it was to have him appear, Volcker quipped, to big laughs, that he supposed it'd "be even more of a privilege if you could hear me," and then provided the gravity of a bona fide public-sector bigfoot of the sort America had not recently seen:

"You know, a good many years have passed since I last appeared be-fore this committee, but during all of that time there's never been a more critical time for the American economy and particularly for financial sta-bility. And that's true not just in the United States, but globally. To put it starkly, we are in a serious recession with no end clearly in sight. The financial system is broken. It's a serious obstacle to recovery. There is no escape from the imperative need for the federal government to come to the rescue to right the economic and financial ship of state. The hard fact is several trillions of dollars will be necessary to be committed in a combination of budgetary expenditures and various guarantee and insurance programs and extensions of credit by the Federal Reserve."

Several trillions of dollars. A true and stunning figure that no one had bothered, up to this point, to fix precisely.

After a few minutes, he turned to the young nominee, with an elegantly parsed endorsement. "Now, I can't reasonably claim that any one person is absolutely indispensable, but as you address this nomination—as you address his nomination, consider that Mr. Geithner brings unique qualifications in terms of hands-on experience, recognition in financial markets, and the confidence in which he is held by the new president of the United States."

Over the next two hours, there were times when Geithner clearly wished his mic had been off as well. He was conspicuously unprepared for prime time. Despite his demonstrable knowledge of regulatory process, he was squirrelly and inarticulate. In private, one-on-one, he could be charming, witty, and thoughtful, but in public, he was surprisingly arrhythmic, sometimes even fumbling over the basic financial lexicon.

It was understandable if his nerves were already frayed. For the past two weeks a senior Obama aide, Jim Messina, just named deputy chief of staff under Emanuel, had been locked in negotiations with his former boss, Max Baucus, over Geithner's future. Messina was once chief of staff to Montana's conservative Democratic senator, who now chaired Finance and often said he considered Messina "like a son." That history would now prove crucial. Geithner owed back taxes, something revealed the previous October to Obama's team as they vetted him as a prospective appointee. He'd improperly reported compensation when he worked from 2001 to 2004 for the IMF. He'd also deducted his children's summer camps as a dependent expense. In sum, he had failed to pay $34,000 over a several-year period. Such oversights for an official slated to oversee the IRS would have been fatal for any number of past Treasury secretary appointees—raising the fire-or-ice choice of having to admit to either fraud or incompetence. Geithner went with the latter, saying he'd filled out his taxes using the software program TurboTax and had simply made a mistake.

In the midst of an economic crisis, however, it was time to cut deals. Baucus kicked off the hearing by preemptively relieving Geithner of responsibility in his tax mishandlings, calling them "innocent mistakes" and "sufficiently corrected," and then pushed the discussion along to the substantive issues framed by Volcker.

But Geithner soon found himself in deep waters.

One committee member who wasn't interested in cutting any deals with the White House waited to pounce. Washington's progressive Democrat Maria Cantwell, a former businesswoman who was once a top executive with Internet media streaming giant RealNetworks, had learned the hard way about lax regulation and the destructive possibilities of "financial innovation."

Not long after she arrived in the Senate in January of 2001, Cantwell was drawn into a local dispute that soon went global. Enron, the darling of Wall Street when she took office, was managing the world's energy markets using many of the same derivatives strategies and trading tricks that would, years hence, collapse the real estate markets. Enron had, in essence, created a host of proprietary platforms for the trading of energy derivatives, complex securities that derived their value from assets such as barrels of oil and cubic feet of natural gas, or the anticipation of such hard assets from oil and gas leases. Acting as the middleman—market maker, proprietary trading adviser, manager of electronic derivatives exchanges—the company exerted enormous, and enormously profitable, influence over the world's energy market. Washington state's energy producers, who saw stunning price hikes (which Enron profited from), thought this influence was improper. Cantwell, fighting on behalf of the companies and the state's strapped ratepayers, was told countless times by Enron and its Wall Street "efficient market" supporters "that this was too complicated," she'd recall, "for anyone like me to understand. That 'anyone' meant a woman."

It also might have meant "a senator." Cantwell was virtually alone in those days fighting Enron. In late 2001 the company collapsed in the largest fraud in U.S. history, having used its market might to pump up earnings, cook its books, and defraud parties on all sides of the trades it controlled. Enron kept many of these activities hidden with the use of SPVs, or special-purpose vehicles, held off the balance sheet in much the same way that CDOs were kept in off-balance-sheet SPVs and funded by repos.

"In a ten-year-period of time, with one major regulatory loophole, derivatives have grown from being a $95 trillion industry to a $683 trillion industry . . . in ten years! This is what we are in America now," she said, a huge derivatives market.

Of course, Enron was just the start. Cantwell's state would take one of the most serious blows from the next crisis to emerge from derivatives trading and financial hubris. On September 25, 2008, with Paulson's TARP proposal on the table, the government seized the bank holding giant Washington Mutual and placed it into receivership of the FDIC. The catalyst for the action was an old-fashioned bank run in which $16 billion in deposits were withdrawn over a ten-day period, at that time nearly 10 percent of the bank's total deposits. JPMorgan Chase, ever proactive in the public-private dance, purchased WaMu's bank subsidiaries from the FDIC for $1.9 billion.

The following day, September 26, WaMu formally filed for Chapter 11, sending shock waves from Cantwell's state to the wider country.

Cantwell was incensed. In her mind, Paulson's tough-love approach with WaMu was politically motivated. Allowing the bank to fail gave lawmakers a taste of the tumult that accompanied bankruptcy in the "too big to fail" era. She felt it was a ploy, albeit drastic, to sell TARP to Congress.

"They were basically picking winners and losers," she'd say later about the Paulson-Bernanke-Geithner trio. "They blew up WaMu . . . I'm not saying WaMu did everything right. But I'm listening to Jamie Dimon talk about how he's going to make 27 percent profit in one year and basically take all the good assets and leave all the bad assets to be cleaned up. They won't even offer to pay retirement benefits [to WaMu employees]. The whole thing is just a catastrophe."

But now she'd get one of that trio at the hearing table, with his nomination on the line.

Summers's rule for Geithner, "don't admit to mistakes," was the first of two. The other rule, in answering questions, was "don't make policy."

Cantwell's goal was to undercut the latter proviso. She was displeased, as were several Democratic leaders, with the choice of Geithner and Summers. "The best tactic was to get them to say [in confirmation hearings] what they were willing to support, so that we could hold their feet to the fire [later]," she said, adding that she expected Geithner and

Summers eventually to cave in to Wall Street, at which point she could start "raising hell about their lack of backbone."

In concert with a cadre of progressives, Cantwell began her campaign to use the confirmation hearings to shape financial reform. When her turn came around, she grilled Geithner on exactly what he was planning to do to reregulate the financial industry, pressing him for specifics that left other committee members checking their briefing materials.

On her second turn, an hour later, she moved in for the kill. Cantwell noted that the previous fall, after the market's meltdown, former SEC chairman Arthur Levitt admitted that the Commodity Futures Modernization Act, which Clinton-era regulators pushed through in 2000 to prevent the regulation of derivatives—over the objections of then–Commodities Futures Trading Commission chairwoman Brooksley Born—"was a mistake." In fact, Summers, who was at the conference where Levitt made that admission, had followed Levitt out the door, chiding him, "You should never have said she (Born) was right!"

Now Cantwell pressed Geithner.

CANTWELL: *I want to go back to the regulatory reform issue, because it's so important. A former SEC chairman, Mr. Levitt, basically describes the CMFA, the credit—I mean the Commodities [sic] Futures Modernization Act—as—at least in the way he was talking about derivatives and credit default swaps—as a failure. Would you agree?*

GEITHNER: *Senator, I—a lot—a lot can . . .*

CANTWELL: *I'm sorry. I'm sorry. He used the word "mistake."*

GEITHNER: *It was a mistake? I don't think I agree with that, but I do agree that we're going to have to take a very careful look at the whole comprehensive framework of requirements, regulations, constraints, and incentives that exist for the institutions that play a central role in those markets.*

We want to make sure that the standardized part of those markets moves into a central clearinghouse and onto exchanges as quickly as possible.

Clearinghouses and exchanges. No one seemed to take much note, and Cantwell pressed forward to her next question.

Later that afternoon, in his temporary office at the Treasury Department, Gary Gensler trolled the newswires about the Geithner hearings.

Gensler knew that the White House would put all its weight behind the confirmation of Geithner and Summers. Their nominations might be called "too big to fail" in a time of crisis. For Gensler, only limited political capital would be expended.

Once a top economic adviser to Hillary Clinton, Gensler had been hustling to get a key spot on the Obama team since a few days after Clinton's concession in June 2008. If nothing else, since then, Gensler had been scoring high marks for indefatigable effort, having worked to raise money for Obama on Wall Street, gathered endorsements from nearly three hundred CEOs, and, after the election, rushed to Chicago to help in any way he could with the transition.

Beyond his long history with Hillary, Gensler's problem was he carried the scarlet letters "GS" on his chest: Goldman Sachs. Just as academia had watched Larry Summers rise meteorically through its ranks, the banking industry had seen in Gensler its own shooting star. By age thirty, after an MBA from Wharton, he'd made partner at Goldman, one of the youngest in the firm's history. His eighteen-year career at the firm would wrap up by the time he was forty, as co-head of all Goldman's financial operations. That's when, in 1997, his longtime mentor, Treasury secretary Bob Rubin, persuaded him to come to Washington as, first, assistant secretary for financial markets, then undersecretary of domestic finance—jobs that oversaw the U.S. financial markets, government-sponsored enterprises such as Fannie and Freddie, federal lending, and the government's fiscal affairs.

One notch above Gensler, throughout, was Larry Summers. Down the hall, as a peer, was Tim Geithner. But Gensler had experience, having actually run the profit-gulping machinery of Goldman, that neither man could match. So, in 1998, when a Greenwich, Connecticut, hedge fund called Long-Term Capital Management—boasting two Nobel Prize winners—found itself on the wrong side of gargantuan derivatives bets on foreign currencies, it was Gensler who raced from a Rosh Hashanah dinner in Washington to get on a plane. What he found, of course, was a first harbinger of coming disasters. He called Rubin, then Treasury secretary, to tell him that the exposure of the rest of Wall Street to losses from LTCM could collapse credit markets. Soon, Wall Street titans gathered and agreed to share losses from LTCM and avert a widening crisis.

But Gensler, also involved in the late-1990s actions undercutting Glass-Steagall and the regulation of derivatives, was, by 2002, moving against the Clintonites' antiregulatory stance. Already independently wealthy, he assisted a longtime friend, Maryland senator Paul Sarbanes, in constructing what would become the Sarbanes-Oxley Act, legislation—reviled across corporate America—that mandated rigor and CEO accountability in the public filing for companies and heavy fines in the event of failure.

This long record of public service and enthusiastic recent efforts on behalf of Obama was just enough to boost Gensler, the son of a vending machine operator from Baltimore, to a modest slot on the ladder of appointments: chairman of the Commodity Futures Trading Commission, or CFTC.

The commission, originally created in 1974, was designed to take over responsibilities housed in the Department of Agriculture to regulate the trading of futures and options on a wide array of commodities, from cotton, corn, and wheat to meats and precious metals. The trading of futures contracts—which would eventually grow into the vast derivatives market of financial instruments—has a long history, with citations about the future delivery of products at a certain price dating back to Aristotle. In nineteenth-century America, when shortages or surpluses of agricultural products caused chaotic fluctuations in price, Chicago businessmen developed a market that allowed grain merchants to trade "cash forward" or "to arrive" contracts that they could use to insulate, or hedge, themselves against price changes. The problem with such contracts, which at the time were often handled as private, two-party agreements, is that they wouldn't be honored by a buyer or a seller if a price fluctuation were not to their liking. The Chicago Board of Trade was formed in 1848 to be an open, transparent market where such contracts could be traded and legally honored, and soon the contracts—which derived their value from some underlying asset, such as bales of wheat—were themselves standardized.

While futures exchanges such as the Chicago Board of Trade established transparent and orderly platforms for trading these contracts, a separate issue of later "clearing" the trades (much in the way parties at a title company meet to "close" on the sale of a house) was taken up, starting in 1883, by clearinghouses, for-profit firms that then proliferated. Clearinghouses (or, in a few instances, the exchanges themselves) stepped briskly into a natural role, assuming, for a fee, the "risk" of a trade by first ensuring that the parties to a transaction had enough capital—money that they'd often have to post with the clearinghouse—to cover any foreseeable outcome on the trading floor.

This structure, which stayed sound and largely unchanged for nearly a century—even with some wild panics and swings in the prices of everything from gold to pork bellies—began to change in the 1970s with the development of financial futures. These allowed the trading of contracts on future fluctuations in interest rates. This market grew in fast evolutionary leaps for two decades, spreading to all manner of financial products, as the CFTC, built to deal with futures on the bales or barrels that eventually got delivered to someone, at a designated price, struggled to keep up.

A showdown of sorts occurred in 1998, when the CFTC's commissioner, Brooksley Born, said that something must be done to better regulate that already sizable world of financial derivatives. Born, once a pioneer in her own right as the first female editor of the *Stanford Law Review*, found herself across the table from a group of unsympathetic men: virtually every senior financial figure or regulator of that era, from Rubin and Summers to Alan Greenspan and then-SEC chairman Arthur Levitt. The financial services industry had been fighting with strength and success for more than a decade to keep their flash-fire terrain of financial derivatives separate from the rules—such as collateral and clearing requirements or standardized contracts and open trading exchanges—that governed the trading of sleepy "tangible" products. As the Internet was exploding, the financial services industry was developing its own virtual world of bets and swaps and hedges on the future prices of anything that could be stamped as having financial value, from a piece of paper to a promise. Born was unconvinced by their pitch of having created a brave new world. A financial product was still a product, she asserted, every bit as sensitive to issues of price discovery, fair dealing, credit and collateral, shortages, gluts, and market panics as were silver or soybeans. Larry Summers, leading a regulatory vanguard of men, disagreed and was soon on the phone, from his office as deputy Treasury secretary, "with thirteen bankers." He brusquely lectured Born, telling her that her ideas for regulating financial derivatives were "going to cause the worst financial crisis since the end of World War Two!" The next meeting was face-to-face with all the men—including the trio of Greenspan, Rubin, and Summers—who said she must cease and desist. They said a golden age was dawning, in which sophisticated investment houses had created new, ingenious ways to manage risk. Born stared them down, quiet, sober, and unmoved. She'd spent her whole life as the lone woman in rooms of supremely confident men; she wouldn't budge. After the meeting, the Clinton administration's regulatory barons, egged on by Wall Street, went to Congress and had her agency neutered.

What followed was a Cambrian explosion of derivatives traded OTC, or "over the counter," in the dark pools managed by the investment banks, large commercial banks, and related financial firms. The derivatives could be crafted—by teams of beautifully compensated lawyers—to fit the needs of any company's balance sheet or the performance expectations of any fund, and then sold off to others as "investments," opening the way for enormous leverage and speculation to flow, often unwittingly, into the financial system. The firms were the matchmakers, finding one party whose need fit another's desire, and then charging each counterparty a fortune.

———————

Gensler was now sitting in Born's chair—his second day on the job—though, before confirmation, he'd be in a temporary office inside Treasury. He understood as well as anyone in government the ins and outs of what they'd done in the late 1990s, and what drove the derivatives bonanza. Gensler always felt a touch of competitiveness with Geithner. They were friends who'd come up together under Clinton but had taken different paths, and if Hillary had won, Gensler might now have been in Geithner's shoes. What's more, after all his hustling, a hard fact—noted in the transition team's secret blueprint for regulatory reform—was the new administration's stance on the CFTC: that it should be folded into the larger SEC.

In short, Gensler was hustling for a job that had been slated for termination. And the displeasure that Maria Cantwell voiced to the administration weeks before about the nomination of Geithner was even more acute on the subject of Gensler, a Goldman Sachs alumnus who would now be overseeing the derivatives market that Goldman had so profitably, and disastrously, gamed.

Then something caught Gensler's eye: a passing reference in a wire report about how Geithner had said, in response to Cantwell, that he was fully supportive of moving the standard part of those derivatives markets onto central clearinghouses and exchanges as soon as possible.

Gensler did a double take. Exchanges? Clearinghouses were in the regulatory blueprint they'd come up with during the transition. But not exchanges.

What Gensler knew was that Wall Street felt it could manage the "central clearing" that Geithner had mentioned that morning. Customers, or end users, trading financial derivatives would have to turn to clearinghouses, just like traders and hedgers of traditional commodities, to settle transactions and trading positions at day's end. This would mean that the issue of collateral would come up, especially if some counterparty were dangerously exposed on the wrong side of a trade, derivatives contract, or swap. This ensured a bustling growth curve for clearinghouses, accountants, lawyers, and the like. Though the clearinghouses would still operate in the dark pool, regulators would have a chance to nose around in their books to spot a perilous exposure that could melt the financial system, the sort of "systemic risk" Gensler found that day in 1998 when he visited Long-Term Capital Management.

But to force financial derivatives onto exchanges? Though it sounded innocuous, a push to standardize derivatives and force them onto open trading platforms is what Wall Street secretly, and rightly, feared.

If the particulars and prices of derivatives contracts and trades were posted like transactions on the New York Stock Exchange, it would destroy the fat margins banks made charging fees on these derivatives deals. As it stood now, only the middleman banks knew both sides of any deal, and this information advantage was powerful. Where buyer and seller were blind, the banks ruled, and they profited wildly—estimated to generate nearly $40 billion in profits a year—from their stranglehold on the derivatives cartel. The market for the most lucrative, customized over-the-counter derivatives was controlled by five large banks.

This opaque arrangement, the very opposite of an "efficient market," is what made derivatives so profitable—which cartels often are—and dangerous. It was also the information advantage, the financial equivalent of classified information, that prevented regulators, and the wider marketplace, from seeing the depth and nature of various banks' exposure. This information could well have laid bare the ballooning problem of mismanaged risk, which in turn could have led to preemptive actions that would have headed off the financial crisis. Instead, invisible risk grew, impelling Warren Buffett to call derivatives "financial weapons of mass destruction." Like their battlefield equivalent, they combined secrecy with terrible destructive capability. Forced to be standardized and placed on exchanges, derivatives would soon be conventional products and Wall Street would lose its most prized profit center.

Gensler sat at his desk wondering what to do. Geithner and Summers, like many seasoned regulators and economists of this era, often appeared to understand the financial markets better than they actually did.

Did Geithner realize he'd just declared war on Wall Street? Even if it hadn't been picked up in the press, it was certainly something the lobbyists for the big banks wouldn't miss.

He walked a few doors down to Geithner's office.

"Tim, got a moment?"

In the late 1990s, Geithner would sometimes double-check his grasp of financial market intricacies against Gensler's long experience with an "oh, by the way" nonchalance.

Now it was Gensler with the question.

Geithner looked up: "Yeah, what's up?"

"I saw a wire story where you had that give-and-take with Cantwell. On the derivatives, you said you wanted derivatives in clearinghouses and trading on exchanges. Is that right?"

Geithner nodded. "Yeah."

"Great. I just wanted to make sure you said both, because I'll need to say the same thing."

"That's what I said," Geithner replied, and then turned back to his work.

———

Back in her office in the Dirksen Senate Office Building, Maria Cantwell huddled with her top aide on financial reform. Leaving the confirmation hearing that morning, he'd turned to her and said, "Did you hear what he said—he said clearing and trading on exchanges. That's huge." Cantwell was perplexed, unaware of the distinction and not sure she'd heard the word "exchanges" in any event.

Now the two of them looked over the transcript. There it was: "exchanges." Her aide then briefed Cantwell on the nuances of what it meant to try to standardize the customized world of derivatives and push them onto transparent trading platforms. It would kill Wall Street's margins. The sunlight of exchanges would cut out the middleman: firms could simply post their "ask" on some standardized derivatives contract—just like someone buying or selling stock—and see what kind of offer they got. They could compare prices and take the lowest one. The handcrafted derivatives product itself would be demystified and out in public, which would kill some of its less-than-pure appeal to clever corporate treasurers or fund managers.

Cantwell immediately got it. The next day, as the Finance Committee was about to convene to vote on whether they would recommend Geithner's confirmation to the full Senate, she called up Geithner's office.

"Yesterday, when you were testifying, did you really mean to say you want to push derivatives onto exchanges?" she asked.

Geithner paused. "No, actually I didn't," he said sheepishly.

Cantwell laughed under her breath. "Well, at least you're honest—I respect that."

Of course, she had Geithner testifying to mandatory exchanges under oath, as a condition of his confirmation, and now she could press Gensler to say the same when his turn came.

The Finance Committee hearing soon started. Though Baucus had cut his deal with a wildly popular president, some of the members couldn't resist speaking their minds.

"I am disappointed that we are even voting on this," said Senator Michael Enzi, the Wyoming Republican who, in general, had good relationships across the aisle. "In previous years, nominees who made less serious errors in their taxes than this nominee have been forced to withdraw."

Even Kent Conrad said that he would have voted against Geithner in normal times, but "these are not normal times."

So, in the latest twist of an improbable journey, Tim Geithner, af-

ter many disastrous instances of commission and omission in both the
Clinton Treasury and the New York Fed, would now be saved from the
ignominy of a failed nomination by the crisis itself.

As for Maria Cantwell, she voted yes as well—helping to recommend
Geithner's confirmation to the full Senate by a vote of 18 to 5—because
he admitted to a mistake. Not on the big issues of altering regulation
in the late 1990s, which had helped unleash financial demons, but on a
smaller issue of not knowing what he was saying under oath.

———

Less than a week into office, Barack Obama knew he had to make a decision. The promise he'd made to Peter Orszag and others about fundamental health care reform being his top priority for year one needed to
be reexamined.

The earth was shifting quickly beneath the White House, as it was
beneath the feet of every American. Figures showed that the U.S. economy had lost nearly six hundred thousand jobs in December. January
was looking just as bad.

It was an emergency the weight of which Obama felt acutely from
the minute he first stepped into the Oval Office. The best-laid plans of a
candidate anticipating victory, or even a president-elect, now needed to
be seen through the new eyes of a sitting U.S. president in the midst of a
worsening crisis. The world looked different from Pennsylvania Avenue.

With negotiations on the stimulus under way, and passage of something resembling the administration's package looking like a foregone
conclusion, a meeting was set in the Roosevelt Room to discuss whether
health care would still be job one.

And if not health care, then what?

There were two primary factions: the camp in favor of leading with
financial regulatory reform, considering that a financial collapse would
trigger economic catastrophe and that a full recovery, and sustained
prosperity, could be possible only if the stimulus package were matched
with a refashioned financial system; and the camp in favor of leading
with health care reform, the multigenerational goal of liberals, and key to
both balancing the federal budget and restoring America's middle class.
There was also a smaller, third camp, led by Carol Browner, the EPA
chief under Clinton and now Obama's energy and environmental czar,
in favor of leading with a bold environmental agenda, especially in at-

tacking global warming, integrated with the building of a sustainable energy future.

Pressing the issue was a matter of the federal budget. By early February, Obama needed to decide what to include in his 2010 fiscal year budget. Whatever decisions he made, they would need to be reflected in the budget, a signal of the administration's policy intentions to Congress and the wider public.

But two of Obama's main voices on health care, senior adviser Pete Rouse and Tom Daschle, Obama's Health and Human Services designee, would not be in attendance. Rouse, though a Colby College graduate, had been born in New Haven and was an avid Yale hockey fan. He was missing the meeting to see his team play, his single concession to something other than work.

Like any good aide, Rouse did a little recon on what Obama could expect on health care.

"Mr. President, the deck is stacked against you."

He was referring to the people who *would* be there—principally the economic team, several of whom had been on the fence about whether to begin with a health care battle. Now they were in concert: given the current economic crisis, it was a bridge too far.

Tom Daschle, the prime proponent of making health care reform a first-year mission, was unable to make it because his brother, Greg, was ill with brain cancer—a strain similar to the one afflicting Ted Kennedy. Daschle had been at the Duke University Hospital for the last few days, including Inauguration Day, sitting in the hospital room as Obama delivered his speech.

With Daschle out of town, Obama had lost more than an adviser. He'd lost the most ardent advocate of pursuing health care reform as quickly as possible.

In his stead was an array of economic advisers who were there to discuss how the fledgling president could hedge his plan to lead with health care.

The specific issue was over what sort of placeholder the president should put in his proposed budget for health care reform. Should it be left blank, or undesignated; should it be designated as a "middle ground" of $650 billion, or should it be a trillion? "Mr. President, you know I support health care reform, I've been passionate about it for years," Peter Orszag said, appealing to sensibilities he and Obama had long shared.

"But until the deficit is below three percent of GDP, it may be fiscally problematic."

This was particularly difficult for Orszag, who'd all but made health care reform in year one a precondition for his leaving CBO. But one of the reasons Orszag was always drawn to fundamental health care reform was budgetary: he believed that cost saving, using evidence-based breakthroughs and comparative effectiveness, would drive down health care expenditures and save the federal budget. Like fighting a war while cutting taxes, however, launching a new huge social program during a recession might be considered fiscally imprudent. The economic downturn was already prompting a decrease in tax receipts, while costs, for unemployment insurance and related programs, were skyrocketing. This meant that even without health care reform, albeit an essential repair for the country but not yet a day-to-day crisis, the deficit was due to rise.

Summers and Geithner echoed this concern, but Obama cut in.

"Who here does think we should include health care in the budget?" he asked.

Mark Childress, Daschle's chief of staff, meekly raised his hand.

"Thank you, Mark. I want you to channel Daschle."

But, after a few minutes, it was clear that Childress was no match for the heavyweights in the room. Every point he made was mercilessly dissected, with the triumvirate of Summers, Geithner, and Orszag parsing the fabric of his argument and then eviscerating it with numerical data.

After a while, Obama had seen enough of the bloodbath. "Okay, enough, enough . . . I'll be Daschle."

The president immediately addressed all the trio's arguments head-on, analyzing their weaknesses and strengths. Even professional interlocutors and trained debaters such as Summers were impressed. Obama thought that this reform was the ideal match for the stimulus: a temporary boost coupled with a long-term restructuring of every kitchen table's budget, and that of the federal government. He summed it up with issues of how to restore the underlying confidence of a people who lived with too little security and too much fear in their lives.

By the time the meeting was over, no one was challenging Obama. The other alternatives, such as financial regulatory reform or a sweeping environmental energy program, had barely been discussed.

Health care would be included in the proposed budget, with a placeholder of $650 billion. After so many meetings during the transition, where the president-elect tried, sometimes futilely, to guide his advisers toward consensus, this time he "channeled" his mentor, Daschle, and made up his own mind.

But the president knew what virtually no one else in the room realized: Daschle was in big trouble. Rouse and Obama had been talking in the past few days about their common friend. Daschle's recent history as a lobbyist for Alston & Bird left him vulnerable to attack if someone had enough desire. And Max Baucus did. He and Daschle were longtime rivals, and he was digging into everything he could find. After losing his Senate seat in 2004, Daschle also lost his crack staff, led by Rouse, and the precise and affectionate care they afforded him in managing every detail of his life. His last four years of private life, with residences in Washington and South Dakota, and a Bismarck accountant, had left behind plenty of loose ends. The one that Baucus joyously pulled was $128,000 in undeclared compensation for the use of a private car from a friendly corporation while Daschle was in D.C.—a detail soon to be released, spelling Daschle's demise.

Had the revelation of Daschle's tax problems preceded the more serious IRS shortfalls of Geithner, he might well have survived, and Obama would be looking for a new nominee for Treasury. But Baucus held the cards and dealt them with an eye toward a bigger prize: commanding the central position on any health care initiative, rather than being upstaged, once again, by the soft-spoken but unflinching Daschle.

What was clear to Obama, as he was whipping into line a group of savvy, argumentative advisers, is that he'd have to go forward without Daschle: his friend, guide, and teacher. It was no surprise that he played him with such force and passion in this important meeting. The practical result was that health care reform would now be the first priority of the Obama presidency. A lifelong consensus builder had stumbled into the first, and often most difficult, lesson of every new president: advisers advise, presidents decide.

On January 29, after Wall Street reported a robust $18 billion in bonuses for 2008, about the same level as the profitable year of 2004, the president became incensed.

"How is this possible that they're paying themselves these bonuses when it was the government that bailed them out!" he said at the

9:30 a.m. daily briefing with his senior economic team. It was a rare moment, when his voice rose in true anger.

Obama, a man with little experience wielding power but the fastest of learners, said he wanted to make a statement. Soon there were cameras in the Oval Office. He spoke from the edge of his seat, eyes wide, with Geithner and Bernanke on either side, calling the bonuses "the height of irresponsibility—it is shameful."

"Part of what we're going to need is for the folks on Wall Street who are asking for help to show some restraint, some discipline, and some sense of responsibility," he said, clearly agitated. "There will be a time for them to make profits and a time for them to get bonuses. This is not the time."

Ben Bernanke, sitting next to Obama, was not so much outraged at the bankers' behavior; he'd been living and working in the midst of high-compensation bankers for years. As one of his aides said later, he was just upset that their taking such big bonuses, prompting outrage, could make his job of extending almost unlimited federal largess to the financial sector even more difficult.

Similarly nonplussed was Tim Geithner, on the president's other flank. During his confirmation hearings, Geithner mentioned that the administration was preparing rules to require that executives at companies receiving taxpayer money agree that any compensation above a certain amount—he did not specify how much—be "paid in restricted stock" that could not be liquidated or sold until the government had been repaid.

It was a low priority. Geithner didn't believe in compensation limits. In his experience, he'd never seen any that worked. On Wall Street, any firm with compensation barriers would just have its employees stolen by a competitor who was not similarly restricted.

What Geithner hadn't told Obama in their many hours together was that there was, not far away, a ticking time bomb on these explosive matters of compensation.

Bonuses of $165 million were due to be paid to AIG executives in mid-March. In the fall of 2008, Geithner presided over the issues of how—and how much—AIG would be permitted to compensate its employees, claiming that the payouts were "retention" bonuses to keep aboard employees who might be helpful in unwinding the derivatives mess AIG had helped weave.

Though Geithner later said he didn't remember any specifics about the AIG bonuses, the issue was being actively managed in February in the upper reaches of his Treasury Department. All across the capital, after all, legislators were impelled to action by the president's angry words. One of them was Chris Dodd, the Connecticut Democrat and chair of the Senate Banking Committee, who inserted an amendment sharply limiting executive bonuses for firms that had received bailout money into the nearly completed American Recovery and Reinvestment Act, the stimulus bill. It would sharply limit the bonuses for executives at institutions that had received TARP funds until those funds were fully paid back. As the stimulus bill crested toward passage, with surprising bipartisan support, a call came to Dodd from Geithner's office. The suggestion: How about only restricting those bonuses agreed upon after the bill's passage that month? Their point was that to vitiate a contract retroactively would undercut the very sanctity of contracts everywhere. Any such new compensation provisions should be for contracts yet to be written. The move, however, would exempt those explosive AIG compensation contracts signed the previous year. Dodd quietly made the change.

Meanwhile, the president was looking for ways to turn his forceful words into action, to find expressions of his will, and outrage, in concrete policy. His venue for this search was the daily economic briefing, something that was announced two days after the inauguration as proof of his concern over the unfurling recession. Across many administrations since the end of World War II, there was a tradition of daily briefings about matters of intelligence and national security. It fell under a president's central responsibility of upholding the national defense.

It was Obama's idea that the economic security of Americans, at this time of crisis, was imperiled, meriting its own designated briefing.

But whereas the intelligence briefing, for instance, rests on a long-standing structure of teams inside CIA and Defense Intelligence upstreaming recommendations through a vetting and distilling process— now run by the relatively new office of the Director of National Intelligence—there was no similar process on the economic front. Not that there wasn't an available entity. The National Economic Council was designed to be a corollary to the decades-old, heavily staffed National Security Council, which has a formalized process in which deputy principals (often number twos at departments) meet to discuss matters that are then upstreamed to the NSC principals, the heads of the major arms of government engaged in security, along with the highest-ranking domestic appointee, the Treasury secretary, all of whom help the president arrive at policy recommendations shaping America's role in the world.

The NEC, with a modest staff, had never matched that sort of process or rigor, partly because economics is not a neat fit for literal assessments of national security or the related analyses of gathered intelligence.

In fact, the productivity and effectiveness of the NEC were often the direct result of the organizational and conceptual abilities of its chief. Rubin, setting the mark early, was a generalist on economic and financial matters, with a talent for bringing in competing perspectives and synthesizing them into coherent recommendations.

Though these were not Summers's strong suits, he was now in charge of a crucial morning slot on the president's schedule each day—at least for a few weeks or, at most, a few months. That's what Emanuel anticipated. Rather than a session to hammer out policy, these daily economic briefings, he felt, were as much as anything for show—a statement of hourly purpose about the president's central commitment to battling the economic crisis. They'd be phased out, Rahm figured, in a month or so.

But Emanuel showed up, along with almost everyone with a senior role in domestic policy—at that point, almost entirely about the economy slide and financial collapse. Geithner, Orszag, and Romer all attended, along with Joe Biden's economic policy chief, the progressive economist Jared Bernstein. Axelrod usually attended as well, as did the vice president.

Of course, the meetings were run by Summers, who set the agenda and worked up briefing materials for the president to read, which the latter often did late the night before, after the girls were tucked in.

And the president did his homework. Compared to the economic meetings during the transition, where he took notes and asked the infrequent question, Obama, now as president, was quite engaged. He was ready to own the key concepts and debate them, in the aim of arriving at what he called "best possible plans."

He ran into a united front, philosophically, of Summers and Geithner. Both men viewed the U.S. economy as a sick patient, but one with strong, and often improbable, recuperative powers. One of Summers's favorite phrases—often echoed by Geithner—was that, as policy makers, they should rely on Hippocrates' dictum "first, do no harm."

By early February it was clear that what the president hoped would be a debate society, organized by Summers but presided over—like a judge in a moot court competition—by Obama himself, was turning into Larry Summers's economics seminar.

The meetings often seemed impromptu, with the tenor of a free-form search for solutions, but Summers, knowing the well-worn steps of dozens of economic debates, seemed to guide discussion toward some waiting item on his syllabus. The NSC-style process of debating concepts through deputies and principals to arrive at some distillation of choices for a presidential decision, was, in essence, being done in Larry Summers's head.

This cribbing of Hippocrates was a formidable rhetorical stance and subtly difficult to refute. Virtually any action on a grand scale would carry unintended consequences, and maybe even intended ones, that would create damage to the short-term interests of some constituency. Meandering discussions about whether the intended consequences would outrun the unintended ones would quickly slip into theoretical guesswork, while underselling the variable of how strong execution or persuasion—or, more succinctly, leadership—could help push proposals to surprisingly strong outcomes.

Obama's response to this cul-de-sac: outside readings. Rather than "first, do no harm," by the first week in February his preferred phrase was "Sweden not Japan."

Though neither country's experience is cleanly applicable to that of the United States, by far the world's largest economy, the experience of each country seemed to present a set of choices.

Sweden had deregulated its financial industry in the early 1980s, much like the United States, creating a bonanza of speculation in new securities tied to housing, and inflating a massive real estate bubble that finally burst in 1991. In circumstances that were eerily similar to those in the United States, credit then froze in an economy that was heavily overleveraged with debt. Values plummeted, from both a crisis of liquidity and a massive correction in inflated prices.

After two rounds of bank bailouts, which seemed at first to be working only to prove inadequate, Sweden temporarily nationalized its banks. Shareholders were wiped out, management teams were generally ousted, troubled assets were auctioned off, and the banks reemerged with the government as a large equity owner. Crucially, though, confidence in the system was quickly restored. Sweden, with this tough-love approach, roared back to strong growth throughout the decade. The government reduced its ownership in the banks, year by year, as they slowly returned to health and sound practices. In essence, Sweden restored its banks by a kind of enforced prudence.

At the same time, half a world away, Japan was experiencing a similar set of disasters from the bursting of its 1980s real estate bubble. The major difference? What Sweden had started—and then reversed—Japan kept doing: it kept bailing out its insolvent banks with government support and cash infusions. There were ups and downs across years, times when the banks seemed to be on the mend, and then fell back. The idea was for the banking system to stay intact and earn its way back to health by slowly reducing its toxic assets as it resumed lending. This never happened. Japan limped along for what was called its "lost decade," the 1990s, with virtually no economic growth, a situation of sluggish economic activity that continues up until the present day.

New York Times columnist Paul Krugman had been developing both edges of the analogy since a few weeks after the September 2008 meltdown, when he wrote on his widely read blog that a temporary nationalization of the banks, as the Swedes had successfully done, was the only sound remedy to the crisis, but one that "won't be possible until January 21"—when, he hoped, Obama would be president.

Just as Obama was firmly opening a mid-October lead that would all but assure him the presidency, Krugman also won a prize, the Nobel Prize for Economics, which gilded the columnist with a rarified credibility ideally suited to the moment. While Krugman's longtime competitor, Summers, assumed the role of senior economic adviser, Krugman was suddenly the voice, twice weekly, of the progressive alternative. While in Stockholm in mid-December to accept the prize, Krugman warned that the "scenario I fear is that we'll see, for the whole world, an equivalent of Japan's lost decade, the 1990s—that we'll see a world of zero interest rates, deflation, no sign of recovery, and it will just go on for a very extended period," a bleak outcome that might result if the United States followed Japan's path of largely unconditional support for "too big to fail" banks.

"Each morning at the economic briefing it was like we were debating

Krugman," said one attendee of the meetings. "Clearly Obama was reading Paul's columns and related materials on this Sweden-versus-Japan
split, and it made sense to him as both analysis and a guide for action."

All of which put Summers and Geithner—both of whom thought the
country comparisons were overly facile and of limited application—in a
bind. This was especially the case for Geithner, who was busy working
through alternatives for a plan, any plan, to fix the financial system, a
plan Obama was anxious to unveil.

It wasn't going to look much like Sweden. He and his thinly staffed
Treasury considered one plan after another, including guaranteeing the
assets of the banking system against extreme losses—a proposal whose
price tag could approach $1 trillion—or forming an "aggregator bank"
that would start buying toxic assets from banks with a large portion of
the $350 billion currently left in TARP. The problem: Treasury officials
estimated there may be as much as $2 trillion in toxic assets throughout
the system. No one had that kind of money.

The remedies were all asset-based. How, in short, to remove or nullify
enough of the toxic assets on bank balance sheets—most of them securities tied to or backed by mortgages, many quite complex—so banks
could begin to lend again, but do it in a way that didn't seem like another
massive government grant to help them earn their way out of a disaster
they'd largely caused.

With only a few days before Obama was due to offer news of
Geithner's solution at his first presidential press conference, Geithner's
team—at that point, pulling all-nighters—settled on a program the Fed
had developed the previous fall: a public-private buyout fund. Investors'
capital would be leveraged up at about ten to one with loans from the
government, which would act as a co-investor. If there were profits, the
investors would do well; if not, their losses would be limited, but their
involvement in what was clearly a sweet deal would help move the toxic
fare out of banks and into a marketplace where it could be priced. At
least, that was the idea.

When Obama stepped into the East Room on the evening of February 9, he was carrying the surety of a man fast establishing his bearings.
With approval ratings in some polls notched above 70 percent—CNN's
was a 76—he could now offer a display of strength in an area of weakness
for his predecessor: the prime-time presidential press conference. View-

ership was high, a 42 household rating. Just three weeks after the historic events on the Mall, people wanted to see the man they'd elected in action, and the live theater of thrust and parry with the Washington press corps is as close as the public tends to get. Obama was pumped up and ready. He'd been training for this for much of his adult life and, stepping to the lectern, he was brimming with explanations for how the world worked and what he was planning to do about it. For the first question—about whether his rhetoric about the economy was too bleak—he went with Japan: "The federal government is the only entity left with the resources to jolt our economy back to life," he said, alluding to the soon-to-be-passed stimulus, and then warned that a failure to act "boldly and swiftly" in handling the failed banks could leave America looking like Japan. "They suffered what was called the 'lost decade,' where essentially for the entire nineties, they did not see any significant economic growth."

As to the specifics of those bold and swift actions—crucial to avoid Japan's fate—he said the country would be hearing the next morning from his right-hand man.

"Tomorrow, my Treasury secretary, Tim Geithner, will be announcing some very clear and specific plans for how we are going to start loosening up credit once again. And that means having some transparency and oversight in the system. It means that we correct some of the mistakes with TARP that were made earlier, the lack of consistency, the lack of clarity in terms of how the program was going to move forward. It means that we condition taxpayer dollars that are being provided to banks on them showing some restraint when it comes to executive compensation, not using the money to charter corporate jets when they're not necessary. It means that we focus on housing and how we are going to help homeowners that are suffering foreclosure or homeowners who are still making their mortgage payments, but are seeing their property values decline."

Obama was just warming up, mentioning a moment later how "my immediate task is making sure that the second half of that money, $350 billion, is spent properly. That's my first job. Before I even think about what else I've got to do, my first task is to make sure that my secretary of the Treasury, Tim Geithner, working with Larry Summers, my national economic adviser, and others, are coming up with the best possible plan to use this money wisely."

The president had not actually done that, at least not yet. There'd been discussions in the morning briefings about guiding principles and the president's view about how policy should be shaped—views that Obama expressed eloquently, several times, across the coming hour.

Principles, however, were not policies, and well along in the questioning, the *New York Times'* Helene Cooper, who understood Obama better than most other reporters in the corps, pressed for specifics: "On the next bank bailout, are you going to impose a requirement that the financial institutions use this money to loosen up credit and make new lending? And if not, how do you make the case to the American people that this bailout will work when the last one didn't?"

The question was a bull's-eye. Obama, for the umpteenth time across an hour, deferred to his Treasury secretary, who, of course, didn't believe in imposing requirements on how financial institutions decide to apply their capital. "Again, Helene, I'm trying to avoid preempting my secretary of the Treasury. I want all of you to show up at his press conference as well," Obama said to hearty laughter. "He's going to be terrific."

The next morning, a standing-room-only crowd gathered in the high-ceilinged Cash Room at Treasury. Geithner was anything but terrific. The plan for government to encourage investors to buy up toxic assets— a program that would eventually be called PPIP, for Public-Private Investment Program—was offered only in generalities. It was so hastily assembled that Geithner's team hadn't worked out the crucial logistics, such as how the assets would be valued, using what yardsticks, or what terms would apply to investors. There were rumors that Geithner would address the fundamental issues on the sellers' side of this equation— whether banks would get a reprieve in "mark-to-market" accounting for the assets they sold to the new fund. Without that, banks would have to take huge write-downs from such asset sales—forcing them to book heavy losses or even publicly acknowledge their insolvency. No remedy for that meant the public-private partnerships could be a bust.

Geithner offered nothing on that score—no clear policy, after all, had been hashed out—though he did mention, almost in passing, a program for "stress-testing" the banks over the coming months, to show their soundness. But he was hard to listen to. He was sleep-deprived and nervous as hell, and it showed. His demeanor seemed shifty and small. MSNBC's Mike Barnicle memorably described him as having the "eyes of a shoplifter," darting fearfully to and fro.

As laudatory reviews of Obama's fortnight's performance filled the news cycles, a wide and diverse audience now saw Geithner and winced. Minutes after he stepped before two huge American flags, looking like the losing candidate in a student council election, the equity markets began to tank. It didn't stop. The confidence Obama seemed to impel was shattered by the man he'd hired. By 4:00 p.m. the Dow had dropped a stunning 378 points. Geithner was widely cited as the cause.

This dissonance was the first glimpse of a gap between sunlight and shadow, between what the public saw and felt about the president— about his incisive intellect and unflappable demeanor, his command of issues and events, his charm and perspicacity—and what was happening inside the protected realm of the White House.

The next morning, and the ones that followed in the coming weeks, the president would work his Japan-versus-Sweden analogy, as Geithner would parry this line of argument with his gentle verbal quickstep, offering qualifiers about how Sweden was different from America, and Japan was, too. There were many distinctions. Sweden had only six large banks. Japan had structural issues that were unique to its economy.

Meanwhile, Summers backed off, steering clear of offering his own definitive position. The issue of whether to take down banks and restructure them was, after all, primarily the province of the Treasury secretary. Summers knew this: he once had that job, had wanted it again, was passed over in favor of his young friend, and now was waiting patiently for the prized job as Federal Reserve chairman when Bernanke's term came up later in the year. Other than offering general comments about the effects of tighter credit on the wider economy, he gave ground, letting the embattled Geithner stand in the way of Obama's evolving position and ardor.

The president, Summers could see, was trying to establish enough mastery of some very complex issues so that he could act boldly and swiftly and, it was hoped, responsibly, on behalf of the American people.

Summers knew it was better in any debate to let one's opponent fully establish his position before you stepped up to the lectern. In others words, he who goes last usually has an advantage and, eventually, the last word.

Obama, now as president, was busy going first, trying to figure out a way to be Roosevelt in the country's hour of need.

WELL MANAGED

T HE BLACK SEDAN WAS SPEEDING BACK FROM CAPITOL HILL, down Pennsylvania Avenue and toward the White House. Tim Geithner, fresh from testifying before the House Budget Committee, was on the phone, and had been on call over the past few days. Citigroup, the largest diversified financial institution in the United States, was on the verge of collapse. The previous afternoon, in a heated conference call with Ben Bernanke and the other top financial officials in the United States, Sheila Bair, head of the FDIC, was pressing Geithner to "bite the bullet" and, with the FDIC's help, do an orderly "resolution"—essentially, a controlled bankruptcy. Geithner fended her off, and then called Dick Parsons, the former Time Warner chief who was Citi's new chairman—replacing Bob Rubin—to report where things stood. Since then, the situation had continued to deteriorate.

Just that morning, March 5, Citi's stock had dropped below $1 per share—less than the bank's charge for a single ATM transaction. The bank, which had a stock price in the high $40 range in 2007, was now facing an upside-down balance sheet, with hundreds of billions in toxic assets and a market capitalization that was racing toward zero.

If Citi collapsed in an unmanageable "run," other banks would likely follow. It could easily be a Lehman repeat, plunging the economy even deeper into trouble. But it was also a test. The government could either add more capital, bailing out another troubled Wall Street giant, or it could show its ability to soundly unwind a big bank without sending the financial world into spasms. What was clear was that the government couldn't stand by and do nothing.

In the car, Geithner looked at that morning's news. Late that afternoon, there'd be another conference call. Bair would be coming at him again.

Sitting next to Geithner in the car was one of his top deputies, Alan Krueger, now the assistant Treasury secretary for economic policy and—

in a term dating back to the eighteenth century—the "chief economist of the United States." Another holder of that title was Paul Volcker, when he had this job in 1969.

"You've got to fill in for me," the Treasury secretary told Krueger as their sedan pulled onto the White House grounds. "I'll just make a quick appearance, show everyone I was there, and then slip out. I don't have time for this today."

Geithner was talking about the big Health Care Summit taking place at midday in the White House. The secretary, in other words, didn't have time for what his boss considered the most important initiative of his presidency.

A hundred yards away, at the Northwest Gate, John Podesta was pleading with White House security. He was certain his name was on the list.

Sitting in his booth, the guard glanced over again at his computer screen. Sorry, no "Podesta" had been cleared. The former Clinton chief of staff shook his head in disbelief. He had once ruled these grounds. He began dialing numbers on his BlackBerry, one White House extension after the next, looking for someone, anyone, to get him clearance. No answers.

Almost everyone of political consequence was already crowding beneath the gold-inlaid ceiling of the East Room. This morning was the grand opening of Obama's adventure in self-governance: the mission to reform health care in America, a goal that had eluded nearly every president since Teddy Roosevelt. Today it was a combination of theater and intervention, with the new president assuming the role of therapist in chief, bent on saving a town addicted to conflict.

The crowd in the East Room was buzzing with anticipation and nervous energy, like a feuding, far-flung family gathered at a rare reunion. Since word of this leaked out two weeks ago, the issue of who was and wasn't on the guest list had become the stuff of controversy. Representative John Conyers, Detroit's aging liberal African American dean, went so far as to squeeze Obama's arm at an event and ask to be included—to no avail—touching off a flurry of online outrage that finally resulted in an invite.

On the day's schedule was a short speech by Obama, followed by an hour where everyone would break into work groups, and then a return to the East Room to begin sketching a way forward. In his Inaugural Address, Obama had said that in the election, America had chosen "hope over fear," but already the town's mandarins were whispering that he would need both of those important tools to squeeze anything like tangible progress from this rabble.

No one knew this better than Podesta, who—having finally found someone to vouch for him with the guards—slipped quietly into a chair in the last row. He had worked in the White House during the last great battle to change a broken health care system. The Clinton crew, many now settling into roles in the current White House, tended to look back on those days a bit like General Pickett reflecting on his disastrous charge at Gettysburg.

It was a slaughter. President Clinton had called together "the finest minds" and, under the guidance of the First Lady and Ira Magaziner, a Rhodes Scholar buddy, they produced a thousand-page opus on how to repair what was even then 11 percent of the U.S. economy. They had unveiled the plan with great fanfare, flags waving, brilliant men and women in analytical concert marching to Capitol Hill for its passage. The doctors and hospitals, insurers and drug companies, who were not included in the deliberations, waited for their moment and then, in unison, opened fire. It was a bloodbath. Health care reform, having sucked up all the town's oxygen for nearly a year, collapsed instantly in a heap. The fledgling president seemed overmatched and confused, and the Democrats were shellacked in the '94 midterms.

Fifteen years later, Podesta tried to think about what was different this time and what was different between the two presidents. Carrying lessons from one era to another, Podesta said, was not simple math. It was more like calculus, with shifting variables. The key was to draw the right conclusions.

In the early nineties, he said, "there was a real debate about the need for reform, but not anymore." Pursuing the thought, he added, "That's the fundamental change. The business community now comes to the discussion with a real urgency. They're getting killed with what's going on in respect to health inflation. It's imperative that the system change. Everyone agrees on that."

But Podesta's vantage point yielded insight into the most important variable, the central actor: the two-term president he had known intimately, as only a chief of staff can, and the new president, whom he had now seen in more executive actions, as head of Obama's transition, than almost anyone, anywhere.

"Clinton had—or rather has—an ability to synthesize competing positions, to command the room and arrive at ingenious versions of the middle ground, that's often invisible to others," Podesta said. Obama was different, though, and it took him a minute to parse just how, in a way that praised both men equally. "He draws people out of their comfort zone," he said, "but he does it subtly, challenging them with his openness and his commitment to change. He ends up making them rise to the occasion. He doesn't just synthesize and sell a solution. He finds opportunities in the larger body of players to create circumstances where change can happen." He paused, thinking all this over, and then he got it to a single sentence: "He's creating a space where solutions can happen."

Or so it might have seemed. It was clear to those inside Obama's inner circle that the new president was trying to find ways to harness the energy that his stunning election and glowing presence had created. He certainly hadn't been bashful so far, answering the high hopes of his election with an audacious breath of early initiatives. Over the objections of his key advisers, Obama had decided to use his historically strong opening hand to bet on health care reform rather than to focus, night and day, on the disastrous nexus of a collapsed financial system and a sinking economy.

Still, they were all anxious to see how Obama used his vast political capital in a moment he had created: calling this White House summit to push forward his signature initiative. Several advisers were recommending toughness, saying that he needed to scare some sense into these health care stakeholders. They argued that fear was all that they, or anyone in Washington, respected.

Obama went with hope instead. His opening speech laid out the problems: medical costs rising at four times the rate of inflation, crushing kitchen-table budgets, tenuous business balance sheets, and leaving forty-six million uninsured. Then he told those gathered—fifty-five members of Congress, eighty-two representatives of the health care interests—that things were this way because over the years "people in this room failed to act."

As the speech ended, Geithner turned impatiently to Alan Krueger. "I need to leave," he told him, and slipped out a side door.

The assembled then broke into discussion groups led by top officials in the administration. Krueger, in Geithner's stead, ran a breakout group with Nancy-Ann DeParle, the White House's new chief official on health care reform, and then made his way back to the main room, where the larger group was reconvening. Orrin Hatch, the conservative senior senator from Utah, grabbed Krueger's arm.

"Tell your boss, Geithner, he shouldn't be coming to things like this," the senator said. "Someone needs to be working full time on the job of saving the economy."

Clearly the president wasn't. Now, with the precious opportunity of having brought official Washington together for the day in his house, the people's house, Obama spent the next hour conducting a kind of afternoon talk show.

He offered a few passionate remarks about reform, read the highlights of what some people had said in their breakout sessions, and then answered a few questions from the audience. There were some special guests who needed to be cited. Key lobbyists were asked to stand and affirm their commitment to reform. They did, one by one—the lead lobbyist for the hospitals, for the doctors, for the nurses. Then the room quieted.

"Is Karen Ignagni here?" Obama said. "Someone get her a mic."

A smallish women with a blond pageboy stood up. Everyone in the room knew that she and her organization—America's Health Insurance Plans, or AHIP—were the dangerous wild card in the mix. Ignagni, once the head lobbyist for the AFL-CIO and now president and CEO of AHIP, had broken with the hospitals, doctors, drug companies, and other stakeholders in 2007, saying the insurers would agree to reform in exchange for a federally supported individual mandate. Such a mandate would force people to get health insurance, in the same way they needed auto insurance to drive a car. Health insurers—with $12 billion in annual revenues, a modest-size lynchpin in a $2.5 trillion health care industry—had suddenly seemed willing to trade plenty to get forty-six million new customers.

And that was before the election. The fear rippling through the room today was about what health care professionals quietly called the "divide-and-conquer strategy." If the new president could turn Ignagni's grand bargain into a grand alliance and, by some combination of fear or bribery, turn the health insurers into more of a federally directed industry, the administration could use the insurers' key informational advantage of knowing every dollar spent and its value to drive down costs across the medical landscape.

Ignagni now clutched the microphone. "We hear the American people about what's not working," she said. "We've taken that very seriously. You have our commitment to play, to contribute, and to help pass health care reform this year."

Obama raised his hands, cueing the audience. "Thank you, Karen," he said. "That's good news. That's America's Health Insurance Plans!" Then he led the crowd in lusty applause.

For his finale, Obama took the theater of goodwill up one more notch, strolling into the hallway behind the East Room and emerging with a hobbled Ted Kennedy on his arm. Kennedy, Obama's early patron and an advocate of health care reform for nearly forty years, was diminished, dying of cancer. But he said he was "looking forward to being a foot soldier in the battle."

The crowd broke into applause with renewed vigor and rose to its feet, with Obama acting as the narrator of this participatory moment he himself had invented. It was what he did at countless campaign rallies. It was what he did best.

But many in the crowd were beginning to wonder, now six weeks into the Obama presidency, how he would direct his inspirational talents in the act of governance. Obama had tried to lift and engage them today, to level with them, as though he were still a candidate and they were still voters, simply citizens on the receiving end of the U.S. health care system. He had tried to talk to them, in short, as human beings.

Of course, these were lobbyists—many of them compensated quite handsomely not to react as human beings. They were paid to act based on the interests they represented. Filing out, many of them wondered about the point of this big-tent revival, and why Obama hadn't unleashed invective on them, which was clearly what the voters wanted him to do. As they pondered this, they also wondered if there was something in the way Obama and Ignagni had been smiling at each other during their exchange. Had the two already cut some sort of secret deal?

Some of Obama's advisers were puzzled as well.

"Look, it's like the president said, you've got to be hopeful and you've got to include Republicans. You've got to include everyone and take them seriously," Zeke Emanuel, Rahm's older brother and a longtime health care expert, said. He'd been brought on in January to help guide reform and was pushing through the White House's front foyer as he spoke. "The system is dysfunctional. The system isn't working. We need to head in the right direction. Are there different ways of getting there? Absolutely. Do we need to be pragmatic? Yes. I thought the president was pretty clear . . . I mean just look at Orszag's numbers—his cost projections on Medicare and Medicaid. We have no choice!"

If Emanuel sounded like he was talking in circles, it was because he knew something only a few others in the room realized: the White House had secretly shelved the best weapons it had for instilling productive fear in this group.

Though the president had made up his mind in the meeting where he channeled Daschle, and decided to include a $650 billion placeholder in the federal budget for health care, his top advisers subsequently wrestled back significant leverage and latitude. In small group meetings throughout February, Obama's senior staff had "modeled" the health care initiative off of a variety of pregame assumptions. The conclusions, by Rahm Emanuel and others, were that the "public option"—a basic government-sponsored plan that the insurers feared—was a nonstarter, as were significant cuts in medical costs. Peter Orszag, who had been pushing the idea that cost savings should drive the expansion in coverage, was opposed in meetings by Rahm Emanuel, who thought Obama shouldn't even attempt health care reform at a time of economic crisis, much less take on the doctors, hospitals, and drug companies about rising costs. A more ambitious game plan, based on flipping and using the insurers, would demand a kind of strategic sophistication that the White House was already having trouble mustering.

Just a month and a half into his presidency, Barack Obama's White House was slipping into a kind of dysfunction. In a way, it was not all that surprising that a president who had never managed anything beyond his own personal journey had responded to wild expectations, at a time of crisis, by grabbing hold of every intractable dilemma in sight. But the improvisational ebullience, and energy, Obama generated in the first few weeks wasn't being turned into concrete actions or strategies. As the president tried to rise to the demands of his job, the White House was increasingly being directed by a back-channel union between two forceful men: Rahm Emanuel and Larry Summers.

By March they had each begun to establish control of the two main sides to any presidency: policy and politics. Summers, fortifying his position as policy gatekeeper for all things economic, had become something of a domestic policy czar. He attended the important policy meetings and frequently talked to the president in private, framing the intellectual parameters on an array of complex issues. On the other side was Emanuel, who decided what agenda items were politically feasible and constructed the tactical plans for their execution. Emanuel had never been known for his long-range, strategic sensibilities. He was rather a man of decisiveness—or, depending on how you saw it, impulsiveness—and action.

But as important as what either man said directly to the president was what each said to the other. The two met often and talked after meetings with the president or the economic team, with Summers wandering down the hall to the chief of staff's office. Normally, Emanuel was wary of what he disparaged as the "pink-sheeters"—what he called people who, he quipped, read the *Financial Times* and passed time at places such as the Aspen Institute. Summers, with his rhetorical gifts, knew how not to come across that way. He talked tough. He talked politics.

"Larry fancies himself very good at politics," said Christina Romer, "and he wanted to please Rahm. That created problems in terms of how things were decided."

Decided by Summers and Emanuel, with or without the president.

Rahm Emanuel didn't come to the Health Care Summit, but Larry Summers did. He ran one of the breakouts, in fact. As the summit ended, just after 3:00 p.m., he was standing on the grass in front of the White House tapping on his BlackBerry. His comments there revealed the subtle complexities of how he saw the world and framed arguments, with him often taking both sides and then deciding which he liked best.

"We've gone from a moment when we've never had a *less* social-science-oriented group," he said coyly, referring to the Bush administration, "to a moment when we've never had a *more* social-science-oriented group. So . . . we'll see what happens."

As the self-styled leader of this latter camp, Summers expanded on this line of thought, remarking that health care presented "some difficult-to-ponder judgments. You can look at nine different hospitals with some heart procedure, and you can see it's working twice as well in some of them as it is in others. You can see what 'best practice' is, and that should propel the market to separate the best providers—whose services will be in highest demand—from the worst. Of course, hospitals and doctors will resist this sort of accountability," he added. "That's why it's going to be pretty tough. The market is tough. It's going to be a difficult shakeout."

A moment later, though, he said he was unconvinced that even the most heavily vetted evidence on these issues, from places such as Dartmouth, would be adequate to drive action. Nonetheless, he felt that government's role should not go much beyond simply making sure such pertinent information was widely available to the public—that that would have to suffice.

"One of the challenges in our society is that the truth is kind of a dis-equalizer," Summers said. "One of the reasons that inequality has probably gone up in our society is that people are being treated closer to the way that they're supposed to be treated." The hard, disequalizing truth of the past forty years, of course, was that those unfettered free markets had become increasingly borderless—a global regimen that had generally proven profitable for a minority of already advantaged Americans and, on balance, brutal for the majority of the U.S. workforce. The world caught up after several decades of post–World War II American economic hegemony, and the response of large U.S. firms, especially in the deregulated post-Reagan era, was to accept capital, in both investments and fresh debt, to fuel their operations overseas. A decade into the new century, office towers of trademark American companies on both coasts were facing outward, using the cheap labor and lax regulations across the world to make strong profits, which flowed to the top corporate officers at twice the rate of even the 1990s. Meanwhile, they turned their backs on much of what once passed for the U.S. economy. Yes, shareholders were advantaged, but a full 60 percent of Americans held few or no securities, while the greatest beneficiaries of all were the "allocators" of capital in the financial services industry. In 2007, this sector accounted for a star-

tling 41 percent of corporate profits, a feat achieved in large part by accel-
erating the steady inclination toward overseas investment and spreading
elegantly packaged debt across the ever more burdened U.S. landscape.
The notion that this is the way many Americans "are supposed to be
treated" might be seen as a pretty harsh prescription.

But Summers's belief in the efficiency of markets was, and had long
been, focused on the drive to get ever-more-precise and accurate information into the hands of what he still believed were mostly rational actors, and let them do what they would. He continued to view people as
rational, even as the behavioral revolution launched by Daniel Kahneman and his partner, Amos Tversky, and last fall's economic meltdown
showed how irrational and self-destructive people could be.

To help decipher Summers's comments—a snapshot of the complex
brew he was, at this point, serving to the president—were two people
within a stone's throw. One was Billy Tauzin, a lobbyist of similar stature
and craftiness to Ignagni. A long-serving Louisiana representative who
switched from Democrat to Republican in the 1990s, Tauzin had pushed
through one of the most expensive pieces of legislation in American history: the Medicare Prescription Drug Improvement and Modernization
Act of 2003. Costing $500 billion over ten years, it is considered by many
to be a massive handout to the pharma industry, which in return hired
Tauzin as their lead Washington representative.

Tauzin, tellingly, was now in concert with Summers. As he walked
from the White House to his waiting car, he averred that the drug companies were all for evidence-based medicine, but that the data should be
simply a guide, offered up for the marketplace to handle as it pleased.
Even the substantial evidence already available, of course, had had little
effect on medical practice. Nonetheless, Tauzin, like Summers, had great
faith in the market—or at least professed to—and little faith in government acting as an arbiter. On that score he had a new fine-feathered arrow in his quiver: in the past few years he had survived intestinal cancer.

"Listen here," he said. "There are 226 cancer drugs that are not accepted in the UK—based on the 'evidence-based' decisions of their government-run health plan—and one of them is the drug that saved my
life. And if the government starts making life-and-death decisions based
on a claim to perfect knowledge, then it's doing what God does," he said,
laughing, and offering a glimpse of what would soon be the "death pan-

els" attack. For both him and Summers, only the unfettered marketplace could stand in for God's judgments.

———

But there was no one in D.C. with more insight into Summers than Alan Krueger, who slipped outside right before the afternoon's dramatic high point—the introduction of Ted Kennedy—because the Treasury's chief economist felt lightheaded.

A small but telling oversight: the president had invited 137 important guests over to his house for the hours from just after midday until the midafternoon and no one seems to have considered the concept of food.

While Summers was holding forth, Krueger was half a block away, hunched over a Formica table in the basement cafeteria of Treasury. He'd bypassed the special restaurant/lounge for senior staff because he was starving and in an acute rush: he had a pile of work before he was due to attend a 5:00 p.m. meeting of the National Economic Council. It was one he didn't want to miss.

The topic was "too big to fail," and Summers would be there. Krueger, Summers's ablest interpreter and, in some cases, opponent, made a point of never missing a meeting where he might sit with his old chum and onetime mentor. They were first together at Harvard for four years, when Summers was building his reputation on original research, rather than government service, and Krueger, six years his junior, was his star graduate student. After Krueger took his Harvard PhD and went on to become a professor at Princeton, the two remained close, corresponding regularly, seeing each other at every opportunity, playing tennis when possible, and sharing many mutual friends at the top of the economics profession.

As is the nature with old friends, Krueger's affection for Summers is not in spite of his friend's flaws but, rather, because of them, even if it is hard to appreciate the way Summers can frustrate a hard-nosed social scientist like Krueger. When he'd hear Summers doing his "disequalizing" riff—one of Larry's favorites—Krueger would think back to days, in the late eighties, when his friend was forming the view:

"Larry felt that it didn't make sense that while he was being paid well by Harvard, some other professors were being paid in his ballpark. After all, he was Larry Summers, and who the hell were the rest of them? He began to study structures, like unions, that compressed wage distinctions in ways that went against the market. Of course, some of those compressions are meant to soften the blow of such distinctions, mindful of a complex array of factors, many uneconomic, that go into who gets paid what. But that's part of the point. Larry believes that the goal is to make everything more brutally 'truthful'—in terms of the market being basically right in how it values people and trying to make it more so—and that process shouldn't be tampered with unless there is overwhelming, indisputable evidence that the market is not working. After a few decades, Larry has gotten very good at undercutting arguments for any government intervention into free markets.

"If you're the policymaker, you need to show overwhelming evidence that a market is not functioning, in a profound and disastrous way, to merit an intervention. The default is to go back to the first principle, of market efficiency, and to let matters mostly continue as they've been."

As presidents often note in their memoirs, every major decision that arrives at the Oval Office is difficult, filled with imponderables and inconsistencies. Otherwise, it wouldn't hit their desk. But not since Franklin Roosevelt has a president had to face the twin crises, inextricably linked, of the economy's collapse and the rescue of the U.S. financial system.

Despite Obama's clear expression of his will about the primacy of health care reform, most of his senior advisers were in agreement with Orrin Hatch—and not only about someone such as Tim Geithner showing up at the Health Care Summit. Their underlying doubts were about Geithner's boss, the president, and whether he should be conducting such a summit now at all. The fear, growing inside the uppermost reaches of the White House through late February, was not just that this was the wrong ordering of priorities, but that it might ensure that none of the three great battles could possibly be done well, a concern that seemed to be quietly stoked by this long day of performances to launch the health care campaign.

Krueger, like most other senior officials, was happy to get back to what he considered more pressing business. At 5:00 p.m., in the midst of Citigroup's woes, the NEC wrestled with "too big to fail." Taken together, the assets of the largest six banks, which included Citi, were now a stunning 60 percent of the country's overall GDP, significantly more concentration than before the great panic. The issue of systemic risk, of how these still-fragile institutions were linked to one another, was all but impossible to fathom. And no one doubted that if the economy were imperiled by the failure of one of the largest banks, the government would be hard-pressed not to step up for a rescue.

Which is precisely why Tim Geithner came late to the meeting: more trouble at Citi. He was in crisis-management mode. He had to excuse himself early: another call to Bernanke.

Meanwhile, Austan Goolsbee, who was trying to revive some of the spirit of reform that was abandoned after the campaign, pushed a proposal about a tax on bank size: that the big banks start getting taxed on assets above a certain threshold. If the so-called externality—econspeak for the side effect of a company practice—"is size," Goolsbee said, "then you tax it, and it shrinks away."

Members of the legislative affairs team, sitting in, were enthusiastic. Congress, they noted, was looking to forcefully engage with the issue of preventing more bailouts and the threats of systemic risk. This proposal also raised revenue, which meant it was doubly saleable!

Summers listened to Goolsbee—no threat in his diminished role—elegantly sketch out the sort of market intervention he tended to oppose, as did Geithner. But Geithner was gone. Romer and Krueger were with Goolsbee, discussing the mechanics of various taxing techniques. The key with any such intervention was to structure it soundly and tightly, so it did what it was intended to—never an easy task. Of course, the political folks, the legislative team and Rahm, would view intended outcomes through a shorter lens: something that could be pushed through Congress and look like sound policy. Most important, there was the president—not in attendance for this meeting, but still arguing gamely through the end of February for bold action of some kind, still pressing his case that would have America acting more like Sweden than like Japan.

Based on their long history together, and general agreement on principle, everyone in the room felt that Summers—even as he kept his cards close—was in Geithner's camp.

Geithner, though, was quietly beginning to worry by early March that it might be otherwise. What he saw gathering through February was what his deputy, Lee Sachs—a former Treasury official under Clinton who'd worked at Bear Stearns and then ran a hedge fund—later called an "unholy alliance between the hedge funds and the academics, who were all now calling for tough measures on the banking system." Sachs, who'd been brought in during the transition to head "crisis management" of the financial meltdown, had created models to show how government intervention would drive down the already low price of the toxic assets. The fact that the toxic assets were difficult to value didn't mean that, if pressured to, the market wouldn't come up with a price. In a market with few buyers, it would be a low price, making the "hole" the federal government was looking at even deeper. Several reliable estimates of the amount of toxic assets across the banking system put the figure above $2 trillion. "We realized early on that a two-trillion-dollar hole was more than we could fill with the $350 billion left in TARP," said Sachs. "We were going to need to draw in private money with incentives and guarantees that we knew would make us look like we were in the pockets of the banks."

While Romer was talking to the academics, Summers was on the phone to the hedge funds, many of which had built up significant short positions on bank stocks. Any federal intervention into banking would drive down bank stocks. The shorts would clean up. Though Summers would surely know this, the more worrisome issue was the case the hedgers were making about how the government could force the kind of efficiency and shakeout that Summers felt the banking industry needed. In other words, the banking industry—like everyone else—should get what it deserves.

A few days after the Health Care Summit, Summers made his move at a briefing with the president. His "first, do no harm" test had been satisfied, he said. He joined Romer in support of the president's belief that a major federal intervention into the banking system was now needed.

Geithner pushed back.

"The confidence in the system is so fragile still," he said. "The trust is gone. One poor earnings report, a disclosure of a fraud, or a loss of faith in the dealings between one large bank and another—a withdrawal of funds or refusal to clear trades—and it could result in a run, just like Lehman."

Geithner tamped down frustration. Romer, Summers, and even the president couldn't understand what he and Bernanke had lived through—the nights of sleepless panic, terrified phone calls from once-unflappable bankers, secretaries standing in the street holding boxes with paperweights and framed photos. He thought it was unwise for the government to pick a troubled bank and dissolve it, a precedent that would create fear and undermine confidence, rather than promote it.

The president, however, seemed undeterred. In fact, he was enlivened: Summers was now on his side. It wasn't consensus, but it was close. "I think it's time to step up and show what government can do," Obama remarked. "I want to deal with these toxic assets across the entire banking system. Let's do it now, let's do it right."

In certain ways, Obama was reaching for what senior advisers had begun to call that "rare combination" where the president decided that a sound policy was also politically advantageous. When the two came together, Obama acted. His words of anger at Wall Street had not been followed with actions. But now a tough-love approach to the banks—much like what Volcker had talked about with Obama in the months after the Cooper Union speech—could show his words backed up with action.

There were general discussions about how much it might cost: another $500 billion, maybe more. "We'll find the money, somewhere," Obama said. "When you have a crisis, you find the money." Obama mentioned what everyone already knew: that in February they had put a placeholder of an additional $750 billion in the proposed budget for further government interventions into the broken financial system. The Congressional Budget Office had already "scored" the cost of any such allocation at $250 billion (under a calculus that $500 billion of that money would eventually be returned) though no one was anticipating that this just-in-case budgetary "placeholder" was slated to be filled.

No one, now, except Obama.

Geithner, meanwhile, said that many of the president's desires for action could find a home, at much lower costs, in his "stress tests," the planning for which were well underway. Geithner's team at Treasury had been working on the structure of the stress tests, in conjunction with Bernanke, since before Geithner mentioned them in his nightmare early-February press conference. They would empower government to assess the health of the large banks over the next few months, almost the way a rating agency would, and then tell the banks how much more capital they needed to continue as going concerns. The government could then decide whether to give a bank a cash infusion or to take it down, with a ratings system that the markets would consider credible. The question on the table was complex. Should they wait for the results of the stress tests—

which Summers and Romer doubted would be credible—and then decide whether, or how, to take down a few banks that were troubled and unable to raise capital? Or should they move more preemptively, taking several large troubled institutions through "resolution"—a term that implied a controlled bankruptcy and brief government takeover—sooner rather than later? Either way, the president was interested in thinking creatively about how to take down some of the nation's largest banks.

Obama listened. "Okay, we should work this out," he said. "Why don't people pull together their proposals."

Geithner left the meeting incensed. Larry had no idea what he was doing or whom he was up against. A meeting was set for Sunday, March 15, in the Roosevelt Room. That meant the teams from Treasury and the White House would have just a week to pull together their presentations. Staffers in the two buildings immediately started calling it The Showdown.

On the afternoon of March 9, Sheila Bair girded herself for the next conference call. It was almost one a day—she would be the only woman on the phone with an army of men, many of them with close ties to Wall Street or an unshakeable belief in the miracle of the markets, the freer the better.

And she would be the scourge.

Tension between Bair and the men managing the town's other regulatory warships was rapidly looking like a redux of the battles Brooksley Born fought in the late 1990s with the fraternity of like-minded regulators allied with Wall Street over derivatives regulation.

If there was one difference, it was that Born had been alone. Now there was a small but powerful contingent of the sisterhood, and a gender battle, long simmering just beneath the surface of cordial relations among regulatory colleagues, was finally starting to draw notice. With Born, now a Washington lawyer, as their inspirational hero, a team of women—led by Bair; Mary Schapiro, chairwoman of the SEC; Elizabeth Warren, heading the TARP Oversight Panel; and the irrepressible Maria Cantwell—was asserting its primacy. They had virtually all been right, and right early, about the way America's financial system was drifting toward crisis. All of them had been shooed away or shouted down by the men, both those manning Wall Street and those atop Washington's regulatory or economic policy posts, who quietly asserted that high finance might be the final mountaintop stronghold of "man's work."

While 58 percent of college undergraduates are now women, and many of the most prized professions and skill-based industries are approaching gender equality, virtually all the top posts on Wall Street and at the largest national banks have long been held by men. Though most of the men won't say it, they feel that the nexus of math and risk—and the gaming of both, without flinching—is an area of male inclination. In fact, many of the women agree. They say that's part of the problem.

Few could, at this point, challenge the idea that the country's male-dominated financial industries had powerfully self-destructive impulses. But Geithner was just the latest in a succession of regulatory men, many with a past (or a bright future) in managing money and risk, who felt the town's few female regulators often didn't understand them or the way Wall Street's male Mecca really worked—knowledge that is crucial to being an effective regulator who can alter ruinous behavior.

The women's response, of course, was that they understood the men better than the men understood themselves.

History's judgments, of late, seemed to be bending toward the ladies.

––––––––––

Bair, for one, was not bashful about pointing out precisely where she'd been right, across nearly three decades. A Kansas Republican who spent most of the '80s working both in campaign and senior staff roles for that state's avatar, Senator Bob Dole, Bair was named one of three commissioners of the CFTC in 1991 by the first President Bush. In the deregulatory environment of that period, Bair—who was once a bank teller in Kansas and waxes nostalgic about kids' opening passbook savings accounts and the pride people felt in meeting their obligations with each month's mortgage payment—took her first turn as skunk at the garden party. She was especially skeptical of a fast-growing Houston-based firm called Enron, a diversified energy company that was pressing the CFTC to exempt what the firm called its "sophisticated" futures contracts from antifraud provisions, a move that would have shielded Enron's burgeoning exchange-trading business from CFTC oversight. Bair, voted down 2 to 1, offered a scathing dissent: "If we are to rationalize exemptions from antifraud and other components of our regulatory scheme on the basis of the 'sophistication' of market users, we might as well close our doors tomorrow."

When, in 2001, Enron's trading business was exploding into a historic fraud—a harbinger of the derivatives disasters to come—Bair had little time to gloat. At that point, as assistant Treasury secretary for financial institutions, under Bush, she was intensely interested in the growth of "nontraditional lenders," free-floating finance companies, funded by Wall Street speculators, that were offering loans with low "teaser" rates and hidden fees. What struck Bair was that these subprime lenders generally had responsibility for the loans for only ninety days—three months of payments—before the traditional fiduciary bond between lender and borrower dissolved and the loan was "securitized" and sold off to other investors. Bair sensed trouble along many links of this chain, but found that the defaults by borrowers who were encouraged to take out larger mortgages than they could afford were lower than she expected. That's because they were constantly refinancing, at ever lower rates, and often using the proceeds for general purchasing. Her concerns that this couldn't last, and would end badly, were drowned out in the naysaying of Alan Greenspan, his cheap-money policies, and the rising real estate values that were fueling wider consumption.

It wasn't until 2006, though, when Bush unexpectedly selected her to run the FDIC, an independent agency whose director serves a five-year term, that Bair found the freedom to be . . . just Bair. Having spotted early troubles in both the derivatives and subprime markets—and then launching flares that were ignored—she could now be an independent actor. And act she did. She analyzed all the subprime data the FDIC could buy and closed one of the most egregious subprime lenders, the California-based Freemont Investment and Loan, in March 2007. Seeing a wave of defaults on the way, especially as tens of billions in "teaser-rate" loans readjusted upward, she pressed the banking industry to restructure the mortgages, which would make more of them sustainable, even as it shrank the banks' profit margins from the often onerous rates. The banks said they would, but didn't. She unloaded on them at a mortgage industry conference in October 2007: "Moody's recently reported that less than one per cent—less than one per cent—of subprime mortgages that are having problems were being restructured in any meaningful way," she implored them. "We have a huge problem on our hands . . . I think some categorical approaches are needed, and needed urgently."

The fact that no one budged and disaster soon reigned only increased her ire, especially at Citigroup and Bank of America, the industry leaders, which she felt exhibited anything but industry leadership, especially when they should have known better—after all, she herself had warned them of what was ahead.

But by the fall of 2008 she found herself rushing into a place where regulators rightly fear to tread: cutting deals to buy and sell banks, especially in a volatile market where share prices could drop from respectable to abysmal on an errant rumor. The specific case that snagged her was the sale of the failed Wachovia to Citigroup, a transaction, requiring government assistance, that she and Geithner provisionally approved in late September. But when Wells Fargo arrived with a richer offer in November, and one not needing federal assistance, she opted for Wells. Citi's stock summarily plummeted, along with its overall capitalization, pushing it into the arms of regulators and summoning the fierce disdain of a vast community of Citi officials, past and present, from Bob Rubin on down. Bair demurred that she couldn't stop the Wells deal—it was better for Wachovia, an appropriately arm's-length transaction that didn't need help from the government. But former Clinton-era regulators with net worth in Citi stock, many of them now cycling back into the Obama administration, were incensed.

Bair, they cried, just didn't get it—didn't understand how the world, resting on projections of confidence, really worked. All she could talk about was tier-one capital, and how things used to be in the sleepy 1970s. In fact, Sheila Bair, who'd been around long enough to have used Paul Volcker as her role model, had little respect for the "we're all in this together" bond built across three decades between Washington and Wall Street, a relationship of shared interests in which Citi, like Goldman, was a central actor. Her positions on key issues such as shrinking banks to make sure they weren't "too big to fail" and curbing Wall Street's excesses were generally aligned with Volcker's, and her criticisms of Vikram Pandit and Citi's current management were specific and pointed. She thought both should be replaced, and said so publicly.

Geithner's response to a deputy at Treasury: "She keeps up that kind of talk, we'll have a run on Citi—then, I suppose, she'd finally be happy."

If Sheila Bair had especially strong feelings about Citigroup, she had her reasons. Bear Stearns had been rescued, Lehman had failed, Goldman had gamed everyone it met, JPMorgan had avoided the worst of mortgage-backed hell, as much by good luck as good management, but Citigroup was in its own special category. There was, after all, no bank that embodied past disasters and future risks like Citi. It essentially invented the concept of "too big to fail."

Anyone with a desire to understand banking in America need only follow the two-hundred-year arc of this institution, from its start in 1812 in New York to the $2 trillion behemoth that collapsed in 2008, with three hundred thousand employees, two hundred million customer accounts, and operations in one hundred countries.

Citigroup, under its previous name, National City Bank of New York, was the country's largest bank for much of U.S. history, and had been bailed out by the government many times.

Not that the bank didn't pioneer innovations, including checking accounts, negotiable CDs, unsecured loans, compound interest on savings accounts, and, of course, ATMs. It also was an innovator in the 1920s in creating the disastrous investment trusts, that era's CDOs, that were at the center of the 1929 stock market crash and all but prompted Glass-Steagall so that banks, with depositors' money, would never again operate as investment houses.

While many smaller banks failed, National City Bank was propped up by FDR, as were other large banks, for fear that the overall system would collapse without them. But it was more than that. The bank, which was pilloried, along with its CEO, was always seen as a representative institution—what it did, or what was done to it, would serve as an example for others. No doubt other banks were ever attentive, following Citi's lead as it invested in Latin American debt in the early 1990s (another government bailout) and in the late '90s, as it was growing ever larger with acquisitions and mergers, culminating in the 1998 merger of Citicorp and the Travelers Group. That union, orchestrated by Sandy Weill and his deputy, Jamie Dimon, created a huge financial organism that provided virtually every function in the management of money and risk—from insurance to brokerage services, from investment banking to plain vanilla commercial paper, and every conceivable trading activity. Under one umbrella were brand names galore: Primerica, Travelers, Salomon Brothers, Smith Barney, Commercial Credit, with everything stamped "Citi." More than sixty years after National City's behavior helped prompt Glass-Steagall, Citi's merger mania helped finally kill the already eroded separation between commercial and investment banks. Everyone, then, could be like Citi, and other banks didn't disappoint.

Not that this slaked Citi's acquisitive thirst. Since 2003 the bank bought four credit card lenders and five mortgage lenders, ballooning up to $2.2 trillion in assets by 2007, roughly even with JPMorgan Chase and Bank of America—each, itself, a buffet of services and functions, if slightly less varied than Citi.

And starting in 2004, Citi did what almost everyone else did: load up on CDOs, holding nearly $60 billion of them on its books by early 2008.

The key was that the bank, after so many bailouts, was always seen as "too big to fail," and took advantage of every feature that this designation provided, from a lower cost of credit to regulatory favoritism to a "might makes right" latitude in its all but indecipherable web of interlocking businesses. That's what tends to happen, after all, at this size: the entity becomes impossible to manage. Sometimes banks end up on the right side of large market shifts, but often not. To be sure, the way the markets glorified the prowess of Jamie Dimon by the spring of 2009 was how they'd once felt about Sandy Weill.

Citigroup, for its part, was haphazardly managed, going through four CEOs in just under a decade, with the last being Vikram Pandit, who oversaw institutional investments and trading at Morgan Stanley, and then ran a hedge fund, before becoming Citi's CEO in December 2007.

Pandit accepted a government check from Paulson's Treasury the next fall—for $25 billion, like the other large institutions—but distinguished himself and his bank by returning just a month later, on November 24, for another $20 billion. More important, that same day, Treasury guaranteed $306 billion of Citigroup's assets. It asked little in return for any of this—no management changes or restructuring. Just some warrants and preferred stock. This guarantee, so-called ring-fencing, allowed Citi to keep its enormous pile of nonperforming and illiquid assets—mortgage-related assets and a sinking, toxic haul of credit card debts—on its balance sheet and, with this government support, retain the illusion of solvency. Later, when pressed on this, Geithner cited the reason for this government largess, according to a report by TARP's inspector general, "to assure the world that the Government would never let Citi fail."

Four months later, Sheila Bair was stressing that the government should now be sending the opposite message: destructive behavior could still, in some instances, draw a death sentence.

In the conference call with the country's top financial regulators at 3:00 p.m. on March 9, she stated her case, as she had on several such calls over the past week. Last fall's ring-fencing was insufficient. The $306 billion wasn't enough. In the ensuing months, Citi's credit card defaults were rising, while the value of its toxic mortgage-related assets continued to drop. What had been on its balance sheets, after all, was not even the entire mess: many of the toxic CDOs were off the balance sheet, held in SIVs, structured investment vehicles, another Citi innovation from the late 1980s that had spread across the industry.

FDIC analysts who'd examined the bank put the toxic load at roughly $600 billion out of a total of $1.6 trillion in assets. This figure, however, took into account the "intrinsic value" of the mortgage-related fare, rather than the harsher mark-to-market standard that everyone, everywhere, was ducking—and not without some justification. In the wildly oversaturated real estate market, even solid mortgage-backed assets would have trouble drawing a depressed price. The intrinsic standard accounted for some modest stabilization of the market at some point in the future.

Many of those on the conference call—including John Dugan, the lead banking regulator in his role as head of the Office of the Comptroller of the Currency, or OCC; Bill Dudley, Geithner's replacement as head of the New York Federal Reserve; and Ben Bernanke—were fearful that this "give" on the valuation by FDIC was a trap. Geithner, leading the call, felt "the markets wouldn't respond well" to the intrinsic standard. Bair disagreed: it was eminently defendable, would help institutions get out of their bind of not being able to fully recognize the toxic loads on their balance sheets, and, of course, it was from the FDIC, not known for its charitable view on such matters.

If, hypothetically, that $600 billion number were accepted, and Citigroup moved into some form of "resolution," then, Geithner and others asserted, the FDIC would be on the hook for the whole amount. This game of brinksmanship had been another plotline of the conference calls: fine, if the FDIC wanted to take down Citi, it would have to bankrupt its own accounts to do it. The FDIC, which is supported by a tithing from the commercial banks it insures, would be overwhelmed by the cost and have to appeal to Congress for, well, a bailout.

That was not the kind of resolution Bair envisioned. Now rubber was hitting highway. The FDIC's specialty, of course, is shutting down banks. It's been at it, over umpteen weekends, since the 1930s. Citi was huge, but its core was still a bank, and should be treated as such. That meant a prepackaged bankruptcy: the bank would be shut down; management thrown out; equity holders wiped out; troubled assets moved to a "bad," or aggregator, bank; and a smaller but clean "good bank" would emerge, essentially a new entity that could accept investments and get on with business. The key to the equation was that, as in all bankruptcies, creditors would take a haircut. In this case it would be for a few hundred billion, which would lighten the amount of FDIC money that would be required.

This was the key to the equation—to so many equations in this period, where debt had become sustenance and its purveyors on Wall Street the richest community in human history. Geithner, on this point, would not budge. Debt was sacrosanct. No creditor would suffer. Bair was equally intransigent. Secured creditors, of course, wouldn't be wiped out, but they had to face consequences for lending money to an institution whose recklessness had led to its demise. They must, she said, "face some discipline." Her point was that ultimately this would be seen as progress—as when someone finally got a needed operation—which would begin to restore long-term, sustainable confidence in the financial system. Debt was underpriced. Once it was priced properly, the healing could begin.

Bernanke said little. He'd spent more than a year opening the Fed's coffers to guarantee anything that moved to ensure that traditional market corrections, corrections in the pricing of risk, would not commence, at least not yet. Not that his efforts were resulting in the desired easing of credit by banks and other financial firms being supported by Fed dollars. They were just making money from the free money offered by the Fed, and sitting on the profits. Why, after all, would anyone lend when demand was zilch and America was overleveraged, stem to stern? Once the economy ticked up—maybe then. Of course, that couldn't happen unless credit began to flow.

Dugan, a holdover from Bush, whose OCC regulators for years visited banks and, generally, did not make a peep as the banks loaded up CDOs, said he was concerned about "how the markets will respond" to any actions against Citi.

Around they went, gridlocked. Finally, Bair said that at the very least Pandit must go. He was essentially a fixed-income trader and a hedge fund manager. "We need a commercial banker at the top of this bank—someone who knows the business of banking. That's one way to maybe get some lending started. It is mostly a bank, after all."

In terms of some accountability for reckless actions, Bair considered this a starting point. Geithner wouldn't entertain even this fallback position. The government exchanged its $45 billion in direct aid and $306 billion in guarantees for a 36 percent ownership of Citi. Geithner, thinking about how that leverage might be used, said, "Maybe we suggest a few new directors and let them decide."

Dugan said he was concerned about how "the markets will react" to pushing out Pandit.

Geithner, who'd chatted with Pandit a few hours before, added that maybe they could suggest that Vikram hire some more commercial bankers underneath him.

Forty-five minutes passed—that was all for today. The men hung up. Bair, after she heard the clicks, wondered, as usual, what more she might have said.

Geithner sat at his desk and signed forms allowing for various foreign acquisitions or investment in the United States, a system started thirty years before to review such activities through the lens of national security.

A call had been scheduled at 4:05. His secretary asked if he was ready; it's Vikram Pandit. Geithner told Pandit, as he did most days, where things stood.

The next day, Bair got a call from Summers's office. She was surprised. She didn't talk to Summers all that often. Today, though, Summers was gracious and eager, particularly interested in discussing the basics of how a prepackaged bankruptcy might work on a bank like Citi. Bair ran through it.

Summers was circumspect. He didn't tell Bair that he and Romer were now, for the most part, in Bair's camp and that they'd be in a "showdown" Sunday with Geithner about the future of big banks like Citi. He asked how deep the hole was—the hole that some funds, from somewhere, would have to fill if the bank were shut down and reopened. She said it was about $600 billion tops, and explained the "intrinsic value" calculus.

He said Treasury seemed to think it was higher, more like $800 billion—a number so big it made bankruptcy more difficult. That higher number, of course, made Citi too big to fail.

Without context, though, Bair couldn't really discuss how these cost estimates could shape options and policy. She just considered it an informational call and told Summers to call anytime.

———

On March 11, the AIG mess finally caught up with Tim Geithner—and it was ugly.

The insurance giant had been given another $30 billion just several days before, on March 2, to shore up its operations, bringing the government's total contribution to the firm up to a stunning $170 billion. That same day, AIG declared a fourth-quarter 2008 loss of $62 billion, easily the largest loss in U.S. corporate history.

Geithner knew that bad was about to get worse. Soon the firm would be paying out those secret bonuses. Treasury had managed to avoid an incident in early February, by quietly reshaping the bill by Chris Dodd, but now they were coming to an actual payday.

It would be a $165 million bonus dispersal, mostly to AIG's top brass. Out of a total $450 million in bonuses, $55 million of which had already been paid, $230 million had yet to be paid out to AIG employees in 2009.

But it wasn't just the bonuses. Tucked in the disclosures AIG was due to make was a story that would carry another set of explosive numbers. The firm had used its bailout money to pay not just bonuses, but also much larger obligations on its credit default swaps to Goldman and other banks. Congressional committees, enlivened by Obama's strong words of censure, were closing in on this point. On March 5—while Geithner was trying to handle Citigroup's woes, and Obama was running his Health Care Summit—the Federal Reserve's Donald Kohn, Bernanke's number two, had testified before Dodd's committee to the effect that he didn't want to release which counterparties were being paid what with the AIG money because it would undermine "confidence" in the markets.

The Fed in fact was pushing Geithner to keep his proposed stress tests confidential, so no one, except Treasury, would know how various banks had rated. But the dome of silence, central to the confidence game constructed between New York and Washington, was cracking. Bloomberg

News reporters were hot on the trail of the AIG bonuses. Reporters from the *Washington Post* were not far behind.

On Wednesday, May 11, Tim Geithner called Ed Liddy, whom the government, in consultation with Goldman Sachs, had placed atop AIG the previous fall. Liddy, a former Goldman board member, told Geithner that there was nothing to be done. The bonuses had to be paid.

"We have to do something, Ed," Geithner said.

"They're contracts, Mr. Secretary," Liddy responded. "You can't violate a contract."

Liddy said he would write a letter expressing why AIG needed to pay the bonuses, no matter how distasteful this seemed.

Geithner hung up the phone.

He knew he'd be drawn deeply into all this. He was the New York Fed chairman on watch when they had approved the AIG bonuses, the counterparty payments—all of it. The question of why he had let it get to this point, nearly six months after the arrangement was struck, and why he hadn't alerted the president, still hung in the air.

His schedule was also a problem. The stress-test proposals were proceeding apace. His whole team was working on them, led by Lee Sachs. But Geithner had to leave town. He had meetings over the weekend in Sussex, England, with finance ministers from the G20, twenty of the world's strongest economic powers, in preparation of the full meeting with Obama and the others, scheduled for April 2.

No one was more delighted about this than Larry Summers. He booked time with the president on Friday. His tough-love proposals were taking shape. Now he could sell them to the president while Geithner was far away, across the ocean.

On Saturday, Romer's team from the Council of Economic Advisers and Summers's team from NEC met in the latter's office. News of the AIG bonuses was now all over the papers, and it was Armageddon. The outrage at paying out what looked like a king's ransom to executives of the companies whose "irresponsible" and "shameful" behavior, in Obama's parlance, had wrecked the economy—and who had been saved only by taxpayer money—bled in every direction. Citigroup had gotten $50 billion in federal funds; Bank of America, $45 billion; JPMorgan and Wells Fargo, $25 billion each; and there were plenty more.

If anything, the news storm drove the Summers-Romer team even harder. This was precisely the problem, they said, when government forgot that its role was not to support failing businesses or use government funds to create private profits. It was time for a clean break. They spent the afternoon working through their proposal for government's intervention in the financial system.

In this area, Romer had particular strengths. Like Bernanke, she was an expert on the Depression, especially on the ways the Roosevelt administration had restructured the American financial system. The restructuring had yielded a kind of defining clarity to the managing of money and risk across four decades. But now, after thirty subsequent years of drift without this clarity, Obama had a chance to be Roosevelt. With Romer and Summers working in concert, matching her expertise with his rhetorical gifts, this might be the moment.

The tension at this point was, at any rate, acute. Geithner felt that what Summers and Romer were doing was nothing short of reckless and that they were leading Obama down a path to disaster.

Team Summers-Romer dialed up Team Geithner on an overseas call.

Geithner and his deputies were on a plane back from Sussex. The call started cordially, but descended quickly into angry exchanges.

As one of Geithner's deputies told Romer, "Mommy and Daddy are fighting—can't someone help us."

Apparently not.

———————

On Sunday morning, March 15, Alan Krueger ducked his head into Geithner's office.

"Tennis today? It's nice out."

Geithner was a good player—a great athlete in fact, with a *New York* magazine article describing him as a " 'dauntingly fit' stud on the tennis court."

While Obama favored golf, for the small group that managed U.S. economic policy, it was all about tennis. They'd all played high school tennis, some junior tournaments. Summers was a strong player. Gene Sperling, from Treasury, had played at the University of Minnesota. The four often played doubles. Krueger was the best, still able to take games off of top college players.

"I can't tell you how much I'd love to play tennis, Alan," Geithner said wearily. "I'd give anything."

Geithner had a much more important match to prepare for, against Summers, for high stakes. That afternoon Geithner's team gathered to finalize their battle plan. His proposed stress tests had evolved nicely. If the president could see them as forceful action to repair the banking system, and not just one more delay in dealing with this thorniest of issues, the stress tests would become the undisputed government policy.

But it would be a matter of both offense and defense, defend and attack. In his mind, Summers was just marshaling the arguments of amateurs, pundits, and politicians to cozy up to the president. He had no idea what the takedown of a bank looked like, and Bernanke, who did, was with Geithner. They, after all, would have to play an instrumental role in either the stress tests or any wider intervention.

Yet Geithner had other things to worry about. He'd been mentioned in every story on the AIG bonuses. He would have to face the Watergate question: What did he know and when did he know it? Geithner, himself, had become toxic.

And it was none other than Larry Summers who was on several of the Sunday morning talk shows essentially criticizing what Geithner had done, or not done, on the controversial bonuses.

"There are a lot of terrible things that have happened in the last eighteen months, but what's happened at AIG is the most outrageous," Summers said on ABC's *This Week*. He reiterated a similar position that same day on another show, CBS's *Face the Nation*, saying that the administration's priority was safeguarding the American taxpayer. "No one cares about the shareholders of AIG. No one feels the slightest obligation to people who led us into these difficulties."

Some felt that those "people" included Tim Geithner.

By late afternoon, the Roosevelt Room was already crowding up. People had come early to get a good seat. Everyone was there: Summers, Romer, Emanuel, Biden, Geithner, Axelrod, Jarrett, and the political team, folks from Treasury, teams from the CEA and the NEC, assistant to the president Phil Schiliro and his legislative affairs staff.

Geithner and Summers each laid out his case. The stress tests, Geithner asserted, would dispatch uncertainties in the markets and in American business and the wider consumer population, who needed to know if their financial system was secure. If banks failed the tests, it would be clear why; the tests would highlight their deficiencies and allow the government to decide whether to bail them out or take them through a prepackaged bankruptcy. What was more, as the banks worked through the tests, they would have to recognize and frankly assess their own true condition.

For his part, Summers used metaphors: "Tear the Band-Aid off, let the air in, and let the healing begin." He kept up the medical analogies the president favored: "It's time for radical surgery to save the patient, the U.S. economy." He discussed how the "good bank, bad bank" model would work. The government would close down several troubled institutions, take them over for a brief period, and have the toxic assets placed in the bad bank run by the government. The "good bank" would be cleansed, with management and shareholders wiped out, and creditors entering negotiations about what they might recover.

The president, who'd heard Summers's case two days before, cut him off.

Many of the largest banks were sitting on huge piles of toxic mortgage-related assets, he said, which put a drag on the flow of credit and created wider uncertainty in the economy. Meanwhile, he said, it seemed like the U.S. policy was "waiting and hoping," having government support the banks in all sorts of ways, while everyone waited for the value of their assets to slowly recover—or for the banks with strong enough earnings to write them off. It was a riff he used at his first press conference, a month before, now expanded and directed. "As I understand it," the president concluded, "that's Japan."

Well, sort of, Geithner said. But not exactly.

Summers's retort was that, yes, more or less, that's Japan.

Summers and Romer pointed out that the stress tests might be inadequate, easily gamed by banks and proving little; and also that they wouldn't be done until May, too long to dawdle. Summers said Geithner's policy was "watchful waiting," in contrast to the one he and Romer were suggesting, which was "necessary surgery that shouldn't be delayed any longer."

"We're not waiting for anything!" Geithner retorted. "We're not talking about doing nothing. We are acting—with the stress tests!"

Implicit in Geithner's "we" was Bernanke and the Fed, a crucial vote of confidence from one of the most powerful corners of government. But Romer, who had connections in the Fed herself, was ready.

"I've had a fair amount of contact with the Fed governors," she said, "and there's quite a bit of consensus in the Fed system that something needs to be done now, not later, some sort of resolution, along the lines of a 'good bank, bad bank' model."

It was a direct hit on key underpinnings of Team Geithner's strategy, in which the Treasury secretary implied that he was speaking for the Fed. Geithner glared across the table at her.

There was general talk of how much it would cost. No one had a firm figure. That depended on a host of estimates for which data were unavailable—data on the balance sheets of banks and on the depth of toxic assets across the banking system. Numbers were bandied about. A restructuring of the sagging banks could cost $700 billion. The costs could be stretched out across years. Some of the nonperforming assets in the Resolution Trust Corporation, the agency set up in 1989 to handle the savings-and-loan crisis, had been sold off quickly; others had been held for years. In any event, it would be real money, north of half a trillion.

The president's enthusiasm was undimmed. The restructuring of the large insolvent banks, he said, would be a moment where the government could "strike a blow for prudence." It would "begin to change the reckless behavior of Wall Street and show millions of unemployed Americans that accountability flows in both directions."

Obama was finally pushing the argument above the ongoing disputes inside his economic team to a higher moral and ethical plane. Having absorbed the theatrics for several hours, he had seen enough. He said he wanted something large, something that changed the course of the economic ship. It was clear to everyone: he was leaning toward Summers and Romer.

But Geithner and the Treasury team took a new tack in the debate, and Summers engaged. They were still arguing.

"Look," Obama said, with evident frustration. "I'm going to get a haircut and have dinner with my family. You've heard me. When I come back I want this issue resolved."

And with that, he walked out.

Rahm Emanuel waited until the president was fully out of the room and then seized the floor.

"Everyone shut the fuck up. Let me be clear—taking down the banking system in a program that could cost $700 billion is a fantasy. With all the money that already went to TARP, no one is getting that kind of money through Congress, especially with this AIG bonus disaster." He threw a hard glance at Geithner. "Listen, it's not going to fuckin' happen. We have no fucking credibility. So give it up. The job of everyone in this room is to move the president, when he gets back, toward a solution that *works*."

Romer later said she felt like "I'd been punched in the stomach." The president got it. He was striving, at last, in a Rooseveltian way, to take bold action. Emanuel had "waited until he left and then crushed it."

Emanuel's now-famous tactical dictum—"never let a crisis go to waste"—actually applied in this case, she felt. Not really to health care, which was more an issue of unsustainable trends than a true crisis. This was different. This was a real financial crisis, extending into the fortunes of everyone in the broader economy. After all that had happened starting with Reagan and deregulation, and three decades of the unfettered markets not dealing with the fundamental needs and hopes of a growing economy, now was the time—maybe the only time—for the government to step in to make crucial repairs. "This was the crisis that we shouldn't let go to waste," Romer said later. "Right there, Rahm killed it."

Aides ran out to get food for dinner as Emanuel huddled with Geithner and then Summers, and then the both of them.

When the president returned at 8:00 p.m., Summers, on cue, took the floor.

"We had this very good discussion at the beginning of our meeting, but while you were away, Rahm made the point that there's no chance of Congress approving any more TARP funds. So a broader, systemwide solution doesn't seem possible. But it's absolutely possible, Mr. President, to do Citi, just Citi. We can do that with the $200 billion currently sitting unused in the TARP account."

Obama sat quietly, considering this for a moment. "Well, okay, so we do Citigroup and we do it thoroughly and well. That would show everybody that they can trust us in government to do a hard job, and do it right. And then we go back to Congress and get the money to do the wider job that really needs to be done."

As the president processed this, Emanuel jumped in.

"At the same time," he said, "we'll have Tim do his stress tests so he can decide how to support the banks with his 'Hobbit accounts.'" This was Emanuel's catchphrase for programs with acronyms that sounded like something out of a Tolkien novel, such as TALF (Term Asset-Backed Securities Loan Facility) and PPIP (Public-Private Investment Program). Of course "support" was the right word. Emanuel had called it straight: Geithner's plan was to support the existing structure, not change it.

Obama considered all this for a moment. After a long day of discussion and fierce debate, there seemed to be unanimity from his advisers. For the next few hours, as the evening waned, everyone talked through logistics.

After nearly five hours in the Roosevelt Room, the participants saw the weeks of debates settling into action. The stress tests, now well along in their construction, would move forward as the core of the U.S. government's approach. But Treasury would also pull together a plan for how to "resolve" Citigroup as a first step to returning to Congress for money to take down other banks.

Geithner often said, "plan beats no plan." The stress tests were now a plan. But what Summers and Romer were pushing, stoking the President's enthusiasms, was not. It was a proposal, which was all they could muster with their staff and specific expertise. Only Treasury had the horsepower to pull together a plan for such a significant intervention by government. All balls were now in his court.

Obama thanked everyone and told them "to go get some sleep."

The president had been well managed.

THE COVENANT

THERE WAS PERHAPS NO BETTER CASE STUDY FOR HOW THE "systemic" risk posed by the turbulence on Wall Street threatened the broader economy than what was happening six hundred miles west, in Motor City. The crisis in Detroit was ignited by New York. When credit tightened after Bear Stearns' March 2008 fall, auto sales began to decline precipitously from their historic peak of seventeen million units in 2007.

By late March 2009, the question of what to do about the automakers had persisted for more than a year.

One of the hottest expanding markets for debt had long been the asset-backed securities for car loans, which, just like mortgages, had been securitized and swapped. Almost anyone who wanted a car could get a loan. After Wall Street's crash in September, declining sales all but plummeted, dropping to a rate of nearly half the 2007 levels. Automotive CEOs flew to Congress in November in their private jets to plead for bailouts, were roundly reviled for their transportation choice, and later, with showy penitence, drove the eight hours from Detroit to D.C. for another hearing. In December, the Bush administration cleared a first cash infusion of $17.4 billion out of the TARP funds and kicked the matter to the White House's next occupant.

The automakers presented an issue that was, in many ways, more straightforward than the dilemma about how to handle financial giants such as Citigroup. While the banks stood on the soft turf of confidence, subject to the ongoing brinksmanship between Washington and New York, the car companies at least rested on the firm ground of direct action: their fortunes rose or fell based on the sale of tangible goods in the marketplace.

By the early spring of 2009, though, crises in the two kingdoms, auto and finance, presented a wider choice: whether government, in its decisions to support or abandon each teetering industry, would look to correct some of the glaring imbalances that had grown up in American society across decades.

Detroit was still the capital of the country that made things the world wanted. It was, after all, the Mecca of the manufacturing revolution in the United States and, eventually, abroad. The early-twentieth-century assembly line innovations introduced the quintessential American product, a symbol of gleaming mobility, to the global market. The "Growing Together, Growing Apart" charts that Alan Krueger unfurled nearly three years earlier for a long-shot candidate could easily have carried attachments for the central role of cars in building that storied middle class. The seminal insight, in fact, might well be attributed to the petulant and flinty Henry Ford himself, who in 1908 was having trouble drawing men from many machine shops around Detroit to work on his newfangled assembly lines: they felt the work was dehumanizing, turning men into cogs on a wheel. He drew them in with wages they couldn't resist (wages he cut later, once the plants were filled and the machine shops had vanished), along with a flourish of salesmanship, saying that men should be paid enough to afford to buy the product they built. The assembly line's efficiencies dramatically lowered costs, the solid wages created a community of ready buyers, and the foundations of mass production and mass consumption were laid. The subtle codependency tucked within—that the nation and its economy flourish when workers earn enough to be active consumers—became the best-case justification decades later for many of FDR's aid programs, including Social Security, and for the growth of unions, which bargained collectively for the higher wages and benefits that lifted lower-class laborers into the post–World War II middle class.

As is so often the case with progress, every solution creates a new problem, and one presented itself in the 1970s, as the world co-opted and started to improve upon American manufacturing techniques in factories manned with lower-wage workers. Even if Detroit's giants knew how to respond, the slow-footed, legalistic union-management dialogue stood in the way of rapid change.

And that's, of course, what almost every current debate in the White House and beyond was about: rapid change. Accommodating it is one of the great human capacities, but living through it can be the stuff of stress and, often, suffering.

Wall Street's great modern innovation had been to profit from rapid change itself—and often drive it—without the complications of having to worry too much about outcomes.

Detroit, and much of the rest of America, didn't have that luxury. In the cold spring of 2009, many Americans were actively wondering whether the country's financial agents of change would have to start living lives of tough choices and hard consequences. Since late January, when the new president's harsh words seemed to encourage righteous anger against Wall Street, a fair share of the busy public wondered if the new president would see any distinction between those who profited from change and those who were crushed by it, and whether he believed that government's role was to forcefully, but smartly, impede actions of the former and ease the pain of the latter—to keep the American worker, both figuratively and literally, on the assembly line so he could buy what he produced.

What makes the morality play even richer is that Obama, just as he was calling the financial industry payouts "shameful," brought on board a crew of private-equity specialists from Wall Street—led by Steven Rattner, named head of the Auto Task Force—to work alongside his market-oriented economic team to help frame a set of hard choices about what he might do.

By late March those choices were the stuff of fierce debate. The administration's domestic policy was fast becoming a debate society run by Larry Summers. Obama would sit on high, trying to judge if there was any shared ground between the competing debate teams that might coalesce into a policy. The larger question simmering beneath each busy day was whether his growing inclination to seek consensus in these debate tournaments was a model for sound decision making, a crutch to delay, or avoid, the decisions only a president can make, or a recipe for producing half-measures—a pinch of this matched with a scoop of that—masquerading as solutions. After all, if the breadth of perspectives is wide enough to represent the fullest range of views, consensus is unlikely. If consensus is swiftly achieved, it probably means too few voices have been heard.

In the run-up to the big meeting on the auto bailouts, slated for March 26, the breadth of perspectives was actually quite narrow. Almost everyone of consequence considering the fate of General Motors and Chrysler for the past two months had been looking through the shared lens of market-oriented economics and a philosophical school of thought and action loosely called "private equity."

That colorless term had, over the years, been substituted for a host of vivid precursors, such as "corporate raider," "takeover artist," or, in

some cases, "greenmailer"—names for a group of financial provocateurs who emerged in the early '80s to launch the era of financial innovation. Their leader, Michael Milken—like his debentured kindred
Lew Ranieri—formed new ways to turn debt into tradable, highly liquid securities by floating low-grade, high-risk debt called junk bonds
for that era's "special purpose." Specifically, they would pool the capital
into takeover funds to back the assaults by raiders on public companies
or their efforts to "place" highly leveraged capital. Whereas 1980s competitors such as Warren Buffett and Peter Lynch were looking for value
hidden in public companies to "buy and hold" in the conventional effort
to outsmart the markets, buyout firms such as Drexel Burnham Lambert,
Forstmann Little, and Kohlberg Kravis Roberts claimed to be smarter
about various companies than the executives who managed them. Sometimes the attacks would be hostile; other times, more a matter of making senior management offers they could not easily refuse—such as how
to meet stunning performance measures quickly, get rich, or lose your
company; or, for troubled companies, take this expensive capital as a
last chance for your survival, and sign over everything, often including your home, as collateral. Either way, the private-equity play—to sell
off assets, streamline operations, defund anything that wasn't focused
on short-term earnings, and then look to sell the company within three
to five years—became the enduring modus for both takeovers and turn-
arounds. Although the flashy days of corporate raiders largely passed
with the prosecutions in 1990 of Milken and, before him, his kindred
such as Ivan Boesky, Martin Siegel, and Dennis Levine on various types
of fraud, the private-equity model endured, and grew. In 2007, KKR was
the world's fourth-largest employer, if one added up all the companies
that the firm and its investors controlled.

And control is the key concept: a condition for a private-equity place-
ment tends to be conditional employment or ouster of a company's "existing management," to be replaced by handpicked executives who will
have the gumption—some would say ruthlessness—to drive a swift return for the new investors. But as the U.S. economy became less and
less hospitable to quick investment returns in the past decade, private
equity got busy sharpening its model. Charlie Hallac, a top deputy to
Larry Fink at BlackRock and head of the firm's analytical arm, Black-
Rock Solutions, distilled it down with precision: "Of every twenty deals,
the large, aggressive PE firm expects seventeen of the companies to fail

under the added debt. Two have to survive and one has to hit big for the firm to have a fairly strong return on its PE fund. So that's three out of twenty."

It's hard to find any product, save crack cocaine, that causes ruin for 85 percent of its users. Those unfortunate companies—the seventeen out of twenty—had lined up at bankruptcy courts that were thoroughly clogged, since the fall of 2008, and had been unable to get "exit financing" to emerge from restructuring.

Just as Geithner's stress tests were being designed to stand in for Moody's, by rating which banks were healthy enough for new investors, the U.S. government formed an in-house private-equity division to examine how it might get a reasonable return on controlling "investments"—don't call them bailouts—in Chrysler or GM, or both, or let imminent bankruptcy take its course. Washington was becoming Wall Street.

By the third week in March, there was no clear decision on a path for either Chrysler or GM, but several strong options had taken shape. One was for the government to keep Chrysler alive long enough to arrange a sale to Fiat, with various sweeteners provided by the U.S. government. As for GM, the proposal was for a quick bankruptcy, where the manufacturer would be broken into a bad company, with many of the crushing liabilities taken off the current balance sheet, and a good company, which would swiftly emerge from restructuring with a major government investment that it would, it was hoped, someday repay itself.

In other words, two private-equity plays, with the government as lead investor and the automakers standing in a rough parallel to Bear Stearns and Lehman: the smaller of the two, Chrysler, first on the chopping block, with its potential buyer, Fiat, hoping for federal funds or guarantees; and GM, like Lehman, generally viewed as too big to fail, as the largest U.S. automobile company in an economy where roughly one in ten workers worked for an automaker or a company that supplied them.

But while the investment banks were clearly at fault for their own demise—having profited handsomely from the very activities that ruined them—the issues of fault were more complex with the two automakers. Yes, both had been mismanaged in various ways over the past two decades—especially Chrysler, which was bought by Daimler, the German automaker, in 1998 for $36 billion. It limped through nine years of haphazard cost-cutting and shifting strategies until it was purchased in

May 2007 by Cerberus Capital, a private-equity firm named, fittingly, for the three-headed dog that in Greek and Roman mythology guards the gates of Hades. The next year, as credit tightened, was indeed hell for Cerberus, which was frantically slashing and shoring up its positions, and looking for investors into the winter of 2008.

GM was a different story. When Rick Wagoner, a GM lifer, took the reins of the company in 2000, it was suffering from the poor performance of too many brands sold by too many dealerships, and a steep "dependency ratio" of a steadily shrinking number of workers, as a result of layoffs and productivity gains, supporting an ever-larger number of retirees and their benefits. Wagoner accelerated the productivity gains, in the next few years cutting the GM workforce of four hundred thousand nearly in half and bringing the productivity-per-worker of GM plants in line with those from Toyota and Honda. As to the "dependency" imbalances, Wagoner was the lead negotiator on behalf of the Big Three, forging a 2007 agreement with the United Auto Workers on those crushing retiree benefits. With lump-sum payments to the UAW amounting to $32 billion over the next decade, GM would transfer its health care benefits burden to the union to manage, which would release it from the often contentious union-versus-management deadlocks on medical costs and dramatically lighten the company's burdened balance sheet. As for the actual making of cars, the contract allowed new hires for all the Big Three to be paid about half of the $28-an-hour wage that was mandated in the existing contract—creating a lowered unit cost for production of each car. (Wages were about half of overall costs.) This was matched at GM, as at Ford, with a focus on fewer brands and better built models, which were showing steady traction in quality ratings and the wider marketplace.

The big difference was that Ford had engineered a $23 billion cash infusion in 2007, when the markets were still strong. It was a coin toss. Many said that it wasn't necessary and that General Motors, by staying lean, looking to earn its way to economic soundness, had made the right choice.

Neither company, of course, could have predicted the historic Wall Street meltdown stemming from the mortgage mess and sixty-times-capital leverage and the wild extension of credit, loaded up with exotic covenants and traps and hedges. It was a mind-set that long defined private equity and its debt-driven machinations every bit as much as it did repos and CDOs.

But the position of Obama's private-equity officials was, not surprisingly, that Wagoner and GM management were inbred and feckless—the traditional stance of operators in private equity about "existing management" in virtually every industry for three decades. The Auto Task Force's Wall Streeters were the first and last word on the history, status, and culpability of the troubled automakers. As the internal debate crested toward the Oval Office, the dominant view inside the administration was that the car companies were significantly at fault for their own demise, and that the glories of financial engineering provided the only solutions.

Just before the scheduled meeting with the president, eight members of the economic team and the Auto Task Force met in Summers's office to hash out whether Chrysler should be saved or allowed to fail. After a few hours of discussion, Summers asked for a vote. The group was deadlocked. The strong case for liquidation came, surprisingly, from Austan Goolsbee, Obama's longest-standing economic adviser, who made the case that the death of Chrysler would nourish both GM and Ford with new customers and that both companies, pumping up production to meet heightened demand, would hire many of the ousted Chrysler workers. This could save GM. That analysis, with reams of underlying data, would normally have been sufficient to close a private-equity deal. But, suddenly, without a personal profit motive, Rattner and his Wall Streeters balked at the ouster of as many as three hundred thousand workers, the combined employment of Chrysler and its dependent suppliers.

Without a definitive recommendation, this group entered a wider circle, as more than a dozen advisers gathered with the president in the Oval Office on the afternoon of March 26.

Summers, as usual, led with a framing of the issues, until the president cut him off—"I read the memo, Larry"—and the discussion leapt forward to a central question raised in the briefing materials Summers had prepared: If Chrysler were to fail, would GM and Ford in fact profit from feeding off the corpse? Obama was intrigued by this. It was the kind of integrated solution that often caught his eye, where large, dysfunctional systems connect in such a way that one's adversity can be turned to the other's advantage. That stance, clever but ultimately of limited scope, avoids trying to alter the forces of rapid change—many of which, in this case, had resulted in a steady and disastrous drift for the country—in favor of looking for opportunities within those trends. Or, in Wall Street parlance, don't stand in the way of change, but rather use it. When it became clear that Goolsbee was the architect of this proposal, Obama began to look around the room. "Where's Austan?" Of course, Summers, the master of this debating society, had excluded his old rival from the meeting, prompting a frenzied few moments where staffers raced off to find Goolsbee and drag him, panting, into the meeting.

Goolsbee presented his case; Krueger was with him. The analysis was sound. As the two men spoke, Rattner's co-chairman of the Auto Task Force shook his head. Because the proceedings across two months had been about mostly financial engineering, Rattner's singular métier, Ron Bloom had been largely outmaneuvered in his leadership of the task force.

Bloom had precisely the portfolio that was conspicuously absent from the upper reaches of the administration: experience beyond the traditional borders of the professional class. His passport was a collector's item stamped both by Wall Street, from his decade doing deals for Lazard Frères, and by organized labor, where he'd spent another decade as a senior adviser to the United Steelworkers of America, as a key agent of the restructuring of the U.S. steel industry. While he could be brutally frank about the foibles and delusions of the U.S. labor movement, his view of Wall Street's financial engineers was merciless. What's more, he saw a causal relationship between Wall Street's contemporary practices and the woes of the wider economy, in that the draw of highly remunerative financial engineering—rather than invention, innovation, job creation, and the building of sound products sold at a good price—had fundamentally reshaped the country. When he arrived a few months before, he had expected that Obama would do something to reverse that shift. Now he wasn't so sure.

When Goolsbee talked about how Chrysler workers would be "absorbed," Bloom stepped into the fray.

"Mr. President, these are the reasons we can't kill this company. The damage to these communities and people will never be undone," Bloom said, drawing attention to the chasm between economic modeling and on-the-ground realities.

Rattner, having said almost nothing up to that point, mentioned that it had been a close call inside the task force—"it's fifty-one to forty-nine for liquidation" of Chrysler. Obama's secretary, Katie Johnson, then walked into the Oval Office with a note, indicating that the meeting was over. "I can't decide the future of the auto industry in twenty minutes," Obama said, exasperated, and it was agreed that the group would reconvene at 5:30 in the Roosevelt Room.

Now, in that new venue, more people came, including some of the political and communications teams, adding new voices to the debates on economic theory and practice. After a few minutes, Summers, despite his belief that Goolsbee's economic modeling was sound, sensed the tenor of the room and moved immediately—ahead of the president—to break the deadlock. "Mr. President," he said. "It's a close call, but I think we ought to save them."

But it wasn't Summers's decision to make. The economists continued to argue, as Obama looked on silently. Goolsbee continued to stress his position. "We need to do this for GM and Ford," he said. "These people"—meaning Chrysler's fired employees—"will have job substitution."

Bloom, who later commented, "There wasn't one guy in that room who'd spent any serious time having beers with real workers," was furious. "It just doesn't work that way," he said to the group, his voice rising. "Many of these people are nearing fifty and have been working in the auto business for twenty-five years. They get laid off, they won't get rehired—by anyone."

The discussion now broke beyond the bloodless norm of economic colloquy, of speculative predictions about corporate and consumer behavior with countless livelihoods at stake. While polls showed that the public strongly opposed the bailout of the auto companies, Emanuel said a Chrysler shutdown and economic fallout would have political consequences across the Midwest, and he began reeling off the names of congressmen who had Chrysler plants in their districts. Others, like Axelrod, offered comments about what the president's actions meant to people in trouble and equally to those watching from the sidelines.

"The president wasn't elected to be competent and pragmatic in managing policy debates with economists, who won't ever admit what they're doing is often guesswork, with a data sheet attached," Bloom later said, reflecting on the meeting. "He was elected to act decisively in a way that

makes Americans—especially the American worker, who's been left behind for decades—feel something they haven't felt in a while, which is
hope . . . Hope, because someone, finally, is fighting for them."

Bloom felt that this position was finally being heard in the aptly named
Roosevelt Room, from someone who had little currency in the Larry
Summers Debating Society.

"Mr. President, I don't think it's a close call," said Press Secretary
Robert Gibbs, somewhat tentatively. While clearly not claiming expertise on the forces propelling the economy in recent years, Gibbs, along
with Axelrod, was one of the few people present who understood the
forces that had propelled Obama to the Oval Office. "What are we going
to do when a guy walks out of the plant after we've shut it down, and he's
holding a sign that says, 'I Guess I Wasn't Too Big to Fail.'"

With that one line, Gibbs had stumbled on a larger set of questions
than prospective corporate behavior or gaming the financial system.
Whose failure posed a greater threat to the nation: a Wall Street bank or
the American worker? And when given a choice, shouldn't the government side with the powerless?

Obama had heard enough. "I've decided. I'm prepared to support
Chrysler if we can get the Fiat alliance done on terms that make sense
to us." Then, nodding to the Wall Streeters and market-oriented economists in the room, he added, "I want you to be tough, and I want you to
be commercial."

The next day, Rick Wagoner arrived in Washington to work with the
Auto Task Force through the "good company, bad company" design for
GM's restructuring. Creditors of GM would be getting a "haircut"; their
contracts would have been alterable under a bankruptcy proceeding anyway. Shareholders in the old GM would have to swap their shares for
shares in the "good GM," in the hopes that it would someday succeed.
Tens of billions in federal funds would cover the shortfall between assets
and liabilities, and give the government effective ownership of the new
GM that emerged.

The GM restructuring plan was discussed only briefly at the auto
meeting the previous evening, with just a passing mention of a key feature of the plan: that Wagoner, fifty-six, would be let go. The prevailing,
market-centric view in the room—that, to paraphrase Summers, in the

U.S. economy "people get what they deserve"—was so unanimous that no one raised an objection. That included the president. He had approved Wagoner's firing a few days before, on Rattner's recommendation.

Of course, what was in store for GM was similar to what the president had expressed interest in two weeks before for Citigroup. He might well have thought Wagoner's exit offered the appearance of balance, of even-handedness. Citigroup CEO Vikram Pandit—and the chiefs of other banks that the president hoped would, sooner rather than later, be closed and restructured—would likely be on the street soon as well.

In a conversation Wagoner had with Rattner two weeks before, the GM chief graciously said, "I'm not planning to stay until I'm sixty-five, but I think I've got at least a few years left in me . . . But I told the last administration that if my leaving would be helpful in saving General Motors, I'm prepared to do it."

Considering that GM was in the final stages of a massive, eight-year restructuring, clearing away many of the company's longest-standing problems, Wagoner never expected anyone to take him up on the offer.

Which is why he was stunned on the morning of March 27 as Rattner, sitting across from him at a table inside Treasury, slowly unsheathed the knife: "In our last meeting, you very graciously offered to step aside if it would be helpful, and unfortunately, our conclusion is that it would be best if you did that."

For a moment, Rick Wagoner was speechless.

He had just become the first CEO in U.S. history to be fired by a president.

———

At the same time that Rattner was firing Wagoner, a hundred yards due west, thirteen impeccably dressed men were gathering in the reception room for appointments in the West Wing.

They were the CEOs of the thirteen largest banking institutions in the United States.

And they were nervous in ways that these men are never nervous. Many would have had to reach back to their college days, or even grade school, to remember a moment when they felt this sort of lump-in-the-throat tension.

As some of the most successful men in the country, they weren't used to being pariahs. They weren't sure how to act, either, especially in the presence of someone who had power over them, and may well decide to exercise it.

After all, they were indeed *pariahs*. The populist backlash against the financial sector—building steadily since September—was finally beginning to cause grave discomfort on Wall Street. As unemployment ballooned and credit tightened, the country began to look inward, toward the origins of the panic and its disastrous outcomes.

That frustration had grown as details of the crisis began to trickle out. Outraged Americans, feeling proprietary about where their tax dollars had actually gone, were granted a first primer on the nature of credit default swaps. *CDO*—for Collateralized Debt Obligation—had been an acronym bandied to and fro in conversation since the previous fall, but the term's complexities remained murky to almost anyone who hadn't spent years in finance. That seemed to have changed over the winter as the media offered explanations of how the vilified Goldman Sachs had, in essence, been paid $13 billion in bailout funds as a counterparty to AIG on swaps written to cover their CDOs, and another $6 billion from Société Générale, the French bank that Goldman impelled to be a front man so it could write even more swaps with AIG. Nearly $20 billion in tax dollars going to Goldman. CDSs, or Credit Default Swaps, were like insurance policies without reserves, where the holder could also make a wager on the fortunes of almost anything, as long as there was someone else, a counterparty, on the other side of the bet.

But the backlash had reached fever pitch by mid-March, when AIG announced the imminent disbursement of $165 million in bonuses, and news of the full, 100-cents-on-the dollar payments of federal bailout money to AIG's counterparties created a kind of twin scandal that kept swirling over the ensuing two weeks.

Since mid-February there had been buses touring the houses of AIG executives, carrying demonstrators who would emerge to scream epithets and wave picket signs. The same went for the houses of financial industry lobbyists in D.C.: picketers with bullhorns. Proposals came from both sides of the aisle, buoyed by cable provocateurs from both Fox News and MSNBC—a rare example of ecumenical rage.

But the financial industry and its lobbyist protectors were even more aggrieved by how lawmakers were increasingly capitalizing on this outrage. Picketers and crank callers might yell, and several Wall Street banks might subsidize round-the-clock security for executives, but congressmen can pass laws.

Which is what the House did, on March 17, taxing at 90 percent any bonus above $1 million received by an employee of an institution that had received $5 billion or more in TARP funds.

Meanwhile, reports finally emerged, with White House fingerprints, that Senator Chris Dodd, who had taken more money from AIG than any other congressional official, had written and then withdrawn an amendment to the stimulus package in February that would have stopped the AIG bonuses. Dodd's staff retaliated, saying that he'd quietly made the change at the behest of Geithner himself, who then countered a few days later, saying he'd been concerned about the overall legality of retroactively canceling compensation contracts for all the TARP recipients, rather than about the specifics of the AIG bonuses. None of it seemed to track.

Banking CEOs and their lobbyists watched this back-and-forth with intense interest—they saw it as Geithner having stood in the way of reckless congressional behavior—and they opened a fresh dialogue with the White House. Congress, they asserted, was out of control, ready to take actions that would cripple banks and throw the country into a deep depression.

Where the president himself stood was another question. He had just issued a statement that he now wanted Geithner to "use any legal means necessary to rescind the AIG bonuses," a "legal means," if found, that might well be extended to all the major banks. This, combined with Obama's generally frosty language regarding the financial industry, had left the industry unsure of what to make of the new president.

But the lobbyists' fears about the president's strong words were calmed by calls to Treasury in March. Geithner, they found, was also concerned about congressional excesses. An idea was hatched: leading bankers would meet with the president. The bankers talked with the administration about ground rules and what message such a meeting might send—to the benefit of both the bankers and the president.

Which is why thirteen of the world's most powerful financial executives, and a handful of their lobbyists, were milling about the State Dining Room the morning of Wagoner's firing.

Despite Treasury's assurances about Geithner's sympathies, they were worried about what the president would demand simply because the masses wanted blood.

Until Obama arrived, everything was awkwardly convivial. Jamie Dimon, who'd spent years with Geithner in New York, had thought up an icebreaker, a way to keep things light, and handed the Treasury secretary an oversize novelty check made out for $25,000,000,000. Geithner smiled and joked about whether Dimon could make it a cashier's check. Under the public spotlight, Geithner was uneasy, both ingratiating and defensive, speaking in short bursts between pregnant pauses. But here, in a roomful of bankers—his longtime constituents—he was loquacious and at ease. There was good news to report to the CEOs, many of whom he'd worked beside and socialized with for years. Just four days ago he'd unveiled his Public-Private Investment Program, or PPIP—one those "Hobbit" programs, as Emanuel chided—for the government to partner with private investors in a "no-lose" proposition for them to purchase the toxic assets from bank balance sheets. That, combined with the stress tests, which were coming along nicely, would help the banks survive intact, he told a few CEOs, and earn their way to good health.

Then the room quieted. Obama had arrived, and everyone settled around a bare mahogany table, a single glass of water, no ice, before each Queen Anne chair.

The president was cool, not particularly friendly, even though he'd spent many hours with some of the CEOs, such as Dimon, at fundraising extravaganzas during the campaign.

"His body language made it very clear that he was the president, he was in charge," said one of the participants, and that he wanted to hash things out—what he felt, what they saw. The discussion moved swiftly across topics, such as the general soundness of the overall system and how to jump-start lending, before it came around to what was on everyone's mind: compensation.

The CEOs went into their traditional stance. "It's almost impossible to set caps; it's never worked, and you lose your best people," said one. "We're competing for talent on an international market," said another. Obama cut them off.

"Be careful how you make those statements, gentlemen. The public isn't buying that," he said. "My administration is the only thing between you and the pitchforks."

It was an attention grabber, no doubt, especially that carefully chosen last word.

But then Obama's flat tone turned to one of support, even sympathy. "You guys have an acute public relations problem that's turning into a political problem," he said. "And I want to help. But you need to show that you get that this is a crisis and that everyone has to make some sacrifices."

According to one of the participants, he then said, "I'm not out there to go after you. I'm protecting you. But if I'm going to shield you from public and congressional anger, you have to give me something to work with on these issues of compensation."

No suggestions were forthcoming from the bankers on what they might offer, and the president didn't seem to be championing any specific proposals. He had none: neither Geithner nor Summers believed compensation controls had any merit.

After a moment, the tension in the room seemed to lift: the bankers realized he was talking about *voluntary* limits on compensation until the storm of public anger passed. It would be for show.

Nothing to worry about. Whereas Roosevelt had pushed for tough, viciously opposed reforms of Wall Street and famously said, "I welcome their hatred," Obama was saying, "How can I help?" With palpable relief, the CEOs carried the discussion, talking, easily now, about credit conditions and how loan demand was soft because it should be: businesses were already overleveraged. "We don't want to be making bad loans," said one CEO, as his kindred from the more traditional banks, such as Minneapolis-based U.S. Bancorp or NatWest, nodded. "Much of our business is still old-fashioned lending."

Even among this golden thirteen, there were class divisions. JPMorgan's Dimon, Goldman Sachs' Lloyd Blankfein, Morgan Stanley's John Mack, and Citigroup's Pandit stood atop the global behemoths of Wall Street, making much of their money and their stunning compensation on everything but traditional lending. They ran vast trading and financial gaming operations, focused mostly on the largely depersonalized flows of debt. Although Dimon asked the first question, the Elite Four didn't say much over nearly an hour, especially about the divisive issue of compensation.

There was, after all, no question that they and their kindred, who man the snowcapped peaks of private-equity and hedge funds, were the heirs to Milken. And that legacy is all about compensation, as anyone old enough to have been working on Wall Street in 1983—when all these CEOs were just getting started—could attest.

That year, Milken made $125 million. How much of a jump was it? The previous year, it was something of a scandal when John Gutfreund, the CEO of Salomon Brothers, made $3.1 million after, controversially, transforming his firm from a traditional Wall Street partnership, with the partnership's money on the investment table alongside that of its clients, to a publicly traded company investing other people's money.

Many Wall Streeters can remember, decades later, where they were when they read that morning's *Wall Street Journal* about Milken and did a double take. Once their shock subsided, the great migration began to, by any means necessary, "be like Mike," whose pay, incidentally, continued to rise.

The way this compensation frenzy raced through the professional class—from investment managers first, to their client CEOs, paid by complex options triggers and golden parachutes, to the handsomely paid lawyers and accountants who worked to make sure every practice could be defended as legal—is the real story of how America's most precious asset, its human capital, flowed in a torrent across three decades into financial engineering.

Bank of America's CEO, Ken Lewis—who made his money in an older, more linear fashion, by faithfully executing acquisitions for his charismatic boss, Hugh McColl, and then taking over Bank of America himself—glared at the Wall Streeters throughout the meeting. Lewis, who had long pined to use Bank of America's girth in traditional banking to buy a Wall Street firm, got his wish, and more than he bargained for, when Greg Fleming engineered the bank's purchase of Merrill Lynch. Six months later, Lewis's bank was struggling to manage nearly a hundred thousand foreclosures and a host of homeowners' suits, while its Merrill division, already catching the updraft of restored activities on the Street, was beginning to drive the bank's earnings. Not that the Mississippi-raised CEO was expected to issue many quarters from his executive suite. The brusque Lewis, unfamiliar with the signaling system of shared interests between Washington and New York, had famously botched his conversation with Paulson and Bernanke in December, saying he needed more federal money or else he'd back out of the Merrill deal. Lewis, with the ink barely dry on his Wall Street pass, had interpreted matters too literally: New York clearly made money, with Washington as its guarantor, and he wanted his money now—or else. Paulson was incredulous. The "or else" of Bank of America's retreat could make Merrill another Lehman and melt the fragile economy. Washington's support, in any event, couldn't be so bluntly reduced, like some covenant in a buyout deal that hadn't been fulfilled. Lewis got his money, $20 billion, and then a welter of shareholder suits and investigations. He would soon be demoted, from CEO to chairman, and then ousted.

But as the conversation of shared interest moved forward, Lewis couldn't help but blurt out that the banks shouldn't all be painted with the same brush, that "we in traditional banking didn't cause this disaster; it came from Wall Street!"

Silence. The issues of causation or urgent corrections in how the industry's leaders on Wall Street made their money were on Congress's agenda but not the administration's, to the delighted surprise of many of those attending.

The thirteen bankers, terrified an hour before, now closed the discussion with Geithner about what they should say as they emerged into the enormous reportorial scrum gathered outside. Much of this was actually plotted ahead of time between bank lobbyists and the White House. Whatever happened inside the "people's house," they would emerge with the overall message that "we are all in this together." And walking out of the portico, as the press crushed close, they said it, one after another.

That's the one-line version of the covenant between Washington and successive White Houses (that Lewis, clumsily, tried to turn into a cashier's check): "we're all in this together." Money will flow, as trillions of tax dollars had from capital to capital, D.C. to NYC, in the past year, but only under that gentle, inclusive phrase.

And then the CEOs boarded their private jets, convinced that they had nothing to worry about from the angry public and their congressional representatives.

"I think the administration agreed with our view that these crazy congressmen and their proposals to either nationalize the banks or cripple them with heavy taxes or compensation limits would throw the country in a deep depression," said one of the bankers after the meeting. "Lots of drama, but at day's end, nothing much changed."

And that was the goal: not to change the relationship between the U.S. government and the financial industry that had evolved across thirty years.

It was clear to the banks that this special relationship had never been as imperiled as it was in March of 2009, a time in which the industry was still vulnerable and dependent on government.

Add in the scandals of AIG and outrage over counterparty payments, and there was no better time in a generation to deal directly with the way this crossroads industry—with the role of a utility that powers the economy—had grown dizzyingly huge and profitable while disastrously underpricing risk across the American landscape.

Those in Congress who saw this rare opportunity, and reached to seize it, were generally excluded from White House councils and debates. A group of leading Democratic senators led by North Dakota's Byron Dorgan, along with Virginia's Jim Webb, Iowa's Tom Harkin, Michigan's Carl Levin, California's Dianne Feinstein, Vermont's Socialist Bernie Sanders, and Cantwell—the latter two who had put a hold on Gensler's nomination—had pressed to meet with Obama to discuss options for restructuring the collapsed financial industry since his inauguration.

As March arrived, an incensed Dorgan grabbed a speed-walking Emanuel in the halls of the Senate, all but shouting, "Where's my meeting with the president?"

Emanuel promised to get it scheduled, but when Dorgan heard back, he could hardly believe what Rahm was offering instead: a meeting with Summers. The reason Dorgan and others in his group wanted to meet directly with the president was precisely because they felt that it was Summers, Geithner, and Gensler who had been instrumental in creating the antecedents of the current financial crisis. With the expectation of a Treasury white paper on financial reform coming sometime in the spring, Dorgan and the group fired off an angry letter to Emanuel on March 12: "I am reiterating our request to meet with the President so we may have some meaningful and timely input into the formulation of that program . . . We know the President will get plenty of advice from Larry Summers and Secretary Geithner on this subject. We want him to have the benefit of our advice on these matters as well." When the senators finally got their brief meeting in the Oval Office on March 23 and laid out their proposals for rethinking the current regulatory model, Obama listened respectfully, but showed little reaction and offered no hint of the discussions that had transpired in the marathon meeting of March 15.

In fact, the decision he had made in November to choose Geithner and Summers, and his penchant for wanting to convince his advisers of his rightness prior to making a major decision all but guaranteed that any such market interventions would place him in a position of having to out-debate much of his senior staff. That process, labored though it was, seemed to give Obama surety, a kind of hard-won confidence to act. A diverse array of perspectives is what presidents tend to want and, isolated in their White House bubble, often demand. Dorgan and his senators were not the only ones having trouble getting to Obama. As a senior Obama adviser later said, "The president was concerned about showing his uncertainty, or his lack of acquired knowledge on lots of these policies, to his own advisers—much less people from the outside." He was increasingly insulated by the end of March, with requests for meetings with him on domestic policies of all shapes being funneled to Summers. Larry would then decide if the interloper merited an audience with the president.

Of the many voices Obama was not hearing at this point, few might have proven as valuable as a longtime Massachusetts representative named Edward Markey. A thirty-three-year veteran of the House, Markey was chairman of the House Energy Committee and was known for his work on environmental legislation.

On March 19, a week before Obama met with the thirteen bankers, Markey spoke from the House floor as one of three dozen cosponsors of HR 1586, the bill that would levy a 90 percent tax on bonuses for any executive of a company receiving at least $5 billion in TARP funds who made more than $250,000. "This is March Madness," he intoned. "You don't blow the big game and then still get a trophy. Not one single penny of taxpayer funds should be used to reward the reckless executives whose irresponsible risk-taking has done massive damage to our economy. And this bill will ensure that they are not rewarded."

Markey could bid fair claim to being farther ahead of the curve on the financial crisis than almost any elected official in Washington. As the youthful chairman of the House Subcommittee on Telecommunications and Finance from 1987 to 1995, Markey had held five oversight hearings on the risks that financial derivatives posed to the markets, and then introduced the Derivatives Market Reform Act of 1994, which would have regulated derivatives transactions by affiliates of insurance companies such as AIG. It was defeated, as were similar bills he introduced in 1995, 1999, and March 2008—all killed by the financial lobby.

But times had changed. After HR 1586, the bill most reviled and feared by the thirteen bankers, passed the House, Markey, again from the

well of the chamber, added that "by the early 1990s it was already clear
that the derivatives markets were too risky to remain unregulated and
now the chickens have come home to roost. By passing this bill today,
the House is sending a strong signal that this type of behavior will not be
tolerated. What we still need to do, however, is take up a comprehensive
package of financial market reforms to address the recklessness that led
us to our current crisis."

As for the "type of behavior" that "led us to our crisis," Markey could
cite the moment he saw the culture shift, like some geological event.

It was in 1988, after the 1987 stock market crash, and the prosecution of insider trading and various securities frauds was well underway.
"Something very basic, very fundamental, had changed on the Street,
and we on the subcommittee couldn't put our finger on what was different," Markey recalled. So they decided to bring in an expert. Dennis
Levine, one of the major Wall Streeters convicted of securities fraud, was
serving time in New Jersey. Markey's staff got in touch with the Bureau of
Prisons and arranged to have him transported for an afternoon to a subcommittee conference room. Levine, who couldn't be forced to cooperate, was asked what the subcommittee could do to persuade him to come.
He said he'd do it for a McDonald's Big Mac, fries, and a chocolate shake.
Once a self-proclaimed "Master of the Universe," those were the things
he'd found he missed the most. Soon enough, Levine, in prison blues,
was eating his Big Mac and describing how the rewards on Wall Street
had suddenly grown so large, and the opportunities for self-dealing and
misuse of insider information—so-called informational advantage—so
widespread, that it would only get worse. "He said, we were 'just at the
very start,'" Markey recalled, "and that they'd figured out how to turn
the investing of others people's money into a kind of game, where they
were constantly changing the rules in a way that was subtly fraudulent,
against the basic principles of fairness or fiduciary duty. He said that with
this much money to be made for doing very little, it was worth the risk of
getting caught doing what you had to do, but that they were working on
lowering that risk as well, with lawyers working overtime to make sure
many of these activities were legal, or at least hard to prosecute." After an hour, Markey said that he and the committee members had heard
enough and asked the felon what might be done. Levine, sucking on his
shake, thought this over for a minute or two, and then said, "You need to
send out a slew of indictments, all at once, and at three p.m. on a sunny

day, have Federal Marshals perp-walk three hundred Wall Street executives out of their offices in handcuffs and out on the street, with lots of cameras rolling. Everyone else would say, 'If that happened to me, my mother would be so ashamed.'

"Levine was saying we should take a dramatic stand on principle to reverse the direction we were moving in . . . before things progressed any further and the problems got even bigger," Markey said. "Culture is destiny and the only way you create real change is by acting in a way that changes the culture."

Presidents are among the few mortals who are sometimes graced with chances to change a culture. Throughout a windswept March, the country had been working to dislodge some of the era's prevailing certainties about markets being efficient, about people—economically, at least—getting what they deserve, along with the concomitant belief that financial barons are brilliant and indispensable, and manufacturing executives are dinosaurs.

With the eyes of the country on him, Barack Obama ended the month by shielding Wall Street executives against these winds of cultural change, while he fired a man who had effectively managed four hundred thousand workers in their making of seven million cars a year—without ever bothering to meet him. At the same time, he agreed to try to bail out Chrysler, and eventually GM, by adopting the practices and principles of private equity in the use of government funds.

Improbable combinations, blended solutions, the integrating of opposites.

This was the Obama method, in his life and in his work. But he hadn't gotten elected simply to search for this clever version of the middle ground. He'd been elected at a time of peril to change the country's course.

By that measure, it would be easy to conclude that he missed some opportunities to show that America hadn't necessarily gone from a country that makes things to one that makes things up, and that facing the consequences for one's actions, at the heart of both a working democracy and effective capitalism, knows no boundaries. When the bankers arrived in the State Dining Room, sitting under a portrait of a glowering Lincoln, Obama had them scared and ready to do almost anything he said.

An hour later, they were upbeat, ready to fly home and commence business as usual.

The thirteen bankers, and especially the half dozen titans from New York, returned to their corner offices that afternoon with very strong feelings about one man in Washington: Tim Geithner.

"The sense of everyone after the big meeting was relief," said one of the bankers. "The president had us at a moment of real vulnerability. At that point, he could have ordered us to do just about anything, and we would have rolled over. But he didn't—he mostly wanted to help us out, to quell the mob. And the guy we figured we had to thank for that was Tim. He was our man in Washington."

In public life, constituencies are important. Geithner now had one: the powerful but reviled leaders of the nation's largest banks. He'd have been loath to claim their backing, just as they'd have known not to be demonstrative with support. It was, after all, a bond of mutual desperation: both Geithner and his silent backers were fighting for survival. As one banking lobbyist said, "If Tim were fired, we'd be in trouble; we knew that." Of course, he'd have plenty of job offers in New York.

Calls for Geithner's resignation, which first appeared after the February 10 press conference, had grown into a subject of mainstream discussion in the two weeks after mid-March's AIG explosion.

Axelrod and Jarrett looked on warily to see who might be joining the chorus. Geithner was getting attacked from both the far right and the far left—a dangerous combination. And congressional Democrats were on the phone filled with concern. Line it all up—from TurboTax, to the first press conference, to the AIG bonuses—and it was difficult not to pose a question about Obama's judgment in placing so much faith in this man to handle the most important challenges facing the country. Something had to be done. Geithner was hurting the president.

Obama was standing firm behind Geithner, but that clearly wasn't enough. Geithner had to survive, or not, on his own. At 4:00 p.m., a few hours after the bankers had departed—with their "we're all in this together" message looping through the news cycles—a delegation from the White House convened in the small conference room off Geithner's office at Treasury. Axelrod was there, along with Sarah Feinberg, Emanuel's top assistant. Waiting for them were senior officials from Treasury. Geithner had never appeared on one of Washington's signature Sunday morning news shows. For this coming Sunday, March 29, he'd been booked for two of them. ABC's *This Week*, with George Stephanopoulos, would be taping an interview with him at 8:00 a.m. The producers were already touting it as Geithner's first appearance on a Sunday morning show. NBC's *Meet the Press* would have him at 9:00 a.m., calling it his first "live" appearance on a Sunday show. The latter was the tougher venue, with the bigger audience. Geithner would have to stand on his own, under the hottest of lights.

Fortunately, the week had started on a positive note. A few days before, on Monday, March 23, the Public-Private Investment Program was formally released. This, in fact, was a rollout of the many specific details Obama had promised in his February 9 press conference. They weren't ready the next morning, as Obama had advertised—not nearly. It took six weeks to iron out the key features of the program, in consultation with other regulators and, crucially, with Wall Street pros, who offered counsel about what might excite investors.

This time the White House had been integrally involved in the rollout: weekend leaks of the program's strongest selling points to the investors; a column by Geithner in Monday morning's *Wall Street Journal*; and, not incidentally, a very strong set of favorable reactions from top officials at some of the country's largest banks, who were just then in negotiations over their upcoming meeting with Obama. All this, plus the weeks of calls from Treasury to Wall Street, so the program would curry a positive response, seemed to work. The further that one dug into its details, the more PPIP seemed like a giveaway to the banks. It just took a little digging. Geithner said it was a tough program, where investors would take the risk. Wall Street knew better. The market rose a stunning 497 points.

As the team settled that Friday afternoon in the Treasury secretary's conference room—Geithner was finishing up a call in his office—Axelrod reached out for Krueger's hand. "I don't know anything about you," he said, without a smile, "but the fact that you've been nominated and are about to be confirmed shows that you pay your taxes." The comment was, at best, half in jest. As Obama's fiercest protectors, Axelrod and others on Obama's political staff were increasingly concerned that Geithner was a liability who not only stood in the way of tough, and politically advantageous, measures against Wall Street, but also drew the charge that the administration was in Wall Street's back pocket. He was a lightning rod, and the sparks were starting to hit Obama. Their view: botch the Sunday shows and get ready to pack your bags.

Geithner arrived and slumped into a chair. After a rough couple of weeks, he was tetchy and reflective. "Look, I don't want people feeling sorry for me. I don't want sympathy. I don't want anyone sending me Rudyard Kipling poems," he groused. "It's a tough job; I'm doing everything I can." He told them he'd just heard from his mother. "She said, 'Tim, remember the summer you worked at that bar and the owner said you weren't exactly the best bartender? Well, maybe this is like that, and this job just isn't for you.'" He shook his head. "My own mother!"

Treasury's spokeswoman Stephanie Cutter—a longtime operative among the Democrats, who'd worked atop the Kerry presidential campaign—was at her wit's end. She'd taken Geithner to a media trainer to improve his onscreen demeanor to little effect. Before meeting a delegation of reporters and photographers to roll out PPIP earlier in the week, his collar was hopelessly askew. Gene Sperling, an assistant Treasury secretary, offered him a collar stay, but he had only one. One is better than none, Geithner figured, and emerged at half-mast.

"I grew up under Bob Rubin," he'd regularly quip to the staff, "which means I'm in public only when absolutely necessary." But therein lay a key difference: Rubin's appearances, though rare, fit with a set of unspoken assumptions. With the exception of Summers's one-year term in 1999, almost all the Treasury secretaries since the 1970s had been well-polished CEOs, wealthy men. Geithner was a public servant who wore poorly fitting off-the-rack suits and got his hair cut, for less than $20 a pop, at a barbershop—a favorite of African Americans from the area—a few blocks from Treasury. Meanwhile, everyone thought he'd once worked for Goldman Sachs. No, Treasury officials would tell reporters at every turn: he'd been a public servant all his life. But none of it had any effect. Assumptions are powerful once they settle. At a time when the president talked frequently about restoring confidence in the future of the economy and the soundness of the markets, he had a Treasury secretary who offered his own unique counterpoint: as an inarticulate, poorly tailored, uncertain young man—late thirties or so, it seemed—who was walking proof that all you need in life is to have once worked for Goldman Sachs.

After running through some expected questions, and appropriate answers, Axelrod cut to the marrow. "On *Meet the Press*, you'll be asked if you've discussed your resignation with the president."

Geithner was startled.

"Well, I'll say no," he said. "Because I haven't."

On Sunday, Tim Geithner hunched forward across the *Meet the Press* interview table, his large hands in front of him, like someone ready to fend off a blow. He survived twenty minutes of live questioning. At the end, the host, David Gregory, dropped the anvil: about calls for Geithner's resignation.

Tim Geithner was finally ready.

"David, when I came into this job, I knew two things. One is I knew we were starting with a set of enormously complicated challenges and a deep sense of anger and frustration about the burden Americans were bearing because of a long period of excessive risk-taking. And I knew we were going to face really tough choices. We were going to have to do things that are going to be deeply unpopular, hard to understand. We're not going to get it perfect everywhere. But this is a great privilege for me, a great honor to help this president do what it takes to help get this economy back on track."

Gregory nodded as, no doubt, did thirteen bankers, or their strategic aides, watching across the country. He'd passed.

"Secretary Geithner, good luck with your very important work."

UNRESOLVED

IN EARLY APRIL, OBAMA'S ECONOMIC TEAM CONGREGATED IN THE Oval Office for the morning briefing.

All the key players were there, except Geithner. After a few moments, the president talked about a resolution plan for Citigroup as a key item in his arsenal, and wondered how close it was to completion. Christina Romer and Larry Summers glanced at each other. They had been talking for nearly a month about how the Treasury Department seemed to be ignoring the president's clear, unequivocal orders involving Citigroup.

Geithner and his team were moving forward with their own favored policy, the stress tests, but they had done virtually nothing about a plan to wind down Citigroup.

Romer's mind raced. Wouldn't the president want to know if his orders had been ignored? Especially concerning one of the most important crises he would face in office?

"I'm sorry, Mr. President," she said, summoning her courage, "but there is no resolution plan for Citi."

Obama looked at her, stunned. "Well, there better be!" he said.

Romer immediately felt Emanuel's gaze. Something was clearly amiss.

When the meeting ended, Emanuel and Summers huddled. A short time later, Summers took Romer aside.

"You did something very consequential there, telling the president that there was no plan for Citi," Summers said. "Rahm was incensed that you told him that. That Tim wasn't here to defend himself. But I defended you. I told Rahm, 'She's right!'"

Treasury would in fact never move forward to carry out the president's wishes about Citigroup, as a potential first step in a wider restructuring of the banking sector.

The whole point of the executive enterprise is to carry forward the wishes of the president. "He's the duly-elected representative of the people. None of the rest of us are," said a top White House official on the subject. "We're there, at least we're *supposed* to be there, to serve at his pleasure, to carry out his will—because he carries the will of the people. Right around this time, you could see that starting not to happen."

When questioned later about the matter, Geithner initially said that a proposal for possibly closing Citi, as a first step to doing the same for other banks, was never seen as a "real alternative to the stress tests . . . there was no real alternative to the stress tests." The resolution of Citi or other banks was instead an issue to be seriously broached only "if the stress tests didn't work, and they did," and that most of the people in the room on March 15 "don't understand anything of what was happening about the substance of the choice, so they're crafting their memory . . . they're trying to create memory with the benefit of hindsight."

But in a half-hour interview largely on this matter, Geithner began to reveal the strategic complexities of his "plan beats no plan" dictum.

After praising Romer as a fine economist, he said she was of "no value on policy issues" of "financial rescue" and that "Larry and Rahm were the only ones that mattered in the debate. Larry's problem was that he had no alternative, ever," to the stress tests. "He was never willing to commit to an alternative, never came up with an alternative strategy."

But then Geithner went through the chain of events and meetings on this most portentous issue, saying that the consensus recollection "was largely true," from the president's ardor, starting in late February, to look at alternatives to solely relying on the "stress tests"—the only plan under way at that point. "He forced me and everyone to look at this thing from all angles, chew it over" and make everyone "go through that test: what is the alternative plan? Those who don't like it [the stress tests], *what are you for?*"

The problem, of course, was that the policy-making horsepower, in this instance, was at Treasury and the Fed, both of which were in concert to push forward a chosen policy that almost every other key person in the government was concerned about, from the president on down.

Geithner recalled a typical meeting in this period. "We'd be in the Oval Office, the president was worrying, the world was still burning, people wanted to light me on fire, and the president would say, 'Tim, what I want to know is, are you confident this plan [the stress tests] is going to work.'

"Normally, Larry would answer before I answered. He'd say, 'Mr. President, I'm closer to you on this. I want to be tougher.' And I'd say,

'There's nothing certain in life, but I'm very confident that our plan has a much better chance of working than any alternatives.'"

But, as Larry and Christina worked the phones in early March to try to gather the information they'd need to field, at very least, a strong counterproposal—if not the kind of fully rendered alternative plan that only Treasury could provide—Geithner felt the duo accentuated the financial crisis and actually "fed some of the pressure. They were perceived by the market as indulging in a lot of loose talk about haircuts [to investors holding debt in the banks] and that was very damaging to the markets."

When the meeting finally arrived, Geithner acknowledged that the core of the discussion was whether "we should preemptively nationalize and dismember banks" and that, afterward, Treasury didn't come up with a plan to dissolve Citi—but that sort of thing, like AIG, is "hard to preplan." Of course, coming up with a plan to avoid an AIG-style meltdown and "show what government can do" was precisely what the president was seeking. And, yes, at Treasury they were fearful of alerting Sheila Bair.

As to the issue of what the president said to him after he realized that his will had been ignored, and there was no Citibank resolution plan, Geithner said he didn't remember the president being angry at him, noting that "there were a lot of pointed rolling discussions through April," of "where are we, what's next, how's it going, and what's the thinking on alternatives" to only running the stress tests. Another proposal that got some traction was to match the dismissal of GM's Rick Wagoner with the firing of Bank of America CEO Ken Lewis.

But that proposal was more symbolic than substantive. On matters of substance, Geithner—with the implicit backing of Bernanke—held the cards.

Did that mean he inappropriately controlled the game, taking charge of one of the most important decisions of the Obama presidency? Geithner denied the charge, later made in internal White House documents, that "once a decision is made, implementation by the Department of the Treasury has at times been slow and uneven," and that "these factors all adversely affect execution of the policy process." The parlance for that is "slow walking."

"I don't slow walk the president on anything," he said. "People who wanted to do other things often accused me of slow walking, but I would never do that." But Tim Geithner added, with some satisfaction, the battle over restructuring the financial industry "was resolved in the classic way, that plan beats no plan.

"No one else had a plan." Including Barack Obama.

———————

Summers and Romer were deeply concerned. They feared that in Geithner's hands the stress tests would be so easy that they would end up proving nothing, other than the administration's inability, or unwillingness—depending on how you saw it—to demand tough concessions from Wall Street.

On Easter Sunday, April 12, the two trekked to Geithner's conference room at Treasury, where they—along with Geithner and a dozen others, including former bankers such as Lee Sachs—went through the arcana of loan-to-equity ratios, deposits versus assets, and tiers of capital.

It was another marathon meeting. Now they were decidedly on Geithner's turf, and he was prepared. For every concern of Summers and Romer, Geithner and his team had a ready answer.

The discussion focused on so-called tier-one capital, the safest core capital of a bank, its cushion, which was usually in reserves or common shares. The stress tests needed to decide not only what banks could fairly count as tier-one capital but also what level was sufficient to stave off government action. Geithner and his team thought 4 percent of overall assets was fine. Summers and Romer were pushing for 6 percent or even higher, considering the sluggishness of the economy and the heavy load of mortgage-related assets weighing down balance sheets.

"You only get one shot at this," Romer said. "You don't want to shoot low."

"Our credibility is being put on the line," Summers seconded.

The goal, however, was gentle optimism: that a turnaround for the industry could begin with acceptance of a slightly improved version of reality, and that the ensuing confidence—that things will turn out well—encourages actions to make it so. In this regard, the combatants ate chocolate Easter eggs and matzo as they debated matters of resurrection: how much capital banks should have on hand, given present circumstances, to allow the government to stamp them with a slightly improved version of reality. Summers and Romer said there was no way to precisely predict whether there would be a steady upward trend for the U.S. economy. It was wrong to bet the credibility, and the Treasury, of the federal government on such a prediction. If you got it wrong, you would be missing the best and maybe only opportunity to fix these banks so that credit would begin pumping again, in safe fashion.

At 10:00 p.m. the dispute over whether these stress tests were just the government's version of Kick the Can was starting to slow. Treasury had the upper hand. The tests were for them and the Fed to execute and shape. Gene Sperling left the room and returned with another box of matzo. Geithner, famished like the rest of them, shook his head.

"Don't do that," the Treasury secretary said. "Now we'll end up being here for another hour."

But, at this point, the subtext was clear. Deep down, it didn't matter how each bank was assessed in the stress test. The fact that each one would be given a "United States of Moody's" stamp, and told how much money the government recommended it raise, meant that anyone who invested in a bank should feel confident that they would recoup their losses in the event of a bankruptcy, care of Washington. Being able to sell this assurance in the public markets meant banks would quickly raise enough money to pay back their TARP funds and explore new, commanding heights of profit. Whatever else was happening in the economy, the investment bankers in the room, such as Lee Sachs, could not help but sink into delicious fantasies of how the banks would now be able to earn their way to health and beyond.

Romer shook her head. She had too much context to feel celebratory at this prospect.

"After all that happened over the past two months—much less the last ten years," she said, looking back, the idea that the shareholders and executives of Citigroup and other banks "might now get rich with the help of the U.S. government was just unconscionable."

Yale Law School was as impressive today, with its soaring Gothic spires, as it was on the first day Greg Fleming arrived in 1988, fresh off his undergraduate days at Colgate. Now, years later, with two kids and money in the bank, it impressed him as a place where he might rediscover his ethical moorings.

Three and a half months before, on January 1, Bank of America and Merrill shareholders had approved the bank's $50 billion purchase of the investment firm.

It was already being called the "deal from hell."

That price tag, of course, was only half the story. The buyout was supported by $118 billion in government backstops and an additional $20 billion negotiated in the brinksmanship—still largely opaque—between Ken Lewis and the team of Paulson and Bernanke in late December. Lewis pressed his case that Merrill's losses were worse than expected, and after the deal closed, a $15 billion loss was announced for Merrill, now Bank of America's largest division. This drew one round of lawsuits, followed by more, once revelations about Lewis's December ultimatums began to emerge, followed by a "good God, what's next" fear that crushed Bank of America's share price. By late January it had sunk by nearly 80 percent from where it was on Lehman weekend when the Merrill deal was hastily struck and signed, the handiwork of Greg Fleming.

By January, once the deal was inked, the key details, some of them unsavory, began to emerge in rough lockstep with the departures of senior Merrill executives, from John Thain, Merrill's CEO, to Fleming, the number two, and on down.

———

It was after all this, in late January, that word began to slip out—most likely from aggrieved Bank of America employees—about Merrill's last-minute bonuses of $3.6 billion, paid quickly before the brokerage firm changed hands.

Along with his invective about "shameful" practices, the president said that Wall Street should have the decency to "show some restraint."

The words about "shameful" practices and the need for restraint carried force, and stung Fleming. He liked the president and felt he was right: "It is a time for self-restraint," Fleming said, "for taming the 'animal spirits' of the street, and Washington is the only place with the power to make it happen."

Fleming thought often of his phone conversations with Obama from the New York restaurant in 2007. He knew he was now too controversial, as the man who sold Merrill, to merit an audience, but he daydreamed about how such a meeting might go, how he might help with that self-restraint by building a mix of barriers and incentives to get Wall Street refocused on fundamentals, on actually investing in the construction of a stronger American economy.

In fact, over the years, Fleming had built a strong case for how self-restraint might look—and it had cost him. He was paid $34 million in Merrill's bumper year of 2006, but then took no bonus in 2007—a year Merrill CEO Stan O'Neal was paid $161 million—and then nothing from that $3.6 billion bonus pool in 2008. On that last score, Fleming convinced Thain and two other top executives to also go without pay. That last act may have proved to be salvation for the Merrill team in the days after Obama's "shameful" comments, as the fur flew.

In early February, New York attorney general Andrew Cuomo's office, which began investigating the Merrill–Bank of America deal, had subpoenaed Thain—who'd made more headlines by revealing he'd spent more than $1 million redecorating his office. The details, including an $87,000 rug, were tabloid fodder, and he quickly reimbursed the money.

Fleming, who was up next, received a legal letter from Bank of America telling him, in essence, not to cooperate with Cuomo, and that eternal silence was part of his exit agreement. Fleming leaked the letter, thumbing his nose at Bank of America, and then showed up at Cuomo's office on March 9 for a long day of depositions. He felt he could testify, and that he should. He'd forgone tens of millions in bonuses in 2007 and 2008. He was trying now to redeem himself.

And then he vanished to Yale to start a new life.

"Having nothing to hide is going to cost you these days on Wall Street," he said. "And maybe that's part of what went wrong. Look, I'm no prince. I want to make money as much as the next guy. But things got to the point where acting prudently—or, God knows, ethically—got you slaughtered, left behind. It made you the tortoise in a race where the hares were getting paid by the yard. We've got to figure out a way to reward slow and steady, prudence and sure-footedness so, like in that old story, sometimes the tortoise eventually wins."

Part of the battle Obama faced in translating values he espoused in his Inaugural Address—of his desire to usher in "an era of responsibility"—was to change what he and others often called the "culture of Wall Street." The features of that culture had thoroughly permeated the wider American culture. Wall Street's stars were cultural icons. The Street was a destination for the top students graduating from the top colleges for nearly three decades. It was the epicenter of the quick-kill, winner-take-all, by-any-means-necessary ethic.

Fleming, walking the Yale campus, was testing the undertow of that culture and what it might take to break free of its pull.

Escaping the staccato beat of New York, and getting some distance from the past two years, was a first step. The second was having to field questions from law students who were disinterested parties. Some were merciless. He had a buffer; he taught the class with the help of another professor, and brought in others to be lightning rods: a steady procession of Wall Street players. They took the train two hours from New York to New Haven and, in class after class, sat for an hour of truth therapy before returning south.

Today, April 21, there was an array of lawyers and executives from top investment banks. The most consequential, and least imposing of them, was H. Rodgin Cohen, the managing partner of Sullivan & Cromwell. He was a small, soft-spoken man, but also the most powerful lawyer, deal maker, and consigliere in the financial industry. He had joined Sullivan & Cromwell out of Harvard Law School in 1970, become its chairman in 2000, and advised virtually every major bank in the United States and on Wall Street since.

At sixty-four he was hoping for a valedictory flourish to a storied career, with a few years as the deputy Treasury secretary. A Democrat, he had met Obama several times, liked him, given him money, and raised it. "Rodge" was getting close to retirement age at Sullivan; government would be a perfect fit. But last month it had become clear that his confirmation would turn troublesome. It wasn't so much what he had done, or how he'd profited from the past decade of Wall Street's excesses—which, of course, he had—as what he knew. That would be everything. He had advised *everyone*, and had often stood as the last counselor tapped before action. Under oath, he'd been asked about the AIG bonuses, Goldman's $13 billion counterparty payments, what Dick Fuld knew and when he knew it. Claiming lawyer-client privilege would have sounded like taking the Fifth Amendment. So he reluctantly withdrew.

But, sliding down in his chair in a lounge at Yale—students and other visiting Wall Street types crowded in from all directions—Rodge didn't weigh in, as expected, on ethical or moral issues. He was too concerned about the stress tests and too busy advising banks and his friends at Treasury about the perils and possibilities of their course.

"What's going to happen to banks if they are told they need to raise capital?" he proffered, in a reedy voice as soft and earnest as that of TV's Mr. Rodgers. "What will be the impact on a bank's stock price, its debt trading and counterparties?" These banks, he went on to say, will be able to say that if I can't raise capital on acceptable terms, I can turn to the government. But won't these banks be forced to move very quickly to raise capital at a time they are told they are capital deficient? The ultimate danger is that customers and counterparties will disengage, even if there is the assurance of government capital, because who wants to deal with a bank that has been deemed "weaker" than its peer institutions?

This was the position Wall Street had been pressing on Washington in the past two weeks. The government, Rodge said, "will be picking winners and losers," putting its stamp on strong versus weak. The ways this might affect Wall Street were indeed unique. With Chrysler or General Motors—with their tangible liquid assets, definable product lines, and measurable activities—the government's designation of healthy and unhealthy wouldn't make much difference. Stock prices might suffer, but vendor relationships, the key to most manufacturing, would stay intact.

Wall Street was different. The financial products sold by the Street were virtually all the same: commodities, essentially, offered in many flavors by what, at its core, was a kind of capital cartel. The way the firms made money was by building and breaking alliances within this cartel, to gain small advantages and make their menu look freshened and reshaped for clients and customers. When a firm stumbled, customers tended to wake up, snapping out of a trance, to recognize that the real item in this mix was their hard-earned money—not some firm's claim to magical properties that effortlessly turned money into more money. But having nowhere else to turn—that's the way cartels work—these customers would fearfully leap to another firm with the click of a wire transfer. The practical outcome: when the government tags one institution as weak, the others turn on it like piranhas.

Rodge thought all this over for a minute, doing the math.

"Another interesting part of the dynamic," he said, "is . . . not do you need capital, but how many others do as well? If you need it, and nineteen others also need it and take it, not so bad. But if only four or five take capital, it's much more of a winners-and-losers syndrome."

He is no doubt thinking about which of his clients, or other major banks, might fall in which category. Goldman and JPMorgan, for instance, could grow very strong feasting on four or five big banks that might be wounded by the government's vote of no confidence. In fact, both banks were already ahead of where they'd have been otherwise, having fed on the carcasses of Lehman, WaMu, Bear Stearns, and the others. That was why they were already starting to post stronger-than-expected profits.

But what about the weight of toxic assets? One of the students asked. Under pressure to post strong earnings and shore up their capital, won't it be hard for banks to clear away those toxic assets so they can start lending again? Will any of these actions really restore confidence?

"Under the best of circumstances," Rodge concluded, "I think it's optimistic to assume the stress tests will fully restore confidence in the banking industry. Banks must still deal with their toxic assets . . . that's what this whole PPIP thing is all about. The key question is: Will we be able to see clearing prices—prices at which investors are willing to buy the assets—where banks are capable of selling them without creating too large a capital hole?"

The answer to that was probably no. This was the untenable bottom line that Rodge, like those at Treasury he'd been talking with, was having to face. It was, in fact, the underlying problem of the PPIP, the Public-Private Investment Program, and the stress tests more generally. While banks may go out to raise money, there weren't incentives powerful enough, anywhere, for most of them to sell off toxic assets at rock-bottom prices, marking them to market, and then having to reduce the values of entire real estate portfolios—just like when a house sells for a low price in a neighborhood and, as a "comparable," pulls down appraised values up and down the street.

In Japan, banks wrote down the toxic assets at their own discretion—which meant slowly or not at all, even as they were pushed back to profitability by the government. The drag on their balance sheets hardened into a new normal, constraining the flow of credit for years. One of the points that Summers and Romer made in the big meeting on March 15 was, simply, if you give a public company an option, they'll tend to delay the pain rather than face it, especially when they can get all but free money from the Fed and push it into trading activities.

That dilemma would be left for another day. After two hours, Rodge and the others were on their way back to Wall Street. Fleming, too. He had a fund-raising dinner in New York that night—a gala to support New York's food banks, which were overcome with record numbers of hungry people, many of them newcomers to penury. The whole New York economy rested on the financial industry and the cash that had flowed from the pockets of those lucky enough to be part of the industry's bonanza. That the boom had been over for nearly a year meant that, up and down the line—from cooks to masseurs, caterers to the haberdashers—the city's providers of high-end goods and services were suffering.

The hope of the rest of the country—to get the large banks lending again—was not neatly aligned with the interests of New York, which was to get its banks to start earning money, by whatever means necessary.

Stopping by his office after the speech, Fleming was happy to be divorced from such bottom-line concerns. He said he'd begun talking to friends about starting "an institute to examine how to restore ethical standards to investing." He figured he could base it at Yale and continue to draw Wall Streeters north to discuss "how to make prudence sexy again." Not that he wasn't still logging hours on the cell phone to many of his old friends atop Wall Street. They'd come to New Haven to talk about what went wrong, about lessons learned, but they'd also talked with Fleming about Wall Street's hard, cut-to-the-marrow assessments of self-interest.

"What Rodge was really saying at the end is that it's optimistic—foolish, really—to think the banks will clear away what he calls those legacy assets. They'll never do it. There's too much of it, and in a down market the stuff is worthless.

"But even if they did, slowly across ten years, it won't cause them to start lending again, which is what real people in the real economy need. The big houses have too many other ways to make their money. They're going to do what's in their short-term interest, and lending out money into a soft market is not one of them."

He paused, stopping for a moment before getting into his modest car, kids' backpacks littering the seats. Fleming said the betting line from the inside players such as Rodge was that about half of the nineteen would pass the test, half wouldn't.

"Rodge is afraid right now, and so is the industry. That's why they're going down to Washington to try to keep the stress tests as easy as possible. Wall Street does 'greed' on its own; they don't need any help there.

The card in Washington's hand is fear; they still have it. They shouldn't give that card up unless they get a lot in return. In fact, anything they want. This is not personal or about some shared principle. It's about negotiating well. That's all Wall Street, and a lot of people out there, respect."

Then he jumped in his car and headed for downtown Manhattan, to eat caviar and prime rib and write a check to feed the homeless.

Two days later, Fleming's nemesis, Ken Lewis, was blanketing the news. The New York attorney general's office had released transcripts of Lewis's sealed testimony about how the government had bullied him in December to keep the Merrill deal intact, under threat of dismissal for him and his board, and then gave him another $20 billion in TARP funds. The news was explosive, entrancing the news cycles with a glimpse of this strange, secret dance between Washington and Wall Street. Both sides had operated under legal obligations to act in ways that were transparent and accountable on behalf respectively of voters and consumers. But with their shared goal of projecting confidence—with confidence itself being both end and means—transparency was seen as carrying unacceptable risks. As the fears of September 2008 finally began to dissipate, readers and viewers tuning in to the case were treated to a tour of the shadow land where powerful impressions were manufactured. In a key passage that roiled the news cycles, Lewis told Cuomo's investigators that he had been pressured by Paulson to keep silent about the deepening financial distress inside Merrill.

Q: *Were you instructed not to tell your shareholders what the transaction was going to be?*

A: *I was instructed that "We do not want a public disclosure."*

Q: *Who said that to you?*

A: *Paulson.*

Q: *Had it been up to you would you [have] made the disclosure?*

A: *It wasn't up to me.*

Q: *Had it been up to you?*

A: *It wasn't.*

With actions gamed for their effect, rather than the harder accountability that comes with transparency, the tough-minded decisiveness at
the center of both good governance and sound business gets subtly corrupted.

With Lewis's disclosures now in sunlight, Fleming was receiving calls
nonstop.

Of course, in Cuomo's investigation—officially probing the $3.6 bil-
lion in Merrill bonuses—Lewis testified after Thain and before Fleming.
Back in his office at Yale, Fleming offered a view, from the very inside of
the controversial deal, starting with the "material adverse change" clause.

"It's by no means clear that if we had a 'material adverse change' that
they could exercise their rights under that clause. The clause is extremely
complicated and wasn't negotiated well enough. And it's a Merrill-
specific clause. What happened in October, November, and December was much more than Merrill-specific. The world went to hell after
Lehman went down. So there wasn't anything held back in diligence.
Paulson and Geithner made the greatest mistake. The biggest mistake
that was made, in spite of how hard they tried, was letting Lehman fail.

"The clause protects Merrill because [its] problems would need to be
disproportionate. But the whole industry was in turmoil so it could claim
to not be Merrill-specific."

Then Fleming took it another step, putting on his deal hat.

"I don't know why Lewis pushed to do this, didn't turn around and
say [to Paulson], 'Okay, I'm going to do this, but I need to renegotiate and then I need the SEC or somebody to agree on some expedited
revote.' I mean, you had the government at the table! I'm just amazed
that [Lewis] didn't come back and try to renegotiate."

This was a fine rendition of why, several centuries ago, governments
decided to pass laws about the fair and legal conduct of commerce—
and then get the hell out of the way. This was a dispute between two
companies and their shareholders, for better or for worse. The assertion
that "too big to fail" means "too big to exist"—soon to be voiced at a
congressional hearing by a penitent Alan Greenspan—rested on an underlying principle that government shouldn't find itself "at the table," in
Fleming's apt rendering, having to cut deals with banks it couldn't afford
to let fail. Then deal points become destiny, with banks gaining, or losing, competitive advantages based on how successfully they managed

their negotiations with a public entity—a model that undermined the government's fundamental role as defender of practices and principles. Instead, it had become a case-by-case negotiator, with a bank's survival as the only hard-and-fast goal.

That afternoon, April 23, Barack Obama strolled into his Cabinet Room.

Waiting for him were the elite of Congress. Sitting around the huge mahogany table was the Democratic leadership of both the House and the Senate, along with the Republican leadership of both bodies. They were there to discuss the budget, which had been a steadily growing issue, starting in late winter.

Obama's needs were great, but as budgets always command, there were limits.

The huge financial obligations the United States had taken on during the Bush era were now colliding with the crises and diminished tax revenues left to his successor. The audacious agenda assumed by Obama had also meant enormous costs—most of them projected and yet to hit the balance sheet. The TARP fund for repairing the financial system still had, thankfully, $350 billion in it. But that figure was overwhelmed by Obama's $787 billion stimulus package and the combination of rising unemployment benefits and declining tax receipts from the ongoing recession. Tax receipts had in fact flattened in early 2008, just as costs began to dramatically rise. The cost of the war in Iraq was now diminishing, but Afghanistan was more expensive—a wash. Health care costs continued to rise as the population aged and more people moved onto the Medicaid rolls in a depressed economy. The outcome was that the government's expenses were running $1.2 trillion ahead of its revenues for 2009, a number that was sure to continue to grow until the fiscal year's end on September 30. A version of these hard facts was revealed in late February, when the White House released its preliminary budget for 2010. Since then, in the traditional manner of budgetary brinksmanship, the White House's budget had been matched, mirrored, and contested by budgets in both the House and Senate.

Everyone knew audacity wouldn't be cheap, even with Obama's pledges to remain fiscally prudent. There were grand plans in the budget, of course, led by a request for another $750 billion in additional

TARP funds for bailing out and restructuring the financial system and, of course, health care reform, with $650 billion penciled in. On the latter score, Orszag had special advantages. Models he had been working on since he was CBO director in 2007—largely accepted by the current CBO regime—showed that the government's efforts to use Dartmouth's "comparative effectiveness" findings and similar data could both improve care and save costs. Up to a point. When the CBO scored Obama's overall budget in late March, the projections weren't good: a deficit, over ten years, of $2.3 trillion more than the administration had predicted. Beyond that, the Obama administration had committed itself to a deficit cap of 3 percent of GDP, a level that the CBO felt would be exceeded every year until 2019, when it would be 5.7 percent.

Much would be unaffordable, and this meant new scrutiny on the cost of health care reform and the soundness—or "scoreability"—of its financial projections by independent analysts and, ultimately, by the Congressional Budget Office. The prospects were not good.

What the administration was finding, Orszag and others recalled, were the distinctions between campaign talk and governance. You could say all sorts of things during a campaign. In government there was a system—albeit an imperfect one—to "price" expectations, and equally to negotiate, in a step-by-step process, the new laws of the land.

That was what the leaderships of the House and Senate were poised to discuss in the Cabinet Room, and they did so without much headway. The parties were seriously divided. The Republicans were starting to call this the most liberal, big-spending budget in decades. It was a "third wave" of progressivism, said their fiscal guru, Congressman Paul Ryan, to follow FDR's New Deal and LBJ's Great Society. The Democrats, though, still had the leverage. If there was Republican intransigence in the Senate, they could pass the bill through "reconciliation," a provision in which bills pertaining to the budget can be stripped of nonessential features and passed with a simple majority, rather than with the new normal—driven by creative uses of the filibuster—of 60 votes.

Around they went, until a frustrated Obama improvised. Passing this prebudget resolution, a nonbinding next step in the process, he said, "has got to be a bipartisan process. I think we all need to give." Blank stares from around the room. This was just the traditional partisan push and shove. You eventually found some midpoint and nudged the pieces forward on the board. It had been going on since Hamilton and Jefferson. "As a matter of fact," he continued, "here's an example: I think Democrats need to give up on medical malpractice. As an indication of my good faith, I'm willing to put that on the table."

But this was the table marked "budget." Medical malpractice was a completely different debate—conducted in an entirely different realm—about the nature of health care reform. The admirable idea of trading the sacred cow of medical malpractice, considering how strongly the Democrats were supported by the country's trial lawyers, for a sacred cow on the Republican side was the kind of grand bargain that might take a few weeks or months of secret, cross-party meetings. Though this group represented the congressional leadership, most of those here were not their party's point players on health care reform.

This time Obama filled the space and the silence.

"Okay, now, what are you giving?" he challenged the puzzled Republicans. "What is your reciprocal 'give' here?"

Not one person said a thing. One of the participants later said the moment was "odd and surprising, like a scene from that movie *Dave*," where a man off the street suddenly winds up as president. Once the silence had become intolerable, an agitated Obama wrapped things up: "Look, guys, this is making my case. You talk about bipartisanship. Well, I just laid down a very tough deal, and not one of you responded with a similar concession. Bipartisanship is a two-way street!"

Some of what was driving Obama's improvisations was that, unbeknownst to the public, he still wasn't sure what sort of policy he actually wanted as the "top priority" of his presidency. If Obama had indeed created "a space where solutions can happen" at the Health Care Summit six weeks before, it was by now clear, to one and all, that there'd been little forward motion to show since then.

Losing Tom Daschle in early February was a blow that the White House had yet to recover from. With his wide array of skills, a long history in Washington, and a close bond with Obama, Daschle would have been ideally suited to direct the health care battle. After former Kansas governor Kathleen Sebelius was picked to take Daschle's intended place, heading the Department of Health and Human Services, Nancy-

Ann DeParle was hired, on March 2, to lead the initiative from inside the White House. Obama's idea was that they would work as a team. But the result, even after DeParle's arrival, was that no one was in charge. Orszag, arguably the White House's leading expert in this area, had his hands full running OMB and attending each day's morning economic briefings. Nonetheless, he protested to Emanuel in an e-mail: *Listen, I can't run health care, but someone needs to.*

But on Obama's desk this week was a seven-page memo from De-Parle to help the president decide where he ought to stand on the seminal issue of health care. DeParle, a soft-spoken, Tennessee-bred Rhodes Scholar who, under Clinton, had run the Health Care Financing Administration—the entity that oversees vast federal outlays to Medicare and Medicaid, and is now called the Centers for Medicare & Medicaid Services—wasn't the type to meaningfully challenge Orszag or Summers at the conference table. She was a tough-minded expert with very specific opinions. She was respectful of the Dartmouth data that so enlivened Obama and Orszag. But having been a board member for various health care industry firms, she understood how the mountains of stunning data about "comparative effectiveness" built around the Wennberg Variation, of better care at lower cost, were still seen as a declaration of war by most health care providers.

While Obama, and certainly Orszag, seemed ready to fight that war, DeParle's focus was on the lynchpin calculations involved in insurance reform. She directed Obama's attention to the only working model for reform in the country: Massachusetts, whose health care overhaul bill passed in 2005 under a brokered deal between then-governor Mitt Romney and the state's Democratic legislature. Those who viewed the Massachusetts plan as already a compromise of principles, including Ted Kennedy, pointed out that the model—of an individual mandate, where citizens were required to purchase health insurance; of insurance exchanges, where they could choose from a wide array of policy options; and of government support for those who couldn't manage the cost of premiums—had been the "market-driven" Republican position during the Clinton initiative in 1993 and for the decade to follow. What's more, the centerpiece of that program, the individual mandate, was something Obama had drawn up short of endorsing during the campaign, much to the ire of Hillary Clinton, who called him "all talk, no action" on health care.

Now, DeParle, in her memo, stressed that Obama should embrace a plan much like that in Massachusetts, driven by the teeth of a mandate, where individuals would be fined for not having health insurance. Obama, never much for the mandate, was concerned about legal challenges to it but was impressed by DeParle's coverage numbers. Without the mandate, the still-sketchy Obama plan would leave twenty-eight million Americans uninsured; with the mandate, the estimates of the number left uninsured were well below ten million. But the mandate, with its various features, was expensive, adding an estimated $287 billion across ten years to the total cost.

Which is why at the budget meeting on the twenty-third—and in the weeks to come—Obama was looking for lightning-strike gains on cost, such as tort reform. DeParle's focus, like that of the Massachusetts plan itself, was on expanding coverage: how to get everyone in the tent. Obama had often said to Orszag that he believed coverage and cost needed to walk abreast—in an integrated, mutually supportive way—if health care were to work. But this week, as he found himself persuaded by DeParle's plan, he already saw how coverage would edge ahead of cost in the ordering of priorities.

———

The next morning, over at the Treasury Department, Tim Geithner was wild with single-mindedness: "I don't want even one molecule of energy spent on anything other than the stress tests!"

In the large conference room near Geithner's office, Treasury's senior staff looked on, wondering what'd gotten into him. He was never one for locker room speeches, even when a motivational moment arose.

"Actually, I believe energy is measured in 'ergs,'" quipped Krueger, to fill the awkward silence.

"Okay, then," Geithner shrugged. "Not one erg of energy."

His point was clear to all: Treasury had staked everything—including, quite possibly, Geithner's job as secretary—on the stress tests. Not much had worked up to now, from Geithner's clumsy explanation in February of how the rest of the TARP funds would be applied to, in March, the handling of the AIG bonus scandal.

Treasury desperately needed to appear, at long last, as if they could meet this period's crises like professionals, with matters firmly under control.

Friday, April 24, was the official start of that crucible, with the public debut of the stress tests. After living through a series of backroom deals from last fall that had blown up in his face by spring, Geithner was ever more convinced that the stress tests needed to be kept in sunlight. This was far from an issue of consensus. Bernanke and the Fed had recommended that they be kept confidential, just as they had pushed to keep secret how AIG allocated its bailout money, and—still successfully—which banks needed to rely on Fed funds and guarantees. But the distinct institutional mandates of Treasury and the Fed—the former operating under the direct, day-to-day mandates of a duly elected president; the latter, sometimes called the "fourth branch" of government, designed to support the banking system and manage monetary policy with little public oversight—were now creating regular complications in their many joint efforts to right the economy. As public outrage grew about the alliances between Washington and Wall Street, the Fed's tradition of concealment drew deepening suspicion. Even Bernanke had to acknowledge this. Geithner's position—that the markets would respond to the stress tests' findings only if they were at least as transparent as a bond rating agency—ultimately prevailed, though it meant his tests would have to be cleverly constructed not to reveal their many sub-rosa calculations, even under intense scrutiny.

As the official administrator of the stress tests, it was the Fed's role today to offer a lengthy set of descriptions about the standards of measure for determining the soundness of the top nineteen banks, the first round of the process.

But by morning most of those yardsticks had already emerged.

There had been a steady succession of leaks across the preceding week. Each made news, creating enormous interest in the "stress tests," a quick-fire phrase that was fast seeping into common speech. Coverage of what they were, and what they might show, now spread far beyond the business pages to columnists, pundits, and CNBC alerts.

Around town, managers of the marketplace of ideas were duly impressed.

George Stephanopoulos, the former senior adviser to President Clinton who hosted ABC's *This Week*, complimented Stephanie Cutter, Treasury's spokeswoman, on what a brilliant job Treasury had done with "those targeted leaks." Cutter reported this to her bosses, who immediately saw the irony: they'd been bitterly complaining all week about the leaks, which they were sure were coming from sources in Sheila Bair's office and the FDIC.

Bair seemed to be everywhere. At the end of March, two days before Obama met with the thirteen bankers, the Kennedy Library named Born and Bair as the year's Profile in Courage Award winners. The citation noted that "Sheila Bair and Brooksley Born recognized that the financial security of all Americans was being put at risk by the greed, negligence and opposition of powerful and well-connected interests . . . The catastrophic financial events of recent months have proved them right. Although their warnings were ignored at the time, the American people should be reassured that there are far-sighted public servants at all levels of government who act on principle to protect the people's interests."

A moan could be heard that day from Geithner's office. Officially placing Bair in the company of the already celebrated Born—the brilliant and soft-spoken Jeremiah, a decade back, of a coming derivatives crisis—would only serve to embolden the FDIC chief.

But when it came to controlling information, there was one area in which Geithner's office had been successful. Key disclosures of what actually happened in the March 15 "showdown" never leaked. Bair didn't know, and never found out, that the president had been trying to push forward what the FDIC chairwoman was recommending. He wasn't successful, either.

———

Alan Krueger later speculated that one reason Treasury may have dragged its feet on constructing a plan for Citigroup's resolution was Sheila Bair. They would have had to consult the FDIC chairwoman. After all, her agency is in the business of closing banks.

"The fear was that Sheila would leak it," Krueger said, in a comment echoed by others at Treasury. "And there'd be a run on Citi."

He added that this may have been one of many reasons: "It was more than just that. The bottom line is Tim and others at Treasury felt the president didn't fully understand the complexities of the issue, or simply that they were right and he was wrong, and that trying to resolve Citi and then other banks would have been disastrous."

Krueger, though not involved in the Citigroup debate, was due to have lunch that very day with someone uniquely suited to edify him about the resolution of troubled banks: Anders Borg, the Swedish finance minister.

Borg was in town with other finance ministers of the G20, the world's twenty largest economies, for a meeting at the World Bank. Of course, Sweden was the country that Obama said in many meetings he wanted to emulate.

At Equinox, a tony restaurant three blocks north of the White House that had become the destination of choice for lobbyists and their expense accounts, Krueger had Borg run through what Sweden did in 1991, when its financial system collapsed in the midst of an economic crisis, and what they had learned.

Borg, a tall, square-jawed father of three with a short ponytail, an earring, and a dark-suited seriousness, described how Sweden first supported the banks with infusions of cash. In fact, there were two bailouts of this type, supporting the banks and encouraging them to work out their problems and earn their way back to health. This didn't work.

Borg said they were careful about managing the banks' incentives. "You don't want to make the wrong things conditional," he said. In Sweden, the government decided how and when the banks, once they'd emerged from receivership, would pay back the government money. In many cases, the Swedish government retained equity control for a few years until they were certain the banks were truly healthy and stable. In the United States, he noted, the banks were paying back the TARP money as fast as they could even if it meant engaging in behaviors similar to what had gotten them into the crisis, just to wriggle free of the limits on compensation. "The compensation is an issue, but it shouldn't be related to the need for government support and control," he said. "They're separate issues."

He and Krueger discussed compensation issues—how to bring more serious regulation to payouts in the banking system, such as longer-term incentives and "clawback" provisions—and Borg said it was an ongoing problem, something he was working on even as they spoke.

In fact, Borg and former Swedish finance officials were in regular demand since the fall of 2008, when Bo Lundgren, Sweden's minister for fiscal and financial affairs during the 1991 crisis, met with investment bankers and regulators in New York. Obama's recent framing of "let's be like Sweden, not Japan" was becoming a widely embraced analysis in both Europe and the United States.

But by dessert the conversation had shifted from the causes of economic crises in Sweden and America, a bloated and then collapsed financial system, to the lasting effects of economic distress and rising unemployment. During its banking crisis, Sweden's unemployment rate tripled, from 3 percent to 9 percent, in just over a year.

U.S. employers, feeling a pronounced drop in overall demand, were cutting payrolls dramatically, Krueger said, maybe even more than the drop in demand would merit. Some data showed they were "using it as an opportunity to reduce costs," he said, with layoffs as well as wage reductions. Germany, Krueger mentioned, was busy creating tax incentives for employers to keep workers. Yes, Borg agreed, the Germans were indeed acting swiftly, "but we do it differently in Sweden." He described how strong unemployment benefits in Sweden actually freed employers to regularly lay off workers based on merit, job performance, or changes in corporate priorities or direction. Although the social safety net was strong and well funded, there was a social stigma for the able-bodied not to work in Sweden, and the unemployment rate, while not low—it had averaged a respectable 5.3 percent over the past thirty years—was weighted toward short-timers. Borg explained how people didn't like to be nonproductive, and there was no point adding possible destitution to that equation. "What we find is that the people who are fired are the ones who are soon out starting new businesses."

On the way back to Treasury, Krueger thought about this last twist, an inversion of the American model where limited unemployment benefits, usually capped at twenty-six weeks, were believed to stoke the urgency to find new employment—a ticking clock that got louder as the weeks passed.

An eminent economist he knew well, Peter Diamond, from MIT, had for years been short-listed for a Nobel for his work with another economist on the unemployed, especially data that seemed to show that the out-of-work tended to kick into high gear, often finding jobs, right as their unemployment benefits were due to end. These findings had been crucial to the way politicians and public policy experts had for years viewed the unemployed as responsive to desperation.

The previous spring, while still at Princeton, Krueger launched one of the most ambitious unemployment studies in recent years: a plan to assess six thousand unemployed workers in New Jersey, using breakthroughs in behavioral economics to show how their emotional and rational architecture shifted across their full span of joblessness. The study was designed to yield insights into how best to treat the jobless, for both their own long-term well-being and that of the larger economy. After a year of deliberation, New Jersey gave it the green light. Of course, when Krueger first proffered the study in March 2008, unemployment was below 5 percent.

It was just now becoming clear inside the administration's upper reaches that the jobless rate—predicted by Romer, when the stimulus plan was being designed in December, to go no higher than 8 percent for 2009—would clearly rise above that estimate.

How high would it go? Orszag and Summers, who've both called Krueger the top labor economist in the United States, were already turning to him for a prediction, as well as for recommendations about what to do.

But Krueger, walking from the restaurant, was thinking more about the broad issues discussed at lunch, the larger decisions a society makes that shape its character.

Sweden, after two bailout attempts, and billions of kronor being passed to its banks, made a choice that those who had created the financial crisis, who happened already to be the winners in that society, should not be kept whole and pushed toward a next round of profits by the government. Instead, the Swedes expanded benefits to match a trebling in the ranks of the jobless, restructured the banks—bringing a measure of pain that killed off speculation as a business model—and quickly earned a kind of confidence that they didn't have during the boom and bubble of the late 1980s. What did the government's tough-love decision do to the psyches of two out of every three jobless Swedes who lost employment because of a burst investment bubble? It had to be good, Krueger felt, and indeed Sweden's jobless rate fell swiftly from that peak of 9 percent. But America, with its diversity and boldness and headlong verve, wasn't much like Sweden.

Decisions about closing banks, Krueger ultimately felt, were not just about economic calculations. They were about moral choice.

"We lost the country with those AIG bonuses," he said later, and we never won them back. "I think the president was trying to win it back" by considering how to break up some of the biggest banks. In an hour, at 2:30 p.m., the ingeniously designed stress tests—a kind of federal rating agency whose judgments, if acted on by investors, would be backed by an implicit government guarantee—were to be unveiled. Krueger was sure they'd raise a lot of capital for the banks, but at some point the government would still need to step in.

In the meantime, he said, he was thinking about "how many jobless there would soon be and who will be lobbying for them."

When Obama took on three great challenges at once—the economic crisis, financial restructuring, and health care reform—it seemed no one had the temerity to say, "Mr. President, any one of those three would be more than enough to challenge a new president with so little executive experience."

The person who might have done that was not in the administration. He was in his Washington law office, on April 27, saying things he had planned to say to his friend Barack Obama in his role as president.

Tom Daschle was back in a lobbying capacity at Alston & Bird. He knew he'd messed up his taxes, which had meant withdrawing his nomination for the HHS job in early February. Daschle's sins were mostly accounting errors—the IRS was not much interested—but the penalty levied would be stiff: having to watch his nemesis, Max Baucus, move to center stage on health care reform, a move the Montana senator had executed with such force that he might well end up leading the whole town.

Even before the March 5 summit, Baucus was on the move, preempting Obama. Calling Geithner into a Finance Committee hearing on March 4 to talk about funding options to fill Obama's budgetary placeholder of $650 billion for a health care overhaul, Baucus offered proposals from his own "Call to Action" blueprint, and remarked that "the Director of the Office of Management and Budget [Orszag] said that the path to economic recovery is through health care reform. I agree, and I'm pleased that the president's budget addresses reform as an American imperative. This budget makes a good pitch for a down payment on health care reform," he added, but "my concern, frankly, is the viability of the down payment and how it will help Congress contain the costs associated with reforming the health care system."

Daschle, meanwhile, was prepping Obama for his upcoming debut at the summit.

"How do you force the hospitals and doctors and insurers to come together?" Daschle recalled Obama asking him in the prep session. Daschle said he told the president to "talk about American resiliency and *dare*," his voice rose, "somebody to oppose him and DARE"—now the volume was up—"somebody to not be patriotic. He needs to do it first before it gets framed for him!"

Of course, Obama didn't do that.

"He performed admirably," Daschle acceded, "but the problem is that he hasn't been much on follow-through since. And it's gone dead and stale. The only thing he's got is a bunch of people on record that said at the thirty-thousand-foot level they are for it." Daschle has an ability to distill Washington politics into beautiful metaphors, and his airplane analogy is spot-on.

"I look at it in terms of altitude. At the thirty-thousand level everyone is for it. You drop down to twenty-thousand level and you start to see people peel off; by ground level you are alone. That's inevitable. Unless you force them."

Meanwhile, Baucus was working his ground forces, framing the debate. Just a few days before, on April 23, he had launched a series of roundtable "workshops" in his committee room that were drawing overflow crowds, media coverage, and some ire—especially from "single-payer" proponents, who were concerned that Baucus would not be including their voice or proposals in his heavily attended colloquies.

Baucus was also speaking the language of bipartisanship—music, Daschle knew, to Obama's ears. Once an instrumental supporter of Bush's tax cuts, Baucus claimed close relationships with the more moderate Republicans, with whom he was largely indistinguishable on many issues. In this case, Daschle stressed, bipartisanship was a false god.

"I would say you aren't going to get any Republicans," he said. "It's going to be driven largely by the Democrats. I just don't see anyone willing to stay with it. The four or five most likely participants are Chuck Grassley [R-Iowa], just because he and Baucus are so close, Bob Bennett [R-Colo.], because he's worked the issue so long, Mike Enzi [R-Wyo.], because he and Kennedy worked together. And the last two are Collins and Snowe [both R-Maine], but they don't bring anyone with them."

Over ten minutes, he ticked off razor-sharp profiles of his fellow Democrats, from North Dakota's Kent Conrad, the budget committee chair and deficit hawk; to Baucus's fellow Democrat from conservative Montana, Jon Tester; to Virginia's Jim Webb, the pugnacious former navy secretary; and a half dozen others, with what it would take to get them all in line and locked in.

Then the voice of the famously even-tempered Daschle started to quicken, like he was watching a party barge headed for a waterfall.

"But they need to be on the offensive. If they aren't, we lose. Even if it's just the Democrats—all those Democratic swing votes that in a heartbeat will oppose this if it looks like [Obama] is in a defensive posture.

"We could live with failure in '94 or '93, and we could live with it now. But we're going to pay a much higher price for failure this time than we did back then, in terms of cost quality and access. The price of failure keeps going up," he said, in a mirror image of what his protégé said at the summit. But Obama saw the deepening medical cost crisis as nudging the providers toward consensus. Daschle dispatched that swiftly: more to lose, an existential struggle for providers, deeper intransigence. "In some ways, the problems of consensus building become even more difficult as these problems become more severe."

Counterintuitive, but incisive. A tenor of insight that you'd hear only in the advanced class on health care reform, and the kind of advice Obama wasn't getting, certainly not from Daschle. Daschle hadn't spoken to Obama in any meaningful way for seven weeks, since that pre-summit prep session. It had been perhaps the most important month in fifteen years for health care reform—the Democrats' perennial cause and Daschle's passion—and Obama's longtime mentor was on the outside looking in, his nose pressed to the glass.

This left Daschle perplexed and anxious. His attentiveness to Obama was without boundaries. Friends of Daschle's, who wondered if there'd been some sort of breach, got pushback from other wise men around town. Obama wasn't returning any of their calls. And it seemed that Emanuel, as he tightened control around Obama, was the heavy. "He convinced Obama that 'all Rahm, all the time' was all he needed," said one longtime Washington manager. "Obama didn't know how things were supposed to work, and Emanuel, running in every direction, wasn't going to tell him."

But there may have been more to it, something more personal. Having presided over Obama's formation, Daschle understood exactly what Obama knew and didn't know, and what he had yet to learn—and that's not always the person you want to see before you step onstage to meet unreasonable expectations.

That deep knowledge is a blessing and a curse, and hearing Podesta's elegant rendering of how Obama draws people out and creates a "space where solutions can happen," Daschle paused, thinking it over. Yes, Podesta—another, if slightly lesser, Obama expert—had spoken the truth. But Daschle, speaking today with rare candor, spun it. "I'm seeing glimpses of that." He explained that in the campaign "I saw a man who listened. Sometimes people misunderstood that listening as an acquiescence to their point of view" and that, as president, on health care and other issues, "I think that same approach is happening on a larger scale. And again I think people are confusing that. I think what needs to happen is he needs to be very engaged. It really does require constant vigilance so that we can come to closure on some of these things."

Of course, Daschle had no idea that Obama had, that very week, embraced DeParle's Massachusetts-like plan, nudging his grand initiative away from actual health *care* reform—and with it Daschle's longtime passions for reforming the medical delivery system and reining in costs through government-forced efficiencies—and inexorably toward health *insurance* reform.

All the same, he knew, as few others could, how overwhelmed Obama was at this point, and how "he's got ten wars at once. But that's part of leadership: he's gotta sort it out. If he wants health care to be part of his legacy, he's gotta do it. Pay the dues. I know all of these other things are important, but in the next four or five months it's going to be worth it to the country if we focus and stay on the offensive. Because he only has a short window."

A fully animated Daschle was now almost pleading.

"He doesn't have the luxury of coming back to this a year from now."

NOWHERE MAN

Wslew of jilted economists. The group was characterized largely by progressive, Keynesian thinkers, who soon enough began to question whether the stimulus was sufficient, and who launched forward from there in a wide expanse of op-eds, lectures, and interviews assessing and criticizing the president's first one hundred days.

With that milepost just two days away, Obama, on the evening of April 27, invited this Greek chorus of the noisy and moderately disaffected for a dinner at the White House.

For most in this group, a call from the White House, any call, was something to pine for; when it came, they tended to drop everything. Especially Joseph Stiglitz. Generally uninvolved during the campaign, the Nobel-winning economist hadn't heard a peep since Obama became president. His wife, phoned in her Pilates class that morning by Summers's assistant, managed to get the message to Joe—arguably the world's most cited economist—by midafternoon, just in time for him to jump on a train to D.C.

For most of the others, the invites were a bit more decorous—coming a week ahead—and at 7:00 p.m. they gathered around the curve of a table in the residence. A Mensa murderers' row: Stiglitz; Harvard's Ken Rogoff, a specialist in the history of financial collapse; Jeffrey Sachs, Columbia University's globe-trotting guru of globalism; and Paul Krugman, whose daily blog and twice-weekly columns on the *New York Times* editorial page were quickly becoming the platform for a progressive government-in-exile. Across the table were Summers, Geithner, and Romer, protectively clustered around the president. Of course, all the economists knew one another. Krugman, Summers, and Sachs, in fact, were once graduate students together at MIT, where they had to work out the mathematical proof of how three people can each be the smartest person in a room at the very same instant.

Over roast beef and salad, with lettuce that Michelle had grown in the White House's organic indoor garden, they carried on a somewhat tamer, private corollary of a conversation that had been conducted in public for months. This was early, though. Questions—what exactly was Obama thinking?—had started to harden into criticisms only in the past month or so, following the AIG bonus scandal, revelation of the billions in counterparty payments, the unconvincing surprise and then outrage voiced by both Obama and Geithner (who said that he didn't remember much about the bonuses), and the announcement of the coming stress tests.

Several of the economists had all but foretold the financial crisis and felt they'd not been given due credit or, at the very least, thought their precognition earned them the privilege of an audience with the president. The issue of credit was especially acute for Stiglitz. His Nobel, awarded in 2001, was for his work showing how markets can spin out of control when "imperfect information" is shared unequally by parties to a transaction, often giving an unfair advantage to one participant. This is, more or less, the business plan for much of the subprime and derivatives market. Or, in Stiglitz's words, "Globalization opened up opportunities to find new people to exploit their ignorance. And we found them."

But at dinner, the famously acerbic Columbia professor was polite, happy to see Obama again in the flesh, making his points about why the stimulus should have been significantly larger, closer to $2 trillion, to fill the hole in the economy caused by the great crash. That comported with Romer's number about the size of the downdraft back in December, which was what brought her to the original estimate of $1.2 trillion, deriving from the view that each $1.00 of stimulus results in about $1.50 of GDP growth.

Rogoff was putting the finishing touches on a book with University of Maryland professor Carmen Reinhardt called *This Time Is Different: Eight Centuries of Financial Folly*, which looked at the remarkable similarities between bubbles and busts in sixty-six countries across centuries. He described the pattern over the roast beef: politicians ease regulations governing the financial system, which frees banks to use that latitude to lend and borrow money to crank up profits, which draws foreign investors and their cash to the exuberant country, which creates bubbles in commodities or real estate or stocks. Rogoff, on a darker note, mentions data on the aftermath of "financial crisis recessions," and how often policy makers overlook this one particular difference—a real one—in estimating how long and hard a recovery may be. Such estimates were not fully factored in the projections the administration made in December.

But this was Obama's show, and he moved around the table calling on people—Summers and Sachs, then Geithner, then Krugman—sometimes referring back to one of them and what they'd said. He said he mostly wanted to hear from his guests but spoke a bit himself, talking about his urgent desire to help the economy and the financial system, but defaulting to the position of Summers (mostly) and Geithner (always) that "my first principle, is to do no harm."

He then offered, to one and all, his most compelling "good listener" look—the thing that Daschle noted—and, as they spoke, the economists struggled to detect whether they'd gotten through to him, and if he seemed to be agreeing with any of what they'd said. One "yes, you're right!" and maybe the might of government would find a new direction.

That didn't happen. But all of a sudden there was a ruckus, and in loped Paul Volcker, short of breath and mumbling about how long he'd sat on the tarmac in New York. Axelrod, who'd taken Volcker's chair when he didn't show, leapt up, and the giant Volcker slipped in just in time for dessert. Still puffing, he said nothing, and the president continued his rounds, well along into a second loop.

Obama's Socratic approach left one participant feeling slighted. Romer, the sole female economist, reached down for her purse, took out a business card, and scribbled, "Either he acknowledges me soon or I'm leaving." She passed it under the table to Summers, sitting next to her. She knew every one of the economists here. She had sat on panels with them, had spoken at testimonials for some of them, and she might as well have been serving them the food. Summers, who could do his math as well as Romer—they'd run in the same circles for twenty years—read the note and passed it along under the table to Geithner, who read it himself, and then waited for a moment to pass it to Obama.

"Let's see now, Christy," the president said lightly, a moment later. "We haven't heard from you yet."

Romer cooled down quickly, invisibly, and after a moment she queried Krugman, an old friend, about Japan. He had written a column about how Japan, like the United States, had gone to zero interest rates. She knew that the president still felt there was no way to get more bang out of monetary policy, considering that rates couldn't go below zero, and now she egged Paul on to explain that if a fear of inflation can be created, people will expand borrowing at the same low rates, thinking that zero rates won't last much longer. Of course, this is what Romer had explained to the president in her job interview, after he'd surprised her with his opening line that there was little left to do on monetary policy with interest rates at nearly zero. She'd briefed him otherwise. He didn't seem to have retained it.

"That's very interesting, Paul," Obama said, looking with rapt fascination at the contrarian, and a suggestion of policy filled the room.

Two months before, Summers might not have thought to pass Romer's note along, but her grievance, along with those of other senior women, had recently spilled into the open. There was a nascent gender struggle in the White House. The women, Romer included, were tired of preparing for group meetings and watching the men talk to one another. Obama seemed to favor the men—especially Summers and Emanuel—and not the strong and accomplished women sitting nearby.

If Romer appeared to lead what one top official called "the women's movement," it may have been because of the added burdens of her regular exposure to Summers.

Two months earlier, after several key economic meetings from which she was excluded, Romer had gone to Emanuel's office saying she'd have none of it. He assured her she'd be included from that point forward and not have her access to key meetings or to the president interrupted. But many days there were issues. Summers seemed to take joy in trying to humiliate her in the morning economic briefing. "Sometimes it seemed like he was trying to make her lose her composure, and a few times he definitely succeeded," said someone who came to the morning briefs. "The president had a kind of 'now, now, Larry, be nice' response, which seemed to make Christy even angrier."

After one meeting, she stormed out of the Oval Office, letting out an audible gasp of distress in the hallway. Said one observer present: "Whether or not the president heard her, he didn't react."

When a task would come up, Obama would almost reflexively say, "'Tim and Larry will handle that, always Larry and Tim,'" Romer later recalled, "and I sort of wondered, aren't I supposed to be the third leg of the stool?'"

Romer went to Valerie Jarrett, who had recently hosted a dinner for Romer with the First Lady and a few other women on the senior staff.

Jarrett told her that Obama's inner circle during the campaign was mostly men and that, with more women in top positions in the White House, the women's issues were "something we'd have to work through."

It was soon clear that it wasn't just Romer. The president had hired an array of strong-willed, accomplished women who felt the same way Romer did: ignored. Jarrett, one of the few West Wingers who had actual executive experience, started a women's group and opened lines of communication. Soon the complaints started to build. Many focused on Emanuel and Summers, both notoriously brusque, but even more abrupt and dismissive with women, several of the female staffers complained. There was a roundelay of lunches and dinners between several of the women and Larry and Rahm. When Orszag heard his name might have come up, for being dismissive to Nancy-Ann DeParle, he engaged as well.

Orszag, while sympathetic to the concerns of Romer and the other women, added another interpretation: "I think part of the problem was the lines of organization were so jumbled from the start that no one was quite sure of their role, or what they were supposed to be doing. What is the economic team? What is the health care team? What's our financial reform team? Often people weren't sure where they were supposed to be, who was leading some initiative, who should be included or not, consulted or not."

On the morning of May 7, Obama walked with a small contingent from the Oval Office next door to the Eisenhower Executive Office Building—until recently called the Old Executive Office Building. It was time to deliver the federal budget for 2010.

The past was catching up to him, over and over. After a brutal budget season, where he had to cut back on a wide array of priorities, the president faced a final indignity: over the weekend, projections of the deficit had risen one last time, by $90 billion.

For the fiscal year ending September 30, essentially Bush's last budget, the deficit rose from a February projection of $1.75 trillion to $1.84 trillion. For Obama's fiscal year 2010 budget delivered today, the projected deficit rose from $1.17 trillion—a number arrived after the president agreed to what he considered "basic essentials"—to $1.26 trillion.

That amounted to a deficit of 12.9 percent of GDP for the current year and 8.5 percent for next year, 2010—percentages that represented the largest since World War II and well beyond what economists roundly recommend, which are deficits no larger than 3 percent. With the new projections, Obama would now get under 3 percent at the very end of his current term, in 2013.

Each element of the three-part, budgetary equation—the size of the deficit, the projected condition of the economy, and the amount health care costs were expected to rise—was being factored every few days. On the second point, Romer's office issued a preliminary report supporting Obama's claim that the two-year, $787 billion stimulus package would save or create 3.5 million jobs by the end of 2010. In terms of health care, though, the news got worse, as Treasury released revised numbers showing that the administration's major proposal for raising revenue to pay for health care reform—a 28 percent limit on deductions for those in the two top income tax brackets—would only raise $267 billion, about $50 billion less than had been projected.

Obama had explanations for all of this loaded into the teleprompters in the Eisenhower Building's press room, but he was dealing with an audience—the world's bond markets—that didn't really care much for explanations.

That was what was worrying him today. Like so many companies—including many that had faced trouble on Wall Street—the United States had recently become intently focused on the challenge of rolling over its debt. The level of U.S. debt held by foreign countries was unprecedented. The leverage that this might give them, and especially China, over the United States had been a much discussed fear since the Great Panic of '08. Over the past few months, though, another question had arisen: What if the United States held a Treasury auction and no one came? It seemed as though the so-called indirect buyers of T-bills, mostly foreign countries, were not showing up in their usual numbers and the U.S. government was having to pick up the slack.

With today's shifting numbers, Obama was growing concerned. He'd been briefed on the T-bill issue by Orszag, and how the disfavor of foreign T-bill buyers could be disastrous. He remembered, as many did, the notable exchange between Alan Greenspan and Bill Clinton in 1993, revealed in Bob Woodward's book *The Agenda*, when Clinton asked if his presidency would be determined by how he was seen by the bond market.

Greenspan said, in fact, it would. Clinton eventually balanced the federal budget and became a darling of the bond markets, which graced the U.S. economy with about 2 percent in credit costs, which it had been holding back under the assumption that the federal government would never get its fiscal act together. When it did, and interest rates fell, borrowing and economic growth surged.

Now the United States, from the federal government to corporate offices to kitchen tables, was suffering from an inverse equation. With household debt at nearly 130 percent of GDP—up from 68 percent in 1992—sluggish growth, and enormous federal deficits up another $90 billion, what was needed was a massive deleveraging. But not while the economy was limping. With the bad fiscal news he was about to deliver, Obama wondered how the next Treasury auction would go. Maybe no one would show.

As he and five officials from OMB milled about in a waiting room near the press center, Obama turned to Orszag with a request. "I'd really like you to write me a memo." The memo would detail what Obama's options were in the event of a fiscal crisis. What do we do in terms of policy adjustment to restore our credibility? Obama added: "And I'd like you to give it to me directly."

Orszag looked at him quizzically, making sure he'd heard right: the president wanted a memo that wouldn't get read first by Summers or Emanuel, or circulated by the White House's staff secretary, as was traditional process. Orszag's mind raced. He knew that the new president had a great deal to learn, and might be resistant to the training program that both Emanuel and Summers were keeping him bound to.

"I hope that won't cause too much of a problem," Obama said, with a half-smile. "I don't want to get you into trouble."

"No, sir," Orszag said. "Will next week be soon enough?"

Obama nodded and, with a trace of uncertainty, added, "I guess I'm allowed to do this, right, to ask you for a memo?"

"Well," Orszag said, "you *are* the president."

Barack Obama nodded. Yes, he was actually the president. Then he walked into the glare of cameras to deliver that day's dose of bad news.

On May 8 the man hastily selected to be deputy Treasury secretary, after the nomination of Rodge Cohen was withdrawn, sat in front of the

Finance Committee for his confirmation hearing. Neal Wolin, another in the long procession of Bob Rubin acolytes, had spent six years at Treasury during the Clinton administration and, as general counsel, headed up the team of lawyers that drafted Gramm-Leach-Bliley, which officially dismantled Glass-Steagall. His hearing was scheduled for a Friday, which, strategically speaking, is a good time to slip a nominee through: many senators travel to home states on Fridays. This was what Maria Cantwell was planning to do when one of her aides said Wolin was coming up. She was terse: "If I'm going to stay, you'd better pull together some strong material for me to grill him with."

Her aide did, and the next day she started with a frontal assault, contending that the administration was in "statutory violation" of TARP's April 30 deadline for the executive branch to offer reforms to ensure a similar financial catastrophe was not repeated. Then she pressed Wolin to admit that the actions of the Clinton administration to bar regulation of derivatives was a mistake—he wouldn't, saying only there was a need for "more robust regulation"—and pressed him about moving all derivatives onto transparent exchanges. He attempted to dodge the question by saying he agreed with whatever Secretary Geithner had said in his confirmation hearings.

To see that, even in May, another Treasury nominee from the Clinton days was busy ducking and dodging questions from a Democratic senator revealed unresolved issues inside the administration. Despite the president's publicly stated anger at Wall Street and its practices, Summers and Emanuel were sticking to their program, under which former officials from the Clinton era were never to admit to any errors in pushing deregulatory efforts. A counterstrategy, voiced by several of the president's political advisers, was for nominees who served under Clinton to express appropriate contrition, much like Richard Clarke's famous apology for the 9/11 attacks, which would allow for a truly "robust" discussion about what went wrong and how to fix it—a posture that fit with the president's public statements.

Instead, there was a gap between the president's words and the anticipated deeds of former Clinton officials—virtually all of whom, save Geithner, profited mightily from financial services jobs during the Bush years. This had led to questions about where the president actually stood on economic issues that had drawn populist fury from both left and right.

As one Obama aide put it, "This was the height of stupidity. The nom-

Jewel Samad/AFP/Getty Images

UBS-America president Robert Wolf, whose bank was leveraged at more than 50 to 1, sounded a first alert to then-candidate Obama on August 4, 2007, warning that a "market-driven disaster" was on the way. Wolf, pictured here golfing with Obama in 2010, said, "This could be a once-in-a-lifetime kind of thing."

Timothy A. Clary/AFP/Getty Images

In September 2007, Obama delivered a speech on financial reform at NASDAQ. Still a long-shot candidate, 30 points behind Hillary Clinton, he was well ahead of his rivals in warning of the need to reform Wall Street. The speech got little coverage, but Wall Street noticed.

Employees of Lehman Brothers leave their New York offices with their possessions in boxes after the 158-year-old investment bank declared bankruptcy on September 15, 2008. The bankruptcy initiated the most turbulent economic collapse since the Great Depression.

A managing director of Lehman's real estate department, Carmine Visone—after thirty-six years at the firm—saw his "standards of value" under siege by both the real estate boom and his outsized pay. His response was to regularly rent a truck, fill it with groceries, and deliver "something of indisputable worth—food!" to the hungry and destitute on the streets of New York. The financial crisis left the city's food pantries overflowing with the homeless and Visone, his world shattered, considering dire options.

Merrill Lynch president Greg Fleming was in a footrace with Paulson, Geithner, and Bernanke as "Lehman weekend" approached. Both Lehman and Merrill needed to be saved, but Fleming, in a bold stroke, persuaded the only credible suitor, Bank of America, to buy his investment firm. The next day, Lehman collapsed into the government's arms and chaos ensued.

Neilson Barnard/Getty Images

Chip Somodevilla/Getty Images

Treasury Secretary Hank Paulson did little in the year-long run up to Lehman's collapse—fearful of undermining "confidence" in the financial system—then went to Capitol Hill to beg lawmakers to pass the unpalatable bank bailout later known as TARP. Here, in September 2008, with Fed Chairman Ben Bernanke, he warned Congress of impending disaster, as SEC chairman Christopher Cox and Senator Chris Dodd (D-Conn.) look on.

Timothy A. Clary/AFP/Getty Images

The electric moment of the Obama family stepping onto a shining stage in Grant Park etches itself into collective memory. Already, though, Obama—who said "my presidency began in September," as the financial crisis boosted him to an insurmountable lead—was a step removed, feeling the burden of the challenges he faced and trying to tamp down Election Night enthusiasm.

Obama announced his key economic appointments in November 2008. The team, largely replacing his campaign's more progressive group of Volcker-led advisers, would be marred by bitter infighting and constant "relitigation." *From left to right:* Tim Geithner, Christina Romer, Larry Summers, Melody Barnes, and President-elect Obama.

While Chief of Staff Rahm Emanuel's "points on the board" focus never became a coherent managerial strategy, the ensuing drift and confusion often left him and Larry Summers acting in the president's stead. Obama was delighted in September 2010 when an opportunity opened up in Chicago's mayoral race, saving him the prospect of dismissing his top aide.

Two top economic advisers, NEC chairman Larry Summers *(left)* and OMB director Peter Orszag *(right)* clashed frequently after Obama took office, but held a grudging respect for each other's intellect. Summers repeatedly told Orszag that, with Obama as president, "we are home alone," and that "Clinton would never have made these mistakes."

Pool Photograph/Getty Images

A gender divide in the White House immediately struck White House communications director Anita Dunn when she arrived in April 2009. Looking back, she and others considered it a hostile workplace for women. Here Dunn consults with another adviser who spanned both the campaign and administration, Obama's trusted counselor David Axelrod.

Assistant Treasury Secretary Alan Krueger (*right*) said, "We lost the country with the AIG bonuses and never won them back." A leading labor economist, Krueger—seen here with Treasury Secretary Geithner—briefed Obama on ways to reduce unemployment and fought fiercely, though futilely, for a major federal jobs program.

February 2009 / March 2009 / April 2009

Calendar

	Start	End	Category	Description
6 Mar 2009	8:15 AM	8:45 AM		White House Staff Meeting, Roosevelt Room, White House
	8:45 AM	9:00 AM		Economic Meeting with Peter Orszag, Larry Summers, Christy Romer, Gene Sperling, Larry Summers' Office, White House
	9:00 AM	9:45 AM		Meeting with Steve Shafran, Lee Sachs, Matt Kabaker, Secretary's Office
	9:45 AM	10:15 AM		Daily Meeting with Rahm Emanuel with Larry, Gene, Sephanie, Mark, Rahm Emanuel's Office, White House
	10:15 AM	10:30 AM		Meeting with Nancy Lee, Secretary's Office
	10:30 AM	11:00 AM		Troika 1 Call, re: Economic Assumptions, Secretary's Office
	11:00 AM	11:30 AM		Meeting with Deputy Prime Minister and Ministry of Turkey Professor Dr. Nazim Ekren, Secretary's Small Conference Room
	12:00 PM	12:30 PM		Meeting with FED Chairman Bernanke and FED Governor Dan Tarullo, re: reg reform agenda, Federal Reserve Board
	12:30 PM	2:00 PM		Weekly Lunch with FED Chairman Bernanke, Federal Reserve Board
	2:00 PM	3:00 PM		Meeting with Governor of the Bank of Italy and Chairman of the Financial Stability Forum, Mario Draghi, Secretary's Office
	3:00 PM	3:30 PM		
	3:30 PM	5:00 PM		Auto Task Force Meeting, Roosevelt Room, White House
	6:30 PM	7:50 PM		
	7:50 PM	8:20 PM		
7 Mar 2009	8:00 AM	9:00 AM		
8 Mar 2009	8:00 AM	9:00 AM		
9 Mar 2009	6:30 AM	7:45 AM		
	7:45 AM	8:05 AM		
	8:05 AM	8:15 AM		Arrive White House
	8:15 AM	8:45 AM		White House Senior Staff Meeting, Roosevelt Room, White House
	8:45 AM	8:50 AM		Economic Meeting with Peter, Larry, Christy, Gene, Larry Summers' Office, White House
	8:50 AM	8:55 AM		Return to Office
	8:55 AM	9:00 AM		Call from Bill Rutledge, NY Fed
	9:00 AM	9:15 AM		Meeting with Mark, Lee and Matt Kabaker, Secretary's Office
	9:15 AM	9:30 AM		White House Debrief with Mark, Gene, Stephanie, Kim and Neal Wolin, Secretary's Office
	9:30 AM	9:35 AM		Reg Reform Meeting with Ian, Peter, Amias, Laurie Schaffer, Stephanie, Gene, Secretary's Office
	9:35 AM	9:45 AM		Call from Vikram Pandit
	9:45 AM	10:00 AM		Call to Shelia Bair
	10:00 AM	10:40 AM		POTUS Daily Economic Briefing, Oval Office, White House
	10:40 AM	11:00 AM		Return to Office
	11:00 AM	11:45 AM		Senior Staff and Bureau Heads Meeting, Secretary's Large Conference Room
	11:45 AM	11:50 AM		Call to SEC Chairman Mary Schapiro
	11:50 AM	12:00 PM		
	12:00 PM	12:40 PM		Meeting with Dr. Alan Greenspan, Secretary's Office
	12:40 PM	1:00 PM		Candidate Interview with George Madison, GC Candidate, Secretary's Office
	1:00 PM	2:00 PM		Meeting with Lee, Matt Kabaker, Gene Sperling, Neal Wolin, Secretary's Office
	2:15 PM	3:00 PM		Prep for Charlie Rose Interview with Stephanie, Gene, Lee and Alan, Secretary's Office
	3:00 PM	3:45 PM		Principals Phone Call with Bernanke, Dugan, Bair and Dudley, Secretary's Office with Lee and Matt Kabaker
	3:45 PM	3:55 PM		
	3:55 PM	4:05 PM		CFIUS Signing with Andrew Mayock, Jamie Franco, Mark Jaskowiak, Secretary's Office
	4:05 PM	4:20 PM		Call from Vikram Pandit

Treasury Secretary Tim Geithner's jammed schedule for Monday, March 9, 2009. Through the day and evening, he talked to the FDIC's Sheila Bair four times and Citibank chief Vikram Pandit twice. On the 3:00 to 3:45 conference call with Bair, Bernanke, and others, he blocked the FDIC chair's effort to have Citibank's managers fired and the bank restructured. Little more than fifteen minutes later, at 4:05, he was again on the phone briefing Pandit.

BYRON L. DORGAN
NORTH DAKOTA

March 12, 2009

The Honorable Rahm Emanuel
Chief of Staff
The White House
Washington, DC 20500

Dear Rahm:

We must of had a mis-connect the other day when we talked about the meeting we have requested with President Obama.

Following that telephone discussion, I got a call from Larry Summers' office trying to set up a meeting with him.

Attached is the January 28th letter from seven Democratic Senators requesting a meeting with President Obama to talk about the important issue of financial reform.

Yesterday, Secretary Geithner said that the Administration is going to "lay out critical elements of its regulatory reform program before the G20 Summit on April 2." That is a mere three weeks from today.

As I indicated on the phone, I am reiterating our request to meet with the President so we may have some meaningful and timely input into the formulation of that program. It is not just Larry Summers that the seven of us have asked to meet with. We know the President will get plenty of advice from Larry Summers and Secretary Geithner on this subject. We want him to have the benefit of our advice on these matters as well.

I hope you can set up this meeting quickly.

Sincerely,

Byron L. Dorgan
U.S. Senator

Privately Obtained, Nonclassified Document

While Obama focused on health care, the Senate's Democratic leadership—eager to push forward financial reform—was kept at bay. In a terse mid-March letter to Emanuel, North Dakota's Byron Dorgan, representing seven senators, shows frustration over Rahm's attempt to reroute their long-delayed meeting with Obama over to Larry Summers.

After details of AIG's post-bailout bonuses leaked to the press in mid-March 2009, protestors—these in Connecticut—demonstrated. As anti-Wall Street populism reached a fever pitch, the administration quietly approved some of the largest governmental supports for Wall Street and ducked uncomfortable questions.

Goldman Sachs CEO Lloyd Blankfein (*left*) and JPMorgan Chase CEO Jamie Dimon (*center*) talk to reporters after Obama met with the thirteen bankers representing the country's largest banking institutions. After Obama said, famously, to them, "My administration is the only thing between you and the pitchforks," his tone turned conciliatory. "You guys have an acute public relations problem that's turning into a political problem. And I want to help."

Launching his top priority of health care reform, Obama introduced Ted Kennedy, then dying of brain cancer, to cap an inspirational White House Health Care Summit on March 5, 2009. Little was done, though, in the coming months, as the White House lost control of the debate to bickering senators and Tea Party activists.

Former Senate majority leader Tom Daschle, chosen by Obama to head Health and Human Services, was forced to withdraw when a tax scandal surfaced. He tried to advise the president on health care, but was shut out in the crucial early months as the dysfunctional White House came to be known as the "black hole."

The "grand bargain" by health insurers to support universal coverage to bring millions of new customers onto the insurance rolls was a starting point—and, later, most of what remained—of health care reform. The insurers' lead lobbyist, Karen Ignagni, initially broke with other health care providers to join the administration in pushing for dramatic cost controls. Once the White House abandoned that position—its strongest bipartisan stance—the insurers became a convenient scape goat.

In January of 2010, Scott Brown, an upstart state senator, shocked Massachusetts and the country by winning a special election to take Ted Kennedy's seat. His win killed the Democrats' filibuster-proof majority in the Senate and sent health care reform into near chaos.

Despite being excluded early on by White House officials, former Fed chairman Paul Volcker saw his ideas gain in popularity. The administration, reeling from Scott Brown's victory, hastily embraced his "Volcker Rule," an attempt to restructure parts of Wall Street, but "their hearts are not in it," Volcker complained, about making it into law.

FDIC chairman Sheila Bair, unaware of Obama's interest in closing and restructuring Citibank, pushed to execute just such a plan. Her efforts were met with strict resistance from Treasury Secretary Geithner.

BlackRock CEO Larry Fink, often called the King of Wall Street, had over $3 trillion in assets under management and $9 trillion he oversaw, mostly of toxic assets he priced and managed for the government. In September 2010, Emanuel put forward Fink as a replacement for Summers and ushered him into the Oval Office.

Gary Gensler, a former Goldman Sachs executive named chairman of the Commodities Futures Trading Commission, pulled a "Nixon to China" in becoming an outspoken advocate for regulating a vastly profitable derivatives industry at the center of the global financial meltdown. This placed Gensler on a collision course with Wall Street's largest banks and their tens of billions a year in derivatives-related profits.

Summoning Goldman Sachs executives, led by CEO Lloyd Blankfein, to contentious hearings before the Senate in April 2010 recharged the financial reform debate. Here, costumed activists from Code Pink sum up the widespread antipathy toward Wall Street that senators would try to harness.

In spite of overwhelming public support for fundamental financial reforms, the Dodd-Frank bill, signed into law in July 2010, added regulations and capital requirements but left the industry largely as it was in 2007. From left: Vice President Joe Biden, Speaker Nancy Pelosi, Majority Leader Harry Reid, President Obama, Senator Dodd, and Representative Barney Frank (D-Mass.).

Obama holds a Rose Garden press conference with Treasury Secretary Tim Geithner and Harvard Law School professor Elizabeth Warren in September 2010 to announce that Warren would help "stand up" the new Consumer Financial Protection Bureau, but not be its first director. Warren, who came up with the idea herself, became a lightning rod for embracing "the kind of forceful activism," as one White House official later said, "that some people had expected to see in the president."

In spite of the success of his campaign, Obama showed real weakness in managing his own White House. After historic midterm losses in the 2010 election, interim chief of staff Pete Rouse helped restructure the White House to fit Obama's needs. Here, Rouse looks on in January 2011 as the president announces his new chief of staff, Bill Daley.

By early 2011, Obama felt that his understanding of the presidency, and the uses of "confidence," had grown, and that he had grown with it. Debates are sure to rage—and history, finally, to judge—whether this represents evolution or dangerous compromise.

inees could have been leading the charge to make the needed changes, rather than looking like they were testifying under duress." He went on to point out that by simply acknowledging what everyone already knew—that in the last days of Clinton they were under intense pressure from lobbyists, and some of the money they made during the Bush years was probably ill-gotten—"we would have looked like leaders and might have even been about to draw to Washington a few more top Wall Street types" who could admit wrongdoing and then publicly commit to changing what they'd helped create.

One result of this self-protective playbook was to draw resistance from progressive Democratic senators to the prospective nominees, the outcome of which was now painfully clear: Obama had a woefully understaffed Treasury Department during four of the most important months of his presidency, a time when the opportunities were greatest to use a crisis to alter banking and finance in America.

This was a problem that Cantwell and the progressives hoped to resolve by getting past Geithner and Summers to meet directly with Obama. Based on his posture during the campaign, and public statements as president, they felt he was ready to correct long-standing imbalances in the way money and risk were managed—a problem with a host of devils in the details of law, regulation, and practice. In late March, they finally made it to the Oval Office to lay out what they thought financial reform should look like—from executive compensation practices, to the dissolution of systemically dangerous companies, to the fast-growing industry, derivatives trading. But Obama was noncommittal, saying he couldn't speak with that "level of specificity" about reform. He'd left the problem of blocked nominees untended.

By May, after months of playing this game, Cantwell had finally heard enough from the lawyerly Wolin.

"All right. I just want to be clear, because there are certainly a lot of different opinions floating around. In fact, the previous nominee for your position, Mr. Cohen, recently told a crowd in New York, 'As far as I'm concerned, I am far from convinced there was something inherently wrong with this system.' So I want to get it clear. There are a few people in the administration who still cannot say that it was a mistake, and these are the same people I think who are slow-walking, thinking that we are all going to forget about the regulatory reform that is needed. I can assure you, we are not going to forget what is needed. My patience is running out with the administration having to take five months to say that some of these things ought to be regulated, and how they ought to be regulated."

As to Wolin's dodge—that he'd support whatever Geithner had happened to testify about concerning derivatives—Cantwell countered with a bit of her back-channel conversation with the Treasury secretary regarding exchanges.

"I am not clear where the secretary really is on that issue, because in a private conversation after the hearing he said he did not mean exactly what he said at the hearing, and since then he has said to a group of colleagues that the administration still has not come out with" [a] policy.

But the law is the law—as Cantwell pointed out, citing the April 30 deadline—and it was decided that a group of senior administration officials should finally nail down some clear proposals.

Which they summarily did, in the Roosevelt Room. Geithner, Summers, Romer, and Krueger were among those around the table, along with Emanuel. The chief of staff, who was not particularly versed in these regulatory matters and, in any event, was not an elected official, took charge, acting presidential.

After listening to an hour of debate on the matter of what the outlines of reform should look like—just like hour after hour of debates involving the president—Emanuel took control of matters. "Okay, Tim, what the fuck do you need here?"

Geithner, a bit stunned, paused for a moment.

"Well, a systemic risk regulator [someone to watch the landscape for systemic risk inside institutions], resolution authority [the statutory power to take down a problematic institution], and leverage [higher capital requirements to ensure that banks don't over-leverage themselves]. Those three things."

Emanuel nodded. "Okay, let's throw in the consumer financial agency, and everything else can be flushed."

So it was decided. Everyone kind of shrugged. One participant in the deliberations thought about whether Emanuel had, in fact, simply made this decision, or whether he was just carrying out the wishes of the president, then concluded that "the president couldn't have decided these things and told Rahm what to do. At the start of the meeting, there were too many variables to choose from. You would have needed some sort of decision-making algorithm."

What does it take to lead the world's most powerful nation?

That was the question David Axelrod was considering on May 8 in his smallish office in the West Wing.

"Someone said to me the other day that history produces great leaders. But I don't think that's quite right. I think the American people produce great leaders. The fact that they took a guy who was four years out of the Illinois Senate and made him the president, but insist that he run *every mile* of the race to get there, clear every hurdle, run every gauntlet—there's a wisdom in that."

Axelrod, as the intellectual architect of Obama's victory—the first U.S. senator since Jack Kennedy to manage this leap—falls into the camp that believes primary combat, from coast to coast, is an ideal trial by fire. We live, after all, at a time when presidents largely govern from a blindingly lit public stage. A distinct advantage came in being a skinny target, with a public record of choices and outcomes thinner than that of most sitting governors. But the flip side of this, political inexperience, was rarely leveraged by Obama's opponents to good effect. Much credit for this goes to Axelrod's deftness, and rightfully so.

But now, five months along, he and his boss were furiously trying to run up steep and unforgiving learning curves. Which is why Axelrod was expending inordinate effort following Obama to meeting after meeting, assessing how the president's personality traits, his skills, his inclinations, had matched thus far with the dictates of a job that, until a few months ago, was unfamiliar to both of them.

Since arriving in Washington, Obama had told Axelrod he felt it was imperative to keep his connection with the people. "At times of crisis, it's absolutely crucial. He gets ten letters a day and reads them faithfully, passes them around. Because his greatest fear was that he'd lose his ability to relate to the American people."

Axelrod is a rumpled, large, soft-spoken man, unsusceptible to hyperbole except on the subject of his boss. He is sure that Obama will be one of history's seminal presidents. He talked about how Roosevelt's New Deal era reigned from the 1930s until 1980, and how "the last twenty-eight years we've been defined by Reagan. But I believe this is the start of a new era." The key to that happening, he said, is whether Obama "can restore the values he formulated in the Inaugural. I have no doubt he has the bearing and the capacity. The question is, is the system too ossified to allow for change?"

He then talked about how surprisingly difficult the demands of the White House were, how the process of translating ideas into effective, coherent actions was daunting. Axelrod, speaking for Obama, called it a "Sisyphean task," but "we haven't dropped the boulder yet."

At the same time, in his account of Obama's qualities, he said, "One of the things that serves him so well in this job is not only his strong compass but this very sort of broad intellectual curiosity. He just fluidly moves from one thing to another."

This quality, which Axelrod cited as a strength, several senior hands around Obama who'd served other presidents were now convinced was a liability. They seemed to be acting to fill the void, trying to direct Obama or simply acting on their own with whatever presidential legitimacy they could conjure. But what was the goal? In what direction should they be pushing him?

On that score, Axelrod's mom offered assistance.

"When I talk to my eighty-nine-year-old mother about Roosevelt, who was her hero, she doesn't talk about the FDIC or Social Security. She doesn't talk about the New Deal. She says you always felt that there was someone watching over us. You felt like everything was going to be okay because he was . . . there."

Axelrod thought all that over for a moment, as though his mother were sitting on the couch in his office. Channeling her, he'd stumbled upon a working definition of the saving confidence Roosevelt's presence seemed to restore, year by year, across a desperate nation. The complex acts of government were not what Axelrod's mother—twenty-five years old when Roosevelt died—recalled from her formative years, or what resonated with her in all the years to follow.

Are sound policies, enacted and demonstrably effective, a prerequisite for restoring such crucial confidence in this era? Axelrod wondered, as that evocative phrase, "someone watching over us," ran through his head.

"Does the confidence come from the policies themselves, or maybe something more basic?"

He paused, perplexed. "I just don't know."

"How do you deleverage an entire economy?" Paul Volcker asked, in sort of a joke. "Verrrrry carefully."

The hairless giant laughed quite a bit whenever he delivered some tough-love advice. His demeanor was important to his survival in the early 1980s, when he decided what was right and then did it. Inflation was running in the teens then and killing the U.S. economy. Something had to be done. So, with his cockeyed smile, a small, fat cigar, and a grumbling air of "I'm doing this for your own damn good," he squeezed down on the U.S. economy. He was working the large tectonic plates beneath the landscape, tightening the money supply so stridently it pushed the country into the 1981–82 recession—the worst since the Great Depression, until 2007 took the honor. But he managed to tame the inflationary beast.

Now his focus was on the geological shifts of the debate: "the problem is we're replacing private debt with public debt." When people start lending again, and eventually they will, he said, the private debt is likely to be replenished. Then total debt will be even higher. How do you stop this?

"Well, right now, when you have your chance, and their breasts are bared, you need to put a spear through the heart of all these guys on Wall Street that for years have been mostly debt merchants."

Had he told Obama this? Yes, of course. "Every time I say anything reasonably intelligent, the first thing people ask: 'Have you told this to Obama?'

"I tell him whatever's on my mind," Volcker said. "Does he listen? I think so. But he's usually sitting in a crowd."

And, he added, don't get "me started on the stress tests."

It was May 11. A few days before, the Fed released its verdict on the stress tests. Almost half of the banks were listed as needing to raise more capital. Ten of the nineteen largest banks would need to raise, collectively, $74.9 billion in order to withstand the hypothetical scenario posed by the tests. At the top of the list, to no one's surprise, was Bank of America, which alone was undercapitalized by $33.9 billion. Citigroup and Wells Fargo followed not far behind. They'd have six months to raise roughly that amount of capital or face some added action, not clearly specified, by the Treasury.

Still, the results were met with a sigh of relief from many banks. Goldman Sachs and JPMorgan Chase and Morgan Stanley were all deemed "adequate"—signifying that they could withstand the worse of two projected scenarios for a potential recession—and industry heads all seemed to be patting one another on the back.

Ken Lewis, meanwhile, was in the vocal minority of those still aggrieved by the government's role in the financial sector. Having been removed from his board chairmanship the previous week, he was speaking with investors on a conference call, still acting as CEO. "The game plan is to get the government out of our bank as quickly as possible," he said, maintaining that Bank of America had no plans to convert the government stake into common stock. Instead, it would focus on repaying TARP, a feat already accomplished by two of the other three "Big Four banks."

The Fed announced that under the tests' "adverse" scenario, the losses by the nineteen banks could total $600 billion in 2009, the equivalent of 9.1 percent of the banks' total loans.

Volcker was diametrically opposed to the concept.

"Now the bad banks will want money from the government," he said, or will go out and try to raise it "to make themselves whole. And the good ones, with their government stamp of approval, can go out and raise money that everyone will be sure is government guaranteed. Oh, they'll make plenty of money off of that.

"They have their buzzword: 'systemic risk,'" he went on. "They love that one. All the money being spent on these institutions because they have systemic risk, and then you have to rationalize and justify all that money spent, and that's where you get trapped . . ."

His voice trailed off and then he unleashed a big Volckerian idea: "I do not believe in focusing systemic risk on the safety of specific institutions." He said it like a pronouncement, and looked back at the line to make sure it held up. "You focus your energy instead on developments in the marketplace that *carry* systemic risk, developments that cut across institutions and particular markets. The whole use of financial engineering is a systemic risk, in my view. It led among other things to subprime mortgages. That was a systemic risk that was not particular to an institution, though it brought some of them down. Credit default swaps have a systemic component, as do the many ways people leveraged themselves."

Whether this is sound policy—banning certain activities and altering behavior, after all, are never easy—this is what original thinking looks

like. The problem, clear to all, was that institutions that were too big—
too systemically risky—to fail during the Great Panic, were today even
larger and quite possibly more systemically dangerous. These banks,
Volcker said, not only were susceptible to "moral hazard," but worse,
to keep up their earnings in a soft lending market, they'd need to rely,
ever more, on being R&D labs for "financial innovation." On that score,
Volcker was blunt: it was mostly chicanery draped in the alluring obscu-
rities of marketing and complex math. "The last financial innovation by
the banks that really created productivity and efficiency was the ATM.
Ironically, it was Citibank that really got it started."

He laughed, a kind of wheeze where his shoulders pulled up and down:
"It's like what's-his-name in the ad: they have to start making money the
old-fashioned way, they have to actually earn it."

What's-his-name was John Houseman. The long-running ads, for
Smith Barney, were first launched in 1982—just about the time Wall
Street stopped making money the old-fashioned way and compensation began to rise precipitously. Five years later, when Reagan replaced
Volcker for being insufficiently antiregulatory, the former Fed chairman
began serving on corporate boards. By the mid-1990s he had started to
refuse requests to be on compensation committees. Why?

"What I saw happening made me sick."

In a cautionary tale about how regulation can create unintended nightmares if not thought through, he described how a tax code change in
1992 mandated that companies could deduct only $1 million in cash com-
pensation, per employee, as an expense, and any compensation above
that had to show that it represented "value-added." This effort to limit
deductions on high-end salaries prompted companies to put more compensation in stock options . . . right at the start of the strongest decade for
rising stocks in a century. Compensation, already rising fast, accelerated
its ascent in an environment of weak unions and shareholder rights, and
lax ethical boundaries for directors.

"Once this sort of thing starts, it takes some real toughness to stop
it," Volcker said. "But someone should have. Because having people paid
tens of millions for activities of no social or really economic value—or,
as the crash shows, negative value—just tears a society apart, at all levels, top to bottom. Well, maybe not top."

Volcker, at eighty-one, was one of the last strong voices of an older
age, when ethical toughness was honored and adequately rewarded. He

was part of the midcentury's community of "prudent men," referees on the field of play making sure conduct was fair and cheap shots led to real penalties—and to social sanction. Nothing was worth risking that.

At the center of this community of professionals—lawyers, accountants, auditors—were the closely regulated banks, and Volcker felt it was time to restore them, mostly as they had been before that wall between banking and investing was breached in the 1990s.

"I tell you the argument we're having now," he said, "there are those like me who say the heart of this system ought to be the banking system, like it was historically, and it ought to be a service organization to take care of the basic needs for its clients . . . its big job is providing someplace for their money, transferring funds around the country, making loans, helping them with investments and the rest. They shouldn't get off doing hedge funds and equity and trying to make all their money by trading. That's my view. Then you get the banks closely supervised, as they have been historically, and hedge funds can go off and pretty much do their own thing, unless they get so big that they can mess everything up. You don't worry about every hedge fund, or equity fund, and they'll probably not make as much money as they used to, with more competition and without all those bank deposits to play with.

"And, finally," he added, "you have to deal with this business of some sucker gets a bad mortgage and the guy who sold it to him gets a commission, and the guy who sold it to that guy gets one, too. That's just old-fashioned fraud. Now, the other view," he said, summing up much of Geithner and Summers's position, "is treat everybody alike. They're either angels or robbers. You can't tell which, and there's no point making a distinction between the banking system and the others.

"I think that's just fundamentally wrong."

Taking a course like the one he outlined, creating actual structural changes—"explaining it to everyone, doing it, and letting people get on with their business"—he said, takes "a kind of tough love that'll get Wall Street, and plenty of Washington, too, up in arms. But most people on Main Street would understand what you're doing pretty quickly. And they're the ones who actually elect you."

He'd told all this to Obama, in various ways. "I think Obama understands everything intellectually, very easily, near as I can see. What we don't know is whether he has the courage to follow through. He understands it, but does he feel it in the belly?" Then he mumbled, "I don't know."

He said he always liked that thing Obama said, about how the hardest thing to do in government is "to solve tomorrow's problems with today's pocketbook.

"But he doesn't do it!"

What was happening was that Volcker was struggling to overlook the demonstrable facts: that by passing over him and his like-minded kindred for top Treasury and White House posts, Obama had shown his preference, one quite different from Volcker's, on almost all these issues. The president's preference, Volcker felt, was "first, do no harm"—a phrase he'd heard often in 1980, when he began to pinch off the money supply. The "do no harm" school, he said, "always sounds reasonable" in that it calls for delay, until matters worsen to the point "where there'll be consensus that we need to act in a forceful way. But you never get that consensus, because many of the actors, the institutions and so forth, will follow their own self-interest right off a cliff." Every policy of consequence, meanwhile, is going to "do some harm, short term—something government, mind you, can and should help cushion." But there's no other way "to create the larger good, something you look back on with pride."

That idea of accomplishment, something you could be proud of, reminded him of a breakfast he'd gone to a few months before that had helped him "see things more clearly, even at my age." It was a breakfast of "right-thinking citizens" who were worried about the crumbling infrastructure in the country.

"At the end of the breakfast, this gray-haired old man says, 'I know something about this. I'm a professor of civil engineering at Princeton. And I was up at Yale the other day and they've given up teaching civil engineering. There are just two old geezers like me up at Harvard, and once they're gone that'll be it. There's hardly an elite university in the United States that pays attention to civil engineering. What's the result? We hardly know how to build bridges; they tend to fall down. It's cost twice as much to build that new bridge across the Potomac as it would have cost if it was built in Europe . . . I assure you, I know . . . and besides our bridges are ugly and theirs are beautiful.'"

Then something dawned on Volcker that he told the old engineer.

"Well, I said, 'The trouble with the United States recently is we spent several decades not producing many civil engineers and producing a huge number of financial engineers. And the result is shitty bridges and a shitty financial system!'"

Volcker roared with laughter, until his eyes watered, and he took off his glasses to wipe them. Of course, he was talking about something very serious, about the choices people make in their lives, as well as those made by a nation.

"It always used to bother me—not so much anymore, but for a long time—how I spent all my life in government, doing things that were so intangible. What's there to show for it, what's left behind?" he said in a soft grumble. "And I just thought, imagine saying, 'There's a goddamn bridge I built. Or I designed that building, or I shaped that beautiful landscape.'

"I always wanted to build something in my life. All I did was stop inflation."

Volcker and Axelrod's mother, in their words and posture, were both trying to summon a world where humility was rewarded and government—of, by, and for the people—stood above other competing realms in American life. New York, then like now, was the nation's preeminent city. But Washington had, for the long American midcentury, won the title of capital, in a push-and-shove for primacy between the two cities since the founding of the Republic.

That rise was in reaction to one disaster after the next. The first big financial bust of twentieth-century America, the Panic of 1907, resulted in the creation of the U.S. Federal Reserve Bank. The government, dangerously and more than a little embarrassingly, had been forced to turn to banking magnate John Pierpont Morgan to save the financial system. It hoped never to have to again. But it was not until the Great Depression that Washington really got serious about forcing prudence onto markets and into life.

The banking industry of the 1920s had done all it could to undermine the country's faith in it. By merging commercial and investment banks into "bank holding" companies, it had created hugely profitable conflicts of interest, which then in turn precipitated the collapse of 1929. But as destructive as their behavior had been, the economy needed functioning banks. So when Franklin Delano Roosevelt arrived in the White House almost four years later, his most pressing order of business was to restore Americans' confidence in their banks.

After such a dramatic collapse he knew he would have to do more than simply tell people the banks were now safe. Their confidence needed to be earned, not manufactured. So he crafted a grand trade-off: the federal government would insure deposits in those institutions that behaved themselves, that adhered to strict rules and limitations. The Glass-Steagall Act gave deposit insurance to banks that agreed to act like prudent men. At the same time it broke up the poisonous bank holding companies. Investment banks would still exist and could do as they liked, but no longer would they jeopardize the savings, and thus future, of the American people.

The "prudent man" standard came from a landmark nineteenth-century legal decision in *Harvard College v. Armory*, the case of a money manager who had squandered a widow's inheritance. The decision put in place the Prudent Man Rule, which established a fiduciary duty to invest the assets of a trust as a "prudent man" might his own. By applying a similar standard to banks, Roosevelt would help promote the same sort of assurance in them that their fortresslike facades and heavy vault doors were there to inspire.

Of all the changes that occurred on Roosevelt's watch, one of the most important was the government's realization that its role might not be simply to ensure certain rights, but also to protect and promote a kind of desirable balance, a virtuous equilibrium. The reforms enacted under FDR were different from those that had come before and shifted the basic balance of power between Washington and New York—between public and private, worker and owner, saver and speculator. The walls built were not regulatory guidelines, subject to the enforcement and diligence of bureaucrats, but laws tightly drafted and immovable, clear matters of legal and illegal, just as the founders had done with their "checks and balances" within government.

The most oft-quoted line in FDR's First Inaugural Address—"We have nothing to fear but fear itself"—was followed by stern words, all but forgotten to history, for the president's enemies in New York: "Faced by failure of credit, they have proposed only the lending of more money. Stripped of the lure of profit by which to induce our people to follow their false leadership, they have resorted to exhortations, pleading tearfully for restored confidence. They know only the rules of a generation of self-seekers. They have no vision, and when there is no vision the people perish."

There are many ways to understand what "vision" here might mean: the inventor's insight that creates a new technology or medicine, the leader's foresight of his actions' distant consequences, the prudent man's reserve about the extent to which complexity can be mastered and the future known, people's gut-level sense that something better lies down the path of hard work and fair play. The confidence of the nation rests on trust and can endure for years after this trust has been broken. But it cannot endure indefinitely if the foundation of trust is not at some point earned. Confidence is the immaterial residue of material actions: justly enforced laws, sound investments, solidly built structures, the well-considered decisions of experts and professionals. Confidence is the public face of competence. Separating the two—gaining the trust without earning it—is the age-old work of confidence men.

Inside the White House that very day, May 11, President Obama stood at a lectern proud and firm, with a "coalition" of health care industry representatives around him. All the major players were there, all the bigs, from the American Medical Association, the American Hospital Association, the Advanced Medical Technology Association (medical devices), America's Health Insurance Plans, and PhRMA, the drug lobby. Also represented: the Service Employees International Union, or SEIU, the country's largest private-sector union.

The president hadn't done much since the Health Care Summit. Tom Daschle couldn't get an audience. Max Baucus was moving forward in the Senate. Various groups in the House were working up their proposals. This was Obama's next act.

Over the previous week, health care reform czar Nancy-Ann De-Parle, on board now two months, was working with Dennis Rivera, the health reform chief of SEIU, and Karen Ignagni, from the health insurers. They were trying to hammer out a number, a commitment for cost cutting that would serve as a target goal. This sort of thing had a long history. The industry had lined up to promise "voluntary" cost savings, in various coalitions, since Nixon was in office. Nothing had worked. But this time was different. At least everyone felt it was, for better or worse, depending on where they stood in the unfolding debate.

The key distinction from 1993 was that the health care providers and the insurers were not moving in traditional unison. Insurance executives were building on their grand bargain, committing to ending unpopular underwriting practices, such as refusing coverage to those with preexisting conditions, and were encouraging Congress to adopt uniform federal regulations on their industry, which suffered from the logistics of having to craft their plans state by state. But it went deeper than that.

The growth in costs was the beating heart of provider profits, not insurance profits. Higher medical costs, and the pushback against ever-rising premiums, put insurers in a squeeze. Their profit margins were now slightly lower than that of others in the health care community and, during a recession, destined to shrink further. This, and the existential threat that the so-called public option still posed, was nudging their self-interest toward the cost-cutting goals of the White House and consumer groups. Ignagni, to the surprise of Orszag and others, was in fact pushing for a high number on cost cutting and dragging along some of the reluctant providers.

"Karen was pushing for a big number," said a former senior official involved in the talks. "The fact that we didn't seize the potential for a realignment, I think, showed the cost of not having someone like Daschle aboard. We were playing checkers. We needed to be playing chess."

And it was a big number that Ignagni, leading the coalition, hammered out with DeParle and Rivera: $2 trillion in health care cost savings over ten years.

Excitement bubbled up through the White House. Orszag was given a green light to call Krugman. His column in the *New York Times* on May 10 went so far as to say the commitment, to be announced the following day, was "some of the best policy news I've heard in a long time."

After a meeting on the eleventh in the Roosevelt Room with Ignagni and representatives from the providers, Obama officially unveiled the commitment, laid out in a letter signed by the representatives. Strongly worded but vague on details, it asserted that, working together, these groups could save $2,500 a year for a family of four after five years, for a total of $2 trillion for the nation over ten years. Everyone agreed that there'd be no chance for health care reform with costs rising at the currently projected rate of 6.2 percent annually over the coming decade. If the industry could slice 1.5 percent per year from that growth rate, the gross numbers would be huge.

Nailing down this commitment, Obama said, marked "a historic day, a watershed event." The savings, he said, "will help us take the next and most important step: comprehensive health care reform."

Gibbs reiterated Obama's forcefulness, saying the president had told the health care executives in their meeting, "You've made a commitment; we expect you to keep it."

It was textbook political calculus. Use the president's aura to get the reluctant on the record, so that they either had to stick to their words or face humiliation for backing off.

And then all hell broke loose. Leading members of each trade group—heads of hospitals, drug companies, device manufacturers—started calling their Washington representatives. There were heated exchanges as reality set in. Those running these businesses, accounting for 16.5 percent of GDP, said that such cost cuts were untenable. Already the stocks of the publicly traded companies were beginning to drop. The lobbyists countered that those executives out on the hustings didn't just sit with the president. There had been two million people on the Mall four months ago. Something was going to happen, maybe something sweeping, the trade groups responded, and the hospitals, the doctors, the drug companies needed to be at the table to make it as good for each of them as it could be. And, of course, some of them were cursing Ignagni.

It wasn't long before calls started coming to DeParle from the industry associations: this commitment letter might get a few lead lobbyists fired! Soon she, Obama, and the senior staff were huddling. The question was raised about whether the president should offer a follow-up statement, hedging what he'd said. Obama was adamant. He wasn't budging. A commitment is a commitment.

On Wednesday, two days after the initial press conference, Obama was holding his ground. "These groups are voluntarily coming together to make an unprecedented commitment," he said. "Over the next ten years, from 2010 to 2019, they are pledging to cut the rate of growth of national health care spending by 1.5 percentage points each year—an amount that's equal to over $2 trillion."

Health care leaders were now backpedaling as fast as they could, saying that they'd committed to slowing spending gradually and not to specific annual cuts.

"There's been a lot of misunderstanding that has caused a lot of consternation among our members," Richard J. Umbdenstock, the president of the American Hospital Association, told the *New York Times*. "I've spent the better part of the last three days trying to deal with it."

The opposition to meaningful reform was in disarray, "stakeholders" shouting at their trade group chiefs, who were scrambling to back away from their stated positions, and pressure coming directly from an un-yielding president. The mess was receiving plenty of coverage, too. Calls to the White House from providers meanwhile intensified. Their stance: either the president backs off, or there will be a war like was never known during Clinton's day.

It was a moment to embrace Ignagni, who'd been sitting mostly si-lently and seal a divide-and-conquer strategy, with the insurers joining the White House to force cost cuts among the providers.

The interests of the insurers and the providers, of course, had never been neatly aligned. Before modern health insurance was developed in the 1940s, an individual could pay a doctor for his services or she couldn't. When she couldn't, the doctor, either out of an ethical obligation or the Hippocratic oath, would provide the services because it was . . . the right thing to do. Insurance changed all that. It created a buffer, removing mo-rality from the equation. That awkward moment of payment, when the responsibility of health care provider was put front and center, was re-placed by an omniscient third party to whom consumers paid premiums and from whom providers received payment. It was an elegant solution to an inelegant problem.

But, as was the case with financial services, it ultimately created a sev-ering of accountability and very real market inefficiencies. The consum-ers couldn't directly feel the effects of poor pricing. The competition was lost, and an industry was steadily corrupted.

For White House tacticians, like Emanuel, these were not pertinent matters. New polling showed that, unlike the debacle of the 1990s, the principal villain in the 2000s was no longer seen as government bureau-cracy, but rather insurance profiteering. Leaning heavily on polling is common practice in virtually every administration, but as health care began to kick off in earnest, and the stakes were set, Emanuel and the political team became hyper-reliant on the polls.

Joel Benenson, Obama's head pollster, summed it up best in a speech at the Economic Club of Canada. Talking about the proposed "public option," a plan in which the government would set up an autonomous federal insurance program to compete in the market, Benenson said,

"Initial reaction to it [years ago] wasn't as positive as it is now . . . But we figured out that people like the idea of competition versus the insurance company, and that's why you get a number like seventy-two percent supporting it."

From a broader strategic assessment, this should not have been a surprise. As costs and pressures on the health care system rose, anger at the insurers would have to rise as well. That's their business model. They get paid to be the buffer—to be hated—so the doctors and hospitals don't have to be.

Rather than seizing this opportunity, the White House—without a clear strategic model on health care reform—blinked. Using insurers as the tip of their spear to drive down costs—the very thing providers had been fearing since the March summit—was not to be, even now, as Ignagni tried to put the spear in their hands. For the White House to align itself with insurers was seen as politically untenable. Just look at that poll data.

On May 14, DeParle told the *New York Times'* legendary health care reporter Robert Pear that the president, in his forceful statements on both Monday and Wednesday, was confused. "The President misspoke," she said. Then, a few hours later, she called back to say, now it was she who had just misspoken. "I don't think the president misspoke," she now said. "His remarks correctly and accurately described the industry's commitment."

The providers flip-flopped; now the White House had matched them. The hospitals, doctors, drug companies, and device makers were joyous. To them, the message was clear: the White House was not serious about cutting health care costs.

———

Peter Orszag worked several late nights on his specially ordered, back-channel report for the president on the fiscal crisis. The nut of the report: in case of a failed Treasury action driven by fears of a widening and unmet U.S. deficit, the government would immediately need to launch some revenue-generating programs. Those programs would have to be not only potent money raisers, but also seen as prudent by the bond markets. One action that would meet those dictates, Orszag wrote, was a strong tax on certain financial transactions. Though Wall Street was against this, most economists—and "show me the money" deficit hawks in the bond community—thought this was a good idea. Twenty years ago, Larry Summers did, too. So Orszag made sure to cite Summers's old paper in his footnotes.

The president received the report on May 15. It took just a few days for Summers to hear about it. He found out through Emanuel.

Orszag looked up from his desk. Summers had stormed over from the White House to Orszag's office, and his face was red with rage. It looked like he was about to burst a blood vessel.

He told Orszag he'd found out about the paper. He told him that he, Peter, knew the rules, no matter what the president had said. Everything was supposed to go through NEC. Then its chairman, Lawrence A. Summers, blew a gasket.

"What you've done is IMMORAL!" he shouted and stormed out.

———

Gary Gensler quietly caught the 6:00 p.m. train back to Baltimore on May 26 and, like most days, sat alone reading documents on trading strategies, even though it was a big day—maybe one of the biggest days of his life. He had been sworn in as head of the CFTC.

It had been a whirlwind two weeks of backroom deals, starting on the thirteenth. That's when Cantwell lifted her hold on him. It was all part of her final play to use the confirmation process to press forward on key policies. She told the White House that if they wanted her to lift her hold on Gensler, they'd have to affirm that all derivatives, including the over-the-counter derivatives, would have to be moved to open exchanges.

Gensler huddled with Summers, Geithner, Emanuel, and the team at Treasury. Though Geithner had been equivocal on such a move, Gensler had not been: after that first check with Geithner—"did you really mean what you said?"—Gensler stated in his testimony that electronic exchange trading was a key reform, even if it might mean billions in lost revenue to Wall Street. Acting as a liaison between Cantwell's office and the White House, Gensler crafted a position that would be acceptable to Cantwell. Senator Bernie Sanders might fuss—his anger at Wall Street and its many alumni in D.C. was visceral—but he'd eventually go along with Gensler's appointment as well.

In a press conference back on May 13, Geithner released an outline for the financial reforms being contemplated by the administration, including electronic exchanges, with public prices, for derivatives. "Significant gaps in the basic framework of oversight over critical institutions" had helped cause the financial crisis, he told reporters. "A series of comprehensive reforms to create a stronger system, less vulnerable to crisis, with stronger protections for consumers and investors" would now be worked out with Congress.

Finally, after repeated threats from Congress, a policy—on what many argue is among the most complex and crucial issues preventing another financial disaster—took shape.

Cantwell happily lifted her hold on Gary Gensler.

Negotiations between the White House and Bernie Sanders progressed for the next week, but Cantwell had been the tough one. Bernie just needed to take a stand to make a point. His hold was finally lifted, and Gensler was approved by the Senate—the last of Obama's thirty-two major appointments to cross the threshold. The vote was a bipartisan 88 to 6.

The winding drama of Gensler's nomination, stretching back five months, caught the attention of a few reporters, mostly with the business press. But the lack of coverage in such a busy time belied the importance of the issues at hand.

The push-and-shove between the progressive senators Cantwell and Sanders and the White House, and the interplay of interests and personalities, was a lesson in the subtle ingenuity of the American form of government. If Gensler wanted this job, Cantwell made clear, he'd have to speak loudly and clearly. Gensler did. He said, in endless hearings before the Senate Finance Committee, that mistakes were made at the end of the Clinton era, something Summers and Geithner would never say. He said that regulating the $600 trillion derivatives market, where one $50 tank of gas supports $5,000 in derivatives trades, is the most important thing that can be done in this period to change a "Wall Street culture that has permeated" the economic life of the country. He said he'd push this trading out of the back room, the profitable shadow lands of over-the-counter trading, and onto exchanges, where the fundamental laws of transparency—of subjecting products to the tireless comparative judgments of bang-for-your-buck Americans—would reign.

In fact, by day's end he had gone further than any of the surprised progressives expected, especially from someone worth roughly $20 million from his eighteen years at Goldman Sachs. They couldn't quite figure out what had happened.

But those traveling on the Amtrak train out of Washington with Gensler that night might have been granted a clue. On the outskirts of Baltimore, Gensler hopped into a newspaper-and-coffee-cup-littered "station car" and then stopped by a Mexican restaurant for takeout.

His house, looking like an old dowager of plaster and unfulfilled promise, stately but in need of some loving care, sat in the middle of untended fields, ten acres in any direction. "I'm home—dinner!" he shouted, stepping into the dark foyer. Upstairs, stocking feet were already hitting the floor.

The hallways on the way to the kitchen were filled with paintings— large, sweeping canvases—a few of them depicting a raven-haired woman with delicate features. That'd be the mother of the raven-haired teenaged girls, now crowding into the kitchen, talking buoyantly about their day.

The self-portraits were of Francesca, an accomplished artist, before she got sick. She died in 2006 after a five-year battle with cancer, and Gary made sure those paintings were hung where everyone could see them, every day.

People tend not to change much in their productive middle age, especially when they live within certain strong, self-sustaining communities that provide their basic needs, where their friends and livelihoods and core assumptions reside in some workable combination. To take a stand that creates a breach within that community is quite rare. The cost is just too high.

But that's what Gensler was now doing with one of country's most powerful, self-sustaining, play-for-keeps communities: Wall Street. Its ethos and ethics had altered the way people thought about hard work, honesty, self-reliance, and fair practice—what de Tocqueville once called America's admirable and accessible "bourgeois virtues." Wall Street had bet against people who believed in those sleepy mores, and year after year, it had won huge.

That Gensler, once numbered among its leaders, had now publicly turned on the Street was stunning enough; the rarity of such turn-and-fight moments had been a key to Wall Street's long run of success. Anyone credible enough to have a real effect would have to have made a lot of money, which he'd then have to claim was ill-gotten. On top of this he'd have to suffer a "you'll never have lunch in this town again" sanction from bustling New York. A lot to ask of anyone. But Gensler's challenge went beyond even that: if he became a crusader for reregulation, knowing what he knew, he could really hurt Wall Street.

There were those in New York who were already shorting such fears and chalking the whole mess up to naked ambition—something that would surely guide one of their own—by suggesting that Gensler had said whatever he had to say to get the job. That it was all talk.

Yet, if they had been around Gensler's kitchen table that night, a night made for self-congratulatory revelry, they'd have had cause for deep concern.

Because Gary Gensler fell into one of those discrete categories of people who create lasting change in Washington's marketplace of ideas. They tend to be either old and revered, like Volcker, who could use his unassailable credibility, and the freedom of advanced years, to say convincingly what others couldn't; or like Elizabeth Warren, a mold-breaking oddity who'd emerged from nowhere to catch the public's imagination, a bit like Obama himself; or someone whose priorities had been altered by tragedy, and who had become suffused with the heroic zeal that sometimes emerges from grief.

Gensler was in that third category. The best day of his life, he'd often say, was the day he met Francesca, and many of his worst were littered over the five years of running between hospitals, as he learned hard lessons about risks that can't be managed and things even money can't buy.

And that's why, in the past two years, he'd so often be seen running for trains, or grabbing teacher calls midmeeting, pulling himself away from the complex, oh-so-important discussions of Washington's policy mandarins about the economy or the financial system or the endless tinkering with incentives to make people do something unwillingly, or unwittingly, in society's wider interests. In fact, so much of the middling intellectual competitions in Washington's policy shops of this era were about managing risks and the things money could buy, just like those in the competing capital to the north. Many of the analyses that Obama was having difficulty mastering to Summers's dissatisfaction would, no doubt, be in this category.

But adversity had forced Gensler to glimpse something larger. That was why he'd spent a few hours pushing around this morning's swearing-in so that all three girls could be there, and not miss their most important classes; and why he made sure, though he didn't need to, that they'd wear something stylish when they stood next to him as he raised his hand and swore to uphold the Constitution and the laws of the land.

They knew Dad had a big job. But doing those things, and making sure to rush home on his big day to eat quesadillas with them in the messy, momless kitchen, was to make sure his girls knew something that, incidentally, many Americans were hoping to learn from their inspiring leader: no matter what, there would always be someone there watching over them.

Enough was enough, Rahm Emanuel decided. Something needed to be done. He summoned the two competing super-egos, Summers and Orszag, and told them to make peace. After all, they were each responsible for huge swaths of the federal government. And they were fighting at every turn.

After a bit of delicate negotiations, it was decided that they'd meet once a week for dinner and see how it worked.

So, that night, Orszag settled into a white-clothed table at the Bombay Club, a posh Indian restaurant across Lafayette Park, a favorite of lobbyists and White House officials.

Summers walked in, slightly late, but not impolitely so, and met Orszag at the table.

And then it was the two of them.

Orszag hoped that this time the White House would be less fraught with strife than the last go-round during the 1990s. Summers said it kind of came with the territory.

This talk of their shared history seemed to thaw things out. They both grabbed from the plate of flatbreads that everyone gets served—the restaurant is known for it—and tore corners at the discus-size breads.

"You know, Peter, we're really home alone."

Over the past few months, Summers had said this, in a stage whisper, to Orszag and others as they left the morning economic briefings in the Oval Office. The topics varied: taxes, deficits, the economy, economics in general.

"I mean it," Summers stressed. "We're home alone. There's no adult in charge. Clinton would never have made these mistakes."

No "adult in charge" of the world's mightiest nation at its time of peril? It bespeaks a crisis—of a president overmatched, unable to fulfill the duties of his office, and a nightmare no one wants to acknowledge in daylight.

While Orszag wouldn't publicly affirm Summers's critique of the president's abilities—saying later, "I don't want to go there"—he wouldn't disagree, either. He sat in meeting after meeting where the president would cover the same issue, or controversy, or policy dilemma, and "relitigate" it, in the president's parlance, over and over. Decisions were left unmade; policies drifted without direction. It wasn't a matter of intellectual framing. The president seemed to grasp the nature of key policy dilemmas, like a journalist, or narrator, or skilled observer. The problem was in guiding the analysis toward what a president is paid, and elected, to do: make tough decisions.

Still, Orszag admired the president both he and Summers were there to serve. He knew that if he and Summers went down this path, they'd end up fighting.

And they were here, breaking bread, to stop all the fighting. So Orszag nodded, and changed the subject.

FILLING THE VOID

RAHM EMANUEL WAS GETTING ANTSY. THE EMERGENCY ISSUES of pushing through a stimulus package and stabilizing the financial system had, he felt, been accomplished. The $787 billion stimulus was the only big-ticket item they'd be getting through Congress, at least for the foreseeable future. The stress tests, meanwhile, had the desired effect: by receiving the Good Housekeeping seal of approval from the government, an implicit grant of a federal backstop for any new investors, banks that passed the tests quickly raised capital and so did the ones that didn't. They seemed out of danger, if not yet starting to haul in the strong profits that were sure to come.

It was a Monday in late spring when the senior staff, both policy and political, joined the president in the Roosevelt Room. Emanuel had orchestrated the meeting to discuss what "the next big thing" ought to be.

A similar meeting in February—when the president decided to go with sweeping health care reform instead of financial reform or a comprehensive energy and environmental program—had been premature. At least that was Emanuel's view. It was a time of crisis, of having to think day to day—"with no playbook, no blueprint," Emanuel would later recall—of a collapsed financial system and fast-sinking economy. Now, if those twin crises had not necessarily been solved, their situations had at least been stabilized.

Emanuel felt it was the moment to make a choice about priorities. It was no secret that he thought the president had chosen wrong in making health care his top agenda item. But so little of substance had happened since February on health care that it was as though Obama had not chosen at all. That was the unspoken opening premise of the day's discussion: hitting the "Restart" button. It was as though the February discussion were being rerun or, in Obama's parlance, "relitigated."

Teams advocating health care reform and a large energy/environmental program argued their sides. Then Emanuel made his play, one he'd been carefully considering over the past month: financial reform.

"I argued for financial reform for mainly political reasons," he later recalled. "Having done a stimulus and the bank TARP, this was no money" coming from Congress. "Unlike health care or energy," he said, a tough, sweeping plan for fundamental financial reform needed no funding, no "ask" from stingy lawmakers. Emanuel had stepped up in mid-May, with the president otherwise occupied, to get something out in public with the release of Treasury's blueprint. It was Emanuel acting like a president, taking the helm, but it was like pulling teeth. Treasury was understaffed and unenthusiastic, and he'd gotten pushback, with Deputy Secretary Neal Wolin moaning at one point that "this stuff is really hard." Emanuel's response had been fierce. He pointed to a nearby desk and shouted, "Well, Neal, then sit down and start fucking typing."

But the effort opened Emanuel's eyes to what a plan could look like, and as he stressed in the Roosevelt Room, "We know what we have to do [on financial reform], there aren't any great mysteries here."

The president looked on, asking questions about where different policies—health care, environment/energy—might move from here, how an "action plan" might proceed for each. But as the meeting stretched on, the issue of financial reform took center stage. Again, as in the March showdown about restructuring Citi and other large banks, the key interplay was between Emanuel, Summers, and Geithner, three men who, along with Orszag, were firmly guiding the White House. In that earlier instance, Emanuel had sided with Geithner against Summers's enthusiasm, shared by Obama, for a broad and expensive restructuring of the financial system. Now it was Geithner and Summers against Emanuel. Both men said that undertaking financial reform now would "create an overhang of regulatory doubt" that would slow economic activity when they needed a restored and confident financial sector to drive economic activity.

Emanuel, certainly as attentive to Wall Street's needs and concerns as the duo, was unconvinced. Wall Street always had a complaint, and left to its own devices, it probably wouldn't be driving the recovery anyway. This had been a problem since the previous fall, when Paulson offered the first $125 billion in capital infusions to nine of the largest banks. The idea was that they'd lend the money out, which the banks had committed to trying to do. They didn't, and until the economy rebounded, they wouldn't. Maybe even not then, considering how weighted their operations still were toward exotic trading games and overseas investment. In other words, for something that was chimerical, a long shot, Geithner and Summers were sacrificing an opportunity to show bold leadership. The push for really tough financial reform would be political gold, Emanuel said, because it "had a sense of Old Testament justice."

Others echoed this sentiment. Government's role was not to make the banks profitable, but to stabilize them; that had been accomplished. Of course, the financial sector would grouse and moan and conjure fearful scenarios of being paralyzed by "regulatory overhang." But anti–Wall Street sentiment still ran high. Congress was at the ready, offering, in this case, the prospect of bipartisan action. It was a rare moment, with populist energy in the two parties moving in concert, and with even traditionally antiregulatory Republicans saying now was a time for steely-eyed rules of the road for an out-of-control industry. Emanuel said that Republicans such as Alabama senator Richard Shelby, the party's top player on banking issues, would be with them, and other Republicans as well: reforms could be pushed through quickly, possibly with big majorities.

The arguments shifted to and fro. Again Obama sat back, peppering each side with leading questions that might help them square the circle and reach consensus. Of course, there was no consensus. Emanuel, in a rare break from both Geithner and Summers—so often his back-channel partners in shaping White House policy—was offering up a more dynamic, carpe-diem model, where a settled but still weakened banking industry would learn who was boss. He was "thinking about this politically," he said later, and "Old Testament justice" had its own, strong political track record.

As the meeting approached the hour-and-a-half mark, though, it was clear that Obama was leaning toward Summers and Geithner, who felt that regulatory actions would undermine confidence, rather than boost it. Any uncertainty, they felt, risked depressing economic activity. "Tim and Larry both argued against it," Emanuel recalled. They believed "it would take a year at minimum, that the overhang of regulatory doubt would slow everything down, and the president sided with them."

The result was inaction.

"I gave the president my view," he said tersely.

Spend time with anyone who is officially larger than life, and they're bound to be restored, hour by hour, to familiar human proportions.

How that shrinkage is managed, though, is crucial. As with so much else around Obama, this was not managed at all for either the thirteen bankers or the health care providers. Both groups had been granted extended face-to-face exposure to Obama. From there, the journeys of these two most powerful interest groups, each at the center of the two great tests of the Obama presidency, evolved along a similar arc. The health care providers were quaking with readily exploitable fear at the Health Care Summit, as were the thirteen bankers when they walked into their meeting. Obama went with hope and consensus, and then, as Daschle said, didn't do much.

As summer arrived, that fear had gone from both groups. Obama may have created a "space" where solutions could happen, but when members of both interest groups saw him up close, and poked at him a bit, they found he exhibited certain human frailties that might be easily exploited. What they also saw—many of them managers in banking and health care with long experience—were that his words were not being translated into action. In fact, the actions of Obama's top lieutenants often seemed to contradict their boss's strong words and stated intentions.

While in many instances Obama expressed his desire to push forward major reforms to reorder and repair the financial system, the stress tests seemed to indicate otherwise. The banks were offered the sweet deals under Geithner's "Hobbit" programs. The PPIP, or the Public-Private Investment Program, was an arrangement in which the government matched and backstopped private investors who wanted to buy up troubled assets, to get the toxicity off the banks' balance sheets. No one even bothered to sign up. The stress tests had worked too well. With the government's replacement of Moody's and S&P, and with the assumption that anyone who invested in the federally endorsed banks would enjoy an implicit government guarantee, the banks quickly began to raise capital to repair their tier-one common capital shortfalls and pay back the TARP money. The incentives on that last part were quite acute: as soon as a bank paid back TARP funds it would wriggle free of the compensation caps—and steal talent from its competitors. Investing in the U.S. manufacturing or industrial sectors, and even in high tech, remained negligible, and there was no discernible bump in credit. The banks and their financial subsidiaries went back to earning money the way they had for much of the decade: through exotic, often computer-driven, trading.

In health care, Daschle's fears of April—that if Obama didn't step up and frame this debate, others would—became the hard realities of June. After the mishaps of the May letter on health care cost cutting— over what it meant and who'd said what—the realization dawning on the provider community was "What did it matter anyway?" The inability to frame and force acceptance of some of the era's strongest cost-saving ideas, many of them percolating for nearly two decades, meant that the battle between the two sides in the debate—cost versus coverage—was firmly tilted toward the latter. Orszag and Zeke Emanuel continued to push their concept of an "evidence-based safe harbor," an elegant construct where doctors could get by with lower malpractice premiums if they recommended procedures where there was actually evidence of effectiveness. In fact, the entire comparative-effectiveness mission, with its demonstrable cost savings, was under siege, as would be the case with any encampment left undefended. As Orszag, and later Obama, had long been saying, cost efficiencies are what should drive the expansion of coverage.

In an e-mail sent to the senior staff on June 8, Orszag elucidated how the cost argument was dissolving, both inside the White House and beyond it. Mostly, though, he and Zeke were left to watch as the expanded-coverage advocates—including Nancy-Ann DeParle—ascended. The unspoken default was to do coverage first, pushing the moral issue of universal coverage, and at some point in the future, maybe years from now, the expanded mandate would force a cost crisis that would finally bring all combatants to the table to change the way health care was delivered in America.

At that very moment, though, a visit to Max Baucus's office would have shown where the real action was occurring. Baucus had been holding regular hearings that were tapping the providers, insurers, and consumer groups and drawing almost daily media coverage. But the key events were not transpiring during the long hours of demonstrative debate in the committee's hearing room. They were happening in Baucus's warren of staff offices: providers were slipping in and out of there at all hours of the day.

Coordinating the action from the White House was Jim Messina, Baucus's former chief of staff, who was now deputy chief of staff under Rahm Emanuel. Messina's familiarity with Baucus and his people, seen as an advantage by the White House, had the effect of granting him wide latitude to cut deals. Baucus's interests and those of the White House, however, were not clearly aligned. The effect was forcefulness, but largely being led by Baucus.

Leading the way for the providers was, not surprisingly, Billy Tauzin. In June, Tauzin stood in Baucus's outer office waiting to iron out some details inside. Indeed, he had just cut a ten-year deal whereby PhRMA would provide $80 billion in cost reductions to ensure that no one from government, in the forthcoming plan, had any say over pharmaceutical costs. Other providers were right behind him. The receptionist gave Tauzin his cue to proceed inside. He smiled. "Still cancer-free. Lucky me!" Indeed.

On June 16 at the White House, David Axelrod reached for the remote and turned up the volume. Obama was doing a press conference outside, about a hundred yards away. The first question was, not surprisingly, about Iran. The streets of Tehran had been exploding for the past week in violent demonstrations about President Mahmoud Ahmadinejad and his allies' tampering with the current election. But beneath the bloody events was a startling subtext. Just ten days before, Obama had gone to Cairo to give one of his best, forward-leaning speeches. It was, in its way, a global corollary to the possibilities granted him on the domestic terrain at the start of his presidency. With demonstrations breaking across the globe, including in many Muslim-majority countries, when he won the election and, again, when he was sworn in, this was the speech everyone had been waiting for. It just was delayed, not happening until June 3.

Much like it was in the United States, the stunning speech was not followed with any carefully considered policy shifts. But what was clear was that the Iranians were leaping violently into some of the space Obama had created.

Those on the streets of Tehran, getting slaughtered by the hard-liner Ahmadinejad's security forces, were clearly looking for some signal from Obama: some strong words of support, a suggestion that the United States was with them. The possibility that Obama could shape events across the world, especially in the Muslim world, with his words, was a victory that Americans had long been waiting for. In the global hearts-and-minds struggle, what could be more important?

The one question for a reporter was one word—"Iran?"—and the great hungry eye of the news turned to Obama. Everyone knew the sub-text, and the news commentators, those who were actually paid to provide narration, could handle that. But just for good measure, Obama, as has so often been the case, decided to do a little narration himself.

"It was only—let's see—I think seven hours ago or eight hours ago when I—I have said before that I have deep concerns about the election," he began. "And I think that the world has deep concerns about the election. You've seen in Iran some initial reaction from the Supreme Leader that indicates he understands the Iranian people have deep concerns about the election. Now, it's not productive, given the history of U.S.-Iranian relations, to be seen as meddling—the U.S. president meddling in Iranian elections. What I will repeat and what I said yesterday is that when I see violence directed at peaceful protestors, when I see peaceful dissent being suppressed, wherever that takes place, it is of concern to me and it's of concern to the American people. That is not how governments should interact with their people."

Obama paused as he crafted his finale.

"And my hope is, is that the Iranian people will make the right steps in order for them to be able to express their voices, to express their aspirations. I do believe that something has happened in Iran where there is a questioning of the kinds of antagonistic postures towards the international community that have taken place in the past, and that there are people who want to see greater openness and greater debate and want to see greater democracy. How that plays out over the next several days and several weeks is something ultimately for the Iranian people to decide. But I stand strongly with the universal principle that people's voices should be heard and not suppressed. Okay? All right. Thank you, guys."

Axelrod turned down the volume. The president, given a golden opportunity to use his bully pulpit to direct global events, had decided, instead, to do a bit of exposition about someone—a character named Barack Obama—who actually had no strong personal views on a rare democratic eruption in one of the world's two or three most strategically important dictatorships. The broader problem, of course, was the administration's lack of follow-through, where a stirring speech, Obama's strongest suit, was not integrated into any plan of action.

While the president suddenly seemed to be of many minds about Iran, his top political adviser was single-minded, thinking about the possibilities of "moral energy." "Clearly," Axelrod said, "the president has been in a conversation with those people on the streets in Tehran, certainly and powerfully since his Cairo speech." But, he wondered, was it possible to summon "a similar kind of moral energy on the domestic landscape, especially with health care. The question is how the president can talk over the heads of the interest groups and elected officials in Washington, right to the people, and make clear that health care is a moral issue."

A few minutes later, in his tiny office across the alleyway from the White House in the Eisenhower Executive Office Building, Zeke Emanuel was considering his day.

The eldest of the Emanuel brothers, Zeke was such a renowned student that his two younger brothers, Rahm and Ari—the latter a power agent in Hollywood upon whom a central character in the show *Entourage* is modeled—decided "Why bother?" Now Zeke, a doctor with a PhD in medical ethics, faced the odd denouement of being seen as a threat, as unmanageable, by many in the White House run by his brother. It was soon clear why: Zeke had spent several decades arriving at his conclusions on health care. He had trouble giving them up.

And one of the hard truths about health care was that most Americans were reasonably satisfied with their current situation and fearful of change in an area of such consequence. He explained that most people who had coverage, sadly, didn't care all that much about the one in eight who didn't—folks who mostly just went to the emergency rooms, at great expense, for their basic care.

Zeke looked down at his schedule. He'd had a Health Care Reform Team meeting at 11:00 and had just gotten back from lunch with Jon Kingsdale, founder of the Massachusetts Health Connector, an agency that had helped implement that state's 2005 reform. He'd go over legislative strategy in congressional liaison Phil Schiliro's office at 5:00 and then meet with Vermont senator Bernie Sanders. He tore the schedule off the spindle and drew a bell curve, with A plus B on one side of the high hump and C down at the far tail.

"Do you know any chemistry? You know what that is? That might not be great art. This is the potential energy variant of a chemical reaction . . . so A plus B goes to C. But you need to add some energy to get over this hump, even if C is in a better space and it's more stable and it's

better and everything is more hunky dory. Getting over this [hump]—
the question is, in our system, can we get over this pain, to get to C?"

Where would this energy come from?

"The president . . . it's the fact that everyone is scared of what we do if
we don't reform, how bad it will be. Being scared of losing coverage . . .
or my kid won't have coverage. It's all those things; that's the key. But
you also need to believe in C." That, of course, would be a clear, vivid,
and credible representation of what the future would look like.

As the president sat down for his morning economic briefing on June 18,
there was a self-congratulatory air in the Oval Office. The day before,
with the release of Treasury's eighty-eight-page white paper and a host
of appearances and interviews by senior officials, the administration had
taken its first, nascent steps on financial regulatory reform.

The president had led the brigade, with an interview on CNBC. "We
want to do it right. We want to do it carefully. But we don't want to tilt at
windmills," he said, in a comment that led the morning's papers.

No windmill tilting, meaning nothing too dramatic, despite most
news establishments swallowing the president's top line about "the most
sweeping set of regulations since the Great Depression." There hadn't
really been any since then, so the bar was low. And it was further clear
that the president wouldn't be engaging forcefully with Congress or expending political capital on the matter.

The plan was not deep, but it was wide, touching on almost every part
of the nation's vast financial industry, from mortgages to capital requirements for banks, insurance regulation, and derivatives trading. It would
give added regulatory authority to the Federal Reserve, create a new
consumer financial products agency, like the one proposed by Elizabeth
Warren, give the government power to take over troubled bank holding companies and investment firms, and require banks to keep a share,
albeit only 5 percent, of the mortgage-backed securities they created and
sold.

But early criticisms pointed out that the changes were around the
margins, rather than fundamental or structural. There were no limits on
size, no breaking up of large financial institutions, and no remedy for
the "too big to fail" dilemma. Standard, plain-vanilla derivatives were

destined for clearinghouses and some to be traded on exchanges, but the large, profitable shadow markets for OTC derivatives—the complex "bespoke" products—remained largely untouched beyond added obligations to have trades reckoned by clearinghouses. Several stories, one in the *Wall Street Journal*, said that Wall Street let out a sigh of relief.

More than the substance of reform, which Obama largely left to Treasury, the president was particularly taken with Elizabeth Warren, whom he'd seen on television. "Wow, she's really something," he said, one telegenic law school professor sizing up another. "Really good. We should get her out there more often." Larry Summers and Anita Dunn, the communications chief, discussed for a moment how to get Warren more TV appearances, while Alan Krueger smiled to himself. It was good Geithner wasn't present. He despised the crusading Warren, head of the commission that oversaw TARP, who had grilled Geithner mercilessly in front of her committee.

Obama nodded to indicate he was ready. Krueger and the other labor specialist among the senior staff, Biden's chief economist Jared Bernstein, had been working with their staffs for weeks on one of the most wrenching briefings of the Obama presidency: the jobless recovery.

Bernstein started by defining a jobless recovery as a situation where unemployment remains high or even rises after the official National Bureau of Economic Research date that marks the bottom of a recessionary trough. So, what do you guys think? Obama asked them. Both felt that a jobless recovery was highly likely, and said that others in the administration agreed. A fresh internal forecast of the so-called Troika—Treasury, OMB, and Council of Economic Advisers—was predicting a whopping unemployment rate at 9.8 percent in 2010.

It was a grim glimpse of the future for the Obama presidency: unemployment in 2010 of nearly 10 percent. Obama was pensive. Economics had never been his strong suit, but he could do the political math. That, at least, would mean a disastrous midterm. Unemployment so high would also be a drain on the budget, with a loss of tax revenues, a rise in unemployment benefits, and the cost of added services. Clearly, he said, that stimulus wasn't enough. No one needed to answer.

"All right, let's argue it out," he said, as Krueger passed out a one-page briefing sheet. He knew, at this point, how Obama liked it. Not a dense analysis or lots of charts, but rather a few top-line ideas he could use to shape a discussion. It was titled "Jobless Recovery? Pro or Con," with "pro" bullet points: record low number of hours worked; record high number of permanent layoffs; last two recoveries were jobless. For "con," only one item: "companies are very lean, will find they are too lean and may want to hire."

"Larry, why don't you take that side," Obama said, and three economists hashed it out as Obama listened, throwing in a question or two.

Bernstein emphasized that the number of unemployed workers relative to vacancies had surged and that interest rates implied that aggregate demand would likely be low. Krueger talked about how many key industries—construction and state and local government—might end up shedding more jobs. When demand picked up, hours would rise, but with work hours at a record low, it wouldn't impact job numbers. He then posited that Americans might put up with European-style work hours after the recession. Maybe they'd even want them.

"No, no," Obama interjected. "Here people want the longer hours, because they want the money."

Summers cited Mark Zandi, Moody's chief economist, who'd been predicting a strong bounce-back. He brought in business cycle data, a few behavioral observations, and a few data points indicating that employers were already too lean.

After a bit, Obama shut it down. "Look, I hope Zandi's right that we'll have a quick bounce-back, but we clearly can't count on that." He ran through some obvious items: make sure Recovery Act money is doled out quickly with benefits for job creation; figure out ways to spur further infrastructure investment; look for other ways to increase job growth, such as clean energy. "But we should start talking about it, about a jobless recovery, so we're out in front of this thing."

Obama got up heavily. "Larry, if your arguments about a quick bounce-back turn out to be right, and I don't think they will be, I'll give you a $10 bonus."

Axelrod tried to get some shtick going: "You've offered the bonuses to Larry before. Don't think you've ever paid."

"Sure would be nice to pay this time," Obama said, quietly, almost to himself.

Now, with budgets tight, if these projections were accurate, Obama could be facing real trouble. Of course, more Americans would be too.

A few weeks later, the secretive matter of who would replace Ben Bernanke, or whether he'd be replaced at all, was slowly moving toward a conclusion. The selection process had been delegated to Geithner in the late spring. Someone in Summers's role might otherwise have been involved, but Summers was the leading candidate to replace Bernanke. Larry felt it was knitted into his initial agreement to take the NEC job: barring extraordinary circumstances, he'd be a top choice for Bernanke's position. Maybe the president had said that, maybe he had just implied it. Maybe it was a case, as Daschle said often happened, of someone reading things into Obama's attentive acknowledgments that weren't always there. In any event, Summers was counting on the Bernanke job. It would be the triumphant capstone of his comeback and the high perch from which to complete his long career. Geithner, from the start, handled it deftly. He had the ever-popular Krueger solicit opinions about candidates from far and wide, including from Krugman and Stiglitz, and assembled a list of potential appointees. Summers was not concerned, even though he and Geithner were not getting along all that well. The March "showdown" meeting, and the disputes in its aftermath about the stress tests, had left a residue.

What was more, Geithner's star was rising in Obama's estimation, and on this matter he was the key voice Obama turned to in the Oval Office. The president's question: Whom did Geithner feel he could work with most effectively? Geithner said, according to those familiar with the discussions, that he didn't have a preference between Summers and Bernanke, though he felt Bernanke had done a very strong job, was a terrific partner, and had a great deal of credibility in the financial markets. Obama felt that last point suggested a kind of continuity that would be important for the recently stabilized markets. Winner: Bernanke.

Summers was outraged and petulant. He started to list demands to Rahm: A round of golf with Obama. He wanted to walk into major events, such as signature speeches or the State of the Union, with the cabinet, a privilege not given even to the senior-most advisory posts. And he wanted a car and driver, like Geithner had. The behavior was, for want of a better term, childish, and the Obama team's attitude toward Larry began to shift from frustration, and sometimes fear, to eye-rolling incredulity.

As for the demands, Rahm balked. He could manage everything but the car and driver. No one in the West Wing had that. Summers would have none of it. So, for two weeks, as deputy chief of staff Jim Messina raced between the White House and the Baucus committee, he had to search for a car for Larry Summers. When he came up empty-handed, Summers reluctantly accepted two rounds of golf and preferred seating at the State of the Union as consolation.

But the issue of appeasing Summers went well beyond golf.

He was short-tempered in meetings, even more than usual, and began to launch a rearguard assault for even greater clout, using his broad mandate and closeness to the president to envelop various departments in the executive branch. Summers, who as part of his prenuptial agreement in taking the job had been assured that he would manage "all economic policy" information flowing to the president, was redefining that mandate to include environmental/energy issues, tax policy, and health care. He wanted what he called "content control" from all those departments. That meant any documents, briefing materials, or reports from any of those areas came to him for review, and he'd decide how or whether they upstreamed to the president. In addition, he'd control access to Obama for top officials like energy/climate change czar Carol Browner and health care reform chief Nancy-Ann DeParle. Though Melody Barnes—a widely accomplished scholar, longtime chief counsel to Ted Kennedy, and top domestic policy aide from the campaign—sat atop the Domestic Policy Council (the entity designed to oversee and integrate all domestic policy), she as well was no match for Summers, who now had control of virtually the entire domestic shoreline.

Next stop, Orszag. Summers wanted "content control" over OMB. Anything intended for the president from OMB, as well as all budgetary decisions, would have to be reviewed first by him. Orszag would lose direct access to Obama; he'd have to go through Summers.

It didn't take long for Orszag to show up at Emanuel's office to tell him this was "outrageous." As compared with the departments of czars like Browner or DeParle, OMB's very purpose since its founding under Nixon was to be a kind of management team for the president, distilling actions and options from across the government into their actual costs. Because there was always a limited budget, the OMB directors must keep a president, even with his awesome powers, ever in a conversation with measurable reality. Orszag said he'd be damned if his access was cut off and those choices were served in Summers's rhetorical brew.

Emanuel was sympathetic, but he asked Orszag to be understanding about how difficult it was to manage Summers.

"Come on, Peter, help me out here," he said.

Orszag was incredulous. *Help you out? You're the chief of staff!*

Emanuel finally stepped in, and Summers backed off, at least for that day. But the ongoing push-and-shove atop the administration, without leadership from either the president or the chief of staff, was leaving lines of authority blurred, roles ill defined, and deepening questions of who—at any given moment—was in charge.

The president did not really have a coherent health care plan to sell. By setting overarching goals and then leaving the specifics of any bill largely to Congress, he had nothing to describe or champion as a better future, as Zeke Emanuel's C. It was just a jumble of proposals without a clear model of how to pay for reform and make good on his pledge to keep it "budget neutral."

Several skilled Washington managers—including former Treasury secretary Bob Rubin and former Reagan chief of staff Ken Duberstein, along with Podesta and Daschle—were, by midsummer, starting to offer advice on how to bring a modicum of sound process to the White House. Without that, several of them stressed, an organization of hundreds of political appointees in the White House and across the tops of agencies couldn't possibly move in unison to assist the president in making sound decisions and carrying forward his dictates. Things get lost. Initiatives languish or vanish. Or, as was already the case on a host of issues, the White House gets OBE'd: "overtaken by events." The advice focused mostly on the top, the area they were all most familiar with: how to make certain that issues were debated, with options fully explored, and then distilled into a clear set of choices for the president. Once a decision was made, what would be the agreed-upon model of execution—one that pushes forward with constantly checked progress—to advance the leader's wishes?

They didn't make much headway. Emanuel, with his day-to-day focus on "getting points on the board," scrambled for quick results, trying to win each day's news cycle. As Bob Rubin told one of his many acolytes in the White House during a phone call, "Rahm's more inclined to want to get a bill passed than really be worried about what's in the bill." Only a few people at the very top, such as Summers and Orszag, had begun to ask if the problem wasn't more fundamental. Maybe the issue wasn't just with the loosely organized and impulsive Emanuel, sitting atop a White House where roles, and lines of authority, were fuzzy. Maybe the problem was with the president himself, an inquisitive man who, as Axelrod said, "moved fluidly from one thing to another"—a fox, in the old Isaiah Berlin allegory, who moved lightly from one place of opportunity to another, rather than a hedgehog, who focused intently on a goal and pushed it through.

Either way, someone had to do something. So, in June, Tom Daschle teamed up with John Podesta, in essence, to run a policy process outside the White House. They pulled together a few leading experts on health care funding, carefully constructed a plan to tax high-end health insurance, so-called Cadillac plans, and then worked back channels with the various interest groups, including labor, to get it off the launch pad. Soon enough, the White House had a way to pay for nearly half its health insurance reform.

Meanwhile, more deals were quietly being negotiated with providers. On July 8 the hospitals secretly cut their deal with the team of Baucus, Messina, and now, DeParle, just as Tauzin had for the pharmaceutical companies the month before. They'd accept $155 billion in payment reductions over the coming ten years, provided that the bill had no "public option," which would have reimbursed hospitals at a lower rate than private insurers.

Axelrod and his political team never pulled together much of a plan to go over the heads of official Washington and speak directly to the American people. Not that this had not been suggested for months, since Tom Daschle, at the Health Care Summit, told Obama that if he didn't step forward to frame this debate, someone else would do it for him.

It just took a few months—until summer—for that to happen.

The Tea Party movement, fueled by Fox News, rose out of the heartland and spread. Talk of "death panels," another brilliant bit of rhetorical mischief from the Republican Party, dominated the airwaves. Obama and his surrogates spent much of July trying to wash the smell of death panels off their skin like someone who'd been in a bad run-in with a skunk.

In early August, as news of Tauzin's deal with PhRMA finally leaked out, the Obama team met in the Oval Office. If Obama was on the defensive, he'd lose all the swing votes, Daschle foretold. He was, and the votes were in flight. Even some solid Democratic supporters of health care reform were on the move. Nancy Pelosi felt she had to step in, to set some sort of anchor to keep the debates fixed and focused. Obama had said during the campaign that he was for a basic government-run health insurance plan for those who didn't have private insurance, that a "public option" would be a way "to keep health insurers honest." He hadn't offered much support for the idea since. Emanuel said, internally, that it was a nonstarter and was not a central plank for the internal plans coursing through the White House policy shops. What's more, the core of the deal cut with the hospitals, not yet revealed, had killed the public option.

Pelosi, meanwhile, saw how the public option terrified the insurers—an existential issue that brought them to the bargaining table, and kept them there. She didn't want to give that up, despite opposition from the American Medical Association and other providers. She said that the public option was nonnegotiable—the only way, she felt, for the government to reshape the marketplace.

On balance, it was an utterly incoherent process, where the White House seemed to be of many minds, or none at all, with the House and Senate in open collision, and proposals to significantly reduce health care costs off the table. For opponents of health care reform, the tough decision was whether this should be called ObamaCare or PelosiCare. Both terms seemed to work in stirring up fear and passion. The joyous anger on the right was palpable.

———————

Dr. Jack Wennberg, founder, provocateur, and contrarian of the Dartmouth Atlas Project, prides himself on being precise, punctual, and not easily pleased. Of Norwegian stock, from parents who settled in upstate New York, Wennberg liked to hike (usually alone), read reams of medical data, and be on time.

And today, on a crisp, blue August sundown in the mountains near Hanover, New Hampshire, he was running late.

The event was a Friday evening party at an elementary school near Hanover being thrown by the family of his successor, Dr. Jim Weinstein. Just about everyone he knew would be there. That would include the roughly two hundred people, most from both Dartmouth's Atlas Project—the data-fed analytical engine for revolutionary disruptions in American medical care—and Dartmouth-Hitchcock Medical Center, the huge, modern institute that seemed to have been dropped by some extraterrestrial transport into a notch of hillside just outside of town.

Though it had only been two years since he'd passed the torch to Weinstein, it had nonetheless been a period of transition. When the change was made official in 2007, many of those in the Dartmouth community quipped "it's about time"—Jack, after all, was seventy-three—while appreciating how unimaginable it was that anyone could replace Wennberg.

When he first attempted to publish papers in the late 1960s about the enormous disparities in both the frequency and cost of various procedures—with no discernible difference in outcomes—he was shooed away from established medical journals. When the journal *Science* did publish his work, the problem shifted: he was attacked. Nearly forty years later, he was still being attacked, but now mostly out of frustration. Once Wennberg started the Center for Evaluative Clinical Services in 1988, he began attracting doctors and researchers of every stripe to Hanover as, specialty by specialty, they began to identify wide or stunning variations in medical practice and then "compare outcomes under controlled circumstances." The center began to publish the Dartmouth Atlas, documenting these variations in the way medical resources were used all over the country. One striking example was a thirty-three-fold difference between regions in the frequency of mastectomies and lumpectomies.

When Wennberg and CECS dug into the data on "elective" surgeries they came upon a vast, related line of research: how patients make, or more often don't make, their own decisions—even with elective procedures. Hence the Foundation for Informed Medical Decision Making, an organization that spearheaded the concept, now widely accepted if not often fully implemented, of "shared decision-making"—where patients are helped to actively assess the risks and rewards of procedures, rather than nodding along with a doctor's recommendation.

Each of these ideas, each step forward, was met with skepticism and often open hostility from the medical establishment. As Wennberg tirelessly stresses, the last thirty years has seen the growth of "investor medicine," where Wall Street looked with favor and enthusiasm on hospitals, pharmaceutical companies, and medical device makers. "It's become more about money and less about care," Wennberg said. "For a hospital to do something that may be good for patients but bad for its profits, it risks having its bonds downgraded or having its investors up in arms."

Nonetheless, the data was irrefutable, making the "Wennberg Variation" accepted dogma. Now Wennberg shared stages atop the profession with the likes of Dr. Paul Farmer, cofounder of Partners in Health and builder of hospitals and clinics in some of the most forbidding corners of the globe. Wennberg and Farmer had just won the annual Public Health Heroes Award at University of California, Berkeley, and Wennberg is finally being credited with forever changing American medicine.

But Wennberg's most auspicious contribution may be the man he helped create and was now hugging inside the auditorium of the elementary school, where a fund-raiser for special-needs children was about to start.

Weinstein, twenty years Wennberg's junior, had a tenured chair in orthopedics at the University of Iowa when he came to Dartmouth to do a fellowship in outcomes-based research in 1994. "As an orthopedic surgeon, I often didn't feel that my patients were getting the information they needed to make their decisions," Weinstein said in a recent interview. "They were talking to me, but maybe that wasn't good enough, because I was a surgeon and surgeons do what surgeons do. Maybe they weren't getting a fair shake."

Wennberg soon had another disciple, but one he noticed had a surprising ferocity. Wennberg learned that Weinstein had a daughter, Brianna, then nine, who had been diagnosed with leukemia when she was one. Weinstein had been on the receiving end of what Wennberg called "an uncontrolled experiment in medicine."

It had been hell. There were complications from chemotherapy that had not been well explained. She was given the wrong drugs. And, most tragically, as a toddler she'd been treated with unnecessary radiation that caused extraordinary pain and ongoing disabilities.

What Weinstein had studied at Dartmouth, in terms of unnecessary procedures, he lived when he returned to Iowa. At one point an oncologist threatened to sue him for not accepting a cancer treatment protocol he was recommending. After two years back in Iowa, the Weinstein family moved to Hanover for good in late 1995. Brianna was eleven then. She died a year and a half later.

After her death, Weinstein said, he and his wife "felt it was our obligation to make it better for others. So I decided to try to change the world of medicine from within."

That is where Weinstein began to step beyond his mentor, Wennberg. He became the head of orthopedic surgery at Dartmouth and turned the department on its head. Back surgeries are among the most common, and lucrative, major medical procedures. What Weinstein discovered, using the might of Dartmouth Atlas research and data from within his own hospital, was that many back surgeries offer no lasting benefit to patients. The problem at Dartmouth, like that at hospitals across the country, is what happens once the hard truth is uncovered. There was a department full of surgeons who made their living from these operations. Opting for an array of less intrusive, less expensive, and less profitable alternatives—mostly various kinds of physical therapy—was a formula for economic ruin. Weinstein began what he called "a transition program" to bridge his department to a different model of medical practice. Some doctors left. Others managed on lower incomes. But over the years the situation stabilized. "We simply weren't going to do procedures that had no discernible value—period." Of course, Weinstein, having battled unnecessary treatments with his daughter, carried a tenor of moral authority in this conversation. He could not be opposed. And that made all the difference. "It's Jack's mission and my sadness that came together and gave me direction," Weinstein said. "She was so courageous. She never complained. She fought through all the pain, and the nonsense, and she taught me everything I'd need to know about living this gift of life to its fullest, and with purpose."

Soon Weinstein had gone national, as the principal investigator of the Spine Patient Outcomes Research Trial, one of the largest recent studies funded by National Institutes of Health. The multiyear study examined a wide array of spinal surgeries, including the common surgery for lumbar disk herniation, and has found that nonoperative procedures are often a better choice. Slowly, procedures are beginning to change at many of the leading hospitals.

What Weinstein did for aching backs, along the way saving significant Medicare payments, was what enlivened Orszag and intrigued Obama: the possibility of reshaping medical practice in the United States through the power of evidence-based outcomes and data on comparative effectiveness.

It was, however, a long distance still between theory and practice. Though the data was pleasing to technocrats, it remained threatening to the long-established ways of the medical world. Change is hard, as

Obama often said, and always driven, in Margaret Mead's famous quip, by small groups of committed people. In this case, it was two headstrong men and one brave young girl.

As the sun set, those two men were working hard at having a good time. This was the Tenth Annual Brie Fund Concert and Quilt Raffle, a tradition started by the Weinsteins after Brie's death to celebrate her memory and here—at the elementary school she attended—raise money for children with special needs, physical and cognitive, like those their daughter struggled with after her childhood radiation.

Brianna's younger sister, Shelsey, a senior at Middlebury College and the first cellist in their orchestra, played an original composition and joined other musicians for six selections, ending with the "Song of the Birds," by Pablo Casals, dedicated to her sister.

The day's big money-raiser is always an ample, colorful quilt made by Brianna's mother, Mimi Weinstein, in honor of her daughter. When Shelsey pulled the winning raffle ticket from the bucket, she looked twice at the name, surpressing disbelief, and then called out, "Jack and Corky Wennberg!" A crowded elementary school auditorium of onlookers gasped, then cheered, as one obstinate middle-aged man passed a quilt, a stitched emblem of his inspiration, to an old stick-in-the-mud, and everyone basked in the certainty of what inspiration, and irrefutable data, can achieve.

A team of senior advisers gathered in the Oval Office in August. Rahm Emanuel had been "begging" for a more modest approach to health care reform, dubbed the "Titanic" plan. It would insure more than ten million Americans by widening previous congressional plans to expand coverage for children, and lift the number of single mothers eligible for Medicaid. It could get bipartisan support. "We've always done health insurance in groups: the elderly, the poor," he said, according to a participant in the meeting. "And we can do it again, with a few large groups, like children. That brings us close to everyone."

Obama resisted. The whole enterprise had been badly botched; that was indisputable. But he didn't want to retreat. He was the president, after all. Phil Schiliro, the head congressional liaison, laid out the grim outlines of a Congress in flight. If the swing votes such as Grassley or Enzi, or the Maine twins, Snowe and Collins, had ever been "possibles," they were now reaches. They had all been to town hall meetings in their states, crammed with new enthusiasts of government opposition—many of them self-defined as Tea Partiers, some not. But whatever they were labeled, these dissenters were having an effect. Everyone in the room agreed that health care reform had become a long shot.

Everyone, that is, except the president.

Obama looked around at grim faces, and reached back to see if he could touch the fire—the lightning strike that, as Axelrod said, had propelled a man just four years out of the Illinois Senate into the White House. Whether or not there'd been a "wisdom" to those crowds, in Iowa and everywhere else, Obama had to believe there was.

"Look, I feel lucky," Obama said to the dispirited group. "How can any of you not feel lucky? Just look at me. I was elected president of the United States."

The president had lost control of his White House; he had almost no process to translate his will into policy on the occasions when he could decide on a coherent path. But such decisions were rare. A group of four men, all seasoned Washington hands, had assumed enormous authority in his administration, and the women, who often were more attentive and purposeful in carrying out his wishes, were aggrieved. He was being reviled across much of the country and called a socialist, or worse. His approval ratings, in the 70s in February, had slipped to the signature tipping point of 50 percent, with 43 percent disapproving, in an authoritative Gallup poll of August 24 through August 26.

In a meeting in the Oval Office on September 1, Gibbs quipped about how bad the poll numbers were on health care reform, as others recounted how Obama and his main policy initiative were being framed, far and wide.

"This is about whether we're going to get big things done," Obama said. "I wasn't sent here to do school uniforms."

That barb was directed at Emanuel, who'd been filling the roles left untended by Obama, because someone had to make some decisions. All right, Emanuel said archly, "So, you still feeling lucky?"

"My name is Barack Hussein Obama and I'm sitting here," Obama answered evenly. "So, yeah, I'm feeling pretty good."

What lessons did Obama's days of greatest good fortune hold? When in trouble, dig deep and conjure a defining moment of oratory. It had always worked. It was who he was. As he had prepared his speech for the 2004 convention, some had asked if he was nervous. He laughed, "I've got this. In this, I'm Michael Jordan." He could still give a speech, damn it, and that was exactly what he wanted to do. Emanuel now said he should wait. He'd get only one chance at a big health care speech. If he went for it, and it wasn't well received, it'd be a disaster. He would have dropped the last card in his hand. Obama seemed to say, *How much worse could it get?*

The health care speech, slated as a major address to a joint session on September 9, would have to be written fast, and it would have to be the best of his presidency, Obama told Favreau. This just seemed to fire up both men. It felt like the glory days, and Obama kept everyone at arm's length. Favreau, who had to fly to California for the wedding of another speechwriter on the staff, Ben Rhodes, worked over the long Labor Day weekend, sending Obama pages from a California hotel. Obama hunkered down. Axelrod dove in, too. They had received from Vicki Kennedy a letter Ted had written in the spring, to be released after his death (he died on August 25), calling health care "the great unfinished business of our society," something that was above all "a moral issue," touching "the fundamental principles of social justice and the character of our country." It would be a signature theme in the speech.

The president was suffused with a take-charge forcefulness that was uncommon—he was going to save this thing—and it went beyond what he would say. There had to be substance, so the speech didn't simply lift emotions without lasting effect. He wanted the White House to prepare a detailed plan of where it stood, especially on what he considered the all-important program of evidence-based practice of medicine. In June the president had read a *New Yorker* article by Atul Gawande that essentially applied Dartmouth's model to look at two counties in Texas with enormous variations in health care costs—one of them, the highest-cost county in the United States for Medicare—but negligible differences in the health of their populations. He ordered the entire senior staff to read it. The matter perplexed Orszag, as the article was just a narrative rendering of what he thought the president understood from their frequent discussions on the matter; Axelrod later said putting the latest findings "in that format was eye-opening for him." But it fired up Obama, and he pressed to add new powers to the Center for Medicare & Medicaid Innovation—which would allow them to direct vast annual payments for those programs around principles of comparative effectiveness—to the White House health care plan. And he wanted that plan, the fully articulated position of his administration on health care reform, to be released along with the speech. In a way, it was to be a detailed rendering of what Zeke Emanuel would call C: how health care in America will look when reform becomes real.

But in senior staff meetings without the president attending, Rahm Emanuel dissented. He felt it would be smarter to remain less specific, as the White House had been to that point, and just release a two-page paper, with a few bullet points and no details.

Orszag disagreed. So did Dan Pfeiffer, the deputy communications director. "I can't believe we're releasing a two-page thing when the president keeps talking about releasing his full plan in the speech," Pfeiffer said in one meeting. The White House had a plan pulled together, ready for dissemination.

When Orszag was about to say as much in a meeting with the president, just days before the speech, Emanuel glared at him with what Orszag later recalled as a "do not do that" look. The OMB director put a lid on it.

Meanwhile, the president moved, unaware, thinking his comprehensive proposal was to be released along with the speech, which was turning into a tour de force.

Obama worked furiously on the speech and was still rewriting key passages on Tuesday, the eighth. Emanuel was screaming—they needed to see "at least one final draft before it's delivered." They would get it for only a few hours on Wednesday afternoon before it had to be finalized and printed for the press. This was an adolescent rebellion against the naysayers, such as Emanuel, who were constantly assessing the political landscape and saying what could, and mostly what couldn't, be done. On Wednesday, Obama was adding lines, including a few of the most memorable ones. While the facade of his address to Congress was rooted entirely in pragmatism, its beating heart was something much more profound. The speech confronted a more fundamental question: the identity of government in the modern era.

Unlike at Obama's previous attempts at rhetorical conceptualizing, his audience had become wary. He had to *convince* rather than drum up. At first he appeared to be going through the motions, laying out his case for reform. "The time for bickering is over. The time for games is passed. Now is the season for action," Obama declared, a secure applause line before "Now is the time to deliver on health care!" Midway through, while the president was countering a Republican claim that reform would cover illegal immigrants, a shout came from the audience: "You lie!" It was Joe Wilson, a Republican congressman from South Carolina.

Obama continued undeterred, churning his way slowly toward his dramatic conclusion. The third act of the speech was a show-stopper. Invoking Kennedy, thoughtfulness, and basic decency, Obama made the most compelling case for liberalism that has been made in recent memory. "We did not come to fear the future. We came here to shape it. I still believe we can act even when it's hard. I still believe we can replace acrimony with civility, and gridlock with progress. I still believe we can do great things, and that here and now we will meet history's test."

Still, the speech was light on substance—many proposals were offered, not all of them fitted inside a sweeping, carefully crafted plan. There was no news, about something Obama was strongly for or against, that prompted surprise. But as is the case with leadership, the content of the speech was secondary to the tone. For the first time since Manassas, Obama sounded like a man ready to *lead*. His words were authoritative and moving, making a case not just for health care, but for the community of states and a powerful ethic of shared purpose.

The next morning, Favreau received a note from the president complimenting him on the job. He was sure he knew what the president was thinking. They were all thinking it. They'd recaptured the magic. "Just like the campaign," Favreau wrote back.

———

Barney Frank, trailed by an aide, was standing in front of a church talking to a cop.

"Excuse me, can you tell me where Wall Street is?"

The heavyset cop, gut over his belt, looked this way and that.

"Let me see, I know it's near here somewhere, but . . ."

Frank stormed off in midsentence.

"All these damn cops are from Staten Island. None of them know where the hell Wall Street is."

It was September 14, the one-year anniversary of the Lehman Brothers bankruptcy that set off the Great Panic, and the Washingtonians had descended on Wall Street.

Or close to Wall Street.

Barney Frank, the forceful chairman of the House Financial Services Committee and arguably Congress's most powerful single actor in reforming Wall Street, continued to wander the caverns of Lower Manhattan, talking nonstop.

"This time, we've got 'em, we're gonna get reform, something through, October or November . . . wait a minute, Broad Street? . . . No, Wall Street lost it, they have no clout . . . the only issue is the Consumer Bureau, because that's the one where I have to fight community banks on, they don't like it . . . hold on, where the hell are we? . . . But when it comes to derivatives, and all those other issues, they're done. These people have no clout . . . Okay, I think I'm getting close . . . There'll be some loopholes they can exploit if the FDIC and the SEC don't significantly increase capital requirements . . ."

He could tell he'd hit home, because there was an uncommon ruckus on the street even at 10:00 a.m. The president was due to speak in Federal Hall, the gold-domed neocolonial temple at the corner of Wall and Nassau. It was a summit, of sorts, between America's two great capitals—one of private endeavor, the other of public purpose.

And it was a circus. Barney slipped in the nondescript side entrance of the New York Stock Exchange and soon stepped in front of CNBC's television cameras to talk about the day's events.

The mood on the network was ebullient. The market was back. Wall Street was roaring forward. Trading profits were high. JPMorgan and Goldman Sachs were soon to book record profits for the third quarter, ending September 30. The stock market had risen from 6,600 in early March to 9,000.

Frank said he was ready to start hearings next week to deal, piece by piece, with the major elements of financial reform.

"These issues are complicated," said CNBC's Erin Burnett. "It's tough. Very few people in the industry understand derivatives and what went wrong and how to deal with them. And you may be the only person in Washington who really, some people say, is capable of drafting a reform bill."

Frank, whose considerable ego had been piqued, offered no refutation—some of the derivatives offerings have thousand-page prospectuses, he said—before taking a halfhearted stab at modesty. "I think highly of Geithner and his staff, Ben Bernanke, Sheila Bair . . . um . . . Gary Gensler!"

In his office in Washington, Gary Gensler looked up at the screen. Wall Street's longtime cover story—derivatives and swaps are too complicated for anyone but them to understand—was at the core of "their leave us alone and let us charge whatever we decide" position. Of course, swaps and derivatives could be understood and regulated just like any other product. Gensler, in fact, was betting on it.

He would have killed to be in New York today. He'd bucked for one of the senior appointed jobs, and may have had one if Hillary had won. But in the months since his confirmation, he was beginning to see how his side-step into the regulatory realm, and an agency, the Commodity Futures Trading Commission, that not one person in a hundred could cite, might work out just fine. He was, after all, a regulator—not a political actor, like those appointees close to the president who were, at this moment, snaking through Manhattan traffic in Obama's motorcade, bound for Wall Street.

As a regulator, he could take the lead on issues of his choosing, which is what he'd done over the summer. In June's white paper on financial reform, many of the elements Frank was discussing on CNBC—resolution authority, a systemic risk regulator, a consumer agency—were noted. A key area, as well, was the regulation of derivatives. Despite what Geithner had said in his confirmation hearings, the white paper had not mentioned derivatives exchanges, only clearinghouses.

Geithner might have demurred with Cantwell on the phone as the vote on his confirmation approached, saying he hadn't meant to say he wanted to put derivatives on exchanges. But Gensler never did.

In August, he released a public letter on the position of the CFTC chairman, saying he would push for "transparent exchange trading" of derivatives. He was staking out a position beyond that of the Treasury Department. Geithner expressed displeasure, in his typically passive-aggressive way. "You could have warned me," he reportedly told Gensler.

Barney Frank watched the give-and-take with acute interest. In an interview that summer, he opined about Obama needing someone like a Joe Kennedy, Roosevelt's first head of the newly formed SEC, because "we're short on people who know how to play Wall Street's games." With all the anger at the industry, just about the only one of those people who could manage to slip through confirmation was Gensler. The idea that Geithner or Summers was like Joe Kennedy, something the president would later say, Frank found laughable.

Wall Street was now watching Gensler carefully. When he said he wanted to put derivatives on exchanges, a collective shudder ran through the largest five banks, which controlled nearly 90 percent of the financial industry's most lucrative, and dangerous, product. No matter how hard they pushed Geithner and various leaders of Congress not to tamper with their $40 billion a year in profits from selling shadowy, over-the-counter derivatives—whose secrecy, where buyer and seller were matched by an investment bank but never met, was the key to their profitability—Gensler kept pushing back. There was no way to control him. As a regulator, he was not directly susceptible to political pressure. And, in Gensler's case, he wasn't bucking for some future job on Wall Street. He had all the money he needed.

But it was more than that. To friends and colleagues, Gensler had committed the cardinal sin: suggesting that the money Wall Streeters made was ill-gotten, that the source of the riches was not the "efficient distribution of capital," as financial-sector CEOs liked to earnestly intone, but rather born of inefficiency.

His favored analogy was to an hourglass. Goldman Sachs and one or two other banks, such as Salomon Brothers, figured out a way, in the early 1980s, to begin to capture the shifting sands of capital passing through the U.S. economy in an hourglass. Goldman, in effect, put its hands around the hourglass's chokepoint. For every hundred grains of sand that flowed through the chokepoint, say, they'd take one grain. Other financial firms of all kinds "saw this and said, 'Why should those guys have their hands around the only chokepoint,' and they started to create their own chokepoints above and below. Next thing you knew, there were ten chokepoints, and for every hundred grains, ten grains were being taken out, then twenty." By 2007, when the financial industry accounted for 41 percent of corporate profits in the United States, it was arguable that the figure was up to forty or so grains out of one hundred. The question was where did all those grains go, because at this rate the hourglass would soon be sandless. There was a twist covering that, too. Some of those forty grains went back into the domestic economy, from the consumption of that wealthy army managing the chokepoints. But lots of the wealth went into investments overseas, where returns were

stronger than in the United States. And at the same time, the United
States refilled the hourglass with sand, borrowing from other countries
and going ever deeper into debt as it did.

The profits in this process flowed disproportionately to the chokepoint
kings, who were also called "financial intermediaries." Not only did
this type of intermediation not bring much value or growth to the U.S.
economy, certainly not nearly as much as the intermediaries' dizzying
compensation would suggest, but some, including Volcker, would contend the group had used their positioning and leverage to create a kind
of financial cartel. The huge modern derivatives market, of course, was
among the greatest of the intermediaries' inventions, where buyer and
seller didn't know each other, and no one could figure out the obligations
that each intermediary faced. Systemically speaking, a clot in one of the
forty chokepoints could slow or stop the flow of sand through the other
thirty-nine—meaning the flow of cash and credit through the economy.
That, Gensler said, was more or less what happened in 2007, starting the
first stages of the recession in December and then culminating with the
crisis of the fall of 2008.

What Gensler and Volcker agreed on was that at this point government policy should be focused on how to reduce the might and number of
these financial intermediaries. To use a phrase free-market deficit hawks
had used for years, their idea was to "starve the beast," constraining how
Wall Street made its money and thereby forcing firms to shrink. The
endgame, both Gensler and Volcker agreed, might be to push the intermediaries into a choice: if they wanted to keep their jobs, they would
have to find ways to invest, in patient and meaningful ways, in American
innovation and lasting economic growth.

But Gensler went one step further than Volcker even. That was partly
because, while Volcker had the luxury of moral high ground and the
freedom of old age, Gensler had to do something harder: atone.

"I'm not smarter than other people," he said. "I didn't invent anything, or build anything, or create lots of good jobs for people to make
good lives for themselves in America. I was just lucky enough to be there
early, to get my hands around the chokepoint and hold on tight.

"There are people who are really hurting across the country," he continued quietly. "And to say no one knew, or no one's responsible, or we
were all in this game together so buyer beware, is not right. The people

who helped create the game, and I'm one of them, should say they're sorry and start making amends."

Gensler didn't say that sort of thing publicly, and if a Wall Street CEO had said it, which, speaking frankly, any number of them might have, it would have created havoc. Which is why the Street was handling the Gensler problem very delicately. Their lobbyists had advised them not to make a big stink about what Gensler had proposed, while saying they were in favor of regulation—you bet—and showing enthusiasm for things such as a systemic regulator or resolution authority. Yes, Washington could employ as many new regulators as it needed. But right now, as the industry, with government support, had begun to earn its way out of trouble, Washington shouldn't tamper with the way Wall Street made its money. Not now. What was past was finally past, already being forgotten as confidence returned. Add regulators if you want—regulators can be managed—but don't turn our beloved market principles against us.

"I don't think we can let everything that happened be so easily forgotten," said Gensler, polishing a speech he was due to give in Washington that afternoon, a speech no one would cover, with all of the focus on the goings-on in New York. "I mean, I just don't. I think we have to reform the system. And yes, we're talking in my little world about some paradigm shifts . . . It's okay to talk about paradigm shifts, to bring everything onto transparent electronic markets so people can see where it trades, and see if they're being ripped off, and can get a better price elsewhere. Then everybody says, well, but you'll thwart innovation. I don't think you thwarted innovation back when you had stock trading move to transparent exchanges. What it'll do, like it did then, is kill off some overly fat margins. I call that progress."

Moving between the two capitals, Barack Obama reviewed his Wall Street speech aboard Air Force One.

Another town, another speech. Only a week after the powerful health care address, its effect was already wearing off. In the days before the speech, Obama had repeatedly talked to Baucus—calling him over the weekend, as Baucus trolled Home Depot—asking him how close the Gang of Six was to an agreement on a plan that Obama could claim some ownership of. They'd all worked through the night. After months of waiting, with reporters camped outside Baucus's office, the fabled bipartisan compromise seemed so close, right up until the afternoon of the health care speech. Obama hoped it would be a prize, a bipartisan prize he could deliver from the lectern. It didn't happen. And a week later, it was as though nothing had happened—back to business as usual. Obama and half the Senate were now courting Maine's Olympia Snowe, hoping she'd be the single shining emblem of bipartisanship.

Obama had handed his political capital over to Max Baucus, the vanquisher of Daschle, and now the health care initiative was in shambles. Something might, at some point, emerge. But it would be a long, messy fight, and the dream of harnessing the breakthroughs in comparative efficiencies to reduce costs and expand coverage was mostly gone. In September, Orszag's and Obama's favorite integrated solution—to lower malpractice premiums if doctors used procedures within an evidence-affirmed "safe harbor"—died a quiet death. Doctors didn't like to have their hands tied. At this point, with general disarray, they had plenty of clout to bring over a few of their favorite Democratic congressmen.

But what stung the most was that Obama's powers of oratory and persuasion, at their very best, hadn't moved a single vote in the Senate.

Now it was time for another speech, on the other defining priority of his presidency—one thrust upon him: the financial crisis. At 11:45 Obama and his White House entourage slipped through the side entrance of one of America's most honored and auspicious structures: Federal Hall, a pillared, domed neoclassical temple that was the site, in 1765, where delegates of nine colonies met to challenge the Stamp Act. They drafted a letter to King George III and the British Parliament protesting what they dubbed "taxation without representation." The Continental Congress of the Articles of Confederation had met here; George Washington was inaugurated on the steps, where a twenty-foot bronze statue of him now stands.

As Obama's team, including Geithner, collected themselves in a waiting room, the leaders of Wall Street milled about, convivially, in the main hall, with its marble floors beneath the tall dome. A year after their existential crisis, "too big to fail" had settled into what seemed like a day-to-day repose of "too big to worry." The well-groomed gathering of men, and a spicing of women, chatted about summer vacations to exotic locales, purchases, recent and upcoming, the latest news on shareholder suits (their liability policies would cover them). One prominent banker, who asked not to be named, said, "For Washington to not demand anything when it saved us, even stuff that we know is for our long-term good, was one of the stupidest moves in modern times. I figured Obama understood that—it wasn't a nuanced point—and that he'd act as we started to pull out of the abyss six months ago. But he didn't, and I don't know who to thank. I feel like I should go over and hug Tim. It's a shame we can't pay him, 'cause that's a guy who really earned a big-time bonus."

Not all of Wall Street actually did show up. On this day, an economic equivalent, in the minds of many Americans, to the first anniversary of 9/11, Lloyd Blankfein decided he had something more important to do. Jamie Dimon was also otherwise engaged.

At 12:10, Obama stepped to the lectern to perfunctory applause and delivered a scolding speech that no one much reacted to. Some of the men checked watches. The president's rhetoric, once enough to reduce strong men to tears, had already been shorted. After all, he'd just given a spellbinding address to a joint session of Congress last week and hadn't gotten one vote. With each word, the market value of his rhetorical capacity dropped.

By 12:50 the president was gone, off to a few other meetings in New York before Air Force One left at 3:00 p.m.

The younger men speed-walked to nearby offices or jumped in black sedans, leaving behind the older men, the last generation's titans, who ambled down the long steps to street level. On balance, they'd been pushing for dramatic reforms since last fall. Leading them was Pete Peterson, the billionaire former head of Blackstone and commerce secretary under Reagan, who had spoken publicly and passionately about how moving from partnerships to publicly traded corporations in the early 1980s—allowing partners to take their money off the table and replace it with other people's money, thereby severing the bonds of caution and shared risk—marked the moment Wall Street started to grow into a destructive force. "I know Tim Geithner very well and I've interviewed a lot of top people, in New York and Washington, and they all say that it'll take another crisis before anything changes up here," Peterson said.

Behind him was Volcker, who threw an arm around Pete's shoulder.

"The crisis should have lasted a little longer," he said. "It would have been better if Wall Street didn't pull out of it so soon. Given us more time."

And off they walk together, as reporters yell at them: "Did you like what the president said?" "What should reform look like?"

Scott Talbott, the ubiquitous spokesman for the Financial Services Roundtable, the trade association representing the one hundred largest banks, stood near the feet of George Washington, offering the industry's position. "We solidly agree with the president. We agree with creating a systemic risk authority to oversee the entire industry. We agree with a regulatory authority to resolve non-depository institutions," meaning financial firms as compared to commercial banks. "And we agree with the idea of transparency to protect the consumer, but we don't feel the Consumer Financial Product Agency is the best way to do it."

The many agencies that regulate banks from Washington have their own consumer protection divisions, he elaborated, and those should simply be strengthened. Reporters crowded around and asked about changes in compensation, about making them more closely tied to long-term performance. Talbott said that firms were already doing that voluntarily. When pressed, he acknowledged just one was: UBS.

But if one firm does it and the rest don't, there will be flight from that firm to others.

"Okay, I admit, that is a challenge. But if you force them all to do it, well, that'd be an antitrust violation!" Talbott added with a chuckle, surprising even himself.

A few feet away, belly up to a barricade, a few dozen people with signs held out hope that they might still glimpse the president.

Lynn Safford, with her husband, Dave, an advertising executive, and her son, Matt, was holding up a somewhat understated sign: "Regulate Government Spending." They were from Austin, Texas, and had just come up from Washington, where they'd joined Glenn Beck, Sarah Palin, Michele Bachmann, and assorted Tea Party leaders for the "9/12 March on Washington," a rally that drew tens of thousands of conservative activists to the capital for speeches and a show of political force. It was now clear that the Tea Party, founded a mere seven months before with a televised rant by CNBC's Rick Santelli, about how the government was "promoting bad behavior" by "subsidizing losers' mortgages," was building toward next year's midterm elections. It had already developed a seemingly strong grassroots organization, and was generating ongoing excitement, drawing new members, with media events televised by Fox News.

But the strength, and stickiness, of the movement was more in the excitement of its fast-forming community than in the slavishly transmitted visuals.

It's hard to know what ten letters President Obama was reading every morning, a practice that Axelrod said he did religiously to counter "his greatest fear, that he'll lose touch with the people." But he might have been edified, and forewarned, by reading about Lynn Safford's transformation into an activist.

She was a Glenn Beck watcher. She said she liked his passion, and found herself "checking out some of the things he'd been saying on the Internet, and a lot of it was on the money." This had given her a feeling of both engagement and due diligence, albeit verifying the authenticity of a cable television character with often unsourced Internet data. But after a few months of watching and trolling, she'd asked herself, "How did we get to this place without me knowing it? Nothing was in balance anymore."

One day she ran out of her house in the early evening as her neighbor, a young father named Matt, was coming home from work.

"I said, 'How do you feel about the political arena right now?' He looked at me like 'why are you asking me about that?' I said, 'I'm not gonna sit in my house and scream alone.' Then, you know what Matt said? He said, 'I hate what's going on!'"

Matt and his wife would have joined the Saffords on the trip east, but they had a newborn at home.

The question of why Lynn was screaming and what Matt hated is a complex one. The Tea Party's platform is populist, both conservative and libertarian, endorsing lower taxes, a reduction of national debt, and a reduction in government spending, along with individual rights and an "originalist" interpretation of the Constitution. But Lynn, like a lot of Tea Party activists, didn't offer much in the way of an actual program or coherent policies. Tea Partiers are often against things that are themselves opposites, and against pretty much anything that Obama does.

But policy or ideology doesn't really seem to be as much a driver of the party's growth as its members are themselves, in "being the change that they seek," to adapt Obama's phrase. Lynn had already listed a host of experiences in her weekend of activism, from stunning deals on hotel rooms, to chance, seemingly miraculous encounters with like-minded people—"I felt like she was my sister"—to a moment when she thanked someone who'd said he had never been thanked so warmly before.

This sensation, of a world brimming with possibility, was precisely what waves of Obama supporters had felt as they lifted him to the presidency. A key item of collateral damage from an overcommitted and disorganized White House was the oversight of not creating ways to keep Obama's populist grassroots organization involved in the current array of national debates. Inaction had created a vacuum. In this case, it was clear that populist energy—enlivened by the poor economy, the ravages of Wall Street, and the desire to confront an uncertain future with activism—had settled on the right.

On the evening of the Lehman anniversary, Carmine Visone booked the corner table on the patio at Bice. *His* table.

In the year since he'd stepped back from the window of his Lehman office, he had restored a bit of balance to his life. He wasn't sure what was next. He knew that, a year later, blaming Wall Street was not so simple. Santelli's screed, which had launched the Tea Party, struck Carmine, a lifelong Republican, in a place deep, where his angry, bricklayer father had permanent residence.

"Listen, guy, that house you got, you couldn't afford it. The car you got, the five of them you got, you *knew* you couldn't afford that."

After a year of hearing Wall Street blamed for every ill in America, Carmine channeled his dad on the issue of personal responsibility. It was something of an anniversary present to everyone who found themselves overextended and deep in debt, at the end of Wall Street's thirty-year credit supercycle.

"I submit to you, sir, that not only did you get what you deserve, but you got *more* than you deserve, so be grateful for the free ride that you had, because you never paid for it. So I'm asking you to give back what you didn't use, because you can't pay for everything that you did use, because somebody else is paying for it.

"You never belonged in that house, you never belonged in that car, you never belonged in those shoes, and you never belonged in that restaurant, because you never earned it.

"So don't blame me because I manufacture capital, okay? You, on a personal level, sir, have an obligation to manage your own fucking life, not me. The ocean doesn't get condemned if someone drowns in it, okay? You went in the water, you went in over your head, you didn't know how to swim, you ignored the signs, okay? Don't blame me.

"That's what the ocean does. The ocean floats people and the ocean drowns people, okay? Don't blame the ocean. You did it to yourself. And you wanna know something, too? Somewhere deep down in your soul you knew that going in. And you were trying to get away with it. You know you didn't earn it. No money down. No income verification. Okay? And you figured, 'Well, I figure I can carry the monthly note. It doesn't matter what I paid for it.' You don't look at the cost of these things; you look at the cost to *carry* these things. You're banking on the continuation of your ability to carry. Again, you don't even know what you *paid* for the car. Because you knew what the monthly note was. It didn't matter if you paid $1 million more or less for that house, because all that was an extra $300 in your monthly payment, so you were paying inflated prices, but it didn't matter to you, because the monthly payment was manageable. Until something happened, and all of a sudden the spigot was turned off and whatever it is that you were doing to create that personal income stream level, which, by the way was never ample . . . because you were banking on bonuses that you hadn't earned yet, stock options going up. Today's bills with tomorrow's earnings.

"Not only did you spend money you didn't have at the time, but you were spending money you never even got in the future. You were spending money that wasn't even created yet. You wanna blame me for that? Where's your responsibility? Your self-discipline? I have no sympathy. I have no sympathy because you never should have been there to begin with. You should have exercised restraint every step of the way. Just because the drug dealer is on the corner, you could have walked right past him. You bought the drugs. I didn't sell you the drugs, you bought the drugs."

MAD MEN

THE OBAMA PRESIDENCY DIDN'T END IN THE FALL OF 2009, BUT it came close.

"The worst period of his presidency," was the conclusion of Anita Dunn, reflecting on it more than a year later. "That horrific period in November . . . health care dragging on and on, economy is not looking good, horrible jobless recovery . . . that was a *terrible* time." She added, "Everyone was in a terrible mood."

This inefficacy had started to garner attention from the press. Lofty campaign rhetoric was now being contrasted with a stifling political stagnation. A mid-September poll had Obama's approval rating at just 47 percent, the lowest of his young presidency.

Dunn, the outspoken White House communications director, had been brought in to the West Wing in May to help the president navigate the rocky first few months of his term. "It was a mess," she said. Dunn quickly instigated a better scheduling system and fought, with futility, to heal the growing gender divide. It wasn't the first time she'd been brought in to alleviate such a tense atmosphere.

During the campaign, Dunn was the first female appointed to a serious campaign post. As a senior adviser and communications director, she was shocked to find that in spite of Obama's popularity with female voters, his campaign had more to do with frat house antics than third-wave feminism. Upon being shown a new campaign ad in production, Dunn watched with a quizzical look on her face.

"There isn't a single woman in this ad," she evenly observed. "I was dumbfounded. It wasn't like they were being deliberately sexist. It's just there was no one offering a female perspective."

That was then. The ad was ultimately reshot, and more women were brought into senior campaign roles. But now in the White House, Dunn's concern grew as she saw similar gender issues, this time with even higher stakes and tensions, and plenty of women now in senior roles.

"The president has a real woman problem" was the assessment of an-other high-ranking female official. "The idea of the boys' club being just Larry and Rahm isn't really fair. He [Obama] was just as responsible himself."

The problem at hand was manifold. The schism going back to the campaign manifested itself in two distinct ways. On the one hand was the perception that Obama was a guy's guy, especially in his leisure time. Those coveted moments, not just on the basketball court but between meetings, were times when the president was at his most comfortable.

The second, more aggrieving divide lay in the fact that many women felt that the men, namely Summers and Emanuel, didn't play by the rules. The group of women even coined a term for these transgressions: "pol-icy fouls." That Summers and Emanuel circumvented traditional policy routes and often left other key players out of the loop would alone have been cause for frustration. But when this was coupled with Obama's guy-to-guy attitude and the testosterone aggression that accompanied these "fouls," women in the White House found themselves increasingly frus-trated and feeling worthless.

"I felt like a piece of meat," Christina Romer said of one meeting that she had been deliberately boxed out of by Larry.

But the White House was relying heavily on the disconnect between perception and reality. The public face of the administration was as gender-progressive as any in history. Obama had surrounded himself with smart, assertive women in positions of traditional power. The team, a veritable murderers' row of women of private-sector and academic authority, was greeted with praise from feminist groups for its glass-ceiling-shattering diversity.

By the summer, however, the reality had grown dire. The cabal of men, which in addition to Emanuel and Summers included Orszag, Axel-rod, and Gibbs (the latter two were considered to be "untouchable"), had mitigated the authority of the highest-ranking women officials as a result of their close personal connections with the president. As 2009 wore on, everyone had become cognizant of the internal schism, with Geithner privately concluding, "The perception is that women have real power, yet they all feel like shit."

That characterization, echoed by multiple senior officials, was pain-ful and also unacceptable. The women would do almost anything for the president, and carried on with few complaints. "But looking back," recalled Anita Dunn, when asked about it nearly two years later, "this place would be in court for a hostile workplace . . . Because it actually fit all of the classic legal requirements for a genuinely hostile workplace to women."

At the time, though, they went through the available channels, trying to have their complaints heard. Along with Valerie Jarrett's office, the destination of choice was Pete Rouse's closet-like garret in the West Wing. One after another, the women came in. Rouse is an expert manager with a welcoming disposition. Each one arrived with the same plea: Do something.

Barney Frank got up early on Thursday, September 24. It was a big day. He'd started the week with hearings on key elements of financial reform. Instead of voting the whole package out of his committee at once, the plan was to get key witnesses to stand and deliver on specific areas and then vote each part—derivatives regulation, the proposed Consumer Financial Product Agency, resolution authority, systemic oversight—one by one.

Today was special: he was helping someone with their coming out.

After the president's Lehman anniversary speech ten days earlier, as other dignitaries schmoozed or tried to squeeze in a Manhattan lunch before boarding Air Force One, Barney Frank got to work. He had grabbed a cab north to Rockefeller Center for a secret meeting in Paul Volcker's office.

Frank knew that Volcker was aggrieved. He'd been left out of meetings by Summers. His President's Economic Recovery Advisory Board hadn't even had its first meeting until mid-May, and was already being ridiculed as an afterthought or, even more cynically, a place for Obama to stick all his second-tier donors and campaign advisers who hadn't "made the cut."

But it was more than just access. Frank had spent plenty of time with Geithner and knew that his position on regulating the financial sector was bank-friendly. That was why there had been so little opposition from the banking lobby. The lobby had lost a bit of clout, but it also could live, and maybe live well, with what the administration was proposing. If Frank was going to get something tougher out of his committee, he'd need some leverage. That was why he was sitting with Big Paul. They talked for a few minutes about Volcker's views. These were convincing, and far more activist—more interventionist—than the administration's. Would he consider coming before Frank's committee to speak his mind? Volcker laughed. Both he and Frank knew that the old Fed chairman was too important to Obama's credibility to be fired as head of the PERAB, especially for saying what most progressives, and plenty of old-time Wall Streeters, thought Obama himself should have been saying. So why not see if he could dare the president to be a bit more courageous in taking on the banks?

Which was what he did at 9:30 this morning, in front of Frank's committee. Specifically, he contradicted the testimony of Frank's star witness from the day before, Tim Geithner, who, selling the administration's plan, had said that certain "systemically important" institutions should receive more intense oversight by the Fed.

No, that's a bad idea, said Volcker. "Whether they say it or not, that carries the connotation in the market that they're too big to fail," creating the problem of "moral hazard."

And it wasn't just a single point that Volcker refuted. In a carefully crafted three-thousand-word written statement, which he read aloud, Volcker dismantled much of the regulatory framework put forward by the administration:

"The approach proposed by the Treasury is to designate in advance financial institutions 'whose size, leverage, and interconnection could pose a threat to financial stability if it failed' . . . the clear implication of such designation, whether officially acknowledged or not, will be that such in whole or in part, will be sheltered by access to a Federal safety net in time of crisis; they will be broadly understood to be 'too big to fail,'" he said. "Think of the practical difficulties of such designation. Can we really anticipate which institutions will be systemically significant amid the uncertainties in future crises and the complex interrelationships of markets? Was Long-Term Capital Management, a hedge fund, systemically significant in 1998? Was Bear Stearns, but not Lehman? How about General Electric's huge financial affiliate, or the large affiliates of other substantial commercial firms? What about foreign institutions operating in the United States?"

His recommendation was to restore some version of the Glass-Steagall law, putting commercial banks back in their special category, where they stuck to more traditional banking activities in exchange for the federal guarantee. This would mean they could no longer have hedge funds or private-equity funds beneath their roof, and they would have to stop proprietary trading—that is, trading their own accounts alongside those of their clients.

"The point is not only the substantial risks inherent in capital market activities," he added, in an extraordinary passage. "There are deep-seated, almost unmanageable, conflicts of interest with normal banking relationships—individuals, businesses, investment management clients seeking credit, underwriting, and unbiased advisory services. I also think we have learned enough about the challenges and distractions for management posed by the risks and complexities of highly diversified activities."

In other words, much of what was now called the financial services business was rife with illegal, or quasi-legal, activity. Let's have at least one realm, commercial banks, that are federally insured and not part of that chicanery, rather than federally backing the largest or most audacious actors by terming them "systemically important."

The practical and political effect of all this was an open dispute between the Treasury secretary and the president's most prominent outside economic adviser, the head of his Economic Recovery Advisory Board.

By the time Volcker was in his car to the airport, media requests for interviews were already flooding in. And he was just warming up. He made a note to unearth a quote from the father of modern economics, Adam Smith, who'd wrestled with these same "too big to fail" problems in the eighteenth century: "He said something to the effect of 'I don't know what to do about the problem, except to just keep banks small'—I've got to get that citation." Volcker expressed admiration for Adair Turner, Britain's bank regulatory chief, and his recent statement about the latest breakthroughs in financial engineering, that it was crucial for a society "to recognize that [when] there is some profitable activity so unlikely to have social benefit that we should be voluntarily willing to walk away from it.

"You know, he wrote an essay about the origins of the crisis that ran a hundred and twenty-six pages, critical of what he called the quasi-religious dogma of finance—quite a wordsmith!"

It was Volcker on a tear. At Reagan National Airport, his assistant, Tony Dowd, a retired, fiftyish investment banker, had to run to the ticket desk to get their boarding passes for the 12:30 Delta Shuttle. Volcker was oblivious, ambling forward, saying, "Obama is smart, but smart is not enough. Leadership is another thing entirely, about knowing your mind enough to make real decisions, ones that last." Minutes later, Dowd was running down the breezeway. "Oh, God, I thought I'd lost you," he said, panting. Volcker barely gave him a look. "Over here, here's where we go," Volcker grumbled. After passing through security, he was back on the president, some idea percolating, which hit its boiling point as he reached the gate. "He seems to feel he has all he needs in the clever Mr. Summers. Together they're both so very confident." He flopped into a chair; still fifteen minutes to boarding. Then he hit it, seeing the president plainly: "He's self-confident, too self-confident."

———————

At that moment, Elizabeth Warren was emerging from her testimony before the Senate Banking Committee on issues concerning TARP and its mismanagement. Volcker was, in a way, joining Warren in a new flavor of celebrity—"regulatory dissident"—that Warren had begun working up back in mid-April, when she appeared on Jon Stewart's show. In eight minutes she laid out such a clear, elegant sketch of how Roosevelt-era regulations had been dismantled, unleashing demons, that Stewart basically canceled the rest of the show and just had her talk. She went on for nineteen minutes in all, with periodic breaks, describing changes similar to the ones Volcker recommended. "I know your husband's backstage," Stewart cooed, as the show wrapped up. "I still want to make out with you."

Volcker visited Obama a half dozen times to make his case for tough-love reforms and to argue with Summers. Warren, whose 2007 idea for a Consumer Financial Product Agency was now a central plank of Obama's reform proposal, had not yet been granted such privileges.

Elizabeth Warren speed-walked from Senator Chris Dodd's hearing room to a perch near the great atrium in the Russell Senate Office Building.

Bloomberg Television wanted to interview her about the one-year anniversary of the TARP program and the fact that she had made a cameo appearance in Michael Moore's new movie, *Capitalism: A Love Story*. They opened by running the clip in which Moore asks where the $350 billion in TARP money thus far allocated had gone. Warren responds, "We don't know," at which point Moore does one of his quick cuts, making it sound as if the money was stolen. There is, not surprisingly, a bit more to that story. Warren was leading the charge against the Fed's secrecy oaths to the banks and nonbanks that had received the funds—oaths Treasury supported. Their position was that revealing who got the grants, which amounted to more than the total annual discretionary spending of the U.S. government, would undermine confidence in those institutions.

Bloomberg, hoping to get her to react to Moore, got a bright smile and an evenhanded "there are important issues and I'll talk about them to anyone, anywhere with a camera." Then Warren ran through an artful précis on how the banks were still holding the toxic assets, and how that left them in a default position of continuing to use government grants and funding to do everything but lend money.

Afterward, she ran a few more rounds in the Senate before grabbing a salad in a cafeteria in the basement of Russell.

"What I think about is a whole building of people like me. If we can get this thing off the ground, I'll recruit them. But the idea is out there. They'll come on their own. Because keeping people from getting taken—and they are being taken, just like someone broke into their house and stole their jewelry, or the TV, or the money they were saving for their kids' college—is a way to help people. Really help them. And that's why maybe you forgo some money you might make out in the world of 'make and sell' to come here—because this is public service as something of virtue."

She could have gone on like this all day, but she didn't.

She knew there was no clear precedent for some citizen, even a Harvard Law School professor, coming up with an idea for what government ought to be doing and, soon enough, sitting atop a bona fide federal agency built around her impulse in response to a crisis.

"I know I've become a lightning rod. Oh yes, I'm finding out that I'm drawing strong reactions from people in the administration who you'd figure would be on my team. If I get taken down, that's not a problem. Really, it's not, as long as there's an agency. Then an army will fill it."

Warren, after all, didn't even live in Washington, and soon she was striding down the breezeway at Reagan National, right where Volcker was two hours before. And like Volcker, she came full circle to Obama and Summers.

"You can't run a policy based on a misdirection, on a fiction," she said. "I don't know what the president is thinking. I don't see the president. He meets with bankers. He doesn't meet with me. But if he's involved in this at all, he's got to know that his angry words at Wall Street, at their recklessness and dangerous incentives in compensation, about how they do their business in ways utterly divorced from what's actually good for the economy—that he can't just say that sort of thing, and then dump money in their laps and be credible. Tim and Larry's whole plan is just like Argentina in the 1980s. There was this giant hole marked 'Banks' and the government just dumped money in that hole, as much as they had, while they lied about it. That's what Larry thinks: that the U.S. is Argentina!"

And then Elizabeth Warren started to sing "Don't Cry for Me, Argentina." She was doing this at one of the little standup tables near the gates, people passing by on either side. Several started to applaud, and that seemed to egg her on, working the verse, with Larry Summers in the role of Eva Perón.

She shrugged and let out one of those big laughs. "Why not? He might understand things better as a woman."

––––––––––

By mid-October, all the providers had cut their deals. On the other side of the table was a conjunction of the White House team, led by DeParle; the Baucus team, led by Jon Selib (the senator's chief of staff); and Liz Fowler, a former WellPoint executive now on the Finance Committee's staff. Shuttling between the two groups was Messina. It was a straight pay-for-play arrangement. The subtext was a pricing formula: How much is it worth to you, provider, for the reform package not to deal seriously with the issue of cost, which stands to cripple your profits? Once a price is agreed upon, you pay a portion of it—often by agreeing to certain provisions for your Medicare and Medicaid disbursements—and those federal savings then pay for expanded insurance coverage. These deals were at the heart of the ten-year, $856 billion behemoth of a plan approved by the Baucus group in mid-September and now winding its way through the Senate.

Health care reform had officially become health insurance reform. The providers were no longer up nights worrying, and they certainly had not welcomed Ignagni back into their midst. She and the insurers were on their own. She was alone in saying what no one wanted to hear: that there was little real cost control in any of the bills.

She'd heard that inside the White House, aggrieved that the champions of coverage had killed his dream of containing costs, Orszag was calling Pelosi's House bill a "liberal fantasy" of glut and expansion.

Ignagni set up a meeting with him. The Senate bill, she contended, wasn't all that much better. AHIP had been working on the numbers for weeks, and they showed a significant rise in costs. Orszag could read data points on health care costs as well as anyone. Ignagni's numbers were interesting, no doubt. But as long as her data had the AHIP logo at the top of the page, its findings would be discredited.

So she opted for a third party: PricewaterhouseCoopers. When the accounting firm came back with numbers showing rising costs much like AHIP's, Ignagni contacted DeParle, ready to show her both the AHIP and the PricewaterhouseCoopers numbers. Hoping to stop the release of these figures in a public report, DeParle invited her back to the White House.

Again, Ignagni presented her findings. Obama's health care team was interested, but nothing changed in terms of the basic calculus they and Baucus were using. It was full steam ahead.

On Monday, October 12, amid the Senate's efforts to sell the Baucus proposal, the PricewaterhouseCoopers report was released. The bottom line: by 2019 Baucus's cost projections were undershooting the typical family premium by a whopping $4,000. "The report makes clear that several major provisions in the current legislative proposal will cause health care costs to increase far faster and higher than they would under the current system," Ignagni asserted in a statement.

AHIP, now on the offensive, was prepared to circulate the report in advertisements and memos to congressional leaders. Nancy-Ann DeParle tried her best to deflate the report, snidely undercutting the legitimacy of PricewaterhouseCoopers by remarking that the firm "specializes in tax shelters. Clearly, this is not their area of expertise."

But the report was a potent weapon, easily swung by Republicans and some Democrats. Everyone in the provider community knew the White House wasn't focused on cost. Now that inattention was being called out publicly.

Behind the scenes, the White House expressed its acute displeasure to Pricewaterhouse, which does an enormous amount of business with the U.S. government. Then, on October 13, a day after the report's release, PwC issued a baffling reversal, distancing themselves from the study and

claiming that AHIP had directed the consulting firm to focus on only
certain aspects of the proposed bill.

Ignagni and AHIP were now seen as toying with the cost numbers to
"kill the bill." Ignagni fought back with futility.

That Saturday, after finishing a run in the cold fall morning, Ignagni
returned to her house to hear the president's weekly radio address. With
Afghanistan, the economy, and joblessness all over the news, Ignagni
was eager to hear what the president had to say about anything *but* health
care reform.

"The history is clear: For decades, rising health care costs have unleashed havoc on families, businesses, and the economy," Obama said.
"And for decades, whenever we have tried to reform the system, the insurance companies have done everything in their considerable power to
stop us.

"It's smoke and mirrors. It's bogus. And it's all too familiar. Every
time we get close to passing reform, the insurance companies produce
these phony studies as a prescription and say, 'Take one of these, and call
us in a decade.' Well, not this time."

Ignagni could not understand what she was hearing, literally. She was
legally deaf and required the use of a hearing aid. After picking up her
aid off the kitchen counter and turning up the volume, she listened in
more closely:

". . . those who would bend the truth or break it to score political
points and stop our progress as a country." The president went on to ac-
cuse the insurance industry of broadly "filling the airwaves with deceptive and dishonest ads," deliberately creating reports, such as the PwC
Senate bill study, "designed to mislead the American people."

How had the providers been allowed to walk away from their many
flip-flops on cost-reduction promises? And now this was being used to
demolish insurance? Obama had made his move; the cost-versus-cover-
age debate had shifted completely. Back in February, when the president
first decided to make health care reform his number-one priority, the
view was that attacking rising costs, which were crushing both businesses and families, had the potential to be a truly bipartisan issue. Now
that line of attack, never really tried, had been officially buried. It was
all about expansion of coverage, and the insurers got to play the villain.

It was Ignagni's job in many ways to be the bad actor. That didn't bother her. It would be hard for anyone not paid by the industry to argue with a straight face that insurance companies were not a huge part of the problem. But Ignagni's strategy—to align with, rather than against, the White House—was a missed opportunity to fix the most fundamental issue in health care: cost.

Now the White House could attack someone, the insurers, with an attractively high negative rating. The fact that insurers were talking about rigor on costs was beside the point. They were not to be trusted. That much was now clear.

———————

When Orszag thought of Summers's "home alone" riff, he came back again and again to the morning economic briefings, an anchor of the president's official duties almost every day. "The president thought those morning briefings were the best of the best, the finest economic minds that could be assembled. He'd say it all the time, how he's consulted with the best experts. But it wasn't the case." Orszag found the meetings less and less useful. Some mornings he simply chose not to attend; on those he did, he often felt it was not time well spent.

Krueger—who would sometimes fill in for Geithner, or visit the morning briefing to present a specially tailored research project—remarked that "Larry would frame an argument as A versus B, and that would sound right unless you were someone with deep enough mastery of an area to know that position D represented the real counterpoint and the best policy position was probably C."

The process inside the NEC was not all that strong. This was never Summers's suit. In some instances, the topic for a briefing would be selected late and the materials swiftly and haphazardly prepared. In one such instance, in July, Krueger got a late-afternoon call from Jason Furman, Summers's deputy at NEC. The next morning's briefing was to deal with immigration. Could Krueger pull something together? It was already dinnertime. Krueger said he taught a class on immigration issues, and some of the economic effects, to Princeton freshmen. "I could bring some of those materials," he said. Furman said that would be fine.

Summers, with his rhetorical acrobatics, could paper over such gaps in preparation. This, in fact, was a point of great pride.

Or so he explained in the fall of 2009 to Andrew Metrick, the Yale economist whose father had been number two at Bear Stearns. Metrick had joined Romer's staff as chief economist. One day he found himself walking over to the Treasury Department with Summers, who'd taken a mentor's shine to the youthful Metrick.

"Larry was complaining about the position Treasury was taking on some issue, and how he couldn't dislodge them from their position, that they just wouldn't budge. I said, 'Well, Larry, maybe they're right.' He just looked at me and said, 'That's not an issue. I can win any argument. I can win arguing either side. But then I sit back and think, "Which side did I win more soundly and fairly?" That's usually the right answer.'"

Metrick then recalled stopping and saying, "Larry, that sure places a lot of might on your internal discretion, and what you decide you want to decide."

Obama, propelled to office both through creating and being created by the bold expectations of a terrified nation, could hardly resist the neat fit Summers provided. Larry could win every argument, never flinched. As long as his own ambitions were salved, he'd make sure Obama felt sufficient confidence: that he had mastered the seminal issues, that as a young president he could succeed in office. But it was never enough to make the sweeping decisions that drive history's arc. The president hewed more to a split-the-middle brand of blended solutions: a little of this offset with a little of that.

Of course, Obama, with his great talent for spotting the play of historical forces and distilling it elegantly in his speeches, had to know deep down that blended, split-the-middle solutions allowed for three decades of disastrous drift in the health care and financial sectors and, more broadly, the U.S. economy. The problem now was that he had been found out. A select group of people who'd earned the certainty to make sweeping recommendations—such as Volcker, Warren, and Gensler— had stepped into the breach. All three of them, with their earned confidence and high purpose, raised questions about Obama's claim to either quality.

While Summers wrestled with his discontent, Volcker had been all over the airwaves, and in the magazines, from the day of the Frank hearings on. Summers was opposed to Volcker's idea of banning banks from proprietary trading. He had called around, and friends on Wall Street told him it was untenable to draw such a line with the volume and diversity of a major bank's trading portfolio.

But as Volcker was being lionized in public, Obama began to double back, wondering what his team thought of Volcker's idea. Biden, who was an old friend of Volcker's, stepped in during a White House meeting and said that the banks were strong enough to take some medicine now, even if it wasn't fundamental change. They were making money again, gambling with depositors' funds and with implicit, or explicit, support of the taxpayer. It wasn't right. Obama nodded. Joe had said it, straight and true.

On November 2, at a meeting of the PERAB, Obama called Volcker, Robert Wolf, and Summers together and said he wanted to try Volcker's idea. It was clear that Wall Street was taking advantage of its protected status, drawing free money from the Fed window and making more risky bets with it. "They did this to themselves," Obama said. The logistics of separating a bank's trading accounts from those of its clients was difficult but doable, Wolf said. He'd help to work out the details.

As they left the meeting, Summers turned angrily to Wolf. "You're taking his side!"

Wolf would have none of it. "Larry, I'm telling the president what I think. I'm not taking anyone's side—not yours or Paul's."

On November 5, the women prepared for their big night in the West Wing. After nearly eight months of growing strife in the White House's so-called gender wars, the president was finally engaging.

What had forced the issue? An October 24 *New York Times* story by Mark Leibovich titled "Man's World at the White House?" Several of the women, who generally did not speak for attribution, were aggrieved about a mid-October basketball game held with congressional members and Hill staffers in which no woman was invited to play on either team. Obama immediately called the accusations "bunk," saying that the players were largely drawn from a revolving congressional game, a list that had been reviewed by women on his staff.

The day after the article appeared, Obama invited Domestic Policy Council chairwoman Melody Barnes to join him for a round of golf—the first time he had included a woman in an outing all year—and it was decided that the women would join him for a dinner in the residence to air their concerns.

Several hours before the dinner was to begin on the fifth, the president was confronted with a disaster. Nidal Malik Hasan, an American-born Muslim army major, had allegedly opened fire at Fort Hood, in Texas, killing thirteen and wounding twenty-nine others. Obama, having been briefed throughout the day, spoke at a previously scheduled event at the Department of the Interior and called the attacks "tragic" and "horrific."

"My immediate thoughts and prayers are with the wounded and with the families of the fallen and those who live and serve at Fort Hood," he said. "These are men and women who have made the selfless and courageous decision to risk and at times give their lives to protect the rest of us on a daily basis. It's difficult enough when we lose these brave Americans in battles overseas. It is horrifying that they should come under fire at an army base on American soil."

A dozen women, including virtually all the president's senior female staffers, were sure the dinner would be canceled. But they gathered anyway for cocktails in the residence, a nice opportunity for all of them to be together, only to be surprised, and delighted, when the president managed to arrive twenty minutes late. Their meeting with him was clearly a priority, and it was not the first time Obama had heard directly about the gender issues. In June, the afternoon of the jobless recovery meeting, Valerie Jarrett told the president he needed to meet with Romer and that a space had been cleared on his schedule. Romer talked about the boys' club problem for many of the women—the way they were excluded from key meetings or ignored when they attended; the bullying atmosphere that prevailed—as well as the specific issues for her. "Have you ever tried to get a word in edgewise when Larry and Tim get going?" The president was skeptical about there being a problem, but attentive. Romer brought matters full circle to him: "If you give power to Rahm or Larry," she said, pointedly, "you're responsible for their actions."

Before the dinner, Jarrett approached Anita Dunn, saying she was "worried people are going to be afraid to speak up. Do you mind saying something to get the ball rolling?" Dunn said she would be fine doing that.

As the women settled into their chairs, Obama set the table: "I really want you guys to talk to me about this openly because recently there has been this suggestion that there are some issues here. I'd like to know how you guys feel. Valerie felt this was something we should do, and I want to thank her for putting this together."

Before Dunn had a chance to chime in, Carol Browner, the director of the White House Office of Energy and Climate Change Policy, kicked things off.

"Mr. President . . ."

One by one, the women ticked off examples and frustrations. The problems seemed to be universally agreed upon.

Obama listened awkwardly, as the women tried their best to present their issues without becoming too personal.

"It was so clearly about personalities," said one of the attendees. "And then it ended up being focused around Larry and Rahm, and some Peter. And obviously . . . less about Axe and Gibbs, who were equally guilty but who everybody was terrified of."

The president listened, with a posture of "Okay, I hear you," said another, "though not really offering much in the way of apology or suggestions about what he'd do."

Romer stressed that it wasn't so much overt sexism as "we have a meeting . . . and then . . . discover that after something has been decided at a meeting, Larry sends in a memo. That's not how things are supposed to work."

Romer and others specifically cited situations where Summers would bypass the team, showing his memo to the group before giving it to the president. "You'd get a memo at nine thirty at night saying this is going to POTUS in fifteen minutes, please let me know if you have any input!"

Dunn, who watched in amazement as the women articulated each issue with precision, still had her own analysis.

"There are people feeling that the chief of staff . . . the way he manages the place is one where people don't have the information they need to function," she said. "There are a very small number of people he tasks with other people's jobs."

That assessment was generous. "There was actually very little management at the White House."

At the conclusion of the meal, the president looked around and, in classic Obama fashion, delivered a conclusion that was both placating and earnest.

"You might think because Axe and Gibbs can walk into my office that I don't recognize your value. Not true. You're important to me. You have this perception that they are more important. Just because they are out there doesn't mean I listen to them on your issues."

That explanation was perplexing. Obama seemed to be acknowledging, and tolerating, the problem.

Inferring that some of them thought he should consider dismissing Emanuel and Summers, Obama paused. "Look," he said, evenly, "I really need Rahm."

"That, to me, was one of the more unsatisfying things. 'They are really important to me. I know they are assholes but I need them,'" one of the women said.

"After the dinner we [the women] all decided we'd rather have had dinner just by ourselves."

Later, when Emanuel was asked in an interview about the women's group and their issues, he was succinct. The concerns of women, he said, were a nonissue, a "blip." As to the fact that the White House's women rather strongly disagreed with him on that point, he said, "I understand," and then laughed uproariously.

As the top and bottom of the wider country were pulling in opposite directions, the two capitals, New York and Washington, were at a crossroads.

GDP was moving ahead now, at a measurable pace of between 2 and 3 percent annually, and stocks were up. But unemployment claims were skyrocketing. The unemployment picture was looking worse than the forecasts from the June meeting on jobless recovery. Through October and into November, debates raged in the morning economic briefing. Clearly the stimulus had fallen short. But what to do? There was budgetary pressure: the deficit was huge, and Obama, at heart a deficit hawk, was generally in agreement with Orszag. Showing fiscal responsibility was a top priority.

Romer pressed a counterpoint. Save money from something else; find some funds elsewhere. People were hurting, after all. This was a crisis.

Orszag countered that unless they did something large, applying a significant stimulus, on the order of $700 billion, "it wouldn't jump-start or significantly move the economy"; but $700 billion was politically untenable. In essence, his point was that what they needed to do, they couldn't afford. Romer said this was the wrong approach. By the estimates of her Council of Economic Advisers, at a cost of $100,000 per job, $100 billion would mean one million new jobs. "A million people is a lot of people."

Obama was unenthusiastic. Romer, in meeting after meeting, came back with new plans, new ways either to locate $100 billion or to pitch it to Congress. Her appeals were passionate. She said they were falling into a "the perfect is the enemy of the good" trap. "It's about doing something, anything."

In November, as Obama's political capital began to wane, he took Orszag's position at a briefing, reiterating the OMB chief's view that a small stimulus would be ineffective.

"That is oh so wrong," Romer blurted out, surprising herself, and everyone in the room, with her candor.

"It's not just wrong, it's *oh so* wrong?" Obama queried before launching into an uncharacteristic tirade. "Enough!" he shouted. "I said it before, I'll say it again. It's not going to happen. We can't go back to Congress again. We just can't!"

The room went painfully quiet, as a mortified Romer sat quietly. Obama so rarely raised his voice. "He really came down on me," she later recalled.

After the meeting, Romer, visibly shaken by the president's rant, talked with Dunn and was summoned to talk privately in Jarrett's office. Romer—one of the strongest voices around the president—said less than usual in Oval Office meetings for the next two weeks.

A few weeks later, the economic team was back to the discussion of stimulus versus deficit reduction. The October jobless figures, out in mid-November, were now clear: unemployment had jumped to 10.2 percent. On the issue of finding some sort of small stimulus, even $100 billion, now Summers stepped up, offering, almost word for word, the position Romer had voiced previously. This time Obama listened respectfully: "I know you've got to make this argument, Larry, but I just don't think we can do it."

As they left the meeting, Romer—who was happy to have Summers speak up for a small stimulus rather than leaving it all to her—said, "Larry, I don't think I've ever liked you so much."

"Don't worry," he quipped. "I'm sure the feeling will pass." But then something dawned on Summers, who'd never seemed sympathetic to the women's complaints: "You know, he sure was a lot more generous with me than he was with you."

It was an important moment. "That was the turning point," Romer later said. "After that, [Larry and I] really started to have a decent working relationship."

Both, in fact, were concerned by something the president had said in a morning briefing: that he thought the high unemployment was due to productivity gains in the economy. Summers and Romer were startled.

"What was driving unemployment was clearly deficient aggregate demand," Romer said. "We wondered where this could have been coming from. We both tried to convince him otherwise. He wouldn't budge."

Summers had been focused intently on how to spur demand, and on what might drive a meaningful recovery. Since the summer, in meeting after meeting, he'd ticked off the possible candidates, and then dismissed them—"it won't be construction, it won't be exports, it won't be the consumer." But without a rise in demand, in Summers's view, nothing else would work. What's more, in such a sluggish, low-demand environment, Summers felt that banks probably *shouldn't* be lending. "No one wants banks to offer credit to people who shouldn't be taking on more credit."

But productivity? The implications were significant. If Obama felt that 10 percent unemployment was the product of sound, productivity-driven decisions by American business, then short-term government measures to spur hiring were not only futile but unwise.

The two economists strained their shared memory of dozens of meetings: had they said something he'd misconstrued? At one point, Summers had mentioned how Keynes once wrote in a 1938 letter that the labor movement depressed productivity, and maybe Obama saw that the disruptions in the economy from the Great Panic gave employers an opportunity—an excuse, essentially—to harvest latent productivity gains.

After a month, frustration turned to resignation. "The president seems to have developed his own view," Romer said.

———

By Thanksgiving, the dysfunctions inside the president's economic team, and the policy drift, had grown acute.

On one hand, there was Obama thinking that, despite the pain millions were feeling, this was the way it was supposed to be—a leap forward in productivity that might mean employment problems resistant to any stimulus. On the other hand sat Summers, who believed that without a rise in demand—not expected anytime soon—almost all efforts were futile.

Romer, Bernstein, Krueger, Gene Sperling, and others got to work, putting out proposal after proposal. Summers would shoot them down. The president, though eager for something to work on the jobs front, did little more than say, "Think of something."

The most ambitious proposal was an employer tax credit by Krueger and his team that offered firms a credit for each new job created. The legislative and political teams liked it: as a tax break for business, paid only if they hired, it slipped between the partisan bunkers, appeasing each encampment. The challenge, as with any such stimulus, was a careful design so that the government did not end up paying for something that would have happened anyway.

It was trickier than it looked, and Summers had always sided with the proud claim of businessmen that they never did anything, whether increase hiring or start a new initiative, because of a government handout. But tax credits, properly constructed, could be effective. Krueger was sure of this, and sure the data would bear him out. The problem was that there weren't any pertinent data to be gleaned from inside the government. Without that, Summers wasn't budging. "These things just don't work," he said over and over.

Other members of the team began to coalesce behind Krueger. They had a chance of getting this though Congress, and they knew the dynamic. Summers, the professional contrarian, had done very little original research in two decades. Krueger was still a player, publishing papers that bled with fresh concepts. "There was a little bit of a good and evil thing going on," said one of the regulars at the economic briefing. "Look, everyone loves Alan. Brilliant, of course. World's nicest guy and sort of oddly ego-less when it comes to searching for the right answer. Nothing he likes better than to have the facts, the data, prove him wrong, even if he's invested in the opposing position. Then there's Larry, who is, well, Larry. A gravitational field. The fucking Death Star of 'no,' unless he decides it ought to be 'yes,' which sometimes just has to do simply with what's good for Larry."

And, of course, the two men had their history. As the jobs tax credit languished, Krueger couldn't help but think back on an incident at Harvard, more than two decades before. There was a mathematical sticking point at the heart of a problem the two men were working on. The issue, having to do with GDP growth, was maddeningly complex. Krueger thought Summers's position was wrong—that he was wrong on the math. They argued it for weeks and couldn't agree. Finally, they decided to call in a mathematician, a whiz from Harvard's math department, as an arbiter. He worked the problem for a few days and decided in favor of Krueger. "But even after all that, Larry still wouldn't give," Krueger said, with a chuckle, thinking back on it and seeing how little had changed. "He still thought he was right. Probably still does."

Now, with so much at stake, Krueger trekked back to Princeton, pulled together a team, swiftly tapped into some university funding, and produced a specialized data set showing that if only 10 percent of employers opted to use the tax credit—a figure well below the norm—it would more than pay for itself and have a strong stimulatory effect. He added data that showed distinctions between large employers and small, with the latter, in a significant survey sample, saying they'd use this credit. What's more, the projected cost per hire was about $60,000, much better than the stimulus package projections, in which each added worker cost roughly $100,000 in federal money.

When Krueger presented the data at a morning economic briefing, said one participant, "it was like an intellectual sporting event." Summers gathered himself and began to summon a fresh counterargument. There was a five-on-one revolt. A pile-on. Summers backed off, but only left room for a later counterattack. Meanwhile, the president, with his newfound theories on productivity gains, was bending toward the idea that companies were acting to heighten valuable efficiencies with the layoffs, and might not soon be hiring, government tax credit or not. And around they went, one "relitigation" to the next. Obama was back to square one, dead in the water. He thought of the Economic Summit in February. The Health Care Summit in March. Both events had stirred him up. Maybe he could get something started with jobs. He approved the idea of a Jobs Summit.

Economists and employers flooded into Washington on December 3. Krueger had plenty of supporters in the room, including Princeton's Alan Blinder, the former vice chairman of the Fed. He and others spoke favorably of the jobs tax credit.

In his wrap-up address, Obama said, "Economists seem to like this tax credit, and I suppose I do, too."

The jobs tax credit got the green light.

Hours after Obama left the summit, Romer came to a briefing in the
Oval Office with some terrific news. The economy had only lost eleven
thousand jobs in November, many fewer than economists' projections of
more than ten times that many job losses.

"Does this mean we've turned the corner?" Obama said, looking at
the briefing sheet.

"Maybe so," said Romer. Obama got up and hugged her. And then he
hugged her again.

None of the economists on the president's team wanted to tell him it
could have been a gremlin in the numbers. Neither did Romer. He was a
man reaching for a life preserver. Let him have one.

Obama rushed out to board a plane to Allentown, Pennsylvania. It
was the first of a series of outings that Axelrod dubbed the "White House
to Main Street" tour. It started in the town where, in the words of Billy
Joel, "they're closing all the factories down."

Obama was ebullient, dancing across the stage at Lehigh Carbon
Community College: "This is good news, just in time for the season of
hope."

He was no longer the "no drama" president, looking down from
Olympian heights, thinking about his place among history's giants,
about his legacy. No, he was improvising, reaching back to earlier versions of Barack Obama, all the way to the often-effusive community
organizer, heart on his sleeve. "I've got to admit, my chief economist,
Christy Romer, she got about four hugs when she handed us the report."

The crowd of two thousand erupted in cheers. "But I do want to keep
this in perspective. We've still got a long way to go."

But, of course, he wasn't keeping it in perspective—not in the perspective that had largely defined his presidency. He couldn't afford to.

Alongside the stage, Axelrod leaned against the press riser. "He's
been in the bubble of the White House, arguing policy. The situation in
Washington, with Congress, is gridlocked. And there's not a right answer on policy; it's a roll of the dice. He's not comfortable with that, and
he's starving in there. The idea is to get him out, have him meet people
and remember how he became president, what got him here."

After he effused for twenty minutes, his tenor changed. Unemployment here was officially 10 percent, but real unemployment—including

all those, no longer counted, who'd given up looking for work—was closer to 20.

"I know times are tough," he said softly. "I know." The gymnasium was quiet. There were people packed tight. Some bit their lips. A man in the front row, tattooed, wide as a tree, wiped his eyes. They'd missed this guy, wondered where he'd gone. "Michelle and I were talking the other day—there are members of our families that are out of work. We're not that far removed from struggling to pay the bills. Five, six years ago, we were still paying off student loans. Still trying to figure out, 'If we pay this bill this month, what do we have to give up next month?'

"We're not that far away from there."

Axelrod pocketed his ever-present BlackBerry for a moment and watched from the wings. "That's him, right there. That's him."

PART III

THE EDUCATION OF BARACK OBAMA

LOST AND FOUND

Barack Obama, the master of elegant integration, never managed to bring together Allentown and Washington.

He returned to town, and the bubble, and just fought his way forward through deepening mire.

The ebullience he'd felt, hugging Romer and rushing off to Allentown in early December to tell that hard-hit city the economy had "turned the corner," was being thoroughly mocked by a new set of numbers released this morning, January 8.

Joblessness rose by eighty-five thousand in December. November was an anomaly. Mark Zandi, Moody's sober economist—trusted by both left and right—said he expected unemployment to rise from its current 10 percent to nearly 11 percent in 2010. He pointed out that, adding in those who'd dropped out of the workforce or were underemployed, the current rate was 17.8 percent. Even Zandi, a deficit hawk, was recommending an additional $125 billion in stimulus.

At the noon press briefing, ABC's White House correspondent Jake Tapper, citing the job numbers and new fears by both Stiglitz and Krugman that "the economy is going to contract," tried to get Gibbs to reveal some change in Obama's view from a month ago.

Gibbs would offer none: "He's not an economic prognosticator," he shot back testily. "The president is concerned about the economy, concerned about the stories of people hurting that he has heard for many, many years, and is working to do all that we can to create an environment for businesses, small and large, to hire more people."

Those listening from inside the White House couldn't help but sigh. They were doing little about joblessness, and everybody knew it. Summers's acknowledgment of Krueger's data a month earlier had simply yielded a next subject for debate: how to structure an employer tax credit so it wouldn't simply reward employers for something they were already going to do. The debates inside of the economic team continued to rage, with

Summers standing in the way of almost any proposed stimulus. His underlying position, largely unchanged since the previous summer, was that nothing would be effective if there were not a rise in demand, something the government had little role in effecting, short of another major stimulus package, which Congress wouldn't approve—and around it went.

The president listened, engaged, but wouldn't make a decision. He was still looking for consensus. None was forthcoming.

On the jobs front alone, it had been going on for nearly three months, one "relitigation" after another. By mid-December, Anita Dunn had gone to Pete Rouse and Valerie Jarrett and said someone needed to take control of the economic team, saying that "it's in crisis—it can't go on like this."

By early January she had returned to her job running a political consulting/media firm. She was happy to leave the white building. Of course, she retained enormous affection for Obama, but was dispirited—as so many were—with the shattered, haphazard process of decision making and wildly uneven execution. It was chaos. The situation with the women, for one, hadn't improved. The women's group still met. They'd had their moment with the president and, all together, had made their appeal for action. Several of those at the meeting left feeling unrequited, that the president, with so much on his plate, would not do much more than express attentiveness to the problem. This, to be sure, was the sort of problem that chiefs of staff were generally left to handle. In this case, the chief of staff was at the center of the problem.

But, of course, as the women had stressed at their dinner, the president was responsible. Each president is responsible, after all, for the White House he builds and leads. If there was, in fact, a single operational victory in this period, it involved secrecy: the strife inside the White House was largely kept from public view. Rather than the Cheney-driven secrecy models of the Bush days—where cell phones were White House–issue and where problematic phone numbers, such as those of major newspapers, were regularly searched through shadow directories—the Obama secrecy was born of old-fashioned loyalty. With a few exceptions, it didn't need to be enforced. There was an enveloping adoration of him, still, in the White House, which, month by month, hardened into protectiveness, especially among senior aides who were privy to regular contact. He was indisputably bright and eager; his casual manner, walking through the building, ducking into offices, to get out of what he called his "gilded cage" of the Oval Office, made staffers feel like he never looked down on them. His easy smile and demonstrable charm, even if it came only in brief gusts before he'd settle into his Zen mode, to get down to business, was sometimes forced, but he got an A for effort. What happened on Pennsylvania Avenue stayed on Pennsylvania Avenue. The dozen or so people who'd attended each day's key meeting, the morning economic briefing, would tell stories to anyone who'd listen, and there were plenty: about Obama's brilliance, his strokes of stunning insight, conceptually stitching together cloud formations, or mapping a horizon line. But then, some would comment, there'd be a drift or loss of interest in how an idea would or wouldn't "score" with CBO, or in how to execute it or push it through Congress, or in where an accepted initiative from weeks ago now stood. Meanwhile, within this privileged group, there were whispers and fears, and the kind of growing doubts that continued to undermine Obama's authority.

Of course, Orszag wasn't the only one who heard Summers repeat his "home alone" riff. Others did, too. They'd roll their eyes and look away.

More difficult was what each of them saw in the morning meetings. "Larry would say [to Obama], 'I'll make my argument first; you can go after me,'" Peter Orszag remembered, in a comment echoed by others. "I'm thinking, 'I can't believe he's talking to the president that way.' I don't know why Obama didn't say, 'I made that decision a week ago. Just do what I say.'"

But he didn't. And, over time, some of Obama's more admirable features, his joy of inquiry, his impulse to reach just a bit beyond his grasp, started to get planed down. He was making fewer decisions, and almost none where he couldn't manage to tease some supporting consensus from his senior staff.

At a meeting in January, during one of a dozen arguments over a somewhat confused proposal by Gene Sperling about a small business lending program, Obama, in a voice that was softly dispirited, said, "Well, if you guys can't agree, I mean, we don't have to do it."

Meanwhile, his administration was looking ever more confused and ineffectual. Neither the political nor the policy arm was working effectively, and the two clearly weren't working in any meaningful concert.

The major event scheduled for January 8—cited several times by Gibbs at the noon press briefing—was the granting of $2.3 billion in tax credits to companies involved in high-tech clean-energy manufacturing.

At 3:00 p.m., flanked by Vice President Biden, Tim Geithner, and Steven Chu, the Nobel Prize–winning secretary of energy, the president stepped to the lectern in the East Room to say, portentously, that "building a robust clean energy sector is how we will create the jobs of the future." He went on like that for a bit, as did other officials, talking about the makers of solar panels and wind turbines—143 firms in all—and how they'd form foundations of job growth for the twenty-first century. It was admirable and forward thinking, a bookend to an event in late October where he announced the competition for the grants at a solar panel farm in Arcadia, Florida.

But building capacity for some far-off future was the last thing anyone wanted to hear about. During a brief press availability following his prepared remarks, Obama acknowledged the deflating jobs numbers. They "are a reminder that the road to recovery is never straight," he said soberly. "We have to continue to explore every avenue to accelerate the return to hiring."

Geithner, in his statement, pointed out that the tax credits were expected to draw a match of $5.5 billion in private-sector investments, for a total of $7.7 billion, and eventually create more than seventeen thousand jobs. But the fine points of the program indicated that only a third of the credits were slated to create jobs by the end of the year, which would bring the total to just shy of six thousand jobs in 2010.

Nearly two years before, Goolsbee had told Obama, then an underdog candidate, that hiring from a clean-energy initiative would be modest. But now the White House was offering official pronouncements and fanfare, presenting the president and his top officials, for six thousand jobs? The economy had lost seven million jobs in the last two years of recession; economists agreed that unless it added a hundred thousand a month, the unemployment rate wouldn't budge. In the scheme of things, the clean-energy grants—which some inside the White House were already dubbing the "science fair"—were a rounding error. They fit into a broader category of programs that flowed from Obama's famous line, during the campaign and since, that the hardest thing in Washington was "to solve tomorrow's problems with today's dollars." Trenchant and true. But over the first year, it yielded an array of what were commonly referred to in the White House as "S and S" programs, for "somehow, some way."

Which was the unintended point being made today in the East Room:

the president was occupied with S and S programs, which would not bear fruit for years, while the economy listed forward, with the highest levels of unemployment since the Great Depression.

The most sweeping of those "somehow, some way" programs was, of course, health care. In any version of reform now being contemplated, significant reforms wouldn't take hold until 2014. Not that, after a year of presidential engagement, anyone could actually claim a specific, hard-edged proposal from the White House. Emanuel's initial, and under-standable, fear that an articulated health care plan from the White House would open up Obama to a flurry of slings and arrows, as Clinton's thousand-page proposal had in 1993, never really evolved with changing circumstances. Now it was January—nearly a year after he had taken the oath—and Obama was still engaged in the act of earnest brokering between warring houses of Congress.

Which is what would now thoroughly occupy the president's January schedule, even more than it had, month to month, over the past year. After the press conference on the future of clean energy, Obama picked up briefing materials for a quiet weekend in the White House. On Monday he would begin a bout of negotiations to try to reconcile the bills that the House and Senate had finally passed on health care reform, the latter having passed just before Christmas.

The Senate bill was funded largely by a tax on the so-called Cadil-lac coverage insurance, which was just about the only life feature shared by high-income individuals and some of the more privileged industrial workers. In bitter labor negotiations across decades, the strong coverage was often a replacement for wage increases, and union leaders were fly-ing to Washington to meet with the president on Monday to lodge protest as a start to the reconciliation efforts between the two bills.

But the White House's internal poll numbers from the previous fall showed something surprising: the drop in the president's approval rat-ings over the summer was not significantly due to the "death panel" at-tacks. It was primarily because he'd allowed the congressional wrangling over the shape of health care reform—and especially the widely covered "sausage making" deliberations under the auspices of Max Baucus—to limp forward through the summer and fall.

Of course, the bickering continued through the winter and had now officially migrated down Pennsylvania Avenue. In Washington it was seen as progress. There were, after all, now bills passed by both the

House and the Senate, even if there were wide gaps and distinctions between them. Reconciling the two was now the next step in the legislative process.

To the wider public, anxious about the sliding economy, it was just sound and fury with bills that were hard to comprehend and still had yielded no final legislation to be voted into law.

Even with its poll data about the public's distaste for such sausage making and the poor outcomes of the November governors' races in Virginia and New Jersey, there was no anticipation of a political backlash.

Through the summer and fall and now the winter, it was always the same refrain from Rahm: once they finish health care, they'll take the acquired political capital from that victory and apply it to everything else. "But the clock had run out," said a senior White House official, "and, somehow, we didn't even realize it."

Certainly Republicans had spotted opportunity and were moving forcefully to seize it.

By December, it was clear the race to fill Ted Kennedy's open seat was turning into a close contest, with enormous national stakes: the Democrats' fragile, one-party control of Washington, arguably the greatest bequest of Obama's rise, was on the line.

Since Minnesota's Al Franken was sworn in the previous July, after many recounts and court battles by his Republican opponent, Norm Coleman, the Democrats had a filibuster-proof 60-vote lock on the Senate. But now its soft underbelly was exposed.

In early December, Tea Party activists, supported by Republican fund-raisers, were starting to trickle into Massachusetts, which was holding a special election to fill the U.S. Senate seat that had been held by Ted Kennedy. Martha Coakley, the state attorney general, was treating the race as if it were hers for the taking. She was busy meeting with Bay State power brokers in labor, business, and politics to weave together a like-minded coalition that would help her to be effective as a senator after the special election on January 19.

Her opponent, a telegenic Republican state legislator named Scott Brown, was busy, meanwhile, driving the state in his aging pickup truck.

With populist anger bubbling through the electorate—especially against Wall Street and against backroom deals, of all kinds, cut in Washington—it was an ideal moment for an upset.

A mid-December poll by the Republican Senatorial Campaign Committee showed Brown only 3 points behind among likely voters. In a way, it wasn't a great surprise. Though the current governor, Deval Patrick, was a Democrat, for sixteen years before him Massachusetts had been led by Republican governors, including popular social liberal William Weld and corporate centrist Mitt Romney. The state was more purple than deep Democratic blue.

With the core of its first-year agenda on the line, the White House did nothing. A brief reading of the Boston papers would have sounded an alarm. Coakley was clearly a lackluster candidate, dismissive of voters and smug. Brown, meanwhile, handled like a pro an early controversy over his posing for a *Cosmopolitan* magazine centerfold as a law student, and being paid $1,000. Dealing with issues like that is the sort of thing, campaign managers say, you can't teach. He said he'd needed the money, working his way through law school, and, "I wish I still looked that good." That was it, nice and neat; everyone laughed. They checked out the photo on the Internet. And, of course, Brown, at forty-six, still looked terrific and seemed like a guy you'd want to laugh with over beers. As Obama and his team knew so well, surviving controversies—and even turning them to your advantage—is what people look for in candidates. Coakley took off a week at Christmas, went on vacation. Brown worked twenty-hour days, dominating the airwaves.

"To not see this coming, and not start to act, even back in November, after we got slaughtered in the governors' races, wasn't an asleep-at-the-switch issue," said a close aide to Obama. "It was utter incompetence. This is what political aides get paid for. This is their job." In January—with two weeks, still, until the day of the special election—the White House called Coakley's campaign strategist, Dennis Newman, to see what help Washington could offer. He said they were fine. Nothing was done.

Two weeks was once enough for the Obama campaign to blanket a state, with an artful mix of media buys, troops on the ground, and targeted events by the candidate. Now, with so much at stake, they sat idle. A public poll on Saturday, January 9—a day after the bleak jobs report and Obama's energy policy event in the East Room—showed Brown with a 1-point lead.

The dilemma, at that juncture, had two edges. Do anything necessary, at any cost, to win Massachusetts; and use the threat of a loss, and the loss of the filibuster-proof majority in the Senate, to get an emergency reconciliation, in a matter of days, of the two competing health care bills.

The White House did neither. Obama met with the union leaders on Monday. He was reasonable, as usual, working through disputes and competing positions. Pelosi and Reid were dug in, and the union leaders bounced between them. People worked hard and earnestly, but it was just a bit of an uptick, not a moment of urgency.

The question—"What would Lyndon have done?"—had been bubbling up around town for months, as health care started running off the rails the previous summer. Several senators passed volumes of Robert Caro's signature three-part biography hand to hand. Barney Frank was reading Caro's second volume, *Master of the Senate*, in the fall, as he wrestled with obstinate conservative Democrats opposed to financial regulation. The way Lyndon Johnson, as senator, had pushed the foundations of civil rights legislation through a resistant Republican Senate in the late 1950s held tactical clues. Now, inside the White House, aides pined for what one called "a Lyndon moment."

"A few of us joked that we should just get Robert Caro's book on Lyndon Johnson, highlight a few pages, and leave it on the president's desk," the aide said. "Sometimes a president just needs to knock heads. It's kind of what the combatants secretly want. [Johnson] twisted their arm, they had no choice—he was going defund them, ruin 'em, support their opponent, whatever the fuck—and the deal was cut. It lets them off the hook. They had no choice. I mean, for fuck's sake, he's the goddamn president."

On Thursday, January 14, Axelrod called Massachusetts and it was decided that Obama would make a last-minute visit on Sunday.

Meanwhile, negotiations between the House and Senate, many of them conducted into late nights at the White House, brought the two sides closer, but key divisions remained.

Obama asked the House and Senate teams to each suggest $70 billion in cuts. The senators ordered pizzas in Max Baucus's office and, with each senator giving up something, created a list.

Back at the White House, later that night, the teams gathered in the Cabinet Room. The House had cut nothing. It felt it had already made all the concessions it could and still have a bill that could pass. The teams separated again, to rooms in the White House, and then returned.

They were still $20 billion apart.

It was closing in on midnight. Even if they had come to some agreement, the logistics of getting the blended bill through Congress would have been daunting, maybe even futile.

Obama's method, now clear to all participants, was to sketch overarching principles, wait until others had painted in those outlines with hard proposals, and then, at day's end, step down from his above-the-fray perch to close the deal. Of course, the distance between overarching principle and concrete policy can be so vast that the former becomes invisible. As for the latter, others were left to bloody themselves with the hard negotiating over actual policy.

The result: everyone was exhausted. Obama offered his own suggestions, interesting but mostly fliers, to bridge the last $20 billion.

Henry Waxman, chairman of the House Energy and Commerce Committee, feeling an urge to affirm the president's effort, said, "I don't speak for the House, but you, Mr. President, have put forward a serious set of numbers."

Pelosi just shook her head. "Mr. President, I agree with Henry on two points," she said acidly, turning to Waxman. "The president put out a set of numbers, and you, Henry, don't speak for the House of Representatives."

Now she glared at Obama, and laced into him over the whole mess: an already stripped-down pair of bills, with Republican proposals, such as the health care exchanges, and competing, maybe irreconcilable models for how to pay for the widened coverage, much less actually control costs. It was another strong woman lecturing Obama.

"Well, what do *you* suggest, Nancy?" Obama replied, brimming with frustration.

Pelosi shook her head. She felt she'd been making suggestions for a year. She'd pushed a proposal through the House nearly six months before and then watched the Senate dither. She'd been waiting for the White House—and, more specifically, the president—to take the lead. He never had.

Now it was too late. She had nothing to give.

Obama stormed out of the room, telling aides to clean up the mess.

On Sunday he flew to Boston and appealed to the crowds to recapture the enthusiasm of the campaign. It was a campaign speech . . . for an office he already occupied. It had little to do with Coakley, who stepped up to the lectern as any enthusiasm rushed from the room. The polls were clear. In two days, Scott Brown would be elected to the U.S. Senate.

The next morning, Monday, Obama called his senior staff together.

"What is my narrative?" he all but shouted. "I don't have a narrative."

Of course, he was right. The extraordinary story of Barack Obama—a boy, so truly African American, who was blown between countries and households before finding his solid stance in the United States and then racing upward through its meritocracy—no longer seemed pertinent to almost anything he was doing. It was, no doubt, always a narrative of "up ahead," a dream of what would be: of how he would bind the country into an enlarged ideal of shared purpose, integrating its dissonant chords into a melody as elegant and surely struck as he, himself, appeared to be.

Instead, he had vanished into a cloud of endless policy debates and irreconcilable factions, of bold words—still hoping to summon the magic—so often divorced from measurable deeds.

Bit by bit, month by month, that first narrative had faded, even if plenty of people still felt its presence, like the ghost of a lost limb.

"He was right," one of the participants that morning recalled. "He had no narrative. No story. For someone like Obama, that's like saying I don't know who I am. That I've lost my way."

Nature abhors a vacuum, and now the narrative was being written for him.

The specific issues in Massachusetts were much more than the Tea Party's involvement, despite what the movement's cheerleaders on Fox News were crowing. Exit polls showed a desire by independent voters in Massachusetts to stop Obama's push to bring about health care reform. And this from a state that had a health system that included features from both House and Senate bills: a universal-coverage program that generally received strong reviews from the Massachusetts residents. It was a loss of faith in the president.

Internally, Joe Biden wisely counseled the senior staff to "take a deep breath"; that once everyone got their bearings, opportunities would present themselves.

None seemed to. In the days after the election, health care stalled. All sides just stopped, and sat down, trying to figure out where they stood and what, if anything, to do next.

Almost like a bad joke, what many felt should have been the president's first priority—financial reform, related as it was to the broader issues of the economic crisis—filled the new hole.

No news of progress on that score. Financial reform had been stalled in Congress since the late fall, when Barney Frank, charging forward in the weeks after Volcker's appearance, got a package of reforms through his committee that was then approved by the House and went beyond what the White House had recommended. Now Frank, and everyone else, was waiting on the Senate, which had been left to its own slow-footed devices for six months, without interference from the White House or Treasury. With the filibuster-proof majority gone, financial lobbyists around town were rejoicing. Delay and obstruction had worked, and now it would be that much harder to pass any meaningful financial reform.

The news cycles, meanwhile, were occupied, as they had so often been, with a hard, over-the-shoulder gaze back at the still-smoking disaster of September 2008. Throughout January there'd been a steady ticktock of disclosures about e-mailed memos written the previous fall by lawyers at the New York Fed. The reason that the release of the memos, which were subpoenaed in October by the Republican's investigative bulldog, Representative Darrell Issa, was delayed for three months was clear as soon as they were delivered: one of them showed Fed lawyers telling attorneys at AIG to block disclosure of the insurer's controversial 100 cents on the dollar counterparty payments to Goldman and others—made, of course, with the $182 billion in bailout money. Who was requesting that information? The SEC. Evidence of the Fed telling AIG to hide some of the era's most controversial financial disclosures from the SEC—in the wake of a financial catastrophe enabled by obfuscations from the very financial firms now being bailed out—was more than even Barney Frank, a friend of the White House, could take. Geithner had to make account.

Which is what he did, after some resistance, on January 27, before the House Oversight Committee, in a pile-on that, again, proved to be a brief, shining moment of bipartisanship. Geithner, denying knowledge of anything in the e-mails or many of the particulars of the counterparty payments, was met with open derision: "It stretches credulity for us to believe that you had no role in this and didn't know anything about it when your attorneys were sending e-mails around everywhere," said Representative Dan Burton (R-Ind.).

But Democrats seemed to carry the strongest ire. Pointing out that while the Treasury Department "scalped the folks at Bear Stearns, 2 cents on the dollar, Goldman got 100 cents!" Stephen Lynch, a Massachusetts Democrat, said it "stinks to high heaven what happened here" and "it makes me doubt your commitment to the American people." Geithner countered that his choice was between paying in full or having the contracts slip into legal default, which would have caused AIG's overall collapse, imperiling the entire financial system and millions of insurance policyholders across the globe. Lynch wasn't buying the legal argument. "You were creating new facilities every week. We were changing the rules day by day. We had leverage, and we chose not to do it!"

What wasn't disclosed that day, or at any time since, is that UBS offered to take a haircut—saying it was customary, and only right and what the banks were expecting—but Treasury and the New York Fed literally turned them away.

The Treasury Department, to shore up their leader's "knows nothing and never did" position, was busy saying publicly that Geithner had signed a recusal agreement once he was nominated for the Treasury job in November 2008—to screen himself from the messy workings of his lawyers at the Fed. Marcy Kaptur, another Democrat—she, from Ohio—got Geithner to admit he had signed no such agreement. Well, did he or didn't he? No, he didn't. So did the secretary instruct his deputies to lie? No response.

A White House official who was watching the televised hearings—and also attended the seminal March 15, 2009, meeting, when the president said he wanted to "show accountability flows in every direction" by restructuring the banks that caused the meltdown—said, "Watching it, I couldn't help but think about that big meeting, and Rahm yelling, 'We have no fucking credibility!' Seeing Democrats and Republicans going at the same unresolved issues, side by side, highlighted that this might have been the only area of actual bipartisanship—the kind of bipartisanship the president was searching endlessly for. But here was our guy getting pilloried."

That guy's boss, meanwhile, was busy considering, and reconsidering, many of the decisions he'd made, attempting to reset his course by trying out various public statements, just to see, it seemed, how they sounded.

In the days after the Massachusetts vote, he found himself saying he understood, affirming—and somehow even elevating—the disaster by noting that "Scott is just like me," as though he'd just glimpsed his successor. On health care, in the first days of February, he seemed to say one thing and then another about the future of health care.

Several key House Democrats, including Barney Frank, declared the prospects of passing health care reform completely DOA.

Obama's approval ratings continued to slide.

The question: Who was to blame? The first shot across the bow came on February 3, with a piece by Edward Luce, Washington correspondent with the *Financial Times*. The story—filled with pointed, though mostly unattributed, comments—was the first to begin digging into dysfunction at the White House. The piece said that Obama was captive of the "Fearsome Foursome"—Emanuel, Axelrod, Jarrett, and Gibbs, and more or less in that order—supporting a thesis that "the Obama White House is geared for campaigning rather than governing."

A few days later, the New America Foundation's Steve Clemons, on his influential *Washington Note*—one of the town's most read blogs—wrote about the backroom flurry the Luce story had prompted, as the mainstream media mostly ignored it, for fear of losing White House access, even as they were forced to recognize that "this once mesmerizing Camelot-ish operation" may soon be seen, to paraphrase Churchill, as a case in which "never have so many talented people managed to achieve so little with so much."

Pete Rouse read all the articles from inside the West Wing. He had been in Washington long enough, nearly thirty years, to have read enough stories of palace intrigue to easily paper his tiny office.

Rouse had always been the quiet man with a clear sense that it was important for the elected official to receive the attention, hopefully of a favorable cast, and not the adviser—a basic precept often overlooked by ambitious Washington counselors.

Sticking to this old-school principle in an era when presidential advisers increasingly trafficked in celebrity—with television appearances, speeches, and eventually book contracts—often created gaps between appearance and reality. Rouse, who was generally seen as among the inner circle but not driving events in the West Wing, liked it that way.

He could move freely, at the president's behest, and get done what was needed. His nickname in the White House was Mr. Wolfe, after Winston Wolfe, the character played by Harvey Keitel in the iconic movie *Pulp Fiction*, whose motto was "I solve problems."

And that's what he did through the first year: quietly solve problems, while attending all the key meetings, starting with the 7:30 a.m. gathering of Obama's highest-ranking deputies: Emanuel, Axelrod, Gibbs, Jarrett, Biden, Rouse, Schiliro, and, since August, as part of his demands for not getting the Bernanke job, Summers. Rouse didn't generally say very much, in any meeting. He'd save it for his private sit-downs with Obama. That's where the two old friends could confide in one another and Rouse could do whatever the president needed to get done.

On their agenda was the "annual review." This was something Rouse had done, under different rubrics, from his first days with Obama in 2004. He was suited by disposition, education, and experience to be a powerful memo writer. With graduate degrees from the London School of Economics and Harvard's John F. Kennedy School of Government, the self-effacing Rouse also shared what were frequently cited as Obama's cool-eyed, Zen sensibilities; his grandparents came from Japan and spent time in an internment camp during World War II. His ability to step back and assess complexity nourished two particular memos—"the Strategic Plan" written in 2005, which had astutely guided the new senator through the halls of Congress, and 2008's "Campaign Plan," which had helped shape Obama's electoral rise—that were sure someday to have their own glass cases in the Obama Presidential Library.

Now Rouse was facing his weightiest and most delicate task: turning the annual review into a treatise that looked back, assessing the past year, in order to look forward. The problem: the White House. The solution: reshape it into one that his friend, formerly Senator Obama, needed to run the country most effectively.

Rouse decided to do it in parts over the coming weeks and months. It could be kept largely between him and the president, though Emanuel, at least, would have to get "read in." They'd have to work carefully, and of course he'd be able to discuss privately his findings and recommendations with the beleaguered president.

He knew Obama wasn't made of stone or ice, and that he wasn't some incarnation of King or Gandhi, as his fan club, including Axelrod, would often suggest. He was, in fact, a man wrestling with enormous burdens—a weight he felt getting up each morning, a pressure not to show doubt, or uncertainty, or lack of appropriate knowledge, even to his senior-most staff. What Rouse knew was something presidents often learn slowly—in some cases, against their will: good process creates good outcomes. When a staff of thousands is designated to express the will of a single man, bad process can spell disaster, no matter the clarity of best intentions.

As Anita Dunn said, "The President is such a capable guy, he thought he could master these organizational issues. I don't think he understood how important they were."

He was understanding now.

Beginning a memo dated February 11, Rouse laid out his plan to save the Obama presidency.

This memo addresses management/personnel and structural issues that affect White House operations. The purpose is to stimulate discussion of organizational refinements that may be advisable as we enter the second year of the Obama administration. The observations and ideas outlined are in no way meant to suggest criticism of the work ethic or commitment of individual staff but rather are aimed at improving the efficacy of the collective operation.

This organizational exercise can be broken into two categories, process challenges and structural response. The objectives of our process review are to tighten the policy development process across disciplines inside and outside the white house. Two: To redefine the relationship between the White House strategic planning process and day-to-day tactical execution including definition of what we want to convey to the American people. Three: To improve the communication of decisions among the senior staff. Four: To enforce accountability of the implementation of the policy and message decisions. Process adjustments will impact White House personnel and structure, they will require changes in operating procedures that will likely cause some discomfort within senior staff, thus the various potential ramifications of specific adjustments should be thoroughly thought through and the views of affected senior staff should be solicited before organizational changes are finalized.

All four items struck directly at responsibilities—coordinating policy development, creating a strategic plan to guide and shape day-to-day tactics, communications between top advisers, and the crucial task "to enforce accountability of the implementation of the policy and message decisions"—that amount to a job description for the chief of staff.

Though many actors had contributed to the current state of affairs, including the president, each area had fallen into disarray under Rahm Emanuel's watch.

Rouse's second memo, on February 17, lowered the boom on Emanuel's partner in shaping both policy and politics, Larry Summers, as well as the other key player in the economic realm, Tim Geithner.

Domestic policy far overwhelmed foreign policy in the first year—in terms of both the president's time and the nation's priorities—and virtually all domestic policy was, in some way, related to the economy. The memo, designed "to lay out and enforce clearer operating procedures for the economic team," cited how "tension within the economic team and philosophical differences within the White House have often frustrated our policy process."

Rouse had been taking notes, unobtrusively, in meeting after meeting for more than a year. In four sentences, he laid out his findings:

> First there is deep dissatisfaction within the economic team with what is perceived to be Larry's imperious and heavy-handed direction of the economic policy process.
>
> Second, when the economic team does not like a decision by the President, they have on occasion worked to re-litigate the overall policy.
>
> Third, when the policy direction is firmly decided, there can be consideration/reconsideration of the details until the very last moments.
>
> Fourth, once a decision is made, implementation by the Department of the Treasury has at times been slow and uneven. These factors all adversely affect execution of the policy process.

In the lean, bloodless prose of management consulting, Rouse articulated what would traditionally be seen as insubordination, certainly in terms of the second and fourth items. The idea of an adviser working to reopen and "relitigate" policies because he disagreed with a presidential decision, or, as was the case with Citibank, ensuring that "implementation" was sufficiently "slow and uneven" to kill a presidential decision—

or, in Rouse's terse term, "adversely affect execution"—amounted to fireable offenses. They had been willful.

The memo went on to discuss various remedies for the problems, including replacing Summers, and laid out the case both for and against:

> *Larry Summers' large personality and intellectual brilliance lies at the core of any analysis of this problem. He occupies unique and important space within the administration. A former Secretary of the Treasury, Larry accepted the NEC job, essentially a staff job, with the understanding it would be a short-term appointment. His persona, credibility and expertise are extraordinarily helpful to the new president, and the president relies heavily on Larry's intellect and economic counsel.*

But, the year one review goes on to state:

> *The economic team dominated by Larry has too much "rolling dialogue" with POTUS on various economic policy matters, which strengthens Larry's power to shape policy. Larry on the other hand believes we have not lived up to our representations to him or established his primacy on the economic team. He dismisses the criticism that he doesn't run "an honest policy process" but rather feels our empowerment of Christie, Peter, Nancy-Ann, Volcker and Carol have complicated his job. To him any deficiency in the economic team is not solved by the addition of new personnel but rather by the establishment of "new rules of the road" that empower him to run the economic team as he sees fit.*

Summers, having built capabilities since childhood for never, under any circumstances, admitting error, was once again embracing a writ of infallibility.

Meanwhile, his partner in shaping the administration's policy/politics calculus, Rahm Emanuel, was everywhere discussing error. Not his own—Emanuel was almost Summers's peer in never acknowledging a mistake he himself had made. No, it was the president's error in holding tight to the ideal of comprehensive health care reform, even after the Scott Brown surprise. Brown, after all, gained plenty of support billing himself as the "41st vote against health care reform," and this in the one

state that had a program much like the plans that had been working their
ways through Congress.

In a host of stories, Emanuel was cited, often through surrogates or
not for attribution, as suggesting—as he had the previous summer—a
scaled-back version of health care. Pelosi was vocal in her opposition
to this, disparaging the chief of staff as an "incrementalist" while vow-
ing that she would only support sweeping reform and calling his version
"kiddie care."

The coup de grâce was a column by Dana Milbank in the *Washington
Post* on Sunday, February 21, headlined "Why Obama Needs Rahm at
the Top." The column was almost a point-by-point rebuttal to criticisms
of Emanuel that had been building inside the White House for a year
but were only now—in the past month—starting to sprout up in news
reports.

Emanuel later said he didn't cooperate with the story—a line seconded
by Milbank—but Rahm could have hardly written the column better himself, laying out his case that, in Milbank's words, "Obama's first year fell
apart in large part because he didn't follow his chief of staff's advice on crucial matters." And that "Emanuel is the only person keeping Obama from
becoming Jimmy Carter." Noting that the "earthy and calculating" Rahm
was the ideal counterpoint to an "airy and idealistic" Obama, the column
listed a host of instances—including the proposal to close the Guantánamo
Bay prison and the trial of 9/11 hijacker Khalid Sheikh Mohammed—
where Obama erred because he ignored Emanuel's advice, culminating
in "Obama's greatest mistake" of "failing to listen to Emanuel on health
care." Then Rahm's "health care lite" position from the previous summer,
of going to "a smaller bill with popular items," like widening coverage for
young adults and children, was laid out, including the endgame of how "a
politically-popular health care bill would have passed long ago, leaving
time for other attractive priorities." Instead, Milbank noted, "the president
disregarded that strategy and sided with Capitol Hill liberals who hoped
to ram a larger, less popular bill through Congress with Democratic votes
only. The result was, as the world now knows, disastrous."

Obama, struggling to publicly clarify his own position on health
care—and having been just treated, days before, to Rouse's latest incisive memo—was livid.

He summarily called Emanuel into his office and "really laid him out,"
according to one source close to the president who was familiar with the

meeting. "The president laced into him along the lines of 'so tell me again how you're right and I'm wrong.'"

Emanuel was contrite. The president had had words with him before, said a senior official familiar with the matter, "but, always, a few weeks later, it was like they'd never talked. Emanuel was back in his usual form. The president's view, in general, was, 'Well, that's Rahm; he can't help himself.'"

Both men, after all, were under a great deal of pressure—something the president saw as born of extenuating circumstances. Just a few months before, in December, as issues both foreign and domestic crowded in on the White House, and no constituency or interest seemed capable of being satisfied, Obama and Emanuel joked that their fantasy was to someday open a T-shirt stand in Hawaii. And the key to their success, and psychic well-being, would be in limiting choices to only one size and one color. Morning meetings would start with Emanuel saying "white" and Obama, with a smile, responding "medium." The next day, they'd switch.

But the blow-up in February changed things.

The combination of Emanuel's public antics and Rouse's incisive memos seemed to have dislodged Obama, to have bumped him forward into uncharted territory, even if it was just a few steps. Save Rouse and a few others, he was beginning to leave his staff behind.

Emanuel, when asked later about the Milbank column and the follow-up meeting in the Oval Office, didn't dispute the basic play of events, before noting simply, "I'm not let go."

"When this history is written, this will be seen as the start of the change," said a senior aide to Obama. "I think the president realized he needed a new senior staff—that he needed to start taking back ownership of his White House—and, for starters, he'd have to figure something out on health care on his own."

In a meeting in the Oval Office, Phil Schiliro suggested options for regaining primacy in the health care debate, one of which was a "meet the enemy" strategy. Obama immediately liked the idea. Just as he'd tried to reach back to the campaign for lessons and ways of engaging that might be useful for him as president, he was now reaching back to the early months of his presidency, when so much was possible. He felt that the summits from year one had gone well. Fine, Obama said, let's try it again, but this time the summit will be a debate. He'd be civil and welcoming as he met the Republicans under hot lights to hash it all out. There was plenty that the two parties agreed about—after all, health care largely comprised what had once been Republican proposals, such as the health exchanges. The areas of differences would be highlighted. It was a way to take control of the debate. A long discussion/debate, like the ones he'd mastered in seminar rooms at law school or community centers on the South Side, was his forte, something he was very good at. His advisers, virtually to a one, were nervous: this could backfire in all sorts of ways.

But desperation had created the seeds for growth. Consensus among his advisers, though desirable, was no longer a prerequisite for action.

On February 22, Obama led the Democratic leaders of both the Senate and the House to Blair House, across from the White House, to meet their opposite numbers in the Republican minority. It went well. Representative Paul Ryan, the rising Wisconsin Republican, and Tennessee's veteran senator Lamar Alexander made strong efforts for the Republicans, fencing with the president. But Obama was in rare form. When McCain offered an arch comment with a partisan edge, Obama dispatched him: "The campaign's over, John," leaving McCain to murmur, "I know it is." It was, however, a glimpse of Obama as the kind of confident public actor many had not seen since the campaign, this time engaging directly with the Republicans on the substance of the health care debate.

Obama was buoyed coming out of the meeting—his confidence up— and he felt the strength to turn to someone who he knew would be mercilessly honest with him: Nancy Pelosi.

She was. From this point, with so much of the original bill gone, they just had to ram home whatever they could preserve. Giving up, or going back to the drawing board, as Rahm's plan would have required, could be politically disastrous. If she and Obama just went for it, without reservation, progressives would support them for their ideological clarity, and moderates would join in, simply having nowhere else to go. It would be messy, but politics is messy—by design. You can't preplay the game, Pelosi urged. Let's just get on the field and start playing.

"You go through the gate. If the gate's closed, you go over the fence," Pelosi said to a group of supporters in San Francisco in late January. "If the fence is too high, we'll pole-vault in. If that doesn't work, we'll parachute in. But we're going to get health care reform passed for the American people."

In the ensuing month, that riff had gone viral. Now Obama and Pelosi were working in concert. "I think [Pelosi] is the one who has kept the steel in the president's back—and I think she represents that to Harry Reid, too," said Pelosi's friend, Representative Anna Eshoo.

Shucking off his White House handlers, Obama lunged forward to see what he could salvage. A bloodbath ensued. The only way forward was through the loophole known as reconciliation, a parliamentary mechanism to force matters when budgets need to be passed to stop a government shutdown. The unpalatable Senate bill, which included a slew of infamous backroom deals (the "Cornhusker Kickback," the "Louisiana Purchase"), would have to be used. With no Republican votes in the Senate, reconciliation allowed Democrats to pass the bill without needing a supermajority. In exchange for safe passage by the House, the Senate adopted amendments to the financing of the bill that required only a simple 51-vote majority.

But there were small skirmishes to be navigated. Bart Stupak led a team of pro-life Democrats in threatening to vote against the bill if it included certain language regarding insurance coverage for abortions.

Pelosi intended to win, at all costs, and began relentlessly culling together votes. On March 12 she dispatched a memo to members of the House caucus saying, "We have to just rip the Band-Aid off and have a vote."

In the last week, Pelosi needed to wrangle together 68 votes. With a March 21 vote scheduled, she got members, one by one, to make private commitments. Obama started politicking harder. He canceled trips, and called or spoke with each of the 68 undecideds, one phone call after another. Perhaps the most dramatic reversal was Dennis Kucinich, the feisty Ohio progressive who had opposed the bill due to its not including a public option. On March 17, with four days to go, he flew with Obama on Air Force One. After the flight, he announced he would vote for the bill.

It was a watershed moment.

Health care had already been stripped to the bone, a shadow of the once-sweeping comprehensive plans in which reductions on health care costs would pay for the moral might of universal coverage.

After all the madness, it was, in fact, just as Daschle had warned in April of 2009, when he said, "You don't want to be doing this a year from now." With no Republicans—as Daschle had also predicted—a stripped-down bill passed the Senate under reconciliation.

After passing the filibuster-proof Senate in December by a margin of 60–39, the bill passed the House on March 21 at midnight, with a vote of 219 to 212. Republicans opposed the legislation in lockstep, denouncing it as socialism, and 34 Democrats joined in voting against it.

Obama called a press conference in the East Room of the White House and delivered his culminating remarks. "After nearly a hundred years of talk and frustration," he said, referring to the first signature attempt to reform health care by Teddy Roosevelt, "we proved we are still a people capable of doing big things."

But by the time it passed, almost no one could feel great about it. The process had been so ugly—and the end product so convoluted—that even its fiercest apologists would acknowledge that it was a bill that was only a *start*.

In Obama's mind, it didn't matter. The bill had passed, and not only had he saved face but the bill "would lead," he'd later say, "to a better system."

———

Two days later, on March 23, Obama raised a pen to accomplish something that had flummoxed presidents for generations.

By signing into law the Patient Protection and Affordable Care Act, comprehensive health care reform, he guaranteed access to coverage for millions of uninsured Americans.

The bill promised to expand coverage to thirty million uninsured by providing subsidies to lower- and middle-class Americans while expanding Medicare.

Perhaps the most important aspect of the reform was the "individual mandate," a component of reform that Obama had vociferously opposed in the primary against Hillary, but had replaced the failed "public option" as the cornerstone of the legislation.

That "mandate" required all Americans to buy insurance—some of whom had voluntarily opted not to—or pay a fine. That stipulation would prove legally problematic down the road, but with the law on the books, Obama had accomplished his goal.

The legislation would be more accurately defined as "insurance" reform than "health care" reform, since the centerpiece was mainly an expansion of the private insurance industry.

The grand ideals of cutting costs while improving care—a promise carried in the Dartmouth data and examples of signature hospitals that had managed this feat by embracing concepts of "comparative effectiveness" and "evidence-based" practice—was left to pilot programs and some new powers accorded to Centers for Medicare & Medicaid Services. CMS, which administered the huge government health programs, had limited authority to use its payments to reward or penalize based on these principles. A prime target of this financial encouragement would be doctors and hospitals that banded together into Accountability Care Organizations, or ACOs, where they could keep the savings resulting from an embrace of "best practices" and related efficiencies in providing care. Of course, it was just a start: the ACOs, in several years, were expected to comprise only 1 percent of overall care.

And so with dignitaries looking on, Obama signed the bill with twenty-two separate pens. He had sacrificed a great deal—some would say too much—but his dream, his "legacy," was carved onto a hard partisan landscape.

––––––––

With health care done, Peter Orszag began to think of "when" rather than "if." When would he leave—how soon and under what terms.

The battle over health care reform, as much as any legislative battle in recent history, had bludgeoned the public discourse so thoroughly that many politicians on both sides of the aisle, as well as everyone in the administration, were simply relieved to have it over.

Orszag would be in that category, even if he was having trouble mustering the enthusiasm that was gushing forth from colleagues in the White House and from many press accounts full of Rooseveltian parallels.

Maybe Orszag was just too close to it. He had come to work for Obama with an almost messianic hope that, finally, comparative effectiveness and efficiencies would bring better health care to America at lower cost, savings that would make universal coverage affordable. Along the way, his beloved federal budget would be saved from its so-called unsustainable future.

The law, at day's end, relied on projections—and no one knew better than Orszag how hard it was to project a year or two into the future, much less ten or twenty. If thirty-two million of the uninsured, out of nearly forty-six million, ended up with insurance after the law's full implementation kicked in in 2014, the power of diversified and distributed risk—the miracle, always, of insurance—would help measurably, if modestly, with overall costs.

The law's newly formed Center for Medicare & Medicaid Innovation, within CMS, would become a vehicle for rewarding best practices in the funding and reimbursement choices made by government for Medicare, Medicaid, and the Children's Health Insurance Program. If so, there was a chance that some of the efficiencies would take hold. The same was true of the accountability care organizations (ACOs), a rather clumsy term for a network of hospitals and doctors and related health care providers that shared the responsibility in caring for a group— with a minimum set at five thousand Medicare beneficiaries across three years. The key incentive is that those ACOs that saved money, while meeting "quality targets," got to keep a part of the savings; the idea was that they'd do this by relying more on the overall wellness of their population and focusing on preventative care, and less on the expensive and exhaustive testing and procedures that defined the fee-for-service model.

At least that was the concept. But the start would be small. The Department of Health and Human Services estimated that, in the first three years, ACOs could save Medicare as much as $960 million. That would amount to less than 1 percent of Medicare spending.

As for Orszag's beloved "safe harbors"—where providers who embraced evidence-based, best practices would qualify for lowered insurance rates—and a related provision for the creation of special medical courts? Pilot programs.

Meanwhile, the law's expansion of coverage was, some critics were already contending, an inverted version of the "starve the beast" concept that far-right Republicans had long embraced: namely, cut taxes, starving the government of revenue, and the ensuing budgetary crisis will force government to make deep cuts and shrink dramatically. Health care reform's version: the widened government mandate to cover everyone—especially as baby boomers aged, by the thousands per day, into Medicare—would soon enough turn the lack of serious cost controls into an existential budgetary crisis for America. Then something drastic would have to be done. The key: it would be government's problem to solve. Somehow finding a way to make universal coverage affordable was now on their ledger, an entitlement.

After nearly twenty years in government, and though only forty-one years old, Orszag had lost his appetite for that battle, or for the American government's ongoing and, it would seem, deepening bouts with budget crises.

And a big one was coming. Since the transition days, he'd warned that if health care reform didn't dramatically bend the "cost curve," rising Medicare and Medicaid costs would combine with deficits from the ongoing recession to make the 2010–2011 fiscal year budget a backbreaker.

The bottom line was that the budgetary issues had been pushed along, Kick the Can style, as the need for stimulus and the attempts to push through sweeping reforms took priority. The administration's pitch was always the same: We'll build a brick wall down the road. It'll be solid and credible and unbudgeable. Until then, the administration will spend freely, as is needed in a recession.

Biden had been brilliant in December, negotiating a raised debt ceiling in exchange for the creation of a bipartisan National Commission on Fiscal Responsibility, headed by retired Wyoming Republican senator Alan Simpson and Erskine Bowles, Clinton's former chief of staff, an all-around responsible appointee, to shape a plan for a sustainable fiscal future.

But Orszag knew that the plan's nonbinding recommendations, due out in December 2010, wouldn't be embraced unless there was a sufficient political rationale at that moment. Brick wall? More like a discussion of where such a wall might be placed, if that.

Orszag decided he wouldn't stick around to fight that battle. Soon, he was sitting in the Oval Office.

Obama said he didn't want him to leave. Orszag stuck with substance. He discussed his concerns that they'd left themselves in a budgetary vise—that delaying the pain of real fiscal rigor, the setting of nonbinding placeholders such as the Simpson-Bowles commission, and Orszag's sense that they'd be ducking the tough choices again—meant he'd "have trouble selling" the coming year's budget. The president looked at him skeptically. He knew Orszag was displeased where things were going on the budget, but, Obama said, "we can work those things out—it's still early."

Then Orszag took it down one more step. "I come in every day with a lump in my chest," he told the president. The tension, the chaos, the infighting, especially the battles with Summers—it had all made life hard to tolerate in the White House, Orszag said. It wasn't that he was unfamiliar with a high-pressure, high-stakes effort, after six years in the Clinton administration. But this was different. "I think there are going to be some changes coming in terms of personnel that'll be helpful with all that," Obama said.

The president had received a few more memos from Rouse. Without giving Orszag the specifics, he wanted to let his OMB director know that there might be some departures among the senior staff that might provide relief. "I don't want you to feel that way, Peter," Obama said, genuinely concerned. "I really don't."

Sitting with Obama, Orszag couldn't help but think of what the president might have accomplished if, as Orszag said, he had a "proper process to fill his needs."

And thinking of the president's fortunes brought him back to Summers's assessment—expressed in many ways until this spring—that they were "home alone."

He'd thought about it, and turned it over in his head countless times, in the tumultuous year and a half since joining the administration.

Orszag felt the president had great "raw ability," but was stymied by a process that Summers, for the most part, oversaw, like "someone stealing gas from your gas tank and then criticizing you for not being able to drive your car."

In economic policy meetings without the president, Summers would joke that they were all caught in "relitigation roulette," where the outcomes of important policies—like a spinning roulette wheel—were left to blind chance.

But Orszag and others said that the quip was something of a misdirection on Summers's part, as Larry stood in a central role in determining those outcomes.

How did he do it? "By willfully ignoring the president's wishes and relitigating again and again decisions the president had made because Larry didn't think they were well informed or this or that. And instead of actually coming back to him with more information, he came back to him with the same information, just repackaged a little."

What issues? Orszag, like others—including many of the women who thought Summers's "debate society" had hijacked their policies—can tick off a long list. Obama wanted to move forward on tough climate change legislation; Summers was opposed, telling Orszag, at one point, "we have to derail this!" It was derailed. A financial transactions tax on banks and financial institutions, to try to tame the trading emphasis that has swept those industries and, along the way, raise money: Obama said, in one meeting, "we are going to do this!" Summers disagreed; it never materialized. The list goes on.

"Larry just didn't think the president knew what he was deciding," said Orszag. Sometimes, the result was just long delay. The president was, from early in the administration, pushing for discretionary freeze on spending. Orszag favored that as well and wanted to make a presentation on the matter. Summers said to him, "You can't just march in and make that argument and then have him make a decision because he doesn't know what he's deciding." In that instance, after long delays, the president did champion the discretionary freeze. But either delay or defeat of the president's wishes generally defined the course of events.

"The fundamental question is did the president want a check on his decisions ex post facto? Did he actually want the relitigation roulette, because he recognized that his instincts weren't correct? Or was this outright and willful" on Summers's part, that "I know more than the president, flat-out. That strikes me as more likely."

Even as Orszag sat with the president on that spring day in the Oval Office, he was perplexed, and all but exhausted with frustration. Word had circulated for months through the West Wing of Rouse's reorganization, with a special focus on an economic team which—with so many domestic crises—was the core operation of the Obama presidency.

"The question is why didn't [Obama] stop it. People knew. People realized the process wasn't working, and they kept saying it. By spring of 2010, when I was saying I just don't want to do this anymore, they kept saying they would fix it. And they set deadlines that were, of course, missed . . . but, the president didn't say, 'Goddammit!'

"He didn't demand that it be changed," Orszag said, reflecting, a year later, on his tenure in the White House. "And that can't be healthy."

Which is why sitting with Obama, in this exit meeting, Orszag felt a kind of sadness. The promise of Grant Park, of the inauguration, of all those grand plans. It now seemed so far away.

"Peter, thanks for your hard work," the president said. "I want you to stay in touch with me."

"Of course, Mr. President."

MIND THE GAP

T HE COST OF NOT "USING THE CRISIS" IN THE EARLY DAYS OF his presidency to retool the financial services industry—the power plant of the U.S. economy and, in large measure, of the American way of life—was being acutely felt by the spring of 2010.

After his interest in restructuring the industry, beginning with Citibank, was sidetracked, Obama fell back to the stance that meaningful reform would arrive as soon as the financial system was stabilized.

The industry managed to play to this conditionality to its fullest— saying it remained "fragile" across nearly a year, even as the largest banks were hauling in record profits.

This drew some angry words from the president, especially after another harvest of year-end bonuses was reported in January 2010. But whereas his opprobrium of the year before, when he called such bonuses "shameful," struck fear into the mercantile hearts of Wall Street, his words now had little effect.

The princes of New York had sized him up. He'd already been shorted by the Street.

While he was able to regain his footing to salvage health reform, winning a measurable victory—albeit far less grand than his Inaugural ambitions—financial reform was different. It always was. An individual's options for health insurance, sticker shock from a hospital bill, or fear of being left sick and not covered in old age always carried visceral relevance to daily life that was missing in regard to reforms of the way money and risk were managed.

Advantage Wall Street. The effects of its actions were pervasive, but felt secondhand, where the distressed party was often made to feel that a bad outcome was his fault.

The only things that carried health care's kind of day-to-day, kitchen-table relevance were low interest rates and the ups and downs of the stock market.

As long as those two, linked issues were in the plus column, people would feel a sense of some forward motion. Bernanke kept rates low. The Dow had rebounded from 6,200, its low in early March 2009, to 10,000 by the early spring of 2010.

The Street still focused on the profitable trading of debt securities. Even with the market's rebound, debt remained king, roaring back with a variety of successful arbitrages.

But, if nothing else, the public at large was beginning to better understand the meaning of the word "arbitrage," long at the center of the Wall Street lexicon. The famous phrase "mind the gap"—long heard on the London Underground system to alert riders to the treacherous little space between train and platform, and now widely used—was particularly instructive. Arbitraging, in its many forms, is about minding the gaps—gaps between the way things are and the way they should be, or soon will be—all over the global economy, and then having the speed and flexibility to profit from them. These gaps, mishaps, irregularities, or, in economic parlance, "inefficiencies," are often small and ephemeral, which makes volume the key. A hundred basis points are nothing much on $1,000. Just 10 bucks. On a $100 million, it's real money; on $1 billion, that much more.

And that's the game, the goal of the relentless hustle: to snatch those few hundred basis points by swiftly pushing lots of capital into tiny cracks in the global markets, and then pulling it out just as fast. This doesn't create much of anything—such as new jobs, the way a company might with a fresh invention or a product launch, or even a service that fills a tangible need. It just profits the customer of the arbitrager, and the arb himself—most, still, are men—who's committed, with every available corpuscle, to find "risk-free profit at zero cost." That's the standard definition of arbitrage: it's also called something for nothing, or something gained from something else going terribly wrong.

The great arbitrage of the Great Panic and crash involved interest rates. The Fed's policy, from 2007 onward, was to depress interest rates, pushing them to the lowest levels on record. This was intended, of course, to spur lending and consumer spending as the country slipped into its deep recession. With household debt at a stunning 130 percent of GDP, low rates were seen as the best way to keep cash in people's pockets, as opposed to paying debt service, so they could spend it. They could refinance their existing debts at a lower rate, maybe pay some of them down, or get new credit at attractive rates to help stave off financial collapse, to keep their balls rolling. All these things happened, but only very modestly. While the cost of funds for banks—something directly controlled by the Fed—dropped to less than 1 percent, the rates for mortgages, consumer credit, and small business loans didn't drop quite as much, and profit margins for the purveyors of debt, of all kinds, grew. But by early 2010 it was indisputable that this had not spurred fresh lending. Banks, both shadow and traditional, asserted that individuals and companies, especially small businesses, were already carrying unsustainable levels of debt, and that quality customers were scarce. Mortgages, the lodestar of risk and reward in the debt world, were defaulting at record rates; car loans and credit card defaults were not far behind. The heightened risk of default meant there was little downward pressure on consumer credit rates, just better spreads on any loans that were being made.

Nonetheless, the Fed kept the spigot open, hoping for a change. It had become history's lowest-cost lender, sending off, between the fall of 2007 and the end of 2009, nearly $3.5 trillion in essentially interest-free money to banks, nonbanks, finance companies, state governments, investment trusts, foreign governments, or anyone hanging out a financial services shingle, many of whom would sign on to an arrangement where recipients could keep any profits gained from putting that money "to work," while the Fed ate any losses. Of course, for Bernanke there was a secondary, and largely unspoken, purpose of unleashing this river of free money: to help anyone in the management of money and risk earn his way out of trouble, and then some. This particularly troubled Paul Volcker. In an Oval Office meeting back in the spring of 2009, he saw this bank-support program launched and complained that government was doing too much to restore the existing, flawed system, and that banks were certain to use all that free money to churn up huge profits. "Does it have to be so frothy?" he queried the room, with evident frustration.

Geithner's position was: to be safe, yes, it does. On that score, the Fed's program, complemented by various grants and guarantees from Treasury, succeeded wildly.

By early 2010 the banks had, in fact, notched their easiest victory in years by simply lending that fresh Fed money back to the planet's largest, safest, and still hungriest customer for debt: the U.S. government itself.

Being handed free money and then, by buying Treasury bonds, lending it back to the U.S. government at 3 percent, generated enormous profits. So, while the Fed waited for the gap to close between its intention, getting credit to the hardest hit parts of the economy, and the hard realities of the debt cycle, the banks hit the arbitrager's mark, each day, notching "risk-free profits at zero cost."

For financial institutions who'd spent decades trying, and so often succeeding, in engineering ways to make something from nothing, this particular arbitrage was helpful in restoring them to the form they'd enjoyed before the crash, only more so.

Lending that free money back to the government was just the largest of the advantages available from a negligible cost of funds. The spread between what banks paid depositors and what they received from all borrowers, and extensions of credit, grew admirably.

How much did this federal support of the banks cost taxpayers? By 2010, credible calculations had started to emerge. With debt of approximately $14 trillion issued by the Fed, Treasury, federal agencies, and municipalities, which was scooped up by banks and other investors worldwide, the distinction between a near-zero rate at present (on short-term Treasury bonds) and the long-standing average of about 3 percent amounts to roughly $350 billion a year.

At the same time, that enormous taxpayer subsidy skewed the market for a key commodity, money, in ways that impelled investors to search for yields in higher-risk instruments than they normally would have sought.

That meant the great trading machine was running fast and clean.

Trading in derivatives booked its strongest year ever, with JPMorgan and Goldman leading the way.

As it was in the early 2000s, when interest rates were lowered by Greenspan to spur the consumer activity following the tech boom's crash, the world's aggregated wealth, in funds of all stripes, was again hungry for yield. The fact that 40 percent of the world's assets had vanished in the crash—that those funds had dropped from the 2007 peak of $70 trillion down to $40 trillion—seemed not to have changed behavior. Those assets moved forcefully into whatever exotic arbitrages (gap plays), derivatives (bets on the future), and swaps (noninsurance insurance) the financial engineers could gin up.

Just as banks had used their lowered cost of funds to increase profit margins, companies, especially large ones, used the downturn to cut costs even more than the sluggish demand merited. Their profit margins widened as well. And by early 2010 they had built up large cash reserves, estimated at more than $1 trillion. They weren't hiring, or expanding. This money, building like a lake above a dam, returned corporate treasurers to their lead roles, reuniting them with the large banks to help move huge sums to and fro in arbitrages of all kinds. The repo market got up and running again. Credit default swaps were bustling as well, with $35 trillion in outstanding swaps in early 2011.

People did make money from the rise in equities, but like the stock fluctuations of the late 1990s, it was largely recouping value that had always been on paper. Even with this surge bringing the stock market back to roughly the precrash level—albeit the same level as in 2000—Ranieri's prediction three decades back seemed to hold. Once the debt securities market takes off, it'll dwarf equities.

————————

It wasn't until the spring of 2010—more than two years after the collapse of Bear Stearns—that the SEC finally made a first move. There had been no significant prosecution or disciplinary action, at that point, by any federal entity. With its first salvo, though, the SEC shot high: in mid-April it accused Goldman Sachs of securities fraud in a civil lawsuit. The SEC charged that the bank created and sold a mortgage security secretly built to explode in the laps of unwitting investors, and then bet against it.

The mortgage-backed security in question, called Abacus 2007-AC1, was among two dozen CDOs that Goldman constructed so the bank and several of its most prized clients could bet against the housing market. The meat of the SEC charge was willful misrepresentation by Goldman, which said that the mortgage securities bundled into Abacus had been chosen by an independent firm, with no ongoing interest in the deal, to perform well under a variety of market circumstances. In fact, they had been selected by John Paulson, the hedge fund manager who built expertise in the mispricing of mortgage risk that resulted in one of the largest hauls in Wall Street history—$3.7 billion in 2007—his early and sizable short positions in the mortgage market. Paulson, in fact, had selected some of the most egregiously mischaracterized mortgage securities he could find: CDOs with triple-A ratings, which were all but certain to default. Two European banks and an array of investors lost more than $1 billion on the Abacus. Goldman and Paulson shorted the securities shortly after they were sold and made out handsomely.

"Goldman wrongly permitted a client that was betting against the mortgage market to heavily influence which mortgage securities to include in an investment portfolio," said Robert Khuzami, the head of the SEC's enforcement division, in a written statement on April 13. Goldman, as expected, denied any wrongdoing.

But a match had been struck. The company's stock plummeted. In the first half hour after the SEC's suit was announced, the company's share price dropped more than 10 percent, wiping out over $10 billion of Goldman's market value.

———

As his former employer was sucked into a prosecutorial vortex, Gary Gensler was thinking of gazelles. They were part of a favorite "way the world works" metaphor—one that Summers and Geithner and other old friends had often heard. "The way Washington works is you often start with what's optimal, a best solution to some complex problem, and, surprisingly, there's often quite a bit of bipartisan consensus on what will actually work, at least in private. That's your herd of gazelles. But you've got to get them across the savanna safely, to a distant watering hole. And the longer it takes, the more you lose. You may end up with very few. You may lose them all. Because there are predators out there, lions and tigers, packs of hyenas, and they're big and fast and relentless—considering how any significant solution to a big problem is bound to be opposed, do or die, by some industries or interests who'd figured out a way to profit from the ways things are, even if they're profoundly busted, and often *because* they're profoundly busted! So that's your challenge: see how many gazelles you can get to the watering hole."

The Goldman prosecution, he was thinking, might turn the tide. Something had to. He'd been losing gazelles for four months, since the House passed a version of financial regulation that included significant loopholes for end users of derivatives.

Those loopholes themselves were victories for the financial lobby. In the Senate it was bound to get worse.

After his girls knocked off, Gensler trolled the financial filings of the large investment banks night after night. He, of course, could read a balance sheet; he'd overseen the drafting of enough of them. Goldman's balance sheet was generally considered a work of accounting arts—some would have said dark arts.

Back in mid-December of 2009 he'd found something that surprised him: Morgan Stanley's filing to the SEC for its third quarter, which ended September 30, had a notation about the company's over-the-counter derivatives portfolio. There it was, on page 139: only 40 percent of the bank's OTC derivatives were collateralized.

After the September crash, the estimations were that the major banks were demanding from one another sufficient posted collateral to back up their swap positions. Uncollateralized OTC derivatives, in the form of CDOs, were, after all, what got AIG in trouble. When the values on the CDOs plummeted, Goldman and JPMorgan made collateral calls on AIG. After making several payments, the insurer—which had not initially set aside sufficient capital—ran out of cash. A chain reaction ensued in which many financial institutions had swap obligations with one another that had, as well, been uncollateralized—they owed collateral, and needed to come up with it, and were owed. Geithner's justification for paying 100 cents on the dollar for AIG's swaps was to stem that panic, rather than, as some later suggested, to try to unwind the insurance-like swaps that linked banks in a disastrous daisy chain. In the backroom dealings on derivatives reform, the banks were stressing that they'd learned their lesson, that they didn't need the great dark pools of OTC derivatives to be forced onto clearinghouses—which demanded sufficient collateral and were themselves backstop trades. Morgan seemed to accidentally undercut such assurances with this tiny notation. The result: nearly 60 percent of Morgan's $80 billion–plus derivatives book was uncollateralized—an exposure of roughly $55 billion.

Gensler did a bit more research, feeling like he was back being a young executive for Goldman, digging through financial filings. Come January, he had a "deliverable" for his ex officio role of deciphering complex trading issues for Summers and, less frequently, Geithner. He had discussed with both men Volcker's suggested ban on proprietary trading by banks; both remained quietly opposed. And in the months since Obama's meeting with Volcker and Wolf, both had succeeded in bringing up logistical issues about how such a rule might be implemented—it was, indeed, complex—and so had successfully "slow-walked" it almost to a dead stop. Obama, otherwise occupied, again didn't follow up on the matter, which was turning into a smaller version of the previous spring's Citibank breakup scandal—a presidential decision slowed to oblivion—and no one the wiser.

What resurrected, of course, was external necessity, Volcker's proprietary trading in the wake of Scott Brown. As the president groped for a narrative, as he'd told staffers darkly, he reached back, not surprisingly, to the campaign and summoned Paul Volcker to stand behind him at a press conference on January 21—Summers and Geithner standing sheepishly nearby—to announce that he had heeded the "tall guy" and would push for a ban on proprietary trading. With Volcker behind him—as done to such winning effect during the campaign—Obama dubbed the provision "the Volcker Rule." Then, like the rest of financial reform, "he staffed it out," according to one senior financial regulator.

Geithner's and Summers's positions didn't change. For Summers, as he'd revealed to Wolf the previous fall when the president said he wanted to do this, it was personal, a lone victory for his vanquished opponent Volcker. Geithner felt it was an imperfect, backdoor way to establish the kinds of Glass-Steagall barriers that didn't fit with banks' needed latitude to respond to whatever the marketplace demanded. Neither one stood in the way when Dodd's committee quietly punched a hole in the hull, saying that any provisions for how to define and enforce a ban on banks' making large trading bets using taxpayer funds to trade could be "modified" by regulators at their discretion.

Obama wasn't much involved with derivatives, either. But the Morgan Stanley data, Gensler thought, might catch his attention. He showed Summers the Morgan exposure and explained its particulars. Summers was startled. "The president is not going to like this," he said emphatically.

But nothing happened—the White House was leaving financial regulation to Geithner's deputies at Treasury and to Congress.

Gensler, who had become something of a one-man show on derivatives, was now being noticed, profiled in the press, and mentioned in the same breath with Volcker and Elizabeth Warren. It was an odd position for a regulator from a sleepy no-name agency, but it fit into a larger concept: that the nature of regulation itself had to change, that the job of regulators such as Warren, if she ultimately ran her consumer agency, and Gensler, at CFTC, was not to be a friend of the industries they oversaw, emerging from them to take the big regulatory jobs and then, returning to some corporate suite once their term was up.

But come spring, as Wall Streeters were busy calling Gensler "the most dangerous man in Washington," he was starting to feel like an imposter. Say what they will, financial lobbyists had the upper hand and were making steady advances.

By mid-April, though, Gensler saw it: a plan to save some gazelles. Senator Blanche Lincoln, a conservative Democrat from Arkansas, had become chairwoman of the Senate Agriculture Committee six months before, when an enfeebled Ted Kennedy ceded his chairmanship of the Senate's Heath, Education, Labor and Pensions Committee to Iowa's liberal lion and longtime agriculture chairman, Tom Harkin. All manner of financial lobbyists considered this a stroke of fortune, especially considering that derivatives issues, and oversight of Gensler's Commodity Futures Trading Commission, were handled by Agriculture—a holdover from the decades when derivatives were called "futures" and dealt solely in commodities such as corn and wheat.

Over the past month, Lincoln had been meeting with the committee's ranking Republican, Georgia's Saxby Chambliss, to work out a derivatives deal that was shaping up to be more favorable to industry than the House legislation. That package, even the proud Barney Frank privately admitted, had to ingest too many exemptions to assure passage, especially for "end users"—such as airlines working derivatives to manage fuel costs—that could be exploited by the four largest banks, controllers of 97 percent of the derivatives market.

But Gensler had a ringer, a plant. When Lincoln became chairwoman, she needed a top staffer with expertise in derivatives. She found one . . . on Gensler's staff. Robert Holifield, an effusive and preternaturally polished thirty-one-year-old, had stayed in close touch with his old boss. His new boss, Lincoln, was meanwhile facing an ever-more-serious primary challenge from Arkansas' progressive attorney general, Bill Halter, who was gaining ground in early April charging that she was soft on Wall Street. Gensler huddled with Treasury and crafted a subtle threat: if Lincoln went with the package she was crafting with Chambliss, the White House would, in essence, take Halter's side by publicly saying her deal was inadequate. This "warning" was delivered to Lincoln on Friday, April 9. She had the weekend to think over her next move.

On April 13, a few hours after early-morning news broke about the SEC's charges against Goldman, Arkansas' senator stepped to the lectern to announce a startling about-face: she wanted all derivatives operations to be removed from banks. They needed to be spun off, so that taxpayers—with their obligations, still, to bail out "too big to fail" banks—wouldn't be on the hook to bail out derivatives activities. Plainly said, banks would have to spin off their most profitable business. There was more: she was also stipulating that the derivatives dealers had to act as "fiduciaries," always putting their clients' interests ahead of their own.

Reaction was swift. Startled Republicans, who'd been counting on Lincoln's acquiescence, were outraged, as were all-but-speechless financial industry lobbyists. But this time they had unlikely kindred. Some reform-minded Democrats and even Sheila Bair thought this idea might be ill-considered. You wouldn't want something as unwieldy and dangerous as derivatives trading to be spun off into an array of subsidiary companies. At least housed within banks, the burgeoning derivatives industry would be inside institutions that submitted to regular—albeit, of late, rather ineffectual—regulatory oversight.

It didn't matter. A week later Gensler, with a staff of seven, arrived early at the Agriculture Committee hearing room. He was carrying a stack of what was fast becoming one of the most consequential documents in the U.S. government. After finding the Morgan data, Gensler had gone back to the files. He needed a way to detail the dangerous ongoing credit exposures in the derivatives market, and the web of interrelationships, in a way that a busy senator could look at and quickly understand. He and his staff worked through several models—graphs, charts, printed PowerPoints.

Finally, he had it: a single page with three pie charts, one for each of the major categories of the $400 trillion over-the-counter derivatives industry: foreign exchange derivatives, single-currency interest rate derivatives, and equity-linked, or commodity, derivatives. Using data his staff had dug up from the Bank for International Settlements, or BIS, he'd produced color-coded charts showing the division of each pie among the three major players in the market: nonfinancial customers, such as Boeing and its fuel; reporting dealers, such as Goldman and JPMorgan; and other financial institutions, such as insurance companies.

The one-pager was a corollary to the Morgan findings from the winter; it showed that more than half of the derivatives market was operating in shadows and was without collateral, just like Morgan was. If there was another systemic risk moment, companies across the world would have to come up with collateral, in almost unfathomable amounts, that they had not already set aside. These so-called dark pools, where no one could be sure of the size and scope of another institution's liabilities, create precisely the fear and uncertainty that helped shut down the flow of money through the global economy. Systemic risk from derivatives, in other words, was still with us, and worse than ever.

In the minutes before the vote, senators from both parties were looking at the pie charts, each and every one, like kids who had just been handed back a failing test paper. The charts showed the financial system still loaded with dangerous interconnections; one meltdown, like a Lehman, could bring it all down.

Lincoln's bill passed the committee 13 to 8, with a surprise vote from Iowa Republican Charles Grassley.

Crowded into the chamber, side by side with representatives from public interest groups, journalists, and assorted onlookers, were Wall Street lobbyists who could scarcely believe what they were seeing.

"This is the way we make our money—they're trying to take away our lifeblood," said one of them, who, like most lobbyists, wouldn't give his name. "Maybe we did this to ourselves, sure, but we're just responding to the way things are. We've gone 'long' on developing markets around the world, and gone 'short' on America, where the whole game is using debt to give people what they haven't been able to earn, and may never earn, and derivatives is a key way we make that possible."

———————

Six days later, on April 27, Michigan's canny seventy-five-year-old Democratic senator, Carl Levin, chairman of the Senate's Permanent Subcommittee on Investigations, was looking to prove in public hearings exactly why Goldman Sachs was under investigation.

A few months before, in January, the independent, blue-ribbon, bipartisan Financial Crisis Inquiry Commission, headed by a former California state treasurer named Phil Angelides, had begun to hold hearings. Slow and steady, they were going at the financial crisis, and the actors involved, piece by piece.

Not Levin. He went with a frontal assault: pull in the most recognizable actors on Wall Street and let them explain how they make their money.

At the hearing table before his committee on April 27 was a procession of Goldman Sachs executives, culminating in a late-afternoon appearance by CEO Lloyd Blankfein.

Throughout the day, Levin offered examples of how giant firms such as Goldman had their many arms moving in a kind of subtle coordination to ensure that, no matter how the market broke, they won.

In questioning Goldman executives, Levin pressed this point without much success. The questions were too technical, and the executives could simply claim they knew only what their department was doing, not other departments.

Levin needed a CEO. Blankfein, atop the much reviled and feared Goldman, was his sterling opportunity.

His committee's investigators had pulled up internal e-mails on the Abacus deal and read them aloud, showing that Goldman traders knew that the securities, freshly painted and buffed for sale, were actually ticking time bombs.

Blankfein stammered and, under hot lights, tried to explain how Goldman could represent the interests of clients who could have conceivably made money on Abacus at the same time that the firm was a "market maker," drawing investors into a liquid market by taking the "other side" of the bet on the securities these traders were interested in, and hoping to crush them.

Finally, Levin had his opening.

LEVIN: *We've heard in earlier panels today in example after example where Goldman was selling securities to people and then not telling them that they were taking and intended to maintain a short position against those same securities. I'm deeply troubled by that, and it's made worse when your own employees believe that those securities are "junk" or "a piece of crap" or a "shitty deal," words that emails show your employees believe about a number of those deals . . . Now there's such a fundamental conflict it seems to me when Goldman is selling securities, which particularly when its own people believes they are bad items . . . Given that kind of a history . . . how do you expect to deserve the trust of your clients? And is there not an inherent conflict here?*

BLANKFEIN: *Our clients' trust is not only important to us, it's essential to us, it is why we are as successful a firm as we are and have been for 140 years. We are one of the largest client franchises in market making in the kinds of activities we're talking about now, and our client base is a pretty critical client base for us, and they know our activities, and they understand what market making is.*

LEVIN: *Do you think they know that you think something is a piece of crap when you sell it to them and then bet against it, do you think they know that?*

BLANKFEIN: *I want to make one thing clear . . . the act of selling something is what gives the opposite position of what the client has. If the client asks us for a bid, and we buy it from them, the next minute we own it and they don't . . . we can cover that risk, but the nature of the principal business in market making is that we are the other side of what our clients want to do.*

LEVIN: *When you sell something to a client, they have a right to believe that you want that security to work for them. In example after example . . . we're talking about betting against the very thing you're selling, without disclosing that to that client. Do you think people would buy securities from you if you said, "you know, we want you to know this, we're going to sell you this, but we're going out and buying insurance against this security succeeding. We're taking a short position" . . . That's a totally different thing from selling a security and no longer having an interest in it . . . Is it not a conflict when you sell something to someone, and then are determined to bet against that same security, and you don't disclose that to the person you're selling to?*

BLANKFEIN: *In the context of market making, that is not a conflict. What clients are buying . . . is they are buying an exposure. The thing that we are selling to them is supposed to give them the risk they want. They are not coming to us to represent what our views are. They probably, the institutional clients we have, wouldn't care what our views are, they shouldn't care. We do other things at the firm . . . where we are fiduciaries.*

LEVIN: *And that's the part that's very confusing to folks . . .*

BLANKFEIN: *I know.*

LEVIN: *. . . because they think you're fiduciaries.*

BLANKFEIN: *Not in the market making context.*

LEVIN: *Yeah, but they are not told that not only are you not a fiduciary, you are betting against the same security that you are selling to them. You don't disclose that. That's worse than not being a fiduciary. That's being in a conflict-of-interest position.*

In the 1970s the financial marketplace held many separate entities with distinct functions. Investment banks were partnerships, ever wary of the downside of investments because the partnership's money, in the event of losses suffered by a client or the firm, was on the line. They advised clients, often being granted "privileged" information, and helped them decide what financial instruments to buy or how to manage their balance sheets or which were the good places to invest their capital. They could partner with a client in a deal, at which point the client's interest and that of the investment bank were identical. Brokerage houses, meanwhile, represented clients, generally individuals, in managing their investments and executing trades. Market makers were involved in the issuance of stocks, standing, when needed, on the other side of trades to "make a market" for a buyer, or seller, in search of a trade. It was more of a technical function. And of course the cornerstone of the system was commercial banks, which took in deposits, paid interest, and, for the most part, made loans to businesses and individuals. When a bank wanted to get some extra yield on deposits that weren't tied up in loans, it could do so only in the safest, sleepiest investments, mostly bonds, as designated by the rating agencies' then-precious triple-A stamp.

Now virtually all these functions are held, in sum or in large part, within a half dozen huge institutions that, together, hold assets that amount to nearly two-thirds of the U.S. GDP. They enjoy enormous leverage over the crafting of law, regulation, and wider acts of governance. They stand at the center of America's vaunted professional class—a human yield, in many ways, of the enormous resources and effort the country commits to education—and have formative relationships with the large industrial and manufacturing corporations that are pistons and flywheels of America's economic engine.

What's fascinating about the public exchange between Levin and Blankfein, among the most illuminating of this period, is how it so clearly elucidated the conflicts of self-dealing irreducibly knitted into the country's largest institutions, and the very latest definition of "arbitrage."

The term had circled back, finally, to its etymological origins, to the French word, dating back to 1704, to denote a decision by an arbitrator or tribunal. An arbiter. A decider.

The large firms are designed to gain "informational advantage" as a fiduciary and, day to day, simply to decide how to use it to crush com-

petitors on the trading floor. After Levin grilled Blankfein about how
Goldman traded for clients, against clients, and often for itself using the
precious information gleaned from clients, computer models, or relationships with the government, Blankfein demurred that "we do other things
in the firm . . . we are a fiduciary," and then had to agree with Levin's
statement that "that is what confuses people." Sitting behind Blankfein in
the hearing room, Goldman's battalion of lawyers gasped—this was the
last place they wanted him to be.

A fiduciary, by a variety of legal definitions dating back to Roman
law, must not put his personal interests before that of the principal, the
person to whom he owes a "duty of care," which, in this case, would
be the Goldman client. And "he must not profit from his position as a
fiduciary," say numerous court opinions, "unless the principal consents."

That last issue of consent, though, is ugly in its complications.

What exists at this point, based on the stunning consolidations and
concentrations of power among a few "too big to fail" institutions, is
an unwritten code: clients are drawn to Goldman or JPMorgan or any
number of large hedge funds not *in spite of* the threat that those firms will
act beyond the edge of propriety, but *because* of it. They're counting on it.

Despite what Levin said, there was no confusion about it at all. *Let
them do whatever they want, just as long as I, as a valued customer, get a piece
of it. And if I can help in any way, I will.*

This is, of course, the way criminal syndicates rise up. It's an issue of
might. If the government, with its power of law and prosecution, can't challenge them, they spread, and their influence deepens. The large banks and
their companions, unregulated hedge funds, had increasingly taken ownership of the trading enterprise, opened new casinos dealing with the more
complex, often shadowy realm of debt, and figured out ways to rig it on
their behalf. For the clients and smaller competitors, this hard reality first
brought frustration, then, year by year, acquiescence, and finally a kind of
furtive participation. If it's not going to change, then why not be part of it?
If they didn't sign on, their competitor would. The aim for clients is to be
large enough, or strategically important enough, that Goldman sees them
as valued partners and protects them or, even better, gives them a cut.

Goldman and JPMorgan act as the arbiter, deciding, in ways both
subtle and overt, which client prospers and which is crushed, with the
goal being, ever and always, the bank's profit. That's called "protecting
a balance sheet." To be sure, the bank's balance sheet.

BUSINESS AS USUAL

G REG FLEMING WASN'T PLANNING TO RETURN TO THE STREET.
He had it all mapped out—the option he'd won, a precious gift:
freedom. At only forty-seven, with enough money to do whatever he
wanted, the options were all his.

When classes commenced at Yale in the fall of 2009, he was already
accustomed to not racing from his home in the New York suburbs to the
city each morning and staying late most nights. He and his wife, Mellissa,
went on a few vacations during the summer. He was spending time with
his son and daughter; he was reconnecting with old friends from college.
Up ahead was his ethics institute. He had another procession of Wall
Streeters on their way to Yale for the fall semester as speakers.

But someone, an old Merrill buddy, had said something that he
couldn't get out of his head: "Is this it, your last time out on the field?"

He had been a member of a community, almost all men, who played,
and played hard, in a storied game. It was social and professional. Their
wives were friends. Finance was all any of the guys talked about. "I just
couldn't bear to think of the disaster at Merrill, even considering how
proud I was to sell the firm—that that would be my last time at bat."

Which is why, come spring, he was far from Yale's Elysian campus
and back to a perch overlooking the skyline of New York. No spring
semester in New Haven for Fleming. In February he took a top job at
Morgan Stanley after an old buddy from Merrill, Morgan CEO James
Gorman, pressed him to get back in the game. Almost immediately,
Fleming was being seen as Gorman's number two, there to whip various
parts of the firm into shape.

Now, looking out a wide window in Morgan's executive suite, forty-
one stories up, Fleming was considering whether he'd done the right
thing. "There are moments when I wonder," he said, waxing about his
year thinking "beautifully disinterested thoughts" at Yale. "I'm entirely
focused on substance these days, the gnashing of the business sector, and

the banks, and it just keeps going on . . . in an environment that is very ugly."

But as reentry shock wore off, he'd begun to feel the native self-interest of New York and its needs. The banking industry's recovery, nine months along, now faced the threat of renewed ardor for financial reform.

Fleming, like much of Wall Street, had recently become a fan of Tennessee's former Democratic congressman Harold Ford, Jr., now at Bank of America/Merrill, who'd been taking on his former colleagues, especially the ones from New York who'd started attacking the Street. "In Texas, no one picks on the oil companies. No one in Michigan picks on the car companies," Fleming said, paraphrasing a recent riff of Ford's. "Why does everyone in the New York congressional delegation think Wall Street is now fair game? We're the people paying taxes, providing the jobs. What industry is in New York—and I mean a real industry, that creates real employment—besides financial services?"

But before a few minutes had passed, Fleming edged into a deeper conflict: a recognition that what was currently good for Wall Street, quarter to quarter, might not be good for the long-term interests of the wider country or its economy.

He talked about the Street's restored trading bonanza, namely in fixed-income debt and especially at firms such as JPMorgan and Goldman, now replenished with free Fed funds to trade enormous volume, and profit accordingly.

Morgan, meanwhile, was trying to call for a "return to fundamentals" strategy, by focusing on traditional lines of business such as its brokerage operations and asset management, along with the mutual funds it pushed through a vast retail operation that included Smith Barney. Fleming was brought back to revamp and refresh those areas, "to create a solid, sustainable revenue stream that acts as a steady counterweight to fixed-income trading," he said. Not that Morgan's earnings were depressed, just less than the trading-fueled earnings of its two major competitors.

"Morgan is now getting whacked for not being aggressive enough in certain areas of exotic trading," he demurred. The firm's stock price was sagging, in the high $20s, making it flat or down for the year, "and there's pressure on James [Gorman] to change course."

Fleming said he was trying to be the voice of caution, of "stay on course." The previous fall, up at Yale, he'd talked about being "like Colin

Powell inside of Merrill, calling the alert on the fixed-income trading in mortgages" in the summer of 2006, when CEO Stanley O'Neal wanted to fire the firm's increasingly alarmed head of fixed income, an old-style risk manager and friend of Fleming's named Jeff Kronthal. "I voiced my disapproval, but I didn't resign. And I should have. If I had taken a stand, Merrill might have not loaded up on CDOs—more than $50 billion of them in the next year—and it might still be there today. But I didn't."

He didn't want to make the same mistake again. "I mean, did we learn anything *or* not?" he said, and ran through a bearish analysis that at times like these, when the underlying economy is sluggish after a crash, and huge fixed-income players are looking for yield, "we've always started to build the scaffolding for the next bubble, the next boom and inevitable bust." He didn't know where the bubble would begin to inflate—"we never do in the first year or two"—but he added that he was regularly checking for volatility in the fixed-income trading records of Morgan and other firms. "That's where you see the first signs."

Just a short time into his job at Morgan, he was testing whether the marketplace—still structured, as it had long been, in terms of quarter-to-quarter yardsticks and short-term incentives—would respect a long-term, steady growth strategy.

The answer: not at all. Unless Morgan quickly expanded and juiced up its fixed-income trading, with the now-familiar brew of complex credit hedges backed by a systemically risky web of credit swaps, he and Gorman might find their days numbered. "The question is will any of us be given enough time to show that we're farsighted."

Thus, Fleming, sitting quietly atop the city, marked the distance between Yale ethics and prudence seminars and the compensation-assisted amnesia of Wall Street.

He thought back over the past four years, over what he'd learned since what he calls his "Colin Powell moment" in 2006, and he came around to Obama, how he had his chance in early 2009, when Wall Street was scared and vulnerable. At that point, Fleming said, Obama "could have instituted compensation reforms because people thought their compensation would never be coming back. But that's over now."

And that means New York, with its mighty industry largely restored by Washington, "will defy any change, even if it's for their own long-term good." Wall Street made its money furiously trading funds "it borrowed from the government at zero interest rates, and for them to take the level of compensation that they now are, and not see that people will say that the government did that for them, is unbelievably tone-deaf."

He recounted a recent conversation he had with an old friend from Goldman. "He said our compensation this year dropped to 42 percent" of earnings, down from the usual split of 50 percent. "I said, 'Yeah, but on the elevated profits, that means 20 million bucks, and what value did you really create for that?'"

As long as that compensation model exists, Fleming concluded, before returning to tend to Morgan's traditional, old-line investment operations, "there will be no replacement businesses built" in America's capital of money and risk.

––––––––––

Fleming's competitor now, as he revamped Morgan's asset-management business, turned out to be one of his oldest friends, Larry Fink. It was a long way since, sixteen years back, Fleming, as a Merrill investment banker, helped Fink break his analytical operation away from Blackstone, the private equity firm, to form BlackRock. A few blocks east of Morgan Stanley, BlackRock now stood like a behemoth. In December it closed its deal to purchase Barclays, making BlackRock the largest asset manager on the planet—larger than Fidelity or Pimco. By early 2010 it was managing $3.9 trillion in assets, including holdings, across its many funds, of a 5 percent or more share of 1,800 companies.

But the ever-more-distinctive feature of BlackRock, and its claim to still being in the lineage of traditional investing, was that it was not a principal. It didn't trade its own account, the way Goldman or JPMorgan or, for that matter, Morgan Stanley did. No proprietary trading desk, betting the firm's money against its customers' accounts, or deciding, if there was a choice between clients, who might end up on the losing end of an arbitrage. There's no doubt that BlackRock leveraged all manner of "informational advantage," but it did it strictly for clients. BlackRock invested other people's money hoping to get a return.

"I don't have a balance sheet to protect," said the loquacious Fink. "Jamie Dimon, everything he does is protecting his balance sheet.

"I have $3 trillion in assets, and my job is to protect the capital markets . . . just do the right thing. I'm not here to suggest that I have all the right opinions, but my motives are pure. I have no personal conflict with the broader good."

That kept BlackRock clear of the conflict-of-interest problems that were currently the subject of congressional hearings for a Goldman or a JPMorgan. Fink had no "Chinese walls" to keep proprietary information straight in his head. He was still in the basic game: investing other people's money in publicly traded securities to get a good return.

Not that booking strong performance had been, or would be, easy. With nearly $4 trillion to move, BlackRock—a bit like Fidelity's giant Magellan Fund in the 1980s—had to beat the market, even as its size had grown to all but span the market. Fink and BlackRock had fought this "as the market goes, so goes BlackRock" problem with what they claimed, to general acknowledgment, was the best analytics in the investing world. BlackRock's specialty, not surprisingly these days, was debt, especially mortgage debt; Fink had been working this terrain longer than almost anyone else. He had the distinction of having invented, along with Lew Ranieri, the basic concepts of securitization, and key early forms of mortgage-backed securities—specifically, collateralized mortgage obligations, a progenitor of CDOs. This meant that, in terms of interpreting mortgage data, with a special focus on repayment and default rates—all that affects those two key actions—BlackRock Solutions, the firm's analytical arm, was an industry leader.

Which was the prime reason Fink was so often on the phone to the Treasury Department from 2008 onward, and why, over the past few years, he had been handed nearly $9 trillion in troubled mortgage assets to manage on behalf of the U.S. government. More than half of those troubled assets were hauls from Fannie and Freddie—$5.5 trillion—along with a lion's share of the government-assumed detritus of Lehman and AIG. Again, his was a fee-based business, and for this management task BlackRock received about $300 million in fees a year. The reward was also an unmatched, data-driven perspective into the abyss of "the country's nationalized mortgage industry," Fink said, "which, of course, is a fucking mess and needs to be turned back to the private sector."

He had expressed this and related points of view to Geithner and others at Treasury in phone calls every few months for several years. "Geithner just listens—doesn't say much," Fink reported, but what worried Fink more, with each passing month, was how "they're just playing a game of Kick the Can."

All this means he knows too much—much too much—about how the fortunes of the government, and the wider economy, are tied to the still-unwinding mortgage debacle.

So, while in one office tower Fleming was thinking about finding ways to challenge the dominance of fixed-income trading and "get the investment houses back in the business of investing in America," Fink, across town, was singing a similar song, that "banks should be in the business of lending, and that will never happen unless the government stops coddling them."

That is more or less what Larry Fink was saying alongside the stage of an investment conference at a New York hotel in late May, as he waited for the crowd, about three hundred equity analysts, to get settled. The conference was sponsored by CLSA, a brokerage, investment, banking, and asset-management firm that is an emblem of how meaningless borders have become: it's based in Hong Kong, specializes in how various investment sectors, such as transportation and clean energy, are expressed in the Asia-Pacific region, and is co-owner of Crédit Agricole, France's largest retail banking group.

CSLA is also known for its investors' conferences: quiet, nonpublic affairs—no reporters allowed—where invited analysts pay dearly to get the insider views from star-studded guests, market makers, and movers in both government and business. Today's rundown included David Rubenstein, the CEO of the Carlyle Group, the powerful Washington-based investment bank and home of former senior government officials; Jon Corzine, the former Goldman chief and New Jersey senator, just a few months past losing his New Jersey governor's seat to a Republican, Chris Christie; Rodgin Cohen, of Sullivan & Cromwell; and Walt Lukken, Gensler's predecessor as head of CFTC, who now ran a large clearinghouse for derivatives that would be extremely profitable if some reforms that Gensler was pushing—the kind of reforms that Lukken long opposed—became law. It's no wonder the conference was oversubscribed: while investing in America is passé—returns are much better overseas—anticipating U.S. regulatory moves and trading accordingly is one of America's signature growth industries. Goldman and JPMorgan made tens of billions buying up distressed mortgage securities by knowing, just a little ahead of everyone else, that the Fed's policy of purchasing mortgage securities to keep asset values from tanking—a program started just after the September 2008 crash and now amounting to $1.2 trillion—would lift all boats marked "mortgage credit." It's not a complicated play: you need a lot of free capital and just a little advance warning. The latter is almost thoughtlessly granted to firms who help the government think through "market-oriented" solutions to this sort of problem. They're arbiters—part of an unofficial tribunal of government and select businesses—who make consequential decisions . . . and get first position on an arbitrage as others hustle to fill the gap between what an insider knows and what the wider world is fast finding out.

Fink, along with Blankfein's team from Goldman and Dimon's from JPMorgan, was part of that select group. Larry advised Paulson, Bernanke, and Geithner to buy up the toxic assets directly from the banks, creating some sort of "resolution/reconstruction" bank to hold, handle, and work them out, rather than hand billions directly to the CEOs. He was outgunned by other voices. But Fink knew that dance: for years he'd seen the many ways banks and investment firms avoided hard actions in their long-term interest—such as disposing of toxic real estate, taking heavy losses, and then moving on—in favor of "wait and see" models that allowed earnings to remain solid, quarter to quarter, while they waited for the market to rebound before working on their toxic asset problem in the flooded basement.

But once the government hands over the money, it is entering into a kind of quiet partnership with the bank's management—almost like an investor, but one who is eager to show that his investment, a vote of confidence in existing management, is sound and not sour, and not demanding another investment of good money after bad.

It's that partnership—and the way banks were hauling in trading profits while letting their troubled real estate portfolios languish—that had been driving him buggy. In several interviews through the winter, he'd done something that he knew was imprudent: talk publicly about the way the government, in the wake of the financial crisis, had written rules to protect the second liens, second mortgages, home equity lines, and the like. These amounted to $450 billion, of which 90 percent were on the books of the top five banks. This reversed the traditional lineup of debt, where a first mortgage was, of course, first: "senior" to all others, and secured by the property. If it defaulted, or got restructured, the secondary liens were often wiped out. The protection of the secondary liens, as a way to protect the big banks, ended up standing in the way of the many large holders of first mortgages, including a significant number of small and midsize banks, keeping them from restructuring first loans that were in default, in some cases for years. For those banks, payments on many defaulted loans might resume, albeit at a reduced level, and a larger share of the four million Americans who were in foreclosure proceedings might eventually be able to stay in their homes.

Before Fink stepped up to the lectern, as friends from various financial houses crowded around, he offered up a prize, a vindication on the matter from none other than John Dugan, the U.S. comptroller of the currency. Fink recounted how, while sitting next to Dugan at a recent meeting of the Bank for International Settlements, he grilled him on "the backdoor bailout of the banks of $450 billion—almost as much as has gone out the door in TARP!" Dugan agreed, Fink said, "but said his office had done an analysis and put the number at closer to $200 billion."

Of course, few people breathing have more credibility assessing the value of a toxic mortgage security than the product's inventor, Fink—"I'd like to see Dugan's model on how much a lien on a mortgage is worth!"—which was why he was the star today, even among the august list of speakers.

And there was concern around the room about what Fink might say about the still-fragile debt markets. At the end of April, the Fed had ended "quantitative easing," a program, started in the fall of 2008, in which the Fed bought Treasury bonds and mortgage-backed securities from banks to inject liquidity into the economy and promote growth. The cash that banks got from these Fed purchases—now totaling a whopping $1.7 trillion—became excess reserves, which should have allowed banks to engage in more lending. The Fed purchasing caused mortgage rates to fall and yields on Treasuries to hit a record low, but bank lending remained sluggish. It gave no one much confidence that the Japanese had attempted a similar quantitative easing program in the late 1980s and early '90s, when its interest rates were near zero—as in the United States currently—and there were fears of deflation. It was a large continuing effort, but it didn't do much beyond drain the Japanese treasury and saddle their central bank with toxic real estate of declining value. Not that this Japanese-style program was now prompting complaints from U.S. banks. They were getting a healthy slice of mortgage securities off their books—at what were generally acknowledged to be inflated prices paid by the Fed—and were now sitting on more than a trillion dollars of reserves—reserves that were not being lent out, certainly not much in demand-deficient America, but rather, were fueling the machine of fixed-income trading on all cuts and slices of debt. A lot of liquidity with nowhere to go, in a low-yield environment, was, of course, the ideal circumstance for lots of speculative, exotic trading games.

Which is why Larry was soon huddling with Greg Fleming, who'd just shown up, and Bill Winters, the former number two to Jamie Dimon, who'd left JPMorgan a few months before. These three, speaking one after the other, would be carrying forward the "Capital Markets" portion of today's festivities. But what they talked about together as the moderator prepared to introduce them was the day's overarching topic: Would ardor for financial reform—now revived in the wake of the health care bill's passage and Goldman's pillorying in front of Congress—slow or stymie the trading machine (the only way, in Fink's mind, for the banks, the investment houses, and the hedge funds to make any real money these days . . . and maybe, for many days to come)?

Of special concern was Blanche Lincoln's move to force the spinning-off of derivatives operations. Fink said, nothing to worry about—"Geithner will never let it happen," and that the spinning-off of derivatives, along with some of the more strident reform proposals, would "be used as bargaining chips." Fleming was not so sure: the linked chain of exotic trading—the securitization and reselling of debt in derivative plays, the credit hedges, and the credit default swaps, all of which bind institutions together in the same webs of systemic risk that caused the collapse—"is what most of these reforms are trying to kill off," he told Fink, "so banks have to get back to their core business, actually lending."

Fink laughed, unconvinced. "Most of them, even if they're passed as they are now, won't have that much effect. Goldman can get around almost everything currently on the table. And if they think banks are going to actually start lending in America, they're dreaming. They'll find other ways to make money."

It was time for the trio to take the stage. Winters first, and then Fleming—each ran through regulatory issues, various expectations for how it all might map out and where investment returns were the strongest: overseas. When Fink came on, to talk about the many burgeoning foreign markets that were most attractive to investors—and that would stay so in the near future—Winters was milling about in the empty area behind the ballroom, a forest of cloth-covered round bar tables littered with empty coffee cups, where the group had just finished its fifteen-minute morning break.

"A lot of muffins get eaten in this town," Winters said, nosing around to see what was left at the buffet table, as Fleming was speaking inside the ballroom. "It'll be nice to be out of all this for a while."

Winters, who built JPMorgan's fixed-income trading business and then moved on to head investment banking—a trajectory that put him on a short list someday to succeed Dimon—was now planning a move to London. He'd been asked to help the British government wrestle with their version of financial reform, with proposals to be first recommended by a special independent committee, organized under the Chancellor of the Exchequer's Office. He'd be one of the members.

Leaning on a waist-high table, he talked about gaining more perspective with each passing month since his departure from JPMorgan last November, and how he'd often thought, lately, of a dinner he had with his extended family back in 2007. It was a big group, led by Bill's father, a World War II veteran, a poor kid from Wheeling, West Virginia, who'd served in the U.S. Navy, came home, got educated on the GI Bill, and then got a job with the National Steel Corporation. His father was "a tough proud guy, very responsible, supported his family" and had grown concerned in the previous few years about how much money he saw his son spending. He didn't know exactly how much Bill was making—Winters earned $22.5 million in total compensation in 2007—but now he saw his son paying for eight people at a fancy restaurant on the Florida coast.

"So he takes me aside and looks at me with real seriousness. This is something he'd been wanting to say for a while. He looks me in the eye, mentions how much money I've been spending, how much a dinner like this costs, and says, 'Bill, is what you're doing legal? I don't see how it can be.'"

Winters shook his head, mulling over his dad's words. "I think a lot about that. Him saying, 'How could this be legal?'"

Inside the ballroom, Fink was now holding the crowd rapt; they hung on each word. He spoke, like everyone else, of the overseas opportunities. Fink was a globalist, joyously, and profitably disrespectful of borders. He'd spent much of the fall tapping sovereign-wealth funds in Kuwait, Saudi Arabia, and across Asia—huge capital troves that could be swiftly directed by the governments that ran them. These funds, like most of the rest of the world's aggregated wealth, were happy to work the vast U.S. debt markets, but didn't generally see equity growth opportunities in an American economy. Despite its size—$15 trillion in GDP, nearly three times the size of China's $6 trillion and Japan's $5 trillion—the United States was viewed as overregulated and maturing fast. The pools of money around the world, led by Wall Street, were being invested in the upside of countries with cheap labor, no regulations, child labor, no union organizing. (Organizing, considered a crime, can bring lifelong incarceration in China.) Everyone was busy buying shares in this bright future. Fink, needing something fresh on this front, mentioned Colombia, with a per capita income of $9,800 and half the population below the poverty line. It was also the third-largest exporter of oil to the United States. Yes, Colombia, Fink said—great growth potential—as the analysts nodded and jotted.

But there was more, one more thing, what they had come to hear: Fink's judgment on the core financial business that defined America, still, as it had for the past decade: packaging the flow of money, much of it foreign money, into debt for all the parts and parcels of America. As an inventor of securitization, manager of the U.S. toxic debt portfolio, and overseer of BlackRock—with its unparalleled analytics in how the American government, corporations, and individuals were faring, day to day, under a still-crushing debt load—Fink was in the best position to say what he, in fact, then said: "Everything correlates."

What did this mean? That the core of all their trading strategies, at all the financial houses, had reasserted itself—strategies that rested on loading mountains of data into various predictive equations, algorithms designed to show how the trading and shifting market values of disparate financial products correlated with the past. BlackRock had a longer tail of data than anyone else, especially on mortgage-related securities, and the longer the tail, the more precise the predictive model. When the actual price of a security strayed from that model, traders, or their trading computers, bought, often in huge volume, in whatever direction, short or long, that predicted a regression back to the bell curve over a designated period of time. The more faith you had in your model, the more leverage you piled into it, so each split-second trade was that much more profitable. Traders called this "picking up nickels in front of the steamroller." Do that with trillions of dollars, you make tens of billions picking up those nickels. Of course those bankers and analysts listening to Fink were jittery, and how could they not be? In 1998, Long-Term Capital Management, run by two Nobel Prize winners, thought its predictive bell curve, mapping the movement of interest rates over the past few years, was sound. It was, until it wasn't, and a unique event—aren't they all?—of Russia defaulting on its debt created a "fat tail," where the flat-bottom edge of the bell curve turned up, as though it were starting a new curve. With housing prices rising for three decades, in a thirty-year bubble inflated by easy credit, the meltdown of the mortgage market would be a surprise times a hundred.

What Fink was saying was "Relax." No more "black swan" moments for a while. You won't have to go back to investing in America, back to finding underappreciated value—the intrinsic worth of something that improves someone's busy day, that excites or comforts them—and spotting it before anyone else in this fast-fire, democratized information age, to be the first to put your money down. That was difficult and actually risky, and harder than ever in what looked like a painfully mature America economy. The trader, with his equations that claimed to represent reality—until they didn't—still ruled. That meant more booms were ahead, along with the inevitable busts. And that's why all concerned parties should stick with BlackRock. Because when the coming bust—the next one, which would be even bigger, as each successive one seemed to be—showed its first perplexing signs, when that first moment came, when things didn't correlate for a passing but significant instant, you should be with Fink rather than Dimon or Blankfein. Why? Because that's when they, Dimon and Blankfein, would make their real killing, making—with their own proprietary, pure-profit capital—a "directional" move against the market, often done invisibly, through intermediaries, or in the "dark pools" of derivatives bets. Before you knew that the world had just listed, just heaved in a new direction, you'd be left with securities that couldn't be sold in a declining market; you'd have to catch the falling knife. BlackRock was as drenched with "informational advantage" as Goldman or JPMorgan, but—and here was the sell—BlackRock would use that advantage to make sure its clients were the ones who leapt away before the steamroller flattened them.

Beyond the partitions, with the empty muffin tins, Bill Winters was still thinking about his father's question—"How can this be legal?"—which was now being asked in coffee shops, in carpools, and in Congress.

There was, institutionally speaking, an entity, or rather, three particular firms, that were designed to act as honest brokers in assessing value rigorously, and publicly, for all to share simultaneously: Moody's, Standard & Poor's, and Fitch. That they'd been stunningly, disastrously, stupefyingly wrong in stamping risky CDOs with their triple-A seal of soundness and safety was one of the most widely acknowledged verities of the great crash. It was also clear that, with all three public companies, they were in conventional competition for profits and primacy, quarter to quarter. The fees for rating CDOs—generally around $200,000 a bundle—were too good to turn away.

But nearly three years after the credit markets began to ice up in 2007, the question of why it had happened, and had there been fraud, still hung like a mist. With no end in sight to Wall Street's impulse for turning financial complexity into cash, and with its powerful, quick-kill incentives unchanged, the rating agencies' role—as a stamped and sealed proxy for actually understanding the next financial gizmo and the one after that—would only grow.

It was thus a twist of good fortune that Bill Winters was suddenly channeling his father, with his plainspoken steelworker's sensibilities. "These were young guys at the rating agencies, making $100,000 a year, one-tenth, or one-fiftieth, what the guy from the investment bank explaining the complex model to him was pulling down," Winters said, as he felt around the contours of it. "He wants to someday be that guy, and maybe he will be, if he plays his cards right. So you take him to a couple of Knicks games, a few fancy dinners, and you'll get your rating."

Carmine Visone wasn't having thoughts of suicide anymore. They came when Lehman fell, and they went. But it was not surprising for a man who looked into oblivion's dark maw, and then jerked away, to keep pulling back across the long life that preceded his brush with self-destruction. That's part of what brought him here to the old neighborhood of Brooklyn—that, and the gravitational pull of life events. His father, the controlling, emotionally penurious bricklayer, whose fierce standards of measuring value are most of what he left to his son, just died—alone in a nursing home—having long since left Carmine's mother, now north of eighty, who still lived in the family's nondescript house on a street near Coney Island.

Not far, in fact, from where Carmine's cobalt blue Mercedes was now weaving, taking the long way, street by street, across the storied realms of Brighton Beach and Sheepshead Bay.

The brick row houses, strips of solid square shops, stone churches built to outlast the "second coming," hadn't changed. It's just everything else that had, or so it seemed to Carmine, as he drove into the past, pointing out what was.

His aunt's flower shop, he said, "was right there, next to the Associated supermarket, right over there, where I was a delivery boy." On the next block, a square box of concrete was "the bank where I opened my first account" with the money he'd made in tips. The shabby supermarket now has staples from the Caribbean and Middle East, and shoppers in dashikis. The bank is gone.

"All gone now," he mumbled, making an illegal right turn near a crowded falafel stand. "A whole world is gone. My world."

This was still called Brooklyn, but the name mattered, really mattered, only to those who gave meaning to such a place with the life they'd lived here, and still did on this spring day. It otherwise belonged to the history of America—from the Dutch settlers in 1643 to the famously noisy twentieth-century brew of Italians and Jews, mostly from Europe and Russia—and the longer history of the world, where people moved to wherever they could to get what they wanted.

If things worked out in America in a way that history tended to work out for the best, there would someday be a sixty-something man from Haiti, Kenya, Libya, Malaysia, or Pakistan, driving whatever decent car was worth buying in 2040, reminiscing about eating falafel at that lunch counter and wondering who the hell all these new people were in "my fuckin' neighborhood."

Carmine was deeply doubtful that history would resolve in this direction.

"Look at them," he said, gazing out at the faces, virtually all black or brown, and many born somewhere far from Brooklyn, *his Brooklyn*. "English here is a third language."

It's the nature of the new immigrant, he said, that troubled him, the way "they come here and create their own ghettos. The new immigrant doesn't want to be an American, he wants to plug into the infrastructure and send the money back home. There's no one giving back to America." The immigrants of his era, who once populated this neighborhood, "were on the same time line" with their "Judeo-Christian values" and shared the "same general desire to take the next step" in America, as opposed, he groused, to this wave of newcomers: "People who worship things and deities that you've never heard of . . . They don't value life the way you value life, because they come from a place where women weren't valued, where horrible things happened to women, where you pissed and threw it out the window . . . and so here they throw the piss out the window."

Carmine, now the major benefactor of the Bowery Mission, the venerable church and shelter serving "skid row's" destitute since 1879, had spent more time with down-on-their-luck minorities than any ten Wall Streeters combined. He socialized regularly with the mission's ebullient director, an African American former drug addict named James MacLynn. "The interracial stuff is child's play," he laughed. "You'll see how fast blacks and whites band together in America as the world keeps arriving on our doorstep."

No, it wasn't race that roiled him, but rather fear that "the middle-class American dream is over," that something unique that created the country he grew up in—an America that coincided with an extraordinary post–World War II surge in confidence and capacity—was gone. He was probably right. No period is ever like any other. But what seemed visible with each glance out his windshield was that a country that once stood atop the world was now bleeding, for better or worse, into the wider world, half of which still lived on less than a dollar a day and most of which was growing ever more impatient—with each passing, image-drenched moment—to grab what it couldn't have, now within clear sight.

By that measure, the old neighborhood of his nostalgic reverie was positively parochial: virtually all émigrés from Europe, their children, or grandchildren, carrying whatever shared history and cultural cues they'd brought across the ocean and then unbundled on these streets.

The same thing, of course, was happening, block by block, in every direction, just with an unwieldy, cacophonous zest that smelled like confrontation to Carmine, a mocking of his identity and the place where it was shaped.

He stopped the car in front of a baseball diamond and got out to inspect a fence he'd helped build as a kid with his father and other men from the neighborhood, along with pouring the concrete and putting up the lights. Carmine painted some scenes, looking through the chain links, of how Brooklyn Dodger legend Gil Hodges dedicated the place,

of summer evenings on the base paths, and of how parents—cops, fire-
men, bakers, bricklayers, like his dad—all knew each other, and one another's kids, "and it was real community with real values."

"But no one gives a shit," he said, back in the car, as he resumed his
loops by the holy sites—the place where Vince Lombardi grew up; Coney Island's parachute jumps, the spot where the bank heist from the
movie *Dog Day Afternoon* happened; the building where mobsters threw
a guy from the fourth-story window; a wailing wall, home of the "greatest handball players in the history of the world—all Jews." Then, the
first building put up by Fred Trump, Donald's father, not far from rows
of empty condos near the beach, new and ghostly.

Carmine understands that the difference between those two structures is that there are, as he said, "two types of development—demand-
driven development and capital-driven development. One is good, one is
bad. Demand-driven means someone actually wants to live there, wants
to rent there, wants to work there, wants to operate there. There's a need
for the space. Capital-driven development is give me capital and I'll build
it. I don't particularly know if anyone wants it. What does it matter?! I'll
make my money by just developing it."

Wall Street figured out how to do that on a vast scale.

But having lived long enough and—in his particular American journey, having crossed more borders than most—Visone knew that the
Brooklyn he loved was built by the rigorous accountability of the former, of all the hustling "demand-driven" merchants, he so fondly recalls,
filling the hard-eyed needs of those crowding these streets. If not, they
went under.

And it was, more or less, the same now. He stopped at a light, as a
lady in flowing African colors dragged along a trio of boys in logoed
T-shirts, proudly sporting the choicest global brands. If he squinted just
so, he could see his mother behind that dashiki, and which of the kids,
skipping behind her, was most like him. He'd rented that truck, after
all, to drive the dark streets of the city, night after night, year after year,
based on the idea that we were all the same, deep down, and we all get
hungry sometimes.

"I don't know, maybe I've lived too long," Carmine Visone said,
quietly—but, then, a smile.

GOD'S WORK

NORTH OF THE CITY, ON A HILLTOP FORTRESS HIGH ABOVE THE Hudson—a setting sun splashing light across its wide expanse—tuxedoed men and gowned women drank champagne from crystal flutes as they fanned out, chatting and strolling, across an endless lawn.

This is the Rockefeller Estate, called Kykuit or, sometimes, Pocantico Hills, but unmistakable as one of the sunlit peaks over the continent's vast firmament. It sweeps up a wide mountain and surrounding cliff inside a discreet electrified fence marking the protected realm of Robber Baron audacities: a main house just a touch smaller than the White House; stables large enough for twenty horses; a courtyard of garages for the parking and repair of a fleet of conveyances, including gas pumps and hydraulic lifts; and a nine-hole golf course.

Tonight, June 11, aging titans of the American Century, or what's left of them, have gathered to honor one another in the quizzical presence of their moneyed, less noteworthy successors.

The event: a black-tie gala for International House, New York's venerable cross-cultural edifice, where seven hundred residents at a time—IHouse fellows from one hundred or so countries—are graced with various enrichment programs and support services, speakers and mixers, while they go about their chosen rigors at entry-level jobs or seek graduate degrees somewhere in the great city. A stately block-wide building on Riverside Drive, built mostly with Rockefeller money in 1924, grew into something of a global networking Valhalla through the midcentury, when borders still mattered, international organizations were scarcer, and the expression "global economy" had not yet been uttered. Though IHouse was early, and its mission—of bringing young people from around the world together—is now so commonplace as to seem conventional, networking never goes out of style. Among the chairmen of IHouse's board have been Dwight Eisenhower, Gerald Ford, and General George C. Marshall, and its graduates include both

Citibank's CEO Vikram Pandit (India) and Morgan Stanley's James Morgan (Australia).

The current chairman: Paul Volcker. Tonight he was to honor past chairmen—namely Henry Kissinger and former Goldman CEO John Whitehead. He was also, as master of the evening's ceremonies, to honor David Rockefeller, upright and sentient at ninety-five, and walking through his house with a smile and an outstretched hand, his carefully tailored tux giving him the top-heavy look of a very old bodybuilder.

As longtime head of the family bank, Chase Manhattan, and heir to America's greatest twentieth-century bonanza, oil, David Rockefeller, or what's left of him, is an auspicious living actor—his generation's ring-leader—of ideals about top-down command and control: the legacy of the behemoth corporations, working in deft coordination, that rose from U.S. soil eventually to span the globe and that lifted small groups of civic-minded men, graced by wealth, who'd gather to solve the world's intractable problems.

It was far from a perfect model, the one Rockefeller helped manage. There was collusion and exclusion, old-boy networks that were all but inpenetrable for the interloper. Day to day, it wasn't nearly as efficient or productive or flexible as the frenetic present tense. But there were rules that were generally heeded, not in spite of the more static and rigid barriers that prevailed, but because of them. If you happened to be born on third base, you generally didn't rub it in the face of the guy who wasn't even born in the stadium, especially after the upheavals of the Depression and World War II. It was unseemly for an office-dwelling boss to take more than ten times the pay of a sweating guy on the loading dock, though no one begrudged the inventor, or builder of corporate giants, their fortunes. They did something special—maybe aided by banker or lawyer or ad executive, who earned just fees, which seemed appropriate. The whole point of the exercise was to make everyone feel the same, like they were all in the race together, even if everyone understood the nature of born, or bred, privileges, and the advantages they bestowed. The epoxy, the way it was all glued together, was with certain agreed-upon standards of right and wrong. An infraction brought shame and ouster. A desire to do the "right thing" yielded credit, and maybe a call to help solve some large dilemma. That would be considered an honor, and self-interest was generally checked at the door with your coat and hat. Could complex problems be managed by these civic-minded actors, working in concert? Up to a point, the answer was yes.

And they'd often gather at this estate. You could almost hear the echoes of midcentury prudent men passing from one room to the next. The National Highway System, the GI Bill, the Marshall Plan—all required such meetings, countless sit-downs in the library, or discussions over nine holes of golf. If some businessman was about to attempt something that would, soon enough, create disaster, the message had to be delivered: if he moved forward with it, he'd be out of the club; if he did the right thing, and subordinated his desires to the greater good, he'd curry gratitude, and that could only amount to something good.

A man who attended his share of such meetings—as an adviser to the Rockefellers and countless others across fifty years—was in fact standing on a crutch in the room, hobbled, broken, but unbowed.

John Whitehead had had his knee replaced just two weeks before, but he wasn't going to miss this night, touted as one of the most auspicious gatherings at Kykuit in nearly twenty-five years.

Whitehead, fit and still handsome at eighty-nine, received one well-wisher after another, looking like an actor hired to play, well, a man like Whitehead: a seasoned repository of experiences and values wrapped neatly into the catchphrase "Greatest Generation." From the time he commanded a landing craft onto Omaha Beach, Whitehead had been busy steering one ship after the next. In 1947, after getting an MBA at Harvard, he joined Goldman Sachs and learned at the knee of the legendary Sidney Weinberg, who'd started as a janitor at Goldman, worked his way to the trading desks, and, after saving the firm from bankruptcy in 1930, to the chairmanship. A few years after Weinberg died in 1969, Whitehead took the top job and, on a yellow legal pad, summarily wrote down Goldman's "14 principles": commonsense guideposts, often called "the commandments" inside the firm, such as the "client comes first," "integrity and honesty are at the heart of our business," and we will be given confidential information that must be "handled with utmost care."

"I didn't come up with them," Whitehead demurred, shifting his weight from crutch to foot and back. "They were principles passed down by Sidney; I just wrote them down. They were part of our tradition."

The pain Whitehead was feeling these days went well beyond his knee. A former Eagle Scout, he had worked his whole life to burnish and protect Goldman Sachs' reputation, and had remained, a quarter century since he left the top job, the firm's emeritus ambassador at large. As a director of civic and nonprofit organizations, including the chairmanship of the 9/11 Memorial Commission, and recipient of numerous honorary degrees for decades of charitable work, Whitehead had seen his value placed, increasingly, in high-profile misdirection: he was now a comforting front man to make people think this was the Wall Street they once knew. Whitehead's ubiquitous presence seemed to keep that other, older Wall Street alive, year after year, like the light from a dead star, even as ethical standards that he, like his mentor Sid Weinberg, had placed at the core of Goldman's franchise were steadily abandoned.

After September 2008 this sleight of hand was untenable. People came, one after another, to Whitehead to step up, to use his stature and credibility to put the financial services business back on course. He took another path—what Fleming would have called the "Colin Powell compromise." He would continue as a key adviser to Blankfein and attempt to alter the wider landscape by guiding Goldman's powerful chief in his words and actions.

As Blankfein whipsawed between cocky and penitent, continued to take bonuses, and effused, in late 2009, about Goldman "doing God's work," Whitehead stuck it out. But the nightmares of April, with the SEC investigation of Goldman and its executives, led by Blankfein, seemed to have finally broken the old man's resolve.

On this night, in the rarified air of Kykuit, he was on dangerous turf. This, after all, was where Whitehead actually spent much of the last quarter century, trying to direct the enormous accrued wealth of America's dynastic families to areas of needs—and especially that of the Rockefellers, with their large, signature foundation and a civic tradition dating from early in the twentieth century.

He said he was trying to be hopeful these days, and how the kids he meets are "more idealistic than we were, trying to do things of meaning rather than just seek money"; and how: often "bad periods" like this one "plant the seeds of good periods that follow. That's what I'm hoping."

Those seeds needed to be "watered and nourished," he acknowledged, to take root, and he thinks every day about what he can do with the time he has left to help that along.

He paused for a moment. There was a story he wanted to tell, about what had happened when the Pennsylvania Railroad went bankrupt in

1970. He explained how Goldman had $60 million of commercial paper outstanding—and technically wasn't obligated to pay it—"but morally I felt we had to be sure everybody got paid back," even though the firm only had a $30 million net worth. In the end, everybody was paid back. It just took a long time. Lesson: Goldman looked beyond its legal obligations to do something larger, something that was right.

Just mentioning Goldman in the current context bore perils, so he mentioned that he remained a regular adviser to Blankfein, which meant he needed "to be delicate" in what he said about Goldman if he were to remain in that role "and continue to have influence over Lloyd."

But tonight there was no stopping him.

He then tacked briskly into the wider issue of some things that need to be discarded, starting with destructive incentives. "The compensation system today is so rewarding of today's results and doesn't encourage anybody to take the long view. It's got to be changed!"

He went on, now getting closer to Blankfein, describing how a CEO shouldn't be able to sell his stock in the company until after he retires . . . long after. He should be paid after he builds the company, not every step of the way.

Sue Weinberg walked up. She is the wife of John Weinberg, Sidney's son, who shared the chairmanship of Goldman with Whitehead. And in this place—a night when the old guard of Wall Street was making one of its last stands—the spirit of Sidney Weinberg, whom the *New York Times* once respectfully called Mr. Wall Street, seemed to inhabit his heir, Whitehead, emboldening him.

"He's so talented and he's so smart: Harvard College, Harvard Law School, top of his class," Whitehead said, finally taking off the gloves, old guard to new, addressing Blankfein directly. "He never thought that if the public is losing their jobs and we're in a recession, it isn't a very good time to talk about the justification for a $60 million bonus. He doesn't get it!"

What happened to America, from one signature generation to its successor? It was there, in Whitehead's voice. "He doesn't get it. He says, 'I'm the CEO of the best financial service firm in the world. And if I'm the CEO, I'm its head man. I deserve to be paid more than anybody else. And I'm prepared to fight for it, and boast about it. Because I'm proud of it.'

"Then, the next month, he says, 'God is on our side.'"

Values define a culture. This was, finally, one set of values speaking sternly to another. Whitehead, on one leg, pushing ninety, was the reedy voice of a vanishing tribe and their something-beyond-profit code of conduct: you should be guided not by what you have a right to do, but by what is right to do.

Across the room, his friend Volcker—another prudent man, old but unbowed, who'd spent the last few years trying to trumpet to the herd about the right thing to do—was being surrounded by middle-aged admirers, men mostly, who'd gained unseemly wealth in financial services. Two hundred people were in attendance tonight and, of the men, most were Wall Streeters and assorted capital jockeys. The place was jammed with them. They admired Volcker, sure—but they also admired themselves. One man, a former fellow at International House now working for the Spanish megabank Santander, just couldn't wait to tell Volcker he spoke four languages, as in "I was an American at IHouse, but I speak four languages!"

"Then you must have felt right at home there," Volcker said acerbically, looking down at the man with disdain. The guy didn't pick up the tone: he was too busy telling Volcker what a fabulous job he was doing at Santander preserving its sterling credit practices: "No, seriously, Paul, no CDOs, none."

It's never easy when your friends die off, or the standards of those you worked to emulate—the code of the "wise men" of the American century such as Averell Harriman or George Marshall; Citibank's old lion Walter Wriston; or William McChesney Martin, Jr., the legendary Fed chairman; all of whom Volcker revered, and patterned his life after—get washed away. Whatever else those men did—and, no, they weren't angels—they didn't take the short money; they didn't calculate the risk of getting caught. They were in it for the eulogy, where someone who really knew them would say what kind of life they'd lived. Volcker, Whitehead, and David Rockefeller will certainly be joining those men sometime in the not-too-distant future, probably before they have the indignity of witnessing another disaster born of craven and careless men.

Both Whitehead and Volcker now needed to be helped down a twisting flight of steps, as the crowd started to make its way toward the "Playhouse." It's a vast room—matching anything at Hearst's San Simeon or Vanderbilt's Biltmore—with twenty elegantly set tables of ten, with flowers and lit candles, arrayed under a vaulted ceiling. The Rockefellers and their guests once put on plays here, hence the name. The motif is neoclassical, the modern age's attempt, across recent centuries, to recapture the intellectual and ethical accomplishments of ancient Greece. Yes, old John D. raped and pillaged to make that fortune. And rather than boast about it—what brilliance, admirable efficiency, and strong management technique—his sons, and then grandsons, such as David Rockefeller, spent their lives making amends.

In the lowlands beneath this hilltop, in every direction, America was furiously showing its particular character as a civilization.

In the hour since the start of this gala, twenty-five thousand gallons of oil had poured into the Gulf of Mexico. The BP disaster was already two months along, having turned into a dark, gushing nightmare of man's penchant for unleashing forces he cannot control. Like so many other disasters in this period, the spill was the result of executives pushing themselves to the very edge of legal limits, and then beyond, in the name of short-term profit. Everywhere were disclosures of endemic regulatory malfeasance—one example after another of "regulatory capture," all but identical to what underpinned the financial meltdown, where energy regulators served the companies they oversaw rather than a wider public interest.

The man who started the empire of oil was, of course, anything but a prince. It took enormous and ongoing effort—from Teddy Roosevelt's trust-busting, breaking up Standard Oil of New Jersey, to Ida Tarbell's fierce journalistic digging into Rockefeller's corruptions—to rein in this prototypical corporate leviathan. Both Presidents Roosevelt—one Republican, the other Democrat—would have said, if they could still walk upright, that government should not be a friend of business; that business can take care of itself; and that government has more important work to do, to carry forward the "greatest good for the greatest number." The Ancient Greeks, in their own unique way, would almost certainly have agreed.

As, suddenly, did much of the U.S. Senate. The triptych of the Goldman investigation, Blanche Lincoln's surprise, and Levin's smackdown of Blankfein seemed to have jerked many of the Democratic senators, and a surprising number of Republicans, out of a trance.

Clearly they were hearing from constituents displaying a surge of populist outrage that, if not quite so raw as it was with the AIG bonuses the previous year, was now more targeted and substantive. It took a while, but the public and the media were finally connecting what had gone wrong across the many years leading up to the financial implosion with what might now be done.

The question: Was it too late? With the House's bill complete and much of the Senate's bill already shaped by long months of lobbyist-encouraged horse trading, panic had taken hold. Democratic senators started filing one amendment after another, in some cases with improbable Republican support.

Ted Kaufman, a lantern-jawed former chief of staff to Joe Biden, who was given the Delaware senator's seat for two years when his old boss became vice president, introduced the SAFE Banking Act. It reined in the size of the largest banks by imposing size caps and limiting leverage. Kaufman, who cosponsored the bill with Ohio's Sherrod Brown, was, by circumstance, a sort of throwback to an earlier era. He was smart about the ways of Washington, a former prosecutor, and he cared not one wit for the political dance of fund-raising and influence management. At the end of the year, he was going home to Delaware. As the Wall Streeters used to say about Volcker and some of the other economic advisers gathered around Obama during the campaign, Kaufman had "no handle," nothing to grab. There was nothing he wanted. No self-interest to twist. The SAFE Banking Act was just a straight-up "too big to fail" amendment legally limiting the size of banks. How would the banks manage this? That was their problem. This was part of the act's immediate appeal: its simplicity.

It imposed a 10 percent cap on any bank holding company's share of the United States' total insured deposits. It limited the size of nondeposit liabilities at financial institutions to 2 percent of U.S. GDP (and 3 percent for nonbank institutions), and, finally, set into law a 6 percent leverage limit for bank holding companies and selected nonbank financial institutions.

The banks immediately cried foul—that the act was unworkable and disastrous, that huge foreign banks would devour the U.S. banking sector, and that the act would dry up credit and banks' ability to serve their customers. All of these were predicate threats to push senators into trying to describe how such a massive restructuring of the banks could be managed without any of these ill effects. This was, of course, a rhetorical strategy that banks and other large corporate "stakeholders" had used with great success for years: gin up fearful consequences, the more wild-eyed the better, and repeated with large marketing and advertising muscle, and then dig in, not budging, until their fears, real or not, were allayed.

All of a sudden it started not to work. Kaufman's and Brown's amendment to the financial reform bill received a glowing affirmation on the *New York Times* editorial page. Dodd and the Senate leadership tried to look the other way—they and the industry had worked all this out, with Geithner and Summers as cheerleaders. But senators started signing on, as the most liberal members, such as Sherrod Brown and Vermont's Bernie Sanders, were joined by none other than Richard Shelby, the ranking Republican on the Senate Banking Committee, and his party's leading voice in the chamber on banking issues; Nevada's John Ensign; and Oklahoma's Tom Coburn, arguably the Senate's most conservative member. The banking lobby called a red alert, charging the chamber and not leaving senators' offices until a deal was cut, and assurances of opposition obtained. The strategy was shock and awe, and then a push for a quick vote. A so-called snap vote on May 6, engineered by Dodd and other Senate leaders, took the amendment down 61 to 33.

Al Franken, a supporter of Brown-Kaufman, was outraged—and it wasn't an act. Having been humbled by his protracted election recount, and wanting to counter his *Saturday Night Live* past with a métier of quiet seriousness, Franken finally stepped up. He had, months before, taken an interest in the role of rating agencies such as Moody's and Standard & Poor's.

As had been widely reported, banks would shop around lousy securities looking for the best rating, paying the rating agency in return for a desired rating. Franken saw the issue, as many did, as a clear conflict of interest. "If a failing student paid their teacher to turn their grade from an F into an A, everyone would agree that what the teacher had done was unethical."

In early May, Franken put forth his proposal, dubbed the "Restore Integrity to Credit Ratings" amendment, and was, as well, greeted with bipartisan support. The amendment called for, among other things, every asset-backed bond issue to be rated by a government-created board, rather than having the bank choose the agency itself.

On May 13, Franken's proposal passed the Senate 64–35. Franken, demonstrably liberal, also drew Republicans, including Grassley, the ranking Republican on Senate Finance; South Carolina's Lindsey Graham; and Alaska's Lisa Murkowski. In all, he managed a whopping 11 Republican votes, making the amendment one of the season's most significant bipartisan votes—and only six months before what was due to be a heated midterm.

Of the four Democrats who voted against it, one was Chris Dodd.

Like Barney Frank, Dodd had played a complex role in the proceedings. Many were critical of the lame-duck senator for not being more aggressive in his reforms, alleging that his interests were inexorably linked with the lobby he so closely served. But Dodd remained steadfast, arguing that he simply wanted to produce the strongest possible bill that could feasibly withstand a vote. It wasn't worth sacrificing reform to make incremental changes in specific amendments.

But no one was in the crosshairs quite like Blanche Lincoln. Banks attacked her in back rooms and hushed lunches with senators as being in "way over her head." Her proposal to spin off derivatives would cause profound disruptions, and many speculated that she'd discard the proposal as soon as she won her primary. But her proposal became something of a third rail, electrified by the populist surge, such that no one could touch it. "This is looking like a democracy," Barney Frank said, even though he had doubts about the amendment. "Publicity has changed the debate."

"Gazelles do better in daylight, that's for sure," Gensler effused.

On May 18, Chris Dodd, who had been working to undercut the Lincoln amendment with an alternative of his own, was forced to remove his proposal under populist anger. It was only two days before the Senate vote, and miraculously the Lincoln amendment remained intact. Lobbyists and both Democratic and Republican members massed for a final fight against the proposal.

But they were fighting on too many fronts. Carl Levin of Michigan and Jeff Merkley of Oregon had discovered that Dodd had discreetly gutted the Volcker Rule, and the two set to work trying to counteract Dodd's efforts.

The Merkley-Levin Amendment articulated Volcker's idea fully— and wrote it as law. No regulatory backsliding, once everything settled down.

There were legislative complications. The Republicans, in early May, invoked the "unanimous consent" rule, which essentially bars the introduction of new amendments until a final vote on the bill. Consequently, the usual process of discussing and vetting components of the amendment would have to wait until the very end of the process.

But now the end was coming fast. Sensing that their amendment would never see the light of day, Merkley and Levin, moving independently of leadership, used an esoteric parliamentary move and attached their amendment to one belonging to Republican senator Sam Brownback. His amendment, already scheduled for a vote, would exempt auto dealers from Elizabeth Warren's Consumer Financial Protection Bureau. It wasn't a pretty solution, but Merkley and Levin were determined to get the Volcker Rule, which did not exist in the House bill, into the Senate version.

Merkley-Levin appeared to be safe on May 20, the day of the Senate vote on the financial regulation package. However, the day before, Republicans, in concert with the Democratic leadership, withdrew the Brownback amendment—killing Merkley-Levin—in exchange for the inclusion of the Brownback proposal during the negotiations for the final reconciled House/Senate bill. The Volcker Rule, with teeth, was dead.

Dodd and Reid then carried it home. The Senate approved its financial-reform bill on May 20, 59 to 39.

The Senate's bill was now placed side by side with the House's bill in one of the most publicized conference committee sit-downs in years. With the Volcker Rule safely reduced, the battle became singularly about the Lincoln Amendment and its ban on traditional derivatives practices.

That amendment was sitting atop a house of cards. For one, Senator Lincoln was embroiled in a heated midterm primary, and many surmised that her ploy was a populist trick to lure progressive voters.

Meanwhile, Republicans across the spectrum had begun denouncing the amendment, specifically section 716, the component that would spin off derivatives trading, and were threatening not to vote for the conference bill if it included such language. Barney Frank, perhaps the most influential person in the conference process, even stated publicly that Lincoln's proposal "went too far."

On June 9 Lincoln had her primary and, after defeating her opponent, systematically began to deconstruct her own amendment. A series of exemptions scaled back her proposal.

Then like an angry zombie, the Volcker Rule wouldn't die. Merkley and Levin were able to persuade the House leadership, under the auspices of Barney Frank, to grant them the same favor as Brownback with his auto dealers' exemption. Their amendment was entered into the deliberative mix-and-match between House and Senate.

But on balance, what was left of the great spasm of springtime amendments, many of which had garnered bipartisan support, was very little.

Franken's rating agency amendment was the last to go, with Frank quietly quashing the proposal in lieu of an SEC-overseen "study group."

The "process" managed by Frank in the House and Dodd in the Senate had prevailed. Now they would largely decide what bill carried their names.

———————

Paul Volcker flew down to Washington a few times during this congressional land war to talk to anyone who'd listen, to do what he could. But mostly he watched it from afar, feeling older than he'd felt in quite a while.

At Kykuit, heading down to the estate's first-floor Playhouse, and the spectacular dinner that awaited him, he had said to his stairway helper, "That Merkley-Levin, that's my amendment. It was a pretty good idea at the start, I thought. We'll see how much of it can be saved."

He'd been watching the slaughter, one amendment after another, each of them, in different ways, trying to restore features, or, at the very least, concepts once housed in Glass-Steagall.

Volcker marveled at how many of those amendments had drawn Republicans and Democrats together. He'd never been much of a partisan, of course—he'd served under presidents of both parties, had friends on both teams. Still, this seemed to warm him, and to harken back, he said, "to a time, I can remember, when we had quite a bit of that sort of thing, where Democrats and Republicans figured things out together, especially on the really important stuff that affects everyone, more or less, equally."

Those last few words had a flaw in them, a fracture that he'd seen grow across nearly thirty years, where some of the very clever men who followed him into public service, and whom he'd see in the restaurants near his office in Manhattan, figured out how to make the "really important stuff" not actually "affect everyone, more or less, equally."

Volcker is no fool—he practically saw this idea get developed, with a winning political strategy attached: that if you can reward a certain group of people in society you'll be developing a very powerful constituency, small in numbers but awesome in might, and they'll do just about anything to make sure you or someone like you is always in power.

Almost all the most meaningful reforms were designed to run counter to this idea of a few people being rewarded at the expense of many. One other thing "all the latest reforms" shared was they were all battered, or already buried, because none of them, including his amendment, "have really been supported by the president—not really."

This left Volcker confused and suppressing a rise of bitterness in his throat. He'd been there for the president, doing whatever Obama wanted, and stepping up a few months ago, duly resurrected, as Obama called this modest attempt to restore sanity, and some safeguards and barriers that had been proven to actually work, "the Volcker Rule."

"They say they're for it, but their hearts are not in it." And this gap between word and deed, between stated intentions and so little action, made Volcker think of a phrase that he knew Summers sometimes used—a couple of people had told him—"that the important thing is just to be caught trying."

He'd always kept Obama and Summers separate—he liked Obama, didn't think much of Summers—but this phrase troubled him, because it seemed to explain some things that he couldn't find other explanations for.

He finally made it down the last step of two flights, and stopped to catch his breath. "I'm not dead yet. I talked to Barney; he's with me."

As for the president, it was back to the same thing Volcker had learned, with some reluctance, over the past two years. If Obama didn't get involved and "show some enthusiasm," Volcker said, the big changes that he, or anyone else, had suggested "just won't happen. It's that simple."

Then Paul Volcker straightened up to his full height—a few inches off his relentlessly cited six foot eight, but just a few. The Playroom, its golden light beckoning from just a few feet ahead, was bustling as the diners, here to celebrate good works, found their tables and settled in.

Tonight, on this mountaintop, he was quite appropriately the master of ceremonies. He wanted to make a good show of it.

On June 17, Gary Gensler was carrying his jammed briefcase through Washington, D.C.'s Union Station, the century-old Beaux Arts landmark that had become a staple of his lengthy commute.

Financial reform was ticking down to zero hour, and already Gensler was preparing to write the new rules for what would be the "teeth" of derivatives reform.

The CFTC chair had become one of the busiest men in Washington, a man on a mission. While making his way through the train terminal, he heard a familiar voice.

"Gary? . . . Gary!"

Gensler paused briefly before placing the man walking toward him—Jon Voigtman, a former Goldman executive—and greeted him warmly.

Encounters like these had multiplied steadily as Gensler's profile had reached mythic status on the Street. Voigtman reverentially treated Gensler as such. Now at the Royal Bank of Canada, the younger Voigtman had come to town for a meeting on mortgage financing at the Treasury.

After a moment of small talk, Gensler began to place Voigtman. He'd been at Freddie Mac in the late '80s, then ran Lehman's mortgage finance operation from the late '90s until 2004, when he moved to Goldman. He was co-head of mortgage financing, the guys who pulled together buyers for all those mortgage-backed securities and helped create the era's famous CDOs and CDSs. Gary, who suddenly realized he was undersecretary of Treasury in 2000 when he'd first met Voigtman, soon launched into an insider's dialogue with a man who'd managed to be at every catastrophe-in-the-making for two decades.

"Let me ask you a question. From when you met me in 2000 to what you saw happen in '05, '06, '07, was it a fundamental change or did it just sort of get . . . bigger?"

Voigtman proffered that the era was marked by people who started entering the structured products in droves but didn't understand the business "coming into the game and [that] it wasn't about mortgages anymore."

Then, under Gensler's prodding, Voigtman got more specific: "2006, that was the year that sent a shudder through the business. Ten percent of the loans that we bought never made their first payments. That was in August '06. You knew by August '06."

"They wouldn't make the *first* payment."

"So," Voigtman continued, "the underwriter who sat down with that borrower forty-five days before got it wrong."

What's more, loans even worse than that 10 percent, the ones Goldman sent back to the underwriter, were "being financed at par," meaning they were being sold to someone else at full value.

Gensler waited before posing the question that Blankfein had repeatedly dodged.

"But by August of '06, when you knew, did you change the underwriting practices?"

Voigtman paused. Gensler was now a leader of the other team, a regulator. But then again, Voigtman was no longer at Goldman. He had left the firm in December of 2006 for his current employer, Royal Bank of Canada. Neither man had a complicating allegiance.

Voigtman shook his head: No, Goldman hadn't changed their underwriting. They took advantage of the unfolding disaster by adding more troops. "It became more competitive. We had more desks on the Street."

Then Voigtman ran through a dissertation on what Goldman knew and when they knew it. Specifically, he described how they knew there was trouble with CDOs long before August 2006.

In fact, it was in 2004 when they first saw underwriting standards start to decline and demand for the CDOs skyrocket. Voigtman explained that with overwhelming demand for the "long side," or upside, someone had to be "the short," taking the downside to "ensure liquidity." Goldman did that as fast as was humanly possible, and then some.

To keep the ball rolling, Goldman began improvising at breakneck speed.

They began fine-tuning the short-play, by helping create the "single-name CDS, which meant they could take out a short position, using the faux insurance of a CDS, on a single item in a bundle of mortgage-backed securities. As bundles were being sold at dizzying speed, Goldman could take out cheap insurance, paying out 100 to 1, on a single weak link inside the bundle. As things heated up in 2005, as demand for CDOs grew with the arrival of large players such as Fannie and Freddie and Pimco, "the deals would be oversubscribed" four times over. Rather than sending the money back to the unrequited buyer, "the smart guys at Goldman said, 'Hey, we can just synthetically fill their order.'" This freed Goldman from the terrestrial obligations of actually needing someone, somewhere, to underwrite an actual mortgage—a process that, even when sped up, couldn't keep up with demand. The bank started to sell, in essence, umpteen CDOs based on a single mortgage.

Even now, as he talked about the moment in Union Station five years later, you could see Voigtman's trader's blood begin to quicken. "The thing I loved about it is you had two views. If you didn't like an underwriting, the only thing you could do before was avoid buying it. But now you could actually have a view and take the short side if someone will take the long side."

Of course, in the frenzy starting in 2004, everyone except Goldman was preferring the long side. Whether or not their justification was "ensuring liquidity," making the market by going short, the fact was that by early 2005, Goldman was more short than long on mortgage securities. That's generally called a "directional bet": the firm's profits were rooted in the market falling as opposed to rising. Goldman's position has been that they were unwitting victims, like so many others. In fact, their desire to short the CDO market was so strong already by 2004 that they'd created the market by building up a huge position on short side of securities most everyone felt were likely to continue their AAA-stamped success. And then they went synthetic. Among those poor everyones would be Goldman clients, of course. At this point, every one of those clients had reason to ask what Goldman knew and when they knew it. Not from December 2007 forward, when Goldman's number two, David Viniar, said the firm first realized mortgage securities were going south, or even from August 2006 onward, when, as Voigtman had just revealed, they were seeing that stunning 10-percent rate of no mortgage payments at all.

But from 2004 onward. Because what Voigtman had just described to Gensler went far beyond the prudent hedging of downside risk. It was Goldman building customized weapons to take advantage of a unique, once-in-a-lifetime market-driven disaster that no one could have foreseen. No one except someone who had helped construct it, by providing the "liquidity" of a burgeoning menu of short-side products, to sate all the "upside" thirst in the world. Should Goldman have told clients, or the general public, its directional bet on CDOs? As a market maker, of course not. They're just making a market for people to follow their trading desires: playing a neutral role. If they have a strong feeling about where that market is headed, they keep that to themselves.

Voigtman had a train to catch, and so did Gensler. Before they parted, Gensler couldn't help but ask Jon if he thought any of the reforms Gensler had been fighting to enact would make any difference. "I think the whole dialogue is very, very healthy," Voigtman said, dodging the question.

Gensler was surprised and deflated. "What about derivatives?"

Voigtman managed to let Gensler down easy: "I honestly don't know what the impact is going to be."

———

Obama was looking relaxed, speaking to the crowded room of dignitaries on the afternoon of July 21. The topic was the economy, and his language was familiar. "For two years we have faced the worst recession since the Great Depression," he started, "a crisis borne of a failure of responsibility from the corridors of Wall Street to the halls of power in Washington."

He was finally signing into law the Dodd-Frank Wall Street Reform and Consumer Protection Act. In an economic briefing that very morning—with unemployment at 9.5 percent—he dismissed proposals to give tax breaks for construction projects as well as a program to create temporary federal jobs at a time when 700,000 census workers were leaving ther jobs. Krueger's small business tax credit, finally proposed in January at $33 billion, was shrunk and folded into a smaller $18 billion hiring stimulus. After nearly a year of internal White House deliberations, with huge Democratic majorities in Congress, that would be the sum of the administration's effort on the jobs crisis. After the briefing he motored over to the Ronald Reagan Convention Center to sign what he called the most comprehensive reforms since Franklin Roosevelt faced down the banks in the 1930s. Financial reform—an issue that had drawn more embedded emotion, following Wall Street's meltdown, than most average citizens ever felt about their health insurance—was being called an empty vessel. Even those in the White House, which had labored for months to demonstrate the boldness of reform, were using more modest language following the act's passage.

"For years," Obama continued, "our financial sector was governed by antiquated and poorly enforced rules that allowed some to game the system and take risks that endangered the entire economy."

To Obama's left were Chris Dodd and Barney Frank, the two men who had guided the bill through to the end. They had maneuvered the legislative process deftly, managing to get the bill passed only months after the debacle of health care reform. Still, critics complained that the most substantial reforms—Merkley-Levin, Brown-Kaufman, Franken, and Blanche Lincoln—had all been systematically gutted during the shadier conference sessions.

Those amendments, complex and esoteric to the passive onlooker, were all variations on the same melody: how to prevent the systemic risk of "too big to fail."

Lincoln's amendment had gone after derivatives, the steroids that fueled exponential growth in banks. Merkley-Levin's "Volcker Rule" spinoff had attempted to ban proprietary trading. Brown-Kaufman had tried to do away with opacity altogether, proposing simply to limit the size that bank holding companies could have.

One by one, in spite of bipartisan support, they had all failed.

The original language of the Lincoln amendment—specifically section 716—articulated that banks would need to spin off their derivatives trading desks, their most profitable business. Lincoln also stipulated that the derivatives dealers had to act as "fiduciaries," removing the conflict of interest similar to that of propriety trading.

An early exemption offered by Lincoln for small community banks was used as a wedge for other exemptions—which now flowed freely, with Lincoln's heated primary victory now behind her. At day's end, banks could move their derivatives operations into "subsidiary units," rather than spin them off. Wide swaths of derivatives—foreign-exchange swaps, interest-rate swaps, cleared CDSs, currency swaps—would operate largely as they had been, meaning that "about 90 percent of the derivatives market was exempted" from meaningful regulation, said derivatives expert Michael Greenberger, once Brooksley Born's deputy. Nonetheless, owing largely to Gensler's effort, most of the systemically dangerous over-the-counter derivatives, especially dealing with debt, would now have to be traded on exchanges, or so-called swap execution facilities, and passed through clearinghouses to make sure one party backstops the trade. This was accomplished by seeming like "middle ground" compared to Lincoln's spinoff derivatives amendment, and by Gensler's literally running in a crouch behind the chairs of congressmen during the conference committee, explaining complex issues in a way that counteracted the expert persuasions of lobbyists. It was a role that drew criticism, but some gazelles were saved.

Meanwhile, the "Volcker Rule," or what was left of it, limped toward the finish line. Having never been given a vote in its first incarnation, the progressive duo of senators had managed to reintroduce language during the conference committee—language that Levin contended was stronger than the "Volcker Rule" originally proposed by the administration.

However, under pressure from Scott Brown, in exchange for his coveted Republican vote, the conference blunted the final push by Merkley and Levin. The rule was changed to allow banks to continue proprietary trading with defined limitations. The agreement ultimately struck would allow a bank to invest up to 3 percent of its tangible equity in hedge and private-equity funds, a stark contrast to the clear-cut separation Volcker had envisioned.

And 3 percent, in the world of behemoth bank holding companies, was no small figure.

Furthermore, several banks, including Goldman and Citi, estimated elements of the rule wouldn't affect them until 2022, a whopping ten years.

Journalist Matt Taibbi and economist Simon Johnson were outspoken in their criticisms. Paul Krugman blogged about the ineptitude of the bill. How could anyone expect such a clunky piece of legislation to properly regulate an industry solely dedicated to finding loopholes? Dodd and New York senator Charles Schumer were lambasted for their backroom deals helping to shield financial interests.

Even Barney Frank, crusading icon of the left, drew criticism. It was, after all, Frank who, with White House support, had gutted both the Franken and Lincoln amendments in conference and pushed against many of the more progressive structural reforms.

Still, in spite of its many flaws, Obama had a lot of items to tout in the law. It expanded the purview of federal regulators significantly, subjecting previously unexamined elements of the financial markets to oversight. It created a panel of federal regulators charged with detecting and implementing policies to prevent a "too big to fail," or "too systemic to fail," problem before it occurred—albeit a difficult mission. Perhaps most notable was Elizabeth Warren's Consumer Financial Protection Bureau, which survived the sausage making weakened but intact.

Obama's rhetoric, though, rested mainly on the intangible aspects of the bill. Wall Street should no longer be coddled by government. Dodd-Frank should be interpreted as a harsh rebuke on the practices that had led to the crisis.

Most of those practices, though, remained intact, and the prevailing sense was one of uncertainty. With an already expected backlash in the coming midterms, there were whispers among conservatives over how they would be able to cut down the bill after November. Hundreds of components of the bill were dependent on the complicated rule-writing process—especially the derivatives reform—that could take years to complete. With Republicans back in power, they would be able to slow and potentially derail many aspects of that reform.

Still, much like health care, it was a start. In one instance, government took on the burden of having everyone insured. Now it took on a mandate to attempt, at the very least, the regulation of the nation's central and signature industry. A titanic crisis, however, had come and gone, and neither Washington nor Wall Street had fundamentally changed. At least not yet.

After concluding his remarks, Obama—noticeably gaunt and appearing short of sleep—sat down and signed the bill as those assembled broke into applause.

Obama made his way to the elder statesman Paul Volcker. The two men hugged as, standing immediately behind Volcker, a clapping Elizabeth Warren cheered them on. Standing nearby was a crowd of people—congressmen, dignitaries, consumer advocates—who were waiting to meet her. They were huge fans.

And after a minute Barack Obama slipped out to get back to the White House.

THE NOISE

I N A MEMO DATED AUGUST 5, PETE ROUSE OUTLINED HIS FINAL recommendations for revamping the White House's administrative structure. The memo, like its six predecessors, portended a clean sweep as soon as possible.

That same evening, Christina Romer, exhausted, announced her departure as chair of the Council of Economic Advisers. She was not the first major exit. Just a week before, Peter Orszag had left his post at OMB. Reports had surfaced that Larry Summers would be leaving by year's end. Obama's B-Team was on its way out.

Replacements for Romer and Orszag were easy. Austan Goolsbee, Obama's old friend and campaign ally, would replace Romer as chair at CEA. Meanwhile, Jack Lew, the man who many felt deserved the OMB post all along, replaced Orszag, having spent a year in purgatory at the State Department.

As members of the old team left and replacements started to fill their chairs, Obama—after six months of intensive managerial review with his trusted senior aide Rouse—started to sense the yield of that effort: a clean slate. An innermost circle around a president sees the man, up close, in ways that no one else can. But, even to this group, he is the president—someone not generally afforded the casual luxuries of doubt or confusion or common human frailty.

During so many days of crisis in his first two years, Obama often felt that performance pressure—having to play the part of president, in charge and confident, each day, in front of his seasoned, combative, prideful team, many of whom had, all together, recently served another president. As he confided to one of his closest advisers, after a private display of uncertainty, "I can't let people see that, I don't want the staff to see that."

And: "But I get up every morning. It's a heavy burden."

By August, there was increasingly little to do on the policy front.

Health care and financial reform, Obama's early legacy, were complete. The midterms, just ahead.

The sound and fury over health care had reached fever pitch, and then passed, as polling began to show that the legislation was unpopular, but only marginally so. The coming midterms were going to hurt, no doubt, but there was an ease in the White House. What was done was done.

The health care debate seemed to co-opt everyone. The process had been so protracted and ugly and partisan that there was almost no one who could claim credibly not to have had a dog in the fight.

Up at Dartmouth, Jim Weinstein had watched the debate rage, while trying to summon impartiality. After all, it had been data from the Atlas Project that had fueled Obama early on in the debate. Going back years, Peter Orszag had been captivated by the data-driven allure of Atlas's findings: Reduce costs now, and you will be able to expand coverage with the savings from an improved health care system. Doing it in reverse involved a diametric opposition impossible to reconcile.

During the summer of 2009, when Atul Gawande published his influential *New Yorker* piece, it seemed that Dartmouth, with Weinstein at the helm, could be the research engine that drove pragmatic reform. And so Weinstein and Wennberg, two outspoken proponents of the need for reform, both ethically and economically, had championed the cause through its most trying hours.

The centrality of the Dartmouth data to the intent, at least, of health care reform is hard to overstate. Weinstein was considered for the surgeon general's job during the Obama transition. The fact that he didn't take it made sense to everyone. As Nancy-Ann DeParle later said, "You're more important to have up at Dartmouth."

In the spring of 2010, Weinstein was called to the White House to help draft the final bill. In it was a section legally mandating that various comparative effectiveness and evidence-based analyses—albeit shrunk, at that point, to mostly pilot programs—rely on Dartmouth's data. It was blocked at the final moment by Massachusetts senator John Kerry, under pressure from Harvard's noted medical centers, so aggrieved were they at how Dartmouth's effectiveness data had revealed flaws, inefficiencies, and unnecessary treatments even at the world's most noted hospitals. Though their data and methodology would prevail, Kerry managed to get the name "Dartmouth" out of the final bill.

Weinstein, who had recently matched his leadership of Dartmouth's Atlas with the lead job at Dartmouth-Hitchcock Medical Center, was excited when the bill became law, as was his predecessor, Wennberg, now nearly eighty.

But in the ensuing months, as he dug into the new law, its features and consequences, he had dropped to ground level.

In early August he was sitting in a diner near Hanover reflecting with painstaking specificity about how bringing the first steps of analytical, outcomes-based rigor to America's bloated fee-for-service medical system was so important "that it should have been the first priority, even above the expansion of coverage."

To spend a "once-in-a-generation" effort on extending coverage to the uninsured—without any real teeth in using evidence about what was effective in reducing unnecessary procedures, and driving down costs— was a "stunning error."

"It's made things worse," he said solemnly.

And then he got frustrated. "I can't believe how wrong they got it. This was our one chance, and we completely blew it."

———

In the weeks following the passage of financial reform, as editorials and online petitions pressed for Elizabeth Warren to be named head of the consumer bureau she'd conceived, the Harvard professor was booked for a round of meetings with the important players of Washington.

First, it was lunch with representatives from the financial services industry, Scott Talbott and Steve Bartlett, a meal for which she needed to write a check for $13, so as not to violate ethics standards.

Next stop, the White House, where she met with Pete Rouse, David Axelrod, and Valerie Jarrett.

Axelrod was a huge fan and was pushing for Warren to be nominated, even if it meant a fight with Congress. Jarrett, also a Warren supporter, was keeping her counsel. Rouse was gaming the issues in Congress, the mechanics of which he knew all too well. A long confirmation battle could keep Warren in limbo for a year, when she wouldn't be able to help shape the agency. He was working on the legislative math.

Then she moved to offices where there were doubts, starting with Christy Romer's, just a few days before Romer cleaned her office to return to Berkeley. Warren could tell that Romer had put real thought into her questions. The two of them sat alone in Romer's office.

"You are coming into something new, that hasn't been regulated," Romer started. "You could come in hard, which has some real benefits. But it has some disadvantages. You could break a lot of things and cause some damage. Or you could come in slow and soft. How are you going to handle that?"

Warren was caught off guard by Romer's intensity, and her thoughtfulness.

When Warren explained her approach—like everything about the CFPB, she could answer the question in intricate detail—Romer immediately pushed back with a counterquestion. Question after question, the two engaged in an intellectual thrust-and-parry, until finally, after Warren forcefully reiterated her desire to be a potent regulator, Romer finally broke her stride.

"Why is it always the women?" Romer said. "Why are we the only ones with balls around here?"

———

That night Warren got a call from Valerie Jarrett. "Wow, you really turned Christy Romer around."

Warren demurred, secretly surprised that Romer had initially opposed her.

"Christy was totally with Larry and Tim," Jarrett continued. "They've been saying we can't bring you in. After you met with her, she walked into a meeting with the president and said, 'Mr. President, I've been pretty strongly opposed, and I was wrong.'"

Summers, shocked by her reversal, was fuming.

This didn't surprise Warren. Her meeting with Summers had been just the opposite. He arrived late, looking disheveled. After asking a couple of simple questions, he told her in a huff that he needed to take a call, and abruptly departed.

The next day, August 13, Warren finally got her meeting with the president. It was her first time in the Oval Office, and she told herself to try to focus and remember every detail.

But she noticed little about the iconic room, as Obama ushered her in and kissed her on the cheek. The president opened the meeting with his familiar line:

"This is not a job interview."

Warren took a seat on the couch as Jarrett sat quietly across the room, taking notes.

"So, Elizabeth, do you think the bill is good?"

"Yes, Mr. President, it has the right tools."

Obama thought for a moment—and then got authentic.

"It just *kills* me that the car lenders are not included," Obama opened up, referencing the Brownback amendment, which exempted dealers from regulation by the protection bureau using an arcane parliamentary trick.

The president then launched into a more personal story. "Michelle and I, when we were younger, decided we were going to lease a car. I went out and shopped around and got a car. When I returned the car four years later, like I was supposed to, it was the first time I realized how expensive that car was," he confided, trying to show Elizabeth his empathy for her cause. "How could anyone understand that? I *really* tried!"

Warren flashed back to her meeting in Cedar Rapids several years before. Obama had used the same personal touch to relate to her. Had it really been three years?

The meeting went on for half an hour, then forty-five minutes. The president offered a long explanation of the complex logistics whereby Warren would stand up the agency and become a special adviser to him. That way she wouldn't spend months, or maybe longer, on ice, as a nominee going through confirmation. He said this would be a new period in his presidency. And then he stopped, as if something had just dawned on him. He said simply, "I want you to help me."

As the president was expressing need, and maybe yearning, to Elizabeth Warren, the carpeted hallways outside the Oval Office had become a battleground.

After months of growing recriminations, Axelrod and Emanuel—friends for thirty years—had descended to a state of open warfare.

The tensions had been building, slowly but steadily, since the first few months of the Obama presidency, as Emanuel, Geithner, Summers, and Orszag established their domain over policy, and Axelrod's hopes for a "movement presidency" steadily evaporated. Now, as the White House's policy operations began to dim their lights, and Obama was facing a slaughter in the midterms, an opening era of promise—maybe promise unfulfilled—was coming to a close.

Today's specific issue of conflict was a strict collision of principle and pragmatism: the heated dispute over a petition by a New York City Islamic organization to place a mosque beside the World Trade Center memorial.

The debate had been boiling in New York for weeks. Obama felt strongly about the issue. Rahm was unyielding: Mr. President, don't get involved!

Axelrod disagreed and, more importantly, so did the president. Obama felt it was an opportunity to state sacred principles.

But, as was often the case in the first two years, Emanuel barred the door. He was saving the president from himself.

It was clear that the dynamic inside the White House had become intolerable. Obama tried to ease the tension—these were two of his top advisers, his friends.

In an interview a few months later, Axelrod said darkly that the president would never again need a chief of staff as powerful as Rahm.

"We clashed a lot because he viewed me as kind of the manifestation of aspects of Obama that frustrated him," of the president's being "excessively idealistic and not pragmatic," Axelrod reflected in another interview. "He's not going to confront the president about that . . . so he and I would have surrogate battles over those things and there's no doubt that there were tensions in many instances."

The frustrations flowed in both directions. The mosque issue brought matters nearly to blows, as Axelrod yelled at Emanuel: "You may think you can keep him from speaking to this, but you're not going to!"

In the estimation of Axelrod and many others who had risen with Obama through the campaign, this is precisely where they felt Emanuel and other powerful advisers had triumphed: in keeping Obama from doing what he really wanted to do.

But not in this case. A few hours after Elizabeth Warren's meeting, Obama stepped to the podium in the East Room after emerging from a dinner celebrating the start of Ramadan.

"As a citizen, and as president, I believe that Muslims have the same right to practice their religion as anyone else in this country," he said.

"I understand the emotions that this issue engenders. Ground zero is, indeed, hallowed ground." But, he continued, "This is America, and our commitment to religious freedom must be unshakable. The principle that people of all faiths are welcome in this country, and will not be treated differently by their government, is essential to who we are."

He was bitterly attacked from across the political spectrum, but within a few days the onslaught was already starting to fade, leaving—to Obama's satisfaction—a statement of principle.

———

Five days later, Robert Wolf, now UBS's CEO, stepped onto a dock on Martha's Vineyard. He was on the island for a reason: the president wanted him there. Obama was on his summer vacation, and Wolf was scheduled for two rounds of golf. He and his sons, both athletes like their dad, also played basketball with Obama in the gymnasium of a local high school.

The two men had stayed close. Obama talked to Wolf on and off and had Wolf, as a member of the PERAB, often give the perspective of Wall Street in briefings with the group.

Part of the key to their relationship, Wolf felt, was that he treated the president just like "one of the guys—which is what he doesn't otherwise get to be." They talked trash, and family and sports.

But Wolf, seeing his friend in distress, wanted to expand the conversation. The president was being roundly criticized for being antibusiness, a charge that Wolf believed to be false, a trumped-up attack to get particular results. Wall Street wanted even more from Obama, and this was the way to get it. Start with an audacious stance, and see if Obama bent toward you, searching for a middle ground. All this made Wolf protective. He wanted to ask Obama if he could help, if he could "be the son-of-a-bitch that a guy like Obama needs." Wolf wanted to sit across the table from the guys on Wall Street and the wider realm of corporate America and say, as he put it, "Don't fuck with my man. If you want to cut a deal, let's talk—about some ways we might help you, but, more importantly, let's talk about what you're going to do for us. Otherwise get outta my face."

Then, from the dock, he saw the nose of a ship rounding a point on the Vineyard.

It was *Le Rêve*. His buddy, Sal Naro, had managed to hold on to it, all 110 feet.

Sal had landed upright. He now ran a company that was sort of like a Moody's for derivatives. It had been an amazing year for Wall Street. Best ever.

Robert Wolf considered his schedule. Maybe tomorrow, when they played golf, he'd have that talk with Obama, man to man.

But now Sal Naro was waiting. Robert Wolf walked purposefully to the end of the dock and stepped aboard *The Dream*.

On Tuesday, September 7, Mayor Richard Daley stunned Chicago with the announcement that he would not be running for reelection when his term expired in early 2011.

"Simply put, it's time," he said at an afternoon news conference at City Hall. "Time for me. And time for Chicago to move on."

For most of the past fifty-six years, the Daleys had run Chicago, starting with Mayor Richard J. Daley, one of America's signature political bosses, who led Chicago from 1955 to 1976 and died in office, soon to be followed by the equally long tenure of his son. Richard M. Daley, elected in 1989, was slated to become the city's longest-serving mayor the day after Christmas.

A few hours after the announcement, Rahm Emanuel released a statement:

"While Mayor Daley surprised me today with his decision to not run for reelection, I have never been surprised by his leadership, dedication, and tireless work on behalf of the city and the people of Chicago."

In an appearance on Charlie Rose's show in April, Emanuel said that being mayor of Chicago had "always been an aspiration of mine, even when I was in the House of Representatives."

Emanuel had long planned to remain the White House chief of staff until June 2011. The idea was that he would take Obama through the midterms, handle the aftermath of whatever occurred, and remain with the president until Obama had firmly passed his second anniversary in office and was five months along and properly launched into the final two years of his first term. Everything rested on that target date. Emanuel's house in Chicago was rented until June 2011. By then his kids would have finished their school year in Washington.

The president was aware of Rahm's plans, as were other members of the senior staff.

But with Rouse having completed his long review, and having just finished meetings with Obama on his final August memo, the president was working through the logistics of a clean sweep.

Daley's announcement, just a day after Labor Day, "was like manna from heaven" and an "elegant thing for everybody involved," said Axelrod, especially considering the coming decimation (already expected by the White House) of a Democratic majority in the House that Rahm helped build in 2006. "The tension of that for him would have been unbearable, and it would have had very negative manifestations for the whole operation."

Another adviser was blunter: "It was total luck. He would have been fired."

Emanuel asserted later that the president wanted him to stay—"I know what the president felt"—but his swift announcement that he'd leave in a few weeks to run for mayor left Obama joyous.

The president then completed his housecleaning, starting with David Axelrod. Obama's senior adviser was, like Emanuel, planning to stay in Washington until the next summer, using roughly the same calculus as his old friend turned adversary.

Obama had other ideas. He felt Axelrod was burned out from his difficult tenure in Washington, which had grown contentious, especially in his battles with Emanuel over the past six months.

Obama said he wanted Axelrod to get out of the building and get out of Washington after the midterms, to be his "eyes and ears" out in the wider country. Most importantly, he wanted his old friend to rest and recharge his batteries until the following summer, when he'd need to be fresh and ready to start on the next campaign.

Obama needed a change. Axelrod's tenure in Washington was over.

It was the same for Robert Gibbs, who'd been at Obama's side on most days, around the clock, since he was hired on to the Senate staff in 2005.

Obama, drawing from his seven months of management review and discussions with Rouse, felt Gibbs's relationship with the press was too contentious, too much like a combative press spokesman in a heated campaign. After the midterms, Obama decided he wanted to try some new public strategies with new faces.

But, as with Axelrod, Gibbs wasn't just an employee, serving "at the pleasure" of his boss, the president. He was a friend who'd been at Obama's side since the very old days, when they were more like Don

Quixote and Sancho Panza than King Arthur and his trusty Galahad.

Just as with Axelrod, Obama thought about himself. But he also thought about what was best for his press secretary.

"He said that this would turn out to be a good move," said a senior adviser familiar with the housecleaning. Gibbs, who'd been in loyal service for eight years, could now be a political media consultant. "It'll be good for Robert to finally go out and make some money."

————————

During the first week of October, Alan Krueger was sitting with people who understood confidence: Jim Clifton, the CEO of Gallup, and Gallup's editor in chief, Frank Newport.

They were fans of Krueger's work on the behavior of workers and recent studies of how people defined well-being. They had all decided to meet for dinner at the Four Seasons in Georgetown.

But Krueger had an interest as well, in a poll Gallup had just released. It was just four weeks until the midterm election, and the poll dissected the defining issue of confidence. Specifically, whether people felt confidence in Barack Obama.

Newport said they didn't. The numbers were dismal. People liked the president, but only 32 percent felt real confidence in him as a leader.

"Confidence is a kind of catchall for a wide array of emotions and responses," Newport said. "It's what you do, it's how you do it, and it's also how people feel afterward."

Krueger asked a few questions, trying to press Newport and Clifton to dig deeper.

"A big issue we find with confidence," Clifton added, "is the question of whether people take ownership of what they say. Look, we all say all sorts of things for all sorts of reasons. But the key is whether, for better or for worse, you take ownership of your words. If you do—or, as a leader, if you make sure your people do—then you usually have a pretty high confidence reading, even if you make mistakes. It's kind of the straight-shooter thing. People like that."

After dinner Krueger made his way back from Georgetown toward the building where he'd been renting an apartment. After a lengthy run working at Treasury, he was finally ready to leave.

It was a warm evening in early October, a good night for walking, especially when life changes were afoot. In a few weeks he would return to Princeton, and he'd been trying to think about the last two years in Washington, and about the Barack Obama he first met in 2007.

He felt there was a clarity of thought and purpose to that earlier version that was increasingly difficult to find in the years he saw the president in his White House environs. He wasn't sure why there had been a change, if in fact there had been, and he was not blaming Obama. But somehow the president had lost ownership of his words and, eventually, his deeds.

After a few blocks of quiet strolling, he thought of all the experiments over the years which had resulted in academic disputes, including a few he'd had with other prominent professors on how questions were asked in surveys, or whether the selection of those being questioned skewed results toward certain responses.

In a particular dispute years back, Krueger eventually found something wrong in the methodology, that the data were being corrupted by the respondents' subtle urge to show the questioner that they were motivated and resourceful, when they actually were often dispirited and without energy.

"What we found was that in the early data, we were relying on seemingly strong responses from those surveyed that were meaningless. We were being misled by thorough but meaningless data. The statisticians call it 'noise.' We were living off the noise."

And that brought him back to present tense, and his past two years in Washington. As he walked, he tried to count the number of times that days or weeks rose up and down, relief to despair, on vast and wildly imperfect data. GDP or unemployment rates—imperfect measurements to start with—are often quietly changed several months after their news cycle-driving "release" has already had a profound effect on politics, public statements, quickly fashioned policies, and, by association, public confidence.

Then, he smiled, a researcher to the last.

"I think that happens to a lot of good people, in these times, when they come to this town. Our president may just be the most recent example. They think they're seeing things clearly. But they're living off the noise."

———

Larry Summers's exit from the White House, scheduled for shortly after the midterms—though it ended up not taking place until early 2011—

provided a certain catharsis. The departure brought finality to the first phase of the Obama presidency.

The degree to which Summers's exit was organic is debatable. The restructuring plan concocted by Rouse starting at the beginning of the year suggested that Summers would need either to leave or accept a modified position, with his far-reaching post at NEC becoming administratively untenable. Summers contended that the exit was beyond amicable and that, in fact, the president pleaded with him to continue in his capacity.

What is not debated is the esteem that Obama continued to hold for Summers. When the announcement of Summers's departure was made public, Obama issued a lengthy statement in admiration of his service:

"I will always be grateful that at a time of great peril for our country, a man of Larry's brilliance, experience and judgment was willing to answer the call and lead our economic team. Over the past two years, he has helped guide us from the depths of the worst recession since the 1930s to renewed growth. And while we have much work ahead to repair the damage done by the recession, we are on a better path thanks in no small measure to Larry's wise counsel. We will miss him here at the White House, but I look forward to soliciting his continued advice and his counsel on an informal basis, and appreciate that he has agreed to serve as a member of the President's Economic Advisory Board."

That public encomium was reflected privately, where Obama showed a begrudging fondness for Summers. Valerie Jarrett, when talking about the conflicts within the economic team, was quick to note, "The president considers Larry to be a friend." Shortly before the midterms, Obama had inadvertently channeled George Bush praising FEMA director Michael Brown following the Katrina disaster, when, in an appearance on *The Daily Show*, he told Jon Stewart that Summers had done "a heckuva job." When the audience scoffed aloud at the connection, Obama quickly, but unconvincingly, recovered, with a forceful "Pun intended!"

Obama's private admiration and public defense of the controversial Summers was made all the more poignant by the not-so-subtle slight Summers had shared with Orszag and others. Every time he riffed about being "home alone" with no one in charge, and declared that "Clinton would never have made these mistakes," he impugned the president's intellect and management skills. These, of course, were the very qualities Obama was publicly praising in Summers.

Later, in an interview, Summers was asked about his "home alone" riff, which was read back to him in full thus: "We're home alone. There's no adult in charge. Clinton would never have made these mistakes." In the interview, Summers at first shouted, "I never said it!" but then it was made clear to him that others had heard it and some—like Orszag—could even cite a specific instance, May 26, 2009, at the Bombay Club, when they'd discussed it. At that point Summers assumed ownership of the acerbic assessment and, after a few moments, offered this response about what he meant when he gave it: "What I'm happy to say is, the problems were immense, they came from a number of very different sources, they were all coming at once, and there were not very many of us, and people were pulled in many many different directions. And we couldn't make . . . That meant it wasn't possible to give—there were five issues at once, that were more important than any issue in a typical year of American economic management, and there certainly weren't five times as many of us. And that's what I must have been referring to."

In their final meeting, the two men had lunch. Obama handed Summers a new sterling-silver putter, saying it was to recognize him as not only a colleague, but a friend. Larry was grateful. Obama, gracious almost to a fault and offering more loyalty to those who'd served him than they often returned, had won over even the thorny Summers.

It wasn't until he left and got to the top of the stairs that Summers saw that the putter had been inscribed: *Thank you, Larry—POTUS*.

"Why doesn't business like me?" That question, pondered by the president privately, had come to a head by the fall of 2010. He was quick to point out that his administration had overseen the complete turnaround of the financial sector. Why, then, was the business community so frustrated with him?

Within the corridors of American business there was a different feeling. Obama was an academic—albeit very smart—who didn't understand, as the Calvin Coolidge quip so acutely summed up, that the "business of America is business."

Larry Fink had previously dismissed the Obama White House as being "all professors." But beyond the policies the Obama administration enacted, Fink felt fatigued at what was perceived to be Obama's Rooseveltian idealism. Any serious conversation about creating jobs needed to start not with federal programs or vouchers, but rather with a focus on how to get the economy growing again.

That point was driven home during a series of perspective-forming meetings through the late fall leading up to the midterms. Rahm Emanuel, before making his grand exit, orchestrated several private one-on-ones for the president and leading business magnates.

First up was Warren Buffett, whom Obama had consulted at various points during the campaign. Buffett was direct, telling Obama that there were gaps in the housing market. There was an imbalance, and it would take at least two years to restore equilibrium, no matter what plans the government proposed.

This leitmotif, the limitations of government, was difficult for Obama to reconcile. Having so eloquently defended liberalism, the humbling recession and the coming shift in American politics meant that an embrace of austerity, and more limited aspirations, would define the next two years.

In a series of meetings with Larry Fink through the fall, Obama wondered aloud what he could do to better align himself with business.

But that wasn't the only reason Fink had been invited to meet with the president. It was an interview of sorts. Summers, with his adoration of Wall Street, had told Krueger that "Fink is the smartest man in the world." Greg Fleming, who had known Fink for years as a close friend and business colleague, would differ with Summers. Fink was smart, but Fleming had learned, he said, that "it's wrong to judge people's intelligence by how much money they have—there's not always a correlation." Nonetheless, when Emanuel asked Summers who he thought would be best to replace him, Summers mentioned Fink. That's all Emanuel needed to hear. He told Obama that Fink was his first choice to head the NEC.

Which is why just a few days before he himself left for Chicago, Rahm Emanuel ushered Fink into the Oval Office for his first meeting with the president.

Through September and October, Fink met with Obama and talked to him on the phone several times. He fretted about whether to take the job. Emanuel suggested that he could be NEC chief for a year, get seasoned in the ways of Washington, and then possibly be in line for Geithner's job.

But as October neared its end, BlackRock entered into negotiations to sell a major portion of its Bank of America shares, and had just raised

$10 billion in equity. With those changes afoot, Fink told Obama it would be "immoral" for him to leave his post at BlackRock at this moment.

Fink's perception of the president had evolved dramatically since an interview he gave the previous November, when he ranted: "I'm frustrated with these academic economists. Goolsbee, Krugman, I haven't spent a moment with the president . . . Not that I've sought it . . . But they don't want to hear it. He's a college professor, he'd reach out to John Sexton [the NYU president] before he reached out to a CEO. We have 3 trillion in assets—they don't care what we think!" After his arrival at the Oval Office, though, he was impressed by the president's grasp of financial arcana, as when he rattled off obscure housing statistics or spoke with Fink about industry jargon such as the "filtering process," a housing term for the passage of houses through the marketplace. As for Obama's policies, Fink said, "The president is much more of a centrist . . . in some ways he might even be called right of what used to be called center."

Grasping policy options had never been difficult for Obama. It was about leadership—and how he could wrangle the mighty universe of American business. Fink and Buffett knew more than anyone about that. But Fink also knew that government and Wall Street were different beasts, and he could be just as critical of his own capital as he was of Washington.

"Wall Street's confidence is buying back your shares; that does not add a job. Wall Street's confidence is doing a merger; that destroys jobs."

———

On Tuesday, November 2, the American electorate showed a lack of confidence in Barack Obama and his Democratic Party. Voters came out in droves for Republicans. They picked up sixty-three seats in the House, the largest swing since 1948. The Republican Party took control of the House, having relinquished it to Nancy Pelosi and the Democrats for only four short years.

A half dozen Senate seats also fell to Republicans, a feat, considering that only a third of the members were up for election.

The counterpoint to Obama's reform period featured a wide swath of characters. Many of the Republicans were business-owning "American Dream" candidates, especially in the congressional races, with the cash to finance juggernaut campaigns. Less prevalent, but still influential, were the Tea Party candidacies, many of whom fell short in the Republican primaries but pushed the nominee further right in the election.

Perhaps most interesting was the strain of Libertarian and Constitutionalist candidates who percolated to prominence in senatorial and gubernatorial elections. Rand Paul of Kentucky and Marco Rubio of Florida, both Senate victors, appeared to be the ones most suited to rise quickly. Young and charismatic, they harnessed support, deep-seated in the conservative psyche, for dramatically limited government. The 2006 midterms had been a referendum on Bush. Republicans were hoping these midterms were a referendum on liberalism.

Of course, this view was myopic. If the election had proven anything, it was that American politics were still a realm of striking volatility. Obama had fallen from historic highs to crushing defeat in just two short years. But it was also a reminder that, from now on, anything could happen.

Speaking at a press conference the day after the election, Obama expressed the unfamiliar emotions of a president coping with defeat.

"I do think that, you know, this is a growth process and—and an evolution. And the relationship that I have had with the American people is one that was built slowly, peaked at this incredible high, and then during the course of the last two years, as we've together gone through some very difficult times, has gotten rockier and tougher.

"And, you know, it's going to, I'm sure, have some more ups and downs during the course of me being in this office."

THE MAN THEY ELECTED

REFLECTING ON THE TWO YEARS LEADING UP TO THE MIDTERM shellacking, President Obama focused most acutely on the portentous early days.

"In the first six months, we were in uncharted territory. When we met every day with our economic team, and the markets are gyrating by hundreds of points every day, and nobody was sure how bad the banking crisis might get, I'm the first one to admit that at that stage, we were constantly working with probabilities. Every day having to make decisions . . . will the stress tests work? What would nationalization look like? Nobody has been through this since the 1930s."

That first six months, from the inauguration through the summer, was, of course, the seminal period in the Obama presidency, when the historic forces that converged on the newly elected president provided both challenges and opportunities. Decisions made, or not made, during that period on the largest issues—financial restructuring, the related issue of jobs, economic recovery, and health care—would, in essence, be the hand he'd have to play right up until the harsh electoral judgment.

"I think at the time we had a spectrum of options," he said about the enveloping crisis of a collapsed financial system. "Nobody wanted to do pure nationalization of the banks. Not only because philosophically that would have been a radical shift for America, but also because if you do it to one bank there would be capital flight, essentially. On the other hand you could end up like Japan. Zombie banks. That's a classic example of where I made a decision based on having heard from everybody and gotten as much factual information as we could have, and then basically having 70 percent probability of this working, and understanding that there was a 30 percent chance it wouldn't work, in which case we would have to go back in and try something new."

But even with those uncertainties, Obama did make a decision, one of the most important of his young presidency, in the seminal meeting on March 15, 2009. The decision was to continue with the stress tests while pulling together a plan to restructure many of the large, troubled banks starting with Citigroup. That directive, he discovered nearly a month later, had been ignored by the Treasury.

When asked about how agitated he was at his Treasury secretary when he found this out, Obama said, "I'll be honest, I don't recall the exact conversations."

Then, recalling the matter—something never publicly disclosed—he said, "Agitated may be too strong a word. But I will say this," he continued. "During this period, what we are increasingly recognizing is that there are no ideal options. And so, on something like a Citibank plan and doing a 'good bank, bad bank' structure, the technical constraints around how to execute are enormous. And typically, in these situations you might have one institution that you are dealing with. Here you had potentially fifty! And if you didn't get it right, it could have made everything else worse."

This is precisely the fear that the president's plan to close and then reopen Citibank was, in fact, meant to address. By handling Citibank effectively, Congress and the American people would see that "government could do this right," as the president asserted that afternoon nearly two years before, killing off fear that if another financial institution failed, it would spark a financial crisis similar to what happened after Lehman. Then the White House could go back to Congress to restructure the banking system properly.

But the Citibank incident, and others like it, reflected a more pernicious and personal dilemma emerging from inside the administration: that the young president's authority was being systematically undermined or hedged by his seasoned advisers. On this issue, a matter perilously close to insubordination, the president was careful in his selection of each word: "What's true is that I was often pushing, hard, and the speed with which the bureaucracy could exercise my decision was slower than I wanted. But I don't think, it's not clear to me—and I'll have to reflect on this at some point—it's not clear to me that that was necessarily because of a management problem, as it was that this is really hard stuff."

In poll after poll, across two years, Americans agreed, without regard to political party, about their most pressing concern: jobs.

This was an area where the dysfunctions of an often leaderless White House were most pronounced. In the period from the fall of 2009 to the spring of 2010—when unemployment was just above or just below 10 percent, the highest level in nearly thirty years—the president and his economic team, led by Larry Summers, were locked in paralysis and constant "relitigation," as the president often groused, over what to do. The policies that emerged from those endless hours were negligible. This was a central result of all the management woes. It wasn't a matter of his policies not succeeding in Congress. Few policies of any real heft were even proposed.

"Some of this was also just compelled by circumstance," Obama said of this particularly frustrating area of drift. "Part of the reason issues would get relitigated is A, that they were just very hard. B, it was because we didn't have a clean story that we wanted to tell against which we would measure various actions. C, the reason that story wasn't as coherent as a principle, up and down the bureaucracy, was because what was required to save the economy might not always match up with what would make for a good story. So, if I wasn't in crisis, or if I had been elected six months later . . . then shaping a story for the American people . . . might have been very different."

A central issue, he added, was the "first, do no harm" stance that Summers and Geithner stressed from the start and that the president, in most cases, affirmed. "We were thinking very practically about how do we get through this crisis without doing permanent damage and hurting taxpayers," he said; if that can't be done then what might be possible? "Precisely because you would never arrive at the perfect technical answer, what [then] are the clear philosophical underpinnings that guide us in sorting through these various decisions?"

He stopped on a dime, at a conclusion: "And that helped lead to a bunch of relitigation."

This president, showing one of the qualities people find most admirable about him, didn't blame his many experienced subordinates, or how they may have mismanaged or misled him. For any failures of his administration, he blamed himself.

Those last few thoughts, accepting responsibility, was a broader summation of his first two years: a frustrating and often futile search for "the perfect technical answer" to each item on a very full plate of complexity—such as job creation or financial restructuring, or even health care, where the original goals of cost cutting were mostly abandoned by July of 2009, leaving a long scramble to push through health insurance reform. Not that there weren't results to show, in health care and elsewhere. Plenty of his proposed policies became law. But there were fewer than there might have been, the president admitted, because of a lack of "clear philosophical underpinnings" to shape policy. There was no narrative, no story to tell, because there was no guiding vision. And that, not incidentally, diminished the creation of policies that could improve the lives of Americans.

———

Barack Obama had originally wanted Pete Rouse to be chief of staff. When he proffered the idea at the "secret summit of chiefs of staff" in Reno, back in October 2007, Rouse demurred—not right for him, not now. Obama said, "Well, maybe later."

"Later" had finally arrived in the fall of 2010, with a vengeance. Rouse officially became interim chief of staff on October 1, after Emanuel's departure. But since his first February memo, he'd been steadily shaping the president's understanding of how the White House needed to be organized and managed.

Now, following the midterms, the president seemed to be assembling the team he'd originally wanted. Austan Goolsbee, the early favorite, from the campaign days, to be chairman of the Council of Economic Advisers, now took that role. Jack Lew, whom Obama had once slated to be head of economic policy process as NEC chairman, was brought into the White House as head of OMB; he was confirmed and at his desk by mid-November.

Though the dispute between Axelrod and Emanuel had seemed to drive troubles within the political and communications staff, Obama, with Rouse's guidance, felt that this was also in need of an overhaul. Erskine Bowles's warning, "leave your friends at home," now became a call to action.

Gibbs would soon be gone. Jim Messina, Emanuel's deputy, would be leaving for Chicago to build the foundations for the next campaign. Axelrod would return to Chicago to do the same. He'd be replaced by the yin to his yang from the glory days, David Plouffe, who would step into Axelrod's role as senior adviser.

"Rahm and Larry especially, but others on senior staff as well, didn't have a strong appreciation of what got [Obama] elected, the power of it and how to harness it. It wasn't just any old election—it was the key to who Obama was and his connection to the American people," one long-time adviser to the president said. "After the midterms, with Rahm gone, Larry due to leave, and many others from the first two years either out the door or soon to be, it was almost as though the president was hitting the Restart button."

The shift in atmosphere inside the White House was so dramatic that those who knew about the Reno meeting couldn't help but wonder what might have transpired over the first two years if Rouse had accepted Obama's original offer.

The biggest change, several top advisers noted, was in the president himself. After a few days of slouching and soul-searching following the midterms—when he gave a sober and downbeat interview saying he'd received a "shellacking" and had "heard the American people, loud and clear"—he seemed to revive.

By mid-November he appeared oddly liberated. It was back to the future . . . but all the way back, to his days in the Senate, when Rouse was his chief of staff and all-purpose guide to Washington.

So many of the senior staff brought aboard after the 2008 election, in fact, were people that Obama—stunned, as everyone was, by the unfolding financial crisis and collapsing economy—felt he needed; the people, like it or not, he was "supposed" to have, seasoned veterans, such as Emanuel, Orszag, and Summers, to help him navigate through the coming storms. Obama, who'd never captained a ship, was naturally hesitant to have any of them spot him practicing his knots belowdecks. The pressure of not letting top advisers see a president's doubt or confusion is something noted by many former presidents, especially concerning their first years in office.

Now that equation was inverted. Rouse knew everything, from the messy start, when Obama stumbled into town like a tourist. There was nothing to hide. Meanwhile, Obama had gained hard-won experience, and insights into how difficult the job really was; how, loyalty and personal affection notwithstanding, his needs, in surrounding himself with a staff to help him govern most effectively, were all that mattered.

Then there was the matter of Rouse himself. Outside of Valerie Jarrett and the Davids—Axelrod and Plouffe—there were few people whom the president felt as comfortable around; and none of them had Rouse's combination of managerial skills and understanding of Washington.

Rouse could sit with his old friend, now the president, and help him recover his balance and bearings. Years before, in the early months of 2008, he told Obama that he needed to "take ownership" of his campaign. Now he helped Obama take ownership of a reconstituted White House.

In mid-November, Biden came to the Oval Office with a full dossier of issues he'd been handling with Congress. He'd been meeting since the midterm with his old colleagues in the Senate, John McCain and Mitch McConnell. Biden, of course, had had relationships with them in the Senate since Obama was in college, and this time, with Biden's guidance, they'd baked a tall layer cake. In it was a wide array of swaps, from the Dream Act, which gave rights to illegal aliens; to the still unratified START II treaty on nuclear weapons reduction with the Russians; to ending "Don't Ask, Don't Tell" in the military in favor of acceptance of gays; to tax giveaways; to the closing of food safety programs that industry opposed.

Obama sat with Biden, going over the package. He had great affection for Biden, who'd been an enormous, and generally unheralded, asset to him, largely because he could act, much like Rouse had, through his own designated channel to the president.

But now Obama said, "No, I'm not going to make some of these trades."

Biden, who'd been waiting for his friend to step up and assert more control, gladly stepped back.

A few weeks later, Obama was on the phone to McConnell. He could do this himself; presidents often do. Over the first weekend of December, he and McConnell cut a deal: exchange the two-year extension of the soon-to-expire Bush tax cuts for high-income Americans, a hot-button issue for the left, for a yearlong extension of unemployment benefits and a payroll tax cut.

By Monday night, December 6, the deal was done. Now Obama— having decided this on his own, consulting no one except his innermost circle, namely Rouse and Biden—had to pull up the curtain and sell it.

The hardest part, of course, would be the front end. The legacy of the Bush cuts, in 2001 and 2003, had become its own atmospheric zone. The cuts, especially the second batch, were opposed by then-Treasury secretary Paul O'Neill. He said to Bush and Cheney that tax cuts were not

as stimulatory as Republican supply-side enthusiasts had long claimed—
that they did not return anywhere near their lost tax revenue—and that
it was "irresponsible" and unprecedented to cut taxes at a time of war.
When O'Neill made this case most strongly in late 2002, the war in Afghanistan and one about to start in Iraq would clearly be costing hundreds
of billions a year. Cheney famously shot O'Neill down, saying, "Reagan proved deficits don't matter; we won the midterms—this is our due."
O'Neill turned out to be even more famously correct: the tax cuts blew
a $2 trillion hole in the U.S. balance sheet, contributing mightily to the
$1.1 trillion annual deficit that Obama inherited when he arrived in office.

But the attacks from the left, that tax cuts were a giveaway to the
wealthy, were true only in part. The total ten-year tab on the cuts was
$2.5 trillion in so-called middle-class tax cuts, which went to most tax-
payers, and $700 billion for those at the top making over $250,000 a year.
During the campaign, Obama had guaranteed that he wouldn't raise
taxes on the middle class. Deep down, his deficit hawk's assessment, as
he now looked at yawning deficits, was clear: that the whole package, the
entire $3.2 trillion, over ten years, would have to go.

On the other hand, the unemployment insurance extension and payroll tax holiday, both opposed by Republicans, amounted to an annual
stimulus of nearly $500 billion for the coming year, a time of need, when
the economy was still sluggish and uneven.

When the deal was unveiled, House Democrats, wounded and outraged in their last few months of control, were unhinged. They were used
to joining Obama in often endless meetings to deliberate and discuss,
as though he were still a congressional colleague. Now they crowded
into the Roosevelt Room as Obama calmly, with his usual patience and
courtliness, defended his position to one delegation after the next. But
a subtle calculus had shifted. Obama's presence, and his openness in
searching for shared interest, still created some "space where solutions
can happen." It was still him; he was still the president. Over the past
two years, of course, he'd been reluctant to fill that space. There were
many reasons: his lack of surety in making decisions, in arriving at what
he felt was an appropriate, defendable stance; the way he'd waited, and
watched, as others, both in Congress and among the wide community of
"stakeholders," filled that space and then claimed squatters' rights. And
then there was the troubling matter of how he'd ceded authority in managing that space to senior staffers, who seemed all too anxious to fill it.

This dysfunction is precisely what had undermined action on the Bush tax cuts across more than two years. During internal debates dating all the way back to the transition, the issue's symbolic power, in terms of the passage of one president to the next, was clear. High-end tax cuts, where the added income often went into investments or savings, were not particularly stimulatory; killing this tax cut's extension could have been readily passed through a Democratic-controlled Congress, even if a 50-vote reconciliation move was needed in the Senate. Fears in 2009 that any withdrawal of stimulus, even this unstimulatory tax cut, prompted the first round of decision delays. Once the economy was limping, though upright, in 2010, that reasoning was moot. At a final White House meeting on the matter in August 2010, it was already clear that the midterms could be the debacle that was, indeed, on the way, where the Democrats could lose the House. Some, such as Orszag, pleaded that now, while the Democrats could still unilaterally decide to kill the extension, was the last chance for the White House at least to swap the tax cuts for something significant. The meeting ended, like so many, with no decision.

Now, less than four months later, Obama had simply taken control of the matter. He was sitting in the space his presidency had created. He owned it. This decision, like so many presidential decisions, was imperfect and filled with unknowns. The economy could move in many directions in the coming two years. The termination of the Bush tax cuts would ultimately rest with the matter of who won the next election. If Obama lost in 2012, the cuts would almost surely be made permanent, and would force deeper cuts across the government that Republicans—suffused with postelection, Tea Party–spiced fervor—said they were eager to make.

But that was another fight for another day. Or so Obama had decided. The country needed stimulus; this was the best way to get it. He'd made his decision. He was the president. After a firestorm from the progressive press, and countless meetings in the Roosevelt Room, the deal easily passed in the House. In mid-December, the Senate voted for it with an overwhelming majority, one not seen on anything of any significance for years: 82 to 18.

History may decide that this was a disastrous compromise for Obama, that what he got in return was not worth what he paid, that he abandoned a core principle. Or not.

The mood in Washington—and surprisingly across much of the country, based on late December poll numbers showing a boost for both Obama and Congress—was different: a subtle boost in confidence.

The future was unknowable. But at least this month, as Christmas neared, there seemed to be a president in the White House.

Pete Rouse still didn't want the job, even after the surprising post-midterm progress he'd helped guide. No dice. He was sixty-one. He was dating a new woman. He could serve the president in many other ways.

On the afternoon of January 6 the entire White House staff, several hundred people, along with assorted notables from around Washington, gathered in the East Room.

President Obama, dapper and looking rested in a crisp white shirt and gray-and-white-striped tie, stepped up to the lectern. To his left was a bald, solidly built man with a steady gaze and feet firmly planted. It was William Daley, the son of the former boss and mayor of Chicago, Richard Daley, and brother of its soon-to-be-departing mayor. Daley, who had also served as a deputy chief of staff under Clinton and as commerce secretary, had been working for the past five years as a top executive at JPMorgan, based in Chicago. He had strong organizational skills, he knew how to delegate, he knew Washington, he knew labor—having worked with them for years in their home base of Chicago—and he knew business. The reviews, just a few days after it was leaked that he'd be named chief of staff, were positive on Wall Street and across party lines.

Of course, Daley had been at the meeting in Reno, too.

On Obama's other side stood Pete Rouse, still looking ruffled, even in his best suit.

Before the president introduced Daley, he said he wanted to say a few words about the media-shy man to his right.

He talked about how Rouse had stepped up in mid-October, after Emanuel left, to take over the White House, as ever reluctantly. Obama said, "When I asked him, Pete said, in the gruff voice we all know, 'Well, Mr. President, my strong inclination is to leave government.'" Obama said this out of the side of his mouth, imitating Rouse, and the crowd reacted with laughter and applause.

It was as if warm air had filled a cold chamber. Obama smiled, and spoke from the heart. He said everyone had heard Rouse say this, heard him speak about his "strong inclinations" when he was asked to do anything over the past six years. "But each time, he saddled up," Obama said, including this last time, when Rouse oversaw the resurgent months since the midterms—a time "people thought would be one of retrenchment that turned out to be one of great progress"—while he "was working to develop a structure and plan for the next two years that will serve us going forward."

Obama reached for summation: "I wouldn't be where I am today without his expert counsel."

Of course, they were there to introduce Daley, as the new boss, which Obama said he'd now do, and let Bill say a few words. But before he did, he wanted to mention one other thing, that he had "prevailed once again on Pete's sense of duty, or guilt—I'm not sure which—and he's agreed to one more tour of duty as my counselor for the next two years."

That last word was barely out when the room—led by Biden, leaping up first in the first row—stood and applauded raucously, cheered, and hooted. After waiting a minute, Obama seemed to cue them with a nod and a shuffling of papers. He needed to introduce Daley, standing, somewhat stunned, by his side. But they wouldn't stop.

After years of wrestling with so many famous and consequential advisers, ambitious men with ambitious plans of their own, Obama looked over at Rouse and smiled, the last hoots finally dying down.

"I cannot imagine life here without him," he said softly. "And I told him so."

Afterward, in the foyer near the East Room, Obama clasped Rouse's shoulder. "Jesus, Pete," said the president, whose capacity for managing his emotions is renowned. "You almost made me pull a Boehner there."

———

Two days later, Arizona representative Gabrielle "Gabby" Giffords strolled to the first of her "Congress on the Corner" gatherings in front of a Safeway just north of Tucson. It was a sunny Saturday morning in suburban Arizona and about thirty residents had gathered to meet Giffords, a so-called blue dog Democrat who'd been elected in 2006. A Jewish onetime Republican, she'd been targeted by the national Republican Party in her wins in 2008 and '10, because her district was affluent, conservative, and had virtually always elected Republican men. She ran counter to that, and was only the third woman elected to the U.S. Congress in Arizona's history. Only forty, Giffords had already made a strong impression politically—as a swing vote on key issues, ranging from supporting health care reform to backing immigration reform, that made her a favorite subject of derision as a "traitor" on conservative blogs and cable.

Maybe for these reasons, maybe not, she was also an object of obsessive interest for Jared Lee Loughner, who witnesses claimed rushed toward the crowd firing an automatic weapon. Six people died, among them a conservative federal judge who had previously received death threats, and another thirteen were injured, including Giffords, who had a bullet tear through her skull. Moments later, Giffords, with her dimpled, girl-next-door smile and long blond hair, became the face of a country that had lost its bearings. Cable channels set up a round-the-clock vigil at the hospital where the congresswoman, the wife of Space Shuttle astronaut Mark Kelly and mother of two young daughters, struggled to stay alive.

On all sides of the human drama emerged petulant debates about what had set off Loughner, who was a regular consumer of political vitriol from the far right. Soon a Sarah Palin citation—in which Palin targeted districts, including Giffords's, on her Take Back America Web site with the insignia of a gun sight—was igniting partisan battles. No one doubted that there was a high quotient of anger across the American landscape. Death threats against Obama that were considered credible by law enforcement were running at nearly four times what they had been against Bush or, for that matter, Bill Clinton. Palin responded that she'd never suggested anyone shoot down the congresswoman on a street corner, but then she attacked those who criticized her tactics as being engaged in a "blood libel," an oddly chosen term, linked exclusively to anti-Semitic charges the Nazis used to justify the Holocaust. A few days later it was clear that Loughner was deeply psychotic, at the very fringe of being able to calculate any premeditation. But everyone, from left to right, was bruised, still shocked and grieving, as regular reports of Gabby's condition, how parts of her skull were removed to relieve pressure from a swollen brain—and guesses on how much of her ebullient personality would be left—dominated the national consciousness.

On the twelfth, Obama boarded Air Force One bound for Tucson. This was, of course, what he'd always thought he'd do as president: help bring the country together. It was, in fact, central to his appeal at the end of the divisive Bush era. Though arriving into the field day of fear that marked the economic decline and financial collapse, he had seemed to step back and opt instead for stability at all costs—bending, in a way, toward Bayard Rustin's old concerns, rather than King's forceful jeremiads and the actions that might have flowed from them. Pushing policies with a focus on technocratic pragmatism was a formula, the president painfully discovered, for division.

But now, trying to restart the presidency as he'd long imagined it, Obama saw a type of crisis he knew how to handle, and he set foot in the Southwest like a thirsty man ready to drink deep from healing waters. He met with the families of the victims, visited Gabby Giffords at the hospital, as she opened her eyes for the first time, and then went to meet ten thousand people gathered at the University of Arizona for a memorial service.

"I have come here tonight as an American who, like all Americans, kneels to pray with you today, and will stand by you tomorrow," the president opened. "There is nothing I can say that will fill the sudden hole torn in your hearts. But know this: the hopes of a nation are here tonight. We mourn with you for the fallen. We join you in your grief. And we add our faith to yours that Representative Gabrielle Giffords and the other living victims of this tragedy pull through."

He quoted scripture, and then—just "as an American," not due any special status—Obama listed the six who'd been slain, saying they "represented what is best in America." He offered affectionate, well-researched renderings of each of their lives, from the conservative judge John Roll, appointed by McCain and the "hardest working judge in the Ninth Circuit"; to George Morris, a former Marine on a cross-country RV journey with his wife of fifty years, who dove to save her but could not, and took a bullet himself; to Gabe Zimmerman, Giffords's young aide, who was struck down just months before he was to be married.

The citation of some individual and his circumstances, often in a story of triumph or resilience, had been a rhetorical standard since Ronald Reagan effectively tried it at his first State of the Union speech in 1981. Obama took it beyond prop, speaking like a dear friend of each of the victims, and many of those injured, to make his transcendent point about how, in all the essential ways, we remain identical to one another, that it is only our inability to see this that holds us back. And then he went a level deeper, as he arrived at the final victim, nine-year-old Christina Taylor Green, who was born on 9/11. As he spoke about her—a dancer, gymnast, an A student, the only girl on a Little League team, who "wanted to be the first woman to play in the majors"—he was talking, his eyes growing moist, about his own girls, and about the man their father hoped to become.

This speech, which he wrote himself, was finally a conversation with the marble busts behind his wing chair back in Washington. He finished it with a reach for the high plane where both King and Lincoln actually lived their headlong, crisis-filled days: "What we can't do is use this tragedy as one more occasion to turn on one another," Obama said. "Rather than pointing fingers or assigning blame, let us use this occasion to expand our moral imaginations, to listen to each other more carefully, to sharpen our instincts for empathy, and remind ourselves of all the ways our hopes and dreams are bound together. After all, that's what most of us do when we lose someone in our family—especially if the loss is unexpected. We're shaken from our routines, and forced to look inward. We reflect on the past. Did we spend enough time with an aging parent? we wonder. Did we express our gratitude for all the sacrifices they made for us? Did we tell a spouse just how desperately we loved them, not just once in a while but every single day? Perhaps we ask ourselves if we've shown enough kindness and generosity and compassion to the people in our lives. Perhaps we question whether we are doing right by our children, or our community, and whether our priorities are in order. We recognize our own mortality, and are reminded that in the fleeting time we have on this earth, what matters is not wealth, or status, or power, or fame—but rather, how well we have loved, and what small part we have played in bettering the lives of others."

The crowd in the field house stood and wept and clapped its hands red, as did countless viewers at home and for weeks on YouTube. It was an Obama who had been elusive—invisible, even—since the campaign. Not that there hadn't been strong speeches since then—the State of the Unions, the health care speech—but they were without a clear framing, based on principles beyond pragmatism: of how America had drifted from its moorings and how it might find a way back. There had been no moral handle for him to hold and lift. Axelrod's hope, in the days after the Cairo speech, that Obama might tap and direct a similar "moral

energy" to reshape the day's pernicious and defining domestic battles—
such as health care, financial reform, and jobs—had never been realized.
In fact, it was barely attempted.

The day after Obama's speech, on January 13, a warrant was filed under
seal in U.S. District Court in Manhattan for the arrest of Vincent Mc-
Crudden, the manager of a small investment fund who had threatened
Gary Gensler, several dozen other employees of the CFTC, and various regulatory officials in a series of mid-December e-mails and post-
ings—including an "execution list"—on his Web site. McCrudden, a
commodities trader and hedge fund manager on Wall Street for twenty
years, was facing several CFTC civil enforcement actions. He posted
threats on his Web site with a $100,000 reward for personal information
on Gensler and others.

When the threatening e-mails hit CFTC in December, Gensler was in
full battle mode, negotiating with other members of the commission—
two Republicans and, including Gensler, three Democrats—over the
controversial issue of how derivatives "bids" could be posted on trading platforms called "swap execution facilities" by a wide array of individuals and firms, and then matched, or answered, by the most attractive
offer. Though Wall Street opposed such a change, and their lobbyists
had literally been camped in front of CFTC for months, it was a feature
that, more than any other, would push the shadowy derivatives market
into sunlight. Trading derivatives would start to look more like trading
stocks on the NYSE. In fact, creating free, open, and transparent access
to the platforms is at the heart of the "trading" function Gensler fought
fiercely to get into Dodd-Frank and that he said was nonnegotiable.
But, that day, he was forced to negotiate, in order to get the votes he
needed to have the specifics of the trading rules firmly delineated. Then a
deputy passed a printed copy of an e-mail to him: "You can tell that fucking corrupt piece of Goldman Sachs shit (G.G.) I am coming after him
as well," McCrudden had written to a senior attorney at CFTC. Soon,
after the FBI was alerted, a security guard appeared at the back door of
the CFTC hearing room.

Gensler got up from his chairman's seat, walked to the back of the
room, shook the hand of the guard—an African American woman—
and thanked her for coming.

A few days before, at the White House Hanukkah party, Gensler—with one of his daughters in tow—shook the president's hand in the receiving line. Though he had one of the most important jobs in government, they'd scarcely met. But Obama was on cue. "How's the rule writing?"

"Great," Gary said, using the three to five seconds one has to say anything as the line pushed forward. He abruptly added, mostly over his shoulder while moving onward, "But don't let them go after our funding!"

Gensler was, indeed, getting it from all sides. Into January, and especially after the Tucson shooting, he thought frequently about the death threats. Regulation, once a sleepy realm of a government that had lost faith in its capacities, had become the stuff of fierce—and even violent—passions.

So he was happy to find out on January 14, the day after the arrest warrant was filed in Manhattan, that McCrudden had been apprehended by the FBI at Newark International Airport. With the arrest, news of the incident was now finally made public, creating plenty of arch comments on financial Web sites about how regulators had, in this era, managed to make themselves targets.

But they are largely unprotected ones—at least in terms of the way the intent of legislation can be thoroughly, and often brilliantly, attacked by an army of lobbyists. Washington was still a town where public purpose only rarely managed to outrun private gain.

Gensler often joked that "gazelles fare better in sunlight," and CFTC's response to the onslaught of literally thousands of lobbyists over the past six months from both Wall Street and Fortune 500 companies—the latter not wanting to post collateral at clearinghouses for their hedges—had been to post each lobbyist's name, their interest, and whom they met with at CFTC. At the same time, he managed to give speeches virtually nonstop and testify to Congress, where the House's newly charged Republican majority was already planning to cut his funding and that of other regulators.

Back at CFTC, the security guard, who he said, "was always a comfort to see in the back of the room," was gone: with the arrest she was no longer needed. Gensler's mid-January schedule was jammed with meetings and speeches. He knew now that he'd miss a late-January deadline for a crucial provision to set position limits on trading, something that Democratic lawmakers were hoping would prevent the big investment firms from gaming the oil markets. But Gensler, a driven man who'd run fifty-mile marathons, remained sanguine about the messy but basic soundness of democracy. "Look, progress is always slow, and uneven, but if you manage to be moving in the right direction—creating something a little better than what we had before—the pain is worth it. That's the trick: you've got to learn to love the pain, to own it, to make sure it doesn't kill you. Day by day, year by year, you get stronger."

———

Up at Dartmouth, Jim Weinstein was fine-tuning his latest outrage. Twelve years ago, Dartmouth and two hospitals that Dartmouth's Atlas identified as leaders in "best practices"—the Mayo Clinic and Utah's Intermountain Medical Center—began to pool data to rigorously test the effectiveness of various medical procedures, a union that helped create continuous improvements of better care at lower cost for all three institutions. Adding hospitals to the trio, though, had not been easy. Many didn't want to have to live by the revealing data and the changes in practice that it might portend. By 2009, it was up to six, including the Cleveland Clinic and Geisinger Medical Center in Danville, Pennsylvania. "The concept, of course, is wherever the data leads, we will follow," Weinstein said, "even if it means forgoing some expensive procedures that are, to be blunt, profitable for our hospitals."

But this was not nearly enough. These hospitals were the ones that Obama, Orszag, and others often cite as models for the rest, ones that have managed to lower costs—for themselves and ultimately the government's insurance programs—while improving care.

What surprised and now agitated Weinstein was that in the past ten months, since the passage of health care reform, fifteen more hospitals, a diverse array of institutions urban and rural, plush and threadbare, had volunteered to join, with another fifteen lined up behind them.

To organize and integrate the measurement and data collection procedures for this many hospitals, especially some with subpar capacities, would take money. "We didn't go after these guys. They knocked on our door, even when they know that some of the conclusions drawn from this much data might mean they'd have to make major changes in the way they practice medicine."

So for weeks he'd been on the phone to Washington. The cost of funding a cooperative with this many hospitals, Weinstein estimated, would be $300 million across five years, or $60 million per year. "It sounds like a lot," he said, but then he broke down the numbers and the offsetting cost reductions in just a single area, back surgery, where he's one of the country's leading experts. The frequency of back surgery at Dartmouth Hitchcock is 2.2 surgeries annually per thousand people; nationally, the frequency is 4.5 per thousand. At Johns Hopkins it's 4.8, and at the Medical Center in Casper, Wyoming, it is 10.5—more than four times Dartmouth's level. Annual funding of $60 million, to include major hospitals that cover 30 million people, would be paid for with savings—roughly about $50 million—on this one procedure. Nationally, bringing spine surgeries in line with Dartmouth's level would save $500 million, annually. "And that's just one procedure," Weinstein exhorts. "But I can't get a call back from Washington."

But then he smiled, thinking of Oregon. This was something that always gave him a lift, something he discovered a few years ago that surprised him. Oregon was the first state to pass a "Death with Dignity Act," in 1994, allowing for physician-assisted suicides in certain limited cases. Since then, the law had been repealed and reinstated, challenged and, ultimately, affirmed in a 2006 Supreme Court ruling.

Nearly 30 percent of Medicare costs are spent on end-of-life care, a stunning figure considering that most beneficiaries arrive into Medicare at sixty-five and the average life expectancy is seventy-nine. In the last year of life, covered medical costs average nearly $30,000.

But here's what made Weinstein smile, thinking about the ferocious debate in Washington. "The Oregon debates, over all these years, helped people see and understand all sides of the issue." Even if they would never consider physician-assisted suicide, "they began to think more clearly and exercise 'shared-decision making' " in their end-of-life care. "When people learn what they need to know, they often surprise you taking charge of their life. They learn, then they act." The result: Medicare costs in Oregon are some of the lowest in the country. And it's largely because of reduced end-of-life costs. "They learned what the doctors didn't want to tell them," Jim Weinstein said with a chuckle. "That in medicine, less is often more. And you—*patient*—are in charge, right until the end."

By late January, Alan Krueger had settled back into his office at Princeton. He was sleeping better, seeing more of his wife and two college-age kids—one at Princeton—and getting back full-time to the research.

The exhaustive study of 6,025 unemployed New Jersey residents was completed. The findings, of which he presented a preliminary glimpse in mid-November at the Federal Reserve Bank of Atlanta, were surprising and, of course, ever more pertinent to a growing national crisis of chronic unemployment.

For the 13.9 million unemployed as of January, the length of their joblessness, on average, was 36.9 weeks, the highest duration since the government began this measurement in 1948 and nearly twice as high as the most recent, comparably serious recession, in 1983, when it was 21.2 weeks. Understanding this group, and why it was so difficult to reduce their number, was on everyone's mind, in both parties. Among Krueger's findings was that the amount of time devoted to job search declined sharply over the spell of unemployment; the exit rate from unemployment was low at all durations of joblessness, and declined gradually as time passed; and also, quite importantly, there was no rise in job search or job finding around the time unemployment insurance benefits expired. This refuted a long-standing study—the centerpiece of public policy actions in handling the jobless and their benefits, for two decades—that recently won its coauthor the Nobel Prize.

But what struck Krueger, poring over the data in his office in late January, was how sad the unemployed were—sadder than data indicated the jobless had been in previous eras—and how they were particularly depressed during episodes of job search.

Economists have long been better at measuring misery than they are at measuring happiness, and the issues that push the unemployed into depression tend to be a complex brew, including a sense of whether society is fair, the length of a person's joblessness, and how they see employment as identity. "Those without a job for an extended period of time seem to lose their identity," Krueger said, "their sense of who they are, and the path they've chosen in life."

A few weeks later, he was standing before seventy or so students, mostly upperclassmen, inside one of Princeton's Gothic stone halls teaching "The Great Recession: Causes, Consequences, and Remedies." His guest that day was Wendy Edelberg, an economist with the Federal Reserve who'd spent much of the past two years on loan to the Financial Crisis Inquiry Commission.

Krueger told the students that the class "was an attempt to teach history in real time" and that they'd have to think clearly about distinguishing "contributing factors from root causes."

Candidates for the latter, he said, might be the housing bubble, "poor choices by consumers in taking on mortgages they couldn't afford," or "money flowing into the financial system and whether the financial system did a bad job of directing that capital." Edelberg talked about the crisis inquiry's views of the matter, focusing mostly on the financial industry's incentives and ultimately destructive activities, while she noted there was general agreement that lack of regulation was a "contributing factor, more than a root cause."

However, after the lecture, with twenty students from one of the class's sections, or precepts, the two teachers themselves were taught a lesson.

After an hour of discussion, Krueger asked the undergraduates to introduce themselves and say something about their plans or their goals. About half were economics majors, but the other half were spread across many disciplines—history, philosophy, biology. One after another, they said they planned on going to Wall Street. All of them. Finally, one student—the last of them—said he wasn't sure what he was going to do.

"You might consider becoming a financial regulator," Krueger said, anxiously. "We're going to need a lot of them going forward."

"Yes," Edelberg implored him. "It's an opportunity to speak truth to power!"

The student seemed unconvinced. The rest of the class looked on, unmoved, as silence filled the seminar room.

A few minutes later, Krueger and Edelberg walked in silence to a nearby cafeteria and sat picking at a pair of salads. A clean sweep for Wall Street. They were stunned. "Can we get any more proof that we're back to the same attitudes of 2007?" Krueger said. Edelberg nodded glumly. Usually a phrase like "speaking truth to power" gets a rise from young adults; at least it once did. "They looked at us like we were walking anachronisms," Krueger said later. "Like we were hippies from the sixties."

On the evening of January 30, Tim Geithner walked down the hall from his office on the third floor of the Treasury Department to the stately Diplomatic Reception Room, restored recently to its nineteenth-century grandeur.

Waiting for him there were six men who understood, better than virtually anyone else on the planet, what it felt like to preside over the U.S. economy.

They were all former Treasury secretaries.

There was a practice in the early years of the American government for the outgoing Treasury secretary to host his successor for dinner— a bit of courtliness, amid the often vicious political dialogue, to ensure continuity in the managing of the financial accounts of the United States. Some things were viewed as too important for partisan bickering. By the twentieth century the dinner had grown into more of an official, cer- emonial welcome. About a year into each new Treasury secretary's term, his predecessor buys dinner for all the former Treasury secretaries to celebrate the arrival of a new member into this exclusive club.

So, on this night, Hank Paulson was the host. He warmly toasted Geithner and treated Bob Rubin, Paul O'Neill, James Baker, Nick Brady, and John Snow to dinner. Federal Reserve chairman Ben Bernanke and deputy Treasury secretary Neil Wolin were asked to attend as well.

Of course, the only schedule that really mattered in the mix was that of the guest of honor. And Tim Geithner was so thoroughly engaged in the crushing weight of successive crises that the dinner had already been delayed a year beyond custom. It floated on his "to do" list month after month. The decision to go forward, oddly enough, was political. Geithner had been hopeful that the president would include recommen- dations of Alan Simpson's and Erskine Bowles' National Commission on Fiscal Responsibility—which in early December had recommended approximately $3 billion in cuts and $1 billion in added revenues over the coming decade—as part of his grand bargain on the Bush tax cuts and stimulus spending with Republicans. The president, cutting that deal himself, dismissed it as too much to attempt.

By early January, Geithner was feeling the clock tick: the U.S. gov- ernment was a few months away from hitting its borrowing capacity. The debt limit would have to be raised in April to avoid a government shutdown—a prospect that was sure to be a matter of pitched combat with the new Republican-controlled House.

And then he remembered the dinner.

Most of the Treasury secretaries who would attend were Republicans. On balance, these were men he could talk to—hailing from a Republi- can Party that, compared to Congress's many new Tea Party warriors, would be considered pragmatic, even progressive. They'd all been stewards of America's finances and understood what it would mean for the United States to slip into default.

He got in touch with Hank. How about that dinner? Then, several of the prospective attendees were contacted by Treasury to engage in the new debt-limit debate, to be spokesmen for probity, writing letters and making calls, especially to congressional Republicans—Treasury secretaries . . . united!

After Hank's toast, Geithner spoke casually and assuredly to his kindred about the state of affairs and especially the debt limit. They all needed to speak as one. This was not something to be left to politics. Anyone who'd have the temerity to "play chicken" with the prospect of the United States defaulting on its obligations was simply irresponsible. Nods all around.

Anyone in the room who could still conjure images of Geithner from two years back, with his darting eyes of a shoplifter at that disastrous first press conference downstairs in the Cash Room, might have wondered where this man came from. Geithner, the last man standing from Obama's original team, was now thoroughly in charge and, it seemed, reconstructed around a set of ideas that had prevailed . . . for better or for worse. Among this constellation of ideas, his North Star was continuity: to keep matters moving forward with as little disruption as possible. It was always an "up ahead" focus: who knew, maybe in the near future they'd encounter improved prospects, new opportunities to seize, surprising twists. When dramatic reform or restructuring was proffered— for Wall Street, for jobs programs, for reregulation of all kinds—he'd often say, let's assess the "Hippocratic risk." The risk, in short, of doing harm. For a new president, with a powerful intellect but little experience, this stance was always available as a sensible course. As Obama learned the limits of pure intellect, in hour after hour of frustrating relitigations, Geithner's posture increasingly felt like a prudential path, rather than a backing away from history's call to arms.

For America's other great center of power—New York and its financial machine—continuity was the path to victory. Wall Street, as it has been constructed in this age of financial miracles, mocks Hippocrates. Doing harm is its business; destruction itself can be quite profitable, properly wrought, especially when the many overwrought parts of the

American economy are on the receiving end. Tim Geithner managed, across two years, to win over two constituencies, as both Wall Street's man and Obama's. He figured it out: Washington could be fearfully prudent so New York wouldn't have to be.

As for his old mentor, Larry Summers, Geithner was coy, sizing up matters from the start, searching out shifts in the key relationships atop the administration. Summers's pride in leading the most academically accomplished, big-brained team since Kennedy's "best and brightest" always carried the scent of peril. That was true for Obama, just like JFK. Geithner, the clever pragmatist, could see this from the start. As the months passed, he mostly observed Larry's debate society, participated only when necessary, and kept his own counsel. Obama arrived with too much faith in intellect's power—with the idea that a collection of smartest people kept in one room could solve almost any problem. While the president learned otherwise, and while his frustration with Summers grew, Geithner held firm, offering the sensible path, feet solidly planted. And when the time came, he said the sensible path would be to reappoint Bernanke. Why make a change? Continuity is a virtue. Deep down, Summers never forgave him.

After Paulson's toast, as the Treasury secretaries drank wine and stood talking before they took their seats, several of the honored guests noticed that a member of their exclusive club was not present. Several of them crowded around Tim. Where's Larry? Geithner had just returned that day from the World Economic Forum in Davos, Switzerland, the first time he'd attended in years. Summers must have been at Davos, too? Geithner nodded, yes, of course.

Then he smiled that coy Geithner smile and offered his trademark shrug, which in no way bespeaks uncertainty. "Larry would rather be in Davos than at dinner with me."

Two weeks later, on February 14, the president meditated on the most important things he'd learned as president, the hard lessons he felt would be most valuable in the days ahead.

"The area in my presidency where I think my management and understanding of the presidency evolved most, and where I think we made the most mistakes, was less on the policy-making front and more on the communications front. I think one of the criticisms that is absolutely legitimate about my first two years was that I was very comfortable with a tech-nocratic approach to government . . . a series of problems to be solved."

This riff about too much policy, too little politics—a point he'd recently made in another interview—he then broadened, searching for a fundamental redefinition of his presidency.

"The irony is, the reason I was in this office is because I told a story to the American people," he said, his voice dropping into that distinctive cadence that takes hold when he's hit a rich vein—slow, steady, but rising to meet the words that matter most. "It wasn't the specifics of my health care plan or my proposals around Afghanistan. The reason people put me in this office is people felt that I had connected our current predicaments with the broader arc of American history and where we might go as a diverse and forward-looking nation. And that narrative thread we just lost, in the day-to-day problem solving that was going on, and that wasn't because of bad execution on any particular issue. I think I was so consumed with the problems in front of me that I didn't step back and remember, 'What's the particular requirement of the president that no one else can do?' And what the president can do, that nobody else can do, is tell a story to the American people about where we are and where we need to go."

While his brilliance in understanding a story and its power—so forcefully expressed in that last aria—was what had lifted him to the White House, his difficulty in finding a story to tell, and tell convincingly, as president was surely tied to the burdens of governance. A candidate can tell a story of what will be. A president, after the first few months in office, must tell a story of what is, and what his presence in the White House has changed for the better.

The "great progress" of the nearly four months since the midterms—a time when Obama's confidence and, according to polls, the confidence the public had in him, had both risen—highlighted what was so often absent in his first two years. The disclosures of his management struggles in making difficult decisions and demanding accountability of his top advisers, and their seeming loss of confidence in him, further stressed gaps about which he is understandably defensive. No president, after all, can afford to acknowledge a lack of confidence; not in this era, when the projection of confidence—justified or not, earned or willed or manufac-tured—remains the coin of the realm.

"I have to say this, though," he added, a touch defensively. "I actually felt very confident through the first year. And if I hadn't felt confident in my second year we would never have gotten health care passed, because after Scott Brown in Massachusetts, people around here were pretty depressed. I was still confident that doing that [health care] was the right thing to do and was right for the Congress."

But he backed away from this "to be sure" defense after a bit. It didn't suit him at this moment. He was struggling to express himself honestly, from a deeper core. Obama, after all, always felt that he was different from the others, from politicians, or Wall Street CEOs, or pitchmen all over America, who met challenges to the country's spirit and capabilities with a smile and a handshake and a feel for saying whatever their audiences wanted to hear.

"Part of what was important in the tax deal was not that my mind was changed around the Bush tax cuts. I still think they were a bad idea. What I think I was able to recognize was that, at this juncture, the country will feel better about itself and that will have important ramifications. If they see Democrats and Republicans agreeing on anything . . . Because right now they are just exhausted with the partisan wars that are taking place. In addition, it turns out that, technically speaking, the most important antipoverty program I can initiate, the most important deficit reduction program I can initiate, is to get the economy growing again."

Ever competitive, Obama's first urge was to try out this fresh construction of a sort of meta-confidence on his peer group, his competitors. At this point it was a mere handful of men, an all-but-extraterrestrial group of a few other presidents he emulated and measured himself against.

"You think about FDR and the New Deal. Three-quarters of the things he did didn't work. But what he was able to project was 'we are going to get through this.' Nobody remembers Kennedy's economic policies. They remember Peace Corps, and they remember a few other New Frontier programs, but basically this job is not about just getting the policy right. It's about getting the American people to believe in themselves, and in our capacity to act collectively to deliver for the next generation."

He sat for a moment. It was all working, integrating nicely, with Kennedy and FDR. But there were other presidents he never wanted to be compared to. "Carter, Clinton, and I all have sort of the disease of being policy wonks," he said, clearly citing this shared characteristic as a liability. But now, with his new self-definition, this improved view, he could distance himself from them. "I think that if you get too consumed with that you lose sight of the larger issue."

This "larger issue"—a larger and ostensibly more effective model of leadership—would be a star to guide him in the years ahead. And, he said, he now had the team to do it: "The reorganization that's taken place here is one that is much more geared to those functions." Almost reflexively, he snapped into a quick take-back, that his old team was "exactly the right team to get a lot of laws passed through Congress," and that he's "incredibly proud" that financial reform has "made the system more stable" and health care reforms "have started what will be a long path toward a more sensible health care system." Then he just swept them, and all the sound and fury, away with a one-liner: "But I have very much internalized the fact that my job is not legislator in chief."

There was one president whom Obama seemed to be speaking directly to, though not yet mentioned. Ronald Reagan's ability to project optimism when there may be no defendable reason to be optimistic was his particular genius, his specialty, and a subject of controversy every day since he left office over twenty years before. Reagan was instrumental in defining confidence, and its many uses, in the modern era. Some say he allowed America to move forward in an age of limits. Others, that he was a charming agent of destruction.

"He was very comfortable in playing the role of president. And I think part of that really was his actor's background," Obama said, betraying, in his tone, a hint of envy. As he edged closer to Reagan, though, Obama seemed to squirm a bit in his chair, trying to get comfortable. Looking back over his life, the president said that he always took pride "in pushing against artifice" and "not engaging in a lot of symbolic gestures, but rather, thinking practically . . . And I think that the evolution that happened in the campaign was me recognizing that if I was going to be a successful candidate, then the symbols and the gestures mattered as much as what my ideas were."

And who could deny Reagan's mastery, his actor's grasp, of symbols and gestures?

No one can know what it's like to be president until they are one, and then they have to decide how much of what they feel, sitting in that lonely cornerless room, they ought to reveal. People, deep down, suspect that the life of a nation, like that of each of us, is shaped by forces well beyond our control, beyond earnest efforts and best-laid plans, just as we all tend to learn at some moment of discovery that those grown-ups who once seemed so assured and certain were neither. As the nation wrestled through a period of maturation, Obama considered how to reconcile his era's hard truths with a working definition of confidence in a world that often merits anything but. The age-old fear, after all, is that we are in fact "home alone," that there is no one responsible in charge. The role of government is to make a convincing case to the contrary, so everyone can get on with their lives and manage a good night's sleep.

Obama, a brilliant amateur, arrived to power's pinnacle believing he'd make his case with a show of demonstrably correct answers to complex problems, solutions he'd competently execute to launch a new "era of responsibility."

It hadn't worked quite as he'd hoped, bruising the preternatural confidence—quite real—that, more than anything, is what got him elected.

Now, firmly along in a more dynamic "I'll just do it myself" model of leadership, he reached for a compass for the course ahead.

"Going forward as president," Obama said, straightening up his chair, "the symbols and gestures—what people are seeing coming out of this office—are at least as important as the policies we put forward."

"I think where the evolution has taken place," Barack Obama said finally, looking into the middle distance, "is understanding that leadership in this office is not a matter of you being confident. Leadership in this office is a matter of helping the American people feel confident."

ACKNOWLEDGMENTS

I T IS ALWAYS A PRIVILEGE TO OFFER OF A FEW PAGES OF GRATITUDE to close a journey of nonfiction. Many people conspire to help a book grow from first idea to a fully realized expression, and with this book there are many people to thank, starting with those who presided over its conception. This is my second book with my friend and trusted guide Tim Duggan, executive editor at HarperCollins, and Jonathan Burnham, the division's publisher.

Across more than two and a half years, from the book's starting point in February 2009, Tim was ever at my side, providing wise counsel and nourishing enthusiasm as the project twisted and spun forward—and sometimes sideways—through many stages. Finally, when it all came together, an able HarperCollins team snapped into action. Assistant Editor Emily Cunningham was a dream, already a seasoned pro, and Tina Andreadis, a publisher's row promotional whiz, leapt into battle.

As with each of the last three books, my agent, Andrew Wylie, was a source of straight talk and sterling advice. He's one of the sanest madmen I know and just about the best corner man you could want.

I wrote a book in the late 1990s about a teenager's heroic rise from a blighted urban high school to the Ivy League, and saw how, along the way, that young man was often seen as both less and more than he really was, and how he was constantly wrestling with "what people wanted to see."

Something similar happened, writ large, with Barack Obama. I, like many Americans, felt a surge of pride when an African American was elected president. It took some time for me to see him simply as a man, with the full complement of gifts and faults, occupying the White House. An opposite, though similar, preconception existed in the early reporting about Wall Street. The emotional shock of the meltdown and the natural urge to uncover malice and affix blame became a barrier to cross.

What helped on both accounts were the many sources who, hour after hour, strove for honesty in helping me understand the complexities of the situation. I can't thank them all here and many, of course, would rather remain anonymous. But I am in their debt. In my efforts across twenty-five years, I've often said that nonfiction writing should dig beneath the alluring, often simplified narratives of heroes and villains in search of a deeper, more resonant rendering of human complexity. If this book has in any way managed that, it is due to hundreds of sources and their faith in being able to understand the times in which we live.

On this project I was particularly fortunate to have as my young deputy Will Kryder, a clear-eyed product of Boston College who signed on for a span that stretched nearly a year beyond initial projections. He didn't flinch. In fact, he rose to meet every challenge—as the number of characters, topics, and disclosures built—and acted as one of my key interlocutors in the shaping of the narrative. My dear friend Greg Jackson dove in to assist at a crunch time and offered fresh eyes for a final read.

The reporting and writing of this book stretched across three summers, and my friends at Dartmouth, where I've been a writer-in-residence since 2000, again provided me with a refuge. During this time, it has been at the John Sloan Dicke Center, led by a brilliant and seasoned diplomat, Ken Yalowitz, who has welcomed me into the company of scholars.

But, in terms of refuge—along with joy and sustenance, I've long been the most fortunate of men. During the nearly three years conceiving, reporting, and writing this book, my sons have grown, firmly, into manhood. Walter, just graduated from college, will read this book with critical faculties sharpened to a fine edge. My younger son, Owen, just off to college, speaks frequently of the nature of courage and friendship, and how "all great journeys are about facing your fears." As with fathers everywhere, I've learned from my sons much more than I could teach them, and those lessons have inspired this effort.

As for my wife, Cornelia, my partner in all things, I simply offer unspeakable gratitude for her support and guidance, with additional acknowledgments remaining firmly off the record.

SOURCES

‖N A PERFECT WORLD EVERYONE WOULD SPEAK FREELY OF THEIR THOUGHTS, feelings, and recollections, on the record, and stand with proprietary regard beside those words. It certainly would make for some very interesting journalism.

Of course, we are far from such a world—maybe farther than ever, with "message," these days, so often trumping truth, analysis, and even action itself. With the large institutions that populate Washington and New York, this is regularly the case: the face they show to the public is crafted, each day, with fastidious ardor.

All of which means that many of the sources that cooperated with this project—in both those two cities and elsewhere—are off the record or do not speak for attribution.

Let me apologize to readers for this. Off-the-record sources are, no doubt, crucial to a journalist's task of discovering what is knowable—George Washington was an active off-the-record source for reporters during the Revolutionary War; as was Thomas Jefferson, during the early days of the country. But sources who identify themselves and speak openly are almost always preferable. Thankfully, many do in this book. They are to be commended.

Many others manage to help with the reconstruction of events of recent history—who said what, at a particular place and time; who was in the room; what preceded an event to suggest what people were thinking before an episode or incident, and what they thought afterward; what is visible now, looking back. The major meetings and scenes rendered in this book are drawn from multiple sources, with only a handful of exceptions. That latter tends to be subjects who recall what they themselves did with no one around. Transcripts of some key meetings were provided, as were documents and e-mails that preceded and followed various gatherings.

Some subjects were interviewed as many as thirty times during the reporting and writing of the book, a period that spanned almost three years. In all, 746 hours of interviews were conducted with more than 200 individuals, including the president of the United States.

A few final notes on the notes. Many books have been written in the past few years about both Wall Street and Washington. Where possible, I've cited instances in which I've drawn from those books, especially the ones that broke news. Though it is my practice to confirm quotations that have appeared elsewhere from subjects—and often have cause to alter them—the first public citation is mentioned first. In any era, the biggest stories tend to be told bit by bit, day by day, with journalists balancing on one another's shoulders to reveal all the public has a right to know. May this group effort continue.

CHAPTER 1

4 unveiled in an article she published in the spring of 2007: Elizabeth Warren, "Unsafe at Any Rate," *Democracy* 5 (Summer 2007): available at http://www.democracyjournal.org/5/6528.php.

6 "This isn't a job interview": A phrase often used by the president, mentioned to several sources. In this context, Elizabeth Warren, interview with the author, September 2010.

6 "Why didn't you put her up for confirmation?": "Obama Announces Appointment of Elizabeth Warren," ABC News, September 17, 2010, video available at abcnews.go.com/Politics/video/obama-announces -appointment-elizabeth-warren-11666764.

7 Krueger is something of an oddity in the upper reaches of government: Alan Krueger résumé available at http://www.krueger.princeton.edu/Krueger12_15_09.htm.

7 the Census Bureau had announced that poverty had hit a fifteen-year high: Carmen DeNavas-Walt, Bernadette D. Proctor, and Jessica Smith, U.S. Census Bureau, *Income, Poverty and Health Insurance Coverage in the United States: 2009*, September 2010, available at http://www.census.gov/prod/2010pubs/p60-238.pdf.

7 Even the *Wall Street Journal*'s: Conor Dougherty and Sara Murray, "Lost Decade for Family Income," *Wall Street Journal*, September 17, 2010, available at online.wsj.com/article/SB100014240527487034406045754956707140696694.html.

8 "Going back to Princeton": Alan Krueger, interview with the author, October 1, 2010, scene and quotes.

10 "We have to get folks off the sidelines": Barack Obama, interview by Jann S. Wenner, *Rolling Stone*, October 14, 2010, available at http://www.rollingstone.com/politics/news/obama-in-command-br-the-rolling-stone-interview-20100928.

11 "Did you think I was kidding": Valerie Jarrett, interview with the author, November 2008.

CHAPTER 2

13 "I stand here knowing that my story is part of the larger American story": Barack Obama, "Keynote Address," 2004 Democratic National Convention, Boston, Mass., July 24, 2004.

14 "We ought not, we will not, travel down that hellish path blindly": Barack Obama, "Speech Against the Iraq War," Chicago, Ill., October 2, 2002, transcript available at www.npr.org/templates/story/story.php?storyId=99591469.

14 Hence the morning's address, given at Washington's Woodrow Wilson Center: Barack Obama, Woodrow Wilson International Center, Washington, D.C., August 1, 2007, speech, available at www.cfr.org/us-election-2008/obamas-speech-woodrow-wilson-center/p13974.

15 An NBC News/*Wall Street Journal* poll . . . showed Hillary Clinton with a 21-point lead: NBC News/*Wall Street Journal* poll, July 2007, Hart/ Newhouse, study #6074, available at http://online.wsj.com/public/ resources/documents/july2007pollv1.pdf.

16 "Growing Together (1947–1973) vs. Growing Apart (1973–2005)": Claudia Golden and Lawrence W. Katz, "Long-Run Changes in the U.S. Wage Structure: Narrowing, Widening, Polarizing," September 2007, available at http://www.economics.harvard.edu/faculty/katz/files/GoldinKatz_ NWP_1107.pdf.

17 household debt, commonly between 30 and 50 percent: Laura Conaway, "Household Debt Vs. GDP," *NPR: Planet Money*, February 27, 2009, available at http://www.npr.org/blogs/money/2009/02/household_debt_ vs_gdp.html.

18 "Okay, in year two of my administration": Interviews by the author with Alan Krueger, Austan Goolsbee, and President Obama, various dates, scene and quotes.

18 *Dreams from My Father*, a book in which he deconstructs himself: Barack Obama, *Dreams from My Father: A Story of Race and Inheritance* (New York: Broadway Books, 2004).

22 "On my 7 hour drive back from Maine": Robert Wolf, "Another way to look at the direction of the markets . . ." message to undisclosed, July 23, 2007, e-mail.

25 "Tonight he can do no wrong": Robert Wolf, interviews with the author, multiple dates.

25 "The world's coming to an end, Wolfie": Sal Naro and Robert Wolf, interviews with the author, multiple dates.

28 "market-driven disaster": Barack Obama, "Oval Office interview," with Ron Suskind, February 14, 2011; as well as interviews with Robert Wolf, multiple dates, 2010–2011.

29 "the contemporary tendency in our society is to base our distribution on scarcity": Martin Luther King, *Where Do We Go from Here: Chaos or Community?* (Boston: Beacon Press, 1968).

29 "One day we will have to stand before the God of history": Delivered at the National Cathedral, Washington, D.C., on March 31, 1968. *Congressional Record*, April 9, 1968. http://mlk-kpp01.stanford.edu/index.php/kingpapers/article/ remaining_awake_through_a_great_revolution/.

CHAPTER 3

31 "Amid a crisis of confidence, Roosevelt called for": Barack Obama, "NASDAQ speech," speech at NASDAQ, New York, September 17, 2007, transcript available at www.nytimes.com/2007/09/17/us/politics/16text-obama.html?pagewanted=print.

32 "I'm really busy with my homework": Valerie Jarrett, interview with the author, November 2008.

33 "Hope is what led a band of colonists": Barack Obama, "Iowa Caucus Victory Speech," Des Moines, Iowa, January 3, 2008, available at www.washingtonpost.com/wp-dyn/content/article/2008/01/03/AR2008010304994.html.

34 "who would often express fears of black men and uttered stereotypes that made me cringe": Barack Obama, "A More Perfect Union," speech, National Constitution Center, Philadelphia, Pa., March 18, 2008, available at www.npr.org/templates/story/story.php?storyId=88478467.

35 on March 16, JPMorgan agreed to buy Bear Stearns: Andrew Ross Sorkin and Landon Thomas Jr., "JPMorgan Acts to Buy Ailing Bear Stearns at Huge Discount," New York Times, March 16, 2008, available at http://www.nytimes.com/2008/03/16/business/16cnd-bear.html.

37 "As I said last fall at NASDAQ": Barack Obama, "Renewing the American Economy," speech at Cooper Union, New York, March 27, 2008, available at www.nytimes.com/2008/03/27/us/politics/27text-obama.html?pagewanted=print.

37 "Barack Obama's speech on the financial crisis was a remarkable break-through": Robert Kuttner, "Obama v. Krugman," American Prospect, March 28, 2008, available at http://prospect.org/cs/articles?article=obama_v_krugman.

40 "I think, based on the way things have gone": Greg Fleming, multiple interviews with the author, June 2010, scene and quotes.

41 Merrill chief Stan O'Neal was abruptly fired after the firm lost $2.3 billion in its third quarter: Thomas Landon Jr. and Jenny Anderson, "Risk-Taker's Reign at Merrill Ends With Swift Fall," New York Times, October 29, 2007, available at http://www.nytimes.com/2007/10/29/business/29merrill.html?ref=estanleyoneal.

41 the Wall Street Journal reported that Merrill had fraudulently handled its derivatives book: Susan Pulliam, "Deals With Hedge Funds May Be Helping Merrill Delay Mortgage Losses," Wall Street Journal, November 2, 2009, available at http://online.wsj.com/article/SB119401977393180546.html?mod=sphere_ts.

45 "Greed, leverage, and lax investor standards": Henry M. Paulson, On the Brink, (New York: Business Plus, 2010).

46 Two top Treasury officials, Neel Kashkari and Phillip Swagel: Andrew Ross Sorkin, Too Big to Fail (New York: Viking, 2009), p. 90.

48 "Now, tell me again what $10 million in advertising [in Ohio] got us": Senior official from Obama campaign, interview with the author, November 3, 2008.

49 "Tonight, more than ever": Hillary Clinton's Pennsylvania victory speech, Philadelphia, Pennsylvania, April 22, 2008, available at http://www.realclearpolitics.com/printpage/?url=http://www.realclearpolitics.com/articles/2008/04/clintons_pennsylvania_victory.html.

50 "I know what I'm good at": Richard Wolffe, Renegade: The Making of a President (New York: Three Rivers Press, 2009), p. 39.

51   "Barack . . . take ownership of this campaign": Peter Rouse, interviews with
     the author, multiple dates.

52   "I distinguish between the campaign and the presidency": Barack Obama,
     interview with the author, February 14, 2011.

55   "He pulled out, plain and simple, because it was *his* money": Carmine Visone,
     interviews with the author, multiple dates, 2009–2011, scene and quotes.

56   If Stockholm gives Shiller the nod: Robert J. Shiller and Karl E. Case. "Is
     There a Bubble in the Housing Market?" Cowles Foundation Paper 1089,
     Cowles Foundation for Research in Economics, Yale University, 2004,
     available at http://www.econ.yale.edu/~shiller/pubs/p1089.pdf.

57   Geithner ignored Shiller's warning: Robert Shiller, interview with the
     author, September 2009.

                              CHAPTER 4

69   "Fannie Mae and Freddie Mac are not in crisis": Barney Frank, Hearing
     of the House Financial Services Committee, September 10, 2003, quote
     available at http://online.wsj.com/article/SB122290574391296381.html.

72   Geithner was getting ready for a wildly busy day: "Geithner's Calendar
     at the New York Fed," p. 462, in *New York Times*, available at documents
     .nytimes.com/geithner-schedule-new-york-fed.

73   "Countrywide had no idea what its exposure was": Timothy Geithner,
     interview with the author, December 15, 2009.

74   "Reducing Systemic Risk in a Dynamic Financial System": Timothy
     Geithner, "Reducing Systemic Risk in a Dynamic Financial System,"
     speech at the Economic Club of New York, June 9, 2008, available at www
     .newyorkfed.org/newsevents/speeches/2008/tfg080609.html.

75   "has judged it necessary to take actions that extend *to the very edge* of its
     lawful and implied power": Paul Volcker, speech at the Economic Club
     of New York, April 8, 2008, available at economics.kenyon.edu/melick/
     Econ391/K-Monetary%20Policy%20During%20and%20After/Volcker_
     Transcript_April_2008.pdf.

75   "The Fed made the judgment": Geithner, "Reducing Systemic Risk in a
     Dynamic Financial System."

76   There was no more mention of clearinghouses: "Statement Regarding June 9
     Meeting on Over-the-Counter Derivatives," Federal Reserve Bank of New
     York, press release, June 9, 2008, available at http://www.newyorkfed.org/
     newsevents/news_archive/markets/2008/ma080609.html.

81   "I haven't been living in this bubble very long": Elizabeth Warren, multiple
     interviews with the author, September 2010, scene and quotes.

82   "innate gender differences": Lawrence Summers, from a speech
     delivered in January 2005, available at http://www.thecrimson.com/
     article/2005/1/14/summers-comments-on-women-and-science.

84   The result of this particular overreach . . . when Harvard lost nearly one-
     third of its endowment: Geraldine Fabrikant, "Harvard and Yale Report

Losses in Endowments," *New York Times*, September 10, 2009, available at http://www.nytimes.com/2009/09/11/business/11harvard.html.

84 Despite spending just one day . . . Summers was paid $5.2 million: Louise Story, "A Rich Education for Summers (After Harvard)," *New York Times*, April 5, 2009, available at http://www.nytimes.com/2009/04/06/business/06summers.html.

84 They were state-of-the-world renderings: Lawrence Summers, "The pendulum swings towards regulation," *Financial Times: Economists' Forum*, October 26, 2008, available at http://blogs.ft.com/economistsforum/2008/10/the-pendulum-swings-towards-regulation/#axzz1SXE1S3n1.

86 "The financial storm that reached gale force": Ben S. Bernanke, "Reducing Systemic Risk," speech, Jackson Hole, Wyoming, August 22, 2008, available at www.federalreserve.gov/newsevents/speech/bernanke20080822a.htm.

88 As fears about the company's exposure to toxic CDOs grew in January and February: Heidi N. Moore, "Can what Happened to Bear Happen to Other Banks?" *Wall Street Journal*, March 18, 2009, available at http://blogs.wsj.com/deals/2008/03/18/repos-just-where-do-the-other-banks-stand/.

89 An odd twist on the repo market: Study by Metrick and Gorton available at http://econ-www.mit.edu/files/3918.

89 "The Panic of 2007": Gary Gorton, "The Panic of 2007," August 4, 2008, available at www.kansascityfed.org/publicat/sympos/2008/gorton.08.04.08.pdf.

90 "I thought my talk went badly": Gary Gorton, interview with the author, October 2010.

CHAPTER 5

92 Of the first fifteen polls covered that month . . . Obama was ahead in just four of them: Presidential polling statistics for the 2008 election available at http://www.realclearpolitics.com/epolls/2008/president/national.html.

92 "Wall Street's Fears": Jenny Anderson and Ben White, "Wall Street's Fears on Lehman Bros. Batter Markets," *New York Times*, September 10, 2008, available at www.nytimes.com/2008/09/10/business/10place.html.

93 "It was one of those situations where you knew an earthquake might happen": Barack Obama, "Oval Office interview," interview with the author, February 14, 2011.

96 "The thing about these Brits is that they always talk and they never close": Andrew Ross Sorkin, *Too Big to Fail*.

97 "The good news is that in fifty-three days": Quotes taken from text of Obama's September 12, 2008, campaign speech in Dover, New Hampshire, available at www.realclearpolitics.com/articles/2008/09/obamas_remarks_in_dover_new_ha.html.

107 "You know what, Greg?": Exchanges with Fleming and Thain based on extensive on-the-record interviews with Fleming by the author, February 2010, as well as others familiar with the deal.

109 "Worse," said Wolf: Robert Wolf, multiple interviews with the author
     2009–2011, scene and quotes.

109 At 1:45 a.m., a few hours into Monday, September 15, Lehman Brothers
     filed: Andrew Ross Sorkin, "Lehman Files for Bankruptcy; Merrill Is Sold,"
     New York Times, September 14, 2008, available at http://www.nytimes
     .com/2008/09/15/business/15lehman.html?pagewanted=all.

109 $40 billion in commercial real estate . . . and other exotic asset-backed
     securities and derivatives: Lawrence McDonald, *A Colossal Failure of
     Common Sense: The Inside Story of the Collapse of Lehman Brothers* (New
     York: Crown Business, 2009), p. 298.

111 He threw the jacket into his box: Carmine Visone, interviews with the
     author, September 2009, scene and quotes.

CHAPTER 6

112 On Tuesday, Moody's and Standard & Poor's downgraded ratings on AIG:
     Hugh Son, "AIG Credit Ratings Cut, Threatening Quests for Funds,"
     Bloomberg, September 16, 2008, available at http://www.bloomberg.com/
     apps/news?pid=newsarchive&sid=aX_zVXoWfK54.

113 Federal Reserve announced it was lending $85 billion to AIG: Edmund
     L. Andrews, "Fed rescues AIG with $85 billion loan for 80% stake,"
     New York Times, September 17, 2008, available at http://www.nytimes
     .com/2008/09/17/business/worldbusiness/17iht-17insure.16217125.html.

113 Speaking in Elko, Nevada: Taken from text of September 17, 2008,
     speech, transcript available at http://www.realclearpolitics.com/
     articles/2008/09/.

114 "This is a one-hundred-year situation": All quotes from the September 18,
     2008, meeting with Paulson, Bernanke, and members of the Senate and
     House of Representatives are based on several accounts of the meeting and
     an in-depth packet obtained by the author April 2009.

116 John McCain was holding a rally in Cedar Rapids, Iowa: McCain speech,
     September 18, 2008, Cedar Rapids, Iowa, available at http://www
     .realclearpolitics.com/articles/2008/09/mccains_economic_remarks_in_
     ce.html.

116 "What we're looking at right now is to provide the Treasury and the Fed":
     Obama remarks on the economy, September 19, 2008, available at http://
     www.washingtonpost.com/wp-dyn/content/article/2008/09/19/
     AR2008091901960.html.

120 "I'd like to hear what Senator McCain has to say": Alter, *The Promise*, p. 11.

121 "When President Bush took office": Quotes taken from speech on the
     House floor, September 29, 2008, transcript available at www.nytimes
     .com/2008/09/30/washington/30pelositranscript.html?pagewanted=all.

125 Eras end with a whisper: Ron Suskind, "Change," *New York Times*, November
     11, 2008, available at www.nytimes.com/2008/11/16/magazine/16change
     .html.

126 "You need to ask yourself *why* you want to do this": David Axelrod, interviews with the author, November 2008.

128 "a single word: tomorrow": Barack Obama, "Speech Before Election Night," Manassas, Virginia, November 3, 2008; the author covered and reported on the speech.

131 "This victory alone is not the change we seek": Barack Obama, "Grant Park Victory Speech," Chicago, Illinois, November 4, 2008.

132 He took her raised hand and gently lowered it . . . Not tonight: The author covered Obama's speech at Grant Park, Chicago, Illinois, on November 4, 2008.

CHAPTER 7

134 "Leave your friends at home": Scene and quotes based on multiple interviews with participants from the meeting, 2011.

136 "Rahm is a little intense": Peter Baker, "The Limits of Rahmism," *New York Times Magazine*, March 8, 2010, available at http://www.nytimes .com/2010/03/14/magazine/14emanuel-t.html.

137 "I'm not into this whole alpha-senator thing": Peter Orszag, interview with the author, August 27, 2010, scene and quotes.

143 "All you economists dress the same!": Peter Orszag, interview with the author, October 2010.

147 had briefly worked with Obama's mother: Alter, *The Promise*, p. 31.

151 Romer . . . listened to Obama invoke FDR's example: Christina Romer, "The Great Crash and the Onset of the Great Depression," *Quarterly Journal of Economics*, August 1990, pp. 597–624, available at http://emlab.berkeley.edu/ users/cromer/CRomerQJE1990.pdf; "What Ended the Great Depression?" *Journal of Economic History*, December 1992, pp. 757–84, available at http://elsa.berkeley.edu/~cromer/What%20Ended%20the%20Great%20 Depression.pdf.

151 "The first thing out of your mouth was 'No, you're wrong'?!": Christina Romer, interview with the author, December 2010, scene and quotes.

151 On Monday, November 24, Obama unveiled his newly minted economic team: November 24, 2008, transcript available at http://www.nytimes .com/2008/11/24/us/politics/24text-obama.html.

152 "whatever happened before, it was okay": Peter Orszag, interview with the author, August, 2010.

152 "He's just not very good at politics": Christina Romer, interviews with the author, December 2010.

153 Romer pushed for a larger stimulus, at around $1.2 trillion: Ryan Lizza, "Inside the Crisis: Larry Summers and the White House Economic Team," *New Yorker*, October 12, 2009, available at www.newyorker.com/ reporting/2009/10/12/091012fa_fact_lizza, in addition to interviews by the author with several senior White House officials.

156 "Reagan spoke to America's longing for order": Barack Obama, *The*

Audacity of Hope: Thoughts on Reclaiming the American Dream (New York: Crown, 2006), p. 31.

158   "What speeches can accomplish": David S. Broder, "Obama Asks Nation to Rise to the Challenge of His Words," *Washington Post*, January 20, 2009, available at http://www.washingtonpost.com/wp-dyn/content/article/2009/01/20/AR2009012002299.html.

CHAPTER 8

162   "no such thing as 'shovel-ready' projects": Peter Baker, "The Education of a President," *New York Times Magazine*, October 12, 2010, available at http://www.nytimes.com/2010/10/17/magazine/17obama-t.html.

162   "A long-term investment program should not be put together hastily": Alice Rivlin, "Budget Policy Challenges," testimony in front of the House Budget Committee, Washington, D.C., January 27, 2009, available at www.brookings.edu/testimony/2009/0127_budget_rivlin.aspx.

164   "You know, a good many years have passed since I last appeared before this committee": Paul Volcker, comments during the confirmation hearing of Timothy Geithner in front of the Senate Finance Committee, Washington, D.C., January 21, 2009, available at www.washingtonpost.com/wp-srv/politics/documents/transcript_geithner_012109.html.

167   "They were basically picking winners and losers": Maria Cantwell, interview with the author, September 2009.

168   "We want to make sure that the standardized part of those markets": Comments during the confirmation hearing of Timothy Geithner in front of the Senate Finance Committee, Washington, D.C., January 21, 2009, available at www.washingtonpost.com/wp-srv/politics/documents/transcript_geithner_012109.html.

174   "I saw a wire story where you had that give-and-take with Cantwell": Scene and quotes based on interviews with members of the transition team, September 2010.

175   "I am disappointed that we are even voting on this": Senator Michael Enzi, Senate Finance Committee Vote on the Confirmation of Tim Geithner, full transcript provided by off-the-record source.

177   "Mr. President, the deck is stacked against you": Scene based on interviews with senior White House officials and meeting attendees.

178   "Thank you, Mark. I want you to channel Daschle": Scene and quotes based on interviews with senior White House officials and meeting attendees, December 2010 and January 2011.

184   The major difference? What Sweden had started . . . with government support and cash infusions: Carmen M. Reinhart and Kenneth S. Rogoff, "Banking Crisis: An Equal Opportunity Menace," paper, December 17, 2008, available at www.economics.harvard.edu/files/faculty/51_Banking_Crises.pdf.

184   "won't be possible until January 21": Paul Krugman, "The Good, the Bad, and the Ugly," from his blog *The Conscience of a Liberal*, in the *New*

York Times, September 28, 2008, available at krugman.blogs.nytimes
.com/2008/09/28/the-good-the-bad-and-the-ugly/.

CHAPTER 9

189 The black sedan was speeding back from Capitol Hill: Alan Krueger, multiple interviews with author, scene and quotes.

192 "He's creating a space where solutions can happen": John Podesta, interview with the author, March 2009.

193 "Tell your boss, Geithner, he shouldn't be coming to things like this . . . job of saving the economy": Alan Krueger, interviews with the author, June 2010.

194 Ignagni now clutched the microphone: Karen Ignagni, transcript of March 5, 2009, White House Summit on Health Care, scene and quotes, available at www.whitehouse.gov/the_press_office/Closing-Remarks-by-the-President-at-White-House-Forum-on-Health-Reform.

195 "Look, it's like the president said, you've got to be hopeful and you've got to include Republicans": Zeke Emanuel, interview with the author, March 2009.

196 "Larry fancies himself very good at politics": Christina Romer, interviews with the author, December 2010.

196 "We've gone from a moment when we've never had a *less* social-science-oriented group": Larry Summers, interview with the author, March 2009.

198 He continued to view people as rational: Daniel Kahneman and Amos Tversky, "Prospect Theory: An Analysis of Decisions under Risk," March 1979, *Econometrica*, vol. 47, no. 2, available at http://www.hss.caltech.edu/~camerer/Ec101/ProspectTheory.pdf.

198 "There are 226 cancer drugs": Billy Tauzin, interview with the author, March 2009.

215 "'dauntingly fit' stud on the tennis court": Jim Impoco, May 1, 2009, available at http://nymag.com/daily/intel/2009/05/tim_geither_is_fleet-footed_tk.html.

219 "Right there, Rahm killed it": Christina Romer, interviews with the author, January 2011.

CHAPTER 10

224 "Of every twenty deals . . . So that's three out of twenty": Interview with Charles Hallac by the author, November 2009.

227 Rattner and his Wall Streeters balked at the ouster: Oval Office meeting on auto bailouts based on interviews with numerous officials attending the auto meetings, 2009–2011.

229 "Many of these people are nearing fifty . . . they won't get rehired—by anyone": Interview by the author with Ron Bloom, July 2009.

233 Which is what the House did . . . taxing at 90 percent any bonus above $1 million: Carl Hulse and David M Herszenhorn, "House Approves 90% Tax

on Bonuses After Bailouts," *New York Times*, March 19, 2009, http://www
.nytimes.com/2009/03/20/business/20bailout.html.

233 Meanwhile, reports emerged, with White House fingerprints: "Dodd:
Administration pushed for language protecting bonuses," *CNNPolitics*,
March 18, 2009, available at http://articles.cnn.com/2009-03-18/politics/
aig.bonuses.congress_1_aig-bonuses-new-language-amendment?_
s=PM:POLITICS.

234 "My administration is the only thing between you and the pitchforks":
Meeting of the thirteen bankers on March 27, 2009, based on interviews with
White House officials and attendees from Wall Street, 2009–2011.

238 "I am reiterating our request . . . plenty of advice from Larry Summers and
Secretary Geithner on this subject": Letter obtained by the author from
a source wishing to remain off the record who was involved closely with
financial reform.

239 "You don't blow the big game and then still get a trophy": Ed Markey,
speaking in front of the House of Representatives, March 19, 2009, available
at markey.house.gov/index.php?option=com_content&task=view&id=
3575&Itemid=244.

243 A few days before . . . the Public-Private Investment Program was formally
released: March 23, 2009, PPIP Treasury press release available at http://
www.treasury.gov/initiatives/financial-stability/investment-programs/
ppip/Pages/publicprivatefund.aspx.

245 "Secretary Geithner, good luck with your very important work": Timothy
Geithner, *Meet the Press*, March 29, 2009, scene and quotes.

CHAPTER 11

249 "Our credibility is being put on the line": Multiple sources present at the
meeting, interviews with the author, scene and quotes.

250 "After all that happened over the past two months . . . was just unconscionable": Christina Romer, interviews with the author, December 2010.

256 "Rodge is afraid right now and so is the industry": The author attended and
spoke, on April 21, 2009, at Mr. Fleming's Yale Law School class.

257 In a key passage that roiled the news cycles . . . keep silent about the deepening
financial distress inside Merrill: Examination of Kenneth Lee Lewis, taken
at the State of New York, Office of the Attorney General, New York, on
February 26, 2009, at 4:30 p.m., before Sara Freund, a shorthand reporter
and a notary public of the State of New York, available at online.wsj.com/
public/resources/documents/ExhibitA-cuomo04232009.pdf.

258 "I don't know why Lewis pushed to do this": Greg Fleming, interviews with
the author, April 2009.

262 *I can't run health care*: E-mails, obtained by the author, between Rahm
Emanuel and Peter Orszag.

263 "I don't want even one molecule of energy spent on anything other than the
stress tests!": Alan Krueger, interview with the author, March 2011.

265 "Sheila Bair and Brooksley Born recognized that the financial security":
     Press release, John F. Kennedy Presidential Library and Museum, March 25,
     2009, available at www.jfklibrary.org/About-Us/News-and-Press/Press-
     Releases/2009-Profile-in-Courage-Award-Recipients-Announced.aspx.

267 The previous spring . . . Krueger launched one of the most ambitious
     unemployment studies in recent years: Alan Krueger and Andreas Mueller,
     *Job Search and Job Finding in a Period of Mass Unemployment: Evidence from
     High-Frequency Longitudinal Data*, Princeton University, January 2011,
     available at http://www.irs.princeton.edu/pubs/pdfs/562.pdf.

272 "doesn't have the luxury of coming back to this a year from now": Tom
     Daschle, interview with the author, April 27, 2009, scene and quotes.

CHAPTER 12

274 Rogoff was putting the finishing touches on a book with . . . Carmen
     Reinhardt: Carmen M. Reinhart and Kenneth Rogoff, *This Time Is
     Different: Eight Centuries of Financial Folly* (Princeton, New Jersey: Prince-
     ton University Press, 2009).

275 Obama's Socratic approach left one participant feeling slighted: April
     27, 2009, economists' dinner based on accounts of several participants in
     interviews in November 2010.

278 He remembered, as many did, the notable exchange between Alan Greenspan
     and Bill Clinton: Bob Woodward, *The Agenda: Inside the Clinton White
     House* (New York: Simon & Schuster, 1994).

279 "you *are* the president": Peter Orszag, interview with the author, January
     2011, scene and quotes.

283 What does it take to lead the world's most powerful nation?: David Axelrod,
     interview with the author, May 2009, scene and quotes.

285 "How do you deleverage an entire economy?" Paul Volcker, interview with
     the author, May 2009, scene and quotes.

293 And it was a big number: May 11, 2009, letter to the president from the
     "Providers" alliance: PhRMA, SEIU, AMA, AHA, AHIP and AdvaMed,
     available   at   graphics8.nytimes.com/packages/pdf/politics/20090511_
     HealthGroups_Letter.pdf.

295 "Initial reaction to it . . . a number like seventy-two percent supporting it":
     Joel Benenson, quotes at the Economic Club of Canada, from July 31, 2009,
     Washington Post, available at www.washingtonpost.com/wp-dyn/content/
     article/2009/07/30/AR2009073001547.html.

296 "The President misspoke": Robert Pear, "Health Care Leaders Say Obama
     Overstated Their Promise to Control Costs," *New York Times*, May 14, 2009,
     available at www.nytimes.com/2009/05/15/health/policy/15health.html.

296 The providers flip-flopped: Providers' debacle based on interviews with
     Karen Ignagni, Peter Orszag, and other, off-the-record, sources, 2010.

297 "What you've done is IMMORAL!": Peter Orszag, interviews with the
     author, August 2010.

297 That's when Cantwell lifted her hold on him: Maria Cantwell, press release, available at http://cantwell.senate.gov/news/record.cfm?id=313039.

297 In a press conference back on May 13, Geithner released an outline: CNN, May 13, 2009, available at http://money.cnn.com/2009/05/13/news/derivatives.fortune/index.htm.

301 there would always be someone there watching over them: Gary Gensler, multiple interviews with the author, scene and quotes.

301 "You know, Peter, we're really home alone": May 26, 2009, scene, and more generally the "home alone" quote, based on interviews on October 15 and November 5, 2010, with Peter Orszag, and on follow-up conversations and e-mails to ensure accuracy.

CHAPTER 13

303 At least that was Emanuel's view . . . "with no playbook, no blueprint": Rahm Emanuel, interview with the author, June 2011.

304 "I argued for financial reform" . . . needed no funding, no "ask": Rahm Emanuel, interview with the author, June 2011.

307 In an e-mail sent to the senior staff on June 8: E-mail obtained by a senior White House official shown to the author on a condition of anonymity.

308 Indeed, he had just cut a ten-year deal: David D. Kirkpatrick, "White House Affirms Deal on Drug Cost," New York Times, August 5, 2009, available at http://www.nytimes.com/2009/08/06/health/policy/06insure.html?adxnnl=1&adxnnlx=1311076743-EixPG5NQJt26HdKzGmE19Q.

310 "The question is how the president can talk . . . make clear that health care is a moral issue": David Axelrod, interview with the author, June 8, 2009, scene and quotes.

310 "Do you know any chemistry? . . . so A plus B goes to C": Zeke Emanuel, interview with the author, June 8, 2009, scene and quotes.

311 The day before, with the release of Treasury's eighty-eight-page white paper: Treasury Release, "A New Foundation," June 17, 2009, available at http://www.cfr.org/united-states/us-treasury-department-financial-regulatory-reform—new-foundation/p19659.

313 "Sure would be nice to pay this time": Scene and quotes based on interviews with several senior White House officials and meeting participants, from 2009 to 2010.

316 Help you out? You're the chief of staff!: Peter Orszag, interview with the author, January 29, 2011, scene and quotes.

323 His approval ratings . . . Gallup poll of August 24 through August 26: Gallup polling data on presidential approval ratings available at http://www.gallup.com/poll/116479/barack-obama-presidential-job-approval.aspx.

CHAPTER 14

338 "Everyone was in a terrible mood": Anita Dunn, interview with the author, April 2011.

339   "I felt like a piece of meat": Christina Romer, interview with the author, December 2010.

340   "this place would be in court for a hostile workplace . . . a genuinely hostile workplace to women": Anita Dunn, interview with the author, April 2011, confirmed by several top administration officials.

342   "The point is not only the substantial risks inherent in capital market activities": Paul Volcker, testimony in front of the House Financial Services Committee, September 24, 2009, available at http://financialservices .house.gov/Media/file/hearings/111/Volcker9_24_2010.pdf.

343   "He's self-confident, too self-confident": Paul Volcker, interview with the author, September 2009.

343   Warren in a new flavor of celebrity—"regulatory dissident": Elizabeth Warren, interview by Jon Stewart, April 15, 2009, available at http://www .thedailyshow.com/watch/wed-april-15-2009/elizabeth-warren-pt--1.

345   "Don't Cry for Me, Argentina": Elizabeth Warren, interview with the author, September 2009, scene and quotes.

346   On Monday, October 12 . . . the PricewaterhouseCoopers report was released: PWC report available at www.americanhealthsolution.org/assets/Reform-Resources/AHIP-Reform-Resources/PWC-Report-on-Costs-Final.pdf.

346   on October 13 . . . PwC issued a baffling reversal: Ezra Klein, "PriceWaterhouseCoopers Backs Away From AHIP," *Washington Post*, October 13, 2009, available at http://voices.washingtonpost.com/ezra-klein/2009/10/pricewaterhousecoopers_backs_a.html.

347   "those who would bend the truth or break it to score political points": Barack Obama, weekly radio address, available at politicalticker.blogs.cnn .com/2009/10/17/president-obama-cites-progress-in-health-care-debate/.

347   It was Ignagni's job in many ways to be the bad actor: Karen Ignagni, interview with the author, January 2010.

350   "You're taking his side!": November 2, 2009, PERAB scene based on off-the-record interviews with attendees of the meeting, November 2009.

350   On November 5, the women prepared: Alter, *The Promise*, p. 307.

350   Obama immediately called the accusations "bunk": Mark Leibovich, "Man's World at the White House?" *New York Times*, October 24, 2009, available at www.nytimes.com/2009/10/25/us/politics/25vibe.html.

351   "My immediate thoughts and prayers are with the wounded and with the families of the fallen": President Obama's remarks on the Fort Hood shootings, November 5, 2009, available at http://www.washingtonpost .com/wp-dyn/content/article/2009/11/05/AR2009110504202.html.

353   "After the dinner we [the women] all decided we'd rather have had dinner just by ourselves": The women's dinner has been widely reported; however, this version includes additional quotes and insights from various sources who attended the dinner.

354   "It's not just wrong, it's *oh so* wrong?": Interview with Christina Romer, December 2010.

354   "You know, he sure was a lot more generous with me than he was with you": Scene and quotes based on interviews with multiple attendees of the November 2009 meeting who asked to remain off the record.

358   "Does this mean we've turned the corner?": Christina Romer, interview with the author, December 2010, scene and quotes.

359   "That's him, right there": David Axelrod, interview with the author, December 15, 2009, scene and quotes.

CHAPTER 15

363   Mark Zandi, Moody's sober economist: Peter S. Goodman, "U.S Jobs Loss in December Dim Hope for Quick Upswing," *New York Times*, January 8, 2010, available at http://www.nytimes.com/2010/01/09/business/economy/09jobs.html?hp.

363   "Economy is going to contract": Paul Krugman, available at http://blogs.abcnews.com/politicalpunch/2009/12/krugman-reasonably-high-chance-the-economy-will-contract.html.

363   Gibbs would offer none: http://whitehouse.gov/the-press-office/briefing-white-house-press-secretary-robert-gibbs-182010.

364   "it's in crisis—it can't go on like this": Anita Dunn, interview with the author, April 2011.

364   "Rather than the Cheney-driven secrecy": The machinations of the Bush White House under Cheney's direction have been reported by the author in his other books, *The One Percent Doctrine* and *The Way of the World*.

365   "home alone" riff: Peter Orszag, interviews with the author, October 15, 2010, and November 5, 2010, as well as e-mails to ensure accuracy.

365   "I'll make my argument first; you can go after me": Peter Orszag, January 29, 2011, characterization of Summers, confirmed by others who attended Oval Office meetings.

366   "building a robust clean energy sector is how we will create the jobs of the future": President Barack Obama, January 8, 2010, "Remarks on Jobs and Clean Energy Investments," available at http://www.whitehouse.gov/the-press-office/remarks-president-jobs-and-clean-energy-investments.

370   "A few of us joked that we should just get Robert Caro's book on Lyndon Johnson": Interviews with senior White House sources, February 2011.

371   "Well, what do *you* suggest, Nancy": Carrie Budoff Brown and Glenn Thrush, "Nancy Pelosi Steeled White House for Health Push," *Politico*, March 3, 2010, accessed June 21, 2011, at www.politico.com/news/stories/0310/34753.html.

372   "What is my narrative?": Meeting and quotes based on interviews conducted with members of the senior White House staff by the author, January 2011.

373   "It stretches credulity for us to believe that you had no role in this": Dan Burton, Steven Lynch, and Timothy Geithner, testimony of Tim Geithner in front of the House Committee on Oversight and Government Reform, January 27, 2010, all quotes.

375   Several key House Democrats, including Barney Frank: Jake Sherman,

"Rep. Anthony Weiner: Health Care May Be 'Dead' if Scott Brown Wins," *Politico*, January 19, 2010, available at www.politico.com/news/stories/0110/31647.html.

375   "the Obama White House is geared for campaigning rather than governing": Edward Luce, "A fearsome foursome," *Financial Times*, February 4, 2010, available at http://www.ft.com/cms/s/0/f65c9a80-1145-11df-a6d6-00144feab49a.html#axzz1ShZ46ZC3.

377   "This memo addresses management/personnel and structural issues": The restructuring memos written by Pete Rouse were circulated among senior staff and given to the author by a senior source wishing to remain off the record.

380   "kiddie care": Sheryl Gay Stolberg, Jeff Zeleny, and Carl Hulse, "Health Vote Caps a Journey Back from the Brink," *New York Times*, March 20, 2010, available at www.nytimes.com/2010/03/21/health/policy/21reconstruct.html.

380   The coup de grâce was a column by Dana Milbank: Dana Milbank, "Why Obama needs Rahm at the top," *Washington Post*, February 21, 2010, available at http://www.washingtonpost.com/wp-dyn/content/article/2010/02/19/AR2010021904298.html.

380   He summarily called Emanuel into his office and "really laid him out": Scene based on conversations with top aides wishing to remain off the record.

381   "I'm not let go": Interview with Rahm Emanuel by the author, June 2011.

382   "The campaign's over, John": Video of the exchange between Obama and McCain at the February 25, 2010, health care summit, available at http://abcnews.go.com/Politics/video/obama-mccain-campaign-9938356.

383   "I think [Pelosi] is the one who has kept the steel in the president's back": Sheryl Gay Stolberg, Jeff Zeleny, and Carl Hulse, "Health Vote Caps a Journey Back from the Brink," *New York Times*, March 20, 2010, available at www.nytimes.com/2010/03/21/health/policy/21reconstruct.html.

384   "After nearly a hundred years of talk and frustration": President Barack Obama, "Obama's Remarks on House Health Bill Passage," March 22, 2010, available at http://www.nytimes.com/2010/03/22/health/policy/22text-obama.html?ref=policy.

389   "Of course, Mr. President": Scene between Orszag and President Obama based on interview with Peter Orszag by the author, January 2011.

CHAPTER 16

390   especially after another harvest of year-end bonuses: "Goldman Reports $4.95 Billion 4th-Quarter Profit," *New York Times: Dealbook*, January 21, 2010, available at http://dealbook.nytimes.com/2010/01/21/goldman-reports-495-billion-4th-quarter-profit/.

394   in mid-April it accused Goldman Sachs of securities fraud: Gretchen Morgenson and Louise Story, "S.E.C. Accuses Goldman of Fraud in Housing Deal," *New York Times*, April 16, 2010, available at http://www.nytimes.com/2010/04/17/business/17goldman.html.

394   The mortgage-backed security in question: Wall Street and the Financial
      Crisis: Anatomy of a Financial Collapse," Majority and Minority Report,
      U.S. Senate Permanent Subcommittee on Investigations, Committee on
      Homeland Security and Governmental Affairs (Carl Levin, chairman),
      Washington, D.C., issued, April 13, 2011, available at hsgac.senate.gov/
      public/_files/Financial_Crisis/FinancialCrisisReport.pdf.
394   The meat of the SEC charge: *SEC v. Goldman Sachs and Co.*, U.S. District
      Court, Southern District of New York, available at www.sec.gov/litigation/
      complaints/2010/comp21489.pdf.
395   "Goldman wrongly permitted a client that was betting against the mortgage
      market": Robert Khuzami, SEC Press Release, April 16, 2010, available at
      http://www.sec.gov/news/press/2010/2010-59.htm.
396   Only 40 percent of the bank's OTC derivatives were collateralized: U.S.
      Securities and Exchange Commission, Form 10-q, for Morgan Stanley,
      September 30, 2009, available at www.morganstanley.com/about/ir/
      shareholder/10q0909/10q0909.pdf.
399   Finally, he had it: a single page with three pie charts: Notes of Gary
      Gensler.
402   "You don't disclose that": From video of "Investment Banks and the
      Financial Crisis, Goldman Sachs Chair and CEO," CSPAN, April 27, 2010,
      available at www.clicker.com/tv/c-span-video-library/investment-banks-
      and-the-financial-crisis-goldman-sachs-chairman-and-ceo-872955/.

CHAPTER 17

408   "there will be no replacement businesses built": Greg Fleming, interview
      with the author, May 2010.
408   "I don't have a balance sheet to protect": Larry Fink, interview with the
      author, November 9, 2009.
409   "Chinese walls": David Segal, "Chinese Walls, Pocked with Peepholes,"
      New York Times, June 12, 2010, available at www.nytimes.com/2010/06/13/
      weekinreview/13segal.html.
410   "banks should be in the business of lending": Larry Fink, interview with the
      author, 2010.
417   "These were young guys at the rating agencies, making $100,000": William
      Winters, interview with the author. The author attended the event; scene
      and quotes based on his reporting.
420   "I don't know, maybe I've lived too long": Carmine Visone, interview with
      the author, 2010.

CHAPTER 18

421   The event: a black-tie gala for International House, New York's venerable
      cross-cultural edifice, where seven hundred residents at a time: The author
      attended and reported on the event; all quotes attributed to his reporting.
423   A few years after Weinberg died in 1969: John Whitehead, "Business

Principles," available at www2.goldmansachs.com/our-firm/our-people/business-principles.html.

425 "He doesn't get it. He says, 'I'm the CEO'": John Whitehead, interview with the author, June 11, 2010.

426 "No, seriously, Paul, no CDOs, none": Paul Volcker, exchange covered by the author. June 11, 2010.

433 "I'm not dead yet. I talked to Barney; he's with me": Paul Volcker, interview with the author, June 2011, scene and quotes.

437 "I honestly don't know what the impact is going to be": Interview with John Voigtman and Gary Gensler, June 2010 as well as interviews July 2011.

437 "For years . . . our financial sector was governed": Barack Obama, remarks by the president at signing of Dodd-Frank Wall Street Reform and Consumer Protection Act, Ronald Reagan Building, Washington, D.C., July 21, 2010.

CHAPTER 19

441 In a memo dated August 5: The restructuring memos written by Pete Rouse were circulated among senior staff and recounted to the author by a senior source who had a copy and wished to remain off the record.

442 During the summer of 2009, when Atul Gawande published: Atul Gawande, "The Cost Conundrum: What a Texas Town Can Teach Us About Health Care," *New Yorker*, June 1, 2009, available at www.newyorker.com/reporting/2009/06/01/090601fa_fact_gawande.

443 "I can't believe how wrong they got it": Jim Weinstein, interview with the author, August 2010.

444 "Why is it always the women?": Elizabeth Warren, interview with the author, September 2010, scene and quotes.

445 "I want you to help me": Elizabeth Warren, interview with the author, September 2010, scene and quotes.

446 "You may think you can keep him from speaking to this": Exchanges between Rahm Emanuel and David Axelrod surrounding the proposed mosque in New York City, based on interviews with both Mr. Emanuel and Mr. Axelrod by the author, on multiple dates, in June 2011.

446 "As a citizen, and as president, I believe that Muslims": President Obama, "Remarks at Iftar Diner," August 13, 2010, available at http://www.whitehouse.gov/the-press-office/2010/08/13/remarks-president-iftar-dinner.

449 "He would have been fired": Obama's contemplating firing Rahm Emanuel, based on various off-the-record interviews with senior White House officials.

451 "I think that happens to a lot of good people, in these times, when they come to this town": Alan Krueger, interviews with the author, October 2010, scene and quotes.

453 *Thank you, Larry—POTUS*: Larry Summers, interview with the author, May 9, 2011, scene and "Home Alone" response.

455 "Wall Street's confidence is buying back your shares; that does not add a job.

Wall Street's confidence is doing a merger; that destroys jobs": Larry Fink, interview with the author, May 2011, scene and quotes.

456 "it's going to, I'm sure, have some more ups and downs during the course of me being in this office": Barack Obama, press conference by the president, East Room, White House, November 3, 2010, available at www.whitehouse .gov/the-press-office/2010/11/03/press-conference-president.

CHAPTER 20

457 Reflecting on the two years leading up to the midterm shellacking, President Obama focused most acutely on the portentous early days: The author interviewed the president in the Oval Office on February 14, 2011. All quotes in this chapter attributed to the president are from that interview. To read the full transcript of the interview, please visit RonSuskind.com.

460 "leave your friends at home": Interview with participants at meeting, January 2011, scene and quotes.

466 "You almost made me pull a Boehner there": Interview with participants at press conference, January 2011, scene and quotes.

468 "I have come here tonight as an American": Barack Obama, speech in Tucson, Arizona, January 13, 2011.

472 "Day by day, year by year, you get stronger": Gary Gensler, interview with the author, May 2011.

478 "Larry would rather be in Davos than at dinner with me": Scene and quotes, of a January 30 dinner, based on interviews with attendees and Treasury officials asking to remain anonymous.

482 "Leadership in this office is a matter of helping the American people feel confident": Barack Obama, interview with the author, February 14, 2011.

INDEX

R ON SUSKIND IS THE AUTHOR OF *THE NEW YORK TIMES* BEST-sellers *The Way of the World: A Story of Truth and Hope in an Age of Extremism*, *The One Percent Doctrine: Deep Inside America's Pursuit of Its Enemies Since 9/11*, and *The Price of Loyalty: George W. Bush, the White House, and the Education of Paul O'Neill*. He is also the author of the bestselling and critically acclaimed *A Hope in the Unseen: An American Odyssey from the Inner City to the Ivy League*. He has written for *The New York Times Magazine* and *Esquire*, and is a distinguished visiting scholar at Dartmouth College. From 1993 to 2000 he was the senior national affairs writer for *The Wall Street Journal*, where he won a Pulitzer Prize. He lives with his wife, Cornelia Kennedy Suskind, in Washington, D.C.